# FOREWORD

When Visual Basic was originally being developed, we immediately thought of The Waite Group. The light touch and high quality of Mitch's books, particularly those on QuickBasic and C, made him an excellent publisher to seed.

Of course we all wondered what the reception to Visual Basic would be, after all the traditional development platform for Windows was C, and Microsoft had thousands of developers working with that language. We were pleased to find that the development community quickly embraced Visual Basic. Quotes from many technical developers and journalists in our industry all agreed: Visual Basic gives "leverage" over Windows programming and provides a full-fledged development system for creating real Windows applications. Compilation is almost instantaneous and the final results are indistinguishable from programs written in C. The core language is based on QuickBasic and modified for the graphics platform with an event-driven programming model which ensures a major host of new programmers can use it.

Rather than write just another tutorial, The Waite Group has given us clever new insights to the Visual Basic language through the extensive use of Windows APIs. The API or Application Programming Interface is the underlying library of over 800 system calls and messages that makes up the Windows programming environment. Visual Basic is designed so that it can easily call these powerful functions. With the *Visual Basic How-To Second Edition* you will learn how to push the environment to its limits.

We're proud to have book authors and publishers in the Visual Basic add-on community. And we're especially proud of the support of Mitch Waite and The Waite Group. The *Visual Basic How-To Second Edition* is a valuable source for all kinds of tricks and tips. I think you'll enjoy this book, and at the same time, it will stretch your appreciation of Microsoft's revolutionary new product. With Microsoft Visual Basic and *The Waite Group's Visual Basic How-To Second Edition,* you can create real Windows applications the fast and easy way.

**Nevet Basker**
Visual Basic Product Manager
Microsoft Corporation

# FOREWORD

In 1987 I wrote a program called "Ruby" that delivered visual programming to the average user. When I showed the prototype to Bill Gates, he said "this advances the state of the art." Little did we know at the time just how far forward it would go. More than two years later, as the project evolved, Ruby was married to QuickBasic, and the result was Visual Basic—the first native programming environment for Windows. And you are the beneficiary. For the first time you can write Windows programs from within Windows without the enormous overburden of code needed with C. And they are real programs, for real customers with real application needs.

When people ask me what is the best way to learn programming or how to use a specific language, I tell them to experiment—write as many small programs as you can, as each one will teach you more—and each one will add another trick to your tool bag. Unfortunately, when a simple "Hello, World" program takes four hundred lines of code, as it can when Windows is programmed with the C language, this prescription is nearly impossible to follow. Well now The Waite Group gives us a book that uses that learning method. First, Visual Basic brings the size of Windows programs down to a manageable level, then *The Waite Group's Visual Basic How-To Second Edition* guides you through dozens of small programs (and some not-so-small) that fulfill the learning prescription admirably.

This book goes considerably beyond reference, without catering to the lowest common denominator of typical tutorials. You can think of it as a guide to enjoyable learning, a mentor for experimentation. The programs in this book are the kind that you can learn with. You can add to them, combine them, extend them and, ultimately, use them in day-to-day computing.

Mitch Waite has been delivering practical, helpful writing for personal computer users since the mid-seventies. He has gathered around him some of the best and most capable writers working today. Their collective expertise with the Basic language and programming in Windows has come together with their understanding of learning and writing. Coupled with Robert Arnson's amazingly strong affinity with Visual Basic, it means the book you now hold in your hands delivers the most useful information available on the subject.

**Alan Cooper**
Director Applications Software
Coactive Computing Corp

*(Alan Cooper is considered the father of Visual Basic)*

# VISUAL BASIC

# HOW-TO

## Second Edition

### The Definitive
### VB3 Problem Solver

**ZANE THOMAS**
**ROBERT ARNSON**
**MITCHELL WAITE**

WAITE
GROUP
PRESS™

Corte Madera, California

**Publisher:** *Mitchell Waite*
**Editorial Director:** *Scott Calamar*
**Managing Editor:** *Joel Fugazzotto*
**Content Editor:** *Heidi Brumbough*
**Technical Reviewer:** *William Potter*
**Production Director:** *Julianne Ososke*
**Design:** *Cecile Kaufman*
**Production:** *Michele Cuneo*
**Cover Design:** *Michael Rogondino*

© 1993 by The Waite Group®, Inc.
**Published by Waite Group Press, 200 Tamal Plaza, Corte Madera, CA 94925.**

Waite Group Press™ is distributed to bookstores and book wholesalers by Publishers Group West, Box 8843, Emeryville, CA 94662, 1-800-788-3123 (in California 1-510-658-3453).

Printed in the United States of America
93 94 95 96 • 10 9 8 7 6 5 4 3 2 1

Arnson, Robert, 1970-
     Visual basic how-to : the difinitive VB2 problem solver / Zane Thomas,  Robert Arnson,
   Mitchell Waite.-- 2nd ed.
       p.   cm.
     Rev. ed. of:  The Waite Group's Visual basic how-to / Robert Arnson ... [et al.]. 1992.
     Includes index.
     ISBN 1-878739-42-5 : $36.95
     1. BASIC (Computer program language) 2. Microsoft Visual BASIC.
I.  Thomas, Zane.  II. Waite, Mitchell.  III. Title.  IV. Title: Waite Group's visual basic how-to.
QA76.73.B3W334   1993
005.4'3--dc20                                                                     93-25454
                                                                                      CIP

# DEDICATION

To my wife Deborah, and my children Zachary, Chelsea, and Alexander.

-Zane Thomas

# ● ACKNOWLEDGMENTS

First I would like to express a special thanks to Mitch Waite. Mitch has the vision and tenacity to consistently produce the best programming books. It has been a tremendously rewarding experience to work with Mitch; he has provided a number of really great ideas for projects to incorporate in this book, and has always been available to provide advice on its style and content.

And to Joel Fugazzotto, the editor of the *Visual Basic How-To Second Edition,* thanks a thousand times over! Joel nursed me through the ups and downs, led me through the visions and revisions, and kept me on course through the sea of details involved in putting together this book. Knowing that Joel has a number of books in process at any given time, it was surprising that I could call him up at any time to ask about this detail or that and find him completely familiar with the material. It was as if he spent all his time thinking about this book alone!

We express our gratitude to first edition co-authors Daniel Rosen and Jonathan Zuck, whose substantial contributions carry over to this edition.

Thanks to Brett Foster for providing a really great custom control and How-To for this book. Brett's TOOLBUTN control makes it really easy to add toolbars to your programs. Like many other great programmers Brett has taken the time to write some really cool code and distribute it free of charge.

We all owe a debt of gratitude to Bill Potter for his excellent technical review of the Visual Basic code. Bill has a great talent for reading and understanding code, no matter how cryptic it may appear at first. Bill located the rough spots in the code and made really great suggestions for how to make it more useful and understandable.

Zane Thomas
September 1993

Dear Reader:

What is a book? Is it perpetually fated to be inky words on a paper page? Or can a book simply be something that inspires—feeding your head with ideas and creativity regardless of the medium? The latter, I believe. That's why I'm always pushing our books to a higher plane, using new technology to reinvent the medium.

I wrote my first book in 1973, **Projects in Sights, Sounds, and Sensations.** I like to think of it as our first multimedia book. In the years since then, I've learned that people want to *experience* information, not just passively absorb it—they want interactive MTV in a book. With this in mind, I started my own publishing company and published **Master C,** a book/disk package that turned the PC into a C language instructor. Then we branched out to computer graphics with **Fractal Creations,** which included a color poster, 3-D glasses, and a totally rad fractal generator. Ever since, we've included disks and other goodies with most of our books. **Virtual Reality Creations** is bundled with 3-D Fresnel viewing goggles and **Walkthroughs & Flybys** comes with a multimedia CD-ROM. We've made complex multimedia accessible for any PC user with **Ray Tracing Creations, Multimedia Creations, Making Movies on your PC, Image Lab,** and three books on Fractals.

The Waite Group continues to publish innovative multimedia books on cutting edge topics, and of course the programming books that make up our heritage. Being a programmer myself, I appreciate clear guidance through a tricky OS, so our books come bundled with disks and CDs loaded with code, utilities and custom controls.

By 1993, The Waite Group will have published 135 books. Our next step is to develop a new type of book: an interactive, multimedia experience involving the reader on many levels.

With this new book, you'll be trained by a computer-based instructor with infinite patience, run a simulation to visualize the topic, play a game that shows you different aspects of the subject, interact with others on-line, and have instant access to a large database on the subject. For traditionalists, there will be a full-color, paper-based book.

In the meantime, they've wired the White House for hi-tech; the information super highway has been proposed; and computers, communication, entertainment, and information are becoming inseparable. To travel in this Digital Age you'll need guidebooks. The Waite Group offers such guidance for the most important software—your mind.

We hope you enjoy this book. For a color catalog, just fill out and send in the Reader Report Card at the back of the book. You can reach me on CIS as 75146.3515, MCI mail as mwaite, and usenet as mitch@well.sf.ca.us.

*Mitchell Waite*

Mitchell Waite
Publisher

Waite
Group
Press™

# ● ABOUT THE AUTHORS

### Zane Thomas

Zane Thomas began programming in the mid 1970s on a 6800 micropro-cessor with a whopping 512 (there really is no K here!) bytes. After a few months he dropped his pursuit of a degree in molecular-biology and started programming full time. He soon found himself at Alpha Microsystems, one of the many startup companies that blossomed during the beginning of the personal-computer revolution. Since then he has programmed using a num-ber of processors, operating systems, and languages.

Zane lives in Washington State with his wife and three children. Zane and his wife Deborah are active in environmental issues in the Pacific Northwest. And, believing that personal commitment and sacrifice are nec-essary to preserve the quality of life for future generations, they have pledged to donate 10 percent of their proceeds from this book to environmental organizations.

### Robert Arnson

Robert Arnson has been programming in BASIC, Pascal, C, and FOR-TRAN for almost a decade. He has developed several large business applica-tions for professional insurance and statement billing, using QuickBASIC versions 2.0 through 4.5 and BASIC compilers 6.0 and 7.0. He is co-author of *The Waite Group's Microsoft QuickBASIC Bible,* and *The Waite Group's MS-DOS QBasic Programmer's Reference,* both published by Microsoft Press.

### Mitchell Waite

Mitchell Waite is President and CEO of The Waite Group, a developer and publisher of computer books. He is an experienced programmer fluent in a variety of computer languages, including Visual Basic, C, Pascal, BASIC, Assembly, and HyperTalk. He wrote his first computer book in 1976, and is co-author of many best-selling computer books including *The Waite Group's C Primer Plus, Microsoft QuickC Programming, Microsoft QuickBASIC Bible,* and *The Waite Group's Master C.*

# INTRODUCTION

## What This Book Is About

If you love Visual Basic and want to do marvelous things with it—things not immediately apparent—this book is for you.

However, if you are looking for a book that shows how to make a beep, tells how to set up a menu with three items in it, or shows how you set the caption of a form, this book may not be for you. For those kinds of things we recommend one of the many introductory books on Visual Basic or the manuals which we think are pretty adequate for first-time learners.

## Takes Visual Basic to Its Limits

Rather than rehash the manuals, *Visual Basic How-To Second Edition* shows you how to take the program to its ultimate limits. We view Visual Basic as a complete stand-alone Windows development system—rivaling the professional Windows SDK used by C programmers. And so we show you how to do things that you would think could only be done in C with the SDK. The bottom line is that our book is chock full of tricks of all kinds.

For example, you'll learn how to size a form's controls automatically, flash title bars, make a button with continuous events, and remember the size and locations of forms so the next time you open them they are in the same place. You'll see how to build a powerful editor that searches for text, make floating pop-up menus, or give an application a NeXT-like graphical interface. There are details on how to scroll objects in a window, align text automatically, ensure numeric-only entry in a text box, even control the rate at which your text caret blinks.

## Uses Windows APIs Extensively

One of the cool things about this book is that it uses many of Windows' built-in Application Programming Interface (API) routines. These powerful routines are what professional Windows developers use to create killer applications. We'll tell you how to use the Windows APIs to draw transparent icons, create a file dialog box, send messages to controls, display the progress of an operation in a bar chart, paint the interiors of complex objects, and build professional line, bar, and pie charts. There is even a complete slide show project that displays Windows bitmaps with special graphics effects.

### Question and Answer Format

The questions and answers are arranged by categories: controls, forms, text and scrolling, mouse and menu, graphics, environment and system, peripherals, custom controls, DLLs, and Windows APIs. Each How-To contains a program solution with complete construction details. All the code, bitmaps, fonts, icons, forms, and DLLs are contained on the enclosed disk.

### Free Custom Controls

*Visual Basic How-To Second Edition* provides more than just solutions—the bundled disk contains free, fully functional custom controls. One of the free custom controls, MSGHOOK.VBX, makes it possible to intercept Windows messages sent to any control. A number of How-Tos in the *Visual Basic How-To Second Edition* show you how to use the MSGHOOK control to read low-level MIDI messages, create "hot-spots" on forms, recieve command completion messages from the Windows Multimedia services, add prompt messages to your menus, and more. TOOLBUTN.VBX provides a control that you can use to create button-bars for your applications. There are also controls that display GIF files and provide access to the Open and Save As Common Dialogs.

### The Fractal DLL

A chapter on Windows DLLs shows how to interface Visual Basic to a custom-made Fractal DLL that is written in C++ and supplied with the book. You'll see how to translate the parameters required by a Windows DLL into Visual Basic Declare statements. Finally, an exhaustive appendix explains Microsoft's WINAPI.TXT Declare file for using Windows APIs. The file is also included on the disk so you can merge it into your programs.

### Expected Level of Reader

No, you don't need to be a genius to use this book. It's really designed for all levels of readers—beginner, intermediate, and advanced. What we have done is give each question and its solution a heading that indicates what the "complexity" level is. If you are just starting out with Visual Basic you can use the beginning How-Tos. These almost exclusively use pure Visual Basic code. If you are somewhat experienced in Basic, you can jump to the intermediate level How-Tos which push the use of Basic and in a few cases use simple APIs. If you are experienced in Visual Basic or C and really want to stretch the code, you should check out the advanced level complexity How-Tos. These almost exclusively use APIs and tricks to do their magic.

## What You Need to Use This Book

In order to use this book you will need a computer capable of running Windows 3.1 and Visual Basic 2.0 or 3.0 (3.0 is preferred), we recommend a VGA display. You should have a mouse hooked up as well. And you probably should get a copy of *The Waite Group's Visual Basic Super Bible* which provides a comprehensive reference to Visual Basic that goes way beyond the manuals.

## How This Book Is Organized

The book is divided into 11 chapters and 4 appendices as follows:

### Chapter 1 Forms

You will probably want to include the techniques in this chapter to make sure your form is centered automatically, and that its controls are adjusted automatically when the form is resized. You'll also learn to ensure that your program's settings, size, and location are saved when you exit the program and restored when you reopen it. This chapter demonstrates ways to attract user attention by flashing the title bar of a form, displaying a hidden or minimized form, and a very cool way of starting your applications with an animated "exploding" look. You will also learn two different ways to secure your programs from unwanted eyes: one to prevent typed text from appearing on the screen, and a method of locking a window or a file so the user needs to enter a password to access it.

### Chapter 2 Controls

This chapter, Controls, reveals little-known secrets of Visual Basic controls by using several powerful Windows APIs. A firm footing is provided in SendMessage, one of the most powerful APIs which allows you to exploit many control properties not found in Visual Basic. One of the projects in Chapter 2, FORMSIZE.MAK, shows you how to use the MSGHOOK control to intercept Windows messages sent to forms. You'll learn how to make a custom check box that uses real checks instead of little Xs, how to add controls at run time, and how to make a file dialog box using APIs. A powerful API-based text editor will be created that allows cut, copy, and paste to the clipboard, as well as a searching list box using APIs. There is a How-To that shows how to make a button with continuous events. And there is a How-To that shows you how to use the TOOLBUTN custom control. Another shows how to set up old-fashioned file dialog boxes that have the directories listed together with the drives.

### Chapter 3 Text and Scrolling

This chapter presents a number of different techniques for scrolling text and graphics using Windows APIs and native Visual Basic code. You'll find How-Tos that scroll when Visual Basic's AutoRedraw property is either enabled or disabled, line-by-line scrolling or "crawl" scrolling like you see in movie credits, and how to accomplish those effects with scroll bars or command buttons. You'll find out how to align text horizontally and vertically, instead of simply left-aligned, and how to create a README file viewer and a simple text editor that searches for text strings. You'll also see how to accept text strings limited to numbers, how to trim null characters from strings, how to modify the speed at which the cursor blinks, and how to preview screen color combinations with scroll bars. And, you'll learn some tricks you can use to make the Grid control more useful, such as editing cell contents and displaying colored text in grid cells. Along the way, we'll corral a few Windows API functions to help make text processing quick and accurate, including the very powerful SendMessage API.

### Chapter 4 Mouse and Menu

This bag-of-tricks chapter shows you how to create more powerful mouse trapping and selection capabilities and how to create more customized, useful, and attractive menus. We will use some very handy Windows APIs to extend Visual Basic's menu-making capabilities: GetMenu, GetSubMenu, GetMenuItem, ModifyMenu. We will also see the versatility of Visual Basic's timer features. Having mastered the fundamentals of the Windows menu APIs you will see how to use the MSGHOOK control to add menu prompts to the programs you write.

### Chapter 5 Graphics

This chapter provides a collection of projects that show how easy it is for Visual Basic to imitate any "look" you wish—from a modern brushed aluminum NeXT-like interface to a Macintosh-style trash can. Other projects show you how to easily draw shapes using the Shape control, create "hotspots" on forms, and play Autodesk animation files. You'll see how to fill complex polygon shapes with patterns and colors, how to draw pictures inside your iconized application, and how to build line, bar, and pie charts that work just like the charts in Excel. There is even a powerful slide show that does dissolves and other special effects for presentations. Throughout the chapter powerful APIs are used and carefully explained.

### Chapter 6 Environment and System

This chapter presents techniques for communicating with DOS, running DOS programs from Visual Basic, and determining the state of various aspects of the Windows environment. You'll learn how to use many APIs for finding the amount of available memory, the version of Windows running on your machine, the names of directories, the type of keyboard your user has, and much more. Many important APIs are covered here, including the WinExec function that lets you shell to DOS but doesn't give error messages if the program can't be found. There are also APIs for determining the class name of an application, as well as a great project that simulates the Windows SDK Spy program that gives important information on all applications running under Windows.

### Chapter 7 Peripherals: Screen, Speaker, and Serial Ports

This chapter will show you how to get Visual Basic to control the various hardware extensions of your PC. You will see how to figure out the color capabilities of any user's video display and printer, how to create sound effects and attach them to your programs, how to create a phone dialer that works with a modem and serial port, and how to build your own Visual Basic communications program. Visual Basic lacks the great PLAY statement that came with QuickBASIC so we'll show you a way to simulate PLAY's complete macro language to play music. Many of the familiar hardware-addressing commands of QuickBASIC or DOS have been left out of Visual Basic. This is because Visual Basic programs are written to run in the Windows multitasking environment, where all hardware interrupts must be processed and parceled out by Windows. This chapter will also show you how to use the Media Control Interface's Command String Interface to play multimedia files such as Wave and MIDI files. Another project will show you how to record low-level MIDI messages using the MSGHOOK custom control. This chapter takes full advantage of a number of Windows APIs to manipulate computer peripherals.

### Chapter 8 The Professional Toolkit

Visual Basic 2.0 Professional Edition introduced a number of new custom controls. Many of the new controls, such as Print and Printer Setup, and File Open and Save As dialogs, are so useful that you will want to use them in almost every program you write. Chapter 8 shows you can easily use the new controls to add standard Windows functionality to your programs. This chapter also shows you how to write a complete installation program by building on the basic tools that are provided with the Professional Edition.

### Chapter 9 Using Visual Basic with DLLs

One of the most powerful aspects of Visual Basic is its ability to use custom dynamic link libraries (DLLs) that greatly extend the power of what you can do. This chapter will show you how to take a DLL written in another language, such as C, and get it working for Visual Basic. It will also point out the advantages of DLLs, how they can be used as black boxes, and the power of Visual Basic to serve as an interface that is completely independent of the DLLs' operation (adaptive programming). In addition you'll learn how to convert between Visual Basic's data types and the data types found in the C language and the extended data types in Windows.

### Chapter 10 Database Controls

Visual Basic 3.0 provides an incredibly powerful set of Database Controls. Using the Database Controls that come with the Standard & Pro Editions of Visual Basic 3.0 you can easily write complete database applications. In Chapter 10 you will learn how to use the standard Database Controls to store and retrieve data. And, perhaps most importantly, you will learn how to extend the functionality of Visual Basic 3.0's Data Controls by linking them to Picture boxes, Option buttons, and other standard controls.

### Chapter 11 Professional Edition Data Access

Using the Professional Edition of Visual Basic 3.0 you can create new databases, add and delete rows and tables from an existing database, and add and modify fields in tables. The projects in this chapter demonstrate how to use the Professional Edition features to do all this and more.

### Appendix A The Annotated Windows API Text Files

Throughout the book, How-To solutions draw on Windows API functions to accomplish tasks that are not built into Visual Basic. Before your Visual Basic program can use a Windows API, the function's parameters, their specific order, and type must be declared in your program. Microsoft supplies files that provide all the information you need to use these APIs but they are cryptic. Appendix A provides explanations about these files to help you more easily use the API functions.

### Appendix B The Visual Basic How-To Disk

The Visual Basic How-To Disk's setup program creates a number of directories on your hard disk. This appendix details the directories and files that will be created on your hard disk during installation.

### Appendix C ANSI Table

This appendix provides a listing of the ANSI characters and their decimal equivalents.

### Appendix D ASCII Table

This appendix provides a list of all IBM-PC ASCII characters, their hexidecimal, decimal, and key equivalents.

# INSTALLATION

## What's on the Disk

The disk bundled with *Visual Basic How-To Second Edition* includes every form, module, control, icon, bitmap, and sound detailed in these pages. All of these files are debugged and ready to run. The disk also includes many powerful add-ons to energize your Visual Basic programs. You'll find the Fractal DLL mentioned in Chapter 9 and the WINAPI.TXT file mentioned throughout the book and detailed in Appendix A. We have also provided a number of free fully functional custom controls. All told, you'll find over a megabyte of Visual Basic code and add-ons on this disk.

## How to Install the Bundled Disk

> Note: Before installing the bundled disk please be sure to read the README.1ST file which you will find in the root directory of the disk. Any last minute changes or advice will be contained in the README.1ST file.

You will need a hard disk with at least 3.5 megabytes free to install all of the files on the bundled disk. You will also need a 3.5" drive to read the bundled disk. In the following directions, we will assume that your PC is configured so that your hard disk is the C: drive and your 3.5" floppy drive is labeled B:. Substitute the correct parameters for your machine, for instance you may have a partitioned hard drive and want to copy these files to drive D:, or your 3.5" drive may be drive A:.

**Figure I-1** Installation directory selection

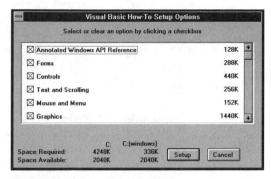

**Figure I-2** Installation options

Use the Windows File Manager's File Run... menu to run A:\SETUP.EXE. After Setup initializes you will see a window like that shown in Figure I-1. You can select the default installation directory by clicking on Continue, or you can modify the installation directory and then click on Continue. After you have clicked on the Continue button you will see a window like that shown in Figure I-2.

This form allows you to select which How-Tos you would like to install. Sections that are checked will be installed when Setup continues. It is not necessary to install every section you want to use at first. You can always run Setup later to install sections not previously installed.

### Navigational Notes

All files have been tested so that they run from the default installation directory. If you use another directory, or copy the files to another disk, you may have to re-link a few of the projects for them to run, and change any hardcoded paths. This is especially true for projects that use the VBHOWTO.BAS file (located in the root directory of the floppy disk) or those that call FILEDLG.FRM. If, when running certain projects, you get a PATH NOT FOUND: message, click the OK button. Then go to Visual Basic's File menu and select the Add File… option. Point to the file in its new location, and double-click. Remember to resave the project after you've re-linked it.

Because actual path names will vary depending upon your hard disk setup, we have intentionally avoided providing path names in each How-To when we tell you to run a project. When you open a project from Visual Basic you will have to navigate to the subdirectory that holds its files.

## Program Note

We have used the $\Leftarrow$ character to indicate program lines that "overflow" onto more than one line in this book. The overflow character means that you should continue to type that line on one Visual Basic line. Do not type the $\Leftarrow$ symbol or a carriage return.

## Windows NT Note

Visual Basic 3.0 programs are not guaranteed to run under Windows NT.

# ● TABLE OF CONTENTS

# TABLE OF CONTENTS

# 1

# FORMS

# How do I...

Forms are the most fundamental building blocks of Visual Basic—it is impossible to program in Visual Basic without a working knowledge of them. Forms hold control buttons, list boxes, picture boxes, and menu bars; they are the multifaceted containers that make Visual Basic programs possible. The tricks and techniques in this chapter are fundamental but versatile. You will probably want to include these techniques in your programs to make sure your form is centered automatically, and that its controls are adjusted automatically when the form is resized. You'll also learn to ensure that your program's settings, size, and location are saved when you exit the program and restored when you reopen it. This chapter demonstrates ways to attract user attention by flashing the title bar of a form, displaying a hidden or minimized form, and a very cool way of starting your applications with an animated "exploding" look. You will also learn two different ways to secure your programs from unwanted eyes: one to prevent typed text from appearing on the screen, and a method of locking a window or a file so the user needs to enter a password to access it.

Although many of these How-Tos are accomplished with surprisingly few lines of code, this chapter relies heavily on the use of Windows APIs including GetWindowRect, GetWindowLong, ShowWindow, SetWindowLong, and the unbelievably versatile SendMessage.

## Windows APIs Covered

| | | |
|---|---|---|
| BringWindowToTop | GetProfileInt | SendMessage |
| CreateSolidBrush | GetProfileString | SetBkColor |
| DeleteObject | GetWindowRect | SetSysModalWindow |
| FlashWindow | GetWindowLong | SetWindowLong |
| GetDC | Rectangle | ShowWindow |
| GetFocus | Release DC | WritePrivateProfileString |
| GetPrivateProfileInt | SelectObject | WriteProfileString |
| GetPrivateProfileString | | |

### 1.1 Automatically center a form on the screen

It is easy to manually center a form on the screen. But how can you tell if your program's user has a different video resolution from the one you designed in, and automatically center your form accordingly? This very simple How-To checks the form's WindowState property, finds out the height and width of the screen, and divides by two. What could be more simple?

### 1.2 Size a form's controls automatically

Windows users have become accustomed to resizing forms on their screen. A professional-looking program will resize the form's controls proportionately on the fly when the form is stretched or reduced. This simple subroutine builds on the How-To in Chapter 3 that sets up a README file reader. It uses the Visual Basic ScaleWidth and ScaleHeight properties to figure out the size of the form and scale its controls.

**1.3**     **Save program settings to a file**

Sometimes you may want to save your program's settings, like a serial number, to a file so that these settings are restored the next time the file is opened. This How-To uses a number of Windows APIs to take care of the "dirty work" of reading and writing data to an .INI file: GetPrivateProfileInt, GetPrivateProfileString, GetProfileInt, GetProfileString, WritePrivateProfileString, and WriteProfileString. In this case, you'll learn how to write your program's settings to the general WIN.INI file.

**1.4**     **Remember the sizes and locations of my forms**

This How-To builds on the previous one to show you how to write additional characteristics of your form to an .INI file. Again we use APIs, in this case GetProfileString and WriteProfileString, but this time we ascertain the size and position of your form's window on the screen. We use Visual Basic's form properties, Left, Top, Width, and Height.

**1.5**     **Flash the title bar of my forms**

A common way to attract a user's attention is to use the PC's speaker to utter a beep, which can eventually become annoying. But there is a more subtle and professional way to draw attention to your form—flash its title bar. By attaching a Windows API, FlashWindow, to Visual Basic's timer event subroutine, you switch back and forth between the title bar's active and inactive colors. This How-To also works on minimized icons.

**1.6**     **Display a hidden form**

Sometimes a form will require attention even if its window is minimized or covered by another application. Two Windows API functions, ShowWindow and BringWindowToTop, can display a hidden window under program control. A Timer event will also make the hidden window visible but not active.

**1.7**     **Start my applications with an animated look**

Have you ever noticed the way Macintosh applications "explode" open when they start up? Essentially, they display a quick succession of gradually increasing zoomboxes before showing the opening window of an application. It is a challenge to duplicate this effect in Visual Basic because the language limits you to drawing objects only on the form itself. This clever How-To uses a number of Windows APIs: GetWindowRect, GetDC, ReleaseDC, SetBkColor, Rectangle, CreateSolidBrush, SelectObject, and DeleteObject to animate a series of expanding boxes on the desktop behind your application. The crucial subroutine in this How-To is written as a separate module so it can be plugged into your other Visual Basic projects.

### 1.8   Prevent text typed in a text box from appearing on the screen

There may be times when you want to shield user input from curious eyes. Perhaps you want to write a telecommunications program that requests a user's password. You could use Visual Basic's KeyPress event to trap keystrokes but there is a more sophisticated and powerful technique using Windows APIs. This How-To uses GetFocus, GetWindowLong, SetWindowLong, and SendMessage to allow Windows to intercept and pass messages. When the user types a text character, a tilde (~) appears in the text box.

### 1.9   Prevent user access to a window or file

Sometimes you may desire more security for your applications than just shielding user input from public view. There may be instances when you want to prevent access to a specific file or window; perhaps you want to create a confidential spreadsheet or document. This intermediate-level How-To uses the APIs we explored in the previous How-To, as well as SetSysModalWindow, to lock a window. This window will not get focus until a user types in the correct password. As an extra precaution, users are only allowed three attempts to type in the password.

### 1.10   Create an MDI-style GIF file viewer

MDI (Multiple-Document Interface) style applications have a main window within which child windows can be created. This How-To shows you everything you need to know to create professional looking MDI style applications. For graphics buffs this How-To uses the Waite Group's free custom control GifBox to load GIF files into the client windows.

## 1.1 ● How do I...                    Complexity: Easy

# Automatically center a form on the screen?

### Problem

How can I automatically center my application's form on the screen? I can manually do it when I design the form, but if a user has a different type of screen than I do, the measurements will be off. What can I do?

### Technique

Remember that one can never assume, in Windows, a computer's configuration—especially the type of video display. You must respect Windows' device independence. (Your Visual Basic application can run on any machine that runs Windows, whether it has a CGA, EGA, VGA, or a display with even more colors and higher resolution. Windows manages all the hardware details for you.) Visual Basic provides plenty of statements that you can use to address aspects of the hardware (such as the screen size) in a device-independent way. Because we can find out the height and width of the screen and of a form, we can simply divide by two to center the form.

### Steps

Open and run AUTOPOS.MAK. There are no controls on the form, but when it loads, it automatically positions itself in the center of the screen. The form isn't locked in the center (you can move the form), but if you resize it, it automatically moves back to the center.

1. Create a new project called AUTOPOS.MAK. Create a new form with no controls. Save it as AUTOPOS.FRM.

2. Place the following code in the Form_Resize event subroutine. The Form_Resize event subroutine ensures that the form is neither minimized nor maximized by checking the form's WindowState property and if it isn't, moves the form to the center of the screen.

```
Sub Form_Resize ()
    If WindowState = 0 Then
        ' don't attempt if form is minimized or maximized
        Move (Screen.Width - Form1.Width) / 2, (Screen.Height  - ⇐
        Form1.Height) / 2
    End If
End Sub
```

### How It Works

The Form_Resize event subroutine checks whether the form is normal—not minimized and not maximized. Minimized forms can't be moved because they're just icons. Maximized forms can't be moved because they already take up the whole screen.

The Move statement does the magic. Subtracting the width of the form from the total screen width gives us the total amount of space on either side of the form. Dividing that by two gives us the same amount of space on either side of the form, horizontally centering it. The same calculations for height can be performed to center the form vertically.

### Comments

Putting the calculations in the Form_Resize event subroutine will recenter the form whenever the form is resized. If you want to center the form only when you first run the application, just put the calculations in the Form_Load event subroutine.

## 1.2  How do I...

## Size a form's controls automatically?

### Problem

Window users want to be able to resize forms and have the controls on those forms shrink or stretch proportionately. Windows PaintBrush works this way. For example, if I expand a form, I'd like my list boxes to take advantage of the increased space available. However, when I resize the form, its controls are "clipped."

### Technique

This resizing is easy to accomplish because a control's properties can be changed on the fly. We can easily query a form's controls to find out its current properties, so all we have to do then to resize a list box is query a form's width and height, then set the list box's matching properties proportionately.

### Steps

Open and run AUTOSIZE.MAK. Scroll bars let you view the entire README file. When you resize a form, the list box resizes right along with it.

1. Create the FileView project as discussed in How-To 3.6. Set up a README file reader, and re-save it as AUTOSIZE.MAK. Then add the following code in the Resize event subroutine of the form object.

```
Sub Form_Resize ()
    List1.Width = ScaleWidth - List1.Left
    List1.Height = ScaleHeight - List1.Top
End Sub
```

### How It Works

The Form_Resize subroutine does all the extra work of resizing the list box. Line 2 of the subroutine sets the Width property of the list box based on the ScaleWidth property of the form, and the current Left property of the list box. This keeps the list box at the current horizontal position but lets it grow toward the right. We used the ScaleWidth property because we want to resize the list box based on the internal width of the form. Line 3 sets the Height property of the list box based on the ScaleHeight property of the form and the current Top property of the list box. This keeps the list box at the current vertical position but lets it grow downward. Again, we use the ScaleHeight property to measure the interior height of the form.

### Comments

The procedure we just outlined assumes that the list box is the "last" control on the form; in other words, there are no controls below or to the right of the list box. If the list box is not the last control, the list box will cover up those other controls.

When the list box resizes itself, the entries in the list box automatically reformat to fit the new size.

## 1.3 ⬤ How do I...

Complexity: Easy

## Save program settings to a file?

### Problem

I want to save some program settings, such as serial numbers and colors, in a file that will read them back the next time I run my application. How can I do this?

### Technique

Many Windows applications save information like serial numbers or window colors in a file and just read them in when the program starts. Have you ever noticed all the files in your Windows directory that have .INI extensions? That's where Windows applications store those kinds of settings. Windows provides the following API functions to do the dirty work of reading and writing those .INI files for you:

- ⬤ GetPrivateProfileInt

- ⬤ GetPrivateProfileString

- GetProfileInt
- GetProfileString
- WritePrivateProfileString
- WriteProfileString

### Steps

Open and run PROFILE1.MAK. The first time you run Profile1, the serial number is 1. You can enter a new serial number, then click on Ok. The new serial number is written to the WIN.INI file and the next time you run Profile1, the new serial number will appear in the text box. If you click on Cancel, nothing is written in the WIN.INI file. Figure 1-1 shows the complete form.

1. Create a new project called PROFILE1.MAK. Create a new form with the properties listed in Table 1-1 and save it as PROFILE.FRM.

| Object | Property | Setting |
|---|---|---|
| Form | Caption | Serial number |
| Label | Caption | Serial number |
| Text box | Name | SerialNumber |
| | Text | <blank> |
| Command button | Name | Ok |
| | Caption | Ok |
| | Default | True |
| Command button | Name | Cancel |
| | Caption | Cancel |
| | Cancel | True |

**Table 1-1** Profile1 project form's objects and properties

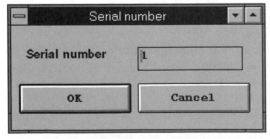

**Figure 1-1** Profile1 form at run time

2. Put the following code in the Declarations section of the form. This code defines some constants for use with the API functions that are declared.

```
Const APPNAME$ = "Profile1"
Const KEYNAME$ = "SerialNumber"

Declare Function GetProfileInt Lib "Kernel" (ByVal lpAppName$, ByVal ⇐
lpKeyName$, ByVal nDefault%) As Integer
Declare Function WriteProfileString Lib "Kernel" (ByVal ⇐
lpApplicationName$, ByVal lpKeyName$, ByVal lpString$) As Integer
```

3. Put the following statement in the Load event subroutine of the form. This statement calls the GetProfileInt API function to read the WIN.INI file and get the serial number currently there. If there is none, the value 1 will be returned.

```
Sub Form_Load ()
    SerialNumber.Text = Mid$(Str$(GetProfileInt(APPNAME$, KEYNAME$, 1)), 2)
End Sub
```

4. Put the following code in the Click event subroutine of the Ok button. This code calls the WriteProfileString API function to write the serial number to WIN.INI. If there is an error, a message box is popped up.

```
Sub OK_Click ()
    SerialNum$ = SerialNumber.Text
    If WriteProfileString(APPNAME$, KEYNAME$, SerialNum$) = 0 Then
        MsgBox "Unable to write profile string", 48, APPNAME$
    End If
    End
End Sub
```

5. Put the following code in the Cancel button's Click event subroutine.

```
Sub Cancel_Click ()
    End
End Sub
```

### How It Works

Luckily, Windows API functions actually do most of the work including reading and writing the WIN.INI file. The Declare Sub statements in the Declarations section give Visual Basic access to the Windows API function DLLs (Dynamic Link Libraries).

The form load event subroutine uses GetProfileInt to retrieve an integer from the WIN.INI file. We then write the string representation of that number into the text box.

The Ok button click event subroutine takes the text and, using WriteProfileString, writes it to the WIN.INI file. If there's a problem, we pop up a message box. Otherwise, we just end the program.

## Comments

Here we're just using the integer versions of the Windows API functions; there are also API functions to read and write strings. You might also want to record the user's name along with the serial number.

The Windows API functions with "Private" in their name read and write data from individual (private) .INI files, rather than from WIN.INI. Using private .INI files is faster than using WIN.INI. Also, because you must give Windows the path name of your private .INIs, they are especially useful on a network. Each user of your application can store his settings in a private .INI file on a local disk. That way, one user's settings won't overwrite all others'.

## 1.4 ● How do I...

**Complexity: Easy**

# Remember the sizes and locations of my forms?

## Problem

My application calls for using multiple forms that users will move around on the screen. I'd like it so when the users quit and then restart the applications the forms appear where they were last.

## Technique

Some Windows applications are "smart" and save and remember the current size and position of their windows. It's easy for you to do the same, using some of Visual Basic's own property keywords.

As mentioned in the previous How-To, Windows supports .INI files—files that store settings on disk so users don't have to enter those settings every time they run an application. One .INI file—WIN.INI—is the "master" .INI file that Windows itself uses to store certain settings, like the type and configuration of your printers. We'll use some Windows API calls to write the size and position of a form to WIN.INI.

## Steps

Open and run PROFILE2.MAK. When you close the window, the size and position of the window will be written to WIN.INI under the section titled [Profile2]. Then, whenever you run Profile2, the window will be sized and positioned to the window's size and position the last time it was closed, as shown in Figure 1-2.

1. Create a new project called PROFILE2.MAK. Create a new form and give it a label and a command button captioned Exit!. Save it as PROFILE2.FRM.

**Figure 1-2** Profile2 form

Put the following code in the Declarations section of the form:

```
Const APPNAME$ = "Profile2"

Declare Function GetProfileString Lib "Kernel" (ByVal lpAppName$, ByVal ⇐
lpKeyName$, ByVal lpDefault$, ByVal lpReturnedString$, ByVal nSize%) ⇐
As Integer
Declare Function WriteProfileString Lib "Kernel" (ByVal
lpApplicationName$, ByVal lpKeyName$, ByVal lpString$) As Integer

Dim iLeft As Single     ' Horizontal size
Dim iTop As Single      ' Vertical size
Dim iHeight As Single   ' Height
Dim iWidth As Single    ' Width
```

2. Put the following code in the Load event subroutine of the form.

```
Sub Form_Load ()
   Temp$ = String$(16, 0)
   i = GetProfileString(APPNAME$, "Left", "1000", Temp$, 16)
   Left = Val(Temp$)

   Temp$ = String$(16, 0)
   i = GetProfileString(APPNAME$, "Top", "1000", Temp$, 16)
   Top = Val(Temp$)

   Temp$ = String$(16, 0)
   i = GetProfileString(APPNAME$, "Width", "1000", Temp$, 16)
   Width = Val(Temp$)

   Temp$ = String$(16, 0)
   i = GetProfileString(APPNAME$, "Height", "1000", Temp$, 16)
   Height = Val(Temp$)
End Sub
```

3. Put the following code in the Unload event subroutine of the form.

```
Sub Form_Unload (Cancel As Integer)
   i = WriteProfileString(APPNAME$, "Left", Str$(iLeft))
   i = WriteProfileString(APPNAME$, "Top", Str$(iTop))
   i = WriteProfileString(APPNAME$, "Width", Str$(iWidth))
   i = WriteProfileString(APPNAME$, "Height", Str$(iHeight))
End Sub
```

4. Put the following code fragment in the Paint event subroutine of the form.

```
Sub Form_Paint ()
   iLeft = Left
   iTop = Top
   iWidth = Width
   iHeight = Height
   Label1.Caption = "Form is" + Str$(iWidth) + "x" + Mid$(Str$(iHeight),⇐
2) + " at" + Str$(iLeft) + "x" + Mid$(Str$(iTop), 2)
End Sub
```

### How It Works

The Windows API functions actually do most of the work for us. The De-clare Sub statements in the Declarations section are very important: They give Visual Basic access to the Windows API function DLLs.

Visual Basic's form properties Left, Top, Width, and Height do all the sizing and positioning for us. We use them in the Paint event subroutine to get the size and position of the form. They are saved to the WIN.INI file in the Unload event subroutine, and reset the size and position of the form in the Load event subroutine.

### Comments

You might want to save other window properties also. Check the WindowState property to save the maximized or minimized property of a window, for example.

## 1.5 ● How do I...

## Flash the title bar of my forms?

### Problem

How can I visually attract my users' attention instead of using some annoy-ing bleeping sound from Windows?

### Technique

Windows provides an API function called, appropriately enough, FlashWindow to briefly flash the title bar of a window. You can key FlashWindow to a timer event subroutine to make a form flash at regular intervals.

### Steps

Open and run FLASH.MAK. The form's title bar will start flashing rapidly. You can stop it from flashing by clicking the Flash checkbox. Figure 1-3 shows the completed Flash form.

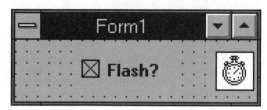

**Figure 1-3** The completed Flash form at design time

1. Create a new project called FLASH.MAK. Create a form with the objects and properties shown in Table 1-2 and save it as FLASH.FRM.

| Object | Property | Setting |
|--------|----------|---------|
| Timer | Name | Timer1 |
| | Enabled | True |
| | Interval | 250 |
| Check box | Name | Check1 |
| | Value | 1 - Checked |
| | Caption | Flash? |

**Table 1-2** Flash project form's objects and properties

2. Put the following code in the Declarations section of the form. This Declare statement lets the program access the FlashWindow Windows API function.

```
Declare Function FlashWindow Lib "User" (ByVal hWnd%, ByVal bInvert%) As ⇐
Integer
```

3. Put the following code in the Check1_Click event subroutine. This code disables the timer that flashes the title bar if the check box isn't clicked.

```
Sub Check1_Click ()
   If Check1.Value = 0 Then
      Timer1.Enabled = 0
      I = FlashWindow(Form1.hWnd, 0)
   Else
      Timer1.Enabled = -1
   End If
End Sub
```

4. Put the following code in the Timer1_Timer event subroutine. This call to the FlashWindow API function flashes the title bar every time the timer goes off (every 250 milliseconds) if the check box is clicked.

```
Sub Timer1_Timer ()
    I = FlashWindow(Form1.hWnd, 1)
End Sub
```

### How It Works

The FlashWindow API function "flashes" the title bar by switching back and forth between the inactive title bar colors and the active title bar colors. It acts just as if you'd clicked the mouse cursor on another window (which makes your form inactive) and then clicked again on your form (which makes it active).

FlashWindow takes just two arguments: a window handle and a flag called bInvert. The window handle is provided by the hWnd property of the form. If the bInvert flag is nonzero, FlashWindow flashes the title bar to the opposite it is at the time of the call (active <-> inactive). If the bInvert flag is zero, FlashWindow returns the form to its original state, active.

In the Check1_Click event subroutine, a call to FlashWindow with bInvert 0 makes the form active again. This code disables the timer, if the Check Box has not been clicked, and prevents the form from flashing.

The Timer1_Timer event subroutine calls FlashWindow with bInvert nonzero (1), which inverts the title bar mode. Since the timer is enabled, the next time the timer interval is activated, the title bar will be re-inverted.

### Comments

FlashWindow also works when the form is minimized to an icon, except that instead of the title bar flashing (which the icon doesn't really have), the whole icon flashes. You must restore the icon to a window before you can click on the form to stop it.

## 1.6  How do I...

## Display a hidden form?

### Problem

How can I let my users know that a Visual Basic form requires attention if it is minimized or covered by another application's window?

### Technique

The Windows API library has a number of functions that will force Windows to display a hidden window. This project demonstrates how a previously hidden window can be displayed under program control.

**Figure 1-4** Topwin form at design time

### Steps

Open and run TOPWIN.MAK. It will look like Figure 1-4. The form will move itself to the lower right-hand corner of the screen and display the current time. If you hide it by running another Windows application, Topwin will pop through to the top. To exit the application, click anywhere on the form. To create the Topwin project, enter the objects and code in the following steps.

1. Create a new project called TOPWIN.MAK. Enter the following constants and Windows API declarations into the Global module and save it as TOPWIN.BAS.

```
Global Const SW_SHOWNA = 8

Declare Sub BringWindowToTop Lib "User" (ByVal hWnd As Integer)
Declare Sub ShowWindow Lib "User" (ByVal hWnd As Integer, ByVal nCmdShow ⇐
As Integer)
```

2. Create a new form with the objects and properties shown in Table 1-3. Save it as TOPWIN.FRM.

| Object | Property | Setting |
|--------|----------|---------|
| Form | FormName | Topwin |
| | Caption | Make Top Window |
| Timer | Name | Timer1 |
| | Enabled | True |
| | Interval | 1000 |
| Label | Name | Label1 |
| | Caption | xx:xx:xx xx |

**Table 1-3** Topwin project form's objects and properties

3. Put the following code in the Form_Load event subroutine.

```
Sub Form_Load ()
' Make Label1 fill entire form.
```

*continued on next page*

*continued from previous page*

```
    Label1.Top = 0
    Label1.Left = 0
    Label1.Width = Scalewidth
    Label1.Height = Scaleheight

' Position form in lower right corner of screen.
    Topwin.Top = Screen.Height - Topwin.Height
    Topwin.Left = Screen.Width - Topwin.Width

' Set up crosshair mouse.
    Topwin.MousePointer = 2
End Sub
```

4. Put the following code in the Timer1_Timer event subroutine. On each timer event, this subroutine will make the form visible and display the current time in the Label1 control. The ShowWindow API call makes the form visible but not active. That is, the currently running application will function normally. The WindowState is set to zero to restore the form to its default size from a minimized or maximized state.

```
Sub Timer1_Timer ()
    ShowWindow Topwin.hwnd, SW_SHOWNA
    Windowstate = 0
    Label1.Caption = Time$
End Sub
```

5. Put the following code in the Label1_Click event subroutine. By clicking the mouse anywhere in the Label1 control, the user can exit the application.

```
Sub Label1_Click ()
    End
End Sub
```

### Comments

The ShowWindow API call displays the specified window but doesn't make it active. To activate the window, simply click on the form's title bar. The BringWindowToTop API call both displays the window and activates it in one step. The declaration for this function is included in the Global module code of Step 1.

You may want to set Topwin's BorderStyle to 0 (None), so that it will take up as little space on the screen as possible.

The form's MousePointer is set to a crosshair as a further indication of when the form is active.

## 1.7  How do I...

## Start my applications with an animated look?

### Problem

I would like to give my forms an "exploding" look when they are first displayed. How can I do this in Visual Basic?

### Technique

You can make your forms appear to expand at startup by displaying a series of expanding boxes behind each form. This will lend an animated feel to your application's startup. The expanding boxes are displayed with code placed in the form's Load event subroutine. This event is called by Visual Basic before the form is first made visible. The boxes are drawn using the Windows API functions since the Visual Basic methods can only draw objects on the form itself.

### Steps

Open and run EXPLODE.MAK. Notice how the window grows until it becomes full-sized, as shown in Figure 1-5. Clicking on the From Center command button will "explode" the form in all directions from its center. Clicking on the From Corner command button will "explode" it from the upper left-hand corner.

The project may be created by entering the objects and code as detailed in the following steps.

1. Create a new project called EXPLODE.MAK. Create a new form with the objects and properties listed in Table 1-4. Save it as EXPLODE.FRM.

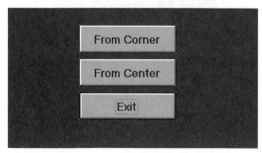

**Figure 1-5** The Explode project as a full-sized window

2. Place the following declarations in the Global module and save it as EXPLODE.BAS.

```
Type RECT
    Left As Integer
    Top As Integer
    Right As Integer
    Bottom As Integer
End Type
```

| Object | Property | Setting |
|---|---|---|
| Form | FormName | Explode |
| | BackColor | &HC0& |
| | BorderStyle | 0 - None |
| Command button | Name | CmdExit |
| | Caption | Exit |
| | FontSize | 12 |
| Command button | Name | CmdCenter |
| | Caption | From Center |
| | FontSize | 12 |
| Command button | Name | CmdCorner |
| | Caption | From Corner |
| | FontSize | 12 |

**Table 1-4** Explode project form's objects and properties

3. Place the following declaration in the Declarations section of the form.

```
Const FALSE = 0
Const TRUE = -1
'
'  Form global flag to expand from corner (false) or
'  center (true).

Dim CenterFlag As Integer
```

4. Place the following code in the CmdExit_Click event subroutine. This command button allows the user to exit gracefully from the application.

```
Sub CmdExit_Click ()
    End
End Sub
```

5. Put the following code in the Form_Load event subroutine to "explode" the form when the application is started.

```
Sub Form_Load ()
   ExplodeForm Explode, CenterFlag
End Sub
```

6. Place the following code in the CmdCenter_Click event subroutine. Setting the CenterFlag variable to True will cause the window to grow from its center.

```
Sub CmdCenter_Click ()
'
' User clicked on from center button, set flag.
' Unload and then load form to trigger Load event.
   CenterFlag = TRUE
   Unload Explode
   Load Explode               ' Simulate startup
End Sub
```

7. Put the following code in the CmdCorner_Click event subroutine. Setting the CenterFlag variable to False will cause the form to expand from its top left corner.

```
Sub CmdCorner_Click ()
'
' User clicked on from corner button, set flag.
' Unload and then load form to trigger Load event.
   CenterFlag = FALSE
   Unload Explode
   Load Explode
End Sub
```

8. Open a new module for this project, using the New Module option from the File menu. This module has the code which gives the form its exploding look at startup. Put the following API declarations into the General section of the module and save the module as EXPLODIT.BAS.

```
Declare Sub GetWindowRect Lib "User" (ByVal hWnd As Integer, lpRect As RECT)
Declare Function GetDC Lib "User" (ByVal hWnd As Integer) As Integer
Declare Function ReleaseDC Lib "User" (ByVal hWnd As Integer, ByVal hDC ⇐
As Integer) As Integer
Declare Sub SetBkColor Lib "GDI" (ByVal hDC As Integer, ByVal crColor As Long)
Declare Sub Rectangle Lib "GDI" (ByVal hDC As Integer, ByVal X1 As ⇐
Integer, ByVal Y1 As Integer, ByVal X2 As Integer, ByVal Y2 As Integer)
Declare Function CreateSolidBrush Lib "GDI" (ByVal crColor As Long) As ⇐
Integer
Declare Function SelectObject Lib "GDI" (ByVal hDC As Integer, ByVal ⇐
hObject As Integer) As Integer
Declare Sub DeleteObject Lib "GDI" (ByVal hObject As Integer)
```

9. Put the following code in the ExplodeForm subroutine of the EXPLODIT.BAS module. This subroutine does the animated drawing on the screen.

```
Sub ExplodeForm (F As Form, CenterFlag As Integer)
Const STEPS = 75
Const TRUE = -1
Dim FRect As RECT
Dim FullWidth As Integer, FullHeight As Integer
Dim I As Integer
Dim X As Integer, Y As Integer, Cx As Integer, Cy As Integer
Dim hDCScreen As Integer, hBrush As Integer, hOldBrush

' If CenterFlag = True, then explode from center of form, otherwise
' explode from upper left corner.
'

' Get current window position (in pixels) and compute width & height.

   GetWindowRect F.hWnd, FRect
   FullWidth = (FRect.Right - FRect.Left)
   FullHeight = FRect.Bottom - FRect.Top

' Get a device context for the whole screen.
' Create brush with Form's background color.
' Select the brush into the device context.

   hDCScreen = GetDC(0)
   hBrush = CreateSolidBrush(F.BackColor)
   hOldBrush = SelectObject(hDCScreen, hBrush)

' Draw rectangles in larger sizes filling in the area to be occupied
' by the form.
   For I = 1 To STEPS
      Cx = FullWidth * (I / STEPS)
      Cy = FullHeight * (I / STEPS)
      If CenterFlag Then
         X = FRect.Left + (FullWidth - Cx) / 2
         Y = FRect.Top + (FullHeight - Cy) / 2
      Else
         X = FRect.Left
         Y = FRect.Top
      End If

      Rectangle hDCScreen, X, Y, X + Cx, Y + Cy

   Next I

' Release the device context and brush to free memory.
' Make the Form visible
   If ReleaseDC(0, hDCScreen) = 0 Then
      MsgBox "Unable to Release Device Context", 16
   End If
   DeleteObject (hBrush)
   F.Visible = TRUE

End Sub
```

## How It Works

The real effort in this program is performed by the ExplodeForm subroutine located in the EXPLODIT.BAS module. This subroutine was written as a separate module so that it can be included in other Visual Basic projects. ExplodeForm draws its series of expanding boxes directly onto the screen, or desktop window. It does this by bypassing the normal window management functions provided by Visual Basic and uses the Windows API directly. It is considered "bad manners" to draw in an area not owned by your application, but, since the area in which we are drawing will eventually be covered by the form itself, potential conflicts are avoided.

To draw on the desktop, we make use of the Windows API functions declared in the General section of the Explodit module. The ExplodeForm subroutine begins by determining the form's size using the GetWindowRect API call. This call loads a form's coordinates into a user-defined structure of type RECT. Each of the elements of RECT: Left, Top, Right, and Bottom, represent the screen coordinates, in pixels, of the form's corners. Because the other API calls in this subroutine use pixels for their drawing coordinates, it is easier to use the GetWindowRect call than to convert Visual Basic's standard unit of measure, twips, to pixels.

To draw a filled object such as a rectangle we must provide Windows with a device context and a brush. The device context identifies on which window the objects will be displayed and their graphics properties, such as the background color. To set a device context's background color, we first create a brush, and then tell Windows to use the brush within a specific device context. Then both the device context and brush must be deleted after use, since Windows can only store internally a limited number of these properties at one time. One of Visual Basic's strengths is that it provides all these functions and services for us when drawing on a form or picture box. However, since Visual Basic's methods cannot be used to draw directly on the desktop, we need to create and delete these items manually.

The GetDC(0) call returns a handle to a device context for the entire screen. With this device context handle, hDCScreen, the Windows API drawing functions can draw anywhere on the display. A brush is created using the API call CreateSolidBrush. Its color is set to match that of the form's background. The SelectObject API call tells Windows to associate the brush with the device context handle passed as the first parameter.

The For...Next loop draws the set of expanding boxes. The variables Cx and Cy contain the width and height, respectively, of each box. If the boxes grow from the center, then the coordinates of the upper left corner, x and y, are set according to Cx and Cy. If the boxes are drawn from the upper left corner, x and y remain fixed.

The Rectangle API function draws a rectangle on the device context passed as its first parameter. The other four parameters are the window coordinates, in pixels, of its four corners. Since the hDCScreen device context has a solid brush associated with it, the rectangles will be drawn with a filled background.

After the boxes are drawn, the device context is released using the ReleaseDC function, and the brush is deleted. If you don't perform these functions, Windows will run out of resources and eventually hang.

To make sure that the form is displayed, the form's Visible property is set to True.

The form exploded on startup as a result of the Form_Load event. When a form is initially loaded, its Form_Load event is called before the form is made visible. Trapping this event and calling the ExplodeForm subroutine lets us get control of the display before Visual Basic initially makes it visible.

The other command button event subroutines take advantage of the Form_Load event by unloading, and then loading, the Explode form. These actions cause a Form_Load event.

### Comments

If you are entering this code manually, save your code often, and be careful about releasing the hDCScreen device context and deleting the brush. Forgetting to do so will cause Windows to hang and require a system reboot.

## 1.8  How do I...

## Prevent text typed into a text box from appearing on the screen?

### Problem

When I ask my users for a password or some other confidential information, I'd like to prevent that text from appearing on the screen as users type it in. Is there some way I can do this?

### Technique

A complex way would be to trap keystrokes using the KeyPress event. Luckily, Windows text boxes can do more than Visual Basic lets them do. Windows text boxes respond to a variety of messages, most of which Visual Basic automatically sends when you use a property like SelText. However, you can access the other messages with the API function SendMessage. One of these

**Figure 1-6** The Password form in action

messages is EM_SETPASSWORDCHAR, which lets you set the character to be displayed.

### Steps

Open and run PASSWORD.MAK. It will look like Figure 1-6. Type any text into the text box. Notice that each character is echoed as a tilde (~), not the actual character that you typed. When you press (ENTER) or click on Ok, what you actually typed is displayed in a message box.

1. Create a new project called PASSWORD.MAK. Create a form with the objects and properties shown in Table 1-5 and save it as PASSWORD.FRM.

| Object | Property | Setting |
|--------|----------|---------|
| Form | Caption | Enter password |
| | FormName | PasswordForm |
| Text box | Name | Text1 |
| | Multiline | False |
| | Text | <none> |
| Command button | Caption | Ok |
| | Name | Ok |
| | Default | True |
| Command button | Caption | Cancel |
| | Cancel | True |
| | Name | Cancel |

**Table 1-5** Password project form's objects and properties

2. Put the following code in the Declarations section of the form. These Const and Declare statements are used to access the Windows API functions that let us send messages to the text box to change its styles.

```
Declare Function GetFocus Lib "User" () As Integer
Declare Function GetWindowLong Lib "User" (ByVal hWnd%, ByVal nIndex%) ⇐
As Long
Declare Function SetWindowLong Lib "User" (ByVal hWnd%, ByVal nIndex%, ⇐
ByVal dwNewLong&) As Long
Declare Function SendMessage Lib "User" (ByVal hWnd%, ByVal wMsg%, ⇐
```

*continued on next page*

*continued from previous page*
```
ByVal wParam%, ByVal lParam&) As Long

Const WM_USER = &H400
Const EM_SETPASSWORDCHAR = WM_USER + 28
Const ES_PASSWORD = &H20
Const GWL_STYLE = -16
```

3. Put the following code in the Cancel_Click event subroutine. This subroutine simply ends the program.

```
Sub Cancel_Click ()
    End
End Sub
```

4. Put the following code in the Form_Load event subroutine. This code changes the text box's styles to suppress displaying the characters as they are typed. Then the SendMessage function tells the text box to use the tilde character (~) instead.

```
Sub Form_Load ()
    Dim StyleFlags As Long  ' Window style for the control

    ' Get current style flags.
    StyleFlags = GetWindowLong(Text1.hWnd, GWL_STYLE)

    ' Set the password style.
    StyleFlags = StyleFlags Or ES_PASSWORD

    ' Change the style flags.
    StyleFlags = SetWindowLong(Text1.hWnd, GWL_STYLE, StyleFlags)

    ' Send message indicating character to print (Chr$(126)=~).
    StyleFlags = SendMessage(Text1.hWnd, EM_SETPASSWORDCHAR, 126, 0&)
End Sub
```

5. Put the following code in the Ok_Click event subroutine. This line displays the actual contents of the Text Box in a message box.

```
Sub Ok_Click ()
    MsgBox Text1.Text
End Sub
```

### How It Works

The Form_Load event subroutine manipulates Windows messages and styles to make a text box display a tilde instead of what the user actually types. Although there are quite a few steps to display multiple lines of text, remember that this is what Visual Basic is doing whenever it encounters a statement like

```
MultiLine = True
```

It's only necessary to resort to sending and processing messages if Visual Basic doesn't provide a keyword to process the text in a non-standard way of your choosing.

Windows sends messages via a window handle, so the GetFocus API function is used to get the window handle of a control.

The Windows message to tell a text box to use another character is EM_SETPASSWORDCHAR, which the WINAPI.TXT file defines as WM_USER + 28. WM_USER is defined as 0x400, or &H400 in Visual Basic hexadecimal lingo. Thus, EM_SETPASSWORDCHAR is actually &H41C.

Windows text boxes have many styles, such as multiple lines. Luckily, most of those styles are selectable by Visual Basic property keywords (such as the Multiline property). One style that Visual Basic doesn't implement is the ES_PASSWORD style, which indicates that a text box will display some character that hides what the user is really typing into the text box.

There might already be several styles applied to the text box, so a call to the GetWindowLong API function returns those styles. The GWL_STYLE constant that is passed as a parameter tells GetWindowLong that all it should return is the current styles of the text box. Visual Basic's bitwise Or operator "adds" the ES_PASSWORD style. Then a call to SetWindowLong updates the text box's styles to include the ES_PASSWORD style.

Once the text box knows a password style is being applied, the box will accept the EM_SETPASSWORDCHAR message, which tells it to change the character it will display as the user types into the text box.

### Comments

Although the Password form example uses a tilde as the password character, you can use any character you like. Asterisks [Chr$(42)] are common, as are underscores [Chr$(95)].

## 1.9 ⬤ How do I...

Complexity: Intermediate

## Prevent user access to a window or file?

### Problem

My users would like to keep their confidential information safe from "prying eyes." I'd like to be able to prevent a user from being able to switch to other windows and get into "confidential" files. Can Visual Basic help me accomplish this?

## Technique

Windows can make any window a system modal window. A system modal window is different from a normal "application modal" window in that it is the only window that is allowed to get the focus. Attempts to switch to another by clicking on it with the mouse or pressing (ALT)-(TAB) to cycle through the windows will have no effect. Even double-clicking on the desktop or pressing (CTRL)-(ESC) to bring up Windows' Task Manager will do nothing.

You can enhance the Password form from the previous How-To (Prevent text typed into a text box from appearing on the screen) to lock the window once the user has typed in a password and only unlock it when the password is typed back in. That way, your users could enter their password to lock the system when they leave for lunch, for example, and reenter the password to unlock the system when they come back.

## Steps

Open and run PASSLOCK.MAK. Be sure to save your work! Enter a password, and don't forget it! The Cancel button will be disabled, so the only way to unlock the system is to enter the correct password and press (ENTER) or click Ok.

1. Create a new project called PASSLOCK.MAK. Create a new form with the objects and properties in Table 1-6 and save it as PASSLOCK.FRM.

2. Put the following code in the Declarations section of the form. These Declare statements are used to access the Windows API functions to make the text box echo back asterisks as the user types the password, and the SetSysModalWindow function, which locks the system.

```
Declare Function GetWindowLong Lib "User" (ByVal hWnd%, ByVal nIndex%) ⇐
As Long
Declare Function SetWindowLong Lib "User" (ByVal hWnd%, ByVal nIndex%, ⇐
ByVal dwNewLong&) As Long
Declare Function SendMessage Lib "User" (ByVal hWnd%, ByVal wMsg%, ByVal ⇐
wParam%, ByVal lParam&) As Long
Declare Function SetSysModalWindow Lib "User" (ByVal hWnd%) As Integer

Const WM_USER = &H400
Const EM_SETPASSWORDCHAR = WM_USER + 28
Const ES_PASSWORD = &H20
Const GWL_STYLE = -16
```

| Object | Property | Setting |
|--------|----------|---------|
| Form | Caption | Unlocked - Enter password to lock |
|  | FormName | PasswordForm |

| Object | Property | Setting |
|--------|----------|---------|
| Text box | Name | Text1 |
| | Multiline | False |
| | Text | <none> |
| Command button | Caption | Ok |
| | Name | Ok |
| | Default | True |
| Command button | Caption | Cancel |
| | Cancel | True |
| | Name | Cancel |

**Table 1-6** PassLock project form's objects and properties

3. Put the following code in the Form_Load event subroutine. This code calls the necessary Windows API functions to set up the password text box and lock the form as the only one that can get the focus.

```
Sub Form_Load ()
   Dim StyleFlags As Long  ' Window style for the control

   ' Get current style flags.
   StyleFlags = GetWindowLong(Text1.hWnd, GWL_STYLE)

   ' Get the password style.
   StyleFlags = StyleFlags Or ES_PASSWORD

   ' Change the style flags.
   StyleFlags = SetWindowLong(Text1.hWnd, GWL_STYLE, StyleFlags)

   ' Send message indicating character to print (Chr$(42)=*).
   StyleFlags = SendMessage(Text1.hWnd, EM_SETPASSWORDCHAR, 42, 0&)

   ' Lock this form as a system modal window.
   I = SetSysModalWindow(PassLockForm.Hwnd)
End Sub
```

4. Put the following code in the Ok_Click event subroutine. This code handles it both when the system is locked and when it's unlocked. When we're locking the system, the Cancel button is disabled, so the only way to unlock the system is by entering the correct password. Also notice how the form's caption is changed to indicate the mode.

```
Sub Ok_Click ()
   Static Password$, Count

   If Password$ = "" Then
```

*continued on next page*

*continued from previous page*

```
        Password$ = Text1.Text
        Text1.Text = ""
        PassLockForm.Caption = "Locked - Enter password to unlock."
        Cancel.Enabled = 0
        Count = 0
    Else
        If Password$ = Text1.Text Then
            Password$ = ""
            Text1.Text = ""
            PassLockForm.Caption = "Unlocked - Enter password to lock."
            Cancel.Enabled = -1
        Else
            Count = Count + 1
            If Count > 3 Then
                MsgBox "Wrong password! Sorry, but you've tried too many ⇐
                    times!", 16
                Ok.Enabled = 0
                PassLockForm.Caption = "Locked - Too many mistyped passwords!"
            Else
                MsgBox "Wrong password! Try again, but remember, you" + ⇐
                    Chr$(13) + Chr$(10) + "only have" + Str$(3 - Count) + " ⇐
                    tries left!", 48
            End If
        End If
    End If
End Sub
```

5. Put the following code in the Cancel_Click event subroutine.

```
Sub Cancel_Click ()
    End
End Sub
```

### How It Works

See the previous How-To 1.8, Prevent text typed into a text box from appearing on the screen, for details on how to prevent the characters being typed into the password text box from being displayed.

The SetSysModalWindow API function locks the window whose handle (hWnd) is supplied as a parameter. The only way to unlock it is by unloading the window. The Cancel_Click event subroutine does just that by executing Visual Basic's End statement.

The Ok_Click event subroutine is where the passwords are handled. There is a Password$ variable declared with Visual Basic's Static statement. The Static statement declares variables that are local to the subroutine where they're defined, and retains their values even after the subroutine ends.

The first If statement checks whether Password$ is equal to the null string. If it is, that means that there is no password, so the system isn't locked yet. Therefore, Password$ gets the text in the text box and the Cancel button is disabled.

If there's already a password, that means the system is locked, so the second If statement compares the password that was previously entered (Password$) with what's in the text box. If they match, the system can be unlocked by re-enabling the Cancel button. If they don't match, it means someone either mistyped the password or someone is trying to break into the system. Since someone might be able to guess the password by just trying random combinations, there should be some way to prevent many random guesses. Another static local variable, Count, keeps track of how many mismatched passwords have been entered. If the user has tried fewer than three times to enter a password, a message box pops up and tells the user that only so many attempts are left. But, if more than three mismatches happen, the Ok button is disabled. The Cancel button was disabled when the password was entered, so this means there's no way to unlock the system except by rebooting it.

### Comments

Remember that a password-protected system is only as secure as the passwords. If your users write their passwords down where other users can find them, someone who wanted to get in could do so easily. A password should be long enough to dissuade the petty hacker yet not so long as to be impossible to remember. Information services like CompuServe and MCI Mail use pronounceable nonsense words like "YAXALUPA" or "HOUSE*DREAM."

As presented, this form can still be closed by double-clicking on the control menu icon in the upper left-hand corner or by pressing (ALT)-(F4). To be extra secure, you should modify the System menu (as shown in How-To 4.4, Modify a form's system menu) to remove the Close item from the system menu.

## 1.10 ⬤ How do I...

**Complexity: Intermediate**

## Make a GIF file viewer?

### Problem

Graphics Interchange Format files are a popular way to distribute and store graphic images. CompuServe's GRAPHICS forum has thousands of GIF files that may be downloaded. To minimize download time and storage space, images are compressed when they are converted to GIF files. The Visual Basic PictureBox and Image controls cannot load GIF files. I would like to write a GIF file viewer. How can I do this using Visual Basic?

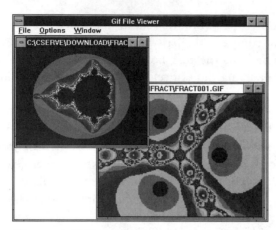

**Figure 1-7** The GifView project in action

### Technique

The sample code diskette included with the Visual Basic How-To contains a fully functional custom control in the file GIFBOX.VBX that was designed to solve this problem. When you add GIFBOX.VBX to your project you can use the Waite Group's GifBox control to display GIF files, as shown in Figure 1-7. The GifBox control is similar to the Visual Basic Image and PictureBox control. To display a GIF file you can simply add a GifBox control to your form and set its Picture property. Like the Image control a GIF image can be displayed using its original size, or it can be stretched (or shrunk) to fill the GifBox. In addition to standard properties such as Top and Left, a GifBox control has the properties listed in Table 1-7. For further information on using the GifBox control you may use the control's on-line help.

This How-To demonstrates using the GifBox control to write a Multiple-Document Interface (MDI) style GIF file viewer. An MDI application has a main form that serves as a container for other forms. Word for Windows and other popular programs use MDI as a technique to allow easy access to multiple documents.

In this How-To, the main form contains multiple forms, each displaying one GIF file. The GIF file forms can be cascaded or tiled within the main form. Each GIF file form can also be individually sized or minimized by the user.

| Property | Meaning |
|---|---|
| BorderStyle | Provides either a single-line border or no border. |
| ImageHeight | Gives the height in pixels of the current GIF file. This property is read-only. |

| Property | Meaning |
|----------|---------|
| ImageWidth | Gives the width in pixels of the current GIF file. This property is read-only. |
| Filename | Assigning a filename to this property during run-time loads the file into the GifBox. This property can only be accessed during run-time. |
| Picture | Used during design-time to load a GIF file into the GifBox. |
| Stretch | When this property is set to True the GIF file will be stretched or shrunk as needed to fit within the dimensions of the GifBox. When this property is set to False the GIF file will be displayed in its original size. If the GIF file is too large to be displayed in the GifBox then not all of it will be visible. |
| XOffset | Used for scrolling a large, unstretched GIF file within the GifBox. Setting XOffset to values less than zero has the effect of scrolling the GIF file image left within the GifBox. Setting XOffset to values greater than zero scrolls the image right. |
| YOffset | Used for scrolling a large, unstretched GIF file within the GifBox. Setting YOffset to values less than zero has the effect of scrolling the GIF file up within the GifBox. Setting YOffset to values greater than zero scrolls the image up. |

**Table 1-7** GifBox Properties

### Steps

Open and run GIFVIEW.MAK. The program initially displays a blank form. Use File Open to open one of the GIF files in the project directory. After you have selected a file to view, a blank form will appear within the main form and the cursor will change to an hourglass. GIF files are compressed, and it takes some time to decompress the file. The amount of time required to decompress a GIF file depends upon the size of the file and the speed of your computer. Loading a 650x350 pixel GIF file using a 25mhz 386 will take about 10 seconds. The GIF file is only decompressed once, so there will not be a delay when you resize the GifBox or redisplay it by some other means.

GIF file forms add Options and Window menus to the main form's menu bar. The Options menu contains Stretch and Keep Aspect menu items. Options Stretch controls whether a GIF file is drawn in its original size or stretched to fit the client area of the form. Options Keep Aspect controls whether the ratio of the GIF file's width to height is preserved when the image is stretched.

The Window menu contains Cascade, Tile, and Arrange Icons menu items. Window Cascade and Tile control the way GIF file forms are displayed on the main form. Arrange Icons arranges the icons for any GIF file forms that have been minimized.

1. Create a new project called GIFVIEW.MAK. Create a new MDI form named GIFVIEW.FRM with the objects and properties listed in Table 1-8. When creating this form be sure to use the Visual Basic File New MDI Form menu item instead of the File New Form menu item.

| Object | Property | Setting |
|---|---|---|
| MDIForm | Caption | "GIF File Viewer" |
| | Height | 5550 |
| | Left | 1020 |
| | Name | MDIForm1 |
| | Top | 1140 |
| | Width | 7485 |
| Picture box | Align | 1 'Align Top |
| | Name | Picture1 |
| | Visible | 0 'False |
| OpenDialog | CreatePrompt | 0 'False |
| | DefaultExt | "gif" |
| | DialogType | 0 'Open Dialog |
| | File | "" |
| | FileMustExist | 0 'False |
| | FileTitle | "" |
| | Filter | "Gif Files(*.gif)|*.gif||" |
| | FilterIndex | 1 |
| | HideReadOnly | 0 'False |
| | InitialDir | "" |
| | Name | OpenDialog1 |
| | OverwritePrompt | 0 'False |
| | PathMustExist | 0 'False |
| | ReadOnly | 0 'False |
| | Title | "Load Gif File" |

**Table 1-8** GIFVIEW.FRM objects and properties

2. Select the Menu Design Window tool and create a menu for GIFVIEW.FRM with captions and names as shown in Table 1-9.

| Control Name | Caption |
|---|---|
| FileMenu | "&File" |
| ----FileOpen | "&Open..." |
| ----FileMenuSep | "-" |
| ----FileExit | "E&xit" |

**Table 1-9** GIFVIEW.FRM menu

3. Create a new form named MDIGIF.FRM with the objects and properties shown in Table 1-10.

| Object | Property | Setting |
|---|---|---|
| Form | BackColor | &H00E0E0E0& |
| | Caption | "Untitled" |
| | Height | 4140 |
| | Left | 2340 |
| | MDIChild | -1 'True |
| | Name | GifViewer |
| | ScaleHeight | 230 |
| | ScaleMode | 3 'Pixel |
| | ScaleWidth | 426 |
| | Top | 2385 |
| | Visible | 0 'False |
| | Width | 6510 |
| VScrollBar | Height | 3180 |
| | LargeChange | 10 |
| | Left | 6105 |
| | Name | VScroll1 |
| | Top | 0 |
| | Visible | 0 'False |
| | Width | 300 |
| HScrollBar | Height | 300 |
| | LargeChange | 10 |
| | Left | 0 |
| | Name | HScroll1 |
| | Top | 3180 |
| | Visible | 0 'False |
| | Width | 6120 |

*continued on next page*

*continued from previous page*

| Object | Property | Setting |
|--------|----------|---------|
| GifBox | Height | 3660 |
| | ImageHeight | 0 |
| | ImageWidth | 0 |
| | Left | -1680 |
| | Name | GifBox1 |
| | Picture | "(none)" |
| | Stretch | 0  'False |
| | Top | -480 |
| | Visible | 0  'False |
| | Width | 7785 |
| | XOffset | 0 |
| | YOffset | 0 |

**Table 1-10** MDIGIF.FRM properties and objects

4. Select the Menu Design Window tool and create a menu for MDIGIF.FRM with captions and names as shown in Table 1-11. Be sure to set the Window List checkbox for the Window menu. When the Window List checkbox is set Visual Basic will automatically append a list of GIF file form items to the Window menu. This enables the user to quickly select a GIF file form from among those that are currently opened.

| Control Name | Caption | Window List |
|--------------|---------|-------------|
| FileNewMenu | "&File" | |
| ----FileOpen | "&Open..." | |
| ----FileClose | "&Close" | |
| ----FileMenuSep | "-" | |
| ----FileExit | "E&xit" | |
| OptionMenu | "&Options" | |
| ----OptionsStretch | "&Stretch" | |
| ----OptionsKeepAspect | "Keep &Aspect" | |
| WindowMenu | "&Window" | True |
| ----WindowCascade | "&Cascade" | |
| ----WindowTile | "&Tile" | |
| ----WindowArrangeIcons | "&Arrange Icons" | |

**Table 1-11** MDIGIF.FRM menu

5. Create a new module named MODULE1.BAS. Add the following to the General Declarations section of MODULE1.BAS.

```
Option Explicit

Global Const CASCADE = 0
Global Const TILE_HORIZONTAL = 1
Global Const TILE_VERTICAL = 2
Global Const ARRANGE_ICONS = 3

Type FormState
    deleted     As Integer
End Type

Global ViewerState() As FormState
Global GifViewers() As New GifViewer
```

6. Add the following subroutine to the General section of MODULE1.BAS. The FileOpen subroutine is called when the File Open menu item is selected from the menu of either the MDIForm1 or GifViewer forms. FileOpen uses the Waite Group's OpenDialog control to easily allow the user to select a file to display. After the user chooses a GIF file to display the subroutine, FindFreeIndex is used to find a free element in the GifViewer form array. Next the GifViewer's GifBox FileName property is set to the filename returned by the OpenDialog control. Finally the GifBox is sized and scroll-bars are added, if needed, by calling the SetUnstretchedSize subroutine.

```
Sub FileOpen ()
    Dim fIndex As Integer
    Dim w As Long
    Dim h As Long
    Dim dialog As Control
    Dim gif     As Control
    Dim newForm As GifViewer

    Set dialog = MDIForm1.OpenDialog1
    '
    ' Setup dialog control for GIF file selection
    '
    dialog.File = ""
    dialog.DialogType = 0
    dialog.Filter = "Gif Files(*.gif)|*.gif||"
    dialog.FilterIndex = 0
    dialog.DefaultExt = "gif"
    dialog.Title = "Open Gif File"
    '
    ' Go get a filename
    '
    dialog.DoIt = True
```

*continued on next page*

*continued from previous page*

```
    '
    ' If some file was selected
    '
    If (dialog.File <> "") Then
        '
        ' Find, or allocate new, form to use
        '
        fIndex = FindFreeIndex()
        Set newForm = GifViewers(fIndex)
        '
        ' Save index so we can free the element when the
        ' form is closed
        '
        newForm.Tag = fIndex
        '
        ' Display the gif filename as the form's caption
        '
        newForm.Caption = dialog.File
        Set gif = newForm.GifBox1
        '
        ' Load the gif file
        '
        gif.FileName = dialog.File
        gif.Top = 0
        gif.Left = 0
        '
        ' Setup scroll bars if needed
        '
        SetUnstretchedSize newForm
        '
        ' Display picture
        '
        gif.Visible = True
    End If
End Sub
```

7. Add the following subroutine to the General section of MODULE1.BAS. The General section of MODULE1.BAS declares an array of GifViewer forms. The FindFreeIndex subroutine first tries to locate an unused element in the array. If there are no unused elements then the array is expanded using ReDim Preserve, and the new element is returned. The Preserve option used with ReDim is new in Visual Basic 2.0. ReDim Preserve lets you change the size of an array without losing its contents. Using ReDim without the Preserve option creates a new array with all of its elements initialized to zero; we wouldn't like that here!

```
Function FindFreeIndex () As Integer
    Dim i As Integer
    '
    ' Search for a free form
    '
```

```
      For i = 1 To UBound(GifViewers)
         If ViewerState(i).deleted Then
            ViewerState(i).deleted = False
            FindFreeIndex = i
            Exit Function
         End If
      Next
      '
      ' If there are no free elements in the GifViewers array then
      ' increase the size of the GifViewers and ViewerState arrays by 1
      '
      ReDim Preserve GifViewers(i + 1)
      ReDim Preserve ViewerState(i + 1)
      FindFreeIndex = i
End Function
```

8. Add the following subroutine to the General section of MODULE1.BAS. The SetStretchedSize subroutine is called after a GIF file is first loaded, or whenever the form is resized and the Stretch property is set to False. SetStretchedSize sizes the GifBox to fit within its GifViewer form. If the GIF image is too large to be displayed in its entirety, horizontal and vertical scroll-bars are added as required.

```
Sub SetUnstretchedSize (f As Form)
    Dim ImageWidth  As Integer
    Dim ImageHeight As Integer
    '
    ' Get frequently referenced properties
    '
    ImageWidth = f.GifBox1.ImageWidth
    ImageHeight = f.GifBox1.ImageHeight
    '
    ' Reset scroll related properties
    '
    f.GifBox1.XOffset = 0
    f.GifBox1.YOffset = 0
    f.HScroll1.Value = 0
    f.VScroll1.Value = 0
    f.HScroll1.Visible = False
    f.VScroll1.Visible = False
    '
    ' If there is an image loaded both imageWidth and
    ' imageHeight will be non-zero
    '
    If (ImageWidth <> 0 And ImageHeight <> 0) Then
       If (ImageWidth > f.ScaleWidth And ImageHeight > f.ScaleHeight) Then
          '
          ' Both vertical and horizontal scroll bars are needed
          '
          f.HScroll1.Visible = True
          f.VScroll1.Visible = True
          f.GifBox1.Width = f.ScaleWidth - f.VScroll1.Width
```

*continued on next page*

*continued from previous page*

```
            f.GifBox1.Height = f.ScaleHeight - f.HScroll1.Height
        ElseIf (ImageWidth > f.ScaleWidth) Then
            '
            ' Only a horizontal scroll bar is needed
            '
            f.HScroll1.Visible = True
            f.GifBox1.Height = ImageHeight
            f.GifBox1.Width = f.ScaleWidth
        ElseIf (ImageHeight > f.ScaleHeight) Then
            '
            ' Only a vertical scroll bar is needed
            '
            f.VScroll1.Visible = True
            f.GifBox1.Height = f.ScaleHeight
            f.GifBox1.Width = ImageWidth
        Else
            '
            ' The image fits on the form, no scroll bars are needed
            '
            f.GifBox1.Height = ImageHeight
            f.GifBox1.Width = ImageWidth
        End If
        If (f.HScroll1.Visible = True) Then
            '
            ' Using horizontal scroll bar ... size it and set
            ' thumb values
            '
            f.HScroll1.Move 0, f.ScaleHeight - f.HScroll1.Height, ⇐
f.GifBox1.Width
            f.HScroll1.Min = 0
            f.HScroll1.Max = ImageWidth - f.GifBox1.Width
        End If
        If (f.VScroll1.Visible = True) Then
            '
            ' Using vertical scroll bar ... size it and set
            ' thumb values
            '
            f.VScroll1.Move f.ScaleWidth - f.VScroll1.Width, 0, ⇐
f.VScroll1.Width, f.GifBox1.Height
            f.VScroll1.Min = 0
            f.VScroll1.Max = ImageHeight - f.GifBox1.Height
        End If
    End If
End Sub
```

9. Add the following code to the FileExit event procedure of MDIForm1. The FileExit event procedure ends the program.

```
Sub FileExit_Click()
   End
End Sub
```

10. Add the following code to the FileOpen event procedure of MDIForm1. FileOpen calls the subroutine FileOpen in MODULE1.BAS to open a new GifViewer form.

```
Sub FileOpen_Click ()
    FileOpen
End Sub
```

11. Add the following code to the Load event procedure of MDIForm1. The Load event subroutine allocates the first element in the GifViewer and ViewerState arrays.

```
Sub MDIForm_Load ()
    ReDim GifViewers(1)
    ReDim ViewerState(1)
    '
    ' Causes FindFreeIndex (in module1.bas) to use the first form
    ' in the GifViewers form array
    '
    ViewerState(1).deleted = True
End Sub
```

12. Add the following code to the General Declarations section of GifViewer.

```
Option Explicit
```

13. Add the following subroutine to the General section of GifViewer. The SetGifBoxSize subroutine is called whenever the GifViewer window size changes. If the GIF image is not being stretched, the subroutine SetUnstretchedSize in MODULE1.BAS is used to size the GifBox and add scroll-bars if needed. If the GifBox property Stretch is set to True then this subroutine sizes the GifBox to fit the client area of the GifViewer.

```
Sub SetGifBoxSize ()
    Dim w       As Integer
    Dim h       As Integer
    Dim r       As Single
    Dim whGif   As Single
    Dim whMe    As Single

    If (GifBox1.Stretch = False) Then
        '
        ' If we're not stretching use subroutine from module1.bas
        ' to setup size and add scrollbars when needed
        '
        SetUnstretchedSize Me
    Else
```

*continued on next page*

*continued from previous page*

```
    '
    ' Otherwise we're stretching the picture to fit, scroll bars
    ' aren't needed
    '
    HScroll1.Visible = False
    VScroll1.Visible = False
    '
    ' And we'll always display the entire picture so
    ' the offsets should be zero
    '
    GifBox1.XOffset = 0
    GifBox1.YOffset = 0
    If (OptionsKeepAspect.Checked = False) Then
        '
        ' Aspect ratio preservation is not required simply
        ' change the size of the GifBox
        '
        GifBox1.Height = Me.ScaleHeight
        GifBox1.Width = Me.ScaleWidth
    Else
        '
        ' Get width/height ratios for both the form and the gifbox
        '
        whGif = GifBox1.ImageWidth / GifBox1.ImageHeight
        whMe = Me.ScaleWidth / Me.ScaleHeight

        If (whMe > whGif) Then
            '
            ' The form is wider relative to its height
            ' than the image, so we can match to GifBox height
            ' to the form height and be sure that the GifBox width
            ' will be less than that of the form
            '
            GifBox1.Height = Me.ScaleHeight
            GifBox1.Width = Me.GifBox1.Height * whGif
        Else
            '
            ' Otherwise we match the form's width and scale the
            ' height accordingly
            '
            GifBox1.Width = Me.ScaleWidth
            GifBox1.Height = GifBox1.Width * (GifBox1.ImageHeight / ⇐
GifBox1.ImageWidth)
        End If
    End If
    End If
End Sub
```

14. Add the following code to the FileOpen event subroutine of GifViewer.

```
Sub FileOpen_Click ()
    FileOpen
End Sub
```

15. Add the following code to the Resize event subroutine of GifViewer.

```
Sub Form_Resize ()
   SetGifBoxSize
End Sub
```

16. Add the following code to the Unload event subroutine of GifViewer. The Unload event procedure deletes the GifViewer array element corresponding to the currently executing instance. Such elements are reused in response to File Open.

```
Sub Form_Unload (Cancel As Integer)
   '
   ' Mark form as available
   '
   ViewerState(Me.Tag).deleted = True
End Sub
```

17. Add the following code to the Change event subroutine of HScroll1. The Change event subroutine scrolls the GIF image horizontally.

```
Sub HScroll1_Change ()
   GifBox1.XOffset = -HScroll1.Value
End Sub
```

18. Add the following code to the Click event subroutine of menu item OptionsKeepAspect.

```
Sub OptionsKeepAspect_Click ()
   OptionsKeepAspect.Checked = Not OptionsKeepAspect.Checked
   SetGifBoxSize
End Sub
```

19. Add the following code to the Click event subroutine of menu item OptionsStretch.

```
Sub OptionsStretch_Click ()
   OptionsStretch.Checked = Not OptionsStretch.Checked
   GifBox1.Stretch = Not GifBox1.Stretch
   SetGifBoxSize
   GifBox1.Refresh
End Sub
```

20. Add the following code to the Change event subroutine of VScroll1. The Change event subroutine scrolls the GIF image vertically.

```
Sub VScroll1_Change ()
   GifBox1.YOffset = -VScroll1.Value
End Sub
```

21. Add the following code to the Click event subroutine of the menu item WindowsArrangeIcons.

```
Sub WindowArrangeIcons_Click ()
   MDIForm1.Arrange ARRANGE_ICONS
End Sub
```

22. Add the following code to the Click event subroutine of the menu item WindowsCascade.

```
Sub WindowCascade_Click ()
   MDIForm1.Arrange CASCADE
End Sub
```

23. Add the following code to the Click event subroutine of the menu item WindowTile.

```
Sub WindowTile_Click ()
   MDIForm1.Arrange TILE_HORIZONTAL
End Sub
```

### How It Works

The subroutines in this How-To can be placed into two categories: subroutines that manage the GifViewer forms and subroutines that manage the GifBox and scroll-bar controls.

MODULE1.BAS declares two dynamic arrays, GifViewers and ViewerState. The GifViewers array contains all open instances of the GifViewer form. The ViewerState array contains FormState variables and is always the same size as the GifViewer array. The GifViewers array is declared using the New keyword. Declaring the array this way tells Visual Basic to create a new instance of a GifViewer form when any element of the array is first accessed. The ViewerState array is used to keep track of which elements of the GifViewers array are being used. When the program first starts executing, both the GifViewers and ViewerState arrays are empty. During the MDIForm1_Load event procedure they are ReDimed so that each array has one element. Since there is one element in each array after they are ReDimed, the MDIForm1_Load event procedure sets the Deleted field of ViewerState(1) to True. When the first GIF file is opened the FindFirstIndex subroutine in MODULE1.BAS will see that the first element of these arrays is not in use (Deleted = True) and will load the GIF file into this element. As new GIF files are opened the GifViewers and ViewerState arrays will be expanded using ReDim Preserve. This command redimensions an array without discarding the current contents. When a GifViewer instance is closed the GifViewer_Unload event subroutine sets the Deleted field of the corresponding ViewerState element to True. This makes the GifViewers element available to be used again.

Visual Basic's MDI form capabilities take care of the management of multiple GifViewers. Using the MDI form's Arrange property makes handling cascade, tiling, and arrangement of minimized icons a breeze. Simulating these capabilities in Visual Basic would take many lines of code.

There are two fundamentally different ways that a GIF file can be viewed with the GIFVIEW program: stretched and not stretched. When a GIF file is being stretched to match the size of the GifViewer client area, there are two cases to deal with. The first case occurs when the Keep Aspect menu item is not checked. This is easy; we simply size the GifBox to fill the GifViewers client area, and the GifBox takes care of drawing the image within that area. When Keep Aspect is checked GifBox sizing is a little more complicated. The goal is to make the GifBox as large as possible while maintaining the relative dimensions of the displayed image, without having any part of it extend beyond the boundaries of form's client area. To do this the width/height ratios of the GifViewer client area and the GIF image are compared. When the width/height ratio of the form is greater than that of the GIF image we can extend the GifBox to the form's height, and scale the GifBox width accordingly. Since the form is wider relative to its height than the GifBox, we can be sure that the scaled GifBox width will not be wider than the form. When the form is taller relative to its width than the GifBox we first set the GifBox width to the form's width and scale its height accordingly.

Displaying an unstretched GIF can result in an image that is too large to display on the GifViewer form. When this happens horizontal and vertical scroll bars are added to the form and the GifBox size is decreased by the size of the added scroll bars. The Max properties of scroll bars are set equal to the number of pixels that cannot be displayed on the form. Setting the Max properties this way makes the scrolling code trivial. To see how this works consider a GIF image that is 100 pixels wider than the GifViewer form's client area. The Max property of HScroll1 will be set to 100. When the HScroll1's Change event subroutine is called we simply move the GIF image to the left by HScroll1.Value pixels.

## Comments

The combination of Visual Basic's simple MDI window capabilities and the Waite Group's GifBox control makes writing this program easy. All of the important features of MDI applications and the GifBox control are used in this project, which can serve as a prototype for other MDI applications. The FormState Type defined in MODULE1.BAS contains only a single field. To maintain information for a more complex MDI application you would probably need to add a number of fields to track things like what file is loaded in a form and whether the form's contents have been modified or not.

# CHAPTER 2

# CONTROLS

# How do I...

This chapter, reveals little-known secrets of Visual Basic controls by using several powerful Windows APIs. A firm footing is provided in SendMessage, one of the most powerful APIs, which allows you to exploit many control properties not found in Visual Basic. You'll learn how to make a custom check box that uses real checks instead of little Xs, how to add controls at run time, and how to make a file dialog box using APIs. A powerful API-based text editor will be created that allows cut, copy, and paste to the clipboard, as well as a "searching" list box using APIs. There is a How-To that shows how to make a button with continuous events. Another shows how to set up old-fashioned file dialog boxes that have the directories listed together with the files.

## Windows APIs Covered

| | | |
|---|---|---|
| GetFocus | GetWindow | SetWindow |
| GetModuleUsage | PutFocus | SetWindowText |
| GetModuleHandle | SendMessage | |

### 2.1 Make a custom check box

You'll begin by learning how to make an Option check box show a real check mark when it's clicked, not just a simple "x." This simple technique can be used to allow any bit-mapped symbol to be used in a check box and uses no APIs.

### 2.2 Add controls at run time

Often you don't know how many of a certain control to put on your form until the program has been run. You'll see how to do this using control arrays.

### 2.3 Set up a drive-directory-file list box combination

### 2.4 Quickly clear a list box

You'll use the SendMessage API described in the previous How-To to make a list box clearing procedure that is much faster than using Visual Basic's RemoveItem method.

### 2.5 Make a file dialog box using APIs

Every program has to open and close files and every program must, therefore, present a File Open and File Save dialog box that lets the user navigate the file system, check for errors, bad file names, and so on. These How-Tos include the pure Visual Basic way to do this, and a more sophisticated method that uses Windows APIs. The API approach gives you greater control over the contents of the files, such as letting you see invisible files.

### 2.6 Make a powerful text editor using APIs

The Microsoft manuals include a Text Editor application written in pure Visual Basic. Unfortunately the code is long and complicated, and spread across three chapters. This How-To shows how to make a MiniEditor that supports cut, copy, and paste, and a single level of Undo. It uses the SendMessage API to manipulate all the controls on the form, as well as the cursor position in the list box containing the edited text. You'll learn how to use the handles property of a control. A simple DLL is included on the distribution disk that lets you get the handle of any Visual Basic control.

### 2.7 Create an old-style file dialog box

The "new" way to create file dialog boxes in Windows puts directory and drive names in different list boxes. In old Windows (pre- 3.1) drives were indicated by the letters [-c-], and scrolled just like directory names. The periods (..) were also shown in the scrolling list box. Visual Basic provides the directory, file, and drive controls and expects you to use all three. If you prefer to give users a classic combo directory/drive dialog box, you'll want this How-To.

### 2.8 Create multiple entries in the Task List

Running multiple instances of your Visual Basic application is a great idea, and with multiprocessing, it gives you a nice way to have several tools running at the same time. However Visual Basic will not give you multiple entries in Windows Task List dialog, making it difficult to maneuver in this environment. This API shows how there is a hidden owner window in Visual Basic, and how this owner window can be manipulated to give the right caption for the Task List.

### 2.9 Make a simple "searching" list box

### 2.10 Make a "searching" list box using APIs

Automatic searching of a list box means that a scrolling list zeros in on the matching line as the user types the name. Windows' Help feature works this way, and so do many file dialog boxes that contain lists to select from. These two How-Tos show you how to create this effect in both pure Visual Basic and then using Windows APIs.

### 2.11 Make a button with continuous events

This How-To shows the technique for making a button that will cause a process to continue all the while the mouse button is pressed. The technique for using DoEvents to allow other Windows processes to run and to avoid hogging processing time is revealed.

### 2.12 Set minimum and maximum sizes for a form

Allowing users to change the size of a form at run time is one of the finishing touches that distinguishes a professional Windows program. For most forms this means that controls need to be sized and positioned when the form's size is changed. For some forms there is either a minimum or maximum size, or both, to which a form can be sized while still being able to reposition controls. This How-To demonstrates adjusting to the user's resizing of a form, and shows how to use the Windows API to prevent the user from changing the size of a form beyond practical limits.

### 2.13 Add a toolbar to Visual Basic programs

Toolbars are a convenient way to invoke commonly used actions of a program. This How-To shows how you can easily add a toolbar to Visual Basic programs using TOOLBUTN.VBX, a free custom control that comes with the *Visual Basic How-To Second Edition*.

## 2.1 ⬤ How do I...

Complexity: Easy

## Make a custom check box?

### Problem
Visual Basic "check boxes" aren't really check boxes; they're X boxes. How can I make a custom check box control where there is a real check mark (✓) in the box?

### Technique
It is possible to create a check box with a real check mark (✓) using Visual Basic's own power. Flipping through a control array of picture boxes will simulate the properties of a check box, with the added ability of being able to use any bitmap for the checked, unchecked, and pressed versions of the box.

None of the icons in Visual Basic's icon library gives the right "look" for the check box, so we provided some on the disk that accompanies this book. Or you can draw your own check box bitmap using the IconWorks sample application provided with Visual Basic.

### Steps
Open and run CUSTOM.MAK. You can click on the check box and observe the three different states of the check box: checked, unchecked, and in the process of being pressed down.

1. Create a new project called CUSTOM.MAK. Create a new form with the objects and properties listed in Table 2-1 and save it as CUSTOM.FRM.

| Object | Property | Setting |
|--------|----------|---------|
| Form | Caption | Custom check box |
| | FormName | CustomCheckbox |
| | BackColor | &HC0C0C0 |
| Label | Caption | Save changes |
| | Name | Label1 |
| Picture box | AutoRedraw | False |
| | AutoSize | True |
| | Name | Checked |
| | Index | 0 |
| | Picture | CHECKOFF.BMP |
| | Visible | False |
| Picture box | AutoRedraw | False |
| | AutoSize | True |
| | Name | Checked |
| | Index | 1 |
| | Picture | CHECKON.BMP |
| | Visible | True |
| Picture box | AutoRedraw | False |
| | AutoSize | True |
| | Name | Checked |
| | Index | 2 |
| | Picture | CHECKPRS.BMP |
| | Visible | False |

**Table 2-1** Custom project form's objects and properties

The form should look like Figure 2-1 when you're finished creating it. Note how the three picture boxes overlap and appear as one. They only differ by their index number and the bitmap they contain. Figures 2-2, 2-3, and 2-4 show an enlargement of the three bitmaps.

2. Place the following code in the Click event of any one of the picture boxes. Because the pictures are part of a control array, Visual Basic runs this code in the Checked_Click event subroutine when any of the picture boxes is clicked. (The Index parameter Visual Basic passes will be the Index property of the picture box that is visible. Thus if Index is nonzero,

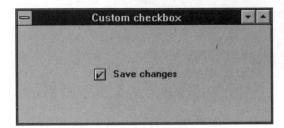

**Figure 2-1** The Custom form in action

**Figure 2-2**
The "Off" bitmap

**Figure 2-3**
The "On" bitmap

**Figure 2-4**
The "Pressed" bitmap

it means the visible picture box is the "checked" picture box so the "unchecked" picture box should become visible.) Otherwise, if Index is 0, it's the "unchecked" picture box that is visible and the "checked" picture box should become visible.

```
Sub Checked_Click (Index As Integer)
   If Index Then
      Checked(0).Visible = -1
      Checked(1).Visible = 0
      Checked(2).Visible = 0
      Print "Changes will not be saved!"
   Else
      Checked(0).Visible = 0
      Checked(1).Visible = -1
      Checked(2).Visible = 0
      Print "Changes will be saved when you exit."
   End If
End Sub
```

3. The following code in the Checked_MouseDown event subroutine causes the "pressed" version of the check box to be displayed while the mouse button is held down.

```
Sub Checked_MouseDown (Index As Integer, Button As Integer, Shift As ⇐
   Integer, X As Single, Y As Single)
   Checked(0).Visible = 0
   Checked(1).Visible = 0
   Checked(2).Visible = -1
End Sub
```

4. Visual Basic runs the following code in the Checked_MouseUp event subroutine when the mouse button is released. The code simply calls the Click event subroutine so the proper picture box is made visible and the "pressed" version is made invisible.

```
Sub Checked_MouseUp (Index As Integer, Button As Integer, Shift As ⇐
    Integer, X As Single, Y As Single)
    Checked_Click (Index)
End Sub
```

## How It Works

Control arrays come to the rescue. Control arrays have a variety of uses; they often solve problems they were not intended to solve. By making the three possible states of a check box (checked, unchecked, and pressed) elements of a control array, we avoid having to write separate routines for each of the possible states.

Normally, Visual Basic Click events occur when the mouse button is pressed and then released. Because controls must often respond when the mouse button is pressed, Visual Basic provides the MouseDown event. Checked_MouseDown intercepts these mouse button presses and makes only the pressed version of the check box visible. Then, when the mouse button is released, Visual Basic runs Checked_MouseUp, which simply calls Checked_Click to display the proper check box bitmap.

If there are MouseDown or MouseUp event subroutines for a control, they "swallow" up the Click event. Visual Basic will not automatically run the Click event subroutine for that control when the mouse button is released, so that's what Checked_MouseUp does.

Checked_Click checks the Index of the picture box that was clicked, and makes the opposite version the only picture box visible. For this example, we only print a message on the form. In a real application, you might set a global variable to True if the checked picture box is made visible or False if the unchecked picture box is made visible.

## Comments

If you don't want to provide a pressed version of the check box, simply delete the picture box whose Index property is 2 and delete the Checked_MouseDown and Checked_MouseUp event subroutines. Visual Basic will invoke the Checked_Click event subroutine when the mouse button is pressed and released over the picture box.

## 2.2 How do I...

## Add controls at run time?

### Problem

When I design forms, I don't always know how many controls will be needed at run time. How can I add or delete controls while an application is running?

### Technique

Visual Basic's control arrays are provided for just this type of situation. When a control is declared to be an object of a control array, you can create as many additional copies of that control as needed under program control.

### Steps

Open and run ADDCTL.MAK. Use the Command-Button menu to create or delete Command1 controls. The Option-Button menu adds and deletes Option1 controls. Figure 2-5 shows the form with multiple new controls added. Clicking on any of the individual command buttons or option buttons will identify the selected control in the label.

The Addctl project may be created by entering objects and code as detailed in the following steps.

1. Create a new project called ADDCTL.MAK. Create a new form with the objects and properties shown in Table 2-2 and save it as ADDCTL.FRM. Make sure that the frame is placed on the right-hand side of the form as displayed in Figure 2-5.

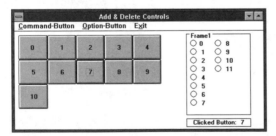

**Figure 2-5** The Addctl form at run time

| Object | Property | Setting |
| --- | --- | --- |
| Form | FormName | Addctl |
| | Caption | Add and Delete Controls |

| Object | Property | Setting |
|--------|----------|---------|
| Command button | Name | Command1 |
| | Caption | 0 |
| | Index | 0 |
| | Height | 735 |
| | Width | 855 |
| Frame | Name | Frame1 |
| Label | Name | Label1 |
| | Alignment | 2 - Center |
| Option button | Name | Option1 |
| | Caption | 0 |
| | Index | 0 |
| | Height | 255 |
| | Width | 735 |

**Table 2-2** Addctl project form's objects and properties

2. Using the Menu Design windows, create a menu for the form with the values in Table 2-3.

| Caption | Name | Index | Accelerator |
|---------|------|-------|-------------|
| &Command-Button | CB | | |
| – – – –&Add | MenuCmdButton | 0 | (CTRL)-(A) |
| – – – –&Delete | MenuCmdButton | 1 | (CTRL)-(D) |
| &Option-Button | OB | | |
| – – – –&Add | MenuOptButton | 0 | (SHIFT)-(F1) |
| – – – –&Delete | MenuOptButton | 1 | (SHIFT)-(F2) |
| E&xit | Quit | | |

**Table 2-3** Addctl menu values

3. Place the following code in the MenuCmdButton_Click event subroutine. This subroutine adds a new command button control to the form or deletes the last one added, depending on the AddDelete parameter.

```
Sub MenuCmdButton_Click (AddDelete As Integer)
Static MaxIndex As Integer            ' # of Command Buttons
Dim CTop As Integer, CWidth As Integer, CLeft As Integer

' AddDelete = 1, Delete the last Command button.
' When adding a new Command button, place to right of previous one.
' If it would overlap frame control, place it at beginning of
'     next line.
```

*continued on next page*

*continued from previous page*

```
' Finally, make control visible; new controls are not visible by default.
    If AddDelete = 1 Then
        If MaxIndex = 0 Then
            MsgBox "Unable to Delete Original Control", 48
            Exit Sub
        End If
'       ------------
        Unload Command1(MaxIndex)        ' Remove the control
'       ------------
        MaxIndex = MaxIndex - 1
    Else
        MaxIndex = MaxIndex + 1
'       ------------
        Load Command1(MaxIndex)          ' Add the control
'       ------------
        CTop = Command1(MaxIndex - 1).Top
        CWidth = Command1(MaxIndex).Width
        CLeft = Command1(MaxIndex - 1).Left + CWidth
        If CLeft + CWidth > Frame1.Left Then
            CLeft = Command1(0).Left
            CTop = CTop + Command1(MaxIndex).Height
        End If
        Command1(MaxIndex).Top = CTop
        Command1(MaxIndex).Left = CLeft
        Command1(MaxIndex).Caption = Str$(MaxIndex)
        Command1(MaxIndex).Visible = -1
    End If
End Sub
```

4. Place the following code in the MenuOptButton_Click event subroutine. This subroutine adds or removes option buttons from Frame1.

```
Sub MenuOptButton_Click (AddDelete As Integer)
Static MaxIndex As Integer
Dim CHeight As Integer, CTop As Integer, CWidth As Integer, ⇐
    CLeft As Integer

' AddDelete = 1, Delete last option button added.
' When adding new option button, place directly below previous one.
' If new button overlaps bottom edge of frame, start a new column.
' Finally, make button visible; new controls are not initially visible.
    If AddDelete = 1 Then
        If MaxIndex = 0 Then
            MsgBox "Unable to Delete Original Control", 48
            Exit Sub
        End If
'       ------------
        Unload Option1(MaxIndex)         ' Remove control
'       ------------
        MaxIndex = MaxIndex - 1
    Else
        MaxIndex = MaxIndex + 1
'       ------------
        Load Option1(MaxIndex)           ' Add control
```

```
'    ------------
     CHeight = Option1(MaxIndex).Height
     CTop = Option1(MaxIndex - 1).Top + CHeight
     CWidth = Option1(MaxIndex).Width
     CLeft = Option1(MaxIndex - 1).Left
     If CTop + CHeight >= Frame1.Height Then
         CLeft = CLeft + CWidth
         CTop = Option1(0).Top
     End If
     Option1(MaxIndex).Top = CTop
     Option1(MaxIndex).Left = CLeft
     Option1(MaxIndex).Caption = Str$(MaxIndex)
     Option1(MaxIndex).Visible = -1
   End If
End Sub
```

5. Place the following code in the Command1_Click event subroutine. Whenever any of the command buttons on the form is clicked, this subroutine will identify which button was selected in the label control.

```
Sub Command1_Click (Index As Integer)
   Label1.Caption = "Clicked Button: " + Str$(Index)
End Sub
```

6. Place the following code in the Option1_Click event subroutine. Whenever any of the option buttons on the form is selected, this subroutine will identify which button was selected in the label control.

```
Sub Option1_Click (Index As Integer)
   Label1.Caption = "Clicked Option:" + Str$(Index)
End Sub
```

7. Place the following code in the Quit_Click menu event. It allows for a graceful exit from the application.

```
Sub Quit_Click ()
   End            ' Exit the Application
End Sub
```

## How It Works

Control arrays are an intrinsic part of Visual Basic and form the basis for a number of features, including the ability to dynamically add controls at run time. A single control is turned into a control array at design time by setting its Index property. In this project we started with an Index of zero for both control arrays.

New controls are added to an array at run time using the Load Name(Index) statement. The Name must previously exist as a control array on the form, and the Index value must not already be in use for that Name. When a new control is added at run time, its Visible property, by default, is turned off, although its position and size will match that of the original control.

In the MenuCmdButton_Click event subroutine, the AddDelete flag indicates whether to add a new control or to delete the previous one. The static variable MaxIndex keeps track of the number of command buttons previously added. Because it is a static variable, MaxIndex retains its value between subroutine calls. When a new control is added, we check whether it can be positioned to the left of Frame1. If it can't, the new control is positioned below the first control of the previous line.

Deleting a control is handled by the Unload Name(Index) statement and by reducing the MaxIndex counter.

The MenuOptButton_Click event subroutine is used to add or remove option buttons. The same variable, MaxIndex, is used here as well to keep track of the number of option buttons. Because MaxIndex is declared at the subroutine level, each subroutine keeps its own, nonshared copy, of the variable. Although the command buttons were added from left to right, we have chosen to add the option buttons from top to bottom. This was done to illustrate the ease of positioning an added control.

The two event subroutines, Command1_Click and Option1_Click, demonstrate how Visual Basic lets you know which control in an array the user selected. The Index parameter is used to differentiate each of the control array elements from the others.

### Comments

This project demonstrates how to add at run time just two of Visual Basic's controls, command buttons and option buttons. However, any of the standard controls can be incorporated into a control array— up to a limit of 255 controls per form. Forms, on the other hand, do not have an Index property and cannot be made into a control array.

Note that when a control is already contained within a container, such as the Option1 control is in this example (in a group box), controls added to that control array will also be positioned in the same container.

## 2.3  How do I...

## Set up a drive-directory-file list box combination?

### Problem

I'd like to incorporate a file selection box so that users can choose and open up a file to work with. How do I go about getting the various controls involved to work together for this purpose?

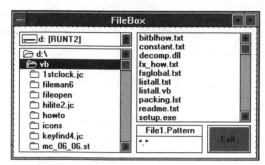

**Figure 2-6** The FileBox project form and its controls at design time

### Technique

The basic functionality for a file selection setup is built into the drive, directory, and file list box objects. All we need to do is enter a little code in the appropriate places to let the individual members of this trio communicate with each other as the user makes changes, and we're up and running! Additionally, we'll add a pattern string so the user can enter the type of files that will be displayed. We'll also include some error checking, so the program won't crash if a user forgets to insert a floppy disk in a drive before selecting it in the drive combo box.

### Steps

Open and run FILEBOX.MAK. The FileBox project can be created by performing the following steps.

1. Create a new project called FILEBOX.MAK. Create a new form with the controls shown in Figure 2-6, then set all the properties as listed in Table 2-4. Any properties not specifically mentioned should be left set to their default values. Save it as FILEBOX.FRM.

| Object | Property | Setting |
| --- | --- | --- |
| Form | FormName | MainForm |
| | Caption | FileBox |
| Drive list box | All Properties | All Defaults |
| Directory list box | All Properties | All Defaults |
| File list box | All Properties | All Defaults |
| Label | BorderStyle | 1 - Fixed Single |
| | Caption | File1.Pattern |

*continued on next page*

*continued from previous page*

| Object | Property | Setting |
|--------|----------|---------|
| Text box | BorderStyle | 1 - Fixed Single |
|  | Text | *.* |
| Command button | Name | ExitDemo |
|  | Caption | Exit |

**Table 2-4** FileBox project form's objects and properties

When they are first dragged onto a form at design time, the contents of drive, directory, and file list boxes reflect the current directory, as would be returned by CurDir$. Thus, the files and directories shown in Figure 2-6 reflect a sample current directory.

2. Place the following code in the Drive1_Change event procedure.

```
Sub Drive1_Change ()
    On Error GoTo Drive1Error
    Dir1.path = Drive1.Drive
    Exit Sub                        'This is normal exit from subroutine
Drive1Error:                        'End up here if an error occurs
    Beep
    If Err = 68 Or Err = 71 Then
        Msg$ = "Error #" + Str$(Err) + "  No Floppy in the Drive!"
        MsgBox Msg$, 48
    Else
        Msg$ = "Error #" + Str$(Err)
    End If
    Resume
End Sub
```

3. Place the following code in the Dir1_Change event procedure.

```
Sub Dir1_Change ()
    File1.path = Dir1.path
End Sub
```

4. Place the following code in the Text1_KeyDown event procedure.

```
Sub Text1_KeyDown (KeyCode As Integer, Shift As Integer)
    If KeyCode = 13 Then            'If Enter key is pressed
        File1.Pattern = Text1.Text
    End If
End Sub
```

5. Place the following code in the ExitDemo_Click event procedure.

```
Sub ExitDemo_Click ()
    End
End Sub
```

**File Selection Hierarchy**

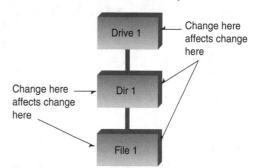

**Figure 2-7** The file selection list box hierarchy

### How It Works

As mentioned previously, the basic functionality for the file-related list boxes is built in. You don't have to write code to have the drive combo box change to a new drive, to have a directory list box update its display when you double-click on a different directory folder, or to have a file list box highlight the file you click on within its borders. These actions occur automatically, courtesy of Visual Basic. The drive-directory-file list box setup can be thought of as having a hierarchical structure, with the drive combo box located on the highest level, the directory list box on the middle level, and the file list box on the lowest level. (Refer to Figure 2-7.)

The small amount of code that must be entered in various event procedures enables the trio of list boxes to stay "in synch" as the user makes changes. A change made on one level generates a Change event for any levels below it. For example, should a user select a different drive in the drive1 combo list box at run time, this will set in motion an updating process courtesy of the Change event procedures for the Drive1combo box and Dir1 list box. When the drive is changed, the path for Dir1 is changed by code in the Drive1_Change event procedure. This action generates a Change event for Dir1, so the Dir1_Change event procedure is called, where code is located to update the path for File1. When a user selects a new directory in Dir1 by double-clicking on it, a Change event is generated for Dir1, so the code in the Dir1_Change event procedure updates the path for File1.

### Comments

If at run time a user selects a floppy drive (such as drive A or B) from the Drive1 combo box, and there is no floppy disk in the drive, the program simply terminates execution (crashes) at that point! By including the error-checking code in the Drive1_Change event procedure, this common pitfall is avoided. With the error-checking code in place, the program displays a dialog box and does not crash. The user is alerted that there is no floppy disk in the drive and can then insert a disk and click the Ok button in the dialog box to continue executing the application.

The standard method of implementing error-checking code in a procedure is to use the "On Error GoTo" statement (located at the beginning of the procedure, after any variable or constant declarations), with the name of a block of code specifically designed to handle errors. The error-handling code comes at the end of the procedure, after an Exit Sub statement, and is not executed unless an error is generated. If an error is generated and the error-checking code is executed, the "Resume" statement will return execution to the statement in the code that generated the error.

The text box is included in the demo for the purpose of allowing a user to change the Pattern property for the File1 list box. (The Pattern property determines the type of files displayed in a file list box.) When a user types a file specification (which, like the value we entered for Text1.Text at design time, can include DOS wildcards) into the text box and presses (ENTER) while the text box has the focus, the Pattern property of File1 will be set to the text in the text box.

When users select Open from the File menu of a Windows application, it is common for the elements of the file selection dialog (drive, directory, and file list boxes, and possibly a Pattern selector) to be displayed on their own form. This demo is set up that way, and the code located in the various event procedures takes care of navigating the file system to get a user to a file. Once there, a file listed in the file list box could be selected by double-clicking on it. Additional code located in the File1_DblClick event procedure would be needed to actually open and process the file.

```
Sub File1_DblClick ()
    'Code here for application to open and deal with selected file!
End Sub
```

## 2.4  How do I...

## Quickly clear a list box?

### Problem
Using Visual Basic's RemoveItem method for clearing a list box is slow. Is there a simple and faster way to do this?

### Technique

Yes, we can use the SendMessageToControl function to do this.

### Steps

Open and run CLEARAL2.MAK. The list box in the form initially loads up to 10 items. If you click once on the form, another 10 items are added to the list box. If you double-click on the form, all the items in the list box are quickly removed using one API call. See Figure 2-8.

1. Create a new project called CLEARAL2.MAK. Create a form with the objects and properties listed in Table 2-5 and save it as CLEARAL2.FRM.

| Object | Property | Setting |
| --- | --- | --- |
| Form | Caption | Form1 |
| | BackColor | &H00C0C0C0& |
| List box | Name | List1 |

**Table 2-5** ClearAl2 project form's objects and properties

2. Add the VBHOWTO.BAS module to your project using Visual Basic's File menu's Add File command. Then add the following code to the VBHOWTO.BAS module.

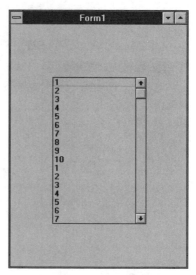

**Figure 2-8** The ClearAl2 form in action

```
Sub ClearListBox (AListBox As Control)
    ' Make sure we're working with a List Box.
    If TypeOf AListBox Is ListBox Then
        ' if so, send the LB_RESETCONTENT message to clear
        I = SendMessage(AListBox, LB_RESETCONTENT, 0, 0)
    End If
End Sub
```

3. Put the following code in the Form_Click event subroutine. This code inserts 10 new items into the list box whenever the form is clicked.

```
Sub Form_Click ()
    For i = 1 To 10
        List1.AddItem Format$(i)  'Put something into List Box.
    Next
End Sub
```

4. Put the following code in the Form_DblClick event subroutine. This code calls the ClearListBox general subroutine whenever you double-click the mouse on the form.

```
Sub Form_dblClick ()
    ClearListBox List1
End Sub
```

5. Put the following code in the Form_Load event subroutine. This code calls the Form_Click event subroutine to insert 10 items into the list box when the form is first loaded.

```
Sub Form_Load ()
    Form_Click
End Sub
```

Figure 2-9 shows the completed ClearAl2 form.

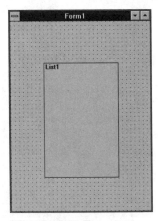

**Figure 2-9** The completed ClearAl2 form

### How It Works

The Windows API function SendMessage, is used to send LB_RESETCONTENT to the list box. If you are using VB version 2.0 or greater you can also use the listbox Clear method to reset the list box contents. The Windows message to remove all the items from a list box is LB_RESETCONTENT, which the WINDOWS.H file in the Windows SDK defines as WM_USER + 5. WM_USER is defined as 0x400, or &H400 in Visual Basic hexadecimal lingo, so LB_RESETCONTENT boils down to &H405.

The ClearListBox general subroutine first ensures that the parameter that was passed is a list box control. If it is, the SendMessageToControl function uses the LB_RESETCONTENT message to clear out the list box.

The Form_Click event subroutine adds 10 numbered items into the list box whenever you click on the form (outside the list box). You can click on the form as many times as you'd like.

The Form_DblClick event subroutine calls the ClearListBox general subroutine, supplying the List1 list box control as a parameter.

The Form_Load event subroutine just calls the Form_Click event subroutine to add 10 items to the list box when the form is first loaded.

### Comments

Before any control can accept Windows messages, it must be visible. Therefore, if you want to use ClearListBox (or SendMessageToControl itself) in a Form_Load event subroutine, you must first make the form visible using Visual Basic's Show method.

## 2.5  How do I...

## Make a file dialog box using APIs?

### Problem

Although there are purely Visual Basic ways to create a File Open dialog box, Windows must offer a more powerful way to do it with API calls. How can I use those API calls in my Visual Basic applications?

### Technique

The file dialog box in How-To 2.7, Create an old-style file dialog box, uses hidden file and directory list boxes to automatically retrieve the file and directory information. Another way to do this uses Windows' messages.

Specifically, Windows list boxes understand a message called LB_DIR, which loads a list box with the file and directory names you specify. You can specify which files to load into the list box two ways. The first is via a wildcard pattern (you've seen wildcards before like "*.*" at the DOS prompt). The wildcard pattern "*.*" will load all available files. The second way to specify files to load into the list box is via a file's attributes; DOS keeps track of several bits of information about the files in a directory:

- If a file has been modified

- If a file can't be changed (the file is read-only)

- If a file isn't normally visible (the file is hidden)

- If a file is a system file (the file is part of DOS)

- If a file is actually a directory

The LB_DIR message lets you load a list box with files with any, or with all of these attributes. The LB_DIR message also lets you load a list box with files that have none of those attributes (also called "normal" files).

We can use the LB_DIR message to create a dialog box that acts just like the dialog boxes of other Windows applications, is just as fast, and does things that in pure Visual Basic would take a lot more code.

### Steps

Open and run FILEDLG2.MAK. The file dialog box will open up with files in the current directory in the list box on the left, and all the subdirectories, directories, and drives in the list box on the right. You can negotiate between directories by double-clicking on a directory name in the right-hand list box. The "[..]" entry backs up to the previous directory. You can also get a list of files on a floppy disk by double-clicking on a drive letter like "[-a-]." Figure 2-10 shows a sample of this style file dialog box.

1. Create a new project called FILEDLG2.MAK. Add the VBHOWTO.BAS module using Visual Basic's Add File menu command (created in How-To 2.4). This module contains several general functions that the file dialog box form uses.

2. Create a new form with the controls listed in Table 2-6 and save it as FILEDLG2.FRM. Put the following code in the Declarations section of the form. This code will give the form's subroutines and functions access to the SendMessage API function.

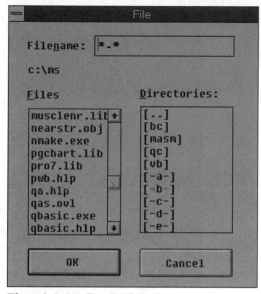

**Figure 2-10** The FileDlg2 form in action

```
Declare Function SendMessage Lib "User" (ByVal hWnd%, ByVal wMsg%, ByVal⇐
wParam%, ByVal lParam$) As Integer

Const WM_USER = &H400
Const LB_DIR = WM_USER + 14
```

| Object | Property | Setting |
|--------|----------|---------|
| Form | Caption | File |
| | FormName | FileDlg |
| | MaxButton | False |
| | MinButton | False |
| | BackColor | &H00C0C0C0& |
| Label | Alignment | 1 - Right Justify |
| | Caption | File&name: |
| | Name | Label1 |
| Text box | Name | FileEdit |
| | MultiLine | False |
| | ScrollBars | 0 - None |
| | TabStop | True |
| | Text | *.* |
| Label | Alignment | 0 - Left Justify |
| | Caption | c:\ |
| | Name | DirLabel |

*continued on next page*

*continued from previous page*

| Object | Property | Setting |
|---|---|---|
| Label | Alignment | 0 - Left Justify |
| | Caption | &Files: |
| | Name | Label2 |
| List box | Name | FileList |
| | Sorted | True |
| | TabStop | True |
| Label | Alignment | 0 - Left Justify |
| | Caption | &Directories: |
| | Name | Label3 |
| List box | Name | DirList |
| | Sorted | True |
| | TabStop | True |
| Command button | Caption | Ok |
| | Name | Ok |
| | Default | True |
| | TabStop | True |
| Command button | Caption | Cancel |
| | Name | Cancel |
| | Cancel | True |
| | TabStop | True |

**Table 2-6** FileDlg2 project form's objects and properties

3. Put the following code in the UpdateListBoxes general subroutine. The form calls UpdateListBoxes whenever something has changed and the list boxes need to be updated.

```
Sub Update_List_Boxes ()

  ' Update current directory label.
  DirLabel.Caption = LCase$(CurDir$)

  ' Clear out the file and directory list boxes.
  ClearListBox FileList
  ClearListBox DirList

  FileList.SetFocus

  ' Get its handle.

  ' Send the message to the control.
  PathPattern$ = FileEdit.Text
  I = SendMessage(FileList.hWnd, LB_DIR, 0, PathPattern$)

  ' Send the message to the control.
  ' &HC010 = subdirectories + drives only
```

```
    I = SendMessage(DirList.hWnd, LB_DIR, &HC010, "*.*")
End Sub
```

4. Put the following code in the Cancel_Click event subroutine. This code sets the filename text box to the null string and hides the file dialog box.

```
Sub Cancel_Click ()
    ' If we select Cancel, we can hide the dialog, because
    ' we don't need it anymore.
    FileEdit.Text = ""
    FileDlg.Hide
End Sub
```

5. Put the following code in the DirList_DblClick event subroutine. This code changes directories and switches drives depending on the item clicked. There's an error routine in case there's no disk in a floppy drive.

```
Sub DirList_DblClick ()
    Const MB_RETRYANDCANCEL = 5
    Const MB_ICONEXCLAMATION = 48

    On Local Error GoTo UhOh

    ' When you double-click on a directory or drive entry,
    ' check whether the selected item is a drive; if so,
    ' change the current drive.
    If Left$(DirList.Text, 2) = "[-" And Len(DirList.Text) = 5 Then
        oldDir$ = CurDir$
        ChDrive Mid$(DirList.Text, 3, 1)
        A$ = CurDir$    ' Check whether the disk is ready;
    ' otherwise, change the current directory.
    Else
        ChDir Mid$(DirList.Text, 2, Len(DirList.Text) - 2)
    End If

    On Local Error GoTo 0

    Update_List_Boxes
    Exit Sub

UhOh:
    If MsgBox("Unable to switch to drive " + Mid$(DirList.Text, 3, 1) + ⇐
        ":", MB_RETRYANDCANCEL + MB_ICONEXCLAMATION, "Visual Basic - ⇐
        FileDlg") = 2
Then
    ' If we press Cancel, go back to the previous drive.
        ChDrive Left$(oldDir$, 1)
    End If

    Resume
End Sub
```

6. Put the following code in the FileList_Click event subroutine. This code puts the filename the user clicked on into the text box.

```
Sub FileList_Click ()
   ' Put the selected filename into the Text Box.
   FileEdit.Text = FileList.Text
End Sub
```

7. Put the following code in the FileList_DblClick event subroutine. This code puts the filename the user clicked on in the text box and hides the file dialog box.

```
Sub FileList_DblClick ()
   ' When we double-click on a filename in the List Box,
   ' set the Text Box to the selected filename and
   ' hide the form, because we've picked the filename.
   FileEdit.Text = FileList.Text
   FileDlg.Hide
End Sub
```

8. Add the following code to the Load event subroutine of Form1. The Update_List_Boxes subroutine is called to initialize the contents of the list boxes.

```
Sub Form_Load ()
   Update_List_Boxes
End Sub
```

9. Put the following code in the Ok_Click event subroutine. This code checks the text in the text box to see whether it contains the * or ? wildcards. If it does, the Update_List_Boxes routine is called to update the list boxes. Otherwise, Ok_Click closes the dialog box, because the user picked a filename.

```
Sub OK_Click ()
   ' If there are wildcards, just update the List Boxes.
   If InStr(FileEdit.Text, "*") Or InStr(FileEdit.Text, "?") Then
      Update_List_Boxes
   Else
      ' Otherwise, there's a real filename, so we can close up shop.
      FileDlg.Hide
   End If
End Sub
```

10. Create another new form and save it as TESTFDIA.FRM. This form will call the file dialog box to test it and show how it works. There are no controls on the form, but give the form the properties listed in Table 2-7.

| Object | Property | Setting |
|--------|----------|---------|
| Form | Caption | File dialog box test |
|  | Name | FileDialogBoxTest |

**Table 2-7** TestFDia project form's objects and properties

11. Create a menu for the form using the Menu Design window as shown in Table 2.8:

| Caption | Name |
| --- | --- |
| &File | File |
| ––––&Open... | FileOpen |
| ––––E&xit | FileExit |

**Table 2-8** TestFDia form's menu

12. Put the following code in the Declarations section of the form. This Const statement declares a constant for the Show method.

```
Const MODAL = 1
```

13. Put the following code in the FileExit_Click event subroutine. The End statement simply ends the Visual Basic application when you select the Exit menu option.

```
Sub FileExit_Click ()
    End
End Sub
```

14. Put the following code in the FileOpen_Click event subroutine. The code sets up the file dialog box and then shows it modally. Then it displays a message box showing you what you selected.

```
Sub FileOpen_Click ()
    FileDlg.FileEdit.Text = "*.*"
    FileDlg.Caption = "File open"
    FileDlg.Show MODAL

    If FileDlg.FileEdit.Text = "" Then
        MsgBox "You hit the Cancel button"
    Else
        temp$ = ""
        For I = 1 To FileDlg.FileList.ListCount
            If FileDlg.FileList.Tagged(I) Then temp$ = temp$ + Chr$(13) + ⇐
                Chr$(10) + FileDlg.FileList.List(I)
        Next

        MsgBox "You selected " + temp$
    End If
End Sub

Sub FileExit_Click ()
    End
End Sub
```

## How It Works

The Update_List_Boxes subroutine updates the contents of all the list boxes as the user changes directories or drives. Using the ClearListBox subroutine developed in How-To 2.4, Quickly clear a list box, both the file and directory list boxes are emptied.

Next, the Windows API function SendMessage is used to send the LB_DIR message to the file list box. A 0 as the wParam parameter tells Windows to load the list box with all "normal" files. (Normal files include all files with no attributes set and ones that have been modified but exclude read-only, hidden, and system files. You can study the WINAPI.TXT file on the distribution disk for the parameter constants to use for other attributes.) For the SendMessage's lParam parameter, the text from the text box is passed. (Note that you can't directly pass the Text property of the text box; although the data type of the Text property is String, Visual Basic won't let an API function change it.)

The same actions are repeated for the directory list box. The difference comes at the SendMessage API function. Instead of passing a 0 as the wParam parameter, we pass &HC010, which tells Windows to load the list box with the subdirectories in the current directory and all the available drives in the system. The subdirectories are automatically enclosed in square brackets (for example, [windows]), and the drives are in the format [-x-], where x is the drive letter.

### Catching Errors

The DirList_DblClick event subroutine is executed whenever the user double-clicks on a directory name or drive letter. It catches any errors that come up (most often, an attempt to switch to a floppy drive with no disk in the drive) with an error handler. Visual Basic will invoke the error handler automatically whenever an error occurs, so we don't have to do any special error checking.

The If statement checks whether the item double-clicked starts with [-. If it does, we know that it's a drive letter and the ChDrive statement will switch to the new drive. Otherwise, it's a directory and the ChDir statement will change to the directory.

If there have been no errors so far, the

```
On Local Error GoTo 0
```

statement disables the error handler. Then a call to Update_List_Boxes updates the list boxes with the filenames and directories for the new drive or directory. Then the Exit Sub statement gets us out of the subroutine.

If some error occurred, however, Visual Basic runs the code at line label UhOh. That code assumes that the error was, in fact, a problem that occurred with switching drives. (That's almost guaranteed to be the cause.) So a message box prompts the user to either retry the operation (after the user inserts a disk in the floppy drive) or cancel it. If the user clicks the Cancel button, the ChDrive statement will switch back to the drive that was current before the user tried to switch.

The Resume statement goes back to retry the statement that caused the error. In this case, it's the

```
A$ = CurDir$    ' Check whether the disk is ready.
```

statement, which is there specifically to try to cause an error. If it succeeds, everything went well.

### Testing the File Dialog

The FileOpen_Click event subroutine in the TestFDia form shows the proper way to use the file dialog box: You can select the files to be displayed in the file list box by setting the Text property of the file text box. You can use any filename, including ones with the DOS wildcards * and ?. If you want all files to be listed, just use *.*. A word processor might use *.DOC to select all files whose extension is .DOC.

Then you should show the file dialog box modally. A constant MODAL equal to 1 is the best way to do that. When the Show method call is complete, you know that the user selected some file or clicked the Cancel button. To determine which actually happened, check the Text property of the file text box. The Cancel_Click event subroutine of the file dialog box sets Text to the null string. If it's not the null string, you know the user selected a filename. You can then use that filename in a Visual Basic Open statement.

### Comments

It's a good idea to set the file dialog box's caption to remind users what they're selecting a file for. In the FileOpen_Click event subroutine, we use

```
FileDlg.Caption = "File open"
```

In a FileSaveAs_Click event subroutine, you might use

```
FileDlg.Caption = "File save as"
```

## 2.6 ● How do I...

# Make a powerful text editor using APIs?

### Problem

Windows controls actually have more features than are made available in Visual Basic. "Messages" are used to access these enhanced features. How do I access the advanced features left out of Visual Basic? Specifically, I am interested in the quickest way to find the current line my cursor is in a text box.

### Technique

It is here that many of the features of Windows controls have been left out of Visual Basic and that accessing those features is accomplished by sending messages.

Nearly all of Visual Basic's control "properties" and "methods" are resolved internally as messages that are sent to the control using the SendMessage API function. However, in order to use messages and the SendMessage API function, we need to pass the "handle" property of a control (called its hWnd property).

Forms in Visual Basic are the only structures that support the hWnd as a property. But actually all controls have hWnds. We will look at two means of determining the hWnd of a control, one of which involves a dynamic link library (DLL) included on the disk.

A DLL is a library of functions, similar to a LIB in QuickBASIC, that can be accessed from Visual Basic. The primary difference between it and a QuickBASIC library function is that DLLs can be linked at run time and as such are never merged into the executable file (.EXE). At this time, Visual Basic is not able to create DLLs. Therefore, CTLHWND.DLL is written in C.

### Steps

The sample program uses a text box to demonstrate the use of SendMessage. The program is the beginning of a utility, similar to Notepad, written almost entirely with the use of messages.

Open and run EDITOR.MAK. You can type text in the editor and the status bar at the bottom will reflect the current line number and the current total number of lines in the editor. (The items in the File menu, such as Open, Save, etc., do not actually function, but they do determine whether the contents of the editor have changed and prompt you accordingly.) The Editor supports full cut and paste and a single level of UNDO. The Edit menu should function just like the one in Notepad.

To create Editor, perform the following steps:

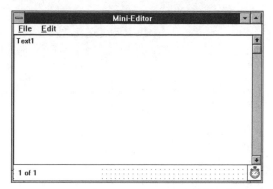

**Figure 2-11** Appearance of the Editor form

1. Create a new project called EDITOR.MAK. Create a new form with the objects and properties in Table 2-9 and save it as EDITOR.FRM. When finished, the form should look like Figure 2-11.

| Object | Property | Setting |
|--------|----------|---------|
| Form | Caption | Mini-Editor |
| Text | Name | Text1 |
| | Multiline | TRUE |
| | Scroll Bar | 2-Vertical |
| Label | Name | Label1 |
| | Caption | 1 of 1 |
| | BorderStyle | NONE |
| Timer | Name | Timer1 |
| | Interval | 400 |
| | Enabled | TRUE |

**Table 2-9** Editor project form's objects and properties

2. Build a menu with choices listed in Table 2-10.

| Caption | Name | Caption | Name |
|---------|------|---------|------|
| &File | FileMenu | &Edit | EditMenu |
| &New | FileNew | &Undo | EditUndo |
| &Open | FileOpen | - | Sep2 |
| &Save | FileSave | Cu&t | EditCut |
| – | Sep1 | &Copy | EditCopy |
| E&xit | FileExit | &Paste | EditPaste |
| | | &Delete | EditDelete |

**Table 2-10** The Mini-Editor menu values

3. Create a new module named TEXTBOX.BAS. Insert the following code in TEXTBOX.BAS.

```
DefInt A-Z

Declare Function SendMessage& Lib "User" (ByVal hWnd, ByVal Msg, ByVal ⇐
wParam, ByVal lParam As Any)

'These constants define the messages we will be sending
Const WM_USER = 1024
Const WM_CUT = 768
Const WM_COPY = 769
Const WM_PASTE = 770
Const WM_CLEAR = 771

Const EM_GETMODIFY = WM_USER + 8
Const EM_SETMODIFY = WM_USER + 9
Const EM_LINEINDEX = WM_USER + 11
Const EM_LINEFROMCHAR = WM_USER + 25
Const EM_UNDO = WM_USER + 23
Const EM_GETLINECOUNT = WM_USER + 10

'Now for each routine, we simply send a different message.
Function TextModified (TBox As Control)
    TextModified = SendMessage&(TBox.hWnd, EM_GETMODIFY, 0, 0&) * -1
End Function

Function TextCurLine (TBox As Control)
    TextCurLine = SendMessage&(TBox.hWnd, EM_LINEFROMCHAR, -1, 0&) + 1
End Function

Function TextLineBegin (TBox As Control, LineNum)
    TextLineBegin = SendMessage&(TBox.hWnd, EM_LINEINDEX, LineNum, 0&)
End Function

Sub TextClean (TBox As Control)
    Ok = SendMessage&(TBox.hWnd, EM_SETMODIFY, 0, 0&)
End Sub

Sub EditUndo (TBox As Control)
    Ok = SendMessage&(TBox.hWnd, EM   NDO, 0, 0&)
End Sub

Sub EditCut (TBox As Control)
    Ok = SendMessage&(TBox.hWnd, WM   UT, 0, 0&)
End Sub

Sub EditCopy (TBox As Control)
    Ok = SendMessage&(TBox.hWnd, WM   OPY, 0, 0&)
End Sub

Sub EditPaste (TBox As Control)
```

```
      Ok = SendMessage&(TBox.hWnd, WM_PASTE, 0, 0&)
End Sub

Sub EditClear (TBox As Control)
      Ok = SendMessage&(TBox.hWnd, WM_CLEAR, 0, 0&)
End Sub

Function TextLines (TBox As Control)
      TextLines = SendMessage&(TBox.hWnd, EM_GETLINECOUNT, 0, 0&)
End Function
```

4. Insert the following code in the Declarations section of Form1.

```
DefInt A-Z

Const MB_CANCEL = 2
Const MB_YES = 6
Const MB_NO = 7
Const CTRL_MASK = 2

Dim OldPos, OldTotal As Integer

Function PromptSave ()
      Title$ = "File has changed"
      Mess$ = "Do you want to save changes?"
      PromptSave = MsgBox(Mess$, 19, Title$)
End Function
```

5. Insert the following code in the FileExit_Click procedure.

```
Sub FileExit_Click ()
   If TextModified(Text1) Then
      Button = PromptSave()
      Select Case Button
         Case MB_CANCEL
            Exit Sub
         Case MB_YES
            'Save file here
      End Select
   End If
   End
End Sub
```

6. Insert the following code in the FileNew_Click procedure.

```
Sub FileNew_Click ()
   If TextModified(Text1) Then
      Button = PromptSave()
      Select Case Button
         Case MB_CANCEL
            Exit Sub
         Case MB_YES
            'Save file here
      End Select
```

*continued on next page*

*continued from previous page*

```
      End If
      Text1.Text = ""
      TextClean Text1
End Sub
```

7. Insert the following code in the FileOpen_Click procedure.

```
Sub FileOpen_Click ()
   If TextModified(Text1) Then
      Button = PromptSave()
      Select Case Button
         Case MB_CANCEL
            Exit Sub
         Case MB_YES
            'Save file here
      End Select
   End If
   Text1.Text = "You have just opened a new file!"
   TextClean Text1
End Sub
```

8. Insert the following code in the FileSave_Click procedure.

```
Sub FileSave_Click ()
   'Save file here
   TextClean Text1
End Sub
```

9. Insert the following code in the EditUndo_Click procedure.

```
Sub EditUndo_Click ()
   EditUndo Text1
End Sub
```

10. Insert the following code in the EditCopy_Click procedure.

```
Sub EditCopy_Click ()
   EditCopy Text1
End Sub
```

11. Insert the following code in the EditCut_Click procedure.

```
Sub EditCut_Click ()
   EditCut Text1
End Sub
```

12. Insert the following code in the EditDelete_Click procedure.

```
Sub EditDelete_Click ()
   EditClear Text1
End Sub
```

13. Insert the following code in the EditPaste_Click procedure.

```
Sub EditPaste_Click ()
   EditPaste Text1
End Sub
```

14. Insert the following code in the Timer1_Timer procedure.

```
Sub Timer1_Timer ()
   CurLine = TextCurLine(Text1)
   TLines = TextLines(Text1)
   If CurLine <> OldPos Or TLines <> OldTotal Then
      Label1.Caption = Str$(CurLine) + " of " + Str$(TLines)
      OldPos = CurLine
      OldTotal = TLines
   End If
End Sub
```

15. Insert the following code in the Text1_KeyDown procedure.

```
Sub Text1_KeyDown (KeyCode As Integer, Shift As Integer)
   If KeyCode = Asc("Y") And Shift  CTRL_MASK Then
     'Find the current row and where it begins
      CurLine = TextCurLine(Text1) - 1
      Text1.SelStart = TextLineBegin(Text1, CurLine)
      LineLen = TextLineBegin(Text1, CurLine + 1) - Text1.SelStart
      Text1.SelLength = LineLen
      Text1.SelText = ""
   End If
End Sub
```

16. Insert the following code in the Form_Unload procedure.

```
Sub Form_Unload (Cancel As Integer)
   If TextModified(Text1) Then
      Button = PromptSave()
      Select Case Button
         Case MB_CANCEL
            Cancel = -1
            Exit Sub
         Case MB_YES
            'Save file here
      End Select
   End If
End Sub
```

### How It Works

The use of SendMessage is dependent on having the handle property of the control to which you wish to send the message. Internally, Windows keeps track of all the controls you create by their "handle." The handle (or hWnd property) is basically like an ID number for a file; it's needed to link a command with a particular control. Internally, handles are simply pointers. If you want to take advantage of any of the built-in functions of the control that can only be accessed via SendMessage, you need the hWnd of that control. Once we have the hWnd to a control, we can then use the Windows SendMessage API function to send a message to that control. The SendMessage API function is a generalized function for sending and retrieving information from a control or form. The Declaration of SendMessage looks as follows:

```
Declare Function SendMessage& Lib "User" (Byval hWnd%, ByVal Msg%, Byval ⇐
wParam%, Byval lParam As Any)
```

all on one line, of course. The handle to the control which receives the message is hWnd%. The message number to be sent is Msg%. The meaning of wParam% and lParam vary depending on the message and sometimes are not used at all, as in the clipboard functions given earlier.

All the parameters to SendMessage are integers with the exception of lParam, which is declared to be As Any. In fact, lParam is always a LONG integer, but sometimes we will want to send a string. When a string is sent by using ByVal to a DLL, it is actually a LONG that is placed on the stack. This LONG is a pointer (known as a "long pointer") to an ASCIIZ string, which is not the native format of Visual Basic strings but the form required by most DLL functions.

Keep in mind that by using the As Any directive, you are effectively disabling parameter checking for that variable in your code. Therefore, you must ensure that you are either sending a LONG integer or a string.

Once you get to this point, the rest is easy. It is simply a matter of knowing which messages a control can receive, and the meaning of wParam and lParam in those contexts. You can refer to *The Waite Group's Windows API Bible*, by Jim Conger (Waite Group Press, 1992), for information on using the correct messages and parameters. For example, the EM_GETMODIFY message determines whether the contents of a text box have changed. The alternative to using SendMessage would be to create a handler for the Text1_Changed procedure that would set a static variable every time it was triggered. Obviously, this would be a waste, because that same status information is already stored by the text control and can be retrieved and set, only when it is needed.

The WM_ Clipboard messages allow you to perform the standard clipboard operations on a text control in one step instead of requiring you to make use of Visual Basic's Clipboard object. The EM_UNDO message would be rather complicated to duplicate in vanilla Visual Basic, requiring a large Select Case block. The TextCurLine, TextLineBegin, and TextLines functions would be almost impossible to create in Visual Basic alone.

The code itself is not really that complex and helps to highlight the sophistication of Windows controls. Each of the clipboard commands is ultimately resolved as one message sent to the controls. Because clipboard capability is inherent in a text box control, operations that might take five or six lines of Visual Basic only take one message. The most sophisticated of these is the EM_UNDO message. Duplicating this with pure Visual Basic code would require managing an "undo buffer" along with information about what operation happened last so you could undo it. This capability, however, is native to the text box control, so we don't need to worry about it.

The file operations demonstrate the use of a hidden "property" of the text box control not available in native Visual Basic. Text box controls maintain a flag that indicates whether the contents have been changed. In the file menu options, we are checking this flag to determine whether or not to prompt the user to save the work in progress. Duplicating this in Visual Basic would require creating a Text1_Change event handler (which would fire *many* times), setting our own flag, and adding unnecessary overhead to the operation of the control. Using SendMessage we can simply retrieve or set this flag at the appropriate time.

### Comments

As you might guess, another reason to be familiar with these messages is to manipulate the controls in other applications. For example, it would not be difficult to activate Notepad and manipulate the text control that gets focus.

## 2.7  How do I...

Complexity: Intermediate

## Create an old-style file dialog box?

### Problem

Users often complain about Visual Basic's separate drive, directory, and file list box threesome (see Figure 2-12). Many would prefer the older style, a file dialog box with a single list box that lists both directories and drives (see Figure 2-13). Additionally, how do I prevent errors when users try to change to a floppy drive that doesn't have a disk inserted or has an open door?

### Technique

Visual Basic provides all the tools you need to modify and re-create the old- style dialog box. Visual Basic's file list box will serve, but we need a way to combine directories and drives into a single list box. You might think the Dir$ function would return directory names, but it does not. Also, unfortunately, there is no Windows API function to combine directories and drives. What you can do is copy all the directories from an invisible directory list box, and all the drives from a drive combo box, into a plain list box.

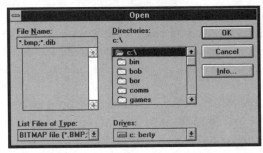

**Figure 2-12** The new, Visual Basic-style file dialog box

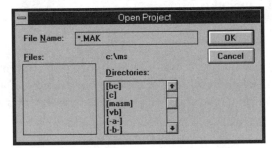

**Figure 2-13** The "old-style" file dialog box

## Steps

Open and run FILEDLG.MAK. You can click on the directories to negotiate the directory tree and click on the drive letters to switch to another drive. You can also double-click on a filename to select that file and close the form. Because this form is ready-to-run, you can simply add it to any project you're working on.

1. Create a new project called FILEDLG.MAK. Create a new form using the properties listed in Table 2-11 and save it as FILEDLG.FRM. Figure 2-13 shows how the form should look when you're finished.

| Object | Property | Setting |
|--------|----------|---------|
| Form | FormName | FileDlg |
| | Caption | File |
| | BorderStyle | 1 - Fixed Single |
| | ControlBox | False |
| | MaxButton | False |
| | MinButton | False |
| | BackColor | &H00C0C0C0& |
| Text box | Name | FileEdit |

| Object | Property | Setting |
|---|---|---|
| Label | Caption | File&name: |
| Label | Name | DirLabel |
| Button | Name | Ok |
| | Caption | Ok |
| | Default | True |
| Button | Name | Cancel |
| | Caption | Cancel |
| | Cancel | True |
| File list box | Name | File1 |
| Label | Caption | &Files: |
| List box | Name | DirList |
| Label | Caption | &Directories: |
| Directory list box | Name | Dir1 |
| | Visible | False |
| Drive combo box | Name | Drive1 |
| | Visible | False |

**Table 2-11** FileDlg project form's objects and properties

2. Now we're ready to enter the code. Most of this code goes in a subroutine called Update_List_Boxes, which goes in the General section of the form. Other event subroutines in this project call Update_List_Boxes whenever the user clicks in one of the list boxes, so any directory or drive changes are immediately reflected.

```
Sub Update_List_Boxes ()
   ' Update current directory label.
   DirLabel.Caption = LCase$(CurDir$)

   ' Update Path of file List Box.
   File1.Path = CurDir$

   ' Update Pattern of file List Box (for wildcard searches).
   File1.Pattern = FileEdit.Text

   ' Clear out the directory List Box
   Do While DirList.ListCount
      DirList.RemoveItem 0
   Loop

   ' Add a [..] (parent directory) if we're in a subdirectory.
   If Right$(CurDir$, 1) <> "\" Then DirList.AddItem "[..]"

   ' Update the hidden directory List Box's Path
```

*continued on next page*

*continued from previous page*

```
    ' to match the actual current directory.
    Dir1.Path = CurDir$

    ' Add each directory in the hidden directory List Box
      ' to the "combined" List Box.
    For I = 0 To Dir1.ListCount - 1
       A$ = Dir1.List(I)

       ' The directories in the hidden directory List Box
       ' are absolute paths; that is, they contain the
       ' complete path name, such as c:\visbasic\icons, and
       ' all we're interested in is the last path--icons--
       ' so strip out the rest.
       For J = Len(A$) To 1 Step -1
          If Mid$(A$, J, 1) = "\" Then
             A$ = Mid$(A$, J + 1)
             Exit For
          End If
       Next

       ' Add the path surrounded by brackets, for example, [icons].
       DirList.AddItem "[" + A$ + "]"
    Next

    ' Add the drives in the hidden drive combo box to the
    ' directory List Box.
    For I = 0 To Drive1.ListCount - 1
       DirList.AddItem "[-" + Mid$(Drive1.List(I), 1, 1) + "-]"
    Next
End Sub
```

3. Place the following code in the Click event subroutine of the Cancel button control to unload the form.

```
Sub Cancel_Click ()
    ' If we select Cancel, we can unload the dialog, because
    ' we don't need it anymore.
    FileEdit.Text = ""
    Hide
End Sub
```

4. Put the following code in the DblClick event subroutine of the DirList list box control. This is where we change directories and switch drives. This is also where we check for errors, because there might not be a disk in a floppy drive.

```
Sub DirList_DblClick ()
    Const MB_RETRYANDCANCEL = 5
    Const MB_ICONEXCLAMATION = 48

    On Local Error GoTo UhOh
```

```
' When you double-click on a directory or drive entry,
' check whether the selected item is a drive; if so,
' change the current drive.
If Left$(DirList.Text, 2) = "[-" And Len(DirList.Text) = 5 Then
   oldDir$ = CurDir$
   ChDrive Mid$(DirList.Text, 3, 1)
   A$ = CurDir$    ' Check whether the disk is ready
' Otherwise, change the current directory.
Else
   ChDir Mid$(DirList.Text, 2, Len(DirList.Text) - 2)
End If

On Local Error GoTo 0

Update_List_Boxes
Exit Sub

UhOh:
   If MsgBox("Unable to switch to drive " + Mid$(DirList.Text, 3, 1) + ⇐
":", MB_RETRYANDCANCEL + MB_ICONEXCLAMATION, "Visual Basic - FileDlg") = 2
Then
   ' If user presses Cancel, go back to the previous drive.
      ChDrive Left$(oldDir$, 1)
   End If

   Resume
End Sub
```

5. Put the following code in the DblClick event subroutine of the File1 file list box control. We set the text of the text box to the file the user selected and unload the form.

```
Sub File1_DblClick ()
   ' When we double-click on a filename in the List Box,
   ' set the edit control to the selected filename and
   ' close the dialog, because we've picked the filename.
   FileEdit.Text = File1.Filename
   Hide
End Sub
```

6. Put the following code in the Load event subroutine of the form and the Click event subroutine of the OK button to update the various list boxes by calling the Update_List_Boxes routine.

```
Sub Form_Load ()
   Update_List_Boxes
End Sub
Sub OK_Click ()
   Update_List_Boxes
End Sub
```

## How It Works

The Update_List_Boxes procedure updates all the list boxes as the user changes directories or drives. The first Do loop empties out the combined list box. Then we add a double periods entry ".." that lets you "back up" to the previous directory (akin to the DOS (CD ..) command). The first For...Next loop adds the entries of the hidden directory list box to the combined list box. Visual Basic's directory list box lists the complete directory path (for example, C:\VB\ICONS), so we have to extract the last part of the complete directory name (ICONS). That's the part we add to the combined directory list box. The second For...Next loop adds the entries from the hidden drive combo box to the combined list box. We mimic the standard format of [-x-] where x is the drive letter.

The DirList_DblClick subroutine manages the selection of a directory and any possible errors that might come up. Constants are set up for the error message box (that's where the MB_ prefix comes from) and a local error handler is set up for any disk error. The If statement checks for the "[-" added to the drive letters to see if there was a double-click on a drive letter. If so, the program switches to the drive using ChDrive. Otherwise, it's a directory and the program switches to the directory using ChDir.

Getting this far means there hasn't been any error, so the error handling routine is disabled, Update_List_Boxes is called to make sure the list boxes get updated with the new drive and directory information, and finally we exit from the subroutine.

If there was any error, the code at line label UhOh gets run and a message box is popped up, as shown in Figure 2-14. If the user clicks on Cancel, we ChDrive back to the drive before we tried to switch (which we know was good). Otherwise, we just use Resume to return to where the error occurred.

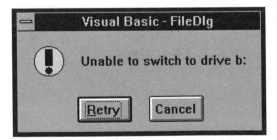

**Figure 2-14** The UhOh message box

## Comments

Note how the LCase$ function is used to make the directory label caption lowercase, so it matches the lowercase filenames. You can omit the LCase$ if you'd prefer your directory names to be uppercase.

This project shows one way to create a file dialog box. The file dialog box presented in How-To 2.5, Make a file dialog box using APIs, is faster than this one, because it uses Windows messages.

The most common use of this form is to provide a dialog box in response to a File Open menu selection. In that case, you may want to change the form's Caption property to "File Open." You can also use it in response to a File Save As menu selection, in which case you might want to set the caption to "File Save." For example,

```
Sub FileOpen_Click ()
    FileDlg.Caption = "Open a file"
    FileDlg.Show MODAL
End Sub
```

## 2.8 ● How do I...

## Create multiple entries in the Task List?

### Problem

I would like to have multiple instances of my application running with different workspaces. When there are multiple instances of other Windows applications running, such as Notepad, the various entries in the Task List reflect the main window caption (such as Notepad—MYFILE.TXT). However, when I run multiple instances of my Visual Basic application, even though I change the Caption property of my main form, all the entries in the Task List are the same: the name of my .EXE file.

### Technique

Visual Basic has the ability to create what appear to be multiple "ownerless" forms. The way Visual Basic achieves this is to create a hidden window that "owns" all the windows that you create. Although rarely an issue, the ownership does matter here, because the caption of that hidden window must change to change the entry in the Task List. Therefore, we must use the GetWindow API function to retrieve the owner of our main form and then the SetWindowText function to set the caption of that window.

### Steps

To try the sample program, an .EXE file must first be generated from our source code. Open and run TASKS.MAK. Select Make.EXE from the File menu and run the resulting program, TASKS.EXE, from the Program Manager.

You will see that the caption of the program is "My Application: X," where X is the "instance" number of the application. As you load and run more copies of the application, this number will be incremented. Now, if you double-click the desktop to bring up the Task Manager, you will see the distinct entries for each instance of the application.

If you enter a new string into the text box on the form and click the command button, you will change not only the caption of the form, but the entry in the Task List, as shown in Table 2-12.

To create the Tasks project, perform the following steps:

1. Create a new project called TASKS.MAK. Create a new form with the following objects and properties and save it as TASK.FRM. When finished, your form should look like Figure 2-15.

| Object | Property | Setting |
|--------|----------|---------|
| Form | FormName | Form1 |
| Text | Name | Text1 |
| Button | Name | Command1 |
| | Caption | Change Task Name |

**Table 2-12** Tasks Project form's objects and properties

2. Insert the following code in the Declarations section of Form1.

```
DefInt A-Z
```

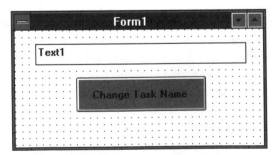

**Figure 2-15** Appearance of the Tasks form

3. Insert the following code in the Command1_Click procedure.

```
Sub Command1_Click ()
    TaskName$ = Text1.Text
    If Len(TaskName$) Then
        SetNewTaskName Form1, TaskName$
        Form1.Caption = TaskName$
    End If
End Sub
```

4. Create a new module called TASKS.BAS and insert the following code.

```
DefInt A-Z
Declare Function GetModuleHandle Lib "Kernel" (ByVal ModuleName$)
Declare Function GetModuleUsage Lib "kernel" (ByVal hModule)
Declare Function GetWindow Lib "user" (ByVal hWnd, ByVal wCmd)
Declare Sub SetWindowText Lib "user" (ByVal hWnd, ByVal WindowText$)

Const GW_OWNER = 4

Sub Main ()
    hModule = GetModuleHandle("TASKS.EXE")
    mCount = GetModuleUsage(hModule)
    TaskName$ = "My Application: " + Str$(mCount)
    Load Form1
    SetNewTaskName Form1, TaskName$
    Form1.Caption = TaskName$
    Form1.Show
End Sub

Sub SetNewTaskName (Frm As Form, TaskName$)
    Wnd = Frm.hWnd
    hOwner = GetWindow(Wnd, GW_OWNER)
    SetWindowText hOwner, TaskName$
End Sub
```

5. Save the form and the project as TASKS.

6. Set Sub Main as the startup form.

7. Create and run the .EXE file.

## How It Works

In Sub Main, GetModuleUsage is used to find the current usage count of the .EXE file, in this case TASKS.EXE. This enables a descriptive task entry to be assigned for each instance of the application that is just in variable TaskName$. The real secret to the technique is in determining that there is a hidden "owner" of the form and that we can use GetWindow to determine the hWnd property of that window. Once we have that information, it is easy to use SetWindowText to assign TextName$ for our Windows caption.

SetNewTaskName is written as a subroutine so it can be called from the form as well as from the module itself.

### Comments

It is indeed possible to use this technique to change the caption and Task List entry for other applications, as well as your own. However, be advised that most applications treat this information dynamically, so your application would have to constantly "check in," using a timer or DoEvents, to see whether another change was warranted.

## 2.9  How do I...

# Make a simple "searching" list box?

### Problem

I'd like to make a text box/list box combination like the one in Windows Help, where as you type in the text box, the matching entry in the list box is automatically scrolled and selected. How can I do this in Visual Basic?

### Technique

Automatically selecting the entries in a text box while typing is a good time-saver for users. The key to implementing this feature in Visual Basic is to use the text box's Change event. That way you don't have to wait until the user presses (ENTER) or clicks on a button.

Once you detect a Change event you can search the entries of the list box, as shown in Figure 2-16. If there's a match, you can select that item in the list box.

### Steps

Open and run SEARCH.MAK. You can type the first letter or two of the city names in the list box. As you type, the appropriate entry will be highlighted. If two names have a similar letter, the highlight will jump to the name as soon as a match occurs. So as you type "San" the highlight bar will fall on "San Jose." If the next letter is a "t," it will jump to "Santa Cruz." When you press (ENTER) or click on the Ok button, the highlighted list box entry will be displayed in a message box.

1. Create a new project called SEARCH.MAK. Create a new form with the controls and properties listed in Table 2-13 and save it as SEARCH.FRM.

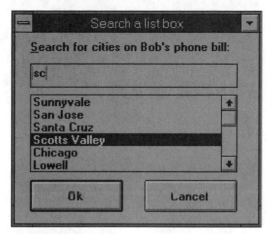

**Figure 2-16** The Search project in action

| Control | Property | Setting |
| --- | --- | --- |
| Form | Caption | Search a List Box |
| | MaxButton | False |
| | BackColor | &H00C0C0C0& |
| Label | Caption | &Search for cities on Bob's phone bill |
| Text box | Name | Text1 |
| List box | Name | List1 |
| Command button | Name | Ok |
| | Caption | Ok |
| | Default | True |
| Command button | Name | Cancel |
| | Caption | Cancel |
| | Cancel | True |

**Table 2-13** Search project form's controls and properties

2. Put the following code in the Cancel_Click event subroutine.

```
Sub Cancel_Click ()
    End
End Sub
```

3. Put the following code in the Form_Load event subroutine. This code simply adds some default items to the list box.

```
Sub Form_Load ()
    List1.AddItem "Sunnyvale"
    List1.AddItem "San Jose"
    List1.AddItem "Santa Cruz"
```

*continued on next page*

*continued from previous page*

```
    List1.AddItem "Scotts Valley"
    List1.AddItem "Chicago"
    List1.AddItem "Lowell"
    List1.AddItem "Roswell"
    List1.AddItem "Cambridge"
    List1.AddItem "Muskegon"
    List1.AddItem "Agoura"
    List1.AddItem "Englewood"
    List1.AddItem "Bellevue"
    List1.AddItem "Anaheim"
End Sub
```

4. Put the following code in the Ok_Click event subroutine. This statement pops up a message box that displays which list box entry was selected, either by clicking on it with the mouse or by typing in the list box.

```
Sub Ok_Click ()
    MsgBox "You selected " + List1.Text
End Sub
```

5. Put the following code in the Text1_Change event subroutine. This is where the actual matching takes place. The For...Next loop goes through the entries in the list box trying to match with what was entered in the text box. If there's a match, the list box's ListIndex property is set and the For...Next loop is aborted.

```
Sub Text1_Change ()
    Search$ = UCase$(Text1.Text)
    SearchLen = Len(Search$)

    If SearchLen Then
        For I = 0 To List1.ListCount - 1
            If UCase$(Left$(List1.List(I), SearchLen)) = Search$ Then
                List1.ListIndex = I
                Exit For
            End If
        Next
    End If
End Sub
```

**How It Works**

Each time the user makes a change to the text box, by typing another character in the text box, or backspacing, the text box's Change event is triggered. So all the code to do searching is in the Text1_Change event subroutine. When doing this search, you don't want the case of the letters to matter, so the string actually searched for is set to all uppercase by using the UCase$ function.

Because you want the search to get more specific as more and more characters are typed, the SearchLen variable holds the length of the text in the text box. Then you can limit the search to the first SearchLen characters in each list box entry. Notice the first If statement. It ensures that the subroutine won't do any searching unless there is text to search for.

The For...Next loop in the SearchLen subroutine goes through each entry in the list box and compares it to the uppercase search string. A match should be made regardless of case, so the UCase$ function is used. Then, because Visual Basic will only match two string variables if they're identical in content and length, the Left$ function is used to make sure the comparison is between strings of the same length as the search string.

If there is a match, the ListIndex property of the list box is set to the examined entry and the For Next loop is exited. If there is no match, the currently highlighted item (the ListIndex property) isn't changed. That's all there is to it. You now have a feature in your application that your users will appreciate.

### Comments

Because the Text1_Change event subroutine searches through the entire list box, the list box doesn't have to be sorted (have its Sorted property set to True).

## 2.10 How do I...

Complexity: Advanced

## Make a "searching" list box using APIs?

### Problem

How-To 2.9, Make a simple "searching" list box, showed how to build a list box that automatically scrolls as it tries to locate the same text the user types. If it finds a matching prefix, it selects that line. Is there a more powerful way to do this using Windows APIs?

### Technique

By using the SendMessage API function, and some tricks, we can build a faster search function. Our goal is to have a sorted list box "track" characters as they are typed into a text box, so the program starts immediately searching for a corresponding prefix in the list box. This technique of searching allows for partial matches, minimizing the typing the user must do to find a particular entry in the list box. The list box always attempts to find a match for as many characters as have been typed in the edit box. If two entries have similar prefixes, the list will jump to the second one as soon as enough characters have been typed in the edit box to distinguish the entries. If matching text is found in the list, we want that line to become the top line in the list. In addition, we want the text in the text box to change to reflect user selections in the list box, as it does in Windows Help.

At first glance, it appears as though a search function of this type can be coded by using the Change event of the text box, then scanning through the list box for matching text and setting the ListIndex property of the list box accordingly. The ListIndex property seems perfectly suited to this task because it can "select" an entry in the list. Unfortunately, setting the ListIndex property in Visual Basic is the same as clicking on the list box. This will trigger another Click event in the list box. Since we would use the Click event handler to change the text in the text box, our application could end up in an endless loop.

The solution is an example of what is known in the object-oriented programming world as "encapsulation." Encapsulation simply means that an object (or control) contains both data and code. Although the search scheme just outlined treats the list box as a mere passive receptacle of data, in fact, the list box contains a great deal of built-in functionality, or methods. One of these built-in Windows methods is the ability to search for a specified text prefix and select the line that contains it. The SendMessage API function, as described in How-To 2.6, Make a powerful text editor using APIs, is used to access these additional list box functions. Using the Windows API search function of the list box is not only faster, but also does not generate the Click event, allowing us to process that separately as a "user driven" event. This means we can send another API message to the list box to make our selection the top of the list.

### Steps

Open and run SEARCH.MAK. You will see that the file box is filled with a list of files. Further, the top line of the file list will be selected and the corresponding text copied to the edit control. If you begin to type, the text in the

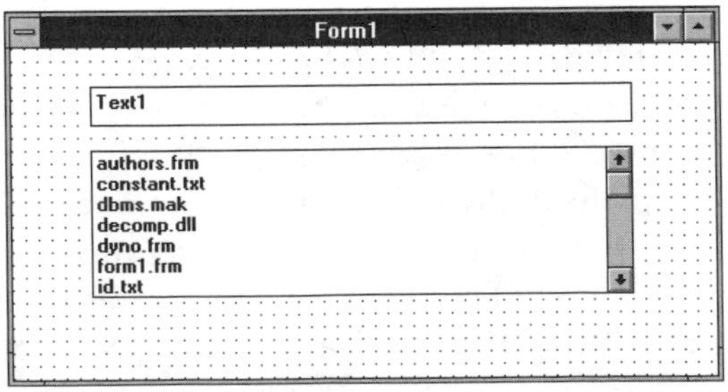

**Figure 2-17** The appearance of the Search form

edit control will be replaced with what you type and, with any luck at all, the list box will "track" your keystrokes.

1. Create a new project called SEARCH.MAK. Create a new form with the objects and properties in Table 2-14 and save it as SEARCH.FRM. When finished, your form should look like Figure 2-17.

| Object | Property | Setting |
|--------|----------|---------|
| Form | FormName | Form1 |
| | Caption | Seach a list box |
| Text box | Name | Text1 |
| FileList | Name | File1 |

**Table 2-14** Search project form's objects and properties

2. Open the Declarations section of Form1 and insert the following code.

```
DefInt A-Z
'Note each Declare statement must fit on one line
Declare Function SendMessage Lib "User" (ByVal hWnd, ByVal wMsg, ⇐
ByVal wParam, ByVal lParam As Any)

'Constants from Windows.h
Const WM_USER - 1024
Const LB_SELECTSTRING = WM_USER + 13
Const LB_SETTOPINDEX = WM_USER + 24
```

3. Put this code in the Form_Load procedure.

```
Sub Form_Load ()
   File1.ListIndex = 0
   Text1.SelStart = 0
   Text1.SelLength = Len(Text1.Text)
End Sub
```

4. Put this code in the File1_Click procedure.

```
Sub File1_Click ()
   Text1.Text = File1.FileName
End Sub
```

5. Put this code in the Text1_Change procedure.

```
Sub Text1_Change ()
   Search$ = Text1.Text
   If Len(Search$) Then
      Index = SendMessage(File1.hWnd, LB_SELECTSTRING, -1, Search$)
      ErrCode = SendMessage(File1.hWnd, LB_SETTOPINDEX, Index, 0&)
   Else
      ErrCode = SendMessage(File1.hWnd, LB_SETCURSEL, 0, 0&)
      ErrCode = SendMessage(File1.hWnd, LB_SETTOPINDEX, 0, 0&)
   End If
End Sub
```

## How It Works

The Form_Load procedure performs an initialization similar to the one used in Windows Help. First, the File1.ListIndex property is set to 0. This is the equivalent of the user clicking on the first row of the file list. Therefore, the File1_Click event handler is triggered. In File1_Click, the Text1.Text property is set to the currently selected FileName in the list. This, in turn, triggers the Text1_Change event. You can see the potential for an endless loop here. What prevents this is that the Text1_Change event handler uses messages instead of the ListIndex property, so it does not trigger a File1_Click event. Finally, the Form_Load procedure selects the text in Text1. The benefit of mimicking this habit of the help system is that "selected" text is easily replaced by the user just by typing, which deletes the existing text and begins a completely new prefix. This technique can't be used if you wish to allow the user to type into the text box holding a filename.

An important procedure is the Text1_Change event handler. Whenever the user changes the contents of the text control, either by adding or removing characters, Text1_Change attempts to find a matching prefix in File1. The Window handle of the file list is obtained using the ControlhWnd function as described in How-To 2.6 Make a powerful text editor using APIs. Next, the LB_SELECTSTRING message is sent to the file list. This message searches the list box for the text prefix and makes the first match the current index, all in one operation and without firing the File1.Click event. The LB_SETTOPINDEX message is sent to the file list to put the selected item on top. The Else clause is optional and is added solely to mimic the behavior of Windows Help. If Text1 is empty, the LB_SETCURSEL messages are sent to make the index of the file list the top line. The LB_SETCURSEL message is functionally equivalent to setting the .ListIndex property without triggering the _Click event.

## Comments

The first thing you are likely to notice when trying this How-To is that sometimes the LB_SETTOPINDEX messages seem to malfunction. The reason is that a list box will not allow itself to be scrolled beyond available data. Therefore, if a list box control has 10 visible lines, contains 20 lines of text, and your search takes you to line 17, LB_SETTOPINDEX will only move item 17 to visible row 7.

In most cases, you will be searching for matches using a normal list box and not a file list. We used the file list here to simplify populating the list for the example. The only code that would need to be changed to use a normal list box instead would be the line in the File1.Click procedure that refers to the .FileName property. Your code would need to refer to the .Text property instead.

Also, you should note that the example passes a value of (-1) as the wParam when sending the LB_SELECTSTRING message. This parameter refers to the starting point of the search and (-1) means to begin from the top. You may optionally begin from a specific index if, for example, you wanted to step through the list box, finding all matching strings.

There may be times when you want a list to perform a search but not to "select" the match. This is accomplished by sending the LB_FINDSTRING (WM_USER + 16) message in place of the LB_SELECTSTRING message.

Interestingly, this search routine works with combo boxes as well as list boxes and file list boxes.

## 2.11 ● How do I...          Complexity: Advanced

## Make a button with continuous events?

### Problem
I want the user to be able to hold down a command button with the mouse and while doing so, have the program perform a continuous operation until the mouse button is released. This would let me create my own custom scrolling number boxes for entering values easily. Command buttons in Visual Basic don't seem to work this way. What is the answer?

### Technique
This effect is easily achieved using a picture box and Visual Basic's DoEvents function. Briefly, the DoEvents function simply delays until all the messages waiting to be processed by your application and all others have been handled, before returning. In other words, DoEvents frees up Visual Basic to allow other messages to be processed. This is equivalent to a C program creating a "PeekMessage loop" and allows for cooperative multitasking under Windows. (For a more detailed description of DoEvents refer to *The Waite Group's Visual Basic Super Bible*, by Taylor Maxwell and Bryon Scott, Waite Group Press, 1992.)

The technique we'll use is to set a static variable to True when the MouseDown event over the button is encountered. Then, the repetitive operation is performed inside a DoEvents loop that checks the status of this global variable to see whether the mouse button is returned down. Finally, the DoEvents loop sets the variable to False when the MouseUp event is encountered.

**Figure 2-18**

Appearance of the
Counter form

Our example creates a simple counter that will go up and down when the buttons are held down. Although this is not the most interesting application of this technique, it is the easiest to present clearly here and should point to more creative uses.

**Steps**

Open and run COUNTER.MAK. If you hold down the mouse button over one of the picture boxes, the counter will change continuously.

1. Create a new project called COUNTER.MAK. Create a new form with the objects and properties in Table 2-15 and save it as COUNTER.FRM. When finished, your form should look like Figure 2-18.

| Object | Property | Setting |
| --- | --- | --- |
| Form | FormName | Form1 |
| | Caption | Counter |
| Text | Name | Text1 |
| Picture | Name | Picture1 |
| | AutoSize | True |
| | Index | 0 |
| | Picture | ARW01LT.ICO |
| Picture | Name | Picture1 |
| | AutoSize | True |
| | Index | 1 |
| | Picture | ARW01RT.ICO |

**Table 2-15** Counter project form's objects and properties

2. Open the Declarations section of Form1 and insert the following code.

```
Dim ButtonDown, Counter As Integer
Const TRUE = -1
Const FALSE = 0
```

3. Put this code in the Picture1_MouseDown procedure.

```
Sub Picture1_MouseDown (Index As Integer, Button As Integer, Shift As ⇐
                   Integer, X As Single, Y As Single)
   Increment = Index * 2 - 1
   ButtonDown = TRUE
   While DoEvents() And ButtonDown
      Counter = Counter + Increment
```

```
      Text1.Text = Str$(Counter)
   Wend
End Sub
```

4. Put this code in the Picture1_MouseUp procedure.

```
Sub Picture1_MouseUp (Index As Integer, Button As Integer, ⇐
                 Shift As Integer, X As Single, Y As Single)
   ButtonDown = FALSE
End Sub
```

### How It Works

The Picture1_MouseDown procedure first determines the increment based on Index passed to the routine. In other words, Increment = Index * 2 - 1 means if Index is 0, Increment is -1; if Index is 1, then Increment is 1. This could just as easily be a Case statement and, in fact, a Case statement is more appropriate for a larger control array, because there would be more than two binary choices of action within the event handler.

The Picture1_MouseDown routine sets the ButtonDown global variable to True. Ultimately, the procedure begins a While...Wend loop that continuously checks both DoEvents and ButtonDown. As stated earlier, we are not checking for any specific value to be returned by DoEvents. The DoEvents function will not return until the message queue under Windows is empty. The very act of checking DoEvents allows all other messages on the system to be processed before continuing, including the MouseUp message.

The MouseUp procedure simply sets ButtonDown to False, causing the test in the While...Wend loop in MouseDown to fail, ending the loop.

### Comments

Windows is based on a system of messages. Every action by the user, and many actions by the system itself, generates messages. If a particular process takes a long time to finish, the messages begin to "queue up." For example, if you open a file, move the mouse, and start typing, Windows queues up each of these events so one can't interfere with another. This is similar to the "type ahead buffer" under DOS. Because Windows, unlike OS/2 Presentation Manager, is not "preemptive," it is possible for applications to misbehave and prevent successful multitasking with other applications. For example, one application can dominate the time slicing so another application doesn't get time to do anything. In fact, if our Picture1_MouseDown routine contained a simple While...Wend loop without the DoEvents function, the application would never free itself up long enough to receive the MouseUp event.

The functionality of DoEvents could be duplicated using a timer but, besides the code being more convoluted, a timer would be slower. The DoEvents loop is the method most often used in Windows programming as it allows the fastest possible execution speed when no other messages are pending.

For this How-To, we used a static variable to hold the state of the buttons. A static variable is available to all the routines within a form. If you choose to use this technique, you might want to add a ButtonDown variable to your global module as you would only need one for each application.

## 2.12  How do I...

## Set minimum and maximum sizes for a form?

### Problem

When the user resizes my application, I would like to be able to adjust the size and positions of controls on the form. This is a problem if the user can make the form either smaller or larger than a reasonable adjustment of the controls will allow. I know that it is possible to reset the size of the form *after* the user has finished resizing it, but I'm looking for a clean way of preventing the user from ever exceeding my preset bounds. How do I control the minimum and maximum sizes that are allowed by Windows for my form?

### Window Messages and the MsgHook Control

To understand the technique used in this How-To, it is first necessary to understand how Windows messages and the MsgHook control work.

Each Windows application has a *message procedure*. Message procedures are similar to Visual Basic event procedures. When Windows has a message for an application, the window procedure for that application is called with four arguments: hWnd, msg, wParam, and lParam. The hWnd parameter contains the handle of the window whose event procedure is being called. The msg parameter is a constant representing the message being sent. The wParam and lParam parameters are used to pass arguments related to the message. For most messages the 6 bytes of the wParam and lParam arguments are enough to hold the message's arguments. When more information than can fit in 6 bytes is required, lParam contains the address of a location in memory where the information is stored. A window procedure always returns a Long, indicating what type of action was taken for a given message.

Visual Basic contains a window procedure that is called for each message sent to a Visual Basic form or control. Visual Basic looks at the msg parameter and takes the appropriate action. For some messages (such as WM_SIZE), Visual

Basic calls the corresponding event procedure (Resize in the case of WM_SIZE). The designers of Visual Basic did not create a corresponding event procedure for other messages.

The MsgHook control, Figure 2-19, can be used to intercept messages sent to any windows application. When it receives a message of interest to your application it fires an event and the message can be examined, changed, modified, or even discarded. The MsgHook properties are listed in Table 2.16.

**Figure 2-19**
The MsgHook control

| Property | Meaning |
|---|---|
| hwndHook | Handle to any window |
| Message | An array of 65536 True/False values, one for each possible Windows message. When an element is set to True the corresponding windows message will generate an event |

**Table 2.16**  MsgHook control's properties

To use the MsgHook control, you first assign a window handle to the hwndHook property of the control. Window handles are available for forms and most of the controls in the hWnd property of the controls. You tell the MsgHook control what messages you are interested in by setting elements of the Message array property. There are 65,536 possible messages in Windows (&H0000 - &HFFFF), and so there are 65,536 elements in the Message array property. The first element of the Message array is 0.

The MsgHook control has only one event procedure, MsgHook_Message. Setting an element of the Message array to True results in the MsgHook_Message event procedure being called when the corresponding window message is received. The MsgHook_Message event procedure has the following declaration:

```
Sub MsgHook_Message (msg As Integer, wParam As Integer, lParam As Long,
action As Integer, result As Long)
```

The msg, wParam, and lParam are the exact same parameters that Windows is passing the hwndHooks message procedure. The action parameter is used by the MsgHook control to determine what to do with a message after the MsgHook_Message procedure is finished. If the MsgHook_Message event procedure sets action to 0, the message will be sent to the window for which it was intended. When the action parameter is set to 1, the MsgHook control does not send the message on to the original recipient and instead the value assigned to result during the MsgHook_Message event procedure is returned to Windows.

The fact that lParam sometimes contains a location in memory where information is stored presents a problem: Visual Basic doesn't provide any way to copy things that are outside of its own variable space. MsgHook provides two subroutines to take care of this problem. The subroutines are declared as follows:

```
Declare Sub MsgHookGetData Lib "msghook.vbx" (ByVal lParam As Long, ByVal
destSize As Integer, destType As Any)
Declare Sub MsgHookSetData Lib "msghook.vbx" (ByVal lParam As Long, ByVal
destSize As Integer, srcType As Any)
```

The first subroutine, MsgHookGetData, is used to copy data from the memory location contained in lParam to the Visual Basic variable destType. MsgHookSetData is used to copy modified data back to the memory location pointed to by lParam. You must be extremely careful when using these functions. Copying too many bytes from the location in lParam can cause a General Protection Fault. If you copy too many bytes back to the location given by lParam, you will be lucky to get a GPF, and you might well expect to crash Windows or hang the machine. Another result could be corruption of Windows-maintained data, with unpredictable and potentially disastrous results. When you write and debug code that uses these functions you should save your project before each run since a GPF will result in termination of Visual Basic and the loss of any unsaved work.

If this all seems a little overwhelming at first, don't worry about it! After you've looked at this How-To, and perhaps some of the many others in the book that use the MsgHook control, go back and reread the previous section.

*Note: Do not call the Windows function SendMessage while executing inside of the MsgHook's Message event subroutine. Calling SendMessage from within the Message event subroutine can cause Windows to become deadlocked. You can call PostMessage to send messages to your own, or other, applications. To be safe, you should do as little as possible within the MsgHook_Message event procedure. Setting and testing global variables is safe. Accessing the properties of other controls is definitely not safe since this can result in messages being sent.*

### Technique

Windows sends the WM_GETMINMAXINFO message to windows whenever it wants to know the minimum and maximum sizes for a window.

Unfortunately, this is one of the Windows messages that does not result in an event. This is where the MsgHook control comes in. By setting the MsgHook.hwndHook property to form1.hWnd and setting MsgHook.Message(WM_GETMINMAXINFO) to True, the MsgHook event procedure will be called whenever the WM_GETMINMAXINFO is sent to the form. The lParam passed with the WM_GETMINMAXINFO message contains the location in memory where information about the window's size is stored. In the MsgHook_Message event routine, MsgHookGetData is used to copy the information into a VB Type variable. Parts of the data are modified and the data is then copied back by using MsgHookSetData

### Steps

Open and run FORMSIZE.FRM. During the Form_Load event procedure, the minimum and maximum sizes for the form are calculated and the form is sized to fall halfway between these sizes. Experiment—try using the mouse to resize the window, and try the minimize and maximize buttons to see how they work, as shown in Figure 2-20.

1. Create a new project named FORMSIZE.MAK. Create a new form with the objects and properties in Table 2-17.

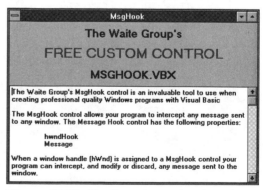

**Figure 2-20** The Formsize project in action

| Object | Property | Setting |
|--------|----------|---------|
| Form | BackColor | &H00C0C0C0& |
| | Caption | "MsgHook " |
| | Height | 5730 |
| | Left | 1035 |
| | Name | Form1 |
| | Top | 1140 |
| | Width | 7620 |
| TextBox | Height | 1095 |
| | Left | 0 |
| | MultiLine | -1 'True |
| | Name Text1 | |
| | ScrollBars | 2 'Vertical |
| | Text | "Text1" |
| | Top | 1680 |
| | Width | 5775 |
| MsgHook | Height | 420 |
| | Left | 120 |
| | Name | MsgHook1 |
| | Top | 3120 |
| | Width | 420 |
| Label | Alignment | 2 'Center |
| | BackStyle | 0 'Transparent |
| | Caption | "The Waite Group's" |
| | FontBold | -1 'True |
| | FontItalic | 0 'False |
| | FontName | "MS Sans Serif" |
| | FontSize | 13.5 |
| | FontStrikethru | 0 'False |
| | FontUnderline | 0 'False |
| | Height | 375 |
| | Index | 0 |
| | Left | 1560 |
| | Name Label1 | |
| | Top | 120 |
| | Width | 2895 |
| Label | Alignment | 2 'Center |
| | BackStyle | 0 'Transparent |
| | Caption | "FREE CUSTOM CONTROL" |
| | FontBold | -1 'True |
| | FontItalic | 0 'False |

| Object | Property | Setting |
|---|---|---|
| | FontName | "MS Sans Serif" |
| | FontSize | 18 |
| | FontStrikethru | 0 'False |
| | FontUnderline | 0 'False |
| | ForeColor | &H000000FF& |
| | Height | 375 |
| | Index | 1 |
| | Left | 1080 |
| | Name Label1 | |
| | Top | 600 |
| | Width | 4935 |
| Label | Alignment | 2 'Center |
| | BackStyle | 0 'Transparent |
| | Caption | "MSGHOOK.VBX" |
| | FontBold | -1 'True |
| | FontItalic | 0 'False |
| | FontName | "MS Sans Serif" |
| | FontSize | 13.5 |
| | FontStrikethru | 0 'False |
| | FontUnderline | 0 'False |
| | Height | 375 |
| | Index | 2 |
| | Left | 1440 |
| | Name Label1 | |
| | Top | 1200 |
| | Width | 3255 |

**Table 2-17** MsgHook project's objects and properties

2. Create a new module named FORMSIZE.BAS. Add the following code to the General Declarations section of the module.

```
'
' Declare subroutines in MSGHOOK.VBX
'
Declare Sub MsgHookGetData Lib "msghook.vbx" (ByVal lParam As Long, ⇐
ByVal destSize As Integer, destType As Any)
Declare Sub MsgHookSetData Lib "msghook.vbx" (ByVal lParam As Long, ⇐
ByVal destSize As Integer, srcType As Any)
'
' Declare Windows API functions
'
```

*continued on next page*

*continued from previous page*

```
Declare Function IsIconic Lib "User" (ByVal hWnd As Integer) As Integer
'
' Declare Windows API type used
'
Type PointApi
    x As Integer
    y As Integer
End Type

Type MinMaxInfo
    ptReserved       As PointApi
    ptMaxSize        As PointApi
    ptMaxPosition    As PointApi
    ptMinTrackSize   As PointApi
    ptMaxTrackSize   As PointApi
End Type
'
' Define value of the WM_GETMINMAXINFO message
'
Global Const WM_GETMINMAXINFO = &H24
```

3. Add the following code to the General Declarations section of Form1.

```
'
' Generate an error if undefined variables are referenced
'
Option Explicit
'
' Maximum size of the window
'
Dim maxWidth    As Integer
Dim maxHeight   As Integer
'
' Top-left corner of maximized window
'
Dim maxLeftPos  As Integer
Dim maxTopPos   As Integer
'
' Minimum size of the window
'
Dim minWidth    As Integer
Dim minHeight   As Integer
```

4. Add the following code to the Load event procedure of Form1.

```
Sub Form_Load ()
    Dim nl    As String
    Dim atab  As String
    Dim s     As String
    '
    ' Initialize crlf and tab strings
    '
    nl = Chr$(13) + Chr$(10)
```

```
atab = Chr$(9)
'
' Build string to put in text box
'
s = s + "The Waite Group's MsgHook control is an invaluable tool "
s = s + "to use when creating professional quality Windows programs "
s = s + "with Visual Basic"
s = s + nl
s = s + nl
s = s + "The MsgHook control allows your program to intercept "
s = s + "any message sent to any window. The Message Hook control "
s = s + "has the following properties:"
s = s + nl
s = s + nl
s = s + atab + "hwndHook" + nl
s = s + atab + "Message" + nl
s = s + nl
s = s + "When a window handle (hWnd) is assigned to a MsgHook control "
s = s + "your program can intercept, modify, or discard any message "
s = s + "sent to the window. "
s = s + nl
s = s + nl
s = s + "The Message property is an array with one element for each "
s = s + "possible Windows message. When an element of the array is set "
s = s + "to True the MsgHook_Message event procedure is called ⇐
whenever "
s = s + "the corresponding message is sent to the window whose handle ⇐
is "
s = s + "in hwndHook"
s = s + nl
s = s + nl
s = s + "And last, but not least, the MsgHook control is a fully ⇐
functional "
s = s + "custom control. As a purchaser of the Waite Group's Visual ⇐
Basic How-To "
s = s + "2nd edition you can distribute the run-time version of the ⇐
control "
s = s + "with your applications, free of charge!"


'
' Assign string to text box
'
text1.Text = s
'
' Use the design-time setting as the maximum window size
'
maxWidth = form1.Width / screen.TwipsPerPixelX
maxHeight = form1.Height / screen.TwipsPerPixelY
'
' Calculate top-left location for form when maximized
'
maxLeftPos = ((screen.Width - form1.Width) / 2) / ⇐
screen.TwipsPerPixelY
```

*continued on next page*

*continued from previous page*

```
    maxTopPos = ((screen.Height - form1.Height) / 2) / ⇐
screen.TwipsPerPixelX
    '
    ' Calculate the minimum window size
    '
    minWidth = (text1.Left + text1.Width + (text1.Left * 2)) / ⇐
screen.TwipsPerPixelX
    minHeight = (text1.top + text1.Height) / screen.TwipsPerPixelY
    '
    ' Initialize the form to be half way between the min and max sizes
    '
    form1.Width = (minWidth + ((maxWidth - minWidth) / 2)) * ⇐
screen.TwipsPerPixelX
    form1.Height = (minHeight + ((maxHeight - minHeight) / 2)) * ⇐
screen.TwipsPerPixelY
    '
    ' Center form on the screen
    '
    form1.Left = (screen.Width - form1.Width) / 2
    form1.Top = (screen.Height - form1.Height) / 2
    '
    ' Initialize the MsgHook control so we can set the MinMax parameters
    '
    MsgHook1.hwndHook = form1.hWnd
    MsgHook1.Message(WM_GETMINMAXINFO) = True
End Sub
```

5. Add the following code to the Resize event procedure of Form1. The controls are resized to fit the form. The Windows API function IsIconic is used here to test whether the form is iconized or not. If the form is iconized, we exit the subroutine without attempting to resize the controls.

```
Sub Form_Resize ()
    Dim i As Integer

    '
    ' We ignore the resize when the window is iconized
    '
    If (IsIconic(form1.hWnd) <> 0) Then
        Exit Sub
    End If
    '
    ' Center the labels
    '
    For i = 0 To 2
        Label1(i).Left = (form1.ScaleWidth - Label1(i).Width) / 2
    Next
    '
```

```
    ' Recalculate size of the text window so it fills the lower part
    ' of the form
    '
    text1.Width = form1.ScaleWidth - (text1.Left * 2)
    text1.Height = form1.ScaleHeight - text1.Top - text1.Left
End Sub
```

6. Add the following code to the Message event procedure of MsgHook1. MsgHookGetData is used to retrieve the message data. The min and max values are set, and MsgHookSetData is used to copy over the message data. The action parameter is set to 1, thus preventing Visual Basic from getting the message.

```
Sub MsgHook1_Message (msg As Integer, wParam As Integer, lParam As Long,⇐
   action As Integer, result As Long)
   Dim info As MinMaxInfo

    '
    ' Use MsgHookGetData to copy the structure pointed to by lParam
    '
    MsgHookGetData lParam, Len(info), info
    '
    ' Set the MinMaxInfo to values calculated during form load
    '
    info.ptMaxSize.x = maxWidth
    info.ptMaxSize.y = maxHeight
    info.ptMaxTrackSize.x = maxWidth
    info.ptMaxTrackSize.y = maxHeight
    info.ptMaxPosition.x = maxLeftPos
    info.ptMaxPosition.y = maxTopPos
    info.ptMinTrackSize.x = minWidth
    info.ptMinTrackSize.y = minHeight
    '
    ' Use MsgHookSetData to copy the structure back to the location pointed
    ' to by lParam
    '
    MsgHookSetData lParam, Len(info), info
    '
    ' Tell the MsgHook control to discard this message
    '
    action = 1
    '
    ' Respond with a zero to the WM_GETMINMAXINFO message. This tells
    ' Windows that we modified the data
    '
    result = 0
End Sub
```

### How It Works

When Windows sends a WM_GETMINMAXINFO message, lParam contains the address of a MinMaxInfo data structure. The MinMaxInfo Type, declared in the General Declarations section of FORMSIZE.BAS, defines the contents of the MinMaxInfo data structure. Each member of the MinMaxInfo data structure has two variables, named x and y. When specifying position, x corresponds to left and y corresponds to top. When specifying sizes, x gives the width and y gives the height.

A C programmer can access the array directly by using the lParam as a pointer to the data in memory. With Visual Basic we use the MsgHookGetData subroutine to copy the data into a Visual Basic variable. After the data has been changed, it is copied back by using MsgHookSetData. Although somewhat inefficient, this approach works well enough; and given that no other alternative exists in Visual Basic, it works very well!

### Comments

The MsgHook control makes an otherwise impossible task easy. The simplicity of the MsgHook control belies its usefulness. Other How-Tos in this book show how to use MsgHook controls to record MIDI music, provide custom mouse cursors, and more!

## 2.13 ● How do I...

### Add a toolbar to Visual Basic programs?

**Complexity: Advanced**

### Problem

Programs like Word for Windows use toolbars to provide easy access to commonly used functions. How can I add a toolbar to my program?

### Technique

TOOLBUTN.VBX contains two custom controls, ToolButton and ContextHelp, that make adding toolbars to Visual Basic programs easy. ToolButton and ContextHelp are fully functional custom controls that you can distribute with your applications, shown in Figures 2-21 and 2-22.

ToolButton is a custom control for Visual Basic that supports command and attribute buttons in toolbars. A command button is used to invoke a

**Figure 2-21**
ToolButton
control

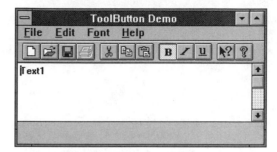

**Figure 2-22** ContextHelp control

command such as File Open. Attribute buttons are used to set and display attributes. A word processor, for instance, would have a File Open command button and Font Bold and Font Italic attribute buttons. Toolbar buttons usually display a small bitmap graphic that indicates its associated function. ToolButton provides standard button images for Edit Cut, Edit Copy, Edit Paste, File New, File Open, File Save, File Print, Help, and Context-Sensitive Help. If none of the standard button images is appropriate for your application, you can supply a custom image by assigning a bitmap to the Picture property of a ToolButton.

The ContextHelp control is used to implement "point-and-click" style context-sensitive help. During run time your application can set the Enabled property of a ContextHelp control to True. This tells the ContextHelp control to capture the mouse and change the mouse cursor to an arrow with a question mark. When the mouse has been captured and is clicked on any control on your form, the ContextHelp control's ControlClick event subroutine is called. The HelpID argument passed to the ControlClick subroutine contains the ContextHelpID property of the control that was clicked on.

### Steps

Open and run TOOLDEMO.MAK. Figure 2-23 shows what the running program looks like. On the toolbar there are four groups of buttons. The first group of buttons provides File New, File Open, File Save, and File Print commands. The second group of buttons provides Edit Cut, Edit Copy, and Edit Paste commands. The third group of buttons is used to set Bold, Italic, and Underlined attributes for text. The fourth group of buttons is used to provide point-and-click help and quick access to Help.

1. Create a new project called TOOLDEMO.MAK. Create a new form with the objects and properties in Table 2-18.

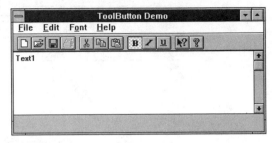

**Figure 2-23** ToolDemo project in action

| Object | Property | Setting |
| --- | --- | --- |
| Form | BackColor | &H8000000F& |
| | Caption | "ToolButton Demo" |
| | ForeColor | &H00C0C0C0& |
| | Height | 3060 |
| | HelpContextID | 101 |
| | Left | 1095 |
| | Name | Form1 |
| | ScaleHeight | 158 |
| | ScaleMode | 3 'Pixel |
| | ScaleWidth | 400 |
| | Top | 1110 |
| | Width | 6120 |
| ContextHelp | Enabled | 0 'False |
| | Left | 364 |
| | Name | ContextHelp1 |
| | Tag | "Left click for help, right click to cancel" |
| | Top | 119 |
| Text box | Height | 55 |
| | HelpContextID | 103 |
| | Left | -1 |
| | MultiLine | -1 'True |
| | Name | Text1 |
| | ScrollBars | 2 'Vertical |
| | TabIndex | 1 |
| | TabStop | 0 'False |
| | Text | "Text1" |

| Object | Property | Setting |
| --- | --- | --- |
| | Top | 33 |
| | Width | 320 |
| Picture box | BackColor | &H8000000F& |
| | BorderStyle | 0 'None |
| | Height | 28 |
| | HelpContextID | 102 |
| | Left | 0 |
| | Name | Picture1 |
| | ScaleHeight | 28 |
| | ScaleMode | 3 'Pixel |
| | ScaleWidth | 317 |
| | Top | 2 |
| | Width | 317 |
| Label | BackColor | &H8000000F& |
| | Caption | "Label1" |
| | FontName | "MS Sans Serif" |
| | FontSize | 8.25 |
| | Height | 16 |
| | Left | 3 |
| | Name | Label1 |
| | TabIndex | 2 |
| | Top | 89 |
| | Width | 46 |
| Line | BorderColor | &H00FFFFFF& |
| | Index | 0 |
| | Name | Line1 |
| Line | BorderColor | &H00808080& |
| | Index | 1 |
| | Name | Line1 |

**Table 2-18** Objects and properties for Form1

2. Add the ToolButton objects and properties listed in Table 2-19 to Picture1. Be sure to create these objects on top of Picture1.

| Object | Property | Setting |
| --- | --- | --- |
| ToolButton | BackColor | &H8000000F& |
| | Height | 22 |

*continued on next page*

*continued from previous page*

| Object | Property | Setting |
|---|---|---|
| | HelpContextID | 200 |
| | HintMessage | "Clears the TextBox" |
| | Index | 0 |
| | Left | 5 |
| | Name | ToolButton |
| | StandardButton | 4 'File New |
| | Top | 60 |
| | Width | 360 |
| ToolButton | BackColor | &H8000000F& |
| | Height | 22 |
| | HelpContextID | 201 |
| | HintMessage | "Reads a file into the TextBox" |
| | Index | 1 |
| | Left | 29 |
| | Name | ToolButton |
| | StandardButton | 5 'File Open |
| | Top | 60 |
| | Width | 360 |
| ToolButton | BackColor | &H8000000F& |
| | Height | 22 |
| | HelpContextID | 202 |
| | HintMessage | "Saves the TextBox to a file" |
| | Index | 2 |
| | Left | 53 |
| | Name | ToolButton |
| | StandardButton | 6 'File Save |
| | Top | 60 |
| | Width | 360 |
| ToolButton | BackColor | &H8000000F& |
| | Enabled | 0 'False |
| | Height | 22 |
| | HelpContextID | 203 |
| | HintMessage | "Prints the textbox (NOT IMPLEMENTED)" |
| | Index | 3 |
| | Left | 77 |
| | Name | ToolButton |

| Object | Property | Setting |
|---|---|---|
| | StandardButton | 7 'File Print |
| | Top | 60 |
| | Width | 360 |
| ToolButton | BackColor | &H8000000F& |
| | Height | 22 |
| | HelpContextID | 204 |
| | HintMessage | "Cuts the selection to the clipboard" |
| | Index | 4 |
| | Left | 101 |
| | Name | ToolButton |
| | StandardButton | 1 'Edit Cut |
| | Top | 60 |
| | Width | 360 |
| ToolButton | BackColor | &H8000000F& |
| | Height | 22 |
| | HelpContextID | 205 |
| | HintMessage | "Copies the selection to the clipboard" |
| | Index | 5 |
| | Left | 125 |
| | Name | ToolButton |
| | StandardButton | 2 'Edit Copy |
| | Top | 60 |
| | Width | 360 |
| ToolButton | BackColor | &H8000000F& |
| | Height | 22 |
| | HelpContextID | 206 |
| | HintMessage | "Replaces the selection with the clipboard contents" |
| | Index | 6 |
| | Left | 149 |
| | Name | ToolButton |
| | StandardButton | 3 'Edit Paste |
| | Top | 60 |
| | Width | 360 |
| ToolButton | BackColor | &H8000000F& |
| | ButtonSource | 1 'Custom |
| | ButtonType | 1 'Attribute |

*continued on next page*

*continued from previous page*

| Object | Property | Setting |
|--------|----------|---------|
| | CustomButton | 1 |
| | CustomCount | 3 |
| | Height | 22 |
| | HelpContextID | 207 |
| | HintMessage | "Sets the TextBox FontBold attribute" |
| | Index | 7 |
| | Left | 173 |
| | Name | ToolButton |
| | StandardButton | 5 'File Open |
| | Value | 1 'Down |
| | Width | 360 |
| ToolButton | BackColor | &H8000000F& |
| | ButtonSource | 1 'Custom |
| | ButtonType | 1 'Attribute |
| | Height | 22 |
| | HelpContextID | 208 |
| | HintMessage | "Sets the TextBox FontItalic attribute" |
| | Index | 8 |
| | Left | 197 |
| | Name | ToolButton |
| | StandardButton | 3 'Edit Paste |
| | Top | 60 |
| | Width | 360 |
| ToolButton | BackColor | &H8000000F& |
| | Name | ToolButton |
| | ButtonSource | 1 'Custom |
| | ButtonType | 1 'Attribute |
| | Height | 22 |
| | HelpContextID | 209 |
| | HintMessage | "Sets the TextBox FontUnderline attribute" |
| | Index | 9 |
| | Left | 221 |
| | StandardButton | 3 'Edit Paste |
| | Top | 60 |
| ToolButton | BackColor | &H8000000F& |
| | HelpContextID | 210 |
| | HintMessage | "Enables context-sensitive help" |
| | Index | 10 |

| Object | Property | Setting |
|---|---|---|
| | Name | ToolButton |
| | StandardButton | 9 'Context-Sensitive Help |
| ToolButton | BackColor | &H8000000F& |
| | HelpContextID | 211 |
| | HintMessage | "Displays the ToolButton help contents" |
| | Index | 11 |
| | Name | ToolButton |
| | StandardButton | 8 'Help |

**Table 2-19** ToolButton controls placed on Picture1

3. Use the Menu Design window to create a menu with the items in Table 2-20.

| Control Name | Caption | Shortcut Key |
|---|---|---|
| ABFile | "&File" | |
| ----MIFileNew | "&New" | |
| ----MIFileOpen | "&Open..." | SHIFT-F12 |
| ----MIFileSaveAs | "&Save As..." | F12 |
| ----MIFileSep1 | "-" | |
| ----MIFilePrint | "&Print" | |
| ----MIFileSep2 | "-" | |
| ----MIFileExit | "E&xit" | |
| ABEdit | "&Edit" | |
| ----MIEditCut | "Cu&t" | CTRL-X |
| ----MIEditCopy | "&Copy" | CTRL-C |
| ----MIEditPaste | "&Paste" | CTRL-V |
| ABFont | "F&ont" | |
| ----MIFontBold | "&Bold" | CTRL-B |
| ----MIFontItalic | "&Italic" | CTRL-I |
| ----MIFontUnderline | "&Underline" | CTRL-U |
| ABHelp | "&Help" | |
| ----MIHelpContents | "&Contents" | |
| ----MIHelpSearch | "&Search for Help On..." | |
| ----MIHelpContext | "Conte&xt-Sensitive" | SHIFT-F1 |
| ----MIHelpUse | "&How to Use Help" | |
| ----MIHelpSep1 | "-" | |
| ----MIHelpAbout | "&About..." | |

**Table 2-20** Tooldemo project's menu

> 4. Create a new module named TOOLDEMO.BAS and add the following to the Global Declarations section.

```
' Catch undeclared variables
Option Explicit
'
' These constants come from the Microsoft Visual Design Guide
'
Global Const BUTTONGAP = 6
Global Const BARHEIGHT = 28

' Minimum size
Global MINWIDTH, MINHEIGHT As Long

' File name for open, save
Global FileName As String

' Pathname of help file
Global HelpPath As String


' ToolButtons
Global Const TB_FILENEW = 0
Global Const TB_FILEOPEN = 1
Global Const TB_FILESAVE = 2
Global Const TB_FILEPRINT = 3
Global Const TB_EDITCUT = 4
Global Const TB_EDITCOPY = 5
Global Const TB_EDITPASTE = 6
Global Const TB_FONTBOLD = 7
Global Const TB_FONTITALIC = 8
Global Const TB_FONTUNDERLINE = 9
Global Const TB_HELPCONTEXT = 10
Global Const TB_HELPCONTENTS = 11

Global Const TB_MAX = 11
'
' Windows Help APIs
'
Declare Sub WinHelp Lib "user" (ByVal hwnd As Integer, ByVal hlHelpFile ⇐
As String, ByVal wCommand As Integer, ByVal dwData As Long)
Declare Sub WinHelpString Lib "user" Alias "WinHelp" (ByVal hwnd As ⇐
Integer, ByVal hlHelpFile As String, ByVal wCommand As Integer, ByVal ⇐
lpstrData As String)
'
' Constants for Windows Help APIs
'
Global Const HELP_CONTEXT = &H1
Global Const HELP_QUIT = &H2
Global Const HELP_CONTENTS = &H3
Global Const HELP_HELPONHELP = &H4
Global Const HELP_KEY = &H101
Global Const HELP_PARTIALKEY = &H105
```

```
'
' Other useful API functions
'
Declare Function GetModuleFileName Lib "kernel" (ByVal hModule As ⇐
Integer, ByVal lpFilename As String, ByVal nSize As Integer) As Integer
Declare Function GetModuleHandle Lib "kernel" (ByVal lpModuleName As ⇐
String) As Integer
```

5. Add the following code to the Declarations section of Form1. The Option keyword is new to Visual Basic 2.0. When Option Explicit is placed in the Declarations section of a form or module, variables must be explicitly declared before they can be used. Visual Basic will generate an error if your program tries to reference an undeclared variable. Without the Explicit option, a misspelled variable is simply treated as a new variable; this makes it difficult to find bugs.

```
'
' Catch undeclared variables
'
Option Explicit
```

6. Add the following code to the ControlClick event subroutine of ContextHelp1. Whenever the Enabled property of ContextHelp1 is set to True, the mouse is captured. When the user subsequently clicks the mouse the HelpContextID property of the control under the mouse pointer is passed to this routine. The Position argument passed to the ControlClick event subroutine will be -1 if no value was assigned to the HelpContextID of the control the user clicked on. There are a number of other possible Position values for a control that has a HelpContextID assigned to it. Generally, the other values for Position indicate what part of a control was clicked on. See the ContextHelp control's online help for further information about Position values.

```
Sub ContextHelp1_ControlClick (HelpID As Long, Position As Long)
    '
    ' Erase the help hint message
    '
    Label1.Caption = ""

    If (Position >= 0) Then
        If (HelpID = 0) Then
          MsgBox "No context-sensitive help available for this control", 48
        Else
            '
            ' For demo purposes, just display the HelpContextID
            '
            MsgBox "HelpContextID =" + Str$(HelpID)
            Exit Sub
            '
```

*continued on next page*

*continued from previous page*

```
                        ' A real application would do this to display help:
                        '
                        Call WinHelp(hWnd, HelpPath, HELP_CONTEXT, HelpID)
                End If
        End If
End Sub
```

7. Add the following code to the Load event subroutine of Form1. When the form is loaded, this code sizes and positions controls. In the loop that positions the ToolButtons, the font italic and font bold attribute buttons are initialized as custom buttons. When you use custom button images, you should use a similar technique.

```
Sub Form_Load ()
    Dim i, hModule, FirstCustom, CustomButton As Integer
    Dim ButtonWidth, NewLeft, NewTop As Single
    Const BUFSIZ = 255
    Dim Buf As String * BUFSIZ
    '
    ' Minimum size set at design time
    '
    MINHEIGHT = Height
    MINWIDTH = Width
    '
    ' The Microsoft Visual Design Guide
    ' gives its measurements in pixels
    '
    ScaleMode = 3
    '
    ' Reposition ToolButtons for device
    ' independence and initialize custom buttons
    '
    FirstCustom = -1
    ButtonWidth = ToolButton(0).Width
    NewTop = (BARHEIGHT - ToolButton(0).Height) / 2
    For i = 0 To TB_MAX
        If (ToolButton(i).ButtonSource = 1) Then
            CustomButton = CustomButton + 1
            If (FirstCustom = -1) Then
                '
                ' Only the first custom button is
                ' initialized at design-time
                '
                FirstCustom = i
            Else
                '
                ' Initialize from first custom button
                '
                ToolButton(i).Picture = ToolButton(FirstCustom).Picture
                ToolButton(i).CustomCount = ⇐
ToolButton(FirstCustom).CustomCount
                '
```

```
            ' Buttons appear in the same order in
            ' the bitmap as on the toolbar
            '
            ToolButton(i).CustomButton = CustomButton
        End If
    End If

    If (i = 0) Then
        ' First button
        NewLeft = BUTTONGAP
    Else
        ' Subsequent buttons
        NewLeft = NewLeft + ButtonWidth - 1
        Select Case i
        Case TB_EDITCUT, TB_FONTBOLD, TB_HELPCONTEXT
            ' Start a new button group
            NewLeft = NewLeft + BUTTONGAP + 1
        End Select
    End If
    '
    ' Reposition this button
    '
    ToolButton(i).Move NewLeft, NewTop
Next i
'
' Reposition other controls for device
' independence
'
picture1.Top = 1
picture1.Left = 0
picture1.Height = BARHEIGHT - 2

line1(0).X1 = 0
line1(0).Y1 = 0
line1(0).Y2 = 0
line1(1).X1 = 0
line1(1).Y1 = BARHEIGHT - 1
line1(1).Y2 = BARHEIGHT - 1
Text1.Top = BARHEIGHT
'
' Toggling AutoSize sets height to minimum
'
Label1.AutoSize = True
Label1.AutoSize = False
Label1.Caption = ""
'
' Figure out where the help file is
'
hModule = GetModuleHandle("TOOLBUTN")
If (hModule <> 0) Then
    i = GetModuleFileName(hModule, Buf, BUFSIZ)
    If (i <> 0) Then
        HelpPath = Left$(Buf, i - 3) + "HLP"
```

*continued on next page*

*continued from previous page*

```
        End If
    End If

    If (HelpPath = "") Then
        '
        ' Custom control DLL not loaded???
        '
        HelpPath = "TOOLBUTN.HLP"
    End If
End Sub
```

8. Add the following code to the Resize event subroutine of Form1. This subroutine makes sure that the window cannot be resized smaller than the size it had at design time.

```
Sub Form_Resize ()
    If (WindowState = 1) Then
      ' Minimized
      Exit Sub
    End If

    If (Width < MINWIDTH) Then
      ' Minimum width set at design time
      Width = MINWIDTH
      Exit Sub
    End If

    If (Height < MINHEIGHT) Then
      ' Minimum height set at design time
      Height = MINHEIGHT
      Exit Sub
    End If

    ' Resize controls to fit window
    Line1(0).X2 = ScaleWidth
    Line1(1).X2 = ScaleWidth
    Text1.Width = ScaleWidth + 2
    Text1.Height = ScaleHeight - Text1.Top - BARHEIGHT
    Label1.Move 6, Text1.Top + Text1.Height + ((BARHEIGHT - Label1.Height)⇐
/ 2), ScaleWidth - 12
End Sub
```

9. Add the following code to the Unload event subroutine of Form1. If help is currently being displayed, the call to WinHelp will close the help window.

```
Sub Form_Unload (Cancel As Integer)
    '
    ' Terminate Windows Help if open
    '
    Call WinHelp(Form1.hWnd, "toolbutt.hlp", HELP_QUIT, 0)
End Sub
```

10. Add the following code to the Click event subroutine of MIEditCopy.

```
Sub MIEditCopy_Click ()
    '
    ' Copy the selection to the clipboard
    '
    Clipboard.SetText Text1.SelText
End Sub
```

11. Add the following code to the Click event subroutine of MIEditCut.

```
Sub MIEditCut_Click ()
    '
    ' Cut the selection to the clipboard
    '
    Clipboard.SetText Text1.SelText
    Text1.SelText = ""
End Sub
```

12. Add the following code to the Click event subroutine of MIEditPaste.

```
Sub MIEditPaste_Click ()
    '
    ' Replace the selection with the clipboard contents
    Text1.SelText = Clipboard.GetText()
End Sub
```

13. Add the following code to the Click event subroutine of MIFileExit.

```
Sub MIFileExit_Click ()
    '
    ' Clean up
    '
    Unload Form1
End Sub
```

14. Add the following code to the Click event subroutine of MIFileNew.

```
Sub MIFileNew_Click ()
    '
    ' Reset filename and clear edit control
    '
    FileName = ""
    Text1.Text = ""
End Sub
```

15. Add the following code to the Click event subroutine of MIFileOpen.

```
Sub MIFileOpen_Click ()
    Dim AskName As String

    '
    ' Get filename
    '
    AskName = InputBox$("Filename:", "Open File", FileName)
    If (AskName = "") Then
```

*continued on next page*

*continued from previous page*

```
        Exit Sub
    End If
    FileName = AskName
    '
    ' Display hourglass cursor while opening and reading the file
    '
    Screen.MousePointer = 11
    '
    ' Attempt to open the file
    '
    On Error GoTo OpenError
    Open FileName For Input As 1
    On Error GoTo 0
    '
    ' Make sure file isn't too big
    '
    If (LOF(1) > 32767) Then
        MsgBox "Selected file is too large", 48, "Open File"
    Else
        '
        ' Read file into textbox
        '
        Text1.Text = Input$(LOF(1), 1)
    End If


    '
    ' We're done, restore cursor and leave
    '
    Close 1
OpenExit:
    Screen.MousePointer = 0
    Exit Sub

OpenError:
    On Error GoTo 0
    MsgBox "Cannot open file '" + FileName + "'", 48, "File Open"
    Resume OpenExit
End Sub
```

16. Add the following code to the Click event subroutine of MIFilePrint.

```
Sub MIFilePrint_Click ()

    MsgBox "File Print not implemented!", 48, "ToolButton"

End Sub
```

17. Add the following code to the Click event subroutine of MIFileSaveAs.

```
Sub MIFileSaveAs_Click ()
    Dim AskName As String

    '
    ' Get filename
```

```
    '
    AskName = InputBox$("Filename:", "Save File", FileName)
    If (AskName = "") Then
        Exit Sub
    End If
    FileName = AskName
    '
    ' Display hourglass cursor while opening and writing file
    '
    Screen.MousePointer = 11
    '
    ' Attempt to open the file
    '
    On Error GoTo SaveError
    Open FileName For Output As 1
    '
    ' Write the file
    '
    Print #1, Text1.Text;
    Close 1
    On Error GoTo 0
    '
    ' We're done, restore the cursor and exit
    '
SaveExit:
    Screen.MousePointer = 0
    Exit Sub

SaveError:
    On Error GoTo 0
    MsgBox "Cannot write file '" + FileName + "'", 48, "Save File"
    Resume SaveExit
End Sub
```

18. Add the following code to the Click event subroutine of MIFontBold.

```
Sub MIFontBold_Click ()
    '
    ' Set/reset bold attribute
    '
    Text1.FontBold = Not Text1.FontBold
    ToolButton(TB_FONTBOLD).Value = Abs(Text1.FontBold)
End Sub
```

19. Add the following code to the Click event subroutine of MIFontItalic.

```
Sub MIFontItalic_Click ()
    '
    ' Set/reset italic attribute
    '
    Text1.FontItalic = Not Text1.FontItalic
    ToolButton(TB_FONTITALIC).Value = Abs(Text1.FontItalic)
End Sub
```

20. Add the following code to the Click event subroutine of MIFontUnderline.

```
Sub MIFontUnderline_Click ()
    '
    ' Set/reset underline attribute
    '
    Text1.FontUnderline = Not Text1.FontUnderline
    ToolButton(TB_FONTUNDERLINE).Value = Abs(Text1.FontUnderline)
End Sub
```

21. Add the following code to the Click event subroutine of MIHelpAbout. The copyright symbol—a small c with a circle around it—can be created by holding down the (ALT) key, pressing the keys (0), (1), (6), (9), and then releasing the (ALT) key.

```
Sub MIHelpAbout_Click ()
    '
    ' Display an About box
    '
    MsgBox "© Brett Foster 1993", 64, "ToolButton Demo"
End Sub
```

22. Add the following code to the Click event subroutine of MIHelpContents.

```
Sub MIHelpContents_Click ()
    '
    ' Invoke windows help
    '
    Call WinHelp(Form1.hWnd, HelpPath, HELP_CONTENTS, 0)
End Sub
```

23. Add the following code to the Click event subroutine of MIHelpContext.

```
Sub MIHelpContext_Click ()
    '
    ' Display a help message
    '
    Label1.Caption = ContextHelp1.Tag
    '
    ' Enable context-sensitive help
    '
    ContextHelp1.Enabled = True
End Sub
```

24. Add the following code to the Click event subroutine of MIHelpSearch.

```
Sub MIHelpSearch_Click ()
    '
    ' Display WinHelp search dialog
    '
```

```
    Call WinHelpString(hWnd, HelpPath, HELP_PARTIALKEY, "")
End Sub
```

25. Add the following code to the Click event subroutine of MIHelpUse.

```
Sub MIHelpUse_Click ()
    '
    ' Display help on help
    '
    Call WinHelp(hWnd, "", HELP_HELPONHELP, 0)
End Sub
```

26. Add the following code to the GotFocus event subroutine of Picture1.

```
Sub Picture1_GotFocus ()
    '
    ' Refuse to accept focus
    '
    Text1.SetFocus
End Sub
```

27. Add the following code to the Change event subroutine of Text1.

```
Sub Text1_Change ()
    Dim SomeText As Integer
    '
    ' Any text in the window?
    '
    SomeText = (Len(Text1.Text) <> 0)

    '
    ' File New and Save enables track empty/not-empty condition of text
    ' box
    '
    If (ToolButton(TB_FILENEW).Enabled <> SomeText) Then
        ToolButton(TB_FILENEW).Enabled = SomeText
        ToolButton(TB_FILESAVE).Enabled = SomeText
        MIFileNew.Enabled = SomeText
        MIFileSaveAs.Enabled = SomeText
    End If
End Sub
```

28. Add the following code to the Click event subroutine of ToolButton1.
    This subroutine uses the ToolButton1 array index to call the menu
    event subroutine corresponding to the button pushed.

```
Sub ToolButton_Click (Index As Integer)
    '
    ' Each ToolButton is equivalent to a menu command
    '
    Select Case Index
        Case TB_FILENEW
            Call MIFileNew_Click
```

*continued on next page*

*continued from previous page*

```
            Case TB_FILEOPEN
                Call MIFileOpen_Click

            Case TB_FILESAVE
                Call MIFileSaveAs_Click

            Case TB_FILEPRINT
                Call MIFilePrint_Click

            Case TB_EDITCUT
                Call MIEditCut_Click

            Case TB_EDITCOPY
                Call MIEditCopy_Click

            Case TB_EDITPASTE
                Call MIEditPaste_Click

            Case TB_FONTBOLD
                Call MIFontBold_Click

            Case TB_FONTITALIC
                Call MIFontItalic_Click

            Case TB_FONTUNDERLINE
                Call MIFontUnderline_Click

            Case TB_HELPCONTEXT
                Call MIHelpContext_Click

            Case TB_HELPCONTENTS
                Call MIHelpContents_Click
        End Select
End Sub
```

29. Add the following code to the MouseDown event subroutine of ToolButton1. Label1 is used as a status bar to display a tool button's hint message.

```
Sub ToolButton_MouseDown (Index As Integer, Button As Integer, Shift As ⇐
Integer, x As Single, Y As Single)
    '
    ' Display help message associated with this button
    '
    Label1.Caption = ToolButton(Index).HintMessage
End Sub
```

30. Add the following code to the MouseUp event subroutine of ToolButton1. This subroutine clears the hint message when the mouse button is released.

```
Sub ToolButton_MouseUp (Index As Integer, Button As Integer, Shift As ⇐
Integer, x As Single, Y As Single)
    '
    ' Clear the help message
    '
    Label1.Caption = ""
End Sub
```

### How It Works

The tool buttons in the ToolButton1 array have index values that correspond to menu items. Clicking on a tool button calls the ToolButton_Click event subroutine. The Select statement in the Click event subroutine uses the passed index to call the correct menu Click event subroutine for each button.

Point-and-click access to context-sensitive help is made possible by using the ContextHelp control. Clicking on the context-sensitive button in the toolbar sets the ContextHelp1 Enabled property to True. When Enabled is set to True, the mouse is captured by the ContextHelp control and the cursor is changed. The user can now click on any control on your form. The click triggers the ContextHelp control's ContextHelp_Click event subroutine. The HelpID argument passed to the ContextHelp_Click event is the value of the HelpContextID property of the control clicked on.

### Comments

Using the techniques and tools shown in this How-To you can easily add toolbars to your programs. Using an array of ToolButton controls you can even allow your users to customize the toolbar, just like Word for Windows!

CHAPTER **3**

# TEXT
# AND
# SCROLLING

# How do I...

As a programmer, one of the most fundamental aspects of your application to control is the presentation of text. This chapter, Text and Scrolling, provides basic techniques, advanced insight, and programmer's tricks for presenting, receiving, and processing text using Visual Basic. This chapter presents a number of different techniques for scrolling text and graphics using Windows APIs and native Visual Basic code. You'll find How-Tos that scroll when Visual Basic's AutoRedraw property is either enabled or disabled, line-by-line scrolling or "crawl" scrolling like you see in movie credits, and how to accomplish those effects with scroll bars or command buttons. You'll find out how to align text horizontally and vertically, instead of simply left-aligned, and how to create a README file viewer and a simple text editor that searches for text strings. You'll also see how to accept text strings limited to numbers, how to trim null characters from strings, how to modify the speed at which the cursor blinks, and how to preview screen color combinations with scroll bars. Along the way, we'll corral a few Windows API functions to help make text processing quick and accurate, including the very powerful SendMessage API.

## Windows APIs Covered

| | |
|---|---|
| GetCaretBlinkTime | SendMessage |
| GetFocus | SetCaretBlinkTime |
| ScrollDC | SetTextAlign |
| ScrollWindow | UpdateWindow |

### 3.1 Scroll all the objects in a window?

Virtually every professional Visual Basic program needs to move graphics, text, and controls around a form. Often, everything your user needs to see will not fit on the screen at one time. For instance, a text document may have lines that are wider than the window, or you may have a large graphic. This How-To shows how to use the Windows API functions ScrollWindow and UpdateWindow to scroll the contents of an entire screen up, down, left or right.

### 3.2 Scroll text and graphics in a form or picture box

This How-To also demonstrates how the Windows API function library is used to extend Visual Basic. Unlike the APIs used in the previous How-To, theWindows API function ScrollDC allows your program to scroll graphics and text in any of four directions when AutoRedraw is enabled. AutoRedraw saves a bitmap of the screen so that the screen image is refreshed every time an item on the screen is moved, but it takes extra memory and screen painting time. This How-To also allows you to change the position of controls in a window and explains the use of persistent bitmaps.

### 3.3 Make text and graphics roll up the screen

A popular scrolling technique is the slow rolling of text and graphics, similar to "crawling" credits at the end of a movie. This type of scrolling is more gradual and professional looking than scrolling text one line at a time because it bases text movement on pixel size, uses a timer, and places a picture box within a picture box. This technique is accomplished using pure Visual Basic code, no Windows APIs are needed. You will learn the subtle power of object containers.

### 3.4 Scroll a text box under program control

Unlike the previous How-To that allows text to scroll up the screen like movie credits, this project produces smooth scrolling of the contents of a scroll box in any of eight compass directions. Rather than using traditional scroll bars to receive user input about the scroll direction, this project sets up command buttons.The ubiquitous SendMessage Windows API and the GetFocus API are used to receive user input from command buttons to control the direction of text scrolling without the use of scroll bars.

### 3.5 Align text automatically

When a Visual Basic program prints text on a screen, that text is always aligned with the left border of the screen. It is relatively easy to use the SetTextAlign Windows API function to vary the location of a text string in relation to the screen. This project will allow you to also center and right justify text, in addition to changing its vertical alignment in one of three ways. This technique uses the x and y properties of a character string to determine and adjust its location.

### 3.6 Set up a README file reader

In more "primitive" BASIC dialects, or in languages such as C or Pascal, creating a program to read DOS text requires some sort of input statements, PRINT or printf statements, and some way to prevent text from scrolling off the screen. Just a very few lines of Visual Basic code will open up a file and put it in a text box or scrollable view on the screen.

### 3.7 Build a simple editor that searches for text

Many applications can benefit by including a text editor. Visual Basic's text box controls allow a simple text editor that reads text data from a DOS file. A few additional Visual Basic functions can extend this editor's capabilities to load and save files, as well as to search for text. The simplicity of this powerful program, which uses purely native Visual Basic functions and no Windows APIs, shows what a flexible language Visual Basic is.

### 3.8 Ensure a numeric-only entry in the text box

Text and data processing account for the most popular computer tasks; word processors, databases, and spreadsheets are routinely used in home and business. Basic to these functions is the processing of user input. For instance, in database field for zip codes, how can you differentiate between text and data to assure that only numeric input is accepted? This How-To uses KeyPress events to limit user input to a restricted range of numbers.

**3.9    Trim null characters from a string**

When using Windows API functions to process text strings, a null character CHR$(0) may be added to the string. Visual Basic's LTrim$ and RTrim$ functions are effective for stripping spaces from the left and right end of strings, but not embedded null characters. This How-To demonstrates how to write a general Visual Basic function that will delete those null characters.

**3.10    Determine and modify the rate at which a text box's caret blinks**

Drawing user attention to a text box may be accomplished in many ways but generally the more subtle the technique, the more professional it appears. This How-To uses two Windows API functions, SetCaretBlinkTime and GetCaretBlinkTime to provide a variable blink rate for the caret. Caret blink speed can be varied through the Windows Control Panel, but this project shows how your Visual Basic application can do the same. A scroll bar is used to select the amount of time between the blinks.

**3.11    Use scroll bars to select colors**

This How-To emphasizes the "Visual" aspect of Visual Basic. When you are changing the appearance of your text or graphics display, it is nice to have a "preview" mode that will allow you to see effects before you enable them. This is useful, for instance, to prevent text from being printed on the same color background. If you've ever found yourself in that situation, you know that it is similar to being caught in a perpetual loop and you may have to halt program execution. This How-To uses scroll bars to let you see in advance the different blends of red, green, or blue colors on your monitor. Control arrays make it a very simple task to change color combinations on the fly.

**3.12    Highlight important information in the Grid control**

Visual Basic 3.0's Grid control provides the basic functionality you would expect. However a number of useful features, such as the ability to set the foreground and background colors for individual cells, is missing. This How-To shows how to simulate the effect of individual cells having separate foreground and background colors.

**3.13   Allow users to enter data into the Grid control**
Another drawback of the Grid control is that it provides no means for the user to enter data into cells. This How-To shows how to use a text box to give the appearance of entering data into individual grid cells.

# 3.1  How do I...

## Scroll all the objects in a window?

### Problem
I would like to be able to move all the graphics, text, and controls around my form.

### Technique
The Windows API function ScrollWindow can be used to solve this problem. ScrollWindow moves the entire contents of a form—graphics, text, and Visual Basic controls—in any of four directions.

### Steps
Open and run SCRLLWND.MAK. Click on any of the four arrows in the center of the screen to scroll the window in the appropriate direction. The value in the centered text box, as shown in Figure 3-1, is the number of screen pixels to scroll on each click. If the value is set to a negative number, the action of the arrows is reversed. Clicking on the Refresh menu item will

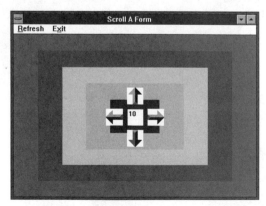

**Figure 3-1** The Scrllwnd form displaying a value of ten screen pixels

redraw the background pattern without changing the current position of the controls.

The Scrllwnd project may be created by entering the objects and code as detailed in the following steps.

1. Create a new project called SCRLLWND.MAK. Create a new form with the objects and properties shown in Table 3-1 and save it as SCRLL-WND.FRM. The placement of the controls is shown in Figure 3-1.

| Object | Property | Setting |
|---|---|---|
| Form | FormName | Scroll |
| | Caption | Scroll a Form |
| | BackColor | &H00C0C0C0& |
| Picture box | Name | Picture1 |
| | Autosize | True |
| | BorderStyle | 0 - None |
| | Picture | ARROW02UP.ICO |
| | Index | 0 |
| Picture box | Name | Picture1 |
| | Autosize | True |
| | BorderStyle | 0 - None |
| | Picture | ARROW02DN.ICO |
| | Index | 1 |
| Picture box | Name | Picture1 |
| | Autosize | True |
| | BorderStyle | 0 - None |
| | Picture | ARROW02LT.ICO |
| | Index | 2 |
| Picture box | Name | Picture1 |
| | Autosize | True |
| | BorderStyle | 0 - None |
| | Picture | ARROW02RT.ICO |
| | Index | 3 |
| Text box | Name | Text1 |
| | Text | 10 |

**Table 3-1** Scrllwnd project form's objects and properties

2. Create a menu for the form using the Menu Design window with the values shown in Table 3-2.

| Caption | Name |
| --- | --- |
| &Refresh | Repaint |
| E&xit | Quit |

**Table 3-2** Menu items for the Scroll form

3. Enter the following Windows API declarations in the Global module and save as SCRLHWND.BAS.

```
Declare Sub ScrollWindow Lib "User" (ByVal hWnd As Integer, ByVal XAmount ⇐
As Integer, ByVal YAmount As Integer, lpRect As Any, lpClipRect As Any)
Declare Sub UpdateWindow Lib "User" (ByVal hWnd As Integer)
```

4. Place the following code in the Form_Resize event subroutine. This code draws a set of concentric colored boxes, filling the form.

```
Sub Form_Resize ()
Dim I As Integer
'
' Draw concentric, colored boxes.
'
    For I = 5 To 1 Step -1
        Boxwidth = I * ScaleWidth / 5
        BoxHeight = I * ScaleHeight / 5
        BoxTop = (ScaleHeight - BoxHeight) / 2
        BoxLeft = (ScaleWidth - Boxwidth) / 2
        Fillcolor = QBColor(I + 8)
        Line (BoxLeft, BoxTop)-Step(Boxwidth, BoxHeight), Fillcolor, BF
    Next I%
End Sub
```

5. Place the following code in the Repaint_Click event subroutine.

```
Sub Repaint_Click ()
    Form_Resize
End Sub
```

6. Place the following code into the Picture1_Click event subroutine. This subroutine scrolls the form's contents in the direction of the arrow that is clicked.

```
Sub Picture1_Click (Index As Integer)
Dim Delta As Integer, Dx As Integer, Dy As Integer
'
' Scroll window in the direction specified.
'
    Delta = Val(Text1.Text)        ' Number of pixels to move
    Select Case Index
        Case 0: Dy = -Delta        ' Move up
```

*continued on next page*

*continued from previous page*

```
        Case 1: Dy = Delta          ' Move down
        Case 2: Dx = -Delta         ' Move right
        Case 3: Dx = Delta          ' Move left
    End Select
    ScrollWindow Scroll.hwnd, Dx, Dy, ByVal 0&, ByVal 0&
    UpdateWindow Scroll.hwnd
End Sub
```

7. Place the following code in the Quit_Click menu event subroutine. This subroutine allows the user to gracefully exit from the program.

```
Sub Quit_Click ()
    End
End Sub
```

### How It Works

Scrllwnd uses the Windows API function ScrollWindow to actually move the objects on the screen. When this project is run, the entire window's contents—text, graphics, and objects—are all moved the number of screen pixels specified by the XAmount and YAmount parameters. When XAmount is positive, the window objects are scrolled to the left; when the value is negative, the objects are scrolled to the right. YAmount scrolls the window up when the parameter is negative or down when positive.

Scrolling is performed in the Picture1_Click event subroutine. Because the four picture boxes are part of the same control array, only one event subroutine is needed. The appropriate parameters to the ScrollWindow subroutine, Dx and Dy, are set depending on the Index of the picture box selected.

Note that after ScrollWindow is called, the UpdateWindow API function statement should be called. This causes Visual Basic to immediately paint the portion of the window exposed by the scrolling action. If Update-Window is not called, the form will be repainted at an indeterminate time in the future. This may cause subsequent screen updates to be overwritten.

### Comments

ScrollWindow is the easiest and fastest way to move data in a window and is ideal for scrolling a form full of text. However, ScrollWindow should not be used when the form's AutoRedraw property is turned on. AutoRedraw causes a window with custom graphics to be updated each time an object is moved. With AutoRedraw enabled, Visual Basic saves an exact copy of the window in what is called a persistent bitmap. The persistent bitmap is a pixel-for-pixel copy of how the control looks when displayed. Whenever a picture box or form needs to redisplay a previously hidden part of itself, and AutoRedraw is true, Visual Basic simply copies the persistent bitmap to the screen. The cost of enabling AutoRedraw is memory and screen refresh speed. ScrollWindow only affects the on-screen copy, not the persistent bitmap. The repaint that takes place after ScrollWindow is called causes Visual Basic to copy the contents of the bitmap back to the screen, thereby overwriting the intended effects of ScrollWindow. The ScrollDC function is more appropriately used when AutoRedraw is enabled, or if you want to change the positions of the controls in a window. The following How-To uses the ScrollDC function.

## 3.2  How do I...

## Scroll text and graphics in a form or picture box?

### Problem
Since I like to include graphics on my form, I prefer to turn on the AutoRedraw property. How can I scroll text and graphics on my forms and picture boxes?

### Technique
The Windows API library provides much of the functionality that was not included directly in Visual Basic. The API function ScrollDC can be used to scroll graphics and text in any of four directions.

### Steps
Load and run SCROLLDC.MAK. Clicking on the Single Step command button will scroll the text up one line. Clicking on the Continuous command button puts the program into a loop, adding new lines to the bottom of the window while existing data scrolls off the top. Figure 3-2 shows this project while scrolling is in progress.

```
┌─────────────── Scroll a Device Context ───────────▼▲┐
│─ playing Counter:                                   │
│ Displaying Counter:  18                             │
│ Displaying Counter:  19                             │
│ Displaying Counter:  20                             │
│ Displaying Counter:  21                             │
│ Displaying Counter:  22                             │
│ Displaying Counter:  23                             │
│ Displaying Counter:  24                             │
│ Displaying Counter:  25                             │
│ Displaying Counter:  26                             │
│ Displaying Counter:  27                             │
│ Displaying Counter:  28                             │
│ Displaying Counter:  29                             │
│ Displaying Counter:  30                             │
│ Displaying Counter:  31                             │
│ Displaying Counter:  32                             │
│ Displaying Counter:  33      ┌──────────────────┐   │
│ Displaying Counter:  34      │ Continuous Scroll │   │
│ Displaying Counter:  35      └──────────────────┘   │
│ Displaying Counter:  36                             │
│ Displaying Counter:  37      ┌──────────────────┐   │
│ Displaying Counter:  38      │  Single Scroll   │   │
│ Displaying Counter:  39      └──────────────────┘   │
│ Displaying Counter:  40      ┌──────────────────┐   │
│ Displaying Counter:  41      │      Exit        │   │
│                              └──────────────────┘   │
└─────────────────────────────────────────────────────┘
```

**Figure 3-2** The ScrollDC form in action, showing scrolling text

The ScrollDC project may be created by entering the objects and code as detailed in the following steps.

1. Create a new project called SCROLLDC.MAK. Create a new form with the objects and properties shown in Table 3-3 and save it as SCROLL-DC.FRM.

| Object | Property | Setting |
|--------|----------|---------|
| Form | FormName | Scroll |
|  | Caption | Scroll a Device Context |
| Command button | Name | Command1 |
|  | Caption | Exit |
| Command button | Name | Command2 |
|  | Caption | Continuous Scroll |
| Command button | Name | Command3 |
|  | Caption | Single Scroll |

**Table 3-3** ScrollDC project form's objects and properties

2. Place the following declarations in the Global module and save as SCROLL.BAS.

```
Global Const NULL = 0

Type RECT
        Left As Integer
        Top As Integer
        Right As Integer
        Bottom As Integer
End Type

Declare Sub ScrollDC Lib "User" (ByVal hDC As Integer, ByVal dx As ⇐
Integer, ByVal dy As Integer, lprcScroll As RECT, lprcClip As RECT, ⇐
ByVal hRgnUpdate As Integer, lprcUpdate As Any)
```

3. Place the following declaration in the General section of the ScrollDC form. The Continue variable is used to stop the Continuous display.

```
Dim Continue As Integer
```

4. Place the following code in the Resize event subroutine of the form.

```
Sub Form_Resize ()
   For I = 1 To 20
      Print "Sample text for Line: ", I
   Next I
End Sub
```

5. Place the following code in the Command1_Click event subroutine. This command button event permits the user to gracefully exit the application.

```
Sub Command1_Click ()
    End
End Sub
```

6. Place the following code in the Command2_Click event subroutine. This subroutine starts continuous printing and scrolling of the ScrollDC form.

```
Sub Command2_Click ()
Dim Counter As Integer, T As Integer, TxtHeight As Integer
'
'  Loop forever scrolling new lines onto the screen from
'  the bottom.
'
    Scalemode = 3              ' To Pixels
    Continue = -1
    Counter = 0
    TxtHeight = TextHeight("A")
    currenty = scaleheight - TxtHeight
    While Continue
        If currenty > (scaleheight - TxtHeight) Then
            ScrollOneLine
            currenty = scaleheight - TxtHeight
            Currentx = 0
        End If
        Print "Displaying Counter: "; Counter
        Counter = Counter + 1
        T= DoEvents()
    Wend
End Sub
```

7. Place the following code in the Command3_Click event subroutine. This command button event scrolls the form up one line. It also turns off the Continue flag in case continuous scrolling is in effect.

```
Sub Command3_Click ()
    Continue = 0
    ScrollOneLine
End Sub
```

8. Place the following code into the ScrollOneLine subroutine. This subroutine is called by the command button events to scroll the form window up one line.

```
Sub ScrollOneLine ()
Dim lprcScroll As RECT
'
```

*continued on next page*

*continued from previous page*

```
'  Scroll the Window line line.
'  Use GetClientRect load get window dimensions.
'  Set Scale to 3 - Pixels, dY = text height.
'  Scroll the window and clear out the erased line.
'
    Scalemode = 3
    lprcScroll.Top = 0: lprcScroll.Left = 0
    lprcScroll.Bottom = ScaleHeight
    lprcScroll.Right = ScaleWidth
    dY = TextHeight("A")
    ScrollDC hdc, 0, -dY, lprcScroll, lprcScroll, 0, ByVal 0&
    Line (0, ScaleHeight - dY)-(ScaleWidth, ScaleHeight), BackColor, BF
End Sub
```

### How It Works

Scrolling text in DOS-based applications is an intrinsic capability of most languages. When text is printed on the last line of a screen, previous lines are moved up to make room for the new line. In Windows and Visual Basic, there is no such built-in capability. It is the responsibility of the application's programmer to scroll screen data and make room for incoming lines. The ScrollDC Windows API function provides the mechanism to do this.

When the ScrollDC project is first run, the Form_Resize event subroutine is automatically called. It will print 20 sample text lines so that the scroll effects can be demonstrated. The Command2_Click and Command3_Click event subroutines are used to initiate the scrolling. Before scrolling, the Command2_Click event subroutine checks whether the next line of printed text will fit onto the screen without scrolling. If it won't, the ScrollOneLine subroutine is called to move the window text up by one line.

The ScrollOneLine subroutine first changes the form's ScaleMode to 3-pixels to be compatible with the ScrollDC call. The RECT structure needed for the lprcScroll and lprcClip parameters are set up to point to the whole window. Table 3-4 lists all of ScrollDC's parameters.

| Parameter | Use |
| --- | --- |
| hDC | Device context of window to scroll. For forms, use <FormName>.HDC; for PictureBoxes, use <Name>.HDC. |
| dx | Number of pixels to scroll horizontally. Positive numbers are used to scroll right, negative numbers to scroll left. |
| dy | Number of pixels to scroll vertically. Positive numbers are used to scroll the window down, negative values to scroll up. |
| lprcScroll | This is a pointer to a RECT structure that defines the size of the scrolling area. For our application, it is set to the entire window. |

| Parameter | Use |
| --- | --- |
| lprcClip | This is a pointer to a RECT structure that will be used to clip the scrolling area. For our application, it is set to the entire window. |
| hRgnUpdate | A handle to an update region. It is not used in our application and is passed as zero. |
| lprcUpdate | If not NULL, the ScrollDC function will update the value of a RECT structure to indicate the area that needs repainting. We don't use this feature, so it is set to NULL. Note the use of the ByVal keyword. |

**Table 3-4** Parameters for the ScrollDC API function

We only want to scroll in the vertical direction, so ScrollDC is called with a zero dX parameter. The dY parameter is set to the text height so that only one line of text is scrolled at a time. ScrollDC moves pixels on the screen as specified but does not clear out the old data. The Visual Basic Line method with the BF (filled box) option clears the area that was occupied by the last screen line.

### Comments

Three Windows API functions can be used to scroll a window. ScrollWindow scrolls everything on a window—controls as well as graphics. However, it does not use a device context and, therefore, can't be used with Visual Basic if AutoRedraw is enabled. The BitBlt routine, like ScrollDC, will also scroll data using the device context, but is slightly slower and more complex to use because of its additional capabilities. ScrollDC will scroll data quickly, and is easy to use.

Be careful in setting the background color of the form when you use this project. When the Line statement draws a box and the background color is not a pure one, the box is bordered in white instead of the background color. Pure colors, other than back or white, are dependent on the type of display card used. Experimentation is required.

## 3.3 How do I...

**Complexity: Easy**

## Make text and graphics roll up the screen?

### Problem

I would like to add a professional touch to my applications by having text and graphics scroll up the screen, similar to the film credits of a movie. How can I make text and graphics roll upward?

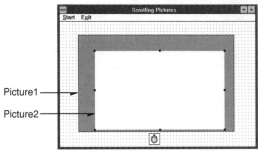

**Figure 3-3** The Scrlpict design time form

### Technique

This project works by changing the position of a picture box control so that the text and graphics drawn on it will move. With the picture box's border removed and its background color changed to match the color of the surrounding container, the text and graphics appear to float on the screen.

To give the program a "film credit" crawl, a Timer control event moves the previously drawn picture box in small increments from the bottom to the top of the screen.

### Steps

Run SCRLPICT.MAK. Select the Start menu option to begin or restart scrolling. Click on the Exit menu to leave the program.

To create the Scrlpict project, enter the objects and code as detailed in the following steps.

1. Create a new project called SCRLPICT.MAK. Create a new form with the objects and properties shown in Table 3-5. Save this form as SCRLPICT.FRM. Note that the Picture2 control must be contained by Picture1 as shown in Figure 3-3. This is done by creating Picture1 first, then drawing Picture2 totally within Picture1's boundaries. When you have done this properly, Picture2 will maintain the same relative position to Picture1 when Picture1 is moved.

| Object | Property | Setting |
|---|---|---|
| Form | FormName | ScrollPicture |
| | Caption | Scrolling Pictures |
| Picture box | Name | Picture1 |
| | Backcolor | &HFF00 |
| Picture box | Name | Picture2 |
| | Backcolor | &HFFFF80 |
| | Border | 0 - None |

| Object | Property | Setting |
|--------|----------|---------|
| Timer | Name | Timer1 |
|  | Enabled | False |
|  | Interval | 5 |
|  | Tag | 2 |

**Table 3-5** Scrlpict project form's objects and properties

2. Using the Menu Design window, create a menu for the form with the parameters in Table 3-6.

| Caption | Name |
|---------|------|
| &Start | Start |
| E&xit | Quit |

**Table 3-6** Menu Design parameters

3. Put the PrintCenter code in the General section of the form. This code centers and prints a string, Txt, on the specified control.

```
Sub PrintCenter (C As Control, Txt As String)
' Display text in the center of the control.
   C.CurrentX = (C.ScaleWidth - C.TextWidth(Txt)) / 2
   C.Print Txt
End Sub
```

4. Place the Timer1_Timer event subroutine in the form. Each time the timer calls this event, the Picture2 control is moved up a few pixels.

```
Sub Timer1_Timer ()
    Delta = Val(Timer1.Tag)
    Picture1.Scalemode = 3
    If Picture2.Top + Picture2.Height > 0 Then
        Picture2.Top = Picture2.Top - Delta
    Else
      Timer1.Enabled = 0
      Picture1.CurrentY = Picture1.ScaleHeight / 2
      Txt$ = "Finished with Scrolling"
      Picture1.CurrentX = (Picture1.ScaleWidth - ⇐
          Picture1.TextWidth(Txt$))/2
      Picture1.Print Txt$
    End If
End Sub
```

5. Put the Start_Click event subroutine in the form. This subroutine starts the action by drawing the text onto Picture2 and enabling Timer1.

```
Sub Start_Click ()
   Timer1.Enabled = 0
   Picture1.Cls
   Picture2.Visible = 0
   Picture2.AutoRedraw = -1
   Picture2.Top = Picture1.ScaleHeight
   Picture2.BackColor = Picture1.BackColor
   Picture2.Height = 5 * Picture1.TextHeight("A")
   Picture2.CurrentY = 0
   PrintCenter Picture2, ""
   PrintCenter Picture2, "Visual Basic"
   PrintCenter Picture2, "makes scrolling"
   PrintCenter Picture2, "of data an easy"
   PrintCenter Picture2, "process"
   Picture2.Visible = -1
   Timer1.Enabled = -1
End Sub
```

6. Place the Quit_Click event subroutine in the form. This routine allows the user to exit the application gracefully by clicking on the Quit menu.

```
Sub Quit_Click ()
   End
End Sub
```

### How It Works

A project like this really highlights the strengths and subtleties of Visual Basic. It takes advantage of object containers to automatically clip windows and selective AutoRedraw to paint text and graphics on nonvisible objects. The program begins when the user clicks on the Start menu, invoking the Start_Click menu event.

Start_Click begins by disabling the timer and clearing the outer of the two picture boxes: Picture1. These two steps are necessary in case the Start menu is clicked again while the program is running.

The Picture2 control is then made invisible and its AutoRedraw property turned on. AutoRedraw is a property of form and picture box controls. When AutoRedraw is True—that is, it has a nonzero value—anything drawn or printed to the control is not only displayed on the screen but also is saved in a persistent bitmap. (See How-To 3.1 Scroll all the objects in a window.) The beauty of Visual Basic is that even when a control is invisible, you can still draw and print to its bitmap. In this project we print four lines of centered text to the nonvisible Picture2 control.

At the end of the Start_Click event, the Picture2 control is made visible again. The timer is started, whose event subroutine, Timer1_Timer, slowly moves the Picture2 control from the bottom to the top of the Picture1 control.

When we drew the controls on the Scrlpict form, Picture2 was drawn inside Picture1, making Picture1 a container for Picture2. When an object is contained inside another, it will not be displayed outside the boundaries of the container. In fact, a contained object's position properties, Top and Left, are relative to the origin of the container. An object can be moved anywhere in a container, yet parts of it that fall outside the container are not displayed. In Windows terminology, this is called clipping.

When Timer1 is enabled, Picture2. is set to the bottom of its container and no part of Picture2 will be visible. Moving the top of Picture2 slowly toward the top of Picture1 creates the crawl effect. The ScaleMode for Picture1 is set to 3 pixels so that the movement of Picture2 will be made in the smallest of screen increments. As mentioned earlier, without a border or contrasting background color for Picture2, there is no visual frame of reference for its text and graphics.

### Comments

The speed at which Picture2 moves is governed by two factors: the timer interval and the number of pixels to move the picture box for each timer event. We set the interval to 5 milliseconds when building the form. The number of pixels to move is kept in the Tag property of the timer. This lets us quickly change these values without altering the code.

## 3.4 ● How do I...

**Complexity: Intermediate**

# Scroll a text box under program control?

### Problem

Although my users can scroll the text in a multiline text box using the scroll bars, is there some way my program can scroll the text automatically? That would be another way I could present a rolling "movie credits" screen, for example.

### Technique

Windows text boxes respond to a variety of messages, most of which Visual Basic automatically sends when you use a property like SelText. However, you can access the other messages with the API function SendMessage.

Windows' EM_LINESCROLL message tells the scroll box to scroll the contents of a multiline text box by the specified number of rows and/or columns like in Figure 3-4.

### Steps

Open and run SCROLL.MAK. You can type any text you'd like in the text box. There are eight command buttons covering the eight compass directions: north, northeast, east, southeast, south, southwest, west, and northwest. See Figure 3-5.

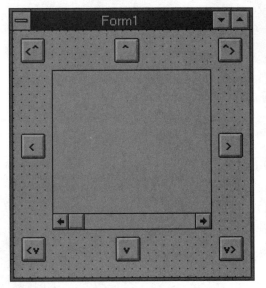

**Figure 3-4** The Scroll form at design time

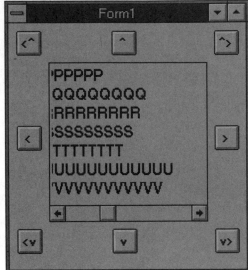

**Figure 3-5** The completed Scroll form

1. Create a new project called SCROLL.MAK. Create a new form with the objects and properties from Table 3-7 and save it as SCROLL.FRM.

| Object | Property | Setting |
|--------|----------|---------|
| Form | Caption | Scrolling text |
|  | FormName | ScrollText |
|  | BackColor | &H00C0C0C0& |
| Text box | Name | Text1 |
|  | Multiline | True |
|  | ScrollBars | Horizontal |
|  | Text | <none> |
| Command button | Name | Scroll |
|  | Caption | <^ |
|  | Index | 0 |
| Command button | Name | Scroll |
|  | Caption | ^ |
|  | Index | 1 |
| Command button | Name | Scroll |
|  | Caption | ^> |
|  | Index | 2 |
| Command button | Name | Scroll |
|  | Caption | > |

| Object | Property | Setting |
|---|---|---|
| | Index | 3 |
| Command button | Name | Scroll |
| | Caption | v> |
| | Index | 4 |
| Command button | Name | Scroll |
| | Caption | v |
| | Index | 5 |
| Command button | Name | Scroll |
| | Caption | <v |
| | Index | 6 |
| Command button | Name | Scroll |
| | Caption | < |
| | Index | 7 |

**Table 3-7** Scroll Project form's objects and properties

2. Put the following code in the Declarations section of the form. These Const and Declare statements let the program access the Windows API functions.

```
DefInt A-Z

Declare Function SendMessage Lib "User" (ByVal hWnd%, ByVal wMsg%, ByVal ⇐
wParam%, ByVal lParam&) As Integer

Const WM_USER = &H400
Const EM_LINESCROLL = WM_USER + 6
```

3. Put the following code in the Form_Load event subroutine. This code simply loads some strings into the text box.

```
Sub Form_Load ()
   For I = 1 To 26
      Text1.Text = Text1.Text + String$(I, 64 + I) + Chr$(13) + Chr$(10)
   Next
End Sub
```

4. Put the following code in the Scroll_Click event subroutine. This code handles the clicks for all the command buttons and scrolls the text in the text box via the SendMessage API function.

```
Sub Scroll_Click (Index As Integer)
   Dim lParam As Long

   Select Case Index
```

*continued on next page*

*continued from previous page*

```
        Case 0
            hScroll = -1    ' Left
            vScroll = -1    ' Up
        Case 1
            hScroll = 0
            vScroll = -1    ' Up
        Case 2
            hScroll = 1     ' Right
            vScroll = -1    ' Up
        Case 3
            hScroll = 1     ' Right
            vScroll = 0
        Case 4
            hScroll = 1     ' Right
            vScroll = 1     ' Down
        Case 5
            hScroll = 0
            vScroll = 1     ' Down
        Case 6
            hScroll = -1    ' Left
            vScroll = 1     ' Down
        Case 7
            hScroll = -1    ' Left
            vScroll = 0
    End Select

    lParam = 65536 * hScroll + vScroll
    I = SendMessage(Text1.hWnd, EM_LINESCROLL, 0, lParam)
End Sub
```

### How It Works

Once again, control arrays come to the rescue. Rather than having eight command button event subroutines, one will do the job. The way the form was designed, the Index of each command button increases by one step each clockwise.

The Windows message that scrolls a text box is EM_LINESCROLL, which the WINAPI.TXT file in the Windows SDK defines as WM_USER + 6. WM_USER is defined as 0x400, or &H400 in Visual Basic hexadecimal lingo. So EM_LINESCROLL is equal to &H406.

The Form_Load event subroutine code loads the text box with multiple strings of varying length, some of which are wider than the width of the text box. This gives the feel of scrolling both vertically and horizontally.

The Scroll_Click event subroutine gets a parameter that's the Index of the command button that was clicked. (Remember that the Index goes from 0 to 7, starting at the upper left-hand corner and going clockwise.)

The Select Case statement block goes through each of the possible Index values for the command button. Each index value sets the hScroll and vScroll variables to -1, 0, or 1. A value of -1 means to scroll up vertically or

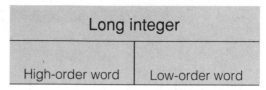

| Long integer | |
|---|---|
| High-order word | Low-order word |

**Figure 3-6** An lParam Long integer packed with two pieces of information

left horizontally. The value 0 means no scrolling in either direction. 1 either means to scroll down vertically or right horizontally. Depending on which command button was pressed, either or both hScroll and vScroll variables are set.

The diagonal scroll command buttons (northeast, southeast, southwest, and northwest) set both of the variables, since scrolling diagonally is the same as scrolling vertically and horizontally at the same time. For example, to scroll northeast one position is the same as scrolling north one position and east one position. The "straight" scroll command buttons (north, east, south, and west) only set one variable and set the other to zero.

The EM_LINESCROLL message expects the number of columns to scroll in the high-order word of the message lParam and the number of rows to scroll in the low-order word. (See Figure 3-6.) Because lParam is a Long integer, multiplying by 65536 will move the hScroll value into the high-order word. There's nothing special required to put a value in the low-order word, so it's just added in.

### Comments

Notice in Figure 3-5 that the text box has a horizontal scroll bar. If a multiline text box doesn't have a horizontal scroll bar, Visual Basic automatically wraps the text at the right edge of the text box, meaning that there is nothing to be scrolled horizontally.

## 3.5  How do I...

Complexity: Easy

## Align text automatically?

### Problem

The Visual Basic Print method always left justifies text at the current location. To center or right justify a string requires calculating a new position using the TextWidth method. Is there any way to do this automatically?

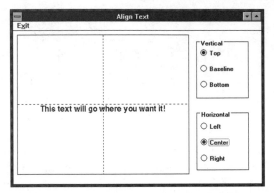

**Figure 3-7** The Aligntxt form with sample text

### Technique

The Windows API library includes a function, SetTextAlign, for automatically aligning text. Calling SetTextAlign before printing will provide your applications with a variety of horizontal and vertical alignments.

### Steps

Open and run ALIGNTXT.MAK. A line of sample text will be displayed at the center of the picture box as shown in Figure 3-7. The intersection of the dashed lines indicates the alignment point. Click on the different option buttons to have SetTextAlign change the alignment of the sample text. This project can be created by entering the objects and code in the following steps.

1. Create a new project called ALIGNTXT.MAK. Create a new form with the objects and properties listed in Table 3-8. Save it as ALIGNTXT.FRM.

| Object | Property | Setting |
|---|---|---|
| Form | FormName | AlignText |
| | Caption | Align Text |
| Picture box | Name | P |
| Frame | Name | Frame1 |
| | Caption | Vertical |
| Frame | Name | Frame2 |
| | Caption | Horizontal |

**Table 3-8** Aligntxt project form's objects and properties

2. Place the option buttons listed in Table 3-9 inside the Frame1 control.

| Object | Property | Setting |
|--------|----------|---------|
| Option button | Name | VertOpt |
| | Caption | Top |
| | Index | 1 |
| Option button | Name | VertOpt |
| | Caption | Baseline |
| | Index | 2 |
| Option button | Name | VertOpt |
| | Caption | Bottom |
| | Index | 3 |

**Table 3-9** Frame1 control's objects and properties

3. Place the option buttons listed in Table 3-10 inside the Frame2 control.

| Object | Property | Setting |
|--------|----------|---------|
| Option button | Name | HorzOpt |
| | Caption | Left |
| | Index | 1 |
| Option button | Name | HorzOpt |
| | Caption | Center |
| | Index | 2 |
| Option button | Name | HorzOpt |
| | Caption | Right |
| | Index | 3 |

**Table 3-10** Frame2 control's objects and properties

4. Create the menu listed in Table 3-11 for the form using the Menu Design window.

| Caption | Name |
|---------|------|
| Exit | Quit |

**Table 3-11** Menu items for the ALIGNTXT form

5. Enter the following declarations into the Global module and save it as ALIGNTXT.BAS.

```
' Text alignment options.
Global Const TA_LEFT = 0
Global Const TA_RIGHT = 2
Global Const TA_CENTER = 6

Global Const TA_TOP = 0
Global Const TA_BOTTOM = 8
Global Const TA_BASELINE = 24
Declare Sub SetTextAlign Lib "GDI" (ByVal hDC As Integer, ByVal wFlags ⇐
As Integer)
```

6. Enter the following code in the Form_Paint event subroutine. This subroutine will draw and align the sample text.

```
Sub Form_Paint ()
Dim wFlags As Integer, HFlag As Integer, VFlag As Integer
    P.Cls
    P.FontSize = 12
    P.DrawStyle = 2
    P.Line (0, P.ScaleHeight / 2)-Step(P.ScaleWidth, 0)
    P.Line (P.ScaleWidth / 2, 0)-Step(0, P.ScaleHeight)

    If VertOpt(1).Value Then VFlag = TA_TOP
    If VertOpt(2).Value Then VFlag = TA_BASELINE
    If VertOpt(3).Value Then VFlag = TA_BOTTOM
    If HorzOpt(1).Value Then HFlag = TA_LEFT
    If HorzOpt(2).Value Then HFlag = TA_CENTER
    If HorzOpt(3).Value Then HFlag = TA_RIGHT
    wFlags = VFlag Or HFlag

    P.Currentx = P.ScaleWidth / 2
    P.Currenty = P.ScaleHeight / 2
    SetTextAlign P.Hdc, wFlags
    P.Print "This text will go where you want it!"
End Sub
```

7. Enter the following code in the VertOpt_Click event subroutine. This subroutine will redraw the sample text whenever one of the VertOpt option buttons changes.

```
Sub VertOpt_Click (Index As Integer)
    Form_Paint
End Sub
```

8. Place the following code in the HorzOpt_Click event subroutine. This subroutine will redraw the sample text whenever one of the HorzOpt option buttons changes.

```
Sub HorzOpt_Click (Index As Integer)
    Form_Paint
End Sub
```

9. Put the following code in the Quit_Click menu event subroutine to allow the user to gracefully exit the application.

```
Sub Quit_Click ()
    End
End Sub
```

### How It Works

When you print text in Visual Basic, it is always displayed relative to the CurrentX and CurrentY properties of the object. The leftmost edge of the text starts at the CurrentX position and the top of the characters align with the CurrentY value. To horizontally center or right justify text, you need to use the TextWidth property as illustrated here:

```
A$ = "Text to Print"
L% = TextWidth(A$)
CurrentX = CurrentX - L%/2%          ' For Centered Text
CurrentX = CurrentX - L%             ' For Right-justified Text
Print A$
```

The Windows API provides a function, SetTextAlign, that automatically justifies all subsequently printed text. In addition to handling horizontal justification, SetTextAlign also permits you to change the vertical alignment of printed text. Figure 3-8 shows the three possible vertical alignments.

The Visual Basic default is to print the top of the character at the CurrentY position. The SetTextAlign function with the TA_BASELINE option is useful when there are multiple sizes of fonts on a line. That function will keep your lines from having a jagged look. The TA_BOTTOM option displays characters with the bottom of the character at the CurrentY position. Be aware that the Visual Basic function, TextHeight, returns the distance between the top and bottom of a character. There is no built-in VB method to retrieve the baseline offset.

The SetTextAlign function takes two parameters, the hDC of the object on which to print, and an integer flag word. The flag word specifies the

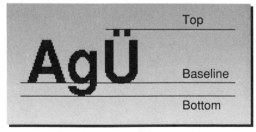

**Figure 3-8** Vertical character alignment alternatives

desired alignment options. The Form_Paint event code shows how the vertical and horizontal alignment options are formed to make the flag word.

### Comments

The alignment capability of the SetTextAlign function will not work properly when you are printing multiple strings in one statement. A Print statement such as Print A$; B$ is treated by Visual Basic as two distinct print commands. This results in unexpected centering or right-justified alignment. To center the two strings, use the Print A$ + B$ statement. This concatenates the strings prior to printing, ensuring that VB and SetTextAlign will treat the entire string as one object.

The hDC property can change whenever VB exits a subroutine, or calls the DoEvents function. Therefore, the SetTextAlign function should be called in each subroutine that needs to align text.

## 3.6 How do I...

**Complexity: Easy**

## Set up a README file reader?

### Problem

As I finish my latest application, I realize that I must provide a way for my users to read late-breaking information after they've installed my application. Normally in DOS you just create the README file on the disk, but this is so unfriendly. What is a better way?

### Technique

This is easy to solve. Simply load the lines of text from a file into a list box. When there are more lines in a list box than will fit on screen, Windows automatically provides scroll bars to let the user view the entire file.

### Steps

Open and run FILEVIEW.MAK. You can then click on any filename (as long as it is an ASCII file).

1. Create a new project called FILEVIEW.MAK. Create a new form using the objects and properties shown in Table 3-12 and save it as FILEVIEW.FRM. It will look like Figure 3-9.

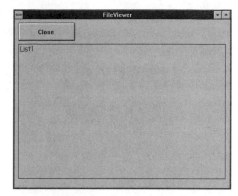

**Figure 3-9** The FileView form that displays ASCII text

| Object | Property | Setting |
|--------|----------|---------|
| Form | Caption | FileViewer |
| | BackColor | &H00C0C0C0& |
| Button | Caption | Close |
| | Name | Cancel |
| List box | FontName | Helv |

**Table 3-12** The FileView project form's objects and properties

2. Put the following code in the Cancel_Click event subroutine of the Cancel button.

```
Sub Cancel_Click ()
    End
End Sub
```

3. Put the following code in the Form_Unload event subroutine of the form.

```
Sub Form_Unload (Cancel As Integer)
    End
End Sub
```

4. Put the following code in the Form_Load event subroutine of the form. This code reads the README file into the list box.

```
Sub Form_Load ()
    fileNum = FreeFile
    Open "README" For Input As #fileNum

    Do Until EOF(fileNum)
```

*continued on next page*

*continued from previous page*

```
      Line Input #fileNum, lin$
      List1.AddItem lin$
   Loop

   Close #fileNum
End Sub
```

### How It Works

The Form_Load subroutine simply opens the README file and reads it, line by line, into the list box using the AddItem method in a Do loop. Notice that we use the FreeFile function to ensure that we have an available file number.

### Comments

You can also use this form as a general-purpose file viewer by just adding a call to a file dialog box (like the FileDlg form).

## 3.7  How do I...

## Build a simple editor that searches for text?

### Problem

I would like to incorporate a file editor in my application. It should follow standard Windows editing techniques for user ease.

### Technique

With Visual Basic, most of the editing functions are provided by the text box control. All you need to do is to load a text box with a copy of a file to provide the standard Windows editing features your users desire. This project also copies entire contents of the text box back to disk to save edits made by the user. Figure 3-10 shows the Editor project.

**Figure 3-10** The Editor in action

### Steps

Open and run EDITOR.MAK. Selecting the File menu displays options that allow you to Open and Save a file or Exit the program. The Search menu selection helps you to locate text. To create the Editor project, enter the objects and code as detailed in the following steps.

1. Create a new project called EDITOR.MAK. Create a new form with the objects and properties shown in Table 3-13 and save it as EDITOR.FRM.

| Object | Property | Setting |
|--------|----------|---------|
| Form | FormName | Editor |
| | Caption | Edit a File |
| Text box | Name | Text1 |
| | FontBold | False |
| | FontName | Courier |
| | FontSize | 10 |
| | MultiLine | True |
| | Text | (blank) |
| | ScrollBars | 3 - Both |

**Table 3-13** Editor project form's objects and properties

2. Create a menu for the form using the Menu Design window, as shown in Table 3-14.

| Caption | Name |
|---------|------|
| &File | FileMenu |
| – – – –&Open | Openfile |
| – – – –&Save | Save |
| – – – –E&xit | ExitProg |
| &Search | Search |

**Table 3-14** Menu design characteristics

3. Place the following code in the OpenFile_Click event subroutine. This code opens the file using the Open_Dlg form, checks the file length, reads its contents, and then loads it into the text box.

```
Sub OpenFile_Click ()
    Open_Dlg.Show 1
    Filename$ = Open_Dlg.Tag
    If Filename$ = "" Then Exit Sub
    Editor.Caption = "Editing: " + Filename$
```

*continued on next page*

*continued from previous page*

```
   Open Filename$ For Binary As #1
   Filelength = LOF(1)
   If Filelength > 40000 Then
      MsgBox "File Too Long to Edit", 16
      Exit Sub
   ElseIf Filelength = 0 Then
      MsgBox "File: " + Filename$ + " not found or empty", 16
      Exit Sub
   End If
   Tmp$ = String$(LOF(1), 0)
   Get #1, , Tmp$
   Text1.Text = Tmp$
   Close #1
   Tmp$ = ""
End Sub
```

4. Place the following code in the ExitProg_Click event subroutine.

```
Sub ExitProg_Click ()
   End
End Sub
```

5. Place this code in the Save_Click event subroutine. It copies the contents of the text box control back to the file.

```
Sub Save_Click ()

' If no filename, prompt use for one.
   1 Filename$ = Open_Dlg.Tag
   If Filename$ = "" Then
      Filename$ = InputBox$("Enter new filename")
      If Filename$ = "" Then
         MsgBox "Filename blank, file not saved.", 48
         Exit Sub
      End If
   Open_Dlg.Tag = Filename$
   End If

' Print TextBox to file.
' Append EOF Chr$(26), if not last char in TextBox

   Open Filename$ For Output As #1
   Print #1, Text1.Text;
   If Right$(Text1.Text, 1) <> Chr$(26) Then Print #1, Chr$(26);
   Close #1

End Sub
```

6. The Form_Resize event subroutine changes the size of the Text1 control to fully cover the face of the form. Because the Resize event is also called when a form initially loads, the Text1 control is expanded at application startup as well.

```
Sub Form_Resize ()
   Text1.Top = 0
```

```
    Text1.Left = 0
    Text1.Width = Scalewidth
    Text1.Height = Scaleheight
End Sub
```

7. No text editor could be considered complete without the ability to search for text. The Search_Click event subroutine prompts the user to enter a search string. If the search string is found, the matching text is left selected.

```
Sub Search_Click ()
  Static Searchstring As String, Newsearchstring As String
'
' Default to previous search string.
' If match is found, leave matching text selected.
'
    Newsearchstring = InputBox$("Enter search string", "", Searchstring)
    If Newsearchstring = "" Then Exit Sub
    Searchstring = Newsearchstring
    T% = InStr(Text1.Selstart + 1 + Text1.Sellength, Text1.Text, ⇐
Searchstring)
    If T% Then
        Text1.Selstart = T% - 1
        Text1.Sellength = Len(Searchstring)
    End If
End Sub
```

8. Open a second form for this project using the New Form selection from Visual Basic's File menu. This form is an Open Dialog box that allows the user to point and choose a file to edit. Enter the objects and properties for this form as listed in Table 3-15 and save the form as OPEN_DLG.FRM. The layout of the controls is shown in Figure 3-11.

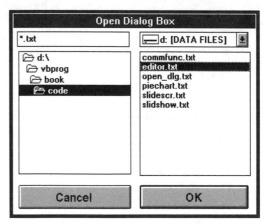

**Figure 3-11** The Open_Dlg form in action

| Object | Property | Setting |
|---|---|---|
| Form | FormName | Open_Dlg |
| | BorderStyle | 3 - Fixed Double |
| | ControlBox | False |
| | MaxButton | False |
| | MinButton | False |
| Command button | Name | Command1 |
| | Cancel | True |
| | Caption | Cancel |
| | FontSize | 12 |
| Command button | Name | Command2 |
| | Caption | OK |
| | Default | True |
| | FontSize | 12 |
| Dir list box | Name | Dir1 |
| Drive list box | Name | Drive1 |
| File list box | Name | File1 |
| Text box | Name | Text1 |
| | Borderstyle | 1 - Fixed Single |
| | Text | *.* |

**Table 3-15** Open_Dlg project form's objects and properties

9. Put the following code in the Drive1_Change event subroutine of the Open_Dlg form. When the user changes drives, this event will send a message to the Dir1 control indicating the new drive.

```
Sub Drive1_Change ()
   Dir1.Path = Drive1.Drive
End Sub
```

10. Put the following code in the Dir1_Change event subroutine of the Open_Dlg form. When the user changes directories, this event will send a message to the File1 control requesting a new directory display.

```
Sub Dir1_Change ()
   File1.Path = Dir1.Path
End Sub
```

11. Put the following code in the File1_DblClick event subroutine of the Open_Dlg form. This code causes a double-click event in the File1 control to be processed the same as clicking on the OK button.

```
Sub File1_DblClick ()
   Command2_Click
End Sub
```

12. Put the following code in the Text1_Change event subroutine of the Open_Dlg form. By responding to changes in the Text1 control, the user can alter which filenames will be displayed by the File1 control.

```
Sub Text1_Change ()
   File1.Pattern = Text1.Text
End Sub
```

13. Put the following code in the Command1_Click event subroutine of the Open_Dlg form. The Command1 button is the Cancel button. This code simply clears the return variable and hides the form.

```
Sub Command1_Click ()
   Open_Dlg.Tag = ""
   Open_Dlg.Hide
End Sub
```

14. Put the following code in the Command2_Click event subroutine of the Open_Dlg form. This is the OK command button which will return the drive, directory, and filename to the calling form.

```
Sub Command2_Click ()
   If File1.Listindex < 0 Then
      MsgBox "No File Selected", 48
      Exit Sub
   End If
   Open_Dlg.Tag = Dir1.Path
   If Right$(Open_Dlg.Tag, 1) <> "\" Then
      Open_Dlg.Tag = Open_Dlg.Tag + "\"
   End If
   Open_Dlg.Tag = Open_Dlg.Tag + File1.List(File1.Listindex)
   Open_Dlg.Hide
End Sub
```

15. Put the following code in the Form_Load event subroutine of the Open_Dlg form. This code positions the dialog form in the center of the screen and sets the default file match pattern.

```
Sub Form_Load ()
   Open_Dlg.Top = (Screen.Height - Open_Dlg.Height) / 2
   Open_Dlg.left = (Screen.Width - Open_Dlg.Width) / 2
   File1.Pattern = Text1.Text
End Sub
```

## How It Works

The text box control provides just the kind of basic editing functions that we need to build a text editor. By adding a few additional functions to load and save a file, and to search for text, our editor becomes fully functional. This program exploits the similarity between the format of text data in a DOS file and how data is kept in a text box Text property. Both are stored as lines of characters, each line ending with carriage return and line feed characters. With a few short lines of code, Visual Basic can copy the contents of a file into a text box control or, conversely, can transfer the text box back to a disk file.

The Openfile_Click event subroutine uses binary input/output to read the entire file with a single Get statement. The user selects the file to open using the Open_Dlg form. After the file is opened, its size is determined using the Lof function (LOF stands for Length Of File). The Tmp$ variable is extended to match the size of the file so that the Get statement will read the entire file in one operation. Copying Tmp$ into Text1.Text moves the data to the text box control and displays it. Tmp$ is cleared so that its memory can be reused by other variables in the form.

Saving the data is even easier. All you need to do is to print the contents of the text box control back to the file. The end-of-file marker [Chr$(26)] is appended to the text.

The Search_Click event subroutine scans from the current position in the text box for characters matching the search string. If a match is found, the text is selected using the SelStart and SelLength text box properties. Note that the InStr function counts characters starting from one, but the SelStart property uses zero to indicate the first character of the Text property.

See How-To 2.6 Make a powerful text editor using APIs for a more full-featured, sophisticated text editor.

## Comments

Because of memory limitations in Visual Basic, the maximum size of a string variable in this program is approximately 40,000 bytes, which limits the maximum size of text files that can be edited. In any event, the maximum number of characters in a text box is limited to 65,000 bytes by Windows itself.

## 3.8 ● How do I...

## Ensure a numeric-only entry in a text box?

### Problem

I need to make sure that a text box control will accept numeric input only. I would also like to restrict input to a specific range of numbers.

**Figure 3-12** Numinput form displaying a numeric character

### Technique

The KeyPress event for a text box control lets your program process each incoming character as it is typed. Nonnumeric keys and out-of-range values can be rejected.

### Steps

Open and run NUMINPUT.MAK or create it according to the following steps.

1. Create a new project called NUMINPUT.MAK. Create a new form with the objects and properties shown in Table 3-16 and save it as NUMINPUT.FRM. A sample of the form appears in Figure 3-12.

| Object | Property | Setting |
|--------|----------|---------|
| Form | FormName | Numinput |
| | Caption | Numeric Input |
| Command | Name | Command1 |
| | Cancel | True |
| | Caption | &Exit |
| | Fontsize | 12 |
| Label | Name | Label1 |
| | Alignment | 1 - Right justify |
| | Caption | Numeric Only |
| | Fontsize | 14 |
| Text box | Name | Text1 |
| | Fontsize | 12 |

**Table 3-16** Numinput project form's objects and properties

2. Put the following code in the Text1_KeyPress event subroutine. The code will analyze each typed character before displaying the character in the text box. If the character is not numeric or would cause the value of the text box to exceed the established minimum and maximum bounds, the character is not passed on for display.

```
Sub Text1_KeyPress (Keyascii As Integer)
Const DECIMAL_OK = -1              ' 0 = no, -1 = YES
Const MIN_VALUE = -999             ' Minimum value
Const MAX_VALUE = 999              ' Maximum value
   Key$ = Chr$(Keyascii)          ' Convert to string
   Select Case Key$
     Case "0" To "9", "-"          ' Numbers and minus signs
       Newvalue = Val(Left$(Text1.Text, Text1.Selstart) + Key$ + ⇐
           Mid$(Text1.Text, Text1.Selstart + Text1.Sellength + 1))
     If Newvalue > MAX_VALUE Or Newvalue < MIN_VALUE Then
         Keyascii = 0
     End If
     Case "."
       If DECIMAL_OK = 0 Or InStr(Text1.Text, ".") Then
         Keyascii = 0
       End If
     Case Chr$(8)                  ' Backspace
     Case Else
       Keyascii = 0
   End Select
   If Key$ = "-" And (InStr(Text1.Text, "-") Or Text1.Selstart <> 0) Then
       Keyascii = 0
   End If
End Sub
```

3. Place the following code in the Text1_GotFocus event subroutine. When the text box receives the focus, the current contents of the control are selected. The first character typed by the user will then overwrite the contents.

```
Sub Text1_GotFocus ()
   Text1.Selstart = 0
   Text1.Sellength = Len(Text1.Text)
End Sub
```

4. Put the following code in the Command1_Click event subroutine to provide a graceful method for ending the application.

```
Sub Command1_Click ()
   End
End Sub
```

## How It Works

The message-based architecture of Windows and Visual Basic makes this type of low-level handling of keyboard input a snap. Each time the user presses a key on the keyboard, a series of messages is sent to the control that has the focus. In Visual Basic, these messages can be trapped and processed as KeyDown, KeyPress, and KeyUp events. The KeyDown and KeyUp events operate at a very low level and would require a lot more work to code. However, the KeyPress event subroutine provides exactly the right data needed for this project.

The Text1_KeyPress event subroutine is called for every printable character typed. Its KeyAscii parameter holds the character's numeric ASCII value. If the KeyPress subroutine changes the value of KeyAscii to zero and exits, the character will not be placed into the text box.

Using a Select Case statement, the code first checks whether the incoming character is numeric (0 to 9) or a minus sign. If the character is either numeric or the minus sign, a simulated insert of the character is made into the text box, and the character's value is taken and compared with the range constants MIN_VALUE and MAX_VALUE. If the new value is out of range, the KeyAscii variable is set to 0, thereby stopping the character from being placed into the text box.

This simulated insert emulates how a text box control actually inserts a character into the Text property. When characters are inserted into a text box, they all are placed at the insertion point (marked on the display by an I-beam caret/cursor) and any currently selected text is replaced by the new character. The text box property SelStart can determine or set the current insertion point. The value of SelStart is the number of characters in the text box that precede the insertion point. The SelLength property keeps count of the number of selected characters. The simulated insert is performed by concatenating the text box characters up to the insertion point with the incoming character (Key$), then appending the remainder of the text box that is not selected. Note that the currently selected characters are not included in the test for the Newvalue.

A quick check is also made to ensure that multiple decimal points and minus signs are not passed on to the text box. The Case Else statement processes all characters that slipped through prior Case statements by setting KeyAscii to 0. The Case Chr$(8) statement is needed so that backspaces are processed.

It is a standard in Windows programs to select the contents of a text box when it receives the input focus. The Text1_GotFocus event subroutine selects all the characters in the control so that the first numeric character the user types overwrites the current contents.

### Comments

If you have multiple text boxes for which you want to have numeric-only input, this routine could be rewritten as a Form-level subroutine with the text box control name passed as a parameter.

## 3.9  How do I...

## Trim null characters from a string?

### Problem

When I use Windows API functions that accept and modify strings, those functions put null characters [Chr$(0)s] into the strings. How can I strip those Chr$(0)s out of the strings?

### Technique

Visual Basic has the LTrim$ and RTrim$ functions to strip extra spaces from the left and right ends of a string, but they don't strip embedded Chr$(0)s. Instead we can write a Visual Basic general function called VBHTTrim$ that will remove them.

### Steps

To use the VBHTTrim$ function, add the module VBHOWTO.BAS to any project using the Visual Basic File menu's Add a file... option. You call the VBHTTrim$ function exactly like you call LTrim$ and RTrim$.

1. Create a new module (with the File menu's New Module option) and add a new function called VBHTTrim$ to it (using the Code menu's New Procedure, Alt+F, to select a function).

2. Add the following code to the VBHTTrim$ function.

```
Function VBHTTrim$ (Incoming$)
   Temp$ = Incoming$
   I% = InStr(Temp$, Chr$(0))
   If I% Then Temp$ = Left$(Temp$, I% - 1)
   Temp$ = LTrim$(RTrim$(Temp$))
   VBHTTrim$ = Temp$
End Function
```

### How It Works

The first line in the VBHTTrim$ function copies the string parameter supplied to the function to a temporary string Temp$.

The second line uses the InStr function to see if there's an embedded Chr$(0). If there is, the third line chops the string at the character immediately before the Chr$(0) using the Left$ function.

The fourth line uses Visual Basic's LTrim$ and RTrim$ functions to trim off any spaces on the left and right ends of the string.

Finally, the last line makes the trimmed temporary string the return value of the function.

### Comments

The VBHTTrim$ function will work with both fixed- and variable-length strings.

## 3.10 How do I...

## Determine and modify the rate at which a text box's caret blinks?

### Problem

I would like to draw my user's attention to a text box by making the cursor blink faster. How can I do this?

### Technique

Your users can pick the cursor blink speed by using the Control Panel's Desktop icon. The Control Panel uses an API function—SetCaretBlinkTime—to change the blink speed to whatever you set it to. A Visual Basic application can do the same thing.

### Steps

Open and run BLINK.MAK. A scroll bar shows the current setting of the cursor blink time. If you change the value, the cursor speed is changed too, through a call to SetCaretBlinkTime.

**Figure 3-13** The Blink form features a horizontal scroll bar to control cursor speed

1. Create a new project called BLINK.MAK. Create a new form with the objects and properties shown in Table 3-17 and save it as BLINK.FRM. See the completed form in Figure 3-13.

| Object | Property | Setting |
|--------|----------|---------|
| Form | Caption | Cursor blink rate |
| | FormName | CursorBlinkForm |
| Horizontal scroll bar | Name | BlinkRate |
| | LargeChange | 50 |
| | Max | 1000 |
| | Min | 1 |

**Table 3-17** Blink form's controls and properties

2. Put the following code in the Declarations section of the form. These Declare statements let the form access the GetCaretBlinkTime and SetCaretBlinkTime API functions.

```
Declare Function GetCaretBlinkTime Lib "User" () As Integer
Declare Sub SetCaretBlinkTime Lib "User" (ByVal wMSeconds As Integer)
```

3. Put the following code in the Form_Load event subroutine. This code will be executed when the form is first loaded, to get the current cursor blink speed and change the scroll bar's value and the form's caption to match it.

```
Sub Form_Load ()
    BlinkRate.Value = GetCaretBlinkTime()
    CursorBlinkForm.Caption = "Cursor blink rate is" +
Str$(BlinkRate.Value) + " milliseconds"
End Sub
```

4. Put the following code in the BlinkRate_Change event subroutine. This code will be executed whenever the user changes a scroll bar value, whether by clicking on the scroll arrows or moving the scroll thumb. This code sets the blink speed based on the new value of the scroll bar and changes the form's caption.

```
Sub BlinkRate_Change ()
    SetCaretBlinkTime (BlinkRate.Value)
    CursorBlinkForm.Caption = "Cursor blink rate is" + ⇐
        Str$(BlinkRate.Value) + " milliseconds"
End Sub
```

### How It Works

One thing to remember is that, in proper Windows terminology, the cursor in a text box is called a caret. So the various Windows API functions that deal with the cursor have "caret" in the name. The (real) cursor is the mouse pointer. Because most people think of the cursor as the blinking rectangle on the screen, that's what we'll call it.

The GetCaretBlinkTime API function returns the time, in milliseconds, between flashes of the cursor. Actually, what is measured is the length of time that the cursor is on, and the length of time it's off.

The parameter supplied to the SetCaretBlinkTime function sets the cursor blink time, in milliseconds.

You can set the blink speed to a value between 1 and 32,767 (the largest possible integer). A blink speed of 1 is dizzying, and one of 32,767 means that the cursor blinks about every 32 seconds.

### Comments

Note that the Control Panel's scroll bar that changes the cursor blink speed is backward from how this application does it. The Control Panel bases the scroll bar on how fast the cursor should blink, but this application bases it on the delay between blinks.

## 3.11 ⬤ How do I...

## Use scroll bars to select colors?

### Problem

Although I understand the RGB (red/green/blue) color scheme of Windows and Visual Basic, it's still confusing to select a unique color other than the primary colors. How can I visualize the way certain combinations of red, green, and blue will turn out?

**Figure 3-14** The ColorScr form in action

### Technique

As with many aspects of a visual development environment, the easiest way to work with colors is to visualize them. Any color in Visual Basic can be specified by the amount of red, green, and blue it contains. Each component color can have a range of 0 to 255, making it perfect to be represented by a scroll bar. Figure 3-14 shows a monochrome picture of a selected color.

### Steps

Open and run COLORSCR.MAK. There are three scroll bars and three text boxes, each of which is red, green, or blue to show which color the scroll bar controls. (Unfortunately, scroll bar color is controlled by Windows and the

Control Panel, so the color can't be changed by an application.) Click on the scroll bars or type a number in the text box, and the background color of the form will change to match the RGB color you specified.

1. Create a new project called COLORSCR.MAK. Create a new form with the objects and properties listed in Table 3-18 and save it as COLORSCR.FRM.

| Object | Property | Setting |
|--------|----------|---------|
| Form | BackColor | &H00000000& (Black) |
| | Caption | Color scroll bars |
| | FormName | ColorScrollBars |
| Scroll bar | Name | ColorBar |
| | Index | 0 |
| | LargeChange | 16 |
| | Max | 255 |
| | Min | 0 |
| | SmallChange | 1 |
| Text box | BackColor | &H000000FF& (Red) |
| | Name | ColorText |
| | Index | 0 |
| | Text | 0 |
| Scroll bar | Name | ColorBar |
| | Index | 1 |
| | LargeChange | 16 |
| | Max | 255 |
| | Min | 0 |
| | SmallChange | 1 |
| Text box | BackColor | &H0000FF00& (Green) |
| | Name | ColorText |
| | Index | 1 |
| | Text | 0 |
| Scroll bar | Name | ColorBar |
| | Index | 2 |
| | LargeChange | 16 |
| | Max | 255 |
| | Min | 0 |
| | SmallChange | 1 |

| Object | Property | Setting |
|---|---|---|
| Text box | BackColor | &H00FF0000& (Blue) |
| | CtlName | ColorText |
| | Index | 2 |
| | Text | 0 |

**Table 3-18** ColorScr project form's objects and properties

2. The code is extremely simple; the form does most of the work. Place the following code in the ColorBar_Change event subroutine. Whenever the scroll bar is moved, this subroutine is executed. Because our scroll bars are elements of a control array, Visual Basic passes the Index of the scroll bar. The code updates the text of the corresponding text box, then uses the RGB function to change the background color of the form with the new value.

```
Sub ColorBar_Change (Index As Integer)
   ColorText(Index).Text = Str$(ColorBar(Index).Value)
   ColorScrollBars.BackColor = RGB(ColorBar(0).Value, ColorBar(1).Value, ⇐
   ColorBar(2).Value)
End Sub
```

3. Visual Basic runs the following code in the ColorText_Change event subroutine whenever the user types any character in any of the text boxes. If the new value in the text box is within range, we change the value of the scroll bar to that value. This invokes the ColorBar_Change event subroutine to update the background color. If the new value is greater than 255, though, the text is changed to 255 to avoid Visual Basic run-time errors.

```
Sub ColorText_Change (Index As Integer)
   Select Case Val(ColorText(Index).Text)
      Case Is < 0
         ColorText(Index).Text = "0"
      Case 0 To 255
         ColorBar(Index).Value = Val(ColorText(Index).Text)
      Case Else
         ColorText(Index).Text = "255"
   End Select
End Sub
```

### How It Works

This example shows how easy control arrays can make some programming tasks. By using control arrays, we avoid having to write three almost identical routines for both the scroll bars and the text boxes. Visual Basic tells us which scroll bar or text box has been changed with the Index parameter, which is the same as the Index property.

Visual Basic runs the code in the ColorBar_Change event subroutine whenever the scroll bar is changed, either by clicking on the scroll arrows or moving the scroll thumb. Also, the scroll bar is changed in the ColorText_Change event subroutine when the user types in one of the text boxes.

The code updates the Text property of the corresponding text box to the Value property of the scroll bar. This will give a running value of the red, green, and blue components of the form's background color.

Finally, ColorText_Change calls the RGB function with the value of each scroll bar and assigns the number that RGB returns to the form's BackColor property.

Visual Basic runs the code in the ColorText_Change event subroutine whenever the user types any character in any of the text boxes. Normally, the form would have an OK button to press before the changes take effect. Using the Change event, though, makes the changes take effect immediately, as the user types them, without having to click on a button or press (ENTER).

Because the component red, green, and blue colors must be within the range from 0 to 255, there's an If statement in the code to ensure that the user doesn't try to exceed that range. If the text box's value is okay, the Value property of the corresponding scroll bar is changed to that value. Changing a scroll bar's value automatically invokes its Change event subroutine. In this example, the ColorBar_Change event subroutine updates the background color.

If the user tries to enter a text box value for a color component greater than 255, the If statement sets the Text property of the text box to "255" so Visual Basic won't complain with an Overflow error.

## Comments

Certain color combinations result in pure colors. For example, RGB(0,0,0) creates black and RGB(255,255,255) creates white. Other combinations like RGB(255,128,255) should give a nice mauve shade on a monitor that supports it. Unfortunately, Visual Basic doesn't support more than 16 colors, so Windows will attempt to dither a matching color. (Dithering means to make a dot pattern that closely matches the requested color.)

## 3.12  How do I...

# Change the colors of individual cells in a grid?

### Problem

The Grid control's foreground and background properties affect all of the cells on the grid. How can I change the colors of selected cells to highlight important information?

### Technique

This project takes advantage of the Grid control's picture property to give the programmer greater control over the appearance of cells in a grid. An endless variety of special effects are possible by creating the desired cell contents in a picture box and then assigning the contents to a cell's picture property.

### Steps

Open and run COLORCEL.MAK. Select a cell in the grid and then choose foreground and background colors, as shown in Figure 3-15. By selecting cells and choosing different combinations of colors, you can compare the appearance of different color combinations.

1. Create a new project called COLORCEL.MAK. Create a new form with the objects and properties listed in Table 3-19 and save it as COLORCEL.FRM.

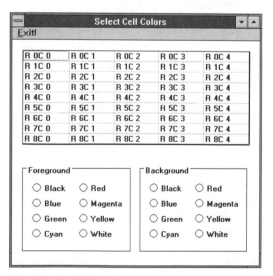

**Figure 3-15** The ColorCel project in action

| Object | Property | Setting |
|---|---|---|
| Form | BorderStyle | 3 - 'Fixed Double |
| | Caption | "Select Cell Colors" |
| | Height | 5955 |
| | Left | 1035 |
| | Name | CellColorSelector |
| | Top | 1140 |
| | Width | 5940 |
| Picture box | AutoRedraw | True |
| | Height | 255 |
| | Left | 4800 |
| | Name | Canvas |
| | Top | 2520 |
| | Visible | False |
| | Width | 495 |
| Frame | Caption | "Foreground" |
| | Height | 2055 |
| | Left | 240 |
| | Name | ForegroundFrame |
| | Top | 2880 |
| | Width | 2535 |
| Frame | Caption | "Background" |
| | Height | 2055 |
| | Left | 3000 |
| | Name | BackgroudPicture |
| | Top | 2880 |
| | Width | 2535 |

**Table 3-19** Colorcel project's objects and properties

2. Place the array of option buttons listed in Table 3-20 on the ForegroundFrame control. Since the options buttons all have the same width, height, and name properties, they are only listed once.

| Object | Property | Setting |
|---|---|---|
| Option button | Caption | "Black" |
| | Height | 375 |
| | Index | 0 |
| | Left | 240 |

| Object | Property | Setting |
|--------|----------|---------|
| | Name | ForeColor |
| | Top | 360 |
| | Width | 1095 |
| Option button | Caption | "Blue" |
| | Index | 1 |
| | Left | 240 |
| | Top | 720 |
| Option button | Caption | "Green" |
| | Index | 2 |
| | Left | 240 |
| | Top | 1080 |
| Option button | Caption | "Cyan" |
| | Index | 3 |
| | Left | 240 |
| | Top | 1440 |
| Option button | Caption | "Red" |
| | Index | 4 |
| | Left | 1320 |
| | Top | 360 |
| Option button | Caption | "Magenta" |
| | Index | 5 |
| | Left | 1320 |
| | Top | 720 |
| Option button | Caption | "Yellow" |
| | Index | 6 |
| | Left | 1320 |
| | Top | 1080 |
| Option button | Caption | "White" |
| | Index | 7 |
| | Left | 1320 |
| | Top | 1440 |

**Table 3-20** ForegroundFrame's objects and properties

3. Place the array of option buttons listed in Table 3-21 on the BackgroundFrame control. Since the option buttons all have the same width, height, and name properties, they are only listed once.

| Object | Property | Setting |
|---|---|---|
| Option button | Caption | "Black" |
| | Height | 375 |
| | Index | 0 |
| | Left | 240 |
| | Name | BackColor |
| | Top | 360 |
| | Width | 1095 |
| Option button | Caption | "Blue" |
| | Index | 1 |
| | Left | 240 |
| | Top | 720 |
| Option button | Caption | "Green" |
| | Index | 2 |
| | Left | 240 |
| | Top | 1080 |
| Option button | Caption | "Cyan" |
| | Index | 3 |
| | Left | 240 |
| | Top | 1440 |
| Option button | Caption | "Red" |
| | Index | 4 |
| | Left | 1320 |
| | Top | 360 |
| Option button | Caption | "Magenta" |
| | Index | 5 |
| | Left | 1320 |
| | Top | 720 |
| Option button | Caption | "Yellow" |
| | Index | 6 |
| | Left | 1320 |
| | Top | 1080 |
| Option button | Caption | "White" |
| | Index | 7 |
| | Left | 1320 |
| | Top | 1440 |

**Table 3-21** BackgroundFrame's objects and properties

4. Put the following code in the General Declarations section of Form1.

```
'
' During Form1_Load this array gets filled with the RGB values
' for Black, Blue, Green, Cyan, Red, Magenta, Yellow, and White
'
Dim colors(8) As Long
```

5. Add the following subroutine to the General section of Form1. This subroutine is the heart of this How-To. Clicking on a Color option button calls the subroutine and sets the picture background or foreground property.

```
Sub DrawCell ()
    '
    ' Adjust the size of the picture so we don't clip the text
    '
    canvas.Width = grid1.ColWidth(grid1.Col)
    canvas.Height = grid1.RowHeight(grid1.Row)
    '
    ' Clear any previous image from the picture
    '
    canvas.Cls
    '
    ' Add offsets used by grid control
    '
    canvas.CurrentX = screen.TwipsPerPixelX * 2
    canvas.CurrentY = screen.TwipsPerPixelY
    '
    ' Print cell name into picture and assign it to the cell
    '
    canvas.Print "R" & Str$(grid1.Row) & "C" & Str$(grid1.Col)
    grid1.Picture = canvas.Image
End Sub
```

6. Add the following subroutine to the General section of Form1. This subroutine is called during Form_Load to initialize the cells of the grid using the grid's foreground and background colors.

```
Sub FillCells ()
    Dim Row As Integer, Col As Integer
    '
    ' Fill the cells with RrCc names
    '
    For Row = 0 To grid1.Rows - 1
        For Col = 0 To grid1.Cols - 1
            grid1.SelStartRow = Row
            grid1.SelEndRow = Row
            grid1.SelStartCol = Col
            grid1.SelEndCol = Col
            grid1.Clip = "R" & Str$(Row) & "C" & Str$(Col)
        Next
    Next
End Sub
```

7. Add the following subroutine to the BackColor_Click event subroutine. Clicking on one of the color option buttons calls this subroutine. The color array is initialized so that an option button index selects the correct RGB value.

```
Sub BackColor_Click (Index As Integer)
    '
    ' Background color selected, set picture box background
    ' color and draw cell using current colors
    '
    canvas.BackColor = colors(Index)
    DrawCell
End Sub
```

8. Add the following subroutine to the ForeColor_Click event subroutine. Clicking one of the color option buttons calls this subroutine.

```
Sub ForeColor_Click (Index As Integer)
    '
    ' Foreground color selected, set picture box foreground
    ' color and draw cell using current colors
    '
    canvas.ForeColor = colors(Index)
    DrawCell
End Sub
```

9. Add the following subroutine to the Form_Load event subroutine. This subroutine loads the color array, assigns the grid's font properties to the canvas, sets the column and row widths, and fills the cells with text.

```
Sub Form_Load ()
    Dim Row As Integer, Col As Integer
    '
    ' Initialize color table
    '
    colors(0) = RGB(0, 0, 0)
    colors(1) = RGB(0, 0, 255)
    colors(2) = RGB(0, 255, 0)
    colors(3) = RGB(0, 255, 255)
    colors(4) = RGB(255, 0, 0)
    colors(5) = RGB(255, 0, 255)
    colors(6) = RGB(255, 255, 0)
    colors(7) = RGB(255, 255, 255)
    '
    ' Copy font properties from grid to picture control
    '
    canvas.FontBold = grid1.FontBold
    canvas.FontItalic = grid1.FontItalic
    canvas.FontName = grid1.FontName
    canvas.FontSize = grid1.FontSize
```

```
'
' Adjust column widths
'
For Col = 0 To grid1.Cols - 1
    grid1.ColWidth(Col) = 1057
Next
'
' Fill cells with row/column names
'
FillCells
'
' Select the upper-left cell
'
grid1.Col = 0
grid1.Row = 0
End Sub
```

10. Use the Menu Design window to create an Exit! item named ExitMenu on the form. Add the following code to the ExitMenu_Click event subroutine.

```
Sub ExitMenu_Click ()
    '
    ' User picked Exit menu ... we're done
    '
    End
End Sub
```

### How It Works

Any bitmap or icon can be assigned to the Grid control's picture property. The picture property is usually set by using the LoadPicture function. In this How-To, a picture box is used as a canvas upon which an image is created. The image is then assigned to the grid's picture property.

Selecting a foreground or background color changes the corresponding property of the canvas picture control, and the current cell's contents are redrawn using the new colors.

### Comments

The Grid control that comes with Visual Basic 3.0 has a minimal set of features. This How-To takes advantage of the Grid control's picture property to simulate a feature that probably should have been part of the control itself.

By using the technique demonstrated in this How-To, as well as the text alignment technique demonstrated in How-To 3.5, it is possible to add the full range of font, formatting, and color options used in programs like Excel.

## 3.13  How do I...

# Allow the user to edit cells in a grid?

### Problem

The Grid control doesn't allow a user to directly enter data into cells. One way to get around this is to put code in the Grid control's keyboard event handlers and put the characters into the cell one at a time. This simple approach would work, but falls far short of providing the functionality Windows users expect. What's needed is an easy way to duplicate the functionality of a text control.

### Technique

The easiest way to duplicate the functionality of an Edit control is to use an Edit control! This project shows how to move an Edit control around the grid. The Edit control is sized to fit each cell as it moves, with its border serving as a nice visual indicator of the selected cell. When the Edit control is moved to a cell, the cell's contents are assigned to the text property of the Edit control. Moving the Edit control from a cell assigns the text to its cell's clip property.

### Steps

Open and run EDITCELL.MAK. You can enter strings in a cell, or edit the existing contents of a cell using all of the usual capabilities of the Edit control. By using the (TAB), (SHIFT)-(TAB), (↑), and (↓) keys, you can move the Edit control around the grid.

1. Create a new project called EDITCELL.MAK. Create a new form with the objects and properties listed in Table 3-22 and save it as EDITCELL.FRM.

| Object | Property | Setting |
|--------|----------|---------|
| Form | Border Style | Fixed Double |
| | Caption | "Cell Editor" |
| | Height | 5160 |
| | KeyPreview | True |
| | Left | 1035 |
| | Name | "Form1" |
| | ScaleHeight | 317 |
| | ScaleMode | Pixel |
| | ScaleWidth | 445 |

| Object | Property | Setting |
|--------|----------|---------|
| | Top | 1140 |
| | Width | 6795 |
| Text box | Height | 19 |
| | Left | 16 |
| | Name | "Text1" |
| | TabStop | False |
| | Text | "Text1" |
| | Top | 288 |
| | Width | 33 |
| Grid | Cols | 8 |
| | FixedCols | 0 |
| | FixedRows | 0 |
| | Height | 265 |
| | HighLight | False |
| | Left | 16 |
| | Name | "Grid1" |
| | Rows | 15 |
| | ScrollBars | None |
| | TabStop | False |
| | Top | 16 |
| | Width | 401 |

**Table 3-22** Form1's objects and properties

2. Put the following code in the Declarations section of Form1.

```
Option explicit
'
' These variables track the current position of the text control on the
' grid
'
Dim curCol As Integer, curRow As Integer
'
' This variable is used to track the state of the shift key
'
Dim shifted As Integer

Const KEY_TAB = &H9
Const KEY_UP = &H26
Const KEY_DOWN = &H28
```

3. Add the following subroutines to the General section of Form1. These subroutines are called whenever a (TAB), (SHIFT)-(TAB), (→), or (←) key is pressed.

You may be surprised at first to see that these subroutines do not move the Edit control. The reason for this is that setting the grid's Row or Col properties cause the grid's RowColChange event to be fired. The code in the Grid1_RowColChange subroutine takes care of moving the Edit control to the new location.

```
Sub MoveDownCell ()
    '
    ' Request to move down, do so if not already at bottom
    '
    If (grid1.Row <> grid1.Rows - 1) Then
        grid1.Row = grid1.Row + 1
    End If
End Sub

Sub MoveLeftCell ()
    '
    ' Request to move left, do so if not at upper left corner
    '
    If (grid1.Col = 0) Then
        If (grid1.Row <> 0) Then
            grid1.Col = grid1.Cols - 1
            grid1.Row = grid1.Row - 1
        End If
    Else
        grid1.Col = grid1.Col - 1
    End If
End Sub

Sub MoveRightCell ()
    '
    ' Request to move right, do so if not at bottom right corner
    '
    If (grid1.Col = grid1.Cols - 1) Then
        If (grid1.Row < grid1.Rows - 1) Then
            grid1.Col = 0
            grid1.Row = grid1.Row + 1
        End If
    Else
        grid1.Col = grid1.Col + 1
    End If
End Sub

Sub MoveUpCell ()
    '
    ' Request to move up, do so if not already at top
    '
    If (grid1.Row <> 0) Then
        grid1.Row = grid1.Row - 1
    End If
End Sub
```

4. Add the following subroutine to the General section of Form1. This subroutine is called during Form_Load to set the initial size and position of the Edit control and by the Grid1_RowColChanged subroutine whenever the grid's Row or Col property is changed.

```
Sub MoveEditControl (c As Integer, r As Integer)
    '
    ' Calculate size and location for the edit control
    '
    text1.Width = (grid1.ColWidth(c) / screen.TwipsPerPixelX)
    text1.Height = (grid1.RowHeight(r) / screen.TwipsPerPixelY)

    text1.Left = (grid1.Left - grid1.LeftCol) + (c * (grid1.ColWidth(c) /←
screen.TwipsPerPixelX)) + c + 1
    text1.Top = (grid1.Top - grid1.TopRow) + (r * (grid1.RowHeight(r) /←
screen.TwipsPerPixelY)) + r + 1


    '
    ' Keep track of the current cell and select it
    '
    curCol = c
    curRow = r
    grid1.Col = c
    grid1.Row = r
End Sub
```

5. Add the following code to the Grid1_RowColChange event subroutine. This subroutine selects the cell that has just been moved from and assigns the contents of the Edit control to the Clip property. Next the cell being moved to is selected and its contents are assigned to the Edit control's Text property. Finally the Edit control is moved to the location of the new cell.

```
Sub Grid1_RowColChange ()
    Dim r As Integer
    Dim c As Integer
    '
    ' Save new current column and row
    '
    c = grid1.Col
    r = grid1.Row
    '
    ' Reselect the cell we left
    '
    grid1.SelStartCol = curCol
    grid1.SelEndCol = curCol
    grid1.SelStartRow = curRow
    grid1.SelEndRow = curRow
    '
```

*continued on next page*

*continued from previous page*

```
    ' Assign text from edit control to the cell we left
    '
    grid1.Clip = text1.Text
    '
    ' Reselect the new cell
    '
    grid1.SelStartCol = c
    grid1.SelEndCol = c
    grid1.SelStartRow = r
    grid1.SelEndRow = r
    '
    ' Hide the edit control while it's changing
    '
    text1.Visible = False
    '
    ' Get text from the new cell
    '
    text1.Text = grid1.Clip
    '
    ' Move the edit control to the new cell
    '
    MoveEditControl c, r
    '
    ' Display the edit control
    '
    text1.Visible = True
End Sub
```

6. Add the following code to the grid's GotFocus event procedure. This code ensures that the Edit control always gets keyboard input.

```
Sub Grid1_GotFocus ()
    '
    ' Whenever the grid gets focus we make sure the edit control
    ' is visible and set the focus to it.
    '
    text1.Visible = True
    text1.SetFocus
End Sub
```

7. Add the following code to the Load event subroutine of Form1. The first part of this subroutine takes care of sizing the rows and columns so that they will fill the grid without leaving space at either the bottom or right edges. The last part initializes some variables and moves the Edit control to the upper left cell.

```
Sub Form_Load ()
    Dim Row As Integer, Col As Integer
    Dim ColWidth As Integer, RowHeight As Integer
    '
    ' Adjust the grid dimensions so that the number of rows and
    ' columns will completely fill it.
```

```
    '
    grid1.Width = (grid1.Width / grid1.Cols) * grid1.Cols
    grid1.Height = (grid1.Height / grid1.Rows) * grid1.Rows
    '
    ' Now set the column height and row width to match the grid
    '
    ColWidth = grid1.Width / grid1.Cols
    RowHeight = grid1.Height / grid1.Rows
    '
    ' Adjust the size of each row
    '
    For Row = 0 To grid1.Rows - 1
        grid1.RowHeight(Row) = RowHeight * screen.TwipsPerPixelY
    Next row
    '
    ' Adjust the size of each column
    '
    For Col = 0 To grid1.Cols - 1
        grid1.ColWidth(Col) = ColWidth * screen.TwipsPerPixelX
    Next col
    '
    ' Make final adjustment to size of grid to get exact fit
    '
    grid1.Width = ((grid1.ColWidth(0) + screen.TwipsPerPixelX) * ⇐
grid1.Cols) / screen.TwipsPerPixelX
    grid1.Height = ((grid1.RowHeight(0) + screen.TwipsPerPixelY) * ⇐
grid1.Rows) / screen.TwipsPerPixelY
    '
    ' Start with some text in ROCO
    '
    text1.Text = "HooHa"
    '
    ' Initialize the variables which track the current location of the ⇐
edit control
    '
    curCol = 0
    curRow = 0
    '
    ' Move edit control to its initial position
    '
    text1.Visible = False
    MoveEditControl 0, 0
    text1.Visible = True
End Sub
```

8. Add the following code to the form's KeyDown event procedure. The state of the (SHIFT) key is tracked so that the KeyPress subroutine can tell the difference between a (TAB) and a (SHIFT)-(TAB). An important feature introduced in Visual Basic 2.0 is the form's KeyPreview property. Since we have set this property to True the form gets a chance to look at all keyboard events before they are passed on to the controls.

```
Sub Form_KeyDown (KeyCode As Integer, shift As Integer)
    '
    ' A key has been pressed, keep track of shift state for Form_KeyPress
    '
    If (shift And 1) Then
        shifted = True
    End If
End Sub
```

9. Add the following code to the KeyPress event subroutine of Form1. If the pressed key is a (TAB) then the current cell is moved either left or right according to the state of the keyboard shift state.

```
Sub Form_KeyPress (KeyAscii As Integer)
    '
    ' A key has been pressed. If it's a tab move the edit control
    ' otherwise let the edit control have it.
    '
    If (KeyAscii = KEY_TAB) Then
        If Not shifted Then
            MoveRightCell
        Else
            MoveLeftCell
        End If
        '
        ' Set the received key to zero ... otherwise the
        ' edit control will see the tab and beep.
        '
        KeyAscii = 0
    End If
End Sub
```

10. Add the following code to the KeyUp event subroutine of Form1. In addition to continuing to track the state of the (SHIFT) key this subroutine moves the current cell up or down whenever an unshifted ⬆ or ⬇ key is released.

```
Sub Form_KeyUp (KeyCode As Integer, shift As Integer)
    '
    ' A key has been released. Keep track of shift state and move the
    ' edit control up or down if required, otherwise let the edit
    ' control have it.
    '
    If (Not shift And 1) Then
        shifted = False
    End If

    Select Case KeyCode
        Case KEY_UP
            If Not shifted Then
```

```
            MoveUpCell
        End If
    Case KEY_DOWN
        If Not shifted Then
            MoveDownCell
        End If
    End Select
End Sub
```

11. Add the following code to the GotFocus event subroutine of Text1. Whenever the Edit control gets focus, all of its text is selected. This makes it easy for the user to delete the entire contents of a cell.

```
Sub Text1_GotFocus ()
    '
    ' The edit control has gotten focus, select all of the text
    '
    text1.SelStart = 0
    text1.SelLength = Len(text1.Text)
End Sub
```

### How It Works

The first interesting thing that happens when this project executes is the firing of the Form_Load event. The Grid control does not support design-time sizing of the rows and columns; they must be sized at run time. The sizing is performed in the Form_Load event procedure so that the grid will be correctly sized when first displayed.

After the grid has been sized, the Edit control is initialized and moved to the upper left cell of the grid. The reason that the Edit control text is initialized and the variables curRow and curCol set to 0 may not be obvious at first. The MoveEditControl routine assigns the current value of the edit control to the cell given by curRow and curCol before moving it. Then the contents of the cell at the new location are assigned to the Edit control. Since curRow and curCol are the same as the row and column being moved to, the call to MoveEditControl harmlessly assigns the Edit control to the cell and then copies the cell contents back to the Edit control. If you want to start a program with the Edit control at some location other than row 0 column 0, simply change the values of curRow and curCol to the starting location, assign the appropriate text to the Edit control, and everything will work fine.

### Handling Keyboard Events

Visual Basic 2.0 added the KeyPreview property to forms. By setting this property to True, it is possible to examine most keyboard events before any control sees them. By setting the TabStop property of the Grid and Edit controls to False, we are able to see the (TAB) key as well. These settings prevent the Edit control from using the up and down arrows to move left and right, and prevent the Visual Basic code from using the (TAB) key to move between controls.

### Moving The Edit Control

Two types of user actions can require the Edit control to move on the grid. First, there are the navigation keys (↑), (↓), (TAB), and (SHIFT)-(TAB). Second, whenever the user clicks on a new cell, the Edit control needs to be moved to the newly selected cell.

By using the form's KeyPreview property, it is easy to catch the navigation keys. Whenever one of these keys is pressed, the appropriate subroutine is called. As a typical case, consider what happens when the (TAB) key is pressed. The form's KeyPress routine calls MoveRightCell, which checks to see whether the Edit control can be moved. If the Edit control is not at the bottom right cell, it is moved by calling the MoveEditControl subroutine.

The way mouse clicks are handled, while actually simpler, is not immediately obvious. When you click on a cell of the Grid control, the Row and Col properties are changed to the location of the cell beneath the mouse pointer. Then the grid's RowColChanged event procedure is called. This RowColChanged subroutine copies the contents of the Edit control to the cell that was previously selected, assigns the contents of the new cell to the Edit control, and then moves the Edit control to the new location. Somewhere in all of this, the grid's GotFocus event procedure is called; but the grid never really has the focus for long because it's given to the Edit control by using the SetFocus method.

### Comments

This How-To could be adapted for use as a datafile browser/editor without too much difficulty. With a datafile browser you would probably want to add vertical and horizontal scroll bars. A vertical scroll bar can be used for scrolling through a list of records, and a horizontal scroll bar can be used when there are too many fields in a record to display at one time.

The ease of using the grid's ScrollBar property is attractive, but it cannot be used for this purpose because the Grid control does not have an event that lets you know when it has been scrolled. One way to deal with this is to put scroll bars on the form yourself. Then as the scroll bar's events are fired, you can respond by changing the LeftCol and TopRow properties as required.

# CHAPTER 4

# MOUSE AND MENU

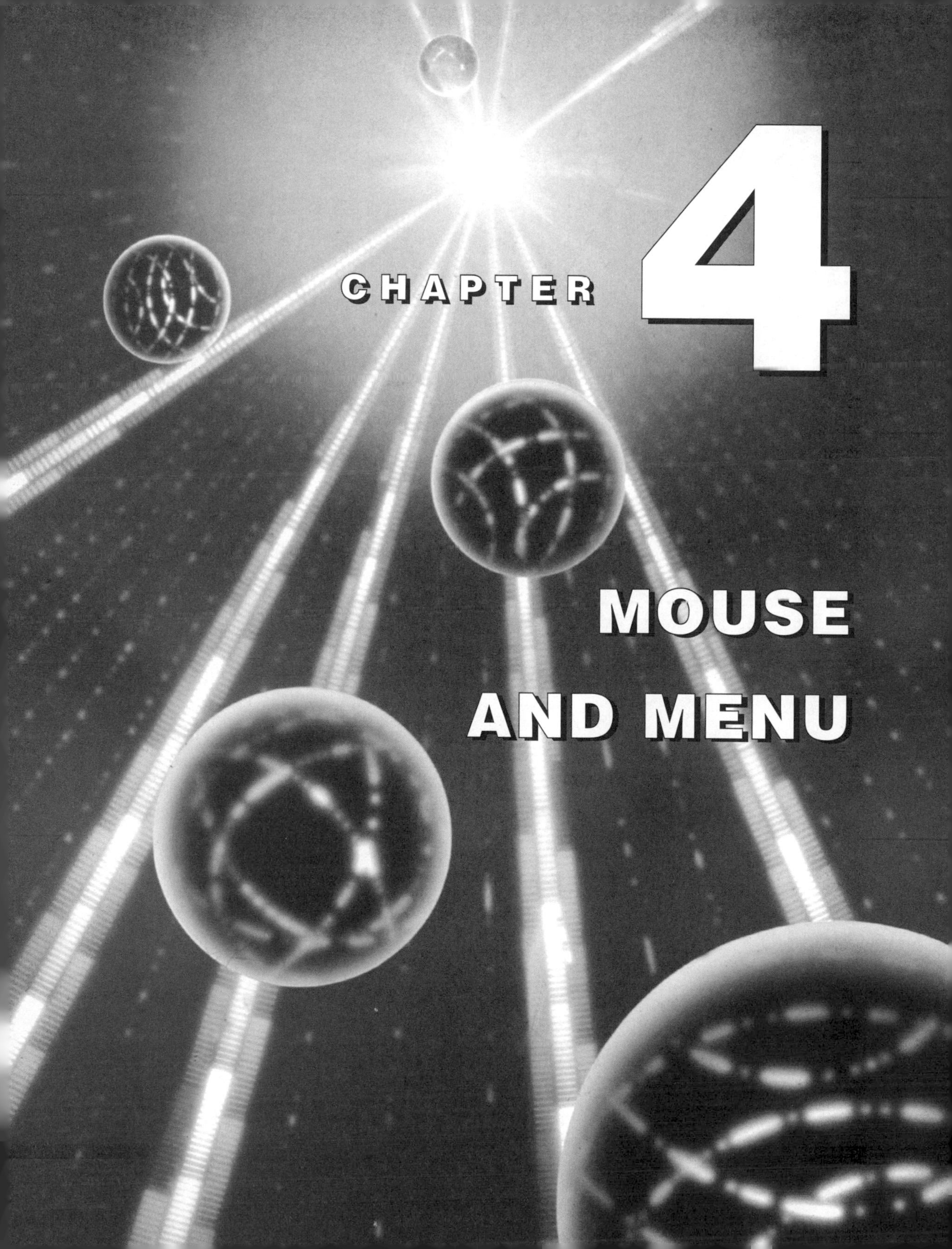

# How do I...

Windows includes many improvements over the DOS operating system, but the most noticeable is the beauty of the user interface. And it has not taken long for faithful DOS command-line users to appreciate the ease of use of the graphical user interface. Most essential to a good user interface are mouse-driven user input and command menus. While Visual Basic makes interface programming a snap with its toolbox and control array features, in some cases this young language is limited. This bag-of-tricks chapter shows you how to create more powerful mouse trapping and selection capabilities and how to create more customized, useful, and attractive menus. We will use some very handy Windows APIs to extend Visual Basic's menu-making capabilities: GetMenu, GetSubMenu, GetMenuItem, and ModifyMenu. We will also see the versatility of Visual Basic's timer features.

## Windows APIs Covered

| | |
|---|---|
| DeleteMenu | GetSubMenu |
| GetMenu | GetSystemMenu |
| GetMenuItem | ModifyMenu |
| GetMenuItemID | TrackPopupMenu |

### 4.1 Draw an animated bounding box

Ease of the user interface is an important issue in a graphically oriented language such as Visual Basic. You may notice that various Windows paint or draw programs use a rotating dashed line to show rectangular areas selected with a mouse. This clever How-To uses the timer to simulate an animated bounding box (or the "marching ants" effect, as it's known to Macintosh programmers). No APIs are required.

### 4.2 Trap both Click and DoubleClick events

Many mouse users are accustomed to clicking and double-clicking to select items, open and close menus, and run applications. Amazingly enough, Visual Basic's capabilities allow you to either trap single Click events or a DoubleClick event, but not both for a single object. One reason for this is that Visual Basic has a hard time distinguishing between two single clicks or one double-click. Waiting for the second half of a double click can slow up your application's performance. This How-To uses the timer to distinguish between the events and allows you to build a more flexible user interface. This project also includes a gauge to display the performance hit that's caused by distinguishing between Click and DoubleClick events.

### 4.3 Make a floating pop-up menu

Visual Basic allows you to easily create menu bars at the top of a form. However, it does not provide the power to create "floating" menus that pop up anywhere at the click of a mouse. This How-To shows you how to use the Windows API functions GetMenu, GetSubMenu, and TrackPopupMenu to display a pop-up menu that allows you to choose a form's background color. This menu will appear anywhere on your screen. You'll also see how to make Windows API functions interpret Visual Basic's "twips" measurement.

### 4.4 Modify a form's system menu

Visual Basic's toolbox allows you to modify most menus, but the System menu seems sacrosanct—it cannot be changed with ordinary Visual Basic control arrays. Sometimes you may want to disable some options of the System menu so users of your program have limited choices. For instance, you may want to restrict the way your users can close an application or to prevent your application from ever being minimized. The Windows APIs GetSystemMenu, ModifyMenu, and DeleteMenu are used in this How-To to get a handle to the System menu and use that handle to delete menu items.

**4.5    Draw a bitmapped picture in a menu**

Visual Basic is a relatively flexible language when it comes to creating menus but it does have its limitations. One restraint is that you cannot put a bitmapped graphic image in a menu with purely native Visual Basic code. Sometimes, however, you may want to spruce up your menus to include icons or custom graphics. For example, a telephone icon could appear next to the word "Dial." This How-To uses the Windows API functions GetMenu, GetSubMenu, and GetMenuItemID to place a bitmapped graphic in a menu, including .BMP (bitmap), .ICO (icon), or .WMF (Windows metafile) file types.

**4.6    Place font typefaces in a menu**

The high-resolution look of Windows 3.0 and 3.1 is causing users to expect a higher standard in the way applications look on the screen. Windows word processors are being touted for their WYSIWYG (What You See Is What You Get) capabilities; you can preview a printed page on your monitor and see the style and size of a font, for instance. The previous How-To demonstrated how to include bitmapped graphics on your menus; this How-To goes further to create a Font menu that displays bitmapped images of the actual font typefaces. Again, the multipurpose Windows APIs GetMenu, GetSubMenu, GetMenuItem, and ModifyMenu API are used for this effect.

**4.7    Display menu prompts**

Most Professional Windows programs include a status bar where short prompt messages are displayed. These prompt messages can be useful for users that basically know what various commands will do, but may need some confirmation or an occasional reminder for some of the less often used commands. Unfortunately, Visual Basic does not fire an event when a menu item is highlighted, only when it has been clicked. The Display Menu Prompts project shows you how to use the MsgHook custom control to intercept the menu select messages. Using the MsgHook control, as shown in this project, you can easily add professional looking menu prompts to your applications.

## 4.1 How do I...

**Complexity: Easy**

# Draw an animated bounding box?

### Problem

I want to offer my users a way to select an area on a form with their mouse. How can I display a rotating bounding box around the area they select?

### Technique

A timer object is useful when you are doing animation. Dotted line boxes can create an optical illusion of movement, as shown in Figure 4-1. Each time the timer goes off, the line can be inverted, which creates the illusion of the box rotating.

### Steps

Open and run BOUNDING.MAK. You can draw boxes by holding down the mouse button and dragging. Once you release the mouse button, the box will remain rotating on the screen until you drag it on another area. Notice that the box rotates even as you draw it.

1. Create a new project called BOUNDING.MAK. Create a new form with the objects and properties listed in Table 4-1. Save it as BOUNDING.FRM.

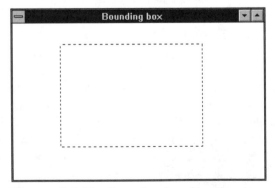

**Figure 4-1** The Bounding form in action

| Object | Property | Setting |
|--------|----------|---------|
| Form | FormName | BoundingBox |
| | Caption | Bounding box |
| | BackColor | &H00FFFFFF& (White) |
| Timer | Name | Timer1 |
| | Interval | 100 |
| | Enabled | True |

**Table 4-1** Bounding project form's objects and properties

2. Place the following code in the Declarations section of the form to define some constants for drawing and global variables.

```
Const DOTSTYLE = 2
Const SOLIDSTYLE = 0
Const INVERTMODE = 6
Const COPYPENMODE = 13
Dim X1 As Single, Y1 As Single, X2 As Single, Y2 As Single
```

3. Put the following code in the form's MouseDown event subroutine to set the box's coordinates to the point where the mouse was clicked. As the user moves the mouse, the coordinates of the lower right-hand corner (X2 and Y2) of the box will change.

```
Sub Form_MouseDown (Button As Integer, Shift As Integer, X As Single, Y ⇐
    As Single)
    X1 = X
    Y1 = Y
    X2 = X
    Y2 = Y
End Sub
```

4. The form's MouseMove event subroutine first checks whether a mouse button is being held down. If so, it erases the previously drawn box, then draws a dotted box at the new coordinates of the mouse with this code.

```
Sub Form_MouseMove (Button As Integer, Shift As Integer, X As Single, Y ⇐
    As Single)
    If Button Then
        DrawStyle = SOLIDSTYLE
        DrawMode = COPYPENMODE
        Line (X1, Y1)-(X2, Y2), BoundingBox.BackColor, B
        X2 = X
        Y2 = Y
        DrawStyle = DOTSTYLE
        Line (X1, Y1)-(X2, Y2), , B
    End If
End Sub
```

5. Timer1's Timer event subroutine draws the inverted dotted box around the current coordinates set by the MouseDown and MouseMove event subroutines.

```
Sub Timer1_Timer ()
    DrawStyle = SOLIDSTYLE
    DrawMode = INVERTMODE
    Line (X1, Y1)-(X2, Y2), , B
End Sub
```

### How It Works

The code in the MouseDown and MouseMove event subroutines handles drawing the box as the user moves the mouse. In the MouseMove event subroutine, the Line statement draws a box using a solid DrawStyle and a dotted DrawMode in the background color of the form. Using the background color erases the last box before drawing the box with the new size.

The key to simulating animation is to be able to invert the box often enough to stimulate continuous motion. A timer causes a timer interrupt to occur every 100 milliseconds, at which point it causes the inverse of the current box to be drawn. Since we used a dotted DrawMode, the inverse of the dot-space pattern will become space-dot. Doing that often enough gives the illusion of a rotating box.

### Comments

Although the MouseMove event subroutine uses a dotted DrawStyle, you could just as easily use another DrawStyle (a dashed box—DrawStyle = 1— also looks attractive). Note that using many timers running on short intervals will slow down your whole system. Be sure to disable timers as soon as you're finished using them. You can safely increase the timer interval, and the bounding box will simply "rotate" more slowly.

## 4.2  How do I... 

Complexity: Intermediate

## Trap both Click and DblClick events?

### Problem

I have seen a number of programs that do one thing when users click on an object and another when users double-click. I can't seem to get this to work in Visual Basic. I can trap either the Click event or the DoubleClick event, but not both. When I create an event procedure for both, the Click handler gets launched in both instances, and my program never hears about the DoubleClick. I know that my DoubleClick procedure works, because if I disable the Click procedure, the DoubleClick procedure works fine. Is there anything I can do?

### Technique

This issue is, in fact, a sore spot with no easy answer for the developers of Visual Basic without a real performance hit. The problem is this: a double-click is technically a series of two clicks in rapid succession. Just how rapid is determined by the system "DoubleClick Time," which can be set by a program, as we will do later in this project, or by using the Control Panel.

When Windows receives the first mouse click, it has no way of knowing whether this will ultimately become a double-click or will remain a single click, so it simply passes on the Click message. (In reality, Windows passes the MouseDown followed by the MouseUp message.) Now, if another click arrives within the specified interval, it is considered the second half of a double-click and the DoubleClick message is sent.

Theoretically, Windows could wait for the duration of the double-click interval before sending the Click message. However, when you consider that the user generates many more clicks than double-clicks, it doesn't make sense to slow the whole system down to make it easier for the few programs that need to trap both events.

The good news is that you can perform this operation yourself, using a timer. The technique is to enable your timer, the interval of which is set to be equal to the "DoubleClick Time," within your Click event handler. Within the Timer event handler, you must first disable the timer and then build in the processing that would normally be contained in the Click event handler. From within the DoubleClick event handler, you simply disable the timer and proceed with normal double-click processing.

### Steps

Open and run CLICKS.MAK. There is a button labeled "Try It!" that you can either click or double-click with the left mouse button. The caption of the form will change to reflect your action as either "Clicked" or "DoubleClicked." As shown in Figure 4-2, the scroll bar is used to set the "DoubleClick Time" and thus the speed with which you must double-click the mouse to have the action register as a double-click in the program. The number below the scroll bar reports the current double-click time in milliseconds. The smaller the number, the faster you have to double-click on the button for it to register as a double-click in the program.

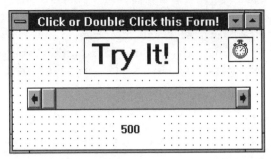

**Figure 4-2** Appearance of the Clicks form

To see that the system-wide double-click time is actually being set, move all the way left on the scroll bar, minimize Clicks, and see whether you can restore it, or try to open any other application by double-clicking it. Luckily, you can select Restore from the System menu to get back into Clicks. When you exit from Clicks, the previous setting for the double-click time is restored.

To create the Clicks program, perform the following steps:

1. Create a new project called CLICKS.MAK. Create a new form with the objects and properties shown in Table 4-2, and save it as CLICKS.FRM.

| Object | Property | Setting |
|--------|----------|---------|
| Form | FormName | Form1 |
| | Caption | Click or DoubleClick |
| | BackColor | &H00FFFFFF& (White) |
| Picture | Name | Picture1 |
| | Caption | Try It! |
| | BorderStyle | Fixed Single |
| Timer | Name | Timer1 |
| | Interval | 200 |
| | Enabled | FLASE |
| Scroll | Name | HScroll1 |
| | LargeChange | 10 |
| | Max | 2000 |
| | Min | 100 |
| | SmallChange | 1 |
| Label | Name | Label1 |
| | Caption 500 | |

**Table 4-2** Clicks project form's objects and properties

2. Insert the following code in the Declarations section of Form1.

```
DefInt A-Z

Declare Function GetDoubleClickTime Lib "User" ()
Declare Sub SetDoubleClickTime Lib "User" (ByVal wCount)

Const TRUE = -1
Const FALSE = 0

Dim OldInterval As Integer
```

3. Insert the following code in the Form_Load procedure.

```
Sub Form_Load ()
    OldInterval = GetDoubleClickTime()
    Timer1.Interval = 500
    HScroll1.Value = 500
End Sub
```

4. Insert the following code in the Form_Unload procedure.

```
Sub Form_Unload (Cancel As Integer)
    SetDoubleClickTime OldInterval
End Sub
```

5. Insert the following code in the Label1_Click procedure.

```
Sub Label1_Click ()
    Timer1.Enabled = TRUE
End Sub
```

6. Insert the following code in the Label1_DblClick procedure.

```
Sub Label1_DblClick ()
    Timer1.Enabled = FALSE
    Form1.Caption = "DoubleClicked!"
End Sub
```

7. Insert the following code in the Timer1_Timer procedure.

```
Sub Timer1_Timer ()
    'Click processing here!
    Form1.Caption = "Clicked!"
    Timer1.Enabled = FALSE
End Sub
```

8. Insert the following code in HScroll1_Change procedure.

```
Sub HScroll1_Change ()
    NewInterval = HScroll1.Value
    SetDoubleClickTime NewInterval
    Timer1.Interval = HScroll1.Value
    Label2.Caption = Str$(HScroll1.Value)
End Sub
```

### How It Works

A click is defined as a MouseDown followed by a MouseUp within the same region. After Visual Basic has received both of these messages, it triggers the Click event for a given control. If another Click occurs within the Double-Click Time, Windows sends the DoubleClick message to your application, and the message gets translated into the DblClick event.

What we are doing here is setting a timer, the Interval of which is the same as the DoubleClick Time, which we enable in the Click event handler. This frees up the system quickly enough to avoid swallowing the DblClick event. If the DblClick event occurs within the specified interval, we immediately disable the timer and process the DblClick event. However, if the timer gets a chance to fire, it means that a second click did not manage to occur within the DoubleClick Time, so we process the first click by itself.

### Comments

You can see by scrolling the interval gauge all the way to the right just what sort of performance slowdown can result from always trapping both events. This is why this sort of trapping is not supported natively in the Windows API. However, it is not too complicated to implement such a feature for your own use.

One issue that might arise is that you want to be able to trap both events for a number of controls. This is most easily accomplished with a control array. If the controls are all in an array, then the index of the array could simply be saved in a static variable. This way, when the Timer event occurs, it can execute specific code based in the index in the static variable.

## 4.3  How do I...

**Complexity: Intermediate**

## Make a floating pop-up menu?

### Problem

Is there any way to make my menus pop up anywhere on the screen at the touch of a mouse button? Pop-up menus are a nice way to let users select an object, then click a mouse button rather than having to select a menu item from the top of the form.

### Technique

Although in Windows the menu bar is fixed at the top of the form, individual menus can be popped up anywhere you'd like, even off your form. Windows API functions allow this.

There are API functions that let you get a menu handle (the Windows identification of a menu and its items). Once you have that handle you can use it to manually pop up a menu. You can also control where you want it to pop up. For this example, we'll pop the menu up at the current mouse position.

### Steps

Open and run FLOATING.MAK. Click and hold down the left mouse button. The Color menu will appear next to your mouse pointer. Move the mouse to select a color and release the button. The background color of the form will change.

1. Create a new project called FLOATING.MAK. Create a new form with the objects and properties listed in Table 4-3, and save it as FLOATING.FRM.

| Object | Property | Setting |
|--------|----------|---------|
| Form | FormName | FloatingPopupMenu |
|  | Caption | Floating popup menu |

**Table 4-3** Floating project form's objects and properties

2. Create a menu for the form, as shown in Table 4-4, using the Menu Design window.

| Caption | Name | Index |
|---------|------|-------|
| &Color | ColorMenu | |
| B&lack | Colors | 0 |
| &Blue | Colors | 1 |
| &Green | Colors | 2 |
| &Cyan | Colors | 3 |
| &Red | Colors | 4 |
| &Magenta | Colors | 5 |
| &Yellow | Colors | 6 |
| &White | Colors | 7 |
| - | Separator | |
| E&xit | ColorExit | |

**Table 4-4** FloatingPopUpMenu menu items

3. Put the following code in the Declarations section of the form. This code declares several API functions and a global variable.

```
DefInt A-Z
Declare Function GetMenu% Lib "User" (ByVal hWnd%)
Declare Function GetSubMenu% Lib "User" (ByVal hMenu%, ByVal nPos%)
Declare Function TrackPopupMenu% Lib "User" (ByVal hMenu%, ByVal wFlags%, ⇐
ByVal X%, ByVal Y%, ByVal nReserved%, ByVal hWnd%, ByVal lpReserved&)
```

4. Once you've created the menu, you can add the code that goes with the menu items. Put the following code in the ColorExit_Click event subroutine.

```
Sub ColorExit_Click ()
    End
End Sub
```

5. Put the following code in the Colors_Click event subroutine.

```
Sub Colors_Click (Index As Integer)
    BackColor = QBColor(Index)
End Sub
```

6. The Form_MouseDown event subroutine is used to call the API functions to pop up the menu. Because Visual Basic automatically passes to MouseDown event subroutines, we'll convert the x- and y-coordinates to pixels using the figure we calculated in the Form_Load event subroutine.

```
Sub Form_MouseDown (Button As Integer, Shift As Integer, X As Single, Y ⇐
   As Single)
    PopupX = (X + Left) / Screen.TwipsPerPixelX
    PopupY = (Y + Top) / Screen. TwipsPerPixwlY
    hMenu = GetMenu(hWnd)
    hSubMenu = GetSubMenu(hMenu, 0)
    I = TrackPopupMenu(hSubMenu, 0, PopupX, PopupY, 0, hWnd, 0)
End Sub
```

### How It Works

Figure 4-3 shows what the pop-up Colors menu will look like at run time. The Declare statements in the Declarations section give Visual Basic access to the Windows API functions we'll need. Windows APIs that affect graphics devices generally expect coordinate arguments to be expressed in pixels. Since our form's ScaleMode is set to twips, the Form_MouseDown event procedure must convert the mouse coordinates from twips to pixels. The Screen object variables TwipsPerPixelX and TwipsPerPixelY allow us to perform this conversion easily. (A twip, by the way, stands for a twentieth of a point. A point, used by typographers, is 1/72nd of an inch. So a twip is

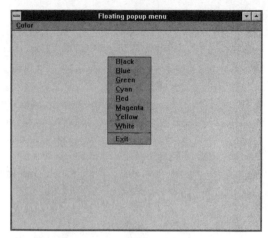

**Figure 4-3** The FloatingPopupMenu form showing a menu to select color

1/1440th of an inch. However, in Visual Basic, an inch on the screen depends on what size and resolution monitor is attached. On a printer, though, an inch is an inch.)

We use a control array's index value to our advantage. The indexes from the Colors menu will be from zero to seven, which correspond exactly to the first eight color codes that QuickBasic uses. Visual Basic has the QBColor function to convert from the QuickBasic color codes to the RGB codes that Visual Basic itself uses. So we'll use it to change the background color of the form by simply saying BackColor = QBColor(Index).

The Form_MouseDown event subroutine calls up the Colors menu. First, the location of the mouse pointer must be calculated using the twips-to-pixels ratio provided by the Screen object's TwipsPerPixelX and TwipsPerPixelY variables. Then Windows' requirement to get a handle on everything must be satisfied by using the GetMenu and GetSubMenu API functions. Finally, the TrackPopupMenu API pops up the menu and lets you select an item. Notice that even though we're using a Windows API function to call the menu, Visual Basic still intercepts the menu access and calls the Colors_Click event subroutine just as if the menu were at the top, where it normally is.

## Comments

Note that the menus are still available, as you'd expect, from the menu bar at the top of the form. The menu only pops up when you click on the "surface" of the form.

## 4.4 How do I...

## Modify a form's system menu?

### Problem

Not all the features of the System menu (the square in the upper left-hand corner of windows) are needed for my application. I would like to both remove some System menu items and modify others, like Visual Basic's toolbox does. Although I can modify a form's normal menu items using control arrays, that method doesn't seem to work on the System menu. I'd like to prevent the user from closing the application except through the File menu's Exit option.

### Technique

Once again, you can use Windows API functions to extend the power of Visual Basic. The API GetSystemMenu is a function that returns a handle to the System menu. Remember, handles are integer values (IDs) that Windows uses to identify elements like menus and windows. Once we have a handle for the System menu, we can use other API functions like ModifyMenu and DeleteMenu to modify it.

### Steps

Open and run SYSMENU.MAK. You'll be presented with a blank form once you access System menu. You'll see the changes that Form_Load has made to the System menu as seen in Figure 4-4.

1. Create a new project called SYSMENU.MAK. Create a new form with no controls on it, and save it as SYSMENU.FRM.

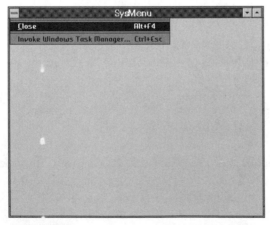

**Figure 4-4** The SysMenu form and menu

2. Add the following Declare statements to the Declarations section of the form. They declare the Windows API functions that will be used later.

```
DefInt A-Z
Declare Function GetSystemMenu Lib "User" (ByVal hWnd, ByVal bRevert)
Declare Function ModifyMenu Lib "User" (ByVal hMenu, ByVal nPosition, ⇐
ByVal wFlags, ByVal wIDNewItem, ByVal lpNewItem$)
Declare Function DeleteMenu Lib "User" (ByVal hMenu, ByVal nPosition, ⇐
ByVal wFlags)
```

3. Put the following code in the Form_Load event subroutine. It declares constants to use in the API function calls. It gets a handle to the System menu and then uses the handle to change the menu and delete some menu Items.

```
Sub Form_Load ()
    Const MF_BYCOMMAND = 0
    Const MF_BYPOSITION = &H400
    Const SC_TASKLIST = &HF130
    Const ICON_STOP = 16

    Dim hSysMenu As Integer

    hSysMenu = GetSystemMenu(hWnd, 0)

    NewMenuItem$ = "Windows Task Manager--" + Chr$(9) + "Ctrl+Esc"
    If ModifyMenu(hSysMenu, SC_TASKLIST, MF_BYCOMMAND, SC_TASKLIST, ⇐
        NewMenuItem$) = 0 Then
        MsgBox "Can't modify system menu item!", ICON_STOP
    End If

    For I = 0 To 4
        If DeleteMenu(hSysMenu, 0, MF_BYPOSITION) = 0 Then
            MsgBox "Unable to delete system menu item!", ICON_STOP
        End If
    Next
End Sub
```

### How It Works

The Declare statements in the Declarations section of the form provide access to the Windows API functions. GetSystemMenu is the API function that returns a handle to the System menu. ModifyMenu lets you change the text of a menu item. DeleteMenu deletes items from a menu, not the whole menu as its name would imply.

The Form_Load subroutine manages the modification process for the System menu. The first couple of lines define some Windows constants for the various API functions. (The MF_ prefix means "menu flags," and SC_ means "system menu commands.") MF_BYCOMMAND specifies to modify a menu item based on its message ID, whereas SC_TASKLIST is the actual message ID of the SwitchTo item on the System menu. MF_BY-POSITION indicates that a menu item should be modified based on its position within the menu.

We call the GetSystemMenu to get the handle of the System menu. We use Visual Basic's hWnd property to give the form's window handle, which GetSystemMenu requires.

Note the use of Chr$(9), the tab character; a tab is used in this menu item to tab over to the right side of the menu. In the Windows interface, that's where you tell users what key to press to get the same result as selecting the menu item. Here, we specify (CTRL)-(ESC) to get to the SwitchTo selection.

By using MF_BYCOMMAND and the same message ID (SC_TASK-LIST) in the call to the ModifyMenu function, we're telling Windows not to change the message ID, just the text of the menu item. If ModifyMenu returns 0, Windows was for some reason unable to make the requested change, so we display a message box with the error. (Windows should always be able to change a menu, unless very little memory is available, but it's better to be safe than sorry.)

The For…Next loop deletes five of the standard System menu items. Actually, we specify to delete by position (MF_BYPOSITION), item 0 five times. Because item 0 is always the topmost item, Visual Basic deletes the top five items. DeleteMenu also returns 0 if there was an error, so we check for it and display a message box if necessary.

### Comments

If you're modifying the text on the System menu, you should always be sure to put the keyboard equivalent in the text. In the previous example, the Form_Load event subroutine uses Chr$(9)-(CTRL)-(ESC) because that was the original key of the SwitchTo item.

Be aware that if you delete an item from the System menu, you won't be able to do the function performed by the deleted item. For example, if you delete the Move item, you won't be able to move it around the screen with either the mouse or the keyboard.

## 4.5 How do I...

# Draw a bitmapped picture in a menu?

### Problem

I want to make my application as graphical as possible. Unfortunately, the part of my application my users must deal with the most is lackluster text: the menu. What can I do to spice up this menu?

### Technique

The use of graphical icons is very important in today's applications. Fortunately, there is a way to place bitmap Images into a menu using Windows APIs.

### Steps

Open and run BITMAPS.MAK. Notice the two picture boxes (as shown in Figure 4-5). They will be hidden when you run the application. Select the Security menu and see how it looks when you mix text and graphics on the same menu.

1. Create a new project called BITMAPS.MAK. Create a new form with the objects and properties listed in Table 4-5, and save it as BITMAPS.FRM.

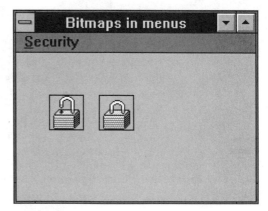

**Figure 4-5** The BitMapMenu form at design time

| Object | Property | Setting |
|---|---|---|
| Form | FormName | BitmapMenu |
| | Caption | Bitmaps in menus |
| | BackColor | &H00C0C0C0& (50% gray) |
| Picture box | Name | Unlocked |
| | AutoSize | True |
| | Picture | \VB\ICONS\MISC\SECUR02A.ICO |
| | Visible | False |
| Picture box | Name | Locked |
| | AutoSize | True |
| | Picture | \VB\ICONS\MISC\SECUR02B.ICO |
| | Visible | False |

**Table 4-5** BitMap project form's objects and properties

2. Create a menu for the form as shown in Table 4-6, using the Menu Design window.

| Caption | Name |
|---|---|
| &Security | SecurityMenu |
| O&ff | SecurityOff |
| O&n | SecurityOn |
| E&xit | SecurityExit |

**Table 4-6** Bitmaps menu

3. Because we need to declare some API functions and API constants, put the following code in the Declarations section of the Form object.

```
DefInt A-Z

Declare Function GetMenu% Lib "User" (ByVal hWnd%)
Declare Function GetSubMenu% Lib "User" (ByVal hMenu%, ByVal nPos%)
Declare Function GetMenuItemID% Lib "User" (ByVal hMenu%, ByVal nPos%)
Declare Function ModifyMenu% Lib "User" (ByVal hMenu%, ByVal nPosition%, ⇐
ByVal wFlags%, ByVal wIDNewItem%, ByVal lpNewItem&)

Const MF_BYCOMMAND = 0
Const MF_BITMAP = 4
Const MF_CHECKED = 8
Const FALSE = 0, TRUE = Not FALSE
```

4. The Form_Load event subroutine manages placing the bitmaps in the menu. Because Windows only allows changes to a menu via its menu

handle (an integer number that Windows uses to identify menus), you'll need to use the GetMenu and GetSubMenu API functions to access those handles from Visual Basic. Also, you'll need to use the GetMenuItemID API function to be able to put a bitmap in the individual menu item.

```
Sub Form_Load ()
    ' Get the form's menu handle.
    hMenu = GetMenu(hWnd)

    ' Get the menu's Security (submenu 0) submenu handle.
    hSubMenu = GetSubMenu(hMenu, 0)

    ' Make sure Picture gets the bitmap handle from Image property.
    UnLocked.Picture = UnLocked.Image
    ' Get the Windows menu message ID of Off item.
    menuId = GetMenuItemID(hSubMenu, 0)
    ' Put the "unlocked" bitmap into the menu.
    J = ModifyMenu(hMenu, menuId, MF_BYCOMMAND Or MF_BITMAP Or ⇐
        MF_CHECKED, menuId, UnLocked.Picture)

    ' Make sure Picture gets the bitmap handle from Image property.
    Locked.Picture = Locked.Image
    ' Get the Windows menu message ID of On item.
    menuId = GetMenuItemID(hSubMenu, 1)
    ' Put the "locked" bitmap into the menu.
    J = ModifyMenu(hMenu, menuId, MF_BYCOMMAND Or MF_BITMAP, menuId, ⇐
        Locked.Picture)
End Sub
```

5. Put the following code in the SecurityExit_Click event subroutine.

```
Sub SecurityExit_Click ()
    End
End Sub
```

6. Place the following code in the SecurityOff_Click and SecurityOn_Click event subroutines. This code simply prints a message and then puts a check mark next to the menu item you picked.

```
Sub SecurityOff_Click ()
    Print "Security has been deactivated"
    SecurityOn.Checked = FALSE
    SecurityOff.Checked = TRUE
End Sub

Sub SecurityOn_Click ()
    Print "WARNING: Security has been activated"
    SecurityOn.Checked = TRUE
    SecurityOff.Checked = FALSE
End Sub
```

## How It Works

The Declare and Const statements in the Declarations section give Visual Basic access to the various Windows API functions that we'll be using to manipulate the menu.

The Form_Load event subroutine does the work of placing the bitmaps from the hidden picture boxes into the menus. The Picture property of a picture box is what Windows is expecting as a handle to a bitmap.

Windows uses handles extensively. A Windows handle is just an integer that Windows uses to identify elements like menus and bitmaps. In the Form_Load event subroutine, a call to the GetMenu and GetSubMenu API functions gets the handles to the main menu and the Security menu.

The Windows API functions don't let you change the properties of a menu item without knowing its message ID (something that we Visual Basic programmers don't have to fuss with), so we call GetMenuItemID to get it and store it in a variable. Next, we give the handle back to Windows in the ModifyMenu call.

Notice the expression MF_BYCOMMAND Or MF_BITMAP Or MF_CHECKED. These are all constants (defined in the Declarations section) that tell Windows how to process the change in the menu. (The MF_ prefix stands for menu flags.) MF_BYCOMMAND tells Windows we want to identify the menu item with its message ID. MF_BITMAP says we're going to be providing a handle to a bitmap rather than the plain text that was there. MF_CHECKED tells Windows to place a check mark next to the bitmap to show that it's selected. We could have modified the Checked property as we do in the SecurityOn_Click and SecurityOff_Click event subroutines; either method works. Also notice how we use the Or operator with the menu flag expressions. Here, Or is a bitwise operator that combines the bits of all three constants, so Windows knows we want to combine them. In other words, the Or expression doesn't mean one MF_ constant or another, it means all three bits are used.

## Comments

Although in this How-To the bitmaps are preloaded into the form, we could also use the LoadPicture function to load any .BMP bitmap file, .ICO icon file, or .WMF metafile into the picture boxes. That way you could display any graphic you wanted to at run time.

## 4.6 How do I...

### Place font typefaces in a menu?

**Figure 4-6** Fonts in a menu

### Problem

Many users would like to see samples of the fonts before they select them from a menu. Is there any way that Visual Basic can place font typefaces in a menu?

### Technique

As shown in How-To 4.5 Draw a bitmapped picture in a menu, you can place simple icons into a menu. Using the same techniques, we can place graphical text in a menu.

### Steps

Open and run FONTSIN.MAK. After a short pause that occurs while Visual Basic creates the menu with all the fonts in your system, you'll be presented with a blank form. Click on the menu of fonts. Your screen should resemble the menu shown in Figure 4-6. You may select any font from the menu as you would normally expect, and a brief message will be printed in the font you selected.

1. Create a new project called FONTSIN.MAK. Create a new form with the objects and properties listed in Table 4-7, and save it as FONTSIN.FRM.

| Object | Property | Setting |
| --- | --- | --- |
| Form | FormName | MenuFontsForm |
| | Caption | Fonts in a menu |
| | FontBold | False |
| | FontSize | 12 |
| Picture box | AutoRedraw | True |
| | BackColor | &H80000004& |
| | Name | FontPicture |

*continued on next page*

*continued from previous page*

| Object | Property | Setting |
|--------|----------|---------|
| | FontBold | False |
| | FontSize | 9.75 |
| | ForeColor | &H80000008& |
| | Index | 0 |
| | Visible | False |

**Table 4-7** FontsIn project form's objects and properties

2. Using the Menu Design window, give the form a menu with the characteristics in Table 4-8.

| Caption | Name | Index |
|---------|------|-------|
| F&ont | FontMenu | |
| First font | FontMenuList | 0 |

**Table 4-8** FontsIn project form characteristics

3. Put the following code in the Declarations section to declare the required Windows API functions and the constants that those functions use.

```
DefInt A-Z

Declare Function GetMenu% Lib "User" (ByVal hWnd%)
Declare Function GetSubMenu% Lib "User" (ByVal hMenu%, ByVal nPos%)
Declare Function GetMenuItemID% Lib "User" (ByVal hMenu%, ByVal nPos%)
Declare Function ModifyMenu% Lib "User" (ByVal hMenu%, ByVal nPosition%, ⇐
ByVal wFlags%, ByVal wIDNewItem%, ByVal lpNewItem&)

Const MF_BYCOMMAND = 0
Const MF_BITMAP = 4
Const MF_CHECKED = 8
Const FALSE = 0, TRUE = Not FALSE
```

4. Place the following code in the FontMenuList_Click event subroutine to switch to the font you selected from the menu and print a brief message.

```
Sub FontMenuList_Click (Index As Integer)
   FontName = Screen.Fonts(Index)
   Print "You have selected " + FontName
End Sub
```

5. The Form_Load event subroutine does all the magic. First, it uses API functions to get menu handles, because those handles are required by the other API functions used to put the fonts in the menu. Second, the first

For…Next loop creates enough new elements in the menu and picture box control arrays to hold all the fonts in your system.

Then, the second For…Next loop goes through each font and prints the name of that font in the picture box, adjusting the width and height of the box to fit. Then, because the ModifyMenu API function needs to know the menu message ID, a call to the GetMenuItemID API function gets it. Finally, a call to ModifyMenu tells Windows to put the font bitmap from the picture box into the menu.

```
Sub Form_Load ()
    ' switch to hourglass cursor
    Screen.MousePointer = 11

    ' get the form's menu handle
    hMenu = GetMenu(hWnd)

    ' get the menu's Font (submenu 0) submenu handle
    hSubMenu = GetSubMenu(hMenu, 0)

    ' create new menu items and picture boxes
    For I = 1 To Screen.FontCount - 1
        Load FontMenuList(I)
        Load FontPicture(I)
    Next

    For I = 0 To Screen.FontCount - 1
        ' switch font
        FontPicture(I).FontName = Screen.Fonts(I)
        ' set width & height to match
        FontPicture(I).Width = FontPicture(I).TextWidth(Screen.Fonts(I))
        FontPicture(I).Height = FontPicture(I).TextHeight(Screen.Fonts(I))
        ' and print font name in picture box
        FontPicture(I).Print Screen.Fonts(I)
        ' make sure Picture gets the bitmap handle from Image property
        FontPicture(I).Picture = FontPicture(I).Image
        ' get the Windows menu message ID of current item
        menuId = GetMenuItemID(hSubMenu, I)
        ' put the font bitmap into the menu
        J = ModifyMenu(hMenu, menuId, MF_BYCOMMAND Or MF_BITMAP, menuId, ⇐
CLng(FontPicture(I).Picture))
    Next

    ' switch to normal cursor
    Screen.MousePointer = 0
End Sub
```

### How It Works

The Declare statements in the Declarations section of the form provide access to the Windows API functions. GetMenu is the API function that returns a handle to the menu. GetSubMenu gets a handle to an individual top-level menu (Fonts, in this example). GetMenuItemID gets the message ID that Windows uses for each menu item (something Visual Basic takes care of for us). ModifyMenu lets you change a menu item; the Form_Load event subroutine will use it to put the font bitmap in the menu.

Notice that we use the ByVal modifier for all the parameters, which instructs Visual Basic to simply pass the actual value of the parameter, rather than the address of a variable (the default). Note the declaration for ModifyMenu, which declares the last parameter ByVal lpNewItem$. When Visual Basic sees ByVal next to a string parameter, it passes (in C lingo) a long pointer to a null-terminated string, the type of string that Windows normally expects. Luckily, that's not something we have to worry about—Visual Basic takes care of it.

The Form_Load event subroutine does all the work of putting the fonts into the Font menu. It uses the GetMenu and GetSubMenu API functions to get the requisite menu handles.

You'll notice that both the picture box and font menu item are defined as elements in a control array, because their Index property is 0, instead of just being left blank. This was necessary because it's impossible to know at design time how many fonts are available on your users' machines. With font managers such as Adobe Type Manager (ATM), it's possible to have dozens of fonts. (Refer again to Figure 4-5.)

The first For…Next loop creates enough new elements in the control arrays to hold all the fonts in the user's system using Visual Basic's Load statement.

The second For…Next loop goes through each screen font, switches to the font, and prints the name of that font in the picture box that holds the fonts before they go in the menu. The loop's code then adjusts the width and height of the box to fit using the picture box's TextHeight and TextWidth properties. The TextHeight and TextWidth properties are very useful, because they let you adjust the width of the picture box before there's any text printed there. Windows automatically adjusts the width of the entire menu to fit the largest width of all the fonts in the menu, but it won't change the height of individual fonts in the menu.

The ModifyMenu API function expects a handle to a bitmapped image (an HBITMAP), which the picture box provides in its Image property.

Finally, because ModifyMenu needs to know the menu message ID, a call to the GetMenuItemID API function gets it. A call to ModifyMenu tells Windows to put the font bitmap from the picture box into the menu. Notice the two menu flag (MF_) constants, MF_BYCOMMAND and MF_BITMAP. They tell Windows that we're modifying the menu by its menu message ID with a bitmapped image.

### Comments

On a system that includes a large number of fonts, it can take a fair amount of time for the Form_Load event subroutine to go through all the fonts. It may take 25 seconds for 33 fonts. You might display a "please wait—fonts loading" message to assure your user that nothing is wrong. Notice the use of the hourglass cursor in the Form_Load() subroutine.

## 4.7  How do I...

## Display menu prompts?

### Problem

Many Windows programs use a status bar to display a short description of each menu as it is selected. Menu controls don't have an event that lets me know when a menu has been selected. What do I need to do to display menu prompts in a status bar?

### Technique

When Windows selects a menu, it sends a WM_MENUSELECT message to the menu owner's window. The wParam parameter that is sent with the WM_MENUSELECT message identifies the menu, or menu item, that is being selected. You can use the Waite Group's MsgHook control, a fully functional custom control included with the *Visual Basic How-To Second Edition,* to intercept the WM_MENUSELECT message. Then, using wParam to determine which menu has been selected, you can display a message in a status bar.

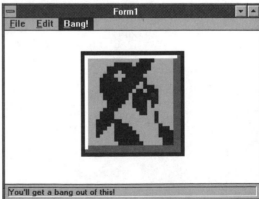

**Figure 4-7** MENUPRMT with the Bang! menu item selected

## Steps

Open and run MENUPRMT.MAK. After the program is running, press and release the (ALT) key. The File menu will now be selected and a prompt will be displayed in the status bar. You can use the arrow keys or the mouse to select various menu items. As each menu or menu item is selected, a different message is displayed in the status bar. Figure 4-7 shows MENUPRMT after (ALT) has been pressed and the (→) key used to select the Bang! menu item.

1. Create a new project named MENUPRMT.MAK. Add the objects and properties shown in Table 4-9 to Form1.

| Object | Property | Setting |
|---|---|---|
| Form | Caption | "Form1" |
| | Height | 4560 |
| | Left | 2310 |
| | Name | Form1 |
| | ScaleHeight | 3870 |
| | ScaleWidth | 5025 |
| | Top | 1140 |
| | Width | 5145 |
| MsgHook | Name | MsgHook1 |
| Line | BorderColor | &H00FFFFFF& |
| | Name | Line2 |
| | X1 | 3960 |
| | X2 | 3960 |
| | Y1 | 3600 |
| | Y2 | 3810 |
| Line | BorderColor | &H00FFFFFF& |
| | Name | Line1 |
| | X1 | 90 |
| | X2 | 3990 |
| | Y1 | 3810 |
| | Y2 | 3810 |
| Label | BackColor | &H00C0C0C0& |
| | BorderStyle | 1 'Fixed Single |
| | Caption | "" |
| | Height | 225 |
| | Left | 60 |

| Object | Name | Label1 |
| | **Property** | **Setting** |
| **Object** | | |
| | TabIndex | 0 |
| | Top | 3600 |
| | Width | 3915 |
| Shape | BackColor | &H00C0C0C0& |
| | BorderColor | &H00404040& |
| | FillColor | &H00C0C0C0& |
| | FillStyle | 0 'Solid |
| | Height | 375 |
| | Left | -30 |
| | Name | Shape1 |
| | Top | 3540 |
| | Width | 7425 |
| Image | Height | 2400 |
| | Name | Image1 |
| | Left | 1110 |
| | Picture | SPYGUY.BMP |
| | Stretch | -1 'True |
| | Top | 570 |
| | Width | 2400 |

**Table 4-9** Objects and properties for Form1

2. Use the Menu Window to create a menu for Form1 with settings shown in Table 4-10.

| **Menu Name** | **Caption** | **Shortcut Key** |
| --- | --- | --- |
| FileMenu | &File | |
| ---FileExit | E&xit | |
| EditMenu | &Edit | |
| ---EditCut | Cu&t | ^X |
| ---EditCopy | &Copy | ^C |
| ---EditPaste | &Paste | ^V |
| ---EditDelete | &Delete | (DEL) |
| BangMenu | &Bang! | |

**Table 4-10** Menu for Form1

3. Create a new module named MENUPRMT.BAS. Add the following

code to the General Declarations section of MENUPRMT.BAS.

```
'
' Message sent by windows when a menu is selected
'
Global Const WM_MENUSELECT = &H11F
'
' Windows API Functions
'
Declare Function GetMenu Lib "User" (ByVal hWnd As Integer) As Integer
Declare Function GetMenuItemID Lib "User" (ByVal hMenu As Integer, ⇐
ByVal nPos As Integer) As Integer
Declare Function GetSubMenu Lib "User" (ByVal hMenu As Integer, ByVal ⇐
nPos As Integer) As Integer
'
' Used to locate prompt string for a menu
'
Type MenuPromptMap
   menuId  As Integer
   prompt  As String
End Type
'
' Room for 100 menu prompts
'
Global menuPrompts(100) As MenuPromptMap
'
' Contains index of last menu prompt string added to array
'
Global iMenuPrompts     As Integer
```

4. Add the following code to the General Declarations section of Form1.

```
Option Explicit
```

5. Add the following code to the Load event subroutine of Form1. First, the Form_Load event subroutine initializes the MsgHook control. Next the menuPrompts array, declared in MENUPRMT.BAS, is initialized. Each menu and menu item has a unique identifier. The identifiers for each menu and menu item are stored in menuPrompts along with the string that is displayed when the menu or menu item is selected.

```
Sub Form_Load ()
   Dim hMenu       As Integer
   Dim hSubMenu    As Integer

   MsgHook1.HwndHook = Me.hWnd
   MsgHook1.Message(WM_MENUSELECT) = True
   hMenu = GetMenu(Me.hWnd)
   '
   ' Load File menu prompts
   '
   hSubMenu = GetSubMenu(hMenu, 0)
   AddPrompt hSubMenu, "File operations"
   AddPrompt GetMenuItemID(hSubMenu, 0), "Exit program"
```

```
'
' Load edit menu prompts
'
hSubMenu = GetSubMenu(hMenu, 1)
AddPrompt hSubMenu, "Edit operations"
AddPrompt GetMenuItemID(hSubMenu, 0), "Cut selection to clipboard"
AddPrompt GetMenuItemID(hSubMenu, 1), "Copy selection to clipboard"
AddPrompt GetMenuItemID(hSubMenu, 2), "Paste clipboard contents"
AddPrompt GetMenuItemID(hSubMenu, 3), "Delete selection"
'
' Load Bang! menu prompt
'
hSubMenu = GetMenuItemID(hMenu, 2)
AddPrompt hSubMenu, "You'll get a bang out of this!"
End Sub
```

6. Add the following subroutine to the General section of Form1. The AddPrompt subroutine is called by Form_Load to add a menu ID and prompt string to the global menuPrompts array.

```
Sub AddPrompt (menuID As Integer, prompt As String)
   menuPrompts(iMenuPrompts).menuID = menuID
   menuPrompts(iMenuPrompts).prompt = prompt
   iMenuPrompts = iMenuPrompts + 1
End Sub
```

7. Add the following code to the Message event subroutine of MsgHook1. The menuPrompts array is scanned for a menu ID matching the menu ID passed in wParam. If a match is found, the menus prompt string is displayed and the For...Next loop is exited. If there is no match, then the previous prompt string, if any, is cleared.

```
Sub MsgHook1_Message (msg As Integer, wParam As Integer, lParam As Long,⇐
   action As Integer, result As Long)
   Dim i     As Integer
   Dim found As Integer

   '
   ' Got a menu select message ... see if it's for one of our menus
   '
   For i = 0 To iMenuPrompts - 1
      If (menuPrompts(i).menuID = wParam) Then
         '
         ' One of our menus ... display prompt message
         '
         Label1.Caption = menuPrompts(i).prompt
         found = True
         Exit For
      End If
   Next
   '
   ' Blank prompt message when no menu selected
   '
   If (found <> True) Then
      Label1.Caption = ""
   End If
```

```
End Sub
```

8. Add the following code to FileExit's Click event procedure.

```
Sub FileExit_Click ()
    End
End Sub
```

9. Add the following code to the Resize event subroutine of Form1. This subroutine resizes and rearranges the visible controls on Form1 whenever the form's size changes.

```
Sub Form_Resize ()
    '
    ' Center Image control slightly above mid-line
    '
    Image1.Top = (Form1.ScaleHeight - Shape1.Height - Image1.Height) * ⇐
    .85 / 2
    Image1.Left = (Form1.ScaleWidth - Image1.Width) / 2
    '
    ' Move Shape control and resize
    '
    Shape1.Top = Form1.ScaleHeight - Shape1.Height
    Shape1.Left = -screen.TwipsPerPixelX
    Shape1.Width = Form1.ScaleWidth + (2 * screen.TwipsPerPixelX)
    '
    ' Move Label and resize
    '
    Label1.Top = Shape1.Top + ((Shape1.Height - Label1.Height) / 2)
    Label1.Left = Label1.Top - Shape1.Top
    Label1.Width = Form1.ScaleWidth - (Label1.Left * 2)
    '
    ' Move and resize 3D effect lines
    '
    Line1.Y1 = Label1.Top + Label1.Height - screen.TwipsPerPixelY
    Line1.Y2 = Line1.Y1
    Line1.X1 = Label1.Left
    Line1.X2 = Label1.Left + Label1.Width - screen.TwipsPerPixelX
    Line2.Y1 = Label1.Top
    Line2.Y2 = Label1.Top + Label1.Height
    Line2.X1 = Line1.X2
    Line2.X2 = Line1.X2
End Sub
```

### How It Works

This How-To uses the Windows API calls GetMenu, GetSubMenu, and GetMenuItemID to get Form1's menu handles and menu item IDs. The GetMenu API function takes a window handle as its argument and returns a handle to the Windows menu bar. Once GetMenu has been used to get

Form1's menu handle, the GetSubMenu API function can be used to get handles to the individual menus on the menu bar.

GetSubMenu takes a menu bar handle and an index as arguments and returns a handle to a menu. In this project, the File and Edit menus are submenus, the index argument ranges from 0 to 1 less than the number of menus. In this project the menus File and Edit have indexes 0 and 1.

Once we've gotten a menus handle, we use the GetMenuItemID API function to get the menu ID for each menu item on the menu. GetMenuItemID takes a menu handle and an index and returns the corresponding menu item ID.

You may have noticed that the Bang! menu item is not handled the same as the File and Edit menus. That is because Bang!, having no menu items, is a menu item not a submenu. The menu ID for Bang! is retrieved using the GetMenuItemID API function with Form1's menu handle and an index of 2, Bang!'s position on Form1's menu.

Form_Load retrieves the handle for each menu, and the menu IDs of its menu items using the API calls described above. As each menu and menu item ID is retrieved, it and a corresponding prompt string are placed in the menuPrompts array. Also during Form_Load, the MsgHook control is initialized so that it will fire its Message event whenever a WM_MENUSELECT message is sent to Form1.

When the MsgHook_Message event is fired, the event subroutine scans the menuPrompts array to find a menu ID corresponding to the subroutine's wParam. If a match is found, the menu's prompt message is displayed in Label1. If there is no menu item that matches wParam, then Label1 is cleared. This will happen when selection is passing from one of Form1's menus to either the system menu or some other control on Form1.

## Comments

Visual Basic ignores a number of Windows messages, such as WM_MENUSELECT, that are essential for creating a polished Windows application. The MsgHook control can be used to intercept these messages, allowing you to add functionality that simply isn't available using Visual Basic alone.

CHAPTER **5**

GRAPHICS

# How do I...

If you really want your applications to make a lasting impression, turn your attention to graphics. This chapter provides a collection of projects that show how easy it is for Visual Basic to imitate any "look" you wish—from a modern brushed aluminum NeXT-like interface to a Macintosh-style trash can. You'll see how to fill complex polygon shapes with patterns and colors, how to draw pictures inside your iconized application, and how to build line, bar, and pie charts that work just like the charts in Excel. There is even a powerful slide show that does dissolves and other special effects for presentations. Throughout the chapter powerful APIs are used and carefully explained.

## Windows APIs Covered

| | | |
|---|---|---|
| ArrangeIcons | EmptyClipBoard | Polygon |
| BitBlt | FastWindowFrame | PtInRect |
| ClientToScreen | GetBitmapBits | ReleaseDC |
| CloseClipBoard | GetCurrentTask | ReleaseCapture |
| CreateBitmap | GetCursor | SelectObject |
| CreateCompatibleBitmap | GetDC | SendMessage |
| CreateCompatibleDC | GetDesktopWindow | SetBKColor |
| CreateCursor | GetFocus | SetCapture |
| CreateDC | GetObject | SetClipBoardData |
| DeleteDC | GetParent | SetPolyFillMode |
| DeleteObject | GetWindowTask | StretchBit |
| | OpenClipBoard | TaskFindHandle |

### 5.1 Make a brushed aluminum NeXT™ interface
### 5.2 Give my application a three-dimensional look

One of the first things you'll want to do with Visual Basic is create an interface. If you wish that interface to be modern and "sexy," then you should examine these two How-Tos. The first shows how simple it is to make a interface that mimics the look of the NeXT computer by simply passing a control to a subroutine that draws a line around it. The second How-To takes that idea further and creates a more general application that lets you control more details of the 3D look, including such things as the width of the bezel around each control and whether the frame is recessed or raised.

### 5.3 Draw pictures into an iconized running application

This How-To reveals how easy it is to change the default icon that Visual Basic gives your application while the program is running. This can be used to notify your user that some process has completed even though the application is minimized.

**5.4**    **Draw a transparent picture or icon on a form**

One of the first things you might discover about Visual Basic is that when you put a picture box on a form, any graphics or text underneath it are covered and won't show through. Unfortunately picture boxes in Visual Basic are opaque and there is no property for making them transparent…unless you know how to use the BitBlt API. This How-To shows you a simple way to make pictures and icons that are transparent, so you can write games, for instance, that let the background show through. It teaches you the concept of how the pixels in your image can be combined in many different ways with the pixels in the background.

**5.5**    **Preview the DrawMode settings**

There are 16 different ways that you can draw graphics on a form or picture box. Trying to visualize the effects of all these modes is not easy. This How-To lets you experiment with the different modes and see how they affect your bitmaps.

**5.6**    **Separate the red, green, and blue components of a color**

When programming color into your applications you'll frequently run across a long integer value that represents a color. This How-To presents a project that lets you enter the long integer and see immediately what red, blue, and green components of the color are. You'll also learn about hexadecimal math in this How-To.

**5.7**    **Make a screen capture from my running program**

While it is easy to capture screens to the clipboard in Windows using (ALT)-(PRT SCREEN) there is no way to capture a section of your running Visual Basic application. This How-To shows how to capture a screen while your program is running. This could be useful if there are graphics that you want your user to save for manipulating in a Paint program or if you wish to make your own Visual Basic screen capture program. This How-To uses a variety of APIs, such as OpenClipBoard and SelectObject, and also gets you familiar with the concept of Windows' Device Contexts.

**5.8**    **Arrange the icons on the Windows desktop**

Normally you can use the Task Manager to arrange the icons on a cluttered desktop and you could devise a way to use SendKeys so that your Visual Basic application could handle this for you. However the Task Manager is slow and when it suddenly pops up it might confuse users of your program. This project shows how to use the ArrangeIconicWindows API.

**5.9**     **Make a Macintosh-style trash can**

You've heard that Windows is close to the Macintosh interface; here is a project that puts a Macintosh trash can on the desktop. Using pure Visual Basic this How-To lets you drag files to the trash can and delete them from a menu. This How-To will teach you a lot about dragging icons and DragDrop events.

**5.10**     **Display the progress of an operation**

Do you wish you could have a progress bar appear on your form while an operation is busy; one that lets the user know the percentage of the operation that has completed? Here is a How-To project that does just that. Again using the Windows BitBlt API, this project presents a colored bar that grows as the operation is progressing. The center of the bar displays the percentage of the operation that has been completed while the bar grows.

**5.11**     **Fill complex objects**

Visual Basic has powerful graphics functions that let you fill a circle or a rectangle, but there is no built-in function for filling a complex object like a polygon. This How-To uses the Polygon and SetPolyFillMode APIs to let you fill any object with any color. This same routine is used in the pie and bar chart How-Tos that follow.

**5.12**     **Build a line chart**

**5.13**     **Build a bar chart**

**5.14**     **Build a pie chart**

Did you know Visual Basic can create charts just like Excel? This trio of How-Tos reveals all you need to build line, bar, and pie charts into your projects. They feature automatic scaling, text labels, centered legends, custom patterns, colors, and line markers. Multiple series are allowed in the line and bar charts so you can compare sets of data. The polygon and Set-PolyFillMode APIs are utilized to do the drawing and filling of patterns in these charts. Values to be plotted are passed in arrays so communication from your application is very simple.

**5.15**     **Build a video-based slide show**

Here is the ultimate Visual Basic weekend project: a slide show that lets you make a custom video presentation with custom transition effects between screens, and variable delays between each slide. The program can present Microsoft .BMP or .WMF files. There is an editor for arranging and previewing the sequence and a display module that shows the actual simulated slides. A File Open dialog box from the How-To "Build an editor that searches for text" is also used to make locating files a breeze. The BitBlt and SendMessage APIs are used in this How-To.

**5.16     Easily draw shapes on a form**
The Shape control can be used to draw shapes and lines on a form. The Shape control is useful because, unlike the Line and Circle methods, you can position and size shapes on your forms at design time. The Shape control also makes it easy to manipulate shapes at run time. This How-To creates a simple "object-oriented" drawing program using the Shape control.

**5.17     Create a "magnifying glass" for bitmaps**
Getting Windows programs to look right often depends on the correct placement of a few pixels. On today's high-resolution monitors, it can be difficult to distinguish individual pixels without a magnifying glass. This How-To shows how to create a magnifying glass with Visual Basic. The finished program can magnify any area of the screen.

**5.18     Add "hot-spots" to pictures**
Programs sometimes use hyper-text and graphics links to allow the user to navigate through information, or retrieve extra information associated with some visual element on the screen. This How-To demonstrates the basic techniques needed to add this kind of capability to your programs.

**5.19     Play back an animation**
The popularity of Autodesk's Animator programs has resulted in the production of lots of FLI (low-resolution) and FLC (high-resolution) animations. This project shows you how to use Autodesk's AAPLAY.DLL to play FLI and FLC animations on your forms. The AAPLAY is included free with the samples diskette, along with complete documentation of the functions it makes available.

# 5.1  How do I...

**Complexity: Easy**

# Make a brushed aluminum NeXT™ interface?

### Problem
I want to create a Visual Basic application with a modern NeXT-like computer interface. But Visual Basic offers only the old-fashioned (Windows 3) kind of buttons. I want the slick, metal-on-metal look, where the light seems to fall on one side and the buttons seem to be raised off a steel or gunmetal gray panel. (Even Microsoft has adopted the NeXT interface look; compare

Word for Windows 2.0 to 1.0.) I also want to have important text on my screen appear like cool blue light is being emitted, similar to a glowing LED. Is there a simple way to do this?

### Technique

It is actually very easy to create a NeXT-like interface in Visual Basic as the simple example shows in Figure 5-1. For those who are not familar with the NeXT computer, it was created by Steve Jobs, founder of Apple computer, as the "next-step" after the Macintosh. Whether that event ever comes to pass, no one knows, but one thing Jobs did do is alter forever how a computer screen looks. Buttons, text input boxes, labels, and the like resemble a gray slick, brushed-metal look. The NeXT computer has raised and recessed panels, soft blue text, red text for warning, yellow for caution, and cleverly uses subtle shades of gray to achieve its stunning effect.

There are a few secrets to achieving this effect using Visual Basic. One of the main tricks is to use a 50 percent gray background. With such a gray background and a white line to draw the left and top border of a box as well as a black line to draw the right and bottom of a box, the box will appear to sit above the background, with light brightening up the left and top sides, and the right and bottom sides in shadow. It will seem that there is light shining on your screen at a 45-degree angle from the button's corner.

To reverse the effect and make the box look like it is below the surface of the background (recessed), simply reverse the algorithm: Create the black line on the left and top, and the white line on the right and bottom. The blue light-emitting-diode look can be achieved by using cyan for the forecolor of your text, and a dark gray for the backcolor.

The trick to this is to recognize that we can turn off the borders of various objects such as text boxes, pictures, and labels. Then we can draw our own borders. We use Visual Basic's Line method (which is just like QuickBasic 4.5's Line statement) to draw four lines around the perimeter of a rectangular object, such as a picture box, using the right colors (black or white).

To NeXTize an object, you need to be able to turn off all its borders and set its background color carefully. In some cases, such as a label, the background color will be the same as the form or picture it is on, and with no border it is hard to see when you want to select it. See Figure 5-2. Clicking on the object and adjusting its position might not always prove worthy of a NeXT approach. You'll have to be the judge of that.

Another important point about setting up examples with controls is the use of picture controls for frames. Microsoft provided the frame object as a way to create a collection of controls so you can move them around as a group. Unfortunately, the frame does not work as advertised and has coloring and positioning limitations. Instead you can use a picture control, which is not only well behaved but also allows you to insert bitmaps, something a frame can't do.

### Steps

Open and run NEXT.MAK and examine its code. If you run the project (press (F5)), you will get the interface shown in Figure 5-1. To build the form from scratch, do the following, using Figure 5-2 as your guide.

1. Create a new project called NEXT.MAK. Create a new form, give it dimensions of about 2 inches wide and 3 inches tall as shown in Figure 5-2. Save it as NEXT.FRM.

2. Add the objects and properties shown in Table 5-1 to this form. If a property is not listed, its effect is not important and the default is assumed.

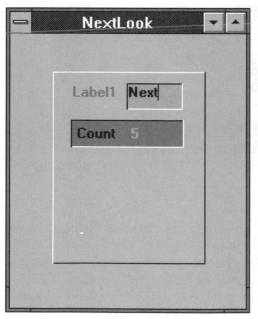

**Figure 5-1** A NeXTized interface in VB

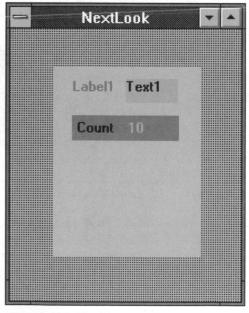

**Figure 5-2** The NextLook Form and Controls at design time

| Object | Property | Setting | |
|--------|----------|---------|---|
| Form | FormName | Form_Next_Look | *Root Control Frame (RCF)* |
| | Caption | NextLook | |
| | BackColor | &H00C0C0C0& (50% gray) | |
| Picture box | Name | Picture1 | |
| | BackColor | &H00C0C0C0& | |
| | BorderStyle | 0 = None | |
| Label | Name | Label1 | *RCF Left Top Control* |
| | Caption | Label1 | |
| | BackColor | &H00C0C0C0& | |
| | ForeColor | &H00808080& (dark gray) | |
| | BorderStyle | 0 = None | |
| Text box | Name | Text1 | *RCF Right Top Control* |
| | Text | Text1 | |
| | BackColor | &H00FFFF00& (cyan) | |
| | ForeColor | &H000000000& (black) | |
| | BorderStyle | 0 = None | |
| Picture box | Name | Picture2 | *Bottom Control Frame (BCF)* |
| | Caption | Label1 | |
| | BackColor | &H00808080& (dark gray) | |
| | BorderStyle | 0 = None | |
| Label | Name | Label2 | *BCF Left* |
| | Caption | Count | |
| | ForeColor | &H00000000& (black) | |
| | BackColor | &H00808080& (dark gray) | |
| | BorderStyle | 0 = None | |
| Text box | Name | Text2 | *BCF Right* |
| | Text | 10 | |
| | ForeColor | &H00FFFF00& (cyan) | |
| | BackColor | &H00808080& (dark gray) | |
| | BorderStyle | 0 = None | |

**Table 5-1**  NEXT project form's objects and properties

3. Add a new module called NEXT.BAS. We will put the two routines BorderBox and BorderBoxRaised in it. By placing this code in a .BAS file, you can easily move it to other projects and it is accessible to all forms in the project. Open the NEXT.BAS form for editing and type the following code in it. You should end up with two individual functions.

```
Sub BorderBox (source1 As Control, source2 As Control)
    'note we can't draw inside a text box so these controls
    'must get their outline drawn on the from or picture
    'box they are inside
    BLeft% = source1.Left - 20  'Get coordinates
```

```
    BTop% = source1.Top - 20
    BWide% = source1.Width + 15
    BHigh% = source1.Height + 15

    ' Draw a recessed border around Source1 control
    source2.Line (BLeft%, BTop%)-Step(BWide%, 0), 0
    source2.Line -Step(0, BHigh%), &HFFFFFF
    source2.Line -Step(-BWide%, 0), &HFFFFFF
    source2.Line -Step(0, -BHigh%), 0
End Sub

Sub BorderBoxRaised (source1 As Control, source2 As Form)
    BLeft% = source1.Left - 20  'Get coordinates and shrink them
                            'to make up for the border
    BTop% = source1.Top - 20
    BWide% = source1.Width + 15 'Make up for existing border on
      BHigh% = source1.Height + 15

    ' Draw a recessed border around Source control.
    source2.Line (BLeft%, BTop%)-Step(BWide%, 0), &HFFFFFF
    source2.Line -Step(0, BHigh%), 0
    source2.Line -Step(-BWide%, 0), 0
    source2.Line -Step(0, -BHigh%), &HFFFFFF
End Sub
```

4. Put this code in the Form_Load procedure of the form.

```
Sub Form_Load ()
    BorderBoxRaised Picture1, Form_Next_Look
    BorderBox Text1, Picture1
    BorderBox Picture2, Picture1
End Sub
```

### How It Works

Examine the first routine called BorderBox. The routine is passed two controls, Source1 and Source2. Thus, we would call the routine with

```
BorderBox Text1, Picture1
```

or

```
BorderBox Picture2, Picture1
```

The first statement passes a text control that is sitting inside a picture control while the second statement passes a picture control that is sitting inside another picture control.

The next four lines set up four variables (BLeft% to BHigh%) for drawing a rectangle around the first control, using the second control as the drawing surface. The drawing is done a few pixels outside the inner control, because you can't draw on a text control with the Line statement (which may be the first control passed to the procedure). So source1.Left% - 20 puts the line to the left of the first control, and so on. The next four lines actually draw the Next rectangle. Refer to *The Waite Group's Visual Basic SuperBible,* Taylor Maxwell and Bryon Scott, Waite Group Press, 1992, for details on how the Line statement works. The first statement draws a line on the control source2 (source2.Line) using the parameters derived from the four variables, BLeft% to BHigh%. The Step option of Line is used to control the width of the box. At the end of each Line statement a value that follows the comma is the color for the line. Here we use 0 for black and &HFFFFFF for white. Thus, we draw a black line on top, a white line on the right side, a white line on the bottom, and a black line on the left side. This makes our box appear to be recessed in the panel.

The next procedure is called BorderBoxRaised. This works like the previous routine except it changes the order of the colors drawn so that the box appears to be white on the left and black on the right. Thus, the box appears to be raised, rather than recessed.

The Form_Load produced simply calls the routines when the program is started and passes the correct names of the parts to the procedures.

### Comments

You don't have to worry about redrawing the form if it is covered with another form or window. Windows remembers the way the screen looks and will repaint things just right.

## 5.2  How do I...

## Give my application a three-dimensional look?

### Problem

In How-To 5.1 Make a brushed aluminum NeXT™ interface, you show a simple technique for making 3-D buttons and controls. Is there a more powerful and more general way to do this, one that gives me better control over the details like the thickness of frames?

### Technique

Adding depth to controls is done using simple optical effects. Light edges on the top and left of an object with corresponding darker colored edges on the bottom and right gives the control a raised appearance, like those in Figure

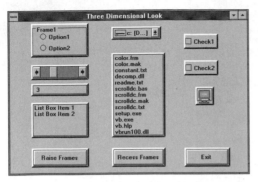

**Figure 5-3** 3D project with raised controls

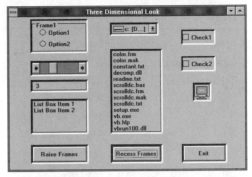

**Figure 5-4** 3D project with recessed controls

5-3. Reversing the light and dark edges causes an object to appear recessed into the form, like those in Figure 5-4. To enhance the effect, coloring the form and object with the same background color gives the edges higher contrast.

### Steps

Open and run 3D.MAK. Click on the Raise Frame button to give all the objects on the form a raised look. Click on the Recess Frame button to have the objects appear recessed. The width of the sculpted frame may be changed by clicking on the horizontal scroll bar arrows. The text box indicates the width, in pixels, of the frames. The three-dimensional project can be created by entering objects and code as detailed in the following steps.

1. Create a new project called 3D.MAK. Create a new form with the objects and properties shown in Table 5-2, and save it as 3D.FRM. Note that one each of the standard Visual Basic objects has been included in this form to demonstrate how it looks in a sculpted frame.

| Object | Property | Setting |
| --- | --- | --- |
| Form | FormName | Form3D |
| | Caption | Three Dimensional Look |
| Command button | Name | Command1 |
| | Caption | Raise Frame |
| Command button | Name | Command2 |
| | Caption | Recess Frame |
| Command button | Name | Command3 |
| | Caption | Exit |
| List box | Name | List1 |

*continued on next page*

*continued from previous page*

| Object | Property | Setting |
|--------|----------|---------|
| Frame | Name | Frame1 |
| Option button | Name | Option1 |
| Option button | Name | Option2 |
| HScrollBar | Name | HScroll1 |
| | Min | 0 |
| | Max | 10 |
| Text box | Name | Text1 |
| Drive list box | Name | Drive1 |
| File list box | Name | File1 |
| Check box | Name | Check1 |
| Check box | Name | Check2 |
| Picture box | Name | Picture1 |
| | AutoRedraw | True |
| | AutoSize | True |
| | Picture | \VB\ICONS\COMPUTER\MONITOR01.ICO |

**Table 5-2** 3D project form's objects and properties

2. Select the Global module, enter the following code and save it as 3D.BAS.

```
Global Const CTLRECESSED = 0      ' Frame is recessed.
Global Const CTLRAISED = -1       ' Frame is raised.
Global Const BKGNDGRAY = 192      ' Background Gray.
Global Const DARKGRAY = 64        ' Dark Gray
Global Const LIGHTGRAY = 255      ' Light Gray (white).
Global Const DEFAULTWIDTH = 3     ' Default Frame Width
Global FrameWidth As Integer      ' Width of 3d frame (in pixels).
```

3. Put the following code in the Form_Load event subroutine. This code sets the form's background color, puts sample data into the text box control, and initializes the default FrameWidth.

```
Sub Form_Load ()
    BackColor = RGB(BKGNDGRAY, BKGNDGRAY, BKGNDGRAY)
    FrameWidth = DEFAULTWIDTH
    HScroll1.Value = FrameWidth
    List1.AddItem "List Box Item 1"
    List1.AddItem "List Box Item 2"
End Sub
```

4. Put the following code in the PaintFrames subroutine in the General section of the form. This subroutine is used to specify which controls have frames around them.

```
Sub PaintFrames (InOut As Integer)

' Convert All forms to Single View.
    Cls  ' Remove Old Frames
    InitCtl Frame1, InOut
    InitCtl HScroll1, InOut
    InitCtl Text1, InOut
    InitCtl List1, InOut
    InitCtl Command1, InOut
    InitCtl Command2, InOut
    InitCtl Command3, InOut
    InitCtl Drive1, InOut
    InitCtl File1, InOut
    InitCtl Check1, InOut
    InitCtl Check2, InOut
    InitCtl Picture1, InOut

' Other elements that need initialization.
    Option1(0).BackColor = BackColor
    Option1(1).BackColor = BackColor
    Picture1.Refresh                ' Repaint Picture Box
End Sub
```

5 Put the following code into the InitCtl subroutine in the (General) section of the form. InitCtl eliminates run-time errors in setting the background color of a scroll bar.

```
Sub InitCtl (C As Control, InOut As Integer)
    If TypeOf C Is HScrollBar Then      ' No BackColor for Scroll bars
    Else
        C.BackColor = C.Parent.BackColor ' Set to Form's Backcolor
    End If
    HighLight C, InOut
End Sub
```

6. Enter the following code into the Form_Paint event subroutine. This subroutine is called automatically at application startup or whenever the system needs to repaint the contents of the form.

```
Sub Form_Paint ()
    PaintFrames CTLRAISED
End Sub
```

7. Place the following code in the Command1_Click event subroutine.

```
Sub Command1_Click ()
    PaintFrames CTLRAISED
End Sub
```

8. Place the following code in the Command2_Click event subroutine.

```
Sub Command2_Click ()
   PaintFrames CTLRECESSED
End Sub
```

9. Place the following code in the HScroll1_Click event subroutine. Clicking the scroll bar arrows will change the width of the sculpted frames from 0 to 10 pixels.

```
Sub HScroll1_Change ()
   FrameWidth = HScroll1.Value
   Text1.Text = Str$(FrameWidth)
End Sub
```

10. Place the following code in the Command3_Click event subroutine. This button allows the users a graceful way to exit the application.

```
Sub Command3_Click ()
   End
End Sub
```

11. Create an additional module for this project by selecting New Module from the File menu. Put the following subroutine in the General section of the module and save the module as 3D_DRAW.BAS. This subroutine draws the sculpted frame around the control passed as the first parameter. The InOut parameter indicates whether the frame is to be raised or recessed.

```
Sub HighLight (C As Control, InOut As Integer)

' Convert ScaleMode of form to pixels.
' Set up colors for borders on InOut. For recessed control:
'     top & left = dark, bottom & right = left
'     opposite for raised controls.
   C.Parent.scalemode = 3
   If InOut = CTLRAISED Then
      TLShade& = RGB(LIGHTGRAY, LIGHTGRAY, LIGHTGRAY)
      BRShade& = RGB(DARKGRAY, DARKGRAY, DARKGRAY)
   Else
      TLShade& = RGB(DARKGRAY, DARKGRAY, DARKGRAY)
      BRShade& = RGB(LIGHTGRAY, LIGHTGRAY, LIGHTGRAY)
   End If

' Now draw the Frame Around the Control, on the Parent Form.
   For I% = 1 To FrameWidth
      T% = C.Top - I%
      L% = C.Left - I%
      H% = C.Height + 2 * I%
      W% = C.Width + 2 * I%
      C.Parent.Line (L%, T%)-Step(0, H%), TLShade&     ' Left side
      C.Parent.Line (L%, T%)-Step(W%, 0), TLShade&     ' Top
```

```
        C.Parent.Line (L% + W%, T%)-Step(0, H%), BRShade& ' Right side
        C.Parent.Line (L%, T% + H%)-Step(W%, 0), BRShade& ' Bottom
    Next I%
End Sub
```

### How It Works

Sculpted frames are easy to draw once you understand how they are formed. The HighLight subroutine does the work of drawing a sculpted frame around any control. Its first parameter is the name of the control to frame; the second parameter is a constant that determines whether the frame is raised or recessed.

HighLight's first task is to set the ScaleMode of the control's parent, or Form, to 3 - pixel mode. Using the parent property enables the HighLight subroutine to work in multiform projects. ScaleMode "3" is used, because a screen pixel is the smallest visible unit of measure. This ensures that each frame line will be drawn directly adjacent to the previous one. The TLShade& (Top-Left Shading) and BRShade& (Bottom-Right shading) variables are set to the appropriate gray colors. Note that equal levels of red, green, and blue for the RGB function will always produce a gray shade. Higher values for each color result in lighter shades.

The global variable FrameWidth specifies the number of lines in each frame. Starting at the existing object border, a successive series of frame lines is drawn on each of the object's four edges. Each frame line is two pixels longer then the previous one giving the frame a beveled look.

The PaintFrames subroutine initiates the drawing for each of the controls on the form. If you add or remove a control from the form, the PaintFrames code will need to be updated.

### Comments

You can change the size of the frame by clicking on the horizontal scroll bar. If you pick an extremely wide frame, greater than six or seven pixels, the frame effect will be exaggerated, creating less visual appeal. When you lay out a form with sculpted frames, be sure to leave enough blank space around each control to draw the frame.

## 5.3 ⬤ How do I...

# Draw pictures into an iconized running application?

### Problem

If a user minimizes my application's form, how can I change the icon that appears at the bottom of the screen from the default "form with shadow" icon that Visual Basic puts there for me?

### Technique

There are several ways to change a form's icon. The first is to specify an .ICO icon file for the Icon property when you design your form. Then, when you make an .EXE executable file using the Visual Basic File menu's Make EXE File option, you can pick an icon for the entire application.

The second is to use the LoadPicture function. You can assign the return value of the LoadPicture function to a form's Icon property, like this:

```
Icon = LoadPicture(NET11.ICO)
```

There is another option, related to the second. Let's say a form was processing some lengthy job and didn't need any user input (for example, an accounting application has to post numerous general ledger entries to a chart of accounts). You would probably want to perform such a job in the background so the user could continue doing other work. It would make sense to minimize the form that is doing the work and place it out of the way when the user switches to other forms or applications. But you'd want to notify the user how the job is progressing and when it is complete. How can you do that when the form is minimized (iconized) at the bottom of the screen?

Visual Basic, of course, provides the option of drawing on the surface of the icon, regardless of its size (icons for a standard VGA screen are 32 by 32 pixels). Assigning the return value of the LoadPicture function with no arguments to a form's Icon property will clear out the form's icon and let you draw on it as if it were a normally sized form.

### Steps

Open and run DRAWICON.MAK. This is a simple example of some graphical output tied to a timer control. Note that the graphics continue to be drawn, even if you click the icon and bring up its System menu.

1. Create a new project called DRAWICON.MAK. Create a new form with the controls and properties shown in Table 5-3, and save it as DRAWICON.FRM.

| Control | Property | Setting |
|---------|----------|---------|
| Timer | Name | Timer1 |
|  | Interval | 50 |

**Table 5-3**   DrawIcon form's controls and properties

2. Put the following code in the Declarations section of the form. The DefInt statement ensures all variables will be integers and the Dim statement defines some variables that will be shared with subroutines in that form.

```
DefInt A-Z

Dim X, Y, Z, Clr
```

3. Put the following code in the Form_Load event subroutine. This code prepares the form's icon to be drawn on, minimizes the window, then finally sets two of the form variables declared in the Declarations section.

```
Sub Form_Load ()
   Icon = LoadPicture()      ' clear out icon
   WindowState = 1           ' iconize window
   Show                      ' show the form so we can
   X = ScaleWidth            ' get the width of the icon
   Clr = 1                   ' start with blue
End Sub
```

4. Put the following code in the Timer1_Timer event subroutine. This code simply draws lines that approach each other from opposite corners of the icon. Once the lines meet, the color used to draw the lines is changed.

```
Sub Timer1_Timer ()
   Line (Z, 0)-(0, Z), QBColor(Clr)
   Line (X - Z, X)-(X, X - Z), QBColor(Clr)

   Z = (Z + 2) Mod X
   If Z = 0 Then Clr = (Clr + 1) Mod 16
End Sub
```

### How It Works

Normally, Visual Basic provides an icon for every form. This icon is unaffected by Cls; it's always in the background. A special feature of the LoadPicture function lets you blank out a form's icon. If you put

```
Icon = LoadPicture()
```

somewhere in your application, that form's icon will be blank. Then you can use normal graphics statements to draw small graphics on the icon.

The WindowState property controls whether a form is normal size (the size that you gave it when you designed the form), maximized (full-screen), or minimized (to an icon).

The statement

```
WindowState = 1
```

is the same as clicking on the down-arrow minimize button in the upper right corner.

Although most icons are 32 by 32 pixels (the standard icon size for VGA monitors), icons for different monitors (like CGA, EGA, or 8514/a monitors) are different sizes. It's important, therefore, to adapt your program to whatever the current icon size is. The Show method in Form_Load displays the icon on the screen, which is necessary before your application tries to get its width with the ScaleWidth property.

The Clr variable keeps track of the color used to draw the current line. In the Timer1_Timer event subroutine, the QBColor function converts the Clr variable to the RGB color that Visual Basic is expecting. The first Line method draws a line in the upper left corner and the second Line method draws a line in the lower right corner. These lines approach and meet each other in the center of the icon.

The first Mod operator is used to prevent Y from overflowing the X width of the icon.

The second Mod operator prevents Clr from going beyond 15, which is the highest value that the QBColor function expects.

The Timer Interval property is set to 50, which causes the lines to be drawn very quickly. You can set the Interval property to whatever value you'd like.

### Comments

You can also use Print methods to print text on the icon; just be sure to set the CurrentX and CurrentY properties to values that are within the width and height of the icon. (CurrentX=0 and CurrentY=0 indicate the upper left corner of the icon.)

## 5.4 ⬤ How do I...

# Draw a transparent picture or icon on a form?

### Problem

I want to draw an icon or picture on the screen, but when I do, the picture always appears as an opaque rectangle covering everything under it. Is there any way around this?

### Technique

The normal way of displaying icons won't work if what you want is transparency. Figure 5-5 shows several pencil icons drawn on a complex bit map. The rectangular 32 by 32 area that surrounds all icons would normally be erased if we used Visual Basic's built-in commands to draw an icon. Instead, these were drawn with Windows BitBlt API function, which is faster and more powerful than any of the graphics keywords built into Visual Basic.

BitBlt lets us blast color bitmaps from one location to any other location on any picture or form. BitBlt needs the size and name of its destination, and other details, but it essentially draws images. BitBlt comes with a large number of possible options that control how it copies the bits when there are existing bits in a background. The secret of drawing without erasing the background is to use the exclusive OR (XOR) mode for the copying.

When using XOR with BitBlt, you must first create a mask of the icon. There will be two icons for each image: the full color image and the mask of the image. All pixels in the original image that are to be reproduced like the original are set to black in the mask. All pixels in the original image that are to be transparent are set to white in the mask. All the pixels in the original that are to be transparent should be made black. So, the original white area around the pencil is changed to black.

Once you have the mask, you are ready to draw your image. You first draw the mask using SCRAND logic. Next you draw the original image using SCRINVERT logic. Using AND for a black (0) pixel in the mask image with any pixel in the background turns that pixel to black. Using AND for any white pixel in the mask does not affect the pixel in the background. So after we draw the mask, the area around the pencil will be unaffected, while the area defined by the pencil will be black.

Next when we OR the original image with the changed background, any pixels that are black in the image will allow the pixels in the background to show through. Thus, the entire area around the pencil will show. Any col-

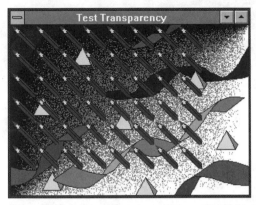

**Figure 5-5** The pencil icon drawn with BitBlt

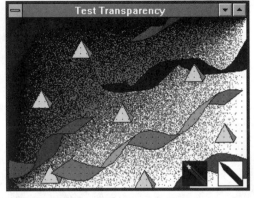

**Figure 5-6** The form for the BitBit project

ored pixels in the original image that are ORed will appear on the background. In this case, the pencil area is all black, so the pixels become those of the original image. It actually sounds more complicated than it really is.

### Steps

Open and run MASK.MAK. When you click on the form 48 little red pencil icons will be drawn on top of the background as shown in Figure 5-5.

1. Create a new project called MASK.MAK and a new form as shown in Figure 5-6. Save the form as MASK1.FRM. There are two icons to be placed on the form and a background bitmap that is supplied with Windows called PARTY.BMP. This can be any bitmap you want, including any of the wallpaper bitmaps supplied with Windows.

Set the properties and objects on it as shown in Table 5-4.

| Object | Property | Setting |
| --- | --- | --- |
| Form | FormName | MaskForm1 |
| | Caption | Test Transparency |
| | Picture | PARTY.BMP |
| | Scalemode | 3 - Pixel |
| Picture box | Name | Pencil_Image |
| | Visibility | False |
| | autoSize | True |
| | autoRedraw | True |
| Picture box | Name | Pencil_Image_Mask |
| | Visibility | False |

| Object | Property | Setting |
|---|---|---|
| | autoSize | True |
| | autoRedraw | True |

**Table 5-4** BitBlt project form's objects and properties

Select an icon to use for the test. It should be one with a lot of uncluttered background so that we can see behind it and so it's easy to modify and make a mask for. We chose one of the pencil icons that is stored in the Visual Basic WRITING subdirectory (PENCIL9.ICO). We renamed it as PENCILA.ICO and then moved it to the same directory as this How-To.

2. Open this icon into an icon editor program, like ICONWRKS that comes with Visual Basic, or into a paint program like PBRUSH.EXE that is supplied with Windows. Duplicate the pencil icon in a new file and store it as PENCILB.ICO. This will be our mask icon. You can do this from DOS using the COPY command or you can do it by saving under a new name in ICONWRKS.

3. Now fill in all the white areas around PENCILA.ICO with black. Make all the colored areas of PENCILB.ICO black; leave the white areas white. According to the technique we'll use, anything that is black in the image and white in the mask will allow the background to show through. Figure 5-7 shows the pencil image after its outer areas have been painted black, and Figure 5-8 shows how the mask for the pencil icon should look.

4. Now you will add the necessary code. The main code will go in the Form_Click procedure of the form.

**Figure 5-7** The PENCILA.ICO icon

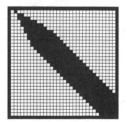

**Figure 5-8** The PENCILA.ICO mask icon

```
Sub Form_Click ()
    'Draw the Image With XOR.
    Cls
    For Y = 1 To Height \ 20 Step 32
    For X = 1 To Width \ 20 Step 32
    R = BitBlt(MaskForm1.hdc, X, Y, 32, 32, Pencil_Mask.hdc, 0, 0, SRCAND)
    R = BitBlt(MaskForm1.hdc, X, Y, 32, 32, Pencil_Image_Mask.hdc, 0, 0, ⇐
        SRCINVERT)
    Next X, Y
End Sub
```

5. Put the following code in the General procedure of the form object.

```
DefInt A-Z
Declare Function BitBlt Lib "Gdi" (ByVal destHdc, ByVal X, ByVal Y, ByVal ⇐
w, ByVal h, ByVal srcHdc, ByVal srcX, ByVal srcY, ByVal rop As Long)
Const SRCCOPY = &HCC0020
Const SRCAND = &H8800C6
Const SRCINVERT = &H660046
```

6. Put the following code in the Load procedure of the form object.

```
Sub Form_Load ()
    'Center the window,
    Move (Screen.Width - Width) \ 2, (Screen.Height - Height) \ 2
    DestPicture.Width = 32: DestPicture.Height = DestPicture.Width
End Sub
```

7. Now run the project by pressing (F5). When you click on the form, a matrix of icons will appear as shown in Figure 5-5. Notice how only the pencil covers the background.

### How It Works

The code is amazingly simple. When the form is started up, it is centered on the screen by the routine in the Form_Load procedure. Use this code in all your applications.

The code for defining the BitBlt function so that Visual Basic can use it is placed in the General procedure of the form object. The ByVal keyword tells Windows that the values will be passed by value, not by reference. A Windows API function that expects the value of a variable will not perform as expected if the variable is passed by reference. This is because passing a variable by reference doesn't actually pass the value of the variable, it passes a reference to a location in memory where the variable is stored. When a variable is passed by reference to a Windows API function that expects the variable to be passed by value, the variable's memory location is used as the value. This almost always results in the called function performing incorrectly, and can even cause a General Protection Fault. The Const statements set up the hex values needed for simulating the proper mode of the BitBlt.

These Const statements come from the file WINAPI.TXT that is documented in Appendix A.

In the Form_Click procedure, we have a simple For...Next loop that increments the variables X and Y, between 1 and the Height and Width of the Form divided by 20. The reason for dividing is to convert twips to pixels. The loop thus gives us a matrix of 32 by 32 pixels.

### Comments

You can repeat the experiment with larger drawing objects, and you can have overlapping regions with transparency working in all layers. As long as you use the SRCAND and SRCINVERT modes with a mask, this process will work.

## 5.5  How do I...

### Visualize the DrawMode settings?

#### Problem

When drawing on forms and picture boxes with Visual Basic, you can set the DrawMode property to control how pixels in the drawn object interact with the pixels on the form or picture box. While the default mode simply copies pixels onto the form, there are a total of 16 different modes with strange names like Whiteness, Merge Pen Not, and so on. Is there some simple way to learn what these modes mean?

#### Technique

A good way to see the effect of these different modes is to draw a bitmap onto the entire form with the different DrawModes selected from a menu. The Visual Basic LoadPicture function can be used to load a bitmap, icon, or metafile into a picture box. The 16 menu items can be a single menu array and the value of the index will exactly correspond to the mode value!

#### Steps

Open and run DRAWMODE.MAK. Select File/Open to load a bitmap into the large picture box. Try one of the wallpaper bitmaps provided with Windows. You can then select any item from the DrawMode menu to see what effect that DrawMode setting has. File/Restore reverses any changes you've made.

**Figure 5-9** The DrawMode form

1. Create a new project called DRAWMODE.MAK. Create a new form with the objects and properties listed in Table 5-5, and save it as DRAWMODE.FRM. See Figure 5-9 for what this form will look like.

| Object | Property | Setting |
|--------|----------|---------|
| Form | FormName | Draw_Mode |
| | Caption | DrawMode |
| | BackColor | &H00C0C0C0& |
| Picture box | Name | Picture1 |

**Table 5-5** DrawMode project form's objects and properties

2. Create a menu for the form using the Menu Design window with the attributes shown in Table 5-6.

| Caption | Name | Index |
|---------|------|-------|
| &File | FileMenu | |
| &Open… | FileOpen | |
| &Restore | FileRestore | |
| E&xit | FileExit | |
| &DrawMode | DrawModeMenu | |
| Blackness | Mode | 1 |
| Not Merge Pen | Mode | 2 |
| Mask Not Pen | Mode | 3 |
| Not Copy Pen | Mode | 4 |
| Mask Pen Not | Mode | 5 |

| Caption | Name | Index |
|---|---|---|
| Invert | Mode | 6 |
| Xor Pen | Mode | 7 |
| Not Mask Pen | Mode | 8 |
| Mask Pen | Mode | 9 |
| Not Xor Pen | Mode | 10 |
| Nop | Mode | 11 |
| Merge Not Pen | Mode | 12 |
| Copy Pen | Mode | 13 |
| Merge Pen Not | Mode | 14 |
| Merge Pen | Mode | 15 |
| Whiteness | Mode | 16 |

**Table 5-6** The DrawMode project menu

3. Put the following code in the Declarations section of the form.

```
Const MODAL = 1
Dim BitMap$
```

4. Put the following code in the LoadBitMap subroutine in the General section of the form.

```
Sub LoadBitMap ()
    Caption = "DrawMode: " + BitMap$
    Picture1.Picture = LoadPicture(BitMap$)
End Sub
```

5. Put the following code in the FileExit_Click event subroutine.

```
Sub FileExit_Click ()
    End
End Sub
```

6. The following code in the FileOpen_Click event subroutine calls up the FileDlg form (from How-To 2.5 Make a file dialog box using APIs). Make another type of file dialog box to get a bitmap to load into the picture box.

```
Sub FileOpen_Click ()
    FileDlg.FileEdit.Text = "*.BMP"
    FileDlg.Show MODAL
    BitMap$ = FileDlg.FileEdit.Text
    If InStr(BitMap$, "*") = 0 Then LoadBitMap
End Sub
```

7. Put the following code in the Click event subroutine of the FileRestore button.

```
Sub FileRestore_Click ()
    LoadBitMap
End Sub
```

8. If you resize the DrawMode form, its Form_Resize event changes the width and height of the picture box to match the form's. (See How-To 1.2 Size a form's controls automatically, for more details.) Put the following code in the Form_Resize event subroutine.

```
Sub Form_Resize ()
    Picture1.Height = Draw_Mode.ScaleHeight - Picture1.Top * 2
    Picture1.Width = Draw_Mode.ScaleWidth - Picture1.Left * 2
End Sub
```

9. The Mode_Click event subroutine handles all the various DrawMode settings. Because the menu is a control array, the Index parameter tells us the DrawMode setting.

```
Sub Mode_Click (Index As Integer)
    Picture1.DrawMode = Index
    Picture1.Line (Picture1.ScaleLeft, Picture1.ScaleTop)- ⇐
    (Picture1.ScaleLeft + Picture1.ScaleWidth, Picture1.ScaleTop + ⇐
     Picture1.ScaleHeight), , BF
End Sub
```

### How It Works

It's no coincidence that we're using a control array for the menu items. The Index property for each menu item represents the numeric value of a DrawMode setting. When you click the menu item, the corresponding control array index sets the picture box's DrawMode property. Then a filled box is drawn using Line,,BF.

The FileOpen_Click event subroutine calls up the file dialog box from How-To 2.5 Make a file dialog box using APIs. When you click on the file dialog box's OK button, FileOpen_Click calls the LoadBitMap subroutine, which loads the file into the picture box using Visual Basic's LoadPicture function.

We cheat a little bit for the Restore button. Instead of undoing the changes that might have been made, we just call the LoadBitMap subroutine again to reload the unchanged picture file from disk.

### Comments

Although the file dialog box defaults to using .BMP bitmap files, you can also load .ICO icon files and .WMF metafiles. Visual Basic's LoadPicture function used in the LoadBitMap subroutine understands all three formats.

## 5.6  How do I...

# Separate the red, green, and blue components of a color?

### Problem

Visual Basic gives us the RGB function that lets you specify values for a color. However, given a combined color made of a single long integer, how do you separate its individual red, green, and blue values?

### Technique

A color value is a long integer that contains the separate red, green, and blue color components. It's a fairly straightforward mathematical operation to separate the three colors from the composite color value. The color value can best be represented as a hexadecimal number, like this:

&Hrrggbb

where rr is the red color component, gg the green, and bb the blue.

### Steps

Open and run COLORVAL.MAK. You can enter a color value in the text box (as a long decimal integer) and a message box will display the red, green, and blue color components it represents.

1. Create a new project called COLORVAL.MAK. Create a new form with the objects and properties shown in Table 5-7, and save it as COLORVAL.FRM. See Figure 5-10 for the form's design.

| Object | Property | Setting |
| --- | --- | --- |
| Form | Caption | Color value separator |
| | FormName | ColorValue |
| | BackColor | &H00C0C0C0& |
| Command button | Name | Ok |
| | Caption | Ok |
| | Default | True |
| Command button | Name | Cancel |
| | Caption | Cancel |
| Label | Name | Label1 |
| | Alignment | Right justify |
| | Caption | Color Value |
| Text box | Name | ColorText |

**Table 5-7** Controls and properties

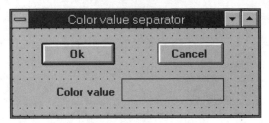

**Figure 5-10** The ColorVal form design

2. Put the following code in the GetRed general function. This code retrieves the red color component from the combined color value.

```
Function GetRed (ColorValue As Long) As Integer
   GetRed = (ColorValue And &HFF0000) \ 65536
End Function
```

3. Put the following code in the GetGreen general function. This code retrieves the green color component from the combined color value.

```
Function GetGreen (ColorValue As Long) As Integer
   GetGreen = (ColorValue And &HFF00&) \ 256
End Function
```

4. Put the following code in the GetBlue general function. This code retrieves the blue color component from the combined color value.

```
Function GetBlue (ColorValue As Long) As Integer
   GetBlue = ColorValue And &HFF&
End Function
```

5. Put the following code in the Cancel_Click event subroutine. The End statement simply ends the application.

```
Sub Cancel_Click ()
   End
End Sub
```

6. Put the following code in the Ok_Click event subroutine. This code gets the value of the text in the text box and retrieves the color components using the GetRed, GetGreen, and GetBlue general functions. Then a MsgBox statement displays the different component values.

```
Sub Ok_Click ()
   Static ColorVal As Long, R As Integer, G As Integer, B As Integer

   CRLF$ = Chr$(13) + Chr$(10)
   ColorVal = Val(ColorText.Text)
   R = GetRed(ColorVal)
   G = GetGreen(ColorVal)
   B = GetBlue(ColorVal)
```

```
    MsgBox "Red component=" + Format$(R) + CRLF$ + "Green component=" +
Format$(G) + CRLF$ + "Blue component=" + Format$(B)
End Sub
```

### How It Works

A combined color value is a long integer that contains the separate red, green, and blue color components packed in a simple format as shown in Figure 5-11. By representing the color value as a hexadecimal number like &Hrrggbb, you can see that each color component ranges from 0 to 255 (or &H00 to &HFF in hexadecimal) and occupies different positions in the long hexadecimal value. You can separate out the component colors by using Visual Basic's bitwise And operator. (See *The Waite Group's Visual Basic Super Bible,* Taylor Maxwell and Bryon Scott, Waite Group Press, 1992.) Figures 5-12 and 5-13 show examples of how the bitwise And operator works.

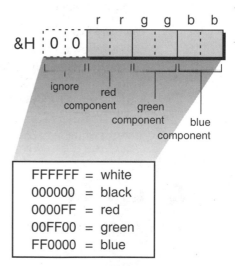

FFFFFF = white
000000 = black
0000FF = red
00FF00 = green
FF0000 = blue

**Figure 5-11** Interpreting the color value long integer

| | AND | |
|---|---|---|
| A | B | C |
| 0 | 0 | 0 |
| 0 | 1 | 0 |
| 1 | 0 | 1 |
| 1 | 1 | 1 |

**Figure 5-12** Bitwise And logic

| | decimal | hex | binary |
|---|---|---|---|
| | 300 | 12C | 100101100 |
| AND | 255 | FF | 011111111 |
| | 44 | 2C | 000101100 |

**Figure 5-13** And-ing multidigit numbers

To extract the red component, the color value is And-ed with &H00FF0000 to zero out the green and blue components. For example, a color value of 16,777,215 is &HFFFFFF, which is the color white. If we bitwise And &H00FF0000 and &HFFFFFF, you'll get &H00FF0000, or 16,711,680, not &HFF. Unfortunately, the bitwise And operator zeroes out the green and blue components and leaves the red component in the same place. Dividing the value by 65536 (&H10000) will move the red component to the low-order byte.

The same problem applies for the green color component. When you bitwise And the color value with &H0000FF00, the red and blue components are zeroed out, but the green component isn't in the low-order byte. Simply dividing by 256 will move it there.

Luckily, the blue component is already in the low-order byte, so simply bitwise And-ing the color value with &H000000FF will remove the red and green components.

### Comments

You might want to add the GetRed, GetGreen, and GetBlue functions to a separate module of your most-used functions and add that module to your projects using the Visual Basic File menu's Add File... options. (We use VBHOWTO.BAS for the functions in this book.)

Using these functions will make it easy for you to increase, say, the amount of red in a color.

## 5.7  How do I...

**Complexity: Easy**

## Make a screen capture from my running program?

### Problem

In Windows, it's a little known secret that pressing (ALT)-(PRT SCREEN) copies the current active window to the Clipboard. The Clipboard can then be viewed with the Windows' CLIPBRD.EXE utility. But suppose I want to capture a specific x/y area of the screen while my Visual Basic application is running. Is that possible?

### Technique

Making such a screen capture is actually quite easy from Visual Basic. The key is to get Windows to provide a display context (DC) for the whole screen. A Display Context is a sort of data structure that contains important information about your particular video hardware. This can be accomplished using the CreateDC API function and passing "DISPLAY" as the driver name.

**Figure 5-14** Appearance of the ScrnCap form

Once you receive the display context, you can manipulate the screen just as you would any other bitmap.

### Steps

Open and run SCRNCAP.MAK. Alternatively, you may create a stand-alone .EXE file and run ScrnCap from the Program Manager. We set up our example so it captures the entire screen, but you can change the rectangle's corner values to capture any area. To capture the screen to the Clipboard once the program is running, simply click on the Capture button. To create the screen capture utility, simply do the following:

1. Create a new project called SCRNCAP.MAK. Create a new form with the objects and properties in Table 5-8, and save it as SCRNCAP.FRM. When finished, the form should look like Figure 5-14.

| Object | Property | Setting |
|---|---|---|
| Form | FormName | Form1 |
| | Caption | Screen Capture |
| | BackColor | &H00FFFFFF& |
| Command button | Name | Command1 |
| | Caption | Capture |

**Table 5-8** Scrncap form's objects and properties

2. Insert the following code in the Declarations section of Form1.

```
DefInt A-Z

Declare Sub ReleaseDC Lib "User" (ByVal hWnd, ByVal hDC)
Declare Sub OpenClipBoard Lib "User" (ByVal hWnd)
Declare Sub EmptyClipBoard Lib "User" ()
Declare Sub SetClipBoardData Lib "User" (ByVal CBFormat, ByVal hBitMap)
Declare Sub CloseClipBoard Lib "User" ()
Declare Sub SelectObject Lib "GDI" (ByVal hDC, ByVal hObj)
Declare Sub DeleteDC Lib "GDI" (ByVal hDC)
Declare Sub BitBlt Lib "GDI" (ByVal DestDC, ByVal X, ByVal Y, ByVal ⇐
BWidth, ByVal BHeight, ByVal SourceDC, ByVal X, ByVal Y, ByVal Constant&)

Declare Function CreateDC Lib "GDI" (ByVal Driver$, ByVal Dev&, ByVal ⇐
O&,_ByVal Init&)
Declare Function CreateCompatibleDC Lib "GDI" (ByVal hDC)
Declare Function CreateCompatibleBitmap Lib "GDI" (ByVal hDC, ⇐
ByValBWidth,_ByVal BHeight)

Const TRUE = -1
Const FALSE = 0

Sub ScrnCap (Lt, Top, Rt, Bot)
    rWidth = Rt - Lt
    rHeight = Bot - Top
    SourceDC = CreateDC("DISPLAY", 0, 0, 0)
    DestDC = CreateCompatibleDC(SourceDC)
    BHandle = CreateCompatibleBitmap(SourceDC, rWidth, rHeight)
    SelectObject DestDC, BHandle
    BitBlt DestDC, 0, 0, rWidth, rHeight, SourceDC, Lt, Top, &HCC0020
    Wnd = Screen.ActiveForm.hWnd
    OpenClipBoard Wnd
    EmptyClipBoard
    SetClipBoardData 2, BHandle
    CloseClipBoard
    DeleteDC DestDC
    ReleaseDC DHandle, SourceDC
End Sub
```

3. Insert the following code in the Command1_Click procedure.

```
Sub Command1_Click ()
    Form1.Visible = FALSE
    ScrnCap 0, 0, 640, 480  'Use appropriate dimentions
    Form1.Visible = TRUE
End Sub
```

### How It Works

The bulk of the work for the program is in the ScrnCap procedure. First, a "Source" device context called SourceDC is created. This is used to create a copy of the DC for manipulation. This is accomplished with the Create-CompatibleDC API function. You then need to create a bitmap in memory. You want this bitmap to be of the same size and palette as the display context that you want to copy. The easiest way to accomplish this is with the Create-CompatibleBitmap API function, which returns a handle to an empty bitmap. SelectObject closes this bitmap as the object of the device context. You can then use BitBlt to copy the contents of the screen display context to the memory bitmap in DestDC.

Now that you have memory bitmap that contains the contents of the screen, it is a simple matter to assign this bitmap to the Clipboard. First, a handle to the currently active screen form is obtained. Then OpenClipboard establishes our application as the "owner" of the Clipboard and allows accessing of the information stored there. A call is made to EmptyClipboard to ensure that the Clipboard is empty of information left there by other applications. The Clipboard can store multiple data formats—such as text, bitmaps, or metafiles. We then use the SetClipboardData API function to assign the application's memory bitmap handle to the Clipboard. The bitmap is now owned by the the Clipboard. Finally, the Clipboard is closed, the device context is deleted, and the various handles to these devices are released.

### Comments

Since ScrnCap takes a number of parameters: x, y, Width, and Height, it is easy to copy any portion of the screen to the Clipboard.

In addition, you should note that you are free to "draw" on the screen as well as copy, although this is not considered "well behaved." This technique is used by screen-capture programs and screen-saver programs. For example, you might want to use the SetCapture function (described in How-To 6.16 Simulate SPY in Visual Basic) to allow the user to "select" a portion of the screen and then copy just that portion to the Clipboard.

If you wanted to create a screen saver, you would want to create a "backup" of the screen image with the memory bitmap, as described earlier when we used the CreateCompatibleBitmap and the BitBlt functions. You could then use all of the normal GDI functions on the screen to create pictures, animation, and so on. Then, when the user pressed a key, clicked something, or used some other standard exit technique, you would restore the original contents of the screen.

## 5.8  How do I... Complexity: Easy

## Arrange the icons on the Windows desktop?

### Problem

When users iconize my Visual Basic applications and move other icons around the screen, the desktop window can become cluttered. Is there any way I can write code that would automatically arrange all those icons?

### Technique

The first solution that comes to mind is to use SendKeys and Task Manager to do this from Visual Basic. If you double-click on the desktop (background or wallpaper) window or press (CTRL)-(ESC), Task Manager pops up. Task Manager has a command button captioned "Arrange Icons." That button does what you want, so you could use the Visual Basic SendKeys statement, like this:

```
SendKeys "^{ESCAPE}%A"
```

This statement sends the (CTRL)-(ESC) key sequence (which will bring up Task Manager) and (ALT)-(A), which is the shortcut key for the Arrange Icons button. The big disadvantage to doing this is that it takes several seconds for Task Manager to load, and when it does you will see Task Manager's window flash briefly on the screen.

A better way is to use the Windows API function called Arrange-IconicWindows which, naturally, arranges all the icons in a given window. Because we want to arrange all the icons on the desktop window, the API function GetDesktopWindow returns the window handle to the desktop window.

### Steps

Open and run ARRANGE.MAK. When you click on the Arrange Desktop Icons button, all the icons on the desktop will be arranged neatly at the bottom of the screen. Figure 5-16 indicates the "before" icon arrangement, and Figure 5-17 the "after."

1. Create a new project called ARRANGE.MAK. Create a form with the controls and properties listed in Table 5-9 and save it as ARRANGE.FRM. Figure 5-15 shows the completed form.

| Object | Property | Setting |
|---|---|---|
| Form | Caption | Arrange desktop icons |
| | FormName | ArrangeIcon |
| | BackColor | &H00C0C0C0& |
| Command button | Name | Arrange |
| | Caption | Arrange desktop icons! |
| | Default | True |

**Table 5-9** Arrange project form's objects and properties

2. Put the following code in the Declarations section of the form. The Declare statements declare the Windows API functions ArrangeIconic-Windows and GetDesktopWindow.

```
Declare Function ArrangeIconicWindows Lib "User" (ByVal hWnd As Integer) ⇐
As Integer
Declare Function GetDesktopWindow Lib "User" () As Integer
```

3. Put the following code in the Arrange_Click event subroutine.

```
Sub Arrange_Click ()
    DesktopHWnd = GetDesktopWindow()
    If ArrangeIconicWindows(DesktopHWnd) = 0 Then
        MsgBox "There are no icons on the desktop window to arrange!"
    End If
End Sub
```

### How It Works

In this case, Windows APIs encapsulate a lot of the work for us. In the Arrange_Click event subroutine, a call to GetDesktopWindow gets the window handle to the desktop window, which is then stored in the DesktopHWnd variable.

The DesktopHWnd is passed in the call to ArrangeIconicWindows, which tells Windows to arrange all the icons on the desktop window.

**Figure 5-15** The Arrange Icons form

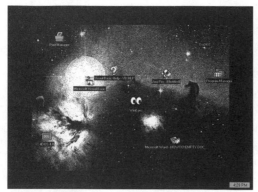

**Figure 5-16** The desktop before arranging the icons

**Figure 5-17** The desktop after arranging the icons

ArrangeIconicWindows returns 0 if there were no icons to arrange, so a call to Visual Basic's MsgBox statement tells the user that.

### Comments
You might want to give your form a Window menu, with an Arrange Icons option, and the following event subroutine.

```
Sub WindowArrangeIcons_Click ()
    DesktopHWnd = GetDesktopWindow()
    If ArrangeIconicWindows(DesktopHWnd) = 0 Then
        MsgBox "There are no icons on the desktop window to arrange!"
    End If
End Sub
```

## 5.9  How do I...

## Make a Macintosh-style trash can?

### Problem
I like the way the Macintosh file managing system uses a trash can. You simply drag the program or document icon you wish to delete over the trash can icon, then select the Empty Trash menu item. Can this be simulated in my Visual Basic application?

### Technique
The Drag method can be used along with the DragDrop and DragOver events to make the trash can change its appearance according to user actions. Moving an item from one list box to another is another underlying function of implementing the trash can.

### Steps
Open and run TRASHCAN.MAK. The Trashcan project can be created by performing the following steps.

1.  The trash can in this project is an icon-sized picture box, and our first step will be to create the different icons necessary for the various states the trash can will have: empty, empty-darkened, full, and full-darkened. Start with the icon for the empty state and modify it for the other three.

    The icon used in the project is located in the ICONS subdirectory of the VB directory, ...VB\ICONS\COMPUTER\Trash01.ICO. If this icon is not available to you, substitute another trash can icon or make one of your own, using the figures shown below as a guide. Open this icon into an icon editor (IconWorks is a great icon editor and comes with Visual Basic), and save it as Empty.ICO to the project directory. Then, to make the job of creating the other icons easier, trim off the shadow in the lower right portion of the icon and save again so it looks like Figure 5-18.

2. Fill in the interior of the trash can until it is completely black, as in Figure 5-19, and save the new, dark icon as Dark.ICO.

3. Open Empty.ICO back in the Editor, save it as Full.ICO, and modify it so it has a bulging appearance, as in Figure 5-20.

4. Now save Full.ICO as Darkfull.ICO and fill in the interior of the fattened trash can until it is completely black, as in Figure 5-21.

You should now have a set of four icons, which will ultimately be used to represent the four trash can states: empty, empty-darkened, full, and full-darkened.

5. Create a new form, place on it the controls shown in Figure 5-22, then set all the properties as listed in Table 5-10. Save the form as MAINFORM.FRM.

**Figure 5-18** (left) The trash can icon TrashO1.ICO before it's modified (Empty.ICO)
**Figure 5-19** (right) The dark trash can icon (Dark.ICO)

**Figure 5-20** (left) The trash can icon modified so it appears full (Full.ICO)
**Figure 5-21** (right) The dark full trash can (Darkfull.ICO)

| Object | Property | Setting |
|--------|----------|---------|
| Form | FormName | MainForm |
| | Caption | TrashCan Demo |
| | BackColor | &H00E0E0E0& (Light Gray) |
| | BorderStyle | 1 - Fixed Single |
| | ControlBox | False |
| | Icon | Empty.ICO |
| List box | Name | SourceList |
| | DragIcon | ...VB\ICONS\COMPUTER\Key06.ICO |
| | Sorted | True |
| | Tag | SourceList |
| Command button | Name | ExitDemo |
| | Caption | Exit Demo |
| Picture box | Name | EmptyTrash |
| | BackColor | &H00E0E0E0& (Light Gray) |
| | BorderStyle | 1 - Fixed Single |
| | DragIcon | Dark.ICO |
| | Height | 495 (twips) |
| | Picture | Empty.ICO |
| | Visible | False |
| | Width | 495 (twips) |
| Picture box | Name | FullTrash |
| | BackColor | &H00E0E0E0& (Light Gray) |
| | BorderStyle | 1 - Fixed Single |
| | DragIcon | Darkfull.ICO |
| | Height | 495 (twips) |
| | Picture | Full.ICO |
| | Visible | False |
| | Width | 495 (twips) |
| Picture box | Name | TrashCan |
| | BackColor | &H00E0E0E0& (Light Gray) |
| | BorderStyle | 0 - None |
| | Height | 495 (twips) |
| | Picture | Empty.ICO |
| | Visible | True |
| | Width | 495 (twips) |

**Table 5-10** Trash can project objects and properties in the MainForm form

6. Create another new form, place on it the controls shown in Figure 5-23, then set all the properties as listed in Table 5-11. Save this form as TRASHFRM.FRM.

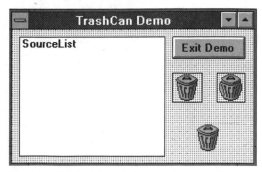

**Figure 5-22** The MainForm form and its controls at design time

**Figure 5-23** The TrashForm form and its controls at design time

| Object | Property | Setting |
|---|---|---|
| Form | FormName | TrashForm |
| | Caption | Trash |
| | BackColor | &H00E0E0E0& (Light Gray) |
| | BorderStyle | 1 - Fixed Single |
| | ControlBox | False |
| | Icon | Empty.ICO |
| List box | Name | TrashList |
| | DragIcon | ...VB\ICONS\COMPUTER\Key06.ICO |
| | Sorted | True |
| | Tag | TrashList |
| Command button | Name | Action |
| | Caption | Close |
| | Index | 0 |
| Command button | Name | Action |
| | Caption | Empty Trash |
| | Index | 1 |

**Table 5-11** TrashForm project form's objects and properties

7. Place the following code in the MainForm.Form_Load event procedure.

```
Sub Form_Load ()
    TrashForm.TrashList.DragIcon = SourceList.DragIcon
    For i = 1 To 12
        Number$ = Format$(i, "00")
        SourceList.AddItem "Source_" + Number$
    Next i
    SourceList.ListIndex = 0                 'Highlight first item in list
End Sub
```

8. Place the following code in the MainForm.SourceList_DragDrop event procedure.

```
Sub SourceList_DragDrop (Source As Control, X As Single, Y As Single)
    If Source.Tag <> "SourceList" Then
        SourceList.AddItem Source.List(Source.ListIndex)
        If SourceList.ListIndex = -1 Then    'If no item highlighted,
            SourceList.ListIndex = 0              'highlight first item
            End If
        SetIndex Source
    End If
End Sub
```

9. Place the following code in the MainForm.ExitDemo_Click event procedure.

```
Sub ExitDemo_Click ()
    End
End Sub
```

10. Place the following code in the MainForm.SourceList_MouseDown event procedure.

```
Sub SourceList_MouseDown (Button As Integer, Shift As Integer, X As ⇐
    Single, Y As Single)
    If SourceList.ListCount > 0 Then            'If list not empty
        If Button = 2 Then                  'If right button down,
            SourceList.Drag 1                   'Begin dragging
        End If
    End If
End Sub
```

11. Place the following code in the MainForm.TrashCan_DblClick event procedure.

```
Sub TrashCan_DblClick ()
    TrashForm.Show
End Sub
```

12. Place the following code in the MainForm.TrashCan_DragDrop event procedure.

```
Sub TrashCan_DragDrop (Source As Control, X As Single, Y As Single)
    If Source.Tag <> "TrashList" Then
        TrashForm.TrashList.AddItem Source.List(Source.ListIndex)
        If TrashForm.TrashList.ListIndex = -1 Then
            TrashForm.TrashList.ListIndex = 0
        End If
        SetIndex Source
    Else
        Beep    'If Source = TrashList
    End If
```

```
        If TrashCan.Picture <> FullTrash.Picture Then
            TrashCan.Picture = FullTrash.Picture
        End If
End Sub
```

13. Place the following code in the MainForm.TrashCan_DragOver event procedure.

```
Sub TrashCan_DragOver (Source As Control, X As Single, Y As Single, ⇐
    State As Integer)
    Select Case State
        Case 0        'If dragged control enters
            If TrashForm.TrashList.ListCount = 0 Then
                TrashCan.Picture = EmptyTrash.DragIcon
            Else
                TrashCan.Picture = FullTrash.DragIcon
            End If
        Case 1        'If dragged control leaves
            If TrashForm.TrashList.ListCount = 0 Then
                TrashCan.Picture = EmptyTrash.Picture
            Else
                TrashCan.Picture = FullTrash.Picture
            End If
    End Select
End Sub
```

14. Place the following code in the TrashForm.TrashList_DragDrop event procedure.

```
Sub TrashList_DragDrop (Source As Control, X As Single, Y As Single)
    If Source.Tag <> "TrashList" Then
        If MainForm.TrashCan.Picture <> MainForm.FullTrash.Picture Then
            MainForm.TrashCan.Picture = MainForm.FullTrash.Picture
        End If
        TrashList.AddItem Source.List(Source.ListIndex)
        If TrashList.ListIndex = -1 Then 'If no item highlighted
            TrashList.ListIndex = 0      'Highlight first item
        End If
        SetIndex Source
    End If
End Sub
```

15. Place the following code in the TrashForm.TrashList_MouseDown event procedure.

```
Sub TrashList_MouseDown (Button As Integer, Shift As Integer, X As ⇐
Single, Y As Single)
    If TrashList.ListCount > 0 Then        'If list not empty
        If Button = 2 Then                 'If right mouse button down
            TrashList.Drag 1               'Begin dragging
        End If
    End If
End Sub
```

16. Place the following code in the TrashForm.Action_Click event procedure.

```
Sub Action_Click (Index As Integer)
    If Index = 1 Then                        'Empty Trash button clicked
        If TrashList.ListCount <= 0 Then 'If trash is empty
            Beep
            Exit Sub
        End If
        Screen.MousePointer = 11            'Hourglass
        For i = 1 To TrashList.ListCount
            TrashList.ListIndex = 0
                'Code here to deal with items in list.
                'This code just clears items from list.
            TrashList.RemoveItem 0
        Next i
        MainForm.TrashCan.Picture = MainForm.EmptyTrash.Picture
        Screen.MousePointer = 0                 'Back to prior value
    Else                                        'Close button was clicked on
        Action(0).SetFocus                      'Set default button to 'Close'
        TrashForm.Hide
    End If
End Sub
```

17. Now create a new module, save it as Gencode.MOD, and add this code to its General Declarations.

```
Sub SetIndex (Source As Control)
    If Source.ListIndex > 0 Then        'If not removing first item in list
        Source.ListIndex = Source.ListIndex - 1
        Source.RemoveItem Source.ListIndex + 1
    Else                                        'If removing first item in list
        Source.RemoveItem Source.ListIndex
        If Source.ListCount > 0 Then  'If list not empty
            Source.ListIndex = 0       'Keep first item highlighted
        End If
    End If
    If Source.Tag = "TrashList" Then
        If Source.ListCount = 0 Then
            MainForm.trashCan.Picture = MainForm.emptyTrash.Picture
        End If
    End If
End Sub
```

### How It Works

Our example allows you to drag items from a scrolling list box into the trash can. A list box responds to a click over an item in its list by highlighting that item and setting its ListIndex property to correspond to that item's position in the list. (The first item in a list box corresponds to a ListIndex value of 0.) Setting SourceList's DragMode property to Automatic would not be a good idea, because once a drag operation on a control is under way all mouse events are ignored. Hence, anytime SourceList was clicked on, dragging would begin, and the ListIndex property could not be changed. Indeed the basic functionality of a list box is impaired by setting its DragMode to Automatic!

Thus, in our example, we left the DragMode property for SourceList set to the default value of Manual. When a user clicks and holds down the *right* mouse button while the mouse cursor is over SourceList, dragging is invoked by code in SourceList's MouseDown event procedure (if the list is not empty). If dragging were simply invoked whenever the user clicked the list box with the left button, then, with a DragMode setting of Manual, the ListIndex property would be set before dragging began. However, a user would not be able to scroll a list by dragging the mouse up and down over its items! Again, basic functionality of the list box would be impaired.

### The Right Mouse Button Drag Trick

Clicking on and dragging the SourceList list box with the right mouse button will begin a drag operation. By itself it won't change the item highlighted in the list (set the ListIndex property of the list box). In this project our drag operations are designed to move the highlighted item in a list box, so the user can first highlight an item with the left mouse button by clicking on it, then drag it with the right mouse button or, because of the way in which a list box deals with MouseDown events, can do both at once by clicking on an item and dragging with both the right and left mouse buttons down. When both buttons are held down, the list box will first process the left mouse button, highlighting an item and setting the ListIndex property, and then the right mouse button, initiating dragging as per our code in the MouseDown event procedure.

The Picture property of the TrashCan picture box is set to the Empty.ICO icon at design time, so that, when our program first appears, the trash can will have the proper look. The appearance of the trash can will change at run time according to whether it's empty and whether a control being dragged passes over it. We need to be able to set the Picture property of the trash can to reflect a total of four different states, so we use the Picture and DragIcon properties of the two picture boxes, FullTrash and Empty-Trash (which are not visible at run time), as storage containers for the four images necessary to accomplish this. Code in the TrashCan picture box's DragOver and DragDrop event procedures changes the look of the trash can by setting TrashCan's Picture property. (As you refer to this code, remember the darkened trash can images are "stored" in the DragIcon properties of our "storage containers.")

### Using the Darkened Icons

If the user drags over the trash can, the picture is darkened according to whether it is empty. If the user then lets up the mouse button while it is still over the trash can, a DragDrop event is generated. Code in the trash can's DragDrop event procedure will remove an item from the SourceList, add an item to the TrashList list box, and change the appearance of the trash can to look full. If the user drags off of the trash can without releasing the mouse button, code in the trash can's DragOver event procedure will reset the Picture property to the proper nondarkened state.

The code located in the SourceList and TrashList's DragDrop event procedures moves an item from one list to the other. Our SetIndex procedure contains code that resets the ListIndex property of a list box after an item has been removed, in a manner befitting the remaining contents of the list box. If this were not done, ListIndex would default to a value of -1 after removal of the highlighted item, and no item in the list would be highlighted. Code in a user defined procedure is local to the form with which it is associated, but code located in a module is global in scope. Thus, we created a new module in which to locate SetIndex so that it could be called from any event procedure in the project, regardless of the parent form.

### Comments

The MainForm's Form_Load event procedure added a number of items to the SourceList, for the purpose of providing items to drag to demonstrate the basic principles of a Macintosh style trash can. Were this an actual application, the items in the SourceList might be filenames of existing files. To fully "empty" the trash, additional code would be needed in the Action_Click event procedure to process the deletion. Our code only removes the items from the TrashList.

## 5.10 ● How do I...

## Display the progress of an operation?

### Problem

A lot of Windows applications use a bar-like horizontal gauge to graphically display the completed percentage of an operation in progress, such as when software is being installed, a file downloaded, or a group of files copied. The shaded portion of the gauge grows to show the progress of the operation, and often text displayed in the gauge (10 percent done, and so on) changes color as the shaded portion passes over it. How can I make such a gauge to include in my own Visual Basic creations?

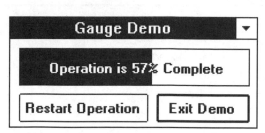

**Figure 5-24** Output of the Gauge project at run time

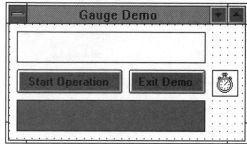

**Figure 5-25** The Gauge project form and its controls at design time

### Technique

The key to making such a gauge lies with the Windows BitBlt API function. You can use it to combine the content of an invisible picture box with that of a visible picture box, which will appear to a user as a gauge being constantly updated.

### Steps

Open and run GAUGE.MAK. It should appear as in Figure 5-24. The Gauge project can be created by performing the following steps.

1. Create a new project called GAUGE.MAK, and create a new form called GAUGE.FRM. Place the controls shown in Figure 5-25 on the form, then set all the properties as listed in Table 5-12. Any properties not specifically mentioned should be left set to their default values. As you can see by comparing the run-time to design-time forms (as shown in Figures 5-24 and 5-25), at run time the gauge's form is resized by code in the Form_Load event procedure around the visible controls.

| Object | Property | Setting |
|---|---|---|
| Form | FormName | MainForm |
| | Caption | Gauge Demo |
| | BorderStyle | 1 (Fixed Single) |
| | ControlBox | False |
| Picture box | Name | Gauge |
| | AutoRedraw | True |
| | BackColor | &H00FFFFFF& (White) |
| | ForeColor | &H00000000& (Black) |
| Command button | Name | StartOp |
| | Caption | Start Operation |

*continued on next page*

*continued from previous page*

| Object | Property | Setting |
|---|---|---|
| Timer | Name | Timer1 |
| | Enabled | False |
| | Interval | 1 (millisecond) |
| Command button | Name | ExitDemo |
| | Caption | Exit Demo |
| Picture box | Name | InvisGauge |
| | AutoRedraw | True |
| | BackColor | &H00FF0000& (Blue) |
| | ForeColor | &H00FFFFFF& (White) |
| | Visible | False |

**Table 5-12** Gauge project form's objects and properties

2. Place the following code in the Global module.

```
Global Const TRUE = -1
Global Const FALSE = 0
Declare Function BitBlt% Lib "Gdi" (ByVal destDC%, ByVal X%, ByVal Y%, ⇐
    ByVal W%, ByVal H%, ByVal srcDC%, ByVal xSrc%, ByVal ySrc%, ⇐
    ByVal RasterOp&)
Global Const SRCCOPY = &HCC0020
```

3. Place the following code in the General section of the Form object.

```
Sub GaugeDisplay (HowMuch!)
    Percent$ = "Operation is " + Format$(HowMuch!, "0%") + " Complete"
    Gauge.Cls                          'Clears previous content
    InvisGauge.Cls
    Gauge.CurrentX = (Gauge.Width - Gauge.TextWidth(Percent$)) / 2
    InvisGauge.CurrentX = Gauge.CurrentX 'Can do because same size
    Gauge.CurrentY = (Gauge.Height - Gauge.TextHeight(Percent$)) / 2
    InvisGauge.CurrentY = Gauge.CurrentY
    Gauge.Print Percent$               'Prints same string in both Picture
    InvisGauge.Print Percent$          'Boxes in same relative location
    OldScaleMode% = Gauge.Parent.ScaleMode
    Gauge.Parent.ScaleMode = 3              'Set to Pixels for BitBlt call
    R% = BitBlt(Gauge.Hdc, 0, 0, InvisGauge.Width * HowMuch!,
    InvisGauge.Height, InvisGauge.Hdc, 0, 0, SrcCopy)
    Gauge.Parent.ScaleMode = OldScaleMode%   'Resetting to prior value
End Sub
```

4. Place the following code in the Form_Load event procedure.

```
Sub Form_Load ()
        'This code will shrink the form around the
        'controls that are visible at run time.
    MainForm.Width = (Gauge.Left * 2) + Gauge.Width
```

```
    MainForm.Height = StartOp.Top + (StartOp.Height * 2)
        'This Code insures the two Picture boxes will
        'be exactly the same size
    InvisGauge.Width = Gauge.Width
    InvisGauge.Height = Gauge.Height
End Sub
```

5. Place the following code in the ExitDemo_Click event procedure.

```
Sub ExitDemo_Click ()
    End
End Sub
```

6. Place the following code in the StartOp_Click event procedure.

```
Sub StartOp_Click ()
    StartOp.Enabled = FALSE
    StartOp.Caption = "In Progress "
    Timer1.Enabled = TRUE
End Sub
```

7. Place the following code in the Timer1_Timer event procedure.

```
Sub Timer1_Timer ()
    Static Counter As Integer       'Initial value of 0 when declared
    HowMuch! = Counter / 100        'Percentage of operation completed
    GaugeDisplay HowMuch!
    Counter = Counter + 1
    If Counter = 101 Then
        StartOp.Enabled = TRUE      'Resetting Command Button
        StartOp.Caption = "Restart Operation"
        Timer1.Enabled = FALSE      'This procedure won't be called
        Counter = 0                 'until StartOp is clicked on again
    End If
End Sub
```

## How It Works

In a working application, a gauge is updated as an operation is in progress. In this demo, we simply use a timer to update our gauge by 1% every time the timer's Timer event procedure gets called. The basic principles involved to actually create the gauge itself in either case are identical. Later you will see how the code would differ for a more practical implementation, where you would actually be following an event's progression.

The event procedure of the project's timer is called as long as the timer's Enabled property is set to True. We set the Enabled property to False at design time, so that at run time we can selectively enable the timer by clicking on the StartOp command button. This button has code in its Click event procedure to set the timer's Enabled property to True.

In the Timer event procedure, we declared the integer variable Counter as a Static variable so that it will retain its value in between procedure calls.

When initially declared, Counter has a value of 0 and is incremented by 1 each time the procedure gets called. When Counter's value reaches 101, the code in the If…Then loop at the end of the procedure will be executed, resetting the timer's Enabled property to False and Counter's value to 0. The net effect is that whenever the timer is enabled, its Timer event procedure will be called while Counter's value cycles through the range 0-100.

Within the Timer event procedure, the user-defined subroutine GaugeDisplay is called, with HowMuch! (calculated as the percentage of the operation completed at the time of the call) passed as its sole parameter. Code in GaugeDisplay formats HowMuch! into a character string and incorporates it into the string Percent$, then prints Percent$ centered horizontally and vertically in the Gauge and InvisGauge picture boxes. Because the picture boxes are exactly the same size, the relative position of the text string within each picture box is the same.

The last line of code in GaugeDisplay is a call to the Windows API Function BitBlt (declared in the Global module), which copies a section of InvisGauge to Gauge. In the call, the width of InvisGauge is multiplied times HowMuch! to determine the size (percentage) of the section to copy. Remember that Gauge has a BackColor of white, and ForeColor (the color that text is painted in) of black. InvisGauge has a blue BackColor and a white ForeColor. Because the content of both picture boxes is identical except for the color, the white letters of the text in the section copied from InvisGauge to Gauge by the BitBlt call mesh seamlessly with the black letters in Gauge.

Were this an actual application that used a gauge to graphically track an operation's progress, HowMuch! would represent the percentage of the operation completed at the time of the call to GaugeDisplay. For example, if the Gauge were tracking the progress of a copy operation involving a number of files, after each file was copied a call could be made to GaugeDisplay, as in the following code:

```
Sub CopyFiles (SourceFile$(), FileCount)
    Dim BufSize As Long
    Dim FilePosition As Long
    Dim FileSize As Long
    Dim FileSizeLeft As Long

    Screen.MousePointer = 11            'HourGlass (Waiting)
    GaugeDisplay(0)                     'initially displays gauge
                                        'with 0% completed
    For i = 1 To FileCount
        Open SourceFile$(i) For Binary Access Read As #1
        Open DestFile$ For Binary Access Write As #2
        FileSize = LOF(1)
        FileSizeLeft = FileSize
```

```
        FilePosition = 1
        While FileSizeLeft >= 0
            If FileSizeLeft > 16384 Then
                BufSize = 16384
            ElseIf FileSizeLeft = 0 Then
                BufSize = 1
            Else
                BufSize = FileSizeLeft
            End If
            Buffer$ = String$(BufSize, " ")
            Get #1, FilePosition, Buffer$
            Put #2, FilePosition, Buffer$
            FilePosition = FilePosition + BufSize
            FileSizeLeft = FileSize - FilePosition

        Wend
        Close #1
        Close #2
        GaugeDisplay(i/FileCount)      'Displays gauge with shaded amount
                                       'proportional to amount of
                                       'operation completed

    Next i
    Screen.MousePointer = 0                    'Back to prior value
End Sub
```

### Comments

The Windows BitBlt function is extremely versatile and can be used to copy a source bitmap (or portion thereof) to a destination bitmap in a variety of ways. The exact manner in which the copy is performed is specified by the RasterOp% (last) parameter of the call. Our demo simply did a straightforward copy of a section of InvisGauge to Gauge by using the constant SRCCOPY (defined in the Global module) in the BitBlt call as the value of the RasterOp% parameter.

The height and width parameters in a BitBlt call specifying the dimensions of the source and destination bitmaps need to be in units of pixels. The value of the ScaleMode property of the parent of a control (the form on which the control is located) determines the units in which the Width and Height properties of the control are given. You can verify this at design time by noting the values of the Width and Height properties of a control, say Gauge, then changing the value of the ScaleMode property of the parent of Gauge, MainForm, to Pixels, and then again noting the values of Gauge's Width and Height properties. They will have changed!

Code in GaugeDisplay first saves the value of the ScaleMode property of the parent of the two picture boxes (Gauge and InvisGauge) involved in the BitBlt call in the variable OldScaleMode%, then sets it to Pixels just prior to the call. After the BitBlt call, the ScaleMode property is reset to Old-ScaleMode%, its value prior to the change. In this way, regardless of the value of the parent form's ScaleMode property at run time, we can rest assured that at the time of the call to BitBlt it will be Pixels.

The Interval property of the timer was set to the minimum possible value (1 millisecond) at design time. Since our demo uses the timer as a stand-in for an actual operation, this insures that the gauge will be updated as quickly as the CPU, on which the project is running, can execute all the code (including the call to GaugeDisplay) located within the Timer event procedure.

A certain amount of overhead is involved when a Gauge is used to display an operation's progress. The total time of the operation is increased by the amount of time it takes to update the Gauge times the total number of times the Gauge is updated throughout the course of the operation.

## 5.11  How do I...

**Complexity: Intermediate**

### Fill complex objects?

#### Problem
Visual Basic has powerful graphing functions and ability to draw rectangles and circles filled with any color or pattern. But there are no routines to fill any other kind of closed shape. Is there a way to do this?

#### Technique
It's true that Visual Basic's drawing tools are limited to the Circle and Line statements. Luckily, more complex objects can be drawn using the Polygon function found in the Windows API library.

#### Steps
Open and run POLYGON.MAK. This program draws five filled objects on the picture box as shown in Figure 5-26. Click Exit on the menu to leave the application.

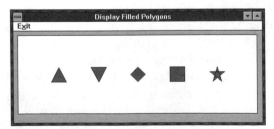

**Figure 5-26** The Polygon project's filled polygons

The project can be built by entering the code and objects as detailed in the following steps.

1. Create a new project called POLYGON.MAK. and create a new form with the objects and properties listed in Table 5-13. Save the form as POLYGON.FRM.

| Object | Property | Setting |
|---|---|---|
| Form | FormName | PolyGon |
|  | BackColor | &H00C0C0C0 |
| Picture box | Name | P |

**Table 5-13** Polygon project form's objects and properties

2. Create a menu for the form using the Menu Design window with the attributes shown in Table 5-14.

| Caption | Name |
|---|---|
| E&xit | Quit |

**Table 5-14** Polygon form menu attributes

3. Select the Global module, enter the following code and save it as POLYGON.BAS. This defines the constants, data structures, and Windows API calls needed to draw the Polygons.

```
Type POINTAPI
     X As Integer
     Y As Integer
End Type

' PolyFill() Modes
Global Const ALTERNATE = 1
Global Const WINDING = 2

Declare Sub Polygon Lib "GDI" (ByVal hDC As Integer, lpPoints As POINTAPI, ⇐
ByVal nCount As Integer)
Declare Sub SetPolyFillMode Lib "GDI" (ByVal hDC As Integer, ByVal         ⇐
    nPolyFillMode As Integer)

'   Shape constants
Global Const PG_TRIANGLE = 1
Global Const PG_INV_TRIANGLE = 2
Global Const PG_DIAMOND = 3
Global Const PG_SQUARE = 4
Global Const PG_STAR = 5
```

4. Enter the following code into the picture box's Paint event subroutine. Whenever Visual Basic needs to paint the picture box, this subroutine will draw the five predefined shapes.

```
Sub P_Paint ()
Dim FColor As Long, Size As Integer
    FColor = QBColor(13)
    P.ScaleMode = 3
    Size = 30

    P.CurrentY = P.ScaleHeight / 2
    P.CurrentX = P.ScaleWidth / 6
    DrawPolygon P, PG_TRIANGLE, Size, FColor

    P.CurrentY = P.ScaleHeight / 2
    P.CurrentX = 2 * P.ScaleWidth / 6
    DrawPolygon P, PG_INV_TRIANGLE, Size, FColor

    P.CurrentY = P.ScaleHeight / 2
    P.CurrentX = 3 * P.ScaleWidth / 6
    DrawPolygon P, PG_DIAMOND, Size, FColor

    P.CurrentY = P.ScaleHeight / 2
    P.CurrentX = 4 * P.ScaleWidth / 6
    DrawPolygon P, PG_SQUARE, Size, FColor

    P.CurrentY = P.ScaleHeight / 2
    P.CurrentX = 5 * P.ScaleWidth / 6
    DrawPolygon P, PG_STAR, Size, FColor
End Sub
```

5. Enter the following code into the Quit_Click menu event subroutine to allow the user to exit the application gracefully.

```
Sub Quit_Click ()
    End
End Sub
```

6. Create a new module by clicking on the File menu's New Module option. Enter the following line of code in the Declarations section and then save the module as POLYLINE.BAS.

```
Dim Ply(10) As POINTAPI
```

7. Enter the following code into the (General) section of the Polyline module. This subroutine will draw the shape on the specified picture box control.

```
Sub DrawPolygon (P As Control, Shape As Integer, Size As Integer, FColor ⇐
    As Long)
Dim nPoints As Integer

'   Draws Different shapes at current location using polygons
'
```

```
'  Save current Scalemode, and Scale Attributes
    SSMode = P.ScaleMode
    SSTOP = P.ScaleTop: SSLeft = P.ScaleLeft
    SSWidth = P.ScaleWidth: SSHeight = P.ScaleHeight


'  Set up Pixel ScaleMode, Fill style, etc.
    P.ScaleMode = 3         ' PolyGon needs everything in pixels
    P.FillStyle = 0         ' Sold fill
    P.fillcolor = FColor    ' Fill color
    P.Drawwidth = 1         ' Border width in pixels

'  Call subroutine to build coordinates for shape
    Select Case Shape
      Case PG_TRIANGLE
        DrawTriangle Size, nPoints

      Case PG_INV_TRIANGLE
        DrawInvertTriangle Size, nPoints

      Case PG_DIAMOND
        DrawDiamond Size, nPoints

      Case PG_SQUARE
        DrawSquare Size, nPoints

      Case PG_STAR
        DrawStar Size, nPoints
    End Select

'  Adjust Points to center shape at current point
'  Set PolyFillMode to fill whole shape
'  Draw polyGon
    For I = 1 To nPoints
        Ply(I).X = Ply(I).X + P.CurrentX - Size / 2
        Ply(I).Y = Ply(I).Y + P.CurrentY - Size / 2
    Next I
    SetPolyFillMode P.Hdc, WINDING
    Polygon P.Hdc, Ply(1), nPoints

'  Restore old ScaleMode
    P.ScaleMode = SSMode
    P.ScaleTop = SSTOP: P.ScaleLeft = SSLeft
    P.ScaleHeight = SSHeight: P.ScaleWidth = SSWidth
End Sub
```

8. Enter the following code in the General section of the Polyline module. This code loads the coordinates for a triangular object.

```
Sub DrawTriangle (Size As Integer, nPoints As Integer)
    Ply(1).X = Size / 2
    Ply(1).Y = 0

    Ply(2).X = Size
    Ply(2).Y = Size
```

*continued on next page*

*continued from previous page*

```
    Ply(3).X = 0
    Ply(3).Y = Size

    nPoints = 3
End Sub
```

9. Enter the following code into the General section of the Polyline module. This code loads the coordinates for an inverted triangle.

```
Sub DrawInvertTriangle (Size As Integer, nPoints As Integer)
    Ply(1).X = 0
    Ply(1).Y = 0

    Ply(2).X = Size
    Ply(2).Y = 0

    Ply(3).X = Size / 2
    Ply(3).Y = Size

    nPoints = 3
End Sub
```

10. Enter the following code into the General section of the Polyline module. This code loads the coordinates for a diamond shaped object.

```
Sub DrawDiamond (Size As Integer, nPoints As Integer)
    Ply(1).X = Size / 2
    Ply(1).Y = 0

    Ply(2).X = Size
    Ply(2).Y = Size / 2

    Ply(3).X = Size / 2
    Ply(3).Y = Size

    Ply(4).X = 0
    Ply(4).Y = Size / 2

    nPoints = 4
End Sub
```

11. Enter the following code in the General section of the Polyline module. This code loads the coordinates for a square shaped object.

```
Sub DrawSquare (Size As Integer, nPoints As Integer)
    Ply(1).X = 0
    Ply(1).Y = 0

    Ply(2).X = Size
    Ply(2).Y = 0

    Ply(3).X = Size
    Ply(3).Y = Size

    Ply(4).X = 0
    Ply(4).Y = Size
```

```
    nPoints = 4
End Sub
```

12. Enter the following code in the General section of the Polyline module. This code loads the coordinates for a five-pointed star.

```
Sub DrawStar (Size As Integer, nPoints As Integer)
    Ply(1).X = Size / 2
    Ply(1).Y = 0

    Ply(2).X = 4 * Size / 5
    Ply(2).Y = Size

    Ply(3).X = 0
    Ply(3).Y = Size / 3

    Ply(4).X = Size
    Ply(4).Y = Ply(3).Y

    Ply(5).X = Size - Ply(2).X
    Ply(5).Y = Size

    nPoints = 5
End Sub
```

## How It Works

To draw graphical shapes, Visual Basic provides you with two methods: Line and Circle. The Line method can be used to draw straight lines or, when used with the BF option, will produce a filled rectangle. More complex objects, with straight edges, can be made up of multiple line segments, but filling the object using Visual Basic statements is tedious and slow. However, the Windows API has a function, Polygon, for drawing and filling complex objects.

The Polygon function takes three parameters as shown in Table 5-15.

| Parameter | Description |
| --- | --- |
| hDC | Device context on which the polygon will be drawn. This could be Form.hDC or, as shown in this project, PictureBox.hDC. |
| lpPoints | An array of a user-defined data type, POINTAPI, which specifies the vertices of the Polygon. lpPoints has two elements, X and Y, which are the coordinates, in pixels, relative to the upper left corner of the device context. |
| nCount | The number of vertices in the PolyGon. |

**Table 5-15** Parameters of the Polygon function

The DrawPolygon subroutine in the Polyline module is used to draw one of the five predefined shapes in a picture box at the current cursor location. Putting the DrawPolygon subroutine into a separate module makes it easy to incorporate it into other projects, such as a Linegrph in How-To 5.12 Build a line chart. Table 5-16 lists the parameters to the DrawPolygon subroutine.

| Parameter | Description |
| --- | --- |
| P | Picture box control onto which the shape will be drawn. |
| Shape | One of five predefined shapes: 1 - Triangle, 2 - Inverted Triangle, 3 - Diamond, 4 - Square, and 5 - Star. |
| Size | Height and Width of the Polygon, in Pixels. |
| FColor | Background FillColor for the object. |

**Table 5-16** Parameters of the DrawPolygon subroutine

DrawPolgygon starts by saving the picture box's current ScaleMode and scale parameters. These values will be restored after displaying the Polygon, just before the subroutine exits. Because the Polygon function uses pixels for its coordinates, the ScaleMode for the control is set to 3 - pixels. A Select Case statement determines the shape of the object. Each object has its own subroutine to load the coordinates of the polygon's verticies.

Using DrawTriangle as an example, the three corners of the shape are stored in the Ply array. The parameter nPoints is returned with the number of corners, or vertices. Note that DrawTriangle doesn't actually draw the object, it only stores the object's coordinates. The For...Next loop adjusts the returned coordinates so that the object is centered around the current position in the picture box. If we didn't do this, the object would always be drawn in the picture box's upper left corner.

The Windows API function SetPolyFillMode determines how complex polygons are filled in. Its second parameter can take one of two values, WINDING or ALTERNATE. The WINDING value specifies that the entire polygon is to be filled in; ALTERNATE only fills in every other enclosed surface. To see the effect of this parameter, change the WINDING constant to ALTERNATE and notice how the five-pointed star (Shape = 5) fill has changed.

DrawPolygon is called from the picture box's Paint event subroutine. Using the Paint event to draw not only displays the shapes automatically at application startup, but also whenever the picture box becomes visible after being minimized or hidden.

### Comments

For nonfilled polygons, the Windows API function, Polyline, can be used instead. It has the same parameters as Polygon.

When an application calls the Polygon function, the entire array of Points needs to be passed as a parameter. To do this with a user-defined data type, you simply use the first element as the function parameter.

## 5.12 ⬤ How do I...

## Build a line chart?

### Problem

How can I draw a Line Chart in Visual Basic similar to the ones created by my Windows spreadsheet program?

### Technique

Visual Basic provides an excellent vehicle for creating all kinds of professional-looking business graphics. The Visual Basic drawing and print methods are used to draw the text, grids, and lines for this application. The Windows API Polygon function in How-To 5.11 Fill complex objects, is used to create the graphical symbols.

### Steps

Open and run LINEGRPH.MAK. It will draw a sample line chart as shown in Figure 5-27. Click on the Exit menu to leave the application.

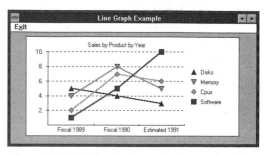

**Figure 5-27** The Linegrph business graphic

The project may be created by entering the objects and code as detailed in the following steps. This project makes use of the code in the Polyline module, entry of which is described in Steps 6 through 13 of the Polygon project.

1. Create a new project called LINEGRPH.MAK. Create a new form with the objects and properties listed in Table 5-17, and save it as LINEGRPH.FRM.

| Object | Property | Setting |
|--------|----------|---------|
| Form | FormName | LineGraph |
| | BackColor | &H00C0C0C0& |
| Picture box | Name | P |

**Table 5-17**  Linegraph project form's objects and properties

2. Using the Menu Design window, create a menu for the form with the attributes from Table 5-18.

| Caption | Name |
|---------|------|
| Exit | Quit |

**Table 5-18**  Linegraph menu attributes

3. Select the project's Global module, enter the following code, and save it as LINEGRPH.BAS. This defines the constants, data structures, and Windows API calls needed to draw the graphic symbols.

```
Type POINTAPI
      X As Integer
      Y As Integer
End Type

'  PolyFill() Modes
Global Const ALTERNATE = 1
Global Const WINDING = 2

Declare Sub Polygon Lib "GDI" (ByVal hDC As Integer, lpPoints As POINTAPI, ⇐
ByVal nCount As Integer)
Declare Sub SetPolyFillMode Lib "GDI" (ByVal hDC As Integer, ByVal ⇐
nPolyFillMode As Integer)

'    Shape constants
Global Const PG_TRIANGLE = 1
Global Const PG_INV_TRIANGLE = 2
```

```
Global Const PG_DIAMOND = 3
Global Const PG_SQUARE = 4
Global Const PG_STAR = 5
```

4. Place the following constant in the Declarations section of the form. The POLYSIZE constant specifies the height and width, in pixels, of the graphical symbols.

```
Const POLYSIZE = 10
```

5. Put the following subroutine in the General section of the LineGraph form. This subroutine contains the data and descriptions used to draw the line graph.

```
Sub Display_Graph ()
Const CATEGORIES = 3
Const Series = 4
Const MAX_VALUE = 10

Static Desc$(CATEGORIES), Values(CATEGORIES, Series), ⇐
   Series_names$(Series)
   P.MousePointer = 11
   Desc$(1) = "Fiscal 1991"
   Desc$(2) = "Fiscal 1992"
   Desc$(3) = "Estimated 1993"
   Display_grid "Sales by Product by Year", CATEGORIES, Desc$(), 5, MAX_VALUE

   Values(1, 1) = 5: Values(1, 2) = 4: Values(1, 3) = 2: Values(1, 4) = 1
   Values(2, 1) = 4: Values(2, 2) = 8: Values(2, 3) = 7: Values(2, 4) = 5
   Values(3, 1) = 3: Values(3, 2) = 5: Values(3, 3) = 6: Values(3, 4) = 10
   Display_Lines CATEGORIES, Values(), Series, MAX_VALUE

   Series_names$(1) = "Disks"
   Series_names$(2) = "Memory"
   Series_names$(3) = "Cpus"
   Series_names$(4) = "Software"
   Display_Legend Series, Series_names$()
   P.MousePointer = 0
End Sub
```

6. Place the following subroutine in the General section of the LineGraph form. This subroutine draws the graphical legend at the right side of the line chart.

```
Sub Display_Legend (NSeries As Integer, Sname() As String)
   P.Fillstyle = 0                              ' Solid blocks
   Theight% = P.TextHeight(Sname(1))      ' Get text height

'   Center Legend in the middle of the Graph height.
'   For each item in the series, draw a small box and the description.
'   Legends are separated by 1.5 times the text height.

   StartY = 50 + (Theight% * 1.5 * NSeries) / 2
   For Series% = 1 To NSeries
```

*continued on next page*

*continued from previous page*

```
      P.FillColor = QBColor(Series% + 8)
      P.CurrentX = 107
      P.CurrentY = StartY - 4
      DrawPolygon P, Series%, POLYSIZE, QBColor(Series% + 8)

      P.CurrentY = StartY
      P.CurrentX = 112
      P.Print Sname(Series%)
      StartY = StartY - Theight% * 1.5
   Next Series%
End Sub
```

7. Place the following subroutine in the General section of the LineGraph form. This subroutine draws the background grid.

```
Sub Display_grid (Title As String, NCategory As Integer, Description() ⇐
As String, Nvalues As Integer, Maxvalue As Single)
Dim I As Integer

' Set scale so graph portion is scaled 0-100 on x- and y-axes.
' Print title in center of the graph grid.
' Draw x-axis and y-axis lines.

   P.Scale (-15, 120)-(140, -15)
   P.CurrentX = (100 - P.TextWidth(Title)) / 2
   P.CurrentY = 105 + P.TextHeight(Title)
   P.Print Title            ' Print bar graph title
   P.Line (0, 0)-(0, 100)   ' Draw x-axis
   P.Line (0, 0)-(100, 0)   ' Draw y-axis

' For each of the grid values, draw a solid tick mark to the left of axis.
' Then draw solid dashed line across entire graph width (0-100).
' Print value of grid line right justified next to tick marks.

   For I = 1 To Nvalues              ' Draw grid lines
      P.Drawstyle = 0
      Yvalue% = 100# * I / Nvalues
      P.Line (-1, Yvalue%)-(0, Yvalue%)    ' y-axis tick marks
      P.Drawstyle = 2
      P.Line (0, Yvalue%)-(100, Yvalue%)   ' y-axis grid dashed grid lines
      Value$ = Format$(Maxvalue * I / Nvalues, "#,##0.#")
      P.CurrentX = -3 - P.TextWidth(Value$)            ' Right justify text
      P.CurrentY = Yvalue% + P.TextHeight(Value$) / 2  ' Center veritcally
      P.Print Value$;           ' y axis values
   Next I

' For each category, draw a small tick mark on x-axis.
' Center and print category description.

   For I = 1 To NCategory       ' Print category descriptions
      P.Drawstyle = 0
      Xvalue = 100 * I / NCategory
      P.Line (Xvalue, -1)-(Xvalue, 2)  ' x-axis tick marks
      P.CurrentY = -2
      P.CurrentX = Xvalue - 50 / NCategory - P.TextWidth(Description(I)) / 2
```

```
      P.Print Description(I)
   Next I
End Sub
```

8. Place the following subroutine in the General section of the LineGraph form. It will compute the line positions and draw them on top of the grid.

```
Sub Display_Lines (NCategory As Integer, Values(), NSeries As Single, ⇐
   Maximum As Single)
  Dim Series As Integer, Cat As Integer
   P.Fillstyle = 0

' For each series in the PictureBox, P, draw the connecting line from
'  previous category to current category.
' Position x-coordinate in center of category, y-coordinate based on value
'  for the point.
' Then draw the ploygon shape to denote the series at left-side of line segment.
' Finally, draw the last shape on a line.
'
   P.DrawWidth = 1
   For Series = 1 To NSeries
     PreviousX = 50 / NCategory
     PreviousY = Values(1, Series) * 100 / Maximum
     For Cat = 2 To NCategory
        NewX = PreviousX + 100 / NCategory
        NewY = Values(Cat, Series) * 100 / Maximum
        P.DrawWidth = 2
        P.Line (PreviousX, PreviousY)-(NewX, NewY), QBColor(Series + 8)
        P.CurrentX = PreviousX
        P.CurrentY = PreviousY
        DrawPolygon P, Series, POLYSIZE, QBColor(Series + 8)
        PreviousX = NewX
        PreviousY = NewY
     Next Cat
     P.CurrentX = PreviousX
     P.CurrentY = PreviousY
     DrawPolygon P, Series, POLYSIZE, QBColor(Series + 8)
   Next Series
End Sub
```

9. Place the following subroutine in the Paint event subroutine of the LineGraph form. The line graph will be displayed whenever the picture box needs to be painted.

```
Sub Form_Paint ()
   Display_Graph
End Sub
```

10. Place the following subroutine in the Quit menu event subroutine of the LineGraph form. This subroutine allows for graceful exit from the application.

```
Sub Quit_Click ()
    End
End Sub
```

11. Add the POLYLINE.BAS file from the directory using the Add File option from Visual Basic's File menu. This module contains the drawing routines for the symbols used on the graph and legend. The code for this module is detailed in steps six through twelve of How-To 5.11 Fill complex objects.

### How It Works

The Display_Graph subroutine is used to set up the data, category, and series descriptions, and invoke the drawing subroutines. These subroutines, Display_Grid, Display_Lines, and Display_Legend, all draw their respective components on a picture box, called "P," forming the complete line graph.

Data in the Display_Graph subroutine is kept by series within each category. Each series is represented by a single line, while categories are sections on the x-axis. In this example, the four series represent sales by class of product while the three categories are fiscal years. Data is stored in the Values array, with category as the first subscript and series as the second.

The Display_Grid subroutine draws the background grid, chart title, and category descriptions. Using Visual Basic's custom scaling capability enables us to draw the graph on any sized picture box. The lines of the graph are drawn within a 100 by 100 unit area, with point 0,0 at the intersection of the x- and y-axes. The actual scaling parameters are set from -15 to 140 for the width and -15 to 120 for the height. The additional scaling units leave room for drawing the chart title, category descriptions, legend, and so on. The subroutine's comments explain the use of each parameter.

The Display_Lines subroutine draws the colored graph lines, one for each of the series. Each line is drawn as a series of lines starting and ending in the middle of each category. The DrawPolygon subroutine draws the graphical symbols. The size of the graphical symbols is determined by the POLYSIZE constant. You can change this constant to alter the symbol size without affecting the rest of the line chart. Note that the values for the QBColor function start at nine to produce a brighter, more colorful graph.

The Display_Legend subroutine also uses the DrawPolygon subroutine to create the graphical symbols.

### Comments

The width of the lines on the chart can be changed by adjusting the number in the P.DrawWidth = 2 statement in the Display_Lines subroutine.

If the drawing is to be done on a monochrome device, you may want to set the DrawStyle property for each series line instead of changing the line's color.

## 5.13  How do I...

## Build a bar chart?

### Problem

Now that I've seen how to do a line chart, I'm ready for a bar graph, one that allows series to be charted. How can I do this?

### Technique

A bar graph is made up of three components: a background grid, the bars themselves, and a legend. Visual Basic's capability to accurately draw and position text, lines, and boxes in a picture box provides all the capabilities needed for this project.

### Steps

Open and run BARGRAPH.MAK. Click on the Display-Graph menu item to draw the sample graph as shown in Figure 5-28. To change the sample data, alter the code in the Display_Graph_Click event subroutine. The Bargraph project may be created by entering the objects and code in the following steps.

1. Create a new project called BARGRAPH.MAK. Create a new form with the objects and properties shown in Table 5-19, and save it as BARGRAPH.FRM.

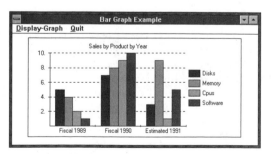

**Figure 5-28** Bargraph project at run time

| Object | Property | Setting |
|--------|----------|---------|
| Form | Caption | Bar Graph Example |
| | FormName | Bargraph |
| Picture box | AutoRedraw | True |
| | Name | P |
| | FontBold | False |
| | FontName | Helv |

**Table 5-19** Bargraph project form's objects and properties

2. Create a menu for the Bargraph form using the Menu Design window with the captions and control names shown in Table 5-20.

| Caption | Name |
|---------|------|
| &Display-Graph | Display_Graph |
| &Quit | Quit |

**Table 5-20** Bargraph menu

3. Put the following code in the Display_Graph_Click event subroutine of the form. This is the name of the routine the menu Display-Graph will call. This subroutine defines all the values that will be drawn, including their descriptions and titles. The constant, CATEGORIES, indicates how many different sets of data will be displayed. In this example, there are three categories, corresponding to the three fiscal years displayed. The SERIES constant is used to specify how many bars will appear in each category. The constant, MAX_VALUE, is used to scale the bars.

```
Sub Display_Graph_Click ()
Const CATEGORIES = 3
Const SERIES = 4
Const MAX_VALUE = 10

Static Desc$(CATEGORIES), Values(CATEGORIES, SERIES),   ⇐
            Series_names$(SERIES)
   Desc$(1) = "Fiscal 1989"
   Desc$(2) = "Fiscal 1990"
   Desc$(3) = "Estimated 1991"
   Display_grid "Sales by Product by Year", CATEGORIES, Desc$(), 5, MAX_VALUE

   Values(1, 1) = 5: Values(1, 2) = 4: Values(1, 3) = 2: Values(1, 4) = 1
   Values(2, 1) = 7: Values(2, 2) = 8: Values(2, 3) = 9: Values(2, 4) = 10
   Values(3, 1) = 3: Values(3, 2) = 9: Values(3, 3) = 1: Values(3, 4) = 5
```

```
      Display_bars CATEGORIES, Values(), SERIES, MAX_VALUE

      Series_names$(1) = "Disks"
      Series_names$(2) = "Memory"
      Series_names$(3) = "Cpus"
      Series_names$(4) = "Software"
      Display_Legend SERIES, Series_names$()
End Sub
```

4. Put the following code in the Display_grid subroutine located in the General section of the form. It will draw the graph's grid, title, and category descriptions in the picture box control.

```
Sub Display_grid (Title As String, Ncategory As Integer, Description() ⇐
      As String, Nvalues As Integer, Maxvalue As Single)
Dim I As Integer

' Set scale so graph portion is scaled 0-100 on x- & y-axis.
' Print title in center of the graph grid.
' Draw x- & y-axis lines.

      P.Scale (-15, 120)-(140, -15)
      P.Currentx = (100 - P.TextWidth(Title)) / 2
      P.Currenty = 105 + P.TextHeight(Title)
      P.Print Title                       ' Print bar graph title
      P.Line (0, 0)-(0, 100)              ' Draw x-axis
      P.Line (0, 0)-(100, 0)              ' Draw y-axis

' For each of the grid values, draw a solid tick mark to the left of axis.
' Then draw solid dashed line across entire graph width (0-100).
' Print value of grid line right justified next to tick marks.

      For I = 1 To Nvalues                    ' Draw grid lines
          P.Drawstyle = 0
          Yvalue% = 100# * I / Nvalues
          P.Line (-1, Yvalue%)-(0, Yvalue%)    ' y-axis tick marks
          P.Drawstyle = 2
          P.Line (0, Yvalue%)-(100, Yvalue%)   ' y-axis grid dashed grid lines
          Value$ = Format$(Maxvalue * I / Nvalues, "#,##0.#")
          P.Currentx = -3 - P.TextWidth(Value$)   ' Right justify text
          P.Currenty = Yvalue% + P.TextHeight(Value$) / 2 ' Center vertically
          P.Print Value$;           ' y-axis values
      Next I

' For each category, draw a small tick mark on x-axis.
' Center and print category description.

      For I = 1 To Ncategory                    ' Print category descriptions
          P.Drawstyle = 0
          Xvalue = 100 * I / Ncategory
          P.Line (Xvalue, -1)-(Xvalue, 2) ' x-axis tick marks
          P.Currenty = -2
```

*continued on next page*

*continued from previous page*

```
      P.Currentx = Xvalue - 50 / Ncategory - P.TextWidth(Description(I)) / 2
      P.Print Description(I)
   Next I
End Sub
```

5. Put the following code in the Display_bars subroutine of the General section of the form. This subroutine draws the bar on picture box, P. Increasing the SEPARATION constant's value will put additional space between each of the category groups.

```
Sub Display_bars (Ncategory As Integer, Values(), Nseries As Single, ⇐
Maximum As Single)
  Const SEPARATION = 25                         ' Percentage to separate bars
  Dim Series As Integer, Cat As Integer
   Catwidth = 100 / Ncategory
   Barwidth = Catwidth * (100 - SEPARATION ) / (100 * Nseries) ⇐
   P.Fillstyle = 0

' For each category compute the starting x position.
' Line function leaves CurrentX at right side of box
' so each bar will display adjacent to the previous one.

   For Cat = 1 To Ncategory
      P.Currentx = Catwidth * Cat - Catwidth / 2 - (Barwidth * Nseries) / 2
      For Series = 1 To Nseries
         P.Currenty = 0                         ' Reset to graph baseline
         P.Fillcolor = QBColor(Series + 8)' Bright colors
         P.Line Step(0, 0)-Step(Barwidth, Values(Cat, Series) * 100 / ⇐
   Maximum), , B
      Next Series
   Next Cat
End Sub
```

6. Put the following code in the Display_Legend subroutine of the General section of the form. This code draws the legend to the left of the bar graph.

```
Sub Display_Legend (Nseries As Integer, Sname() As String)
    P.Fillstyle = 0                             ' Solid blocks
    Theight% = P.TextHeight(Sname(1))           ' Get text height

' Center Legend in the middle of the Graph height.
' For each item in the series, draw a small box, followed by the
' description.
' Legends are separated by 1.5 times the text height.

    Starty = 50 + (Theight% * 1.5 * Nseries) / 2
    For Series% = 1 To Nseries
       P.Fillcolor = QBColor(Series% + 8)
       P.Line (102, Starty)-Step(8, -Theight%), , B   ' Legend Box
       P.Currenty = Starty
       P.Currentx = 112
       P.Print Sname(Series%)
       Starty = Starty - Theight% * 1.5
    Next Series%
End Sub
```

7. Put the following code in the Quit_Click event subroutine so that the user can gracefully exit the program.

```
Sub Quit_Click ()
    End
End Sub
```

### How It Works

This project demonstrates the ease with which Visual Basic can position and draw lines, boxes, and text. The user-defined scale prevents us from having to worry about physical screen dimensions; all graphic and text positioning is performed relative to our own scale.

To keep the project manageable, the program has been divided into four subroutines:

● Display_Graph_Click sets up the values to be graphed, as well as category and series descriptions. It then calls the following three functions.

● Display_grid draws the background axis, title, and category description.

● Display_bars graphs the bars.

● Display_legend displays the legend to the left of the bar graph.

The Display_Graph_Click subroutine is called from the menu. It sets up three data elements: Category descriptions, Series descriptions, and Data values. Categories are groups of data. In our example, there are three categories, each representing a different fiscal year of data. Category descriptions are kept in the Desc$ array. You can change the number of categories by altering the CATEGORIES constant.

The SERIES constant identifies the number of different bars that will be drawn in each category. This example has four series, each representing a different type of computer commodity. The series descriptions are kept in the Series_names$ array.

Each category and series combination requires a data value, to be kept in the Values array. The first subscript is the category number, the second is the series number.

The Display_grid subroutine sets up a user-defined scale so that all positioning of text, lines, and boxes can be done without regard to the picture box's physical screen dimensions. The actual graph portion is scaled to 100 by 100 units. The additional areas on the top, left, bottom, and right are for the graph title, y-axis values, category names, and bar legend, respectively. The balance of the Display_grid function draws the x- and y-axes with solid lines, and grids as dashed lines. The Nvalues parameter determines the number of grid lines to draw. In the example, five grid lines are drawn. The Maxvalue parameter is the maximum y-axis value.

The Display_bars subroutine displays each of the bars by series within category. The SEPARATION constant is the percentage of the category width to leave between bar groups. The sample value of 25 percent means that one-quarter of the category width will be blank. The remaining three-quarters will be occupied by the bar graphs. Increasing SEPARATION will shrink the width of the bars and increase the amount of blank area between each category. Bar colors are picked by using a different QBColor value for each series. QBColors 8 to 15 are used because this will produce brightly shaded bars.

The Display_Legend subroutine draws the legend on the right side of the graph. The legend is centered between the top and bottom of the y-axis. The colors for each series match those used in the Display_bars subroutine.

### Comments

Unfortunately, if the resulting bar graph is to be printed on a black-and-white device (such as a laser printer), the colors will print black. In this case, you might want to include the following code line in the Series% For…Next loop of the Display_bars and Display_Legend subroutines to create different types of fill patterns within the bars.

```
P.Fillstyle = Series%
```

## 5.14  How do I...

## Build a pie chart?

### Problem

I would like to be able to display pie charts as part of my Visual Basic applications. How can this be done without purchasing an add-on graphics package?

### Technique

The Circle function can be used not only to draw complete circles but also to create segments or slices of a circle. By drawing slices of appropriate sizes and filling them with different colors, we can use Visual Basic to draw pie charts.

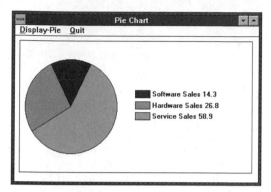

**Figure 5-29** Piechart project

### Steps

Open and run PIECHART.MAK. Click on the Display-Pie menu item to draw the sample chart as shown in Figure 5-29. To change the sample data, alter the code in the Display_Graph_Click event subroutine. The Piechart project may be created by entering the objects and code in the following steps.

1. Create a new project called PIECHART.MAK. Create a new form with the objects and properties shown in Table 5-21, and save it as PIECHART.FRM.

| Object | Property | Setting |
|--------|----------|---------|
| Form | Caption | Pie Chart |
| | FormName | Piechart |
| Picture box | AutoRedraw | True |
| | Name | P |

**Table 5-21** Piechart project form's objects and properties

2. Create a menu for the form as shown in Table 5-22 using the Menu Design window.

| Caption | Name |
|---------|------|
| &Display-Pie | Display_Pie |
| &Quit | Quit |

**Table 5-22** Piechart project menu

3. Place the following constant declaration for PI in the General section of the form.

```
Const PI = 3.141593
```

4. Put the following code in the Display_Pie_Click event subroutine. This subroutine sets up the descriptions and values that will be graphed. The SLICES constant defines the number of segments to chart. The Desc and Values arrays should be changed to reflect the data you want to plot.

```
Sub Display_Pie_Click ()
Const SLICES = 3
Static Desc(SLICES) As String, Values(SLICES) As Single
    Desc(1) = "Software Sales": Values(1) = 8
    Desc(2) = "Hardware Sales": Values(2) = 15
    Desc(3) = "Service Sales": Values(3) = 33
    Draw_circle SLICES, Values(), Desc()
End Sub
```

5. Enter the code for the Draw_circle subroutine. This code calculates the percentages for each slice and draws the slices. It also appends each slice's percentage to its description for display by the Draw_legend subroutine.

```
Sub Draw_circle (Ndata As Integer, Values() As Single, Desc() As String)
Static Newdesc(10)  As String              ' Description with percentages
Dim Total As Single, Startr As Single
Dim N As Integer
    P.Cls
    P.Refresh
    P.Fillstyle = 0
    Total = 0
    Startr = PI / 2

'  Calculate total so we can compute percentage for each pie slice.
'  Calculate percentage of slice, add to description.
'  Draw each slice starting with center of first slice at the top.

    For N = 1 To Ndata
        Total = Total + Values(N)       ' Need total for whole of pie
    Next N
    For N = 1 To Ndata
        Percentage = Values(N) / Total
        Newdesc(N) = Desc(N) + " " + Format$(100 * Percentage, "##0.0") + ""
        Radians = 2 * PI * Percentage
        If N = 1 Then
            Startr = PI / 2 - Radians / 2
            Endr = PI / 2 + Radians / 2
        Else
            Startr = Endr
            Endr = Startr + Radians
        End If
        P.Fillstyle = 0          ' Solid block
        P.Fillcolor = QBColor(N + 8)
        Startr = Adjust_Radians(Startr)
        Endr = Adjust_Radians(Endr)
'
'  Center of Circle is halfway from top, and a little more than one-fifth in.
```

```
'  This will leave room for the legend on the right. Radius is one-fifth
'  of picture box width.
      P.Circle (P.Scalewidth / 4.5, P.Scaleheight / 2), P.Scalewidth ⇐
/ 5, , -Startr, -Endr
   Next N
   Display_legend Ndata, Newdesc$()
End Sub
```

6. Enter the code for the Display_legend subroutine. This subroutine draws legend boxes and displays the description for each of the pie segments.

```
Sub Display_legend (Nseries As Integer, Sname() As String)
Dim Theight As Integer, N As Integer
'  Draws the legend to the left of the circle, centered with the circle.
'  Legends spaced 1.5 times textheight apart.
   P.Fillstyle = 0
   Theight = P.TextHeight(Sname(1))
   Starty = P.Scaleheight / 2 - (Theight * 1.5 * Nseries) / 2
   For N = 1 To Nseries
      P.Fillcolor = QBColor(N + 8)
      P.Line (P.Scalewidth / 2, Starty)-Step(P.Scalewidth / 16, ⇐
Theight),    , B
      P.Currenty = Starty
      P.Currentx = P.Scalewidth / 2 + P.Scalewidth / 14
      P.Print Sname(N)
      Starty = Starty + Theight * 1.5
   Next N
End Sub
```

7. Enter the code for the Adjust_Radians function. This function converts radians that are less than zero or greater than $2*\pi$ into a range of 0 to $2*\pi$.

```
Function Adjust_Radians (Radian As Single) As Single
Dim Pi2 As Single

'  Convert values <0 or > 2 * PI back to be between 0 and 2 * PI
'  If radian = 0 then adjust to small value, circle doesn't like zero
'  radians.
   Pi2 = 2 * PI
   If Radian >= Pi2 Then Radian = Radian - Pi2
   If Radian < 0 Then Radian = Radian + Pi2
   If Radian < .001 Then Radian = .001
   Adjust_Radians = Radian
End Function
```

8. Enter the code for the Quick_Click event subroutine. This function allows a user to exit from the application.

```
Sub Quit_Click ()
   End
End Sub
```

## How It Works

Visual Basic is an excellent tool for developing all kinds of business oriented graphs. This project uses the Circle function to draw the multiple slices of a pie chart in a picture box.

The program starts when the user clicks on the Display-Pie menu. The subroutine associated with this event, Display_Pie_Click, sets up the description and values for each of the pie's slices. The SLICES constant defines the total number of slices to be drawn. Calling the Draw_circle subroutine will actually draw the pie chart.

The real work in this program is handled in the Draw_circle subroutine. Its first order of business is to set up some constants. The constant PI (3.14159) is used extensively in this program and is defined in the General section of the form. The Total variable is set to the sum of the individual values, and will be used to compute the percentages of each slice.

The For...Next loop draws each of the pie slices, putting the center of the first slice at the top of the circle. Because the Circle statement expects its parameters in radians, all arithmetic is performed in that unit of measure. There are $2*\pi$ (6.2832) radians in a circle. If you normally think in degrees, zero degrees is equivalent to zero radians, and 360 degrees is equivalent to $2*\pi$ radians. For the Visual Basic Circle statement, zero radians points to the three o'clock position. Increasing radians move counterclockwise around the circle.

The circumference of each slice is its percentage of the total divided into the circumference of the entire circle, $2*\pi$ radians. The starting position of the first pie slice is centered around the top of the circle, which is $\pi/2$ radians. Each successive slice begins where the previous one left off.

The Circle statement's radian parameters must lie in the range of zero to $2*\pi$. Remember, because radians are points on a circle, $-\pi/2$ radians is equivalent to $3*\pi/2$ radians. The Adjust_Radians function brings the Startr and Endr parameters into range if needed. When you draw a pie slice with the Circle statement, note that the radians must be expressed as negative numbers. This is a required feature of the Visual Basic Circle statement when filling in parts of a circle. For each pie slice, the Fillcolor is set to a different color using the QBColor function. Values 8 through 15 produce attractive, bright colors.

The Display_Legend subroutine draws the legends starting in the right half of the picture box. Like the Draw_circle subroutine, it too adjusts its positioning parameters based on the actual dimensions of the picture box.

## Comments

The Circle statement accepts single-precision floating-point values for the radian parameters. That is why all radian-oriented variables have been declared as Single.

Unfortunately, if the resulting pie chart is to be printed on a black-and-white device (such as a laser printer), each slice will print as a solid black. In this case, you might want to include the following code line after the P.FillColor= statement in the Draw_circle and Display_legend subroutines. This will create different types of fill patterns within each pie slice.

```
P.FillStyle = N%
```

## 5.15  How do I...

Build a video-based slide show?

### Problem

I would like to create a video-based business presentation. The presentation should have that professional look with different types of transition effects between screens, and variable delays between each slide. The program should be able to open Microsoft .BMP or .WMF metafiles.

### Technique

Visual Basic can load and display the graphical image files created by most Windows text, drawing, and paint programs. Using Visual Basic in conjunction with the Windows API function BitBlt, we can manage the way these images are drawn to create a professional-looking presentation.

### Steps

Open and run SLIDSHOW.MAK. A form like that shown in Figure 5-30 will be displayed. Click on the Add command button to bring up a File Open dialog box. Select a graphic file, either bitmap or metafile, to include in the slide show. There are four metafiles on the distribution disk you can practice with. If you are building this from scratch, you could use the PARTY.BMP or CHESS.BMP wallpaper bitmaps in your Windows directory. To change a slide's sequence in the list box, delay, or transition, select

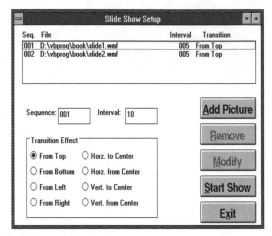

**Figure 5-30** The Slideshow project in action

one of the entries in the list box and alter the appropriate text box or choose a new transition radio button. The new values are posted to the list box by clicking on the Modify button. To remove an item from the list box, select it and then click on the Remove button.

To start the slide show, click on the Start Show command button. Each slide will be drawn on a full screen in the same order as displayed in the list box. The Slideshow form will appear again after the current slide is finished being drawn. To stop the show, click the left-hand mouse button at anytime.

To create the Slideshow project, enter the objects and code as detailed in the following steps. There are three forms involved in this project: the Slide Show form that is used for designing and editing the slide sequence, the display form that shows the actual images, and a File Open dialog box from How-To 3.7 Build a simple editor that searches for text.

1. Create a new project called SLIDSHOW.MAK and a form with the objects and properties shown in Table 5-23. The appearance of the form should match the one in Figure 5-30. Note that a picture box control, Picture1, is not visible. You may place it anywhere on the form as long as it does not cover another control. Its size is not important. Save the form as SLIDSHOW.FRM.

| Object | Property | Setting |
| --- | --- | --- |
| Form | FormName | Slideshow |
| | Caption | Slide show setup |
| Label | Name | Label1 |
| | AutoSize | True |

| Object | Property | Setting |
|---|---|---|
| | Caption | Seq ... File ... Interval .. Transition |
| Label | Name | Label2 |
| | Caption | Interval |
| | AutoSize | True |
| Label | Name | Label3 |
| | Caption | Sequence: |
| | AutoSize | True |
| List box | Name | List1 |
| | Sorted | True |
| Text box | CtlName | TxtSeq |
| | Text | 001 |
| Text box | Name | TxtInt |
| | Text | 010 |
| Frame | Name | Frame1 |
| | Caption | Transition Effect |
| Command button | Name | CmdAdd |
| | Caption | &Add Picture |
| | FontSize | 14 |
| Command button | Name | CmdRemove |
| | Caption | &Remove |
| | FontSize | 14 |
| Command button | Name | CmdModify |
| | Caption | &Modify |
| | FontSize | 14 |
| Command button | Name | CmdStart |
| | Caption | &Start-Show |
| | FontSize | 14 |
| Command button | Name | CmdExit |
| | Caption | E&xit |
| | FontSize | 14 |
| Picture box | IName | Picture1 |
| | Visible | False |

**Table 5-23** SlideShow project form's objects and properties

2. Place the option buttons as shown in Table 5-24 inside Frame1. This is done by selecting Frame1 on the form, choosing the option button control from the toolbox, and then drawing the option buttons inside

Frame1. The option buttons are drawn correctly if they move as a group with their surrounding frame.

| Object | Property | Setting |
| --- | --- | --- |
| Option button | Name | Option1 |
| | Caption | From Top |
| | Index | 0 |
| Option button | Name | Option1 |
| | Caption | From Bottom |
| | Index | 1 |
| Option button | Name | Option1 |
| | Caption | From Left |
| | Index | 2 |
| Option button | Name | Option1 |
| | Caption | From Right |
| | Index | 3 |
| Option button | Name | Option1 |
| | Caption | Horz to Center |
| | Index | 4 |
| Option button | Name | Option1 |
| | Caption | Horz from Center |
| | Index | 5 |
| Option button | Name | Option1 |
| | Caption | Vert to Center |
| | Index | 6 |
| Option button | Name | Option1 |
| | Caption | Vert from Center |
| | Index | 7 |

**Table 5-24** Filefind transition option button controls

3. Select the Global module, enter the following code, and save it as SLIDSHOW.BAS. This defines the API functions and constants as well as Visual Basic variables that are shared between the forms in this project.

```
'
' API Declarations.
'
Declare Sub BitBlt Lib "GDI" (ByVal hDestDC As Integer, ByVal X As ⇐
Integer, ByVal Y As Integer, ByVal nWidth As Integer, ByVal nHeight As ⇐
Integer, ByVal hSrcDC As Integer, ByVal XSrc As Integer, ByVal YSrc As ⇐
Integer, ByVal dwRop As Long)
```

```
Declare Function SendMessage Lib "User" (ByVal hWnd As Integer, ByVal ⇐
wMsg As Integer, ByVal wParam As Integer, lParam As Any) As Long
Global Const WM_USER = &H400
Global Const LB_SETTABSTOPS = (WM_USER + 19)
Global Const SRCCOPY = &HCC0020 ' (DWORD) dest = source
'
'  Visual Basic Declarations.
'
Global TransDesc(7) As String
Global TB As String
Global Const TRUE = -1
Global Const FALSE = 0
```

4. Enter the following code into the Form_Load event subroutine. This code sets up the global values used by the forms.

```
Sub Form_Load ()
'
'  Load constant strings at startup.
   CmdStart.Enable = FALSE
   TB = Chr$(9)
   TransDesc(0) = "From Top"
   TransDesc(1) = "From Bottom"
   TransDesc(2) = "From Left"
   TransDesc(3) = "From Right"
   TransDesc(4) = "Hz to Center"
   TransDesc(5) = "Hz from Center"
   TransDesc(6) = "Vt to Center"
   TransDesc(7) = "Vt from Center"
End Sub
```

5. Enter the following code into the Form_Paint event subroutine. This routine sets up the tab stops in the list box.

```
Sub Form_Paint ()
ReDim ListTabs(3) As Integer
Dim Retval As Long, As Integer
'
' Set tab stops in the list box.
' Disable command buttons that can't be used at this time.
'
   ListTabs(1) = 20
   ListTabs(2) = 180
   ListTabs(3) = 200
   Retval = SendMessage(List1.hWnd, LB_SETTABSTOPS, 3, ListTabs(1))
   CmdRemove.Enabled = FALSE
   CmdModify.Enabled = FALSE
End Sub
```

6. Enter the following code into the CmdAdd_Click event subroutine. This subroutine calls the Open_dlg form to let the user select a file to include in the slide show. The file is checked to ensure that Visual Basic can read it as a picture file.

```
Sub CmdAdd_Click ()
'
' Add a new filename to the ListBox using the Dialog box.
' If LoadPicture() gives error, then file isn't an icon, metafile, or bitmap.
' Default to 10 seconds and Vertical from Center transition.
'
    Open_dlg.Show 1
    If Open_dlg.Tag = "" Then Exit Sub
    On Error Resume Next
    Picture1.Picture = LoadPicture(Open_dlg.Tag)
    If Err Then
        MsgBox "Selected File is not a Picture", 48
        Exit Sub
    End If
    TxtSeq.Text = Format$(List1.ListCount * 10 + 10, "000")
    List1.AddItem TxtSeq.Text + TB + Open_dlg.Tag + TB + TxtInt.Text + ⇐
    TB + TransDesc(7)
 CmdStart.Enable = TRUE
' Disable the Remove and Modify CommandButtons until user selects new entry.
'
    CmdRemove.Enabled = FALSE
    CmdModify.Enabled = FALSE
End Sub
```

7. Enter the following code into the List1_Click event subroutine. This handles the processing when the user selects an item in the list box.

```
Sub List1_Click ()
'
' User has selected an entry to remove or modify.
' Enable Command Buttons.
' Parse the current entry into components and load controls.
' Notice how we set the correct OptionButton.
'
    CmdRemove.Enabled = TRUE
    CmdModify.Enabled = TRUE
    Slide$ = List1.List(List1.ListIndex)
    Firsttab = InStr(Slide$, TB)
    Secondtab = InStr(Firsttab + 1, Slide$, TB)
    Thirdtab = InStr(Secondtab + 1, Slide$, TB)

    TxtSeq.Text = Left$(Slide$, Firsttab - 1)
    TxtInt.Text = Mid$(Slide$, Secondtab + 1, Thirdtab - Secondtab - 1)

    For I = 0 To 7
        If Mid$(Slide$, Thirdtab + 1) = TransDesc(I) Then
            Option1(I).Value = TRUE
        End If
    Next I
End Sub
```

8. Enter the following code into the CmdModify_Click event subroutine. This routine updates the currently selected slide with the values from the text box and option button controls.

```
Sub CmdModify_Click ()
'
' Re-write current value of controls back to list box.
' If nothing selected then exit the subroutine.
'
    If List1.ListIndex < 0 Then Exit Sub
    Slide$ = List1.List(List1.ListIndex)
    FirstTab = InStr(Slide$, TB)
    Secondtab = InStr(FirstTab + 1, Slide$, TB)
    Thirdtab = InStr(Secondtab + 1, Slide$, TB)
    File$ = Mid$(Slide$, FirstTab, Secondtab - FirstTab + 1)
    List1.RemoveItem List1.ListIndex
    For I = 0 To 7
        If Option1(I).Value Then
            Desc$ = TransDesc(I)
        End If
    Next I
'
' Reformat sequence number.
' Rebuild the slide record.
'
    TxtSeq.Text = Format$(Val(TxtSeq.Text), "000")
    Slide$ = TxtSeq.Text + File$ + TxtInt.Text + TB + Desc$
'
' Add item back to Listbox.
' Calculate new sequence numbers.
' Disable Remove and Modify controls.
'
    List1.AddItem Slide$
    ReorderList
    CmdRemove.Enabled = FALSE
    CmdModify.Enabled = FALSE
End Sub
```

9. Enter the following code into the CmdRemove_Click event subroutine. This routine deletes the currently selected line from the list box.

```
Sub CmdRemove_Click ()
'
' Delete selected item from List box.
'
    If List1.ListIndex >= 0 Then
        List1.RemoveItem List1.ListIndex
        CmdRemove.Enabled = FALSE
        CmdModify.Enabled = FALSE
        ReorderList
    End If
End Sub
```

10. Enter the following code into the CmdStart_Click event subroutine. This routine starts the slide show.

```
Sub CmdStart_Click ()
'
' Show other form for show. Use Modal option.
'
    Slidescreen.Show 1
End Sub
```

11. Enter the following code into the CmdExit_Click event subroutine. This code allows the users a graceful way to exit the application.

```
Sub CmdExit_Click ()
    End
End Sub
```

12. Put the following code in the ReorderList subroutine located in the General section of the form. It will update the list box with new sequence numbers.

```
Sub ReorderList ()
Dim I As Integer, FirstTab As Integer
'
' Change the sequence numbers in the List box.
' Increment each line by 10.
'
    For I = 0 To List1.ListCount - 1
        Slide$ = List1.List(I)
        FirstTab = InStr(1, Slide$, TB)
        OldSequence$ = Left$(Slide$, FirstTab - 1)
        NewSequence$ = Format$(I * 10 + 10, "000")
        If OldSequence$ <> NewSequence$ Then
            List1.RemoveItem I
            Slide$ = NewSequence$ + Mid$(Slide$, FirstTab)
            List1.AddItem Slide$, I    ' Specify index to not reorder list.
        End If
    Next I
If List1.ListCount = 0 then CmdStart.Enable = FALSE
End Sub
```

13. Open a second form for this project, using the New Form option from the File menu. This form is used to display the video graphics. Enter the objects and properties for this form as listed in Table 5-25 and save the form as SLIDESCR.FRM. The layout of the controls is shown in Figure 5-31, however, their size and placement are not important.

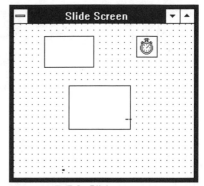

**Figure 5-31** Slidescr form

| Object | Property | Setting |
| --- | --- | --- |
| Form | FormName | Slidescreen |
| | BorderStyle | 0 - None |
| Picture box | Name | P1 |
| Picture box | Name | P2 |
| Timer | Name | Timer1 |

**Table 5-25** Slidescr project form's objects and properties

14. The following code in the Declarations section of the Slidescr form defines the shared variables.

```
Dim SlideCounter As Integer
Dim Transition As String
```

15. Enter the following code into the Form_Load event subroutine of the Slidescr form. This code expands the form and picture boxes to cover the entire screen.

```
Sub Form_Load ()
'
' Resize form to fill entire screen.
' Set background to black.
'
    SlideScreen.Top = 0
    SlideScreen.Left = 0
    SlideScreen.Width = Screen.Width
    SlideScreen.Height = Screen.Height
    SlideScreen.BackColor = &H0
'
' Set PictureBoxes to fill entire screen.
```

*continued on next page*

*continued from previous page*

```
'  P1 is setup box, P2 is display box.
'  P1 is invisible but has a bitmap.
'  P2 is visible but has no bitmap.
'  Set PictureBox scales to 3 - Pixels.
'
    P1.Visible = FALSE
    P1.AutoRedraw = TRUE
    P1.Top = 0
    P1.Left = 0
    P1.Width = SlideScreen.ScaleWidth
    P1.Height = SlideScreen.ScaleHeight
    P1.ScaleMode = 3
    P1.BackColor = &H0          ' Black

    P2.Top = 0
    P2.Left = 0
    P2.Width = SlideScreen.ScaleWidth
    P2.Height = SlideScreen.ScaleHeight
    P2.ScaleMode = 3
    P2.BackColor = &H0          ' Black
'
' Enable Timer and set SlideCounter.
' Timer1.Interval = 1
    Timer1.Enabled = TRUE
' Timer1.Interval = 1
    SlideCounter = 1
End Sub
```

16. Enter the following code into the Timer1_Timer event subroutine of the Slidescr form. This subroutine extracts the next slide name from the list, retrieves the picture, and calls the CopyPicture subroutine to display the slide.

```
Sub Timer1_Timer ()
'
'  Disable Timer so we aren't interrupted.
'  Retrieve next slide from list. Wrap to beginning at end.
'
    Timer1.Enabled = FALSE
    SlideCounter = SlideCounter + 1
    If SlideCounter >= Slideshow.List1.ListCount Then
        SlideCounter = 0
    End If
    Slide$ = Slideshow.List1.List(SlideCounter)
'
'  Parse List into Filename$, Interval, and Transition fields.
'  Load P1 (invisible one) with picture.
'
    Tab1 = InStr(Slide$, TB) + 1
    tab2 = InStr(Tab1, Slide$, TB) + 1
    Tab3 = InStr(tab2, Slide$, TB) + 1
    Filename$ = Mid$(Slide$, Tab1, tab2 - Tab1 - 1)
    Timer1.Interval = Val(Mid$(Slide$, tab2, Tab3 - tab2)) * 1000
```

```
    Transition = Mid$(Slide$, Tab3)
    P1.Picture = LoadPicture(Filename$)
'
' Copy the picture from P1 to P2 using transitions.
' Enable Timer for next picture.
'
    CopyPicture
    Timer1.Enabled = TRUE
End Sub
```

> 17. Put the following code in the CopyPicture subroutine located in the General section of the form. It will copy the new slide to the screen using the desired transition.

```
Sub CopyPicture ()
Dim Pixels As Integer, Row As Integer, Column As Integer, J As Integer
'
' Subroutine to copy from invisible PictureBox (P1) to visible one (P2).
' All routines use BitBlt to copy a line or row at a time.
' Because Windows copies rows faster than vertical lines, Pixels are
' doubled for vertical transitions.
'
    Pixels = 2
    Select Case Transition
      Case TransDesc(0):           ' From Top
        For Row = 0 To P2.ScaleHeight Step Pixels
            BitBlt P2.hDC, 0, Row, P2.ScaleWidth, Pixels, P1.hDC, 0, Row, SRCCOPY
        Next Row

      Case TransDesc(1):           ' From Bottom
        For Row = P2.ScaleHeight To 0 Step -Pixels
            BitBlt P2.hDC, 0, Row, P2.ScaleWidth, Pixels, P1.hDC, 0, Row, SRCCOPY
        Next Row

      Case TransDesc(2):           ' From Left
        Pixels = 2 * Pixels
        For Column = 0 To P2.ScaleWidth Step Pixels
            BitBlt P2.hDC, Column, 0, Pixels, P2.ScaleHeight, P1.hDC, ⇐
                Column, 0, SRCCOPY
        Next Column

      Case TransDesc(3):           ' From Right
        Pixels = 2 * Pixels
        For Column = P2.ScaleWidth To 0 Step -Pixels
            BitBlt P2.hDC, Column, 0, Pixels, P2.ScaleHeight, P1.hDC, ⇐
            Column, 0, SRCCOPY
        Next Column

      Case TransDesc(4):           ' Horizontal to Center
        Pixels = 2 * Pixels
        For Column = 0 To (P2.ScaleWidth + Pixels) / 2 Step Pixels
            J = P2.ScaleWidth - Column
            BitBlt P2.hDC, Column, 0, Pixels, P2.ScaleHeight, P1.hDC, ⇐
```

*continued on next page*

*continued from previous page*

```
                Column, 0, SRCCOPY
            BitBlt P2.hDC, J, 0, Pixels, P2.ScaleHeight, P1.hDC, J, 0, SRCCOPY
        Next Column

      Case TransDesc(5):          ' Horizontal from Center
        Pixels = 2 * Pixels
        For Column = P2.ScaleWidth / 2 To 0 Step -Pixels
           J = P2.ScaleWidth - Column
           BitBlt P2.hDC, Column, 0, Pixels, P2.ScaleHeight, P1.hDC, ⇐
                Column, 0, SRCCOPY
           BitBlt P2.hDC, J, 0, Pixels, P2.ScaleHeight, P1.hDC, J, 0, SRCCOPY
        Next Column

      Case TransDesc(6):          ' Vertical to Center
        For Row = 0 To (P2.ScaleHeight + Pixels) / 2 Step Pixels
           J = P2.ScaleHeight - Row
           BitBlt P2.hDC, 0, Row, P2.ScaleWidth, Pixels, P1.hDC, 0, Row, SRCCOPY
           BitBlt P2.hDC, 0, J, P2.ScaleWidth, Pixels, P1.hDC, 0, J, SRCCOPY
        Next Row

      Case TransDesc(7):          ' Vertical from Center
        For Row = P2.ScaleHeight / 2 To 0 Step -Pixels
           J = P2.ScaleHeight - Row
           BitBlt P2.hDC, 0, Row, P2.ScaleWidth, Pixels, P1.hDC, 0, Row, SRCCOPY
           BitBlt P2.hDC, 0, J, P2.ScaleWidth, Pixels, P1.hDC, 0, J, SRCCOPY
        Next Row
    End Select

End Sub
```

18. Enter the following code into the P2_Click event subroutine of the Slidescr form. This subroutine allows the user to stop the slide show by clicking the mouse.

```
Sub P2_Click ()
'
' Use clicks anywhere on screen to stop the show.
'
   Unload SlideScreen
End Sub
```

19. Add the OPEN_DLG.FRM file from the SLIDSHOW directory. This form is a general-purpose File Open dialog box. Specifications of this form's object, properties, and code are detailed in steps 10 through 17 of How-To 3.7 Build a simple editor that searches for text.

### How It Works

Visual Basic has some exceptional capabilities which enable your application to load and display graphics from bitmap files and Windows metafiles. These graphical files can be created by many Windows applications or even by Visual Basic itself using its SavePicture function. This project enables the user to build a video-based slide show by setting up a list of these graphical files, along with the length of time to display each file, and the transition effect to use between slides. Included in the Visual Basic directory SLIDESHOW are four graphics files, SLIDE1.WMF through SLIDE4.WMF, which can be used with this project.

### Start with the Slideshow Form

When the application starts, the Slideshow Form_Load event subroutine loads the global constants. The Form_Paint event subroutine sets the tab stops in the list box and disables the Remove and Modify command button controls.

When the user clicks the Add button, the CmdAdd_Click event subroutine transfers control to a File Open dialog box. This lets the user select an image file to include in the slide show. An attempt is made to load the selected file into the picture box, Picture1. If an error is not received during the LoadPicture function, the file is considered a valid graphic and it, along with the default interval and transition, is added as a single entry to the list box. Because Picture1 is not visible, this processing takes place without the user noticing it.

To change the sequence number, interval, or transition effect, the user selects one of the items in the list box. The List1_Click event subroutine traps this event and loads the values from the selected item into the text boxes and appropriate radio button. The Remove and Modify controls are then enabled, indicating that the selected item may be deleted or modified. If the Modify button is clicked, the CmdModify_Click event subroutine updates the current list box item with the new values from the controls. When the list is modified or an item removed, the ReorderList subroutine is called to create a new set of sequence numbers for the list.

### Transferring Control to the Display Form

The slide show is started by clicking on the Start button, which transfers control to the Slidescr form. The form is started with the Modal option so that it keeps control until the show is terminated by the user.

There are two picture boxes on the Slidescr form: P1 and P2. Both of these picture boxes and the form itself are expanded in the Form_Load event to fill the entire screen. Note that P1 is made invisible but has its AutoRedraw property enabled. With AutoRedraw turned on, pictures loaded into P1 are stored by Windows in memory even if they aren't displayed on screen.

The Timer1_Timer event subroutine retrieves the next slide description from the SlideShow form list box. The data is parsed into the Filename, Interval, and Transition fields. The invisible picture box, P1, is loaded with the image from the file, and CopyPicture is called to transfer the image from the nonvisible picture box to P2, the visible picture box.

The CopyPicture subroutine moves the image from picture box P1 to P2 using the BitBlt Windows API function. BitBlt is used to copy rectangular areas from one device context to another. Because P1's AutoRedraw is enabled, the device context handle returned by Visual Basic, P1.hDC, points to the in-memory copy of the picture. Each transition effect has its own For...Next Loop and BitBlt call. The parameters for BitBlt are shown in Table 5-26.

| Parameter | Description |
| --- | --- |
| hDestDC | Device context of the destination |
| nX | Upper left corner of destination rectangle. Value in pixels |
| nY | Top of the destination rectangle. Value in pixels |
| nWidth | Width of the rectangle to be copied, in pixels |
| nHeight | Height of the rectangle to be copied, in pixels |
| hSrcDC | Device context of the source |
| nXSrc | Upper left corner of source rectangle. Value in pixels |
| nYSrc | Top of the source rectangle. Value in pixels |
| dwRop | Operation to perform. SRCCOPY is the operation code used to perform a pixel-for-pixel copy from the source to the destination device context |

**Table 5-26** The BitBlt API parameters

### Comments

In the CopyPicture subroutine, each of the different transition effects loops by row or column, copying pixels in picture box P1 to the same location in P2. The Pixels variable determines the copying speed by varying the width of the rectangle being copied. The value of Pixels is doubled when the subroutine is transferring by column, because Windows performs copies by column slower than it does by row. The doubling keeps the copy speed approximately the same for all the different transitions. You may want to experiment with different values for this variable.

## 5.16  How do I...

## Easily draw shapes on a form?

### Problem

I would like to create graphics on my form using simple shapes such as rectangles and ovals. Is there an easy way to create simple graphics with Visual Basic?

### Technique

Visual Basic version 3.0 added a Shape control to the set of standard controls. The Shape control can be used to create rectangles, squares, ovals, circles, rounded rectangles, and rounded squares. Shape controls have a number of properties that can be used to control color, size and location, fill style, and draw mode.

This How-To shows how to use various properties of Shape controls. You can experiment with different shapes and DrawMode settings to see how these properties affect the resulting image using this How-To.

### Steps

Open and run SHAPES.MAK. Select the Add menu and choose one of the listed shapes. The shape you choose will be drawn in the upper left corner of the form. The shape will have six "handles" drawn in a rectangular pattern around the new shape. You will see the mouse cursor change to one of the sizing icons as it is moved over a handle. To "grab a handle" you move the mouse pointer over top of the handle. Once you have grabbed a handle you can resize the selected shape by dragging the handle on the form. You can also move shapes on the form. By pressing and holding down the left mouse button somewhere on the shape you can drag it to a new location. A Shape that you've placed on the form can be selected whenever you want to change its size or location. To select a shape simply click anywhere on the shape, and the selection handles will appear.

Figure 5-32 shows the Shapes project in action. To re-create the image displayed in Figure 5-32, run the Shapes project. Next, add and position the three circles. Then select each circle and use the Color menu to change its color so that the top-most circle is red, the left-most circle is green, and the right-most circle is blue. Finally, select each circle and use the Draw Mode menu to change its draw mode to Xor.

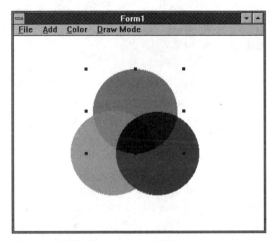

**Figure 5-32** Shapes project in action

1. Create a new project named SHAPES.MAK. Add the objects and properties listed in Table 5-27 to Form1.

| Object | Property | Setting |
|--------|----------|---------|
| Form | BackColor | &H00FFFFFF& |
| | Caption | "Form1" |
| | Height | 5355 |
| | KeyPreview | -1 'True |
| | Left | 1035 |
| | LinkTopic | "Form1" |
| | Name | Form1 |
| | ScaleHeight | 311 |
| | ScaleMode | 3 'Pixel |
| | ScaleWidth | 446 |
| | Top | 1200 |
| | Width | 6810 |
| Shape | BorderColor | &H000000FF& |
| | BorderWidth | 1 |
| | FillColor | &H000000FF& |
| | FillStyle | 0 'Solid |
| | Height | 73 |
| | Index | 0 |
| | Left | 200 |

| Object | Property | Setting |
|--------|----------|---------|
|  | Name | Shapes |
|  | Shape | 3 'Circle |
|  | Top | 104 |
|  | Visible | 0 'False |
|  | Width | 65 |
| Shape | BorderColor | &H00C0C0C0& |
|  | BorderWidth | 2 |
|  | FillColor | &H00000000& |
|  | FillStyle | 1 'Transparent |
|  | Height | 73 |
|  | Left | 184 |
|  | Name | TrackingRectangle |
|  | Top | 104 |
|  | Visible | 0 'False |
|  | Width | 97 |

**Table 5-27** Shapes project's objects and properties

2. Add the array of PictureBoxes in Table 5-28 to Form1. These picture boxes are the handles displayed when an object is selected. Since these picture boxes are sized during the Form1_Load event subroutine, the design-time size is not important.

| Object | Property | Setting |
|--------|----------|---------|
| Picture box | BackColor | &H00000000& |
|  | BorderStyle | 0 'None |
|  | Index | 0 |
|  | MousePointer | 8 'Size NW SE |
|  | Name | Handles |
|  | ScaleMode | 3 'Pixel |
| Picture box | BackColor | &H00000000& |
|  | BorderStyle | 0 'None |
|  | Index | 1 |
|  | MousePointer | 7 'Size N S |
|  | Name | Handles |
|  | ScaleMode | 3 'Pixel |

*continued on next page*

*continued from previous page*

| Object | Property | Setting |
|---|---|---|
| Picture box | BackColor | &H00000000& |
| | BorderStyle | 0 'None |
| | Index | 2 |
| | MousePointer | 6 'Size NE SW |
| | Name | Handles |
| | ScaleMode | 3 'Pixel |
| Picture box | BackColor | &H00000000& |
| | BorderStyle | 0 'None |
| | Index | 3 |
| | MousePointer | 9 'Size W E |
| | Name | Handles |
| | ScaleMode | 3 'Pixel |
| Picture box | BackColor | &H00000000& |
| | BorderStyle | 0 'None |
| | Index | 4 |
| | MousePointer | 8 'Size NW SE |
| | Name | Handles |
| | ScaleMode | 3 'Pixel |
| Picture box | BackColor | &H00000000& |
| | BorderStyle | 0 'None |
| | Index | 5 |
| | MousePointer | 7 'Size N S |
| | Name | Handles |
| | ScaleMode | 3 'Pixel |
| Picture box | BackColor | &H00000000& |
| | BorderStyle | 0 'None |
| | Index | 6 |
| | MousePointer | 6 'Size NE SW |
| | Name | Handles |
| | ScaleMode | 3 'Pixel |
| Picture box | BackColor | &H00000000& |
| | BorderStyle | 0 'None |
| | Index | 7 |
| | MousePointer | 9 'Size W E |
| | Name | Handles |
| | ScaleMode | 3 'Pixel |

**Table 5-28** Array of picture boxes used as handles

3. Use the Menu Design window to create the menus shown in Table 5-29 for Form1.

| Control Name | Caption | Index |
|---|---|---|
| FileMenu | "&File" | |
| ----FileExit | "E&xit" | |
| AddMenu | "&Add" | |
| ----AddShape | "&Rectangle" | 0 |
| ----AddShape | "&Square" | 1 |
| ----AddShape | "&Oval" | ? |
| ----AddShape | "&Circle" | 3 |
| ----AddShape | "Rounded Rec&tangle" | 4 |
| ----AddShape | "Rounded S&quare" | 5 |
| ColorMenu | "&Color" | |
| ----Color | "&Red" | 0 |
| ----Color | "&Green" | 1 |
| ----Color | "&Blue" | 2 |
| ----Color | "&White" | 3 |
| ----Color | "B&lack" | 4 |
| DrawModeMenu | "&Draw Mode" | |
| ----DrawModeSel | "Black" | 0 |
| ----DrawModeSel | "Not Merge Pen" | 1 |
| ----DrawModeSel | "Mask Not Pen" | 2 |
| ----DrawModeSel | "Not Copy Pen" | 3 |
| ----DrawModeSel | "Mask Pen Not" | 4 |
| ----DrawModeSel | "Invert" | 5 |
| ----DrawModeSel | "Xor Pen" | 6 |
| ----DrawModeSel | "Not Mask Pen" | 7 |
| ----DrawModeSel | "Mask Pen" | 8 |
| ----DrawModeSel | "Not Xor Pen" | 9 |
| ----DrawModeSel | "Nop" | 10 |
| ----DrawModeSel | "Merge Not Pen" | 11 |
| ----DrawModeSel | "Copy Pen" | 12 |
| ----DrawModeSel | "Merge Pen Not" | 13 |
| ----DrawModeSel | "Merge Pen" | 14 |
| ----DrawModeSel | "White" | 15 |

**Table 5-29** Menus for Shapes project

4. Create a new module named SHAPES.BAS, and add the following code to the General Declarations section of SHAPES.BAS. This code declares the Windows API functions used by SHAPES.MAK.

```
Declare Function SetCapture Lib "User" (ByVal hWnd As Integer) As Integer
Declare Sub ReleaseCapture Lib "User" ()
```

5. Add the following code to the General Declarations section of Form1. This code declares variables global to Form1.

```
Option Explicit
'
' This variable tells us which shape is currently selected. It is -1 if there
' is no current shape.
'
Dim selected As Integer
'
' This variable is set to True when Form1 has captured the mouse
'
Dim haveCapture As Integer
'
' This variable is set to True when we are moving a shape
'
Dim movingShape As Integer
'
' This variable lets us know what handle has been grabbed
'
Dim handle As Integer
'
' The elements of these arrays are set to either True or False. There is one
' element in each array for each possible shape.
'
Dim shapesInUse(100) As Integer
Dim shapesLoaded(100) As Integer
'
' colorChecked contains the menu index of the currently selected color
'
Dim colorChecked As Integer
'
' modeChecked contains the menu index of the currently selected mode
'
Dim modeChecked As Integer
'
' This array is initialized during the Form1_Load event subroutine to contain
' the RGB values corresponding to the color menu indices
'
Dim fillColors(5) As Long
'
' When a shape is being moved these variables contain the offset of the mouse
' pointer from the upper left corner of the shape.
'
Dim xOffset As Integer
Dim yOffset As Integer
```

6. Add the following code to the Click event subroutine of AddShape. The following code accomplishes two tasks. First, a shape control must be found for the new shape. The arrays shapesLoaded and shapesInUse are used to determine if a deleted shape is available for reuse. If no shape can be reused, then a new one is loaded. Once a shape control has been allocated for the new shape, it is initialized, displayed, and selected.

```
Sub AddShape_Click (Index As Integer)
   Dim i As Integer
   '
   ' Set currently selected shape to none
   '
   selected = -1
   '
   ' Scan loaded shapes looking for a free one
   '
   i = 0
   Do While (i < 100 And selected = -1)
      If (shapesLoaded(i) And Not shapesInUse(i)) Then
         '
         ' Unused, loaded shape ... use it
         '
         selected = i
         shapesInUse(i) = True
      Else
         If (shapesLoaded(i) <> True) Then
            '
            ' No free loaded shapes ... load another
            '
            Load shapes(i)
            shapesLoaded(i) = True
            shapesInUse(i) = True
            selected = i
         End If
      End If
      i = i + 1
   Loop

   '
   ' If we found an available shape, initialize and select it
   '
   If (selected <> -1) Then
      shapes(selected).Shape = Index
      shapes(selected).DrawMode = modeChecked + 1
      shapes(selected).FillColor = fillColors(colorChecked)
      shapes(selected).BorderColor = fillColors(colorChecked)
      shapes(selected).FillStyle = 0
      shapes(selected).Top = 0
      shapes(selected).Left = 0
      shapes(selected).Width = 50
      shapes(selected).Height = 50
      shapes(selected).Visible = True
```

*continued on next page*

*continued from previous page*

```
        HideHandles
        DrawSelectionRectangle
    Else
        MsgBox "All 100 shapes in use."
    End If
End Sub
```

7. Add the following subroutine to the General section of Form1. This subroutine checks the Color and Draw Mode menu items for the currently selected shape.

```
Sub CheckMenus ()
    Dim i As Integer
    '
    ' The Draw Mode menu can be set directly from the shape's
    ' draw mode
    '
    DrawModeSel(shapes(selected).DrawMode - 1).Checked = True
    '
    ' To check the correct color menu item we have to convert
    ' the RGB value into an array index
    '
    For i = 0 To 4
        If (shapes(selected).FillColor = fillColors(i)) Then
            color(i).Checked = True
            Exit For
        End If
    Next
End Sub
```

8. Add the following code to the Click event subroutine of Color. The current selection is unchecked and the new selection is checked. If there is a currently selected shape, its color is changed.

```
Sub Color_Click (Index As Integer)
    '
    ' Uncheck previous menu item, check new one, save current color
    '
    color(colorChecked).Checked = False
    colorChecked = Index
    color(colorChecked).Checked = True
    '
    ' Change color of currently selected shape (if any)
    '
    If (selected <> -1) Then
        shapes(selected).FillColor = fillColors(Index)
        shapes(selected).BorderColor = fillColors(Index)
    End If
End Sub
```

9. Add the following code to the Click event subroutine of DrawModeSel. The current selection is unchecked and the new selection is checked. If there is a currently selected shape, its draw mode is changed.

```
Sub DrawModeSel_Click (Index As Integer)
    '
    ' Uncheck previous menu item, check new one, and save new mode
    '
    DrawModeSel(modeChecked).Checked = False
    modeChecked = Index
    DrawModeSel(modeChecked).Checked = True
    '
    ' If a shape is selected change its draw mode
    '
    If (selected <> -1) Then
        shapes(selected).DrawMode = Index + 1
    End If
End Sub
```

10. Add the following subroutine to the General section of Form1. This subroutine places the handles around the currently selected shape.

```
Sub DrawSelectionRectangle ()
    Dim x As Integer
    Dim y As Integer
    Dim h As Integer
    Dim w As Integer

    x = shapes(selected).Left
    y = shapes(selected).Top
    w = shapes(selected).Width
    h = shapes(selected).Height
    '
    ' Move the handles. We start at the upper-left corner
    ' and move around clockwise.
    '
    handles(0).Top = y - 2
    handles(0).Left = x - 2
    handles(1).Top = y - 2
    handles(1).Left = w / 2 + x - 2
    handles(2).Top = y - 2
    handles(2).Left = x + w - 3
    handles(3).Top = h / 2 + y - 2
    handles(3).Left = x + w - 3
    handles(4).Top = h + y - 3
    handles(4).Left = x + w - 3
    handles(5).Top = h + y - 3
    handles(5).Left = w / 2 + x - 2
    handles(6).Top = h + y - 3
    handles(6).Left = x - 2
    handles(7).Top = h / 2 + y - 2
    handles(7).Left = x - 2

    ShowHandles
End Sub
```

11. Add the following code to the KeyUp event subroutine of Form1. Form1's key preview property is set to True to let us intercept keys typed by the user. Whenever the user presses the (DEL) key (integer value 46), this subroutine deletes the current shape.

```
Sub Form_KeyUp (keycode As Integer, Shift As Integer)
    '
    ' If the delete key is being released and some shape is
    ' selected then zap it!
    '
    If (keycode = 46 And selected <> -1) Then
        shapes(selected).Visible = False
        shapesInUse(selected) = False
        selected = -1
        HideHandles
    End If
End Sub
```

12. Add the following code to the Load event subroutine of Form1. This subroutine sizes the handles and initializes variables.

```
Sub Form_Load ()
    Dim i   As Integer
    '
    ' Initialize selection handles
    '
    For i = 0 To 7
        handles(i).Width = 5
        handles(i).Height = 5
        handles(i).Visible = False
    Next i
    '
    ' Make note that the first shape is loaded
    '
    shapesLoaded(0) = True
    '
    ' Pick black as the default color, copy pen as default draw mode
    '
    colorChecked = 4
    modeChecked = 12
    Color(4).Checked = True
    DrawModeSel(12).Checked = True
    '
    ' Make table to translate menu selection to correct color
    '
    fillColors(0) = RGB(255, 0, 0)
    fillColors(1) = RGB(0, 255, 0)
    fillColors(2) = RGB(0, 0, 255)
    fillColors(3) = RGB(255, 255, 255)
    fillColors(4) = RGB(0, 0, 0)
End Sub
```

13. Add the following code to the MouseDown event subroutine of Form1. This subroutine scans the array of loaded shapes to find one that contains the point identified by the passed arguments x and y. If a shape is located, the trackingRectangle is displayed around the selected shape.

```
Sub Form_MouseDown (Button As Integer, Shift As Integer, x As Single, ⇐
   y As Single)
   Dim i As Integer
   Dim l As Integer
   Dim t As Integer
   Dim w As Integer
   Dim h As Integer

   HideHandles
   '
   ' Assume we won't be moving a shape
   '
   movingShape = False
   '
   ' Now, for each loaded shape
   '
   For i = 0 To 99
      If (shapesLoaded(i) <> True) Then
         Exit Sub
      End If
      '
      ' If the current shape is in use, check to see if the
      ' mouse is in the shapes bounding box.
      '
      If (shapesInUse(i) And x > shapes(i).Left And x < shapes(i).Left + ⇐
      shapes(i).Width) Then
         If (y > shapes(i).Top And y < shapes(i).Top + shapes(i).Height)
Then
            If (selected <> -1) Then
               shapes(selected).ZOrder 1
            End If
            '
            ' Found a shape to select, check appropriate menu
            ' selections for selected shape and move it to the top
            ' of the z-order
            '
            UncheckMenus
            selected = i
            CheckMenus
            shapes(selected).ZOrder 0
            '
            ' Initialize position of tracking rectangle
            '
            t = shapes(selected).Top
            l = shapes(selected).Left
            h = shapes(selected).Height
```

*continued on next page*

*continued from previous page*

```
              w = shapes(selected).Width
              trackingRectangle.Move l, t, w, h
              trackingRectangle.Visible = True
              movingShape = True
              '
              ' Make note of the offset from the mouse pointer to
              ' the upper left corner of the bounding box
              '
              xOffset = x - shapes(selected).Left
              yOffset = y - shapes(selected).Top
         End If
      End If
   Next
End Sub
```

14. Add the following code to the MouseMove event subroutine of Form1. If a handle has been grabbed, haveCapture will be True: and in this case the trackingRectangle's size will be changed. Otherwise, if the trackingRectangle has been moving, the trackingRectangle is moved to follow the mouse's current location.

```
Sub Form_MouseMove (Button As Integer, Shift As Integer, x As Single, ⇐
  y As Single)
  '
  ' The mouse is moving. If capture is set the user has grabbed one
  ' of the handles, so change the shape's size
  '
  If haveCapture Then
     Select Case handle
        Case 0
           MoveNWCorner CInt(x), CInt(y)
        Case 1
           MoveNorthBorder CInt(x), CInt(y)
        Case 2
           MoveNECorner CInt(x), CInt(y)
        Case 3
           MoveEastBorder CInt(x), CInt(y)
        Case 4
           MoveSECorner CInt(x), CInt(y)
        Case 5
           MoveSouthBorder CInt(x), CInt(y)
        Case 6
           MoveSWCorner CInt(x), CInt(y)
        Case 7
           MoveWestBorder CInt(x), CInt(y)
     End Select
  '
  ' Else move the shape if required
  '
  ElseIf movingShape Then
     trackingRectangle.Left = x - xOffset
     trackingRectangle.Top = y - yOffset
```

```
      End If
End Sub
```

15. Add the following code to the MouseUp event subroutine of Form1. If the trackingRectangle has been active (haveCapture = True or movingShape = True), then the current shape is moved or resized to match the trackingRectangle.

```
Sub Form_MouseUp (Button As Integer, Shift As Integer, x As Single, y As ⇐
Single)
    Dim t As Integer
    Dim l As Integer
    Dim w As Integer
    Dim h As Integer
    '
    ' If we have moved or sized a shape finish up and reselect it
    '
    If haveCapture Or movingShape Then
        trackingRectangle.Visible = False
        t = trackingRectangle.Top
        l = trackingRectangle.Left
        h = trackingRectangle.Height
        w = trackingRectangle.Width
        '
        ' Only the tracking rectangle was being changed while the
        ' mouse button was down. Now update the shape's size or location
        '
        shapes(selected).Move l, t, w, h
        DrawSelectionRectangle
        If (haveCapture) Then
            ReleaseCapture
            haveCapture = False
        Else
            movingShape = False
        End If

        shapes(selected).ZOrder 0
    End If
End Sub
```

16. Add the following code to the MouseDown event subroutine of Handles. This subroutine is called when the user presses a mouse button while the mouse is over one of the handles. The handles are then hidden and the tracking rectangle made visible. Finally, the Windows API function SetCapture is used to direct subsequent mouse input to Form1.

```
Sub Handles_MouseDown (Index As Integer, Button As Integer, Shift As ⇐
Integer, x As Single, y As Single)
    Dim wRtn As Integer
```

*continued on next page*

*continued from previous page*

```
    handle = Index
    '
    ' Make handles invisible
    '
    HideHandles
    '
    ' Initialize position of tracking rectangle
    '
    trackingRectangle.Top = shapes(selected).Top
    trackingRectangle.Left = shapes(selected).Left
    trackingRectangle.Height = shapes(selected).Height
    trackingRectangle.Width = shapes(selected).Width
    trackingRectangle.Visible = True
    haveCapture = True
    wRtn = SetCapture(form1.hWnd)
End Sub
```

17. Add the following code to the General section of Form1. This subroutine is used to hide the handles when they are not needed.

```
Sub HideHandles ()
    Dim i As Integer

    For i = 0 To 7
        handles(i).Visible = False
    Next
End Sub
```

18. Add the following subroutine to the General section of Form1. This subroutine is called by Form1's MouseMove subroutine when the user moves the east border of the tracking rectangle.

```
Sub MoveEastBorder (x As Integer, y As Integer)
    If x > trackingRectangle.Left Then
        trackingRectangle.Width = x - trackingRectangle.Left
    End If
End Sub
```

19. Add the following subroutine to the General section of Form1. This subroutine is called by Form1's MouseMove subroutine when the user moves the northeast corner of the tracking rectangle.

```
Sub MoveNECorner (x As Integer, y As Integer)
    Dim w As Integer
    Dim h As Integer

    If (x > trackingRectangle.Left) Then
        If (y < trackingRectangle.Top + trackingRectangle.Height) Then
            w = x - trackingRectangle.Left
            h = trackingRectangle.Height + trackingRectangle.Top - y
            trackingRectangle.Move trackingRectangle.Left, y, w, h
        End If
    End If
End Sub
```

20. Add the following subroutine to the General section of Form1. This subroutine is called by Form1's MouseMove subroutine when the user moves the north border of the tracking rectangle.

```
Sub MoveNorthBorder (x As Integer, y As Integer)
    Dim w As Integer
    Dim h As Integer

    If (y < trackingRectangle.Top + trackingRectangle.Height) Then
        w = trackingRectangle.Width
        h = trackingRectangle.Height + trackingRectangle.Top - y
        trackingRectangle.Move trackingRectangle.Left, y, w, h
    End If
End Sub
```

21. Add the following subroutine to the General section of Form1. This subroutine is called by Form1's MouseMove subroutine when the user moves the northwest corner of the tracking rectangle.

```
Sub MoveNWCorner (x As Integer, y As Integer)
    Dim w As Integer
    Dim h As Integer

    If (x < trackingRectangle.Left + trackingRectangle.Width) Then
        If (y < trackingRectangle.Top + trackingRectangle.Height) Then
            w = trackingRectangle.Width + trackingRectangle.Left - x
            h = trackingRectangle.Height + trackingRectangle.Top - y
            trackingRectangle.Move x, y, w, h
        End If
    End If
End Sub
```

22. Add the following subroutine to the General section of Form1. This subroutine is called by Form1's MouseMove subroutine when the user moves the southeast corner of the tracking rectangle.

```
Sub MoveSECorner (x As Integer, y As Integer)
    Dim w As Integer
    Dim h As Integer

    If (x > trackingRectangle.Left And y > trackingRectangle.Top) Then
        w = x - trackingRectangle.Left
        h = y - trackingRectangle.Top
        trackingRectangle.Move trackingRectangle.Left, ⇐
trackingRectangle.Top, w, h
    End If
End Sub
```

23. Add the following subroutine to the General section of Form1. This subroutine is called by Form1's MouseMove subroutine when the user moves the south border of the tracking rectangle.

```
Sub MoveSouthBorder (x As Integer, y As Integer)
    Dim w As Integer
    Dim h As Integer

    If (y > trackingRectangle.Top) Then
        w = trackingRectangle.Width
        h = y - trackingRectangle.Top
        trackingRectangle.Move trackingRectangle.Left, ⇐
trackingRectangle.Top, w, h
    End If
End Sub
```

24. Add the following subroutine to the General section of Form1. This subroutine is called by Form1's MouseMove subroutine when the user moves the southwest corner of the tracking rectangle.

```
Sub MoveSWCorner (x As Integer, y As Integer)
    Dim w As Integer
    Dim h As Integer

    If (x < trackingRectangle.Left + trackingRectangle.Width) Then
        If (y > trackingRectangle.Top) Then
            w = trackingRectangle.Width + trackingRectangle.Left - x
            h = y - trackingRectangle.Top
            trackingRectangle.Move x, trackingRectangle.Top, w, h
        End If
    End If
End Sub
```

25. Add the following subroutine to the General section of Form1. This subroutine is called by Form1's MouseMove subroutine when the user moves the west border of the tracking rectangle.

```
Sub MoveWestBorder (x As Integer, y As Integer)
    Dim w As Integer

    If (x < trackingRectangle.Left + trackingRectangle.Width) Then
        w = trackingRectangle.Width + trackingRectangle.Left - x
        trackingRectangle.Move x, trackingRectangle.Top, w, ⇐
trackingRectangle.Height
    End If
End Sub
```

26. Add the following subroutine to the General section of Form1. This subroutine is used to display the selection handles.

```
Sub ShowHandles ()
    Dim i As Integer

    For i = 0 To 7
        handles(i).Visible = True
    Next
End Sub
```

27. Add the following subroutine to the General section of Form1. This subroutine makes sure that all items in the DrawModeSel and Color menus are not checked.

```
Sub UncheckMenus ()
    Dim i As Integer

    For i = 0 To 15
        DrawModeSel(i).Checked = False
    Next i

    For i = 0 To 4
        color(i).Checked = False
    Next i
End Sub
```

### How It Works

There are six types of actions that a user may carry out with this program: adding a shape, changing a shape's size, changing a shape's location, changing a shape's color, changing a shape's draw mode, and deleting a shape.

When a shape must be added, the array shapesInUse is used to look for a shape that has been deleted. If no shape has been deleted and fewer than 100 shapes have been loaded, a new shape is loaded. Once an available shape has been located, it is initialized using the menu index passed to AddShape.

Shapes are resized by pressing the mouse button on one of the shape's handles and dragging the mouse to a new location. When the mouse button is first pressed over one of the handles, the Handles_MouseDown event subroutine is called. The handles are hidden and the trackingRectangle is moved to the selected shape and made visible. The menu index is saved in the module-level variable "handle." Later, as the mouse is moved, the saved menu index is used to determine how to change the size of the trackingRectangle. Finally, the Windows API function SetCapture is used to capture subsequent mouse input. This is done so that, regardless of what control the mouse is moved over while the button is held down, Form1's MouseMove event subroutine will be called.

Shapes are moved by pressing the mouse button anywhere inside a shape's selection rectangle and dragging the trackingRectangle to a new location. When the mouse pointer is released, the selected shape is moved to the location of the trackingRectangle.

A shape's color is changed when the user selects one of the items from the ColorMenu. The menu item index serves as an index into an array of RGB values. The contents of the array element are assigned to the FillColor property of the selected object.

DrawModes are set directly by assigning the menu item index + 1 to the DrawMode property of the selected shape. One is added to the menu item index because the DrawModeSel array is 0-based and DrawMode properties are numbered 1 through 16.

To delete the selected shape, its Visible property is set to False. The corresponding element of the shapesInUse array is also set to False. When an element of the shapesInUse array is False, the corresponding element of the Shapes array is available to be reused when another shape is added.

### Comments

This How-To could be used as the starting point for an object-oriented paint program like MS-Draw. Object-oriented paint programs are so named because the user can reselect and modify graphic objects. Contrast this approach with that used by Paintbrush. With the Windows Paintbrush program, the image can have circles and other shapes added to it; but once a shape has been added, it becomes part of a bitmap. It is not possible to adjust the size or location of a shape once it has been added to the bitmap.

## 5.17 ● How do I ...

## Create a "magnifying glass" for bitmaps?

### Problem

Getting the appearance of the user interface to look right often hinges on the placement of a few pixels. This is especially true when creating 3D effects for buttons and other objects. The high resolution of monitors in use today makes it difficult to see individual pixels on the display. I would like to have a "magnifying glass" program that lets me magnify any portion of the screen so that I can see how other programs have created graphical elements.

### Technique

Writing a magnifying-glass program is really pretty simple once you are armed with the right Windows API calls. This How-To uses the Windows function GetDC to get a handle to the screen's Device Context. Then, using this handle, the Windows function StretchBlt copies pixels from the screen and magnifies them for display on the form, as shown in Figure 5-33.

**Figure 5-33** The Magnify project in action

### Steps

Open and run MAGNIFY.MAK. After the form has been loaded, you will see that a portion of the screen has been captured and displayed on the form. The right side of the form contains a scroll bar. By moving the scroll-thumb down, you can increase the magnification of the captured image; moving the thumb up reduces the magnification.

To select a new area of the screen, move the mouse over the form and hold down the left mouse button. Now, while continuing to hold the mouse button down, move the mouse outside of the form. A rectangle will appear as you move the mouse outside of the form, and the image inside the rectangle will be magnified and displayed on the form. Release the mouse button when the form contains the area of the screen you want to examine. You can then adjust the magnification as desired.

To create the magnifying glass program, simply do the following.

1. Create a new project called MAGNIFY.MAK. Create a new form with the objects and properties listed in Table 5-30.

| Object | Property | Caption |
|--------|----------|---------|
| Form1 | Caption | "Magnify Screen" |
| | Height | 2475 |
| | Left | 2460 |
| | LinkTopic | "Form1" |

*continued on next page*

*continued from previous page*

| Object | Property | Caption |
|--------|----------|---------|
|  | ScaleHeight | 138 |
|  | ScaleMode | Pixel |
|  | ScaleWidth | 185 |
|  | Top | 1380 |
|  | Width | 2895 |
| VScroll1 | Height | 74 |
|  | LargeChange | 4 |
|  | Left | 166 |
|  | Max | 32 |
|  | Min | 1 |
|  | Top | 0 |
|  | Value | 4 |
|  | Width | 19 |

**Table 5-30** Form1's objects and properties

2. Create a new module and add the following code to the General Declarations section of the module.

```
'
' Define the Rectangle type used by the Windows API library
'
Type rect
    left As Integer
    top As Integer
    right As Integer
    bottom As Integer
End Type
'
' Define the Point type used by the Windows API library
'
Type POINTAPI
    X As Integer
    Y As Integer
End Type
'
' Define contants used in Windows API calls
'
Global Const DSTINVERT = &H550009
Global Const SRCCOPY = &HCC0020
'
' Declare Windows API library calls used
'
Declare Function GetDC Lib "User" (ByVal hWnd As Integer) As Integer
Declare Function ReleaseDC Lib "User" (ByVal hWnd As Integer, ByVal hDC ⇐
```

```
As Integer) As Integer
Declare Function SetCapture Lib "User" (ByVal hWnd As Integer) As Integer
Declare Sub ReleaseCapture Lib "User" ()
Declare Sub ClientToScreen Lib "User" (ByVal hWnd As Integer, lpPoint As⇐
POINTAPI)
Declare Function StretchBlt Lib "GDI" (ByVal hDC%, ByVal X%, ByVal Y%, ⇐
ByVal nWidth%, ByVal nHeight%, ByVal hSrcDC%, ByVal XSrc%, ByVal YSrc%,⇐
ByVal nSrcWidth%, ByVal nSrcHeight%, ByVal dwRop&) As Integer
'
' Note that FastWindowFrame is an undocumented call used by Microsoft and
' other Windows developers.
'
Declare Function FastWindowFrame Lib "GDI" (ByVal hDC As Integer, lpRect⇐
As rect, ByVal xWidth As Integer, ByVal yWidth As Integer, ByVal dwRop3 ⇐
As Long) As Integer
```

3. Add the following to the General Declarations section of Form1.

```
'
' rectCapture contains the location and extent of the area of the
' screen to capture and magnify
'
Dim rectCapture As rect
'
' rectWidth and rectHeight are based on the size of the form and the value of
' the scroll bar, together these determine the extent of rectCapture.
'
Dim rectWidth As Integer
Dim rectHeight As Integer
'
' MouseLocation is updated as the mouse pointer moves about the screen
'
Dim mouseLocation As POINTAPI
'
' track is set to True whenever the left mouse button is pressed and False
' when the button is later released. As long as track is True each mouse move
' will cause a portion of the screen to be captured and displayed on the
' form.
'
Dim track As Integer
```

4. Add the following subroutine to the General section of Form1. This subroutine calculates the location of the capture rectangle. The mouse location is used as the center of a rectangle having width rectWidth and height rectHeight.

```
Sub CalcCaptureRect ()
    '
    ' Calculate the rectangle to magnify, the rectangle is centered
    ' around the current mouse location
    '
    rectCapture.top = mouseLocation.y - (rectHeight / 2)
    rectCapture.left = mouseLocation.x - (rectWidth / 2)
```

*continued on next page*

*continued from previous page*

```
    rectCapture.right = mouseLocation.x + (rectWidth / 2)
    rectCapture.bottom = mouseLocation.y + (rectHeight / 2)
End Sub
```

5. Add the following subroutine to the General section of Form1. This subroutine calculates the width and height of the rectangular area of the screen to be captured.

```
Sub CalcRectangleExtent ()
    '
    ' Calculate the size of the capture rectangle.
    ' Four pixels are added to the width and height because the capture
    ' rectangle is made from lines that are 2 pixels wide.
    '
    rectWidth = (Form1.ScaleWidth - VScroll1.Width) / VScroll1.Value + 4
    rectHeight = (Form1.ScaleHeight / VScroll1.Value) + 4
End Sub
```

6. Add the following subroutine to the General section of Form1. This subroutine is the heart of the program. After getting a handle to the screen's device context, the Windows API function StretchBlt copies and magnifies the screen contents.

```
Sub CaptureScreen ()
    Dim wRtn As Integer
    Dim hDC As Integer
    Dim ratio As Integer
    '
    ' Get the device context of the desktop and copy from the capture
    ' rectangle to the display rectangle. StretchBlt takes care of the
    ' magnification for us! Two pixels are added to the top and left
    ' coordinates of the source rectangle, and four pixels are subtracted
    ' from the width and height, so that the tracking rectangle will not
    ' be copied to the form.
    '
    hDC = GetDC(0)
    wRtn = StretchBlt(Form1.hDC, 0, 0, Form1.ScaleWidth - VScroll1.Width,⇐
        Form1.ScaleHeight, hDC, rectCapture.Left + 2, rectCapture.Top + 2,⇐
        rectWidth - 4, rectHeight - 4, SRCCOPY)
    wRtn = ReleaseDC(0, hDC)
End Sub
```

7. Add the following subroutine to the General section of Form1. This subroutine draws the tracking rectangle on the screen. The function FastWindowFrame used here is one of the undocumented functions that exist in the Windows API. FastWindowFrame corresponds to a required GDI driver entry point and will likely be supported in the future; however, it can always be replaced with equivalent code if necessary. Using the ROP3 code DSTINVERT tells FastWindowFrame to draw

the rectangle by inverting bits on the screen. Before moving the tracking rectangle, this function is called again; inverting the bits a second time restores the orignal image.

```
Sub drawTrackingRectangle ()
    Dim hDC As Integer
    Dim wRtn As Integer
    '
    ' Get the desktop's device context and draw a frame around the
    ' current mouse location
    '
    hDC = GetDC(0)
    wRtn = FastWindowFrame(hDC, rectCapture, 2, 2, DSTINVERT)
    wRtn = ReleaseDC(0, hDC)
End Sub
```

8. Add the following code to the Load event subroutine of Form1. This subroutine places the form in the upper left corner of the screen and then initializes the mouseLocation variable with the location of the screen's center. After Visual Basic has loaded the form a Resize event is fired. Whenever the magnify form receives a Resize event, the area around mouseLocation is copied to the form. By setting the mouseLocation to the center of the screen, the form will initially capture whatever is at the center of the screen.

```
Sub Form_Load ()
    '
    ' Put the form in the upper left corner of the screen
    '
    form1.Top = 0
    form1.Left = 0
    '
    ' Setting the mouse location to the center of the form
    ' results in capturing the image underneath the form
    '
    mouseLocation.x = (screen.Width / 2) / screen.TwipsPerPixelY
    mouseLocation.y = (screen.Height / 2) / screen.TwipsPerPixelX
End Sub
```

9. Add the following code to the MouseDown event subroutine of Form1. This subroutine begins the tracking process. The current mouse location is used to calculate the location of the capture rectangle and the area within the capture rectangle is copied to the screen. The Windows API function SetCapture is used here to capture the mouse. When an application has captured the mouse, Windows will continue to send MouseMove events even after the mouse has been moved outside of the application's window. This allows us to follow the location of the mouse as it is moved around the screen.

```
Sub Form_MouseDown (Button As Integer, Shift As Integer, x As Single, ⇐
   y As Single)
   Dim wRtn As Integer
   '
   ' track is set to True so we will know to erase and redraw
   ' the tracking rectangle as the mouse is moved.
   '
   track = True
   '
   ' Get the client coordinates passed in and convert them
   ' to screen coordinates
   '
   mouseLocation.x = x
   mouseLocation.y = y
   ClientToScreen Form1.hWnd, mouseLocation
   '
   ' Calculate the location and extent of the rectangle to
   ' display on the form
   '
   CalcCaptureRect
   '
   ' Capture the mouse
   '
   wRtn = SetCapture(Form1.hWnd)
   '
   ' Draw the tracking rectangle at the new location
   '
   drawTrackingRectangle
   '
   ' Copy the screen image to the form
   '
   CaptureScreen
End Sub
```

10. Add the following code to the MouseMove event subroutine of Form1. Each time the MouseMove event is fired with the mouse button held down, this subroutine moves the tracking rectangle and captures the part of the screen within its boundaries.

```
Sub Form_MouseMove (Button As Integer, Shift As Integer, x As Single, ⇐
   y As Single)
   Dim wRtn As Integer
   '
   ' The mouse is moving, if the left button is not down we
   ' ignore the move
   '
   If (Not track) Then
       Exit Sub
   End If

   '
   ' The mouse is moving and the left button is held down,
   ' erase the tracking rectangle by redrawing it at its current
```

```
' location
'
drawTrackingRectangle
'
' Calculate new location for tracking rectangle
'
mouseLocation.x = x
mouseLocation.y = y
ClientToScreen Form1.hWnd, mouseLocation
CalcCaptureRect
'
' Draw the tracking rectangle at its new location
'
drawTrackingRectangle
'
' And finally update the form with the screen image within
' the tracking rectangle
'
CaptureScreen
End Sub
```

11. Add the following code to the MouseUp event subroutine of Form1.
This subroutine executes when the mouse button is released.

```
Sub Form_MouseUp (Button As Integer, Shift As Integer, x As Single, y As ⇐
   Single)
   '
   ' If we haven't been tracking then just return.
   '
   If (Not track) Then
      Exit Sub
   End If
   '
   ' Make note that we are no longer tracking, erase the tracking
   ' rectangle, and release the mouse.
   '
   track = False
   drawTrackingRectangle
   ReleaseCapture
End Sub
```

12. Add the following code to the Resize event subroutine of Form1. After sizing
and positioning the scroll bar, a fresh snapshot of the screen is captured.

```
Sub Form_Resize ()
   '
   ' The form has been resized so we resize the scroll bar
   '
   VScroll1.Height = Form1.ScaleHeight
   VScroll1.Left = Form1.ScaleWidth - VScroll1.Width
   '
   ' Calculate the new display rectangle size
   '
   CalcRectangleExtent
```

*continued on next page*

*continued from previous page*

```
'
' Calculate the new capture rectangle size
'
CalcCaptureRect
'
' And grab a new snapshot of the area inside the tracking
' rectangle
'
CaptureScreen
End Sub
```

13. Add the following code to the Change event subroutine of VScroll1. VScroll1 controls the amount of magnification. When this subroutine executes, it calls subroutines to recalculate the size of the source rectangle and captures a snapshot at the new magnification.

```
Sub VScroll1_Change ()
    '
    ' Magnification change, recalculate the rectangles and
    ' take a new snapshot
    '
    CalcRectangleExtent
    CalcCaptureRect
    CaptureScreen
End Sub
```

### How It Works

The Windows API function StretchBlt is central in this program. Like BitBlt, StretchBlt copies rectangular regions from the bitmap of one device context to the bitmap of another device context. The difference between the two functions is that with StretchBlt you specify the size of both the source and destination bitmaps. When the sizes are not the same, StretchBlt either duplicates or omits bits as they are copied from the source. When the source rectangle is smaller than the destination rectangle, pixels are duplicated as they are copied; this has the effect of magnifying the bitmap being copied.

StretchBlt requires two device contexts, one for the source and one for the destination. Form1's hDC property provides the destination device context. The Windows API function GetDC is used to get the device context of the screen, which we want to use for the source device. GetDC takes a single argument, which can either be a window handle or 0. When 0 is passed as the window handle, GetDC returns the screen's device context.

The Windows API functions FastWindowFrame, SetCapture, and ReleaseCapture are used to provide a visual indication of mouse location. Windows normally sends mouse messages to a window only when the mouse is over the window. When the mouse pointer is over Form1 and the user presses the left button, we call SetCapture to "capture" mouse input.

After SetCapture has been called, mouse input is sent to Form1, regardless of where the mouse is on the screen. When the left button is released, ReleaseCapture is called. This allows Windows to return to its normal mode of sending mouse messages to the window under the mouse pointer. During the time the mouse is captured, the program uses FastWindowFrame to draw a rectangle around the area being captured. This makes it easy to see where the mouse is and what bits are being magnified.

### Comments

Using undocumented functions like FastWindowFrame can have drawbacks. Since they are not documented, there may be circumstances under which they behave unexpectedly. Undocumented functions can also simply disappear in the next release of Windows. FastWindowFrame is not likely to disappear, since it corresponds to one of the required graphical driver interface entry points. The use of this function is well isolated in this program and could easily be replaced by a functionally equivalent set of documented Windows calls. If you need to use this function in a number of different places in a program, it is best to place it in a subroutine and call the subroutine instead. This way, if FastWindowFrame were removed from the API, you would only need to change the code in the subroutine, which would be much easier than locating and changing every use of FastWindowFrame in your code.

## 5.18 ● How do I...

**Complexity: Advanced**

## Add hot-spots to pictures?

### Problem

I've seen programs that let you click on an object in a picture to get information about that object. Objects that invoke an action when clicked-on are often called hot-spots. As a visual indicator that the mouse is positioned over a hot-spot, the mouse pointer is changed to a pointing finger or some other distinct cursor. I would like to add hot-spots to my programs. How can I do this using Visual Basic?

### Technique

Two different problems need to be solved to add hot-spots to a Visual Basic program. First you need to know when the mouse pointer is over a hot-spot. Second, the mouse pointer needs to be changed while it is over a hot-spot.

To solve the first problem, this How-To uses an array of Picture controls. This array, which is named HotSpots, can be thought of as an array of hot-spot controls. During design time each element of the HotSpots array is sized and placed over an object in the main picture, as shown in Figure 5-34.

When the program runs, the area covered by each element of the HotSpots array is copied into the element's bitmap using the Windows API function BitBlt. The image finally displayed is indistinguishable from the original main picture, since each element of HotSpots displays exactly what is underneath it. Now, as the mouse is moved around the screen, the HotSpots controls will receive MouseMove events whenever the mouse is over them. Also, whenever the user double-clicks the mouse over one of the HotSpots, a DblClick event will be executed. So far, so good. What about changing the mouse pointer?

Sometimes a seemingly simple requirement can have a dramatic impact on the code required to get a finished program. So it is with the need to change to an appropriate pointer when the mouse is over a hot-spot. Visual Basic supplies a standard set of mouse pointers through the MousePointer property of many controls. However, none of the available mouse pointers are even close to looking like a pointing finger.

The Visual Basic MousePointer is really what's called a "cursor" in the Windows API. The Windows API function SetCursor(HCURSOR hCursor) can be easily used to change to any cursor, as long as you've got the cursor's handle. Unfortunately, getting a cursor handle from within Visual Basic is far from easy. The Windows API function LoadCursor (HINSTANCE hInstance, LPCSTR cursorName) is used in C programs to get a cursor handle. LoadCursor looks in the executable file for the requested cursor and returns its handle if found. This won't work for us, since we don't

**Figure 5-34** Hot-spots in action

have any way to put cursors in our executable which is VB.EXE! The only other choice offered by Windows is a function called CreateCursor. As you will see later, CreateCursor will serve our purpose, but not without using nearly 20 Windows API functions.

If you were to create a program given the techniques outlined here, you would quickly discover a new problem. You will recall that Visual Basic lets you pick one of a number of cursors for a Picture control. Visual Basic is very persistent in its attempt to make sure that your chosen cursor is used. Even after you explicitly set a cursor, Visual Basic manages to change it back under certain circumstances. For instance, as the mouse moves over one of the hot-spots, Visual Basic sets the cursor it thinks you should be using. Your program can respond by also setting the cursor each time the mouse moves, but this causes a noticeable flicker as the cursor moves over a hot-spot. Similar problems occur whenever the mouse button is pressed.

Visual Basic examines each event sent to a control and takes actions that are usually desirable. In the case of mouse move events, Visual Basic does its best to make sure that the "correct" cursor is always set. What we need is a way to prevent Visual Basic from knowing about the mouse events when we would rather not have the cursor changed.

The Waite Group's free custom control MSGHOOK.VBX, included with the companion disk, lets us handle this problem. MsgHook controls can be used to intercept and examine messages sent to any window in the system before the window receives them. A MsgHook control is used to intercept mouse messages intended for the HotSpots controls. The Message event subroutine of the MsgHook control performs the appropriate action for each mouse message. Then, by setting the Action property of the MsgHook control to Discard, most mouse messages are discarded instead of being sent on to Visual Basic. Since we discard most of the mouse messages sent to a HotSpots control, Visual Basic never sees them and therefore doesn't change the cursor.

## Steps

Open and run HOTSPOTS.MAK. There are three hot-spots on the form: the toucan, the snail, and one of the flowers on the right-side tree. When you move the mouse over one of the hot-spots, the cursor changes to a hand with a pointing finger. Whenever this cursor appears, you can double-click the form and the name of the object will be displayed.

1. Create a new project called HOTSPOTS.MAK. Create a new form with the objects and properties in Table 5-31.

| Object | Property | Setting |
|--------|----------|---------|
| Form | Caption | "Form1" |
| | ClipControls | 0 'False |
| | Height | 6285 |
| | Left | 1020 |
| | LinkTopic | "Form1" |
| | Name | Form1 |
| | ScaleHeight | 392 |
| | ScaleMode | 3 'Pixel |
| | ScaleWidth | 583 |
| | Top | 1665 |
| | Width | 8865 |
| MSGHOOK | Height | 420 |
| | Index | 0 |
| | Left | 0 |
| | Name | MsgHook1 |
| | Top | 6000 |
| | Width | 420 |
| MSGHOOK | Height | 420 |
| | Index | 1 |
| | Left | 480 |
| | Name | MsgHook1 |
| | Top | 6000 |
| | Width | 420 |
| MSGHOOK | Height | 420 |
| | Index | 2 |
| | Left | 960 |
| | Name | MsgHook1 |
| | Top | 6000 |
| | Width | 420 |
| Picture box | AutoRedraw | -1 'True |
| | Height | 615 |
| | Left | 1440 |
| | Name | Picture1 |
| | ScaleHeight | 39 |
| | ScaleMode | 3 'Pixel |
| | ScaleWidth | 40 |

| Object | Property | Setting |
|---|---|---|
| | TabIndex | 0 |
| | Top | 6000 |
| | Width | 630 |
| Picture box | AutoRedraw | -1 'True |
| | DrawStyle | 1 'Transparent |
| | Height | 6375 |
| | Left | 0 |
| | Name | Picture2 |
| | Picture | Bitmap backgrnd.bmp |
| | ScaleHeight | 423 |
| | ScaleMode | 3 'Pixel |
| | ScaleWidth | 583 |
| | TabIndex | 1 |
| | Top | -480 |
| | Width | 8775 |

**Table 5-31** Form1's objects and properties

2. Add the objects and properties in Table 5-32 on top of Picture2. It is important that the objects in Table 5-32 are created on top of Picture2. To do this, select the type of object to add by clicking the appropriate button on the toolbar. Next move the mouse pointer over Picture2. Finally, create the control by pressing and holding down the left mouse button and moving it to size the new control.

| Object | Property | Setting |
|---|---|---|
| Picture box | AutoRedraw | -1 'True |
| | BorderStyle | 0 'None |
| | DrawMode | 11 'Nop |
| | DrawStyle | 1 'Transparent |
| | Height | 1575 |
| | Index | 0 |
| | Left | 1560 |
| | Name | HotSpots |
| | ScaleHeight | 105 |
| | ScaleMode | 3 'Pixel |

*continued on next page*

*continued from previous page*

| Object | Property | Setting |
|--------|----------|---------|
| | ScaleWidth | 65 |
| | TabIndex | 2 |
| | Top | 960 |
| | Width | 975 |
| Picture box | AutoRedraw | -1 'True |
| | BorderStyle | 0 'None |
| | DrawMode | 11 'Nop |
| | DrawStyle | 1 'Transparent |
| | Height | 615 |
| | Index | 1 |
| | Left | 6600 |
| | Name | HotSpots |
| | ScaleHeight | 41 |
| | ScaleMode | 3 'Pixel |
| | ScaleWidth | 33 |
| | TabIndex | 4 |
| | Top | 1560 |
| | Width | 495 |
| Picture box | AutoRedraw | -1 'True |
| | BorderStyle | 0 'None |
| | DrawMode | 11 'Nop |
| | DrawStyle | 1 'Transparent |
| | Height | 495 |
| | Index | 2 |
| | Left | 1440 |
| | Name | HotSpots |
| | ScaleHeight | 33 |
| | ScaleMode | 3 'Pixel |
| | ScaleWidth | 57 |
| | TabIndex | 5 |
| | Top | 5640 |
| | Width | 855 |
| Shape | BorderColor | &H00C0C0C0& |
| | DrawMode | 7 'Xor Pen |
| | FillColor | &H00C0C0C0& |
| | FillStyle | 0 'Solid |
| | Height | 735 |

| Object | Property | Setting |
|--------|----------|---------|
| | Index | 0 |
| | Left | 3360 |
| | Name | Shape1 |
| | Shape | 4 'Rounded Rectangle |
| | Top | 3600 |
| | Visible | 0 'False |
| | Width | 2055 |
| Shape | BackColor | &H00000000& |
| | BackStyle | 1 'Opaque |
| | FillColor | &H00C0C0C0& |
| | FillStyle | 0 'Solid |
| | Height | 735 |
| | Index | 1 |
| | Left | 3240 |
| | Name | Shape1 |
| | Shape | 4 'Rounded Rectangle |
| | Top | 3480 |
| | Visible | 0 'False |
| | Width | 2055 |
| Label | Alignment | 2 'Center |
| | BackStyle | 0 'Transparent |
| | Caption | "Label1" |
| | FontBold | -1 'True |
| | FontItalic | 0 'False |
| | FontName | "MS Sans Serif" |
| | FontSize | 13.5 |
| | FontStrikethru | 0 'False |
| | FontUnderline | 0 'False |
| | Height | 375 |
| | Name | Label1 |
| | Left | 3600 |
| | TabIndex | 3 |
| | Top | 3600 |
| | Visible | 0 'False |
| | Width | 1335 |

**Table 5-32**  Objects and properties placed on Picture2

3. Create a new module and save it as HOTSPOTS.BAS. Add the following
code to the General Declarations section of HOTSPOTS.BAS.

```
'
' Windows API rectangle type
'
Type RECT
    left As Integer
    top As Integer
    right As Integer
    bottom As Integer
End Type
'
' Windows API bitmap information type
'
Type BITMAP
    bmType As Integer
    bmWidth As Integer
    bmHeight As Integer
    bmWidthBytes As Integer
    bmPlanes As String * 1
    bmBitsPixel As String * 1
    bmBits As Long
End Type
'
' Windows API task entry type
'
Type TaskEntry
    dwSize          As Long
    hTask           As Integer
    hTaskParent     As Integer
    hInst           As Integer
    hModule         As Integer
    wSS             As Integer
    wSP             As Integer
    wStackTop       As Integer
    wStackMinimum   As Integer
    wStackBottom    As Integer
    wcEvents        As Integer
    hQueue          As Integer
    szModule        As String * 9
    wPSPOffset      As Integer
    hNext           As Integer
    pad             As String * 1
End Type


' Windows API bitmap functions
'
Declare Function bitblt Lib "GDI" (ByVal hDestDC As Integer, ByVal x As⇐
Integer, ByVal y As Integer, ByVal nWidth As Integer, ByVal nHeight As ⇐
Integer, ByVal hSrcDC As Integer, ByVal XSrc As Integer, ByVal YSrc As ⇐
Integer, ByVal dwRop As Long) As Integer
```

```
Declare Function CreateBitmap Lib "GDI" (ByVal nWidth As Integer, ByVal⇐
Height As Integer, ByVal nPlanes As Integer, ByVal nBitCount As Integer,⇐
ByVal lpBits As Any) As Integer
Declare Function GetBitmapBits Lib "GDI" (ByVal hBitmap As Integer, ⇐
ByVal dwCount As Long, ByVal lpBits As Any) As Long
'
' Windows API device context functions
'
Declare Function SetBKColor Lib "GDI" (ByVal hDC As Integer, ByVal ⇐
crColor As Long) As Long
Declare Function CreateCompatibleDC Lib "GDI" (ByVal hDC As Integer) As⇐
Integer
Declare Function DeleteDC Lib "GDI" (ByVal hDC As Integer) As Integer
'
' Windows API GDI Object functions
'
Declare Function GetObject Lib "GDI" (ByVal hObject As Integer, ByVal ⇐
nCount As Integer, lpObject As Any) As Integer
Declare Function SelectObject Lib "GDI" (ByVal hDC As Integer, ByVal ⇐
hObject As Integer) As Integer
Declare Function DeleteObject Lib "GDI" (ByVal hObject As Integer) As ⇐
Integer
'
' Windows API cursor functions
'
Declare Function GetCursor Lib "User" () As Integer
Declare Function SetCursor Lib "User" (ByVal hCursor As Integer) As ⇐
Integer
Declare Function CreateCursor Lib "User" (ByVal hInstance%, ByVal ⇐
nXhotspot%, ByVal nYhotspot%, ByVal nWidth%, ByVal nHeight%,  ByVal ⇐
lpANDbitPlane As Any, ByVal lpXORbitPlane As Any) As Integer
'
' Windows API mouse functions
'
Declare Sub ReleaseCapture Lib "User" ()
Declare Function SetCapture Lib "User" (ByVal hWnd As Integer) As Integer
'
' Windows API miscellaneous functions
'
Declare Function PtInRect Lib "User" (lpRect As RECT, ByVal lpPoint As ⇐
Any) As Integer
Declare Function GetWindowTask Lib "User" (ByVal hWnd As Integer) As ⇐
Integer
Declare Function GetParent Lib "User" (ByVal hWnd As Integer) As Integer
Declare Function GetFocus Lib "User" () As Integer
Declare Function GetCurrentTask Lib "Kernel" () As Integer
Declare Function TaskFindHandle Lib "toolhelp.dll" (lpTask As TaskEntry,⇐
ByVal hTask As Integer) As Integer
'
' Constants used with bitblt
'
Global Const SRCCOPY = &HCC0020     ' (DWORD) dest = source
Global Const NOTSRCCOPY = &H330008  ' (DWORD) dest = (NOT source)
'
```

*continued on next page*

*continued from previous page*

```
' Mouse messages
'
Global Const WM_MOUSEFIRST = &H200
Global Const WM_MOUSEMOVE = &H200
Global Const WM_LBUTTONDOWN = &H201
Global Const WM_LBUTTONUP = &H202
Global Const WM_LBUTTONDBLCLK = &H203
Global Const WM_RBUTTONDOWN = &H204
Global Const WM_RBUTTONUP = &H205
Global Const WM_RBUTTONDBLCLK = &H206
Global Const WM_MBUTTONDOWN = &H207
Global Const WM_MBUTTONUP = &H208
Global Const WM_MBUTTONDBLCLK = &H209
Global Const WM_MOUSELAST = &H209
```

4. Add the following code to the General Declarations section of Form1.

```
Option Explicit

'
' Handle to our cursor
'
Dim hCursor      As Integer
'
' Used to save previous cursor handle
'
Dim hCursorPrev As Integer
'
' Set when we have captured the mouse
'
Dim haveCapture As Integer
```

5. Add the following function to the General section of Form1. Given a device context handle and a bitmap handle, this function returns the handle of a bitmap suitable for use as the "And Mask" of the Windows API function CreateCursor.

```
Function CreateAndMask (hDC As Integer, hBitmap As Integer) As Integer
    '
    ' Call CreateBitmapMask with appropriate ROP3 code
    '
    CreateAndMask = CreateBitmapMask(hDC, hBitmap, &HFFFFFF, SRCCOPY)
End Function
```

6. Add the following function to the General section of Form1. Given a device context handle and a bitmap handle, this function returns the handle of a bitmap suitable for use as the "Xor Mask" of the Windows API function CreateCursor.

```
Function CreateXorMask (hDC As Integer, hBitmap As Integer)
    '
    ' Call mask generator with appropriate ROP3 code
```

```
'
    CreateXorMask = CreateBitmapMask(hDC, hBitmap, &HFFFFFF, NOTSRCCOPY)
End Function
```

7. Add the following function to the General section of Form1. This function does the work for the previous two functions. Four things need to be done to create the required mask: create a bitmap, create a memory device context, copy bits from the passed bitmap to the new bitmap, and free resources allocated.

```
Function CreateBitmapMask (hDC As Integer, hBitmap As Integer, ⇐
    backgroundColor As Long, Rop3Code As Long) As Integer
    Dim hdcMask       As Integer
    Dim hbmSave       As Integer
    Dim wRtn          As Integer
    Dim bminfo        As BITMAP
    Dim hBmMask       As Integer
    Dim colorSave     As Long
    Dim zero          As Long
    '
    ' Get size of bitmap passed in
    '
    wRtn = GetObject(hBitmap, Len(bminfo), bminfo)
    '
    ' Create a monochrome bitmap
    '
    hBmMask = CreateBitmap(bminfo.bmWidth, bminfo.bmHeight, 1, 1, zero)
    '
    ' Create a compatible device context
    '
    hdcMask = CreateCompatibleDC(hDC)
    hbmSave = SelectObject(hdcMask, hBmMask)
    '
    ' Change the source device context's backgroundColor
    '
    colorSave = SetBKColor(hDC, backgroundColor)

    '
    ' Create mask
    '
    wRtn = bitblt(hdcMask, 0, 0, bminfo.bmWidth, bminfo.bmHeight, hDC, 0,⇐
        0, Rop3Code)
    '
    ' Restore source's background color
    '
    colorSave = SetBKColor(hDC, colorSave)
    '
    ' Reselect default bitmap into temporary dc
    '
    hBmMask = SelectObject(hdcMask, hbmSave)
    '
    ' Delete temporary dc
```

*continued on next page*

*continued from previous page*

```
    '
    wRtn = DeleteDC(hdcMask)
    '
    ' Return handle to bitmap
    '
    CreateBitmapMask = hBmMask
End Function
```

8. Add the following subroutine to the General section of Form1. This function creates the bit masks required by CreateCursor by calling CreateXorMask and CreateAndMask. The bits from the newly created bitmaps are retrieved by calling the Windows API function GetBitmapBits. After calling GetHInstance to get the instance handle of this application, CreateCursor can be called. CreateCursor returns an HCURSOR, which is returned as the value of this function.

```
Function CreateMousePointer (from As PictureBox)
    Dim hInst       As Integer
    Dim andBits     As String
    Dim xorBits     As String
    Dim hbmXor      As Integer
    Dim hbmAnd      As Integer
    Dim wRtn        As Integer
    Dim hbmFrom     As Integer
    Dim hdcFrom     As Integer
    Dim lRtn        As Long
    '
    ' Get handles to source device context and bitmap
    '
    hbmFrom = from.Image
    hdcFrom = from.hDC
    '
    ' Allocate space for mask bits
    '
    andBits = String((32 * 32) / 8, 0)
    xorBits = String(Len(andBits), 0)
    '
    ' Create xor mask and retrieve the bits
    '
    hbmXor = CreateXorMask(hdcFrom, hbmFrom)
    lRtn = GetBitmapBits(hbmXor, Len(xorBits), xorBits)
    '
    ' Create and-mask and retrieve the bits
    '
    hbmAnd = CreateAndMask(hdcFrom, hbmFrom)
    lRtn = GetBitmapBits(hbmAnd, Len(andBits), andBits)
    '
    ' Create and return the mouse pointer
    '
    hInst = GetHInstance()
    CreateMousePointer = CreateCursor(hInst, 1, 10, 32, 32, andBits, ⇐
xorBits)
End Function
```

9. Add the following subroutine to the General section of Form1. This function uses the Windows API function GetCurrentTask to get the task handle of the currently running application (that's this one when it's running!). Then TaskFindHandle from TOOLHELP.DLL is used to retrieve an instance handle. Multiple copies of a program may be run at once under Windows. The instance handle is what Windows uses to keep track of information specific to a given instance of an application.

```
Function GetHInstance () As Integer
    Dim hTask    As Integer
    Dim taskEnt  As TaskEntry
    Dim wRtn     As Integer
    '
    ' Get our task handle
    '
    hTask = GetCurrentTask()
    '
    ' Set the size field so Windows will know we've got
    ' enough memory allocated
    '
    taskEnt.dwSize = Len(taskEnt)
    '
    ' Find our task table entry
    '
    wRtn = TaskFindHandle(taskEnt, GetCurrentTask())
    '
    ' Now, return our instance handle
    '
    GetHInstance = taskEnt.hInst
End Function
```

10. Add the following code to the Load event procedure of Form1. The For...Next loop here takes care of copying into each HotSpot that part of the main picture underneath it. The MsgHook1 control array is also initialized in this loop since there is a one-to-one correspondence between HotSpots and MsgHook controls.

```
Sub Form_Load ()
    Dim hWnd     As Integer
    Dim wRtn     As Integer
    Dim i        As Integer

    '
    ' Center form on screen
    '
    form1.Top = (screen.Height - form1.Height) / 2
    form1.Left = (screen.Width - form1.Width) / 2

    '
    ' Copy parts of picture into HotSpots and initialize message
```

*continued on next page*

*continued from previous page*

```
' interceptor
'
For i = 0 To 2
    wRtn = bitblt(HotSpots(i).hDC, 0, 0, HotSpots(i).Width, ⇐
HotSpots(i).Height, picture5.hDC, HotSpots(i).Left, HotSpots(i).Top, ⇐
SRCCOPY)
    MsgHook1(i).hwndHook = HotSpots(i).hWnd
    MsgHook1(i).Message(WM_MOUSEMOVE) = True
    MsgHook1(i).Message(WM_LBUTTONDBLCLK) = True
    MsgHook1(i).Message(WM_LBUTTONDOWN) = True
    MsgHook1(i).Message(WM_LBUTTONUP) = True
Next
End Sub
```

11. Add the following code to the DblClick event procedure of the HotSpots control array. This code is called whenever the mouse is double-clicked on a HotSpot. The HotSpot index is used to select the correct object name, which is displayed in label1. The two shape controls and the label are made visible whenever a HotSpot is clicked on, creating a pop-up window effect. It is important to note that this event procedure is called from the MsgHook1_Message event routine and not Visual Basic's underlying event dispatcher.

```
Sub HotSpots_DblClick (index As Integer)
'
' A HotSpot has been clicked, display its name
'
Select Case index
    Case 0
        label1.Caption = "Toucan"
    Case 1
        label1.Caption = "Flower"
    Case 2
        label1.Caption = "Snail?"
End Select

shape1(0).Visible = True
shape1(1).Visible = True
label1.Visible = True
End Sub
```

12. Add the following code to the MouseMove event procedure of the HotSpots control array. The interaction between this procedure and the MsgHook1_Message event procedure is fundamental to the cursor handling requirements of the application. This event procedure is called exactly twice each time the mouse moves over a HotSpot.

As the mouse pointer first moves over a HotSpot, the MsgHook1_Message sets its action argument to 0. This causes MsgHook1 to forward the mouse move message to Visual Basic; Visual Basic then fires the MouseMove event. When this happens haveCapture is equal to 0 so the MouseMove event procedure captures the mouse and sets the cursor. Once haveCapture is non-0, the MsgHook1_Message routine looks at each mouse message to see if the mouse pointer is still over the HotSpot. If it is, the message is discarded.

When the mouse pointer moves outside of the HotSpot, the MsgHook1_Message event procedure releases the mouse, restores the previous cursor, and lets Visual Basic have the mouse move message. When Visual Basic receives this message, the MouseMove event procedure is called.

```
Sub HotSpots_MouseMove (index As Integer, Button As Integer, Shift As ⇐
  Integer, X As Single, Y As Single)
    Dim wRtn            As Integer
    '
    ' If we haven't captured the mouse do so
    '
    If (haveCapture = 0) Then
        wRtn = SetCapture(HotSpots(index).hWnd)
        hCursorPrev = GetCursor()
        wRtn = SetCursor(hCursor)
        haveCapture = 1
    '
    ' Otherwise we just released it so hide caption
    '
    Else
        shape1(0).Visible = False
        shape1(1).Visible = False
        label1.Visible = False
        haveCapture = 0
    End If
End Sub
```

13. Add the following code to the Message event procedure of MsgHook1. In addition to watching the mouse pointer to see when it has moved outside of a HotSpot, as discussed in Step 12, this event procedure watches for double-click messages and calls the HotSpots_DblClick procedure when they occur. All mouse down, mouse up, and double-click events are discarded so that Visual Basic will not act on them.

```
Sub MsgHook1_Message (index As Integer, msg As Integer, wParam As ⇐
  Integer, lParam As Long, action As Integer, result As Long)
    Dim wRtn    As Integer
    Dim r       As RECT

    '
    ' Create the mouse pointer if this is our first time here
    '
    If (hCursor = 0) Then
```

*continued on next page*

*continued from previous page*

```
      hCursor = CreateMousePointer(picture1)
   End If

   '
   ' Result is always zero so set it here
   '
   result = 0

   '
   ' Now we'll take a look at the mouse messages of interest
   '
   Select Case msg
      '
      ' Mouse move
      '
      Case WM_MOUSEMOVE
         '
         ' If we have captured the mouse check to see if
         ' the mouse pointer is still over the HotSpot
         '
         If (haveCapture <> 0) Then
            r.Top = 0
            r.Left = 0
            r.bottom = HotSpots(index).Height
            r.right = HotSpots(index).Width
            '
            ' If we're no longer over the HotSpot we release the
            ' mouse and restore the previous cursor, otherwise we
            ' don't let VB get the message (action = 1)
            '
            If (PtInRect(r, lParam) = 0) Then
               ReleaseCapture
               wRtn = SetCursor(hCursorPrev)
               action = 0
            Else
               action = 1
            End If
         Else
            '
            ' Let HotSpots_MouseMove get this one
            '
            action = 0
         End If
      Case WM_LBUTTONDBLCLK
         '
         ' Double-clicked a HotSpot, call subroutine and toss
         ' message so VB doesn't get it
         '
         HotSpots_DblClick (index)
         action = 1
      Case WM_LBUTTONDOWN
         action = 1
      Case WM_LBUTTONUP
```

```
        action = 1
    Case Else
        action = 0
  End Select
End Sub
```

### How It Works

This How-To reaches pretty far into the bag of Windows API tricks; CreateCursor is seldom seen in any Windows program, even those written in C. Creating the cursor and handling mouse messages are two areas of this How-To that make especially heavy use of the Windows API and architecture.

### Creating Cursors

CreateCursor needs two bit-masks to describe the cursor shape and the way it is drawn on the screen. The bits in these two masks are combined with the pixels on the screen using logical-AND and logical-XOR (exclusive-or) functions. The effect that these operations have on the screen can be seen by examining Table 5-33.

| AND mask value | XOR mask value | Result on screen |
|---|---|---|
| 0 | 0 | Black |
| 0 | 1 | White |
| 1 | 0 | Transparent |
| 1 | 1 | Inverted color |

**Table 5-33** Cursor truth table

Figures 5-35, 5-36, and 5-37 show POINT02.ICO, the XOR-mask and the AND-mask respectively. POINT02.ICO is loaded into Picture1 at design time. The masks are created at run time by BitBlting Picture1 into a monochrome

**Figure 5-35**
POINT02.ICO

**Figure 5-36** XOR-mask

**Figure 5-37** AND-mask

bitmap. When a color bitmap is BitBlted into a monochrome bitmap, bits matching the color bitmap's background color become 0 bits, all other bits are copied as 1s. Then once the mask has been BitBlted, GetBitmapBits is used to get the actual mask bits into a string so they can be passed to CreateCursor.

The technique used in this How-To creates an adequate mouse pointer given a suitable image as a starting point. The main problem with this algorithmic approach is that there is no black outline around the hand and finger. The advantage to this approach is that a number of existing icons can be tried out.

It would be possible to write the masks to picture controls, copy them one at a time to the clipboard, and paste them into a bit editor for fine-tuning. Then, after tuning, the masks could be saved in picture controls along with a form. This would provide the best of both worlds; you could try out various icons until you found one you liked, then hand-tune it for the best possible appearance.

### Message Handling

Visual Basic really tries hard to make sure that the correct cursor is set at all times. Usually, that's a good thing, but in this case it's too much of a good thing. It appears that every mouse message to a control results in Visual Basic setting the cursor.

The Waite Group's free custom control MSGHOOK.VBX is what makes this How-To possible. By interrupting the flow of mouse messages when the mouse pointer is over a HotSpot, the application is able to provide a custom cursor that works as smoothly as any. This How-To uses the WM_LBUTTONDBLCLK message to invoke actions. By modifying the Select statement in MsgHook1_Message, it would be easy to handle single-clicks instead, or even to perform different actions for single and double-clicks.

### Comments

The hot-spots How-To can be used as a starting point for a number of interesting applications. Multimedia applications often use hot-spots in graphics as an application navigation tool. By using the techniques demonstrated in this How-To, there is no limit to the actions that can be invoked when a hot-spot is clicked. A point-and-click world atlas with music is just a few bitmaps away!

Another possibility is to use hot-spots as hypertext links. To do this you would place picture controls over selected words in text. When the form loads, you could set the foreground color of the HotSpots to some color (green is often used for this purpose) and print the text into the HotSpots.

For an example of putting text in a picture control see How-To 3.12 Change the colors of individual cells in a grid.

## 5.19 How do I ...

## Play back an animation?

### Problem

I used Autodesk Animator to create an animation that I would like my program to play when it first comes up. How do I play back an animation inside a window? Also, can I let my program's user set animation playback options, such as the number of times the animation loops and whether to use the full screen rather than just a window?

### Technique

Autodesk distributes a dynamic link library (DLL) to play back animation files under Windows. This library lets you play back low-resolution files from Autodesk Animator (FLI files) or high-resolution animations (FLC files, also called *flics*) from Autodesk Animator Pro. The library, AAPLAY.DLL, which also includes routines to play back sound and special script files, is on the *Visual Basic How-To* disk. We've also included VBPLAY.TXT, a text file that contains the complete Visual Basic function and constant declarations for the DLL.

The sample Player project is almost entirely driven by AAPLAY.DLL functions. For example, the function aaGetFile gets a filename from the user, and the function aaPrompt brings up the options dialog in Figure 5-38, which lets the user set playback values for the current animation.

### Steps

Open and run PLAYER.MAK. The main window of this project is the playback window for the animation. To load an animation, click on Load under the File menu. Select an animation to load from the Open File dialog box. The Player demo automatically resizes the window to fit the animation, as shown in Figure 5-39. Click on Play under the File menu to play the animation. By default, the animation loops in the window until you click on the Stop menu item under the File menu. Click on Settings... under the Options menu to change the playback settings. To play the animation only once, set the Loops:Frames parameter to 1. To play back the animation on the full screen, check Use Full Screen. Note: You can also set these values from inside your program; see the end of this section for details.

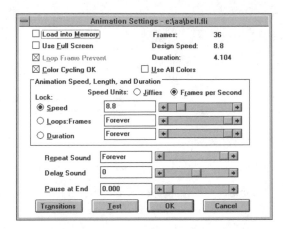

**Figure 5-38** Your program's user can set playback options

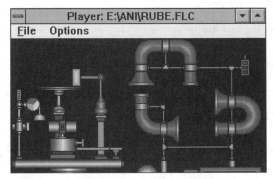

**Figure 5-39** The player demo sizes the window to fit the animation

1. Create a new project called PLAYER.MAK. Open the window for the Global module. Under the Code menu, click on Load Text... and select the file VBPLAY.TXT. These are the global declarations for the AAPLAY.DLL functions and their associated constants. Save the file as VBPLAY.BAS.

2. Create a new form with the objects and properties shown in Table 5-34. Notice that the picture box on this form is the only control, and it won't be visible at run time. It is important that you set the dimensions of this control precisely. Later we'll be using this picture box to measure how much to resize the form to fit the animation.

| Object | Property | Setting |
|--------|----------|---------|
| Form | BorderStyle | 3 - Fixed Double |
| | Caption | Player |
| | FormName | Player |
| | Height | 3756 |
| | ScaleMode | 1 - Twip |
| | Width | 3960 |
| Picture | CtlName | Picture1 |
| | Height | 3012 |
| | Visible | False |
| | Width | 3864 |

**Table 5-34** Player form's objects and properties

3. Using the menu design window, create a menu for the form with the captions and controls shown in Table 5-35.

| Caption | Name | Enabled Setting |
|---------|------|-----------------|
| &File | MMFile | Checked |
| ---- &Load Animation | MMFileLoad | Checked |
| ---- &Play | MMFilePlay | Not Checked |
| ---- &Stop | MMFileStop | Not Checked |
| ---- ———————— | MMFileBar | Checked |
| ---- E&xit | MMFileExit | Checked |
| Options | MMOptions | Checked |
| ---- Settings... | MMOptionsSettings | Not Checked |

**Table 5-35** Player form's menu

4. Enter the following code into the Declarations section of the form.

```
' Variables for this module.
Dim lpzFileName As String   ' Filename of animation, if loaded.
Dim hAa As Integer          ' Handle of current animation.
Dim dummy As Integer        ' Used to call routines when we don't care
                            ' about return value.
```

5. Enter the following code into the Form_Load event subroutine. AAPLAY.DLL must be on the user's system, preferably in WINDOWS\SYSTEM. The function aaOpen() opens the dynamic link library.

```
Sub Form_Load ()
    ' Open the library.
    ' AAPLAY.DLL must be on user's disk drive
    ' in WINDOWS or WINDOWS\SYSTEM or on PATH or in .EXE dir.
    ' AAVGA.DLL must also be present, even though it isn't called directly.
    If aaOpen() = 0 Then
        MsgBox "Error-- Couldn't open AAPLAY.DLL."
        End
    End If
End Sub
```

6. Enter the following code into the Form_Paint event subroutine. This routine is called when the user moves the window. The aaSetParm function sets various animation parameters. In this case, it sets the x-and y-coordinates of the animation inside the window. These values are always 0, which means the top left corner of the animation is always at the top left corner of the window. By re-initializing the x-and-y values, the animation moves with the window. Calling aaPlay again causes the animation to start playing at the point it left off.

```
Sub Form_Paint ()
    ' When the window moves, make sure the animation moves as well.
    ' This procedure is probably called more than necessary,
    ' but it doesn't hurt anything.

    ' Change the x,y window parameters.
    ' This causes the animation to move with the window.
    dummy = aaSetParm(hAa, AA_X, 0, 0)
    dummy = aaSetParm(hAa, AA_Y, 0, 0)

    ' Is the animation currently playing?
    If aaGetParm(hAa, AA_STATUS) = AA_PLAYING Then
        dummy = aaPlay(hAa) ' Set it back in motion.
    End If
End Sub
```

7. Enter the following code into the MMFileLoad_Click event subroutine. This routine hooks into AAPLAY's aaGetFile function to get the name of the animation to play.

```
Sub MMFileLoad_Click ()
    ' Use AAPLAY's built-in GetFile function to prompt the user for a file.
    Dim wFlags, wSizeFile
    wSizeFile = 255

    ' Fill string so aaGetFile won't write past the end of it.
    lpzFileName = String$(wSizeFile, 0)
    wFlags = AA_GETFILE_ANIMATION

    ' If user didn't select Cancel, load animation.
    If aaGetFile(wFlags, lpzFileName, wSizeFile, "", 0) <> 0 Then
        ' Trim null characters.
```

```
    lpzFileName = Left$(lpzFileName, InStr(lpzFileName, Chr$(0)) - 1)
    ' Is there an animation already loaded?
    If hAa <> 0 Then
        ' Is it running?
        If aaGetParm(hAa, AA_STATUS) = AA_PLAYING Then
            dummy = aaStop(hAa) ' Stop it.
        End If

        ' Unload animation.
        dummy = aaUnload(hAa)
        ' Disable Stop/play/settings options.
        MMFilePlay.Enabled = 0
        MMFileStop.Enabled = 0
        MMOptionsSettings.Enabled = 0
        Caption = "Player"
        hAa = 0
    End If

    ' Load the animation
    LoadAnimation

    If hAa = 0 Then
        MsgBox "Couldn't load animation."
    Else
        ' Assign name to window caption.
        Caption = "Player: " + lpzFileName
        ' Enable play menu options
        MMFilePlay.Enabled = -1
        MMFileStop.Enabled = -1
        MMOptionsSettings.Enabled = -1
    End If
  End If
End Sub
```

8. Enter the following general subroutine. This procedure calls aaLoad to load an animation. If the load was successful, it resizes the window so that it is the same size as the animation. The module-wide variable hAa contains the handle of the loaded animation.

```
Sub LoadAnimation ()
' This routine loads an animation using aaLoad(),
' sets the value of hAa (module-wide variable),
' and sets the size of the play window.
' If animation wasn't loaded hAa will be 0.

' Animation is the file named in the module-wide
' variable lpzFileName.

    Dim PlayMode As Integer
    Dim FlicWidth, FlicHeight As Integer
    Dim BeginWidth, BeginHeight As Integer

    ' For possible values of PlayMode, see the AAPlay help file.
```

*continued on next page*

*continued from previous page*

```
    PlayMode = 0
    hAa = aaLoad(lpzFileName, hWnd, PlayMode, 0, 0, 0, 0, 0, 0)
    ' Was it loaded?
    If hAa <> 0 And WindowState = 0 Then
        ' Get dimensions of the animation.
        ' Only do this if user hasn't maximized window.
        FlicWidth = aaGetParm(hAa, AA_WIDTH)
        FlicHeight = aaGetParm(hAa, AA_HEIGHT)

        ' Do some gymnastics to change window size to fit picture
        ScaleMode = 1   ' Change to twips
        BeginWidth = Picture1.Width ' Remember picture's dimensions
        BeginHeight = Picture1.Height

        ScaleMode = 3   ' Switch to pixels
        Picture1.Width = FlicWidth  'Adjust picture to animation size.
        Picture1.Height = FlicHeight

      ScaleMode = 1  ' Back to twips; now we can change window by the same amount.
        Width = Width + Picture1.Width - BeginWidth
        Height = Height + Picture1.Height - BeginHeight
    End If
End Sub
```

9. Enter the following code into the MMFilePlay_Click event subroutine. This routine plays the animation that is currently loaded.

```
Sub MMFilePlay_Click ()
    ' Play the currently loaded animation.
    dummy = aaPlay(hAa)
End Sub
```

10. Enter the following code into the MMFileStop_Click event subroutine. This stops the current animation from playing.

```
Sub MMFileStop_Click ()
    ' Stop the animation.
    dummy = aaStop(hAa)
End Sub
```

11. Enter the following code into the MMOptionsSettings_Click event subroutine. This brings up the AAPLAY settings dialog box. Any options the user selects are applied to the animation automatically by AAPLAY. If you want to set playback options manually, use aaSetParms or aaSetParmsIndirect.

```
Sub MMOptionsSettings_Click ()
    ' Let user adjust animation playback options.
    ' Bring up AAPLAY's settings dialog box.
    dummy = aaPrompt(hAa, lpzFileName)
End Sub
```

12. Enter the following code into the MMFileExit_Click event subroutine. This closes the AAPLAY library and exits the program.

```
Sub MMFileExit_Click ()
    ' Close up the library when done!
    aaClose
    End
End Sub
```

### How It Works

The AAPLAY.DLL handles just about every aspect of playing back animations. In order to run the program, AAPLAY.DLL and AAVGA.DLL need to be on your hard disk, preferably in the WINDOWS\SYSTEM directory. The VBPLAY.TXT text file includes all the declarations you need to call the routines in this library.

The Form_Load event procedure opens the AAPLAY library with the call to aaOpen. If this command fails the program won't continue.

When the user clicks on Load under the File menu, the Player program uses aaGetFile to prompt for a filename. The value of wFlags is AA_GETFILE_ANIMATION, which tells aaGetFile to get an animation file. In addition to .FLI and .FLC formats, AAPLAY can load Windows DIB (device independent bitmap), RLE (run length encoding), and BMP files. Here are the other possible values of wFlags.

```
'    AA_GETFILE_MUSTEXIST    Selected file must satisfy conditions of
'                            OpenFile() flags, else dialog beeps.
'    AA_GETFILE_NOSHOWSPEC   DO NOT show the search spec in the edit box.
'                            Default IS to show the spec.
'    AA_GETFILE_SAVE         Ok button will show "Save".
'    AA_GETFILE_OPEN         Ok button will show "Open".
'    AA_GETFILE_USEFILE      Set the filename to the file in lpszPath
'    AA_GETFILE_USEDIR       Change to the directory in lpszPath
'    AA_GETFILE_SOUND        Get sound file and driver
'    AA_GETFILE_SCRIPT       Get script file
'    AA_GETFILE_ANIMATION    Get Animation File (no scripts)
```

The name of the file the user selected is stored in the module-wide variable lpzFileName. Note that this string is filled with nulls before the function call to prevent aaGetFile from writing past the end of the string. When this call returns, we trim the nulls from the filename.

If there is already an animation loaded, the MMLoadFile_Click routine unloads it, stops it if it is running, and disables the Play, Stop, and Settings menu options. This way, if the load is unsuccessful the menu will behave correctly.

Note the use of aaGetParm in this routine to see if the animation is running:

```
If aaGetParm(hAa, AA_STATUS) = AA_PLAYING Then
    dummy = aaStop(hAa) ' Stop it.
End If
```

This very useful function returns information related to the current animation based on the value of the wType parameter. Possible values are

```
Global Const AA_STATUS = 1              ' Get current status
Global Const AA_FILETYPE = 2            ' Get Type of animation on disk
Global Const AA_MODE = 3                ' Get/Set Animation Flags
Global Const AA_WINDOW = 4              ' Set/Get animation window
Global Const AA_SPEED = 5               ' Set/Get current speed
Global Const AA_DESIGNSPEED = 6         ' Get design speed
Global Const AA_FRAMES = 7              ' Get Number of frames
Global Const AA_POSITION = 8            ' Set/Get current frame position
Global Const AA_LOOPS = 9               ' Set/Get number of loops
Global Const AA_X = 10                  ' Set/Get Pos of display window
Global Const AA_Y = 11                  ' Set/Get Pos of display window
Global Const AA_CX = 12                 ' Set/Get extents of display window
Global Const AA_CY = 13                 ' Set/Get extents of display window
Global Const AA_ORGX = 14               ' Set/Get Origin of display window
Global Const AA_ORGY = 15               ' Set/Get Origin of display window
Global Const AA_WIDTH = 16              ' Get Width of animation
Global Const AA_HEIGHT = 17             ' Get Height of animation
Global Const AA_RPTSOUND = 18           ' Set/Get sound repeats
Global Const AA_PAUSE = 19              ' Set/Get pause time
Global Const AA_DELAYSND = 20           ' Set/Get sound delay time
Global Const AA_TRANSIN = 21            ' Set/Get Transition In type
Global Const AA_TRANSOUT = 22           ' Set/Get Transition Out type
Global Const AA_TIMEIN = 23             ' Set/Get Transition In time
Global Const AA_TIMEOUT = 24            ' Set/Get Transition Out Time
Global Const AA_CALLBACK = 25           ' Set/Get CallBack window
Global Const AA_ANIMWND = 26            ' Get Animation Window Handle
Global Const AA_MODFLAG = 100           ' Set/Get Script is modified flag
Global Const AA_SCRIPTNAME = 101        ' Set/Get Script name
Global Const AA_ANIMATION = 102         ' Get/Set Script Animation
Global Const AA_ANIMATIONCOUNT = 103    ' Get Script Animation Count
Global Const AA_SCRIPTCONTENTS = 104    ' Get Script Contents
Global Const AA_LASTERROR = 1001        ' Get last error code
Global Const AA_LASTERRORMESSAGE = 1002 ' Get/Set last error messsage
```

The MMFileLoad_Click routine calls LoadAnimation, which loads the animation named in the module-wide lpzFileName string. The call to aaLoad assigns the animation handle to hAa. This value is 0 if the load is unsuccessful. If the procedure successfully loads the animation, it resizes the window to fit the animation.

Unfortunately, calculating the window size to fit the animation is rather complicated. The problem is that the animation's resolution is measured in pixels, but we can only resize a window using twips. The technique used here takes advantage of the fact that a picture control, on the other hand, can be measured in either pixels or twips. Here is the code to adjust the window's size:

```
' Get dimensions of the animation.
FlicWidth = aaGetParm(hAa, AA_WIDTH)
FlicHeight = aaGetParm(hAa, AA_HEIGHT)

' Do some gymnastics to change window size to fit picture
ScaleMode = 1   ' Change to twips
BeginWidth = Picture1.Width ' Remember picture's dimensions
BeginHeight = Picture1.Height

ScaleMode = 3   ' Switch to pixels
Picture1.Width = FlicWidth  'Adjust picture to animation size.
Picture1.Height = FlicHeight

ScaleMode = 1  ' Back to twips; now we can change window by the same amount.
Width = Width + Picture1.Width - BeginWidth
Height = Height + Picture1.Height - BeginHeight
```

We start out with a picture that is the same size as the window. When we load an animation, we'll remember the picture's size in twips. Then, we'll find out the animation's dimensions, change the form's scale mode to pixels, and adjust the picture to be the same size as the animation. At this point all we need to do is set the scale mode back to twips and calculate the difference between the picture's old dimensions and its new ones, and change the form's dimensions by that amount.

Once the animation is in the window, the Form_Paint event subroutine ensures that the animation moves when the user moves the window. This routine uses the aaSetParm function to set the x-and y-coodinates of the animation inside the window. aaSetParm uses the same values for wType as the constants listed above for aaGetParm. The x-and y-coordinates are always 0, so that the animation is always in the upper left corner of the window. You might change these values if, for example, you wanted to center the animation inside of a larger window. Form_Paint calls aaPlay to restart the animation at the point it left off.

With the animation loaded, the aaPlay, aaStop, and aaPrompt routines handle all the playback options. Note that if the user changes any of the animation parameters from the aaPrompt dialog box, the changes are assigned to the animation automatically by AAPLAY.DLL. If you want to access the parameters from inside your program, use aaGetParm and aaSetParm. See the VBPLAY constants declarations for more details.

### What About Sound?

Adding animations to your programs may leave your cup half empty. For many applications, you'll want to add sound as well. Fortunately, the AAPLAY.DLL can load and play a sound file using the same straightforward commands you use to play an animation. The settings dialog box can synchronize the animation and sound playback. For example, setting the Loops:Frames value to Sound plays the animation until the sound finishes.

For longer combinations of sound and animation, AAPLAY has a scripting language that lets you (or your program's user) play back sequences of animation and sound files. AAPLAY scripts, which have the extension .AAS, can include instructions to combine the sound and animation files, and to add smooth transitions between the files. AAPLAY loads and plays a script file easily using aaLoad and aaPlay. When a script file is loaded, the aaPrompt command brings up the script editing dialog box shown in Figure 5-40.

### Bug Alert

Autodesk says that there is a known bug in the current version of AAPLAY.DLL that interferes with palette manipulation in Visual Basic 2.0 and may interfere with Visual Basic 3.0. Palette manipulation isn't covered in this How-To.

### Getting Help

Autodesk ships a Windows player program, AAWIN.EXE, that lets you build script files to play back sound and animation in Windows. This program is included on the How-To disk. The AAPLAY.DLL is fully documented under the Help menu of AAWIN. This includes documentation of all the constants, as well as the AAPLAY.DLL functions that are declared in VBPLAY.TXT but unused in this How-To. This Help file also documents the scripting language and shows how to create a script using either a text editor or the script editing dialog box.

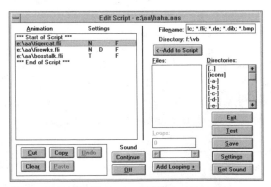

**Figure 5-40** You can edit a script of animation and sound files for AAPLAY

# CHAPTER 6

# ENVIRONMENT AND SYSTEM

# How do I...

This chapter presents techniques for communicating with DOS, running DOS programs from Visual Basic, and determining the state of various aspects of the Windows environment. You'll learn how to use many APIs for finding the amount of available memory, the version of Windows running on your machine, the names of directories, the type of keyboard your user has, and much more. Many important APIs are covered here, including the WinExec function that lets you shell to DOS but doesn't give error messages if the program can't be found. There are also APIs for determining the class name of an application, as well as a great project that simulates the Windows SDK SPY program that gives important information on all applications running under Windows.

## Windows APIs Covered

| | | |
|---|---|---|
| CreatePen | GetModuleFilename | GetWindowText |
| DeleteObject | GetModuleHandle | IsWindow |
| ExitWindows | GetModuleUsage | Rectangle |
| FindWindow | GetNumTasks | ReleaseCapture |
| GDIHeapInfo | GetParent | ReleaseDC |
| GetActiveWindow | GetStockObject | SelectObject |
| GetClassName | GetSystemDirectory | SetActiveWindow |
| GetClassWord | GetVersion | SetCapture |
| GetFreeSpace | GetWindowDC | SetROP2 |
| GetHeapSpaces | GetWindowRect | UserHeapInfo |
| GetKeyboardType | GetWindowsDirectory | WindowFromPoint |
| GetMessagePos | GetWinFlags | WinExec |

### 6.1    Run a DOS program and find out when it's done

One of the most popular uses of Visual Basic is to create interfaces for DOS applications, especially those DOS programs that are crude and expect parameters to be entered on the command line. One of the hurdles that comes up with this approach is communications between your DOS program and the Visual Basic program running under Windows. How do you know, for example, if the DOS program has finished executing some task? This How-To shows a simple way to find the answer to this question using the GetNumTasks API function.

**6.2     Use a more sophisticated method to monitor a DOS program**

While the previous How-To showed that monitoring a DOS process for completion is simple, there are some dangers to using the GetNumTasks API. This How-To illustrates a technique that will guarantee that your Visual Basic application will accurately detect when the DOS process is finished regardless of the number of running applications. Furthermore you will learn how to communicate command-line parameters to a DOS process and learn a little about ray tracing along the way. The GetActiveWindow and IsWindow APIs are used.

**6.3     Exit Windows and return to DOS**

Suppose you want to allow your Visual Basic application to shut down Windows completely, say because you detect the presence of a virus or you just like the idea of an emergency shutdown. This How-To shows off the ExitWindows API to immediately leave Windows and enter DOS.

**6.4     Prevent Windows from shutting down**

When exiting from Windows, many running applications will first ask you if you wish to save your work before Windows quits. Unfortunately, Visual Basic applications do not automatically ask if you want to save and your user will lose all their work if Windows is shut down. This How-To shows a simple way around that. You can use this method with the previous How-To for a safe, emergency shutdown technique.

**6.5     Search an entire disk for a file**

Here is an amazingly useful project that will search the entire hard disk for any file or files specified with a search mask. It builds on the capability of the standard Visual Basic directory list box. As the project searches the file system it automatically adds the files that match the entered specification to a scrolling text box as well as the directories that they are found in. This is a pure Visual Basic project.

**6.6     Use the Shell function without causing run-time errors**

Visual Basic's Shell function allows you to run a DOS program. But if the DOS program is not in the directory you expect it to be you'll get an error message. Then you have to build On Error code into your program to deal with this or else a message will pop up File Not Found and stop your application. Many times you want to shell and not have to write all that code to check for errors. This How-To uses a neat API called WinExec that will not give an error if the DOS application can't be found.

**6.7** **Run a DOS internal command**

Unfortunately the Visual Basic Shell function will not run a built-in DOS command like DIR or TYPE. This How-To presents a trick that lets you directly manipulate the DOS command processor and send it specific parameters that let it run a DOS command. The Environ$ function is used for this purpose along with the COMSPEC setting so this How-To will teach you a lot about DOS.

**6.8** **Prevent multiple program instances from being loaded**

While Windows allows multiple copies of a single application to be run, there are many cases when you would not want a second copy of your application to be started. For example if you're doing telecommunications, a second copy of your application could cause the first to disconnect from the serial port. This How-To shows a safe method that uses the GetModuleHandle and GetModuleUsage APIs to prevent more than one copy of a Visual Basic program to be run.

**6.9** **Find other running applications**

Often you will want to be able to locate other Windows applications and manipulate them from Visual Basic, perhaps via the SendKeys statement. Normally you will enable these applications with the AppActivate statement. However AppActivate relies on the title in the title bar of your window to find its target. Since users can modify this title with a .PIF file your program could lose the target application. This How-To shows how to use the FindWindow and WndPeek APIs to determine the location of a Windows application using the Windows "class name" rather than its title. This is a much more reliable way of activating applications since a program's classname can't be altered.

**6.10** **Determine how many function keys are on my user's keyboard**

A popular way to make your application slick is to enable the function keys on the keyboard to access different features, for instance, (F1) enables Help, (F9) captures the screen to a disk file, and so on. Unfortunately there are several types of keyboards on the market and the number of function keys can vary. There are other differences between keyboards, and some may or may not include the numeric keypad, the (HOME) key, (PGUP), (PGDN), and so on. This How-To shows how easy it is for your Visual Basic program to determine just what kind of keyboard is installed in your user's computer. It uses the GetKeyboardType API.

### 6.11 Determine the directory where Windows is installed

Suppose you are writing an installation routine for your great Visual Basic application. You need to make sure the user has VBRUN300.DLL installed on their hard disk for your Visual Basic application to run, and that the DLL is installed in their Windows directory. How do you find out the name of the Windows directory and the hard disk drive name? This How-To shows how to do that using the GetWindowsDirectory and GetSystemDirectory APIs.

### 6.12 Determine how much memory is available

Often you will want to know how much total RAM memory is available in the user's computer system. This How-To uses the GetFreeSpace API to answer that question and produces an icon that sits on your desktop monitoring memory usage.

### 6.13 Determine system resources

Windows shows a figure called the Free System Resources in the About... dialog box. This figure reflects how much memory is available for storing objects such as controls and windows. If the amount of space allocated for these system resources falls below a certain point, Visual Basic will be unable to load in more controls. This How-To reveals how to determine the amount of memory available to your application via the GetHeapSpaces API.

### 6.14 Determine which version of Windows my application is running on

Microsoft is constantly improving and adding features to Windows. In many cases there are features in newer Windows versions that you would want to access in your Visual Basic programs, yet you don't want to make your application depend on a certain version. The way to handle this is to make your program recognize the version of Windows that is running. Then you can enable or disable features in your program accordingly. This How-To shows how to do that using the GetVersion API.

### 6.15 Find out everything about the system configuration

In the previous How-Tos you saw how to determine the type of keyboard, where the Windows directory is stored, and what version of Windows is running. This How-To creates a single project that summarizes all these functions and provides information on whether a 286 or 386 processor is installed, whether enhanced or standard mode is being run, and whether a math chip is installed in the user's system.

**6.16    Simulate SPY in Visual Basic**

SPY is a very useful utility that ships with the Windows Software Development kit. It is used to trace messages sent to controls and windows so you can debug your program. Most importantly SPY helps you find the class and parent of a window as well as track mouse messages within your form. This How-To builds a program similar to SPY called WndPeek that gives much of the same information. It also highlights windows as the mouse passes over them. Besides being educational, the WndPeek project will help you gauge if you are using too many controls in your application. WinPeek uses the largest number of API calls in this book and is an example of how a Visual Basic program can deftly manipulate Windows as well as any program written in C.

# 6.1 ⬤   How do I...

# Run a DOS program and find out when it's done?

### Problem

Visual Basic is supposed to allow me to wrap a beautiful GUI around a DOS interface. Suppose I have a DOS utility that I have to run occasionally from Windows. I don't want to force users to deal with a Shell to DOS and have to use the command line. What I would like them to be able to do is click on a button and have the DOS utility fire up and do its thing. Also, on the same subject, once I run the DOS process, how do I let my Visual Basic application know that the DOS process is done; in other words how do I communicate between the programs?

### Technique

Being able to wrap a shell around a DOS utility or complex application is a great use for Visual Basic. But there are a number of issues to contend with when communicating between DOS and Windows via Visual Basic. Let's make an example that illustrates some of the caveats.

First, we make a batch file called SHELL.BAT that contains the commands:

```
DIR | SORT /+16 > DIR.TXT
```

This command says do a DIRectory listing on the current drive, then "pipe" the output of the listing into the SORT filter. Results are sorted using the letter in the 16th column, then the output redirected into the file

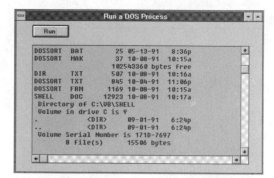

**Figure 6-1** The VB interface for testing the DOS Sort batch file puts the results of the DOS sort into the listing box.

DIR.TXT. The 16th column is the file size column, so this means the files will be sorted by size in the text box.

Next, Shell to this batch file from Visual Basic and run the program as an icon in its minimized state. Then, open the file DIR.TXT from Visual Basic and read its lines into a list box. To the unsuspecting user it appears that Visual Basic did all the work!

However, there is a problem. If we immediately open the file after doing the Shell, the file is empty. This happens because when Visual Basic returns from running the DOS process with Shell, it blindly moves on and executes the next line of code *before* the DOS process is done. We need some way to tell Visual Basic to wait until the DOS process is done (the Shell doesn't offer this—it only tells us if the shell was successful). One simple solution is a Windows API called GetNumTasks. Its use relies on one constraint: that you never begin a second task under Windows until the DOS process run from Visual Basic finishes. That is not really an unrealistic constraint for most users. We'll show you a way around this in the following How-To.

### Steps

Open and run SHELL.MAK. It should look like Figure 6-1 after it's run, assuming all files are in the proper directories.

1. Create a new project called SHELL.MAK. and a form called SHELL.FRM. Give the form the dimensions of about 4 inches wide and 3 inches tall as shown in Figure 6-1 and save it .

2. Add the objects and properties shown in Table 6-1 to this form. If a property is not listed, its effect is not important and the default is assumed.

| Object | Property | Setting |
|---|---|---|
| Form | FormName | Run_DOS |
| | Caption | Run a DOS Process |
| | BackColor | &H00C0C0C0& (50% gray) |
| | Filename | SHELL.FRM |
| Timer | Name | Timer1 |
| | Enabled | False |
| | Interval | 1000 |
| Command button | Name | Cmd_Run |
| | Caption | Run |
| List box | Name | Text1 |
| | ScrollBars | 3 - Both |

**Table 6-1**  Shell project form's objects and properties

3. Now make a .PIF file with the Windows PIF editor. This is important if you expect the Shell styles feature to work. We will specify that the DOS process is minimized and with focus.

The .PIF file filename should be the same as the batch file, with the .PIF extension: SHELL.PIF. The name of the window for the program should be DOS Sort Batch and the startup directory should be set to where the file is located in your system; for instance, C:\VB\SHELL. The Display Usage button should be set to Windowed and Execution set to Background. If you leave this .PIF out, the running DOS batch process will take over the settings in _DEFAULT.DIF.

4. Put the following code in the Declarations section of the general object.

```
Declare Function GetNumTasks Lib "kernel" () As Integer
Dim NumTasks%
```

5. Put this code in the Cmd_Click procedure of the form:

```
Sub Cmd_Run_Click ()
   NumTasks% = GetNumTasks()          'Checks num of tasks running now
   Text1.Text = ""
   ChDir ("c:\vb\shell")
   x% = Shell("shell.bat", 2)
   Timer1.Enabled = -1                'Timer monitors running tasks
End Sub
```

6. Put this code in the Timer1_Timer procedure of Timer1:

```
Sub Timer1_Timer ()
    If GetNumTasks%() <> NumTasks% Then
        Exit Sub
    Else
    ' Slow DOS is finished and we can open the file.
        Open "DIR.TXT" For Input As #1
        Do Until EOF(1)
            Line Input #1, oneLine$
            Text1.SelText = Text1.SelText + oneLine$ + Chr$(13) + Chr$(10)
        Loop
        Close #1
        Timer1.Enabled = 0          ' Disable timer
    End If
End Sub
```

## How It Works

The Declare statement sets up the GetNumTasks API and the Declarations section defines an integer variable called NumTasks that will be global to the form.

Examine the procedure in the single button called Cmd_Run_Click. When the button is clicked, this procedure executes the GetNumTasks API, which returns an integer number that represents the number of tasks running at this moment. Next it clears out any text in the list box and switches to the directory containing our batch file.

Next the Shell command runs the SHELL.BAT file with the window style of 2, which means minimized and focused. This could be a style of 7 also, which is minimized and unfocused; both 2 and 7 work. Finally, the timer is enabled so it starts operating. At this point the DOS process will make a little icon appear on your desktop with the title given by the .PIF file you made. If you would rather your users didn't see this icon you can extend the form so it's larger than the icon, and make the style 7 (unfocused) in the Shell command, so it doesn't pop up on top of the window covering it.

Now examine the code in the Timer1_Timer procedure. This procedure is run every 1000 milliseconds, or 1 second, as set by the value in the timer duration property. The first statement is an If…Then loop that simply examines the current number of tasks with the value stored when we did the Shell. If the number is the same, we can assume that the task is still operating, exit from the subroutine, and do nothing. However, if the task is finished, GetNumTasks will return a lower number than is stored, and the loop will fall through to the next statement. The code that follows is a loop that simply opens the file DIR.TXT for input and reads each line into a variable called oneLine$. The SelText property gives you the current text in the box, so the long statement:

```
Text1.SelText = Text1.SelText + oneLine$ + Chr$(13) + Chr$(10)
```

simply appends a single line to the end of the text block and attaches a carriage return and line feed character to it.

Next we close the file and disable the timer so it doesn't keep checking and we are done!

### Comments

There is a small danger that if the DOS process was a long slow one, your user could go off and start a new program. The SHELL batch file would end, and our program would enter the Timer1 loop looking for the processes to be the same as when we first started the DOS process. But this won't occur until we quit the new application, so for all that time the Visual Basic program would be hung up. For a solution, see How-To 6.2.

## 6.2 ● How do I...

## Use a more sophisticated method to monitor a DOS program?

### Problem

In How-To 6.1 Run a DOS program and find out when it's done, you mention that there could be a problem if another task starts up while the DOS process task is running under Windows. I'd like to know a safer and more sophisticated way to run a process and avoid this hangup. And while we're on the subject of controlling DOS processes, can you give me some tips on running and using Windows and DOS programs in concert? I am particularly interested in making it look like an application is a real Windows application, not a DOS application being run from a shell.

### Technique

There is a better, safer way to know that DOS has finished a process. There are two APIs that can be used: GetActiveWindow and IsWindow. GetActiveWindow returns a handle to the currently active window, the one with the focus. IsWindow returns True if the window exists and False if it no longer exists. Thus, if we use the handle returned by GetActiveWindow for our active DOS process, we can use IsWindow in a loop to check on whether the window is still open. When it is no longer open, the process must have ended, and we can do our next step in Visual Basic, accessing the results from DOS. The DoEvents statement is placed inside the loop that uses IsWindow, so that processing time is given back to Windows. Without DoEvents other processes would not get priority.

We needed a simple interface to control a ray-tracing DOS program called Persistence of Vision Ray Tracer, or just PV. This has all the features of most DOS programs: it is powerful and has an awful interface.

### A Bit About Ray Tracing

A little bit about PV will help you see what we are doing. PV is a ray-tracing program—you feed it a text file that contains a description of a world of objects, spheres, planes, cylinders, light sources, and so on, specified with a simple descriptive language. Objects have locations in a three-dimensional space, have colors and textures, and so on. PV takes light coming from specified light sources and traces how each ray of it would bounce off and pass through the objects in the world. You set up a camera location that represents where your eye is located in a coordinate system of floating point numbers called the universe.

PV makes a 24-bit color Targa (.TGA) file of the image. You can convert this image to a beautiful 256 color .GIF or .PCX file with a shareware program such as PicLab, and you can view the GIF or PCX with PicLab or any popular file viewer. Ray tracing, or rendering, is one of the more important requirements in making photo-realistic scenes and is employed by animation houses that make logos, multimedia presentations, engineering studies, and so on. There is great interest in this subject today, because any 386 machine and a good VGA can perform ray tracing that rivals the computers of Lucas Films, the people that made the movie *Star Wars.*

We won't explain the details of PV and its descriptive language (you can find out more about PV in *Ray Tracing Creations,* Drew Wells and Chris Young, Waite Group Press, 1993). Our goal here is to show you how to run PV from a Visual Basic interface, so that you can extend the idea to any DOS program you like.

PV, as it exists at the time of this writing, has only a command-line interface. You enter the name of the data file you wish to trace, followed by parameters for the ray tracing, such as resolution, antialiasing, and the name of the description file. You have to create the description file with any editor.

All this works well if you are willing to do a little typing and have a good memory, however, the ideal interface for PV would enable you to open any of the description language text files, edit them on screen, set the resolution

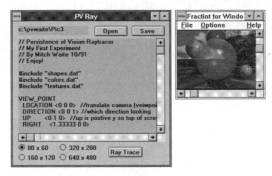

**Figure 6-2** The PV ray tracer with data file open and Fractint for Windows displaying the ray tracing for this data file

of the ray tracing, save the file, and tell the ray tracer to run.

In our example we'll make sure the DOS process runs in a window by setting up a .PIF file, and we'll use the two APIs to monitor when the process has finished. A batch file for PV will also be used that not only runs PV, but also sends the 24-bit Targa output from PV into PicLab and converts it into a 234-color .GIF file that is suitable for viewing under any GIF viewer. Using 234 colors in the map instead of the full 256 means Windows can use the remaining colors for its own interface. If you don't allow for this , you'll get little black holes in your image as Windows steals those colors for its own palette. If you use 234 colors Windows is smart enough to figure out what remaining colors to reserve. Once PicLab finishes the DOS process will end.

At this point we want Visual Basic to bring a GIF viewer—in this case we use the program Fractint for Windows—to the top of the desktop, then automatically open the .GIF file that was just created. This can be done with Visual Basic's SendKeys statement.

Figure 6-2 shows the interface we made for PV and the Fractint for Windows program revealing the small preview of the ray traced scene in file PIC3.DAT. In this How-To we show the exact program names that were used for the PV interface. On the disk provided with this book we substituted batch files that accomplish the same results by simulating the processes without PV.

### Steps

Several files make up this project, as shown in Table 6-2. These files must be in the right directories for this project to work. Besides PV.MAK and PV.FRM, there are PV.BAT and the WINFRACT.BAT batch files, as well as a PV.PIF file.

| File | Description |
| --- | --- |
| *B:\CHAPTER6\6.2* | |
| PV.MAK | |
| PV.FRM | |
| PV.BAT | This is a dummy that represents your DOS program. |
| WINFRACT.BAT | This is a dummy that represents the WINFRACT program. |
| | |
| *WINDOWS directory* | |
| PV.PIF | This .PIF file is needed to make your DOS process run in a window. |

**Table 6-2** PV Files

1. Create a new project called PV.MAK and a form called PV.FRM. Make the form about 4 inches wide and 4 inches tall.

2. Add the objects and properties listed in Table 6-3 to this form. The radio buttons are arranged as an array, with the first button selected by default by setting its Value property to True. The remaining Value properties are set to False.

| Object | Property | Setting |
| --- | --- | --- |
| Form | FormName | PV_Ray |
| | Caption | PV Ray |
| | BackColor | &H00C0C0C0&  (50% gray) |
| Command button | Name | CmdOpen |
| | Caption | Open |
| Command button | Name | CmdSave |
| | Caption | Save |
| Command button | Name | CmdRunPV |
| | Caption | Ray Trace |
| Text box | Name | FldPicName |
| | BackColor | &H00FFFF00& |
| | FontName | Helv |
| | FontBold | True |
| Text box | Name | TxtListing |
| | BackColor | &H00FFFF00& |
| | FontName | Helv |
| | FontBold | True |

*continued on next page*

*continued from previous page*

| Object | Property | Setting |
|--------|----------|---------|
| | ScrollBars | 3 - Both |
| | Text | Listing for the DAT file here |
| Option button | Name | OptReso |
| OptReso(0) | Index | 0 |
| | Caption | 80 x 60 |
| | Value | True |
| OpReso(1) | Index | 1 |
| | Caption | 160 x 120 |
| OptReso(2) | Index | 2 |
| | Caption | 320 x 200 |
| OptReso(3) | Index | 3 |
| | Caption | 640 x 480 |

**Table 6-3** PV project form's objects and properties

3. Now make a .PIF file with the Windows PIF editor and call it PV.PIF. The file, which must be made to use the Shell statement's styles, will be saved in the Windows directory. The DOS process run by Shell has a style of 2, which means a minimized window (iconized) and with focus.

   The .PIF file's filename should be the same as the DOS program, in this case PV.BAT, with the .PIF extension: PV.PIF. Fill out the PIF form as follows: the name of the window for the program should be PV Ray Tracer. The Start-up Directory should be set to where the target file is located in your system, for this book it is B:\CHAPTER6\6.2. The Display Usage button should be set to Windowed and Execution set to Background.

4. Put the following code in the Declarations section of the form. This sets up general variables global to the form and initializes the APIs.

```
DefInt A-Z
Declare Function GetActiveWindow Lib "user" ()
Declare Function IsWindow Lib "user" (ByVal hwnd)
Dim NumTasks%
Dim w As String
Dim h As String
Dim d As String
Dim v As String
Declare Function WinExec Lib "Kernel" (ByVal lpCmdLine As String, ByVal ⇐
nCmdShow As Integer) As Integer
Dim crlf As String
Dim safe As Integer
```

5. Put the following code in the Form_Load procedure of the form.

```
Sub Form_Load ()
    crlf = Chr$(13) + Chr$(10)
    'set default values to 80 x 60 no display verbose mode
    w$ = "80": h$ = "60": d$ = "-d": v$ = "+v"
    'if you don't have winfract substitute a different viewer.
    Er% = WinExec("c:\winfract\winfract.exe", 1)
    safe = 0   'set safe to false
End Sub
```

6. Put the following code in the button CmdRunPV. It is responsible for running the DOS program that does the actual ray tracing.

```
Sub CmdRunPV_Click ()

    PV_File$ = "b:\CHAPTER6\6.2\PV.BAT"
    PV_Para$ = FldPicName.text + " " + w + " " + h + " " + d + " " + v
    X = Shell(PV_File$ + " " + PV_Para$, 2) ' 1 = window with focus, 2 = ⇐
    'minimzed w/focus
    HwndShell = GetActiveWindow()
    While IsWindow(HwndShell)
        X = DoEvents()
    Wend
    ' wait until IsWindow tells us that the iconized DOS window is a
    ' finished process. DoEvents prevents our program from
    ' hogging the system.

    OpenFractint
End Sub
```

7. Put the following code in a procedure called OpenFractint in the Declarations section of the form. This is called whenever the DOS process is finished and control is returned to Visual Basic.

```
Sub OpenFractint ()
    ' Remove comment lines if you have winfract. exe
    ' AppActivate "Fractint for Windows - Vers 16.11"
    ' SendKeys "%(FO)"      'Alt-F Opens File Menu, Alt-O Opens Open Menu
    ' FldPicName.Text is the name in the file box
    ' SendKeys FldPicName.text + ".gif"  ' This is what Piclab made
    ' SendKeys "{ENTER}" 'Open the file and display it with Fractint
End Sub
```

8. Put the following code the OptReso_Click radio button. Since this is a button array, there is only one Click routine.

```
Sub OptReso_Click (Index As Integer)
    Select Case Index
    Case 0
        w$ = "80": h$ = "60"
    Case 1
        w$ = "160": h$ = "120"
```

*continued on next page*

*continued from previous page*

```
    Case 2
       w$ = "320": h$ = "200"
    Case 3
       w$ = "640": h$ = "480"
    End Select
End Sub
```

9. Put the following code in the CmdOpen button subroutine.

```
Sub CmdOpen_Click ()
    TxtListing.text = ""    'clear out the listing box
    Open FldPicName.text + ".DAT" For Input As #1
    Do Until EOF(1)
       Line Input #1, oneLine$
       TxtListing.SelText = TxtListing.SelText + oneLine$ + crlf$
    Loop
    Close #1
    safe = -1  'now okay to save
End Sub
```

10. Put the following code in the CmdSave button subroutine.

```
Sub CmdSave_Click ()
    If safe = 0 Then
       Beep
       Exit Sub
    End If
    SFile$ = FldPicName.text + ".DAT"
    Open SFile$ For Output As #1
       Print #1, TxtListing.text
    Close #1
End Sub
```

### How It Works

The code in the Declarations section of the form sets up the two APIs, as well as several variables global to the form. The WinExec API works just like Visual Basic's Shell command, except it will not make your program halt if an error is returned.

The Form_Load code uses the WinExec API to load the program called WINFRACT.EXE when the Visual Basic application starts. You can replace this with WINFRACT.BAT if you just want to test the routine. The WinExec API will not report an error if the file is missing and, therefore, will not interrupt your program with an error message as Shell does. After opening Fractint for Windows a global variable safe is set to False, which is used later to make sure we don't try to save a program that is empty (which would happen if you pressed Save immediatey after opening the program and running it).

The Form_Load code also sets up the default values for the four important variables that control PV from the command line: w$, which is the entry for ray-tracing width; h$, which is the ray-tracing height variable; d$, which is the display on or off option, and v$, the verbose on or off option.

The PV DOS program is set up so a minus sign (-) in front of an option turns it off, while an addition sign (+) turns it on. So "-d" means the display is turned off (graphics would conflict with Windows), and "+v" means the verbose text output mode is enabled.

### Editing Files

The data files that describe the ray-tracing world are simple ASCII files that can be easily modified. To make it possible to edit the files in Visual Basic, we simply have to load the file contents into a text box. We set its scroll bar property to 3 - Both, so there is both a vertical and horizontal scroll bar. As a quick and dirty way to open and close files, we used a somewhat crude but simple approach. The name of the file is typed into a text box along with its path. When the Open button is clicked, the CmdOpen_Click procedure is called. It attempts to open the file named in the text box, adding the extension .DAT to the file. If the file is found, each line of the file is read one at a time into the list box. When EOF is detected, the loop ends and the file is closed.

The Save button has a similar function but it does the reverse. Clicking on Save takes the entire text box and saves its contents to a serial file with the Print # statement. The routine checks that there has already been a file loaded so that it does not save an empty file. The danger with this approach is that if the filename is wrong the program halts and must be restarted. The next step would be to add a file open and save dialog using one of the several described in this book.

### Doing It

The main code for running the program occurs in the CmdRunPV button. The filename that will be Shelled to is defined as PV.BAT. Next the parameters that will be sent to the PV program are assembled in a string. Finally the Shell statement is executed with the filename PV.BAT and the parameter string. The DOS process is started in a window with focus (that's the purpose of the 2 at the end of the Shell statement). This will let you watch the DOS process run, and will let you interact with it.

Next a handle to the window for this DOS process is obtained in HwndShell, and a DoUntil loop is entered. This loop continues until IsWindow returns False for the active window HwndShell. During the time that the DOS (or icon) window is still active, the DoEvents function assures the Visual Basic program does not hog its Windows multitasking allotment.

At this point, on a 386 computer, you could stop Visual Basic, and your DOS process would keep running. In fact, you may, if it's not a protected mode application, spawn another copy of the DOS process and run two versions of your program at the same time. Once the DOS process stops, the procedure called OpenFractint is called.

### Open My Application or Bring It to the Top

The code for OpenFractint brings the Fractint program to the top of the desktop and instructs it to open our newly created .GIF file. Recall the .PIF file opened earlier in this project. That file must contain the name of the program. The Visual Basic AppActivate function is used to make the program come to the top of the desktop. The name in the string has to exactly match the name in the .PIF file. Next, SendKeys is used to tell Fractint to pull down its File menu and open a file. The extension .GIF is now added to the name of the file in the filename text box (the file we ray traced complete with path). This name is then entered into the name field of Fractint's open file dialog box again using SendKeys. This is followed by sending an (ENTER) keypress, and the image is loaded and displayed.

The OptReso_Click procedure is the way we set the resolution for w$ and h$ variables. A simple Case statement just puts different values in these variables. When the Ray Trace command button is pushed the parameter file is assembled with the current values.

### Comments

Communicating the output of a DOS process to a Visual Basic program running under Windows is not simple. The simple way to accomplish this is by writing information from the DOS process to a file and then reading it with Visual Basic. Another less known way to communicate between a DOS and a Visual Basic program is by using the DOS Intra Application Communications area (IAC) located at 0040:00F0 to 0040:00FF. A single POKE and PEEK DLL would allow Visual Basic to access this area.

## 6.3 How do I...

## Exit Windows and return to DOS?

### Problem

I've written an application that determines whether a virus has attacked a Windows system. If it detects a virus, I'd like to inform the user and then shut down Windows so the virus can't do any damage. Is this possible?

### Technique

Visual Basic's End statement simply terminates the current application. It can't terminate Windows. Luckily, there is a Windows API function—ExitWindows—that will terminate Windows and return to DOS.

Using ExitWindows won't cause you to lose any data. All the applications you have running at the time have the chance to say: "Hey, gimme a minute to save my files!" before Windows will shut down.

### Steps

Open and run EXITWIND.MAK. Click on the Exit Windows! button. If all the other applications running agree to terminate, Windows will shut down and you'll be returned to the DOS prompt.

1. Create a new project called EXITWIND.MAK. and a new form with the controls and properties shown in Table 6-4. Save the form as EXITWIND.FRM. See Figure 6-3 for the appearance of the completed form.

**Figure 6-3** The Exit Windows project design

| Object | Property | Setting |
|---|---|---|
| Form | Caption | Exit Windows |
| | FormName | ExitWindowsForm |
| | BackColor | &00HC0C0C0& |
| Command button | Name | ExitWin |
| | Caption | Exit Windows! |
| | Default | True |

**Table 6-4** ExitWindows project form's controls and properties

2. Put the following code in the Declarations section of the form. This Declare statement gives the form access to the ExitWindows API function.

```
Declare Function ExitWindows Lib "User" (ByVal wReturnCode As Long, By ⇐
Val dwReserved As Integer) As Integer
```

3. Put the following code in the ExitWin_Click event subroutine.

```
Sub ExitWin_Click ()
    If ExitWindows(0, 0) = 0 Then
        MsgBox "Sorry; another application says not to terminate!"
    End If
End Sub
```

This is a call to the ExitWindows API function. If ExitWindows returns 0, a message box pops up and informs the user that another application won't let Windows terminate.

**How It Works**

The Windows API function ExitWindows is used to shut down Windows and all the running applications. ExitWindows will not terminate DOS windows, so if there are any DOS windows, ExitWindows won't shut down all of Windows. ExitWindows tells all Windows applications that someone has requested that Windows be shut down. Those applications can then save any open files. (For example, a word processor would ask the user to save a document.) An application can tell Windows that it can't be terminated at this time, in which case Windows won't shut down.

If all Windows applications agree to terminate, Windows will shut down and you will be returned to the DOS prompt.

The first parameter, wReturnCode, is the return code that Windows will pass back to DOS. The second parameter of the ExitWindows call, dwReserved, isn't used by this version of Windows and must be zero. If you started Windows from a batch file, you can check this return code by using the IF ERRORLEVEL command.

### Comments

You can tell when your Visual Basic application is being terminated by checking for the form's Unload event. If you have some code in the Form_Unload event subroutine, that code will be executed before your application is terminated. For example, you could pop up a message box giving the user a chance to change his mind or to save files.

## 6.4 How do I...

## Prevent Windows from shutting down?

### Problem

If my users exit Windows (by selecting Exit from the Program Manager's File menu), my Visual Basic application will be shut down without a chance to save any work the user has done. Is there some way I can prevent this?

### Technique

Before Windows shuts down, it gives all the running applications a chance to say "Hey! I'm not finished yet." If an application tells Windows not to shut down, Windows stays active at that application.

Usually the reason you won't want Windows to shut down your Windows application is that there is some data that hasn't been saved to a file yet. The most common approach to preventing data loss is to pop up a message box saying "Save this file?". If the user clicks on Yes to save the file, the application saves it, and then tells Windows it's okay to shut down.

In Visual Basic, the event that's triggered by a potential Windows shutdown is the Form_Unload event. (Note that this event is also triggered by the Unload statement.) You can include a call to your form's file save routine in the Form_Unload event subroutine. For example, if you have a File menu with a Save option that saves a file, you might use the following Form_Unload event subroutine:

```
Sub Form_Unload (Cancel As Integer)
    FileSave_Click
End Sub
```

It's traditional Windows practice to ask users whether they really want to save their changes, so you should include a MsgBox function call, too, as follows:

```
Sub Form_Unload (Cancel As Integer)
    If MsgBox("Do you want to save?", 4 + 32) = 6 Then FileSave_Click
End Sub
```

The "4 + 32" parameter in the MsgBox function call tells Visual Basic to include Yes and No buttons (4) and the question mark icon (32). If MsgBox returns a 6, the user selected Yes, so a call to the FileSave_Click event subroutine will save the file.

But what if you don't want Windows to shut down? Some Windows applications give the user the option of aborting the shutdown and to continue working on their applications. You can achieve the same thing in Visual Basic by using a message box with a Cancel button, as follows:

```
Sub Form_Unload (Cancel As Integer)
    Select Case MsgBox("Do you want to save?", 3 + 32)
       Case 6
           FileSave_Click
       Case 2
           Cancel = 1
    End Select
End Sub
```

The "3 + 32" parameter in the MsgBox function call tells Visual Basic to include Yes, No, and Cancel buttons (3) and the question mark icon (32). If MsgBox returns a 6, the user selected Yes, so a call to the FileSave_Click event subroutine will save the file. Otherwise, if MsgBox returns a 2, the user selected Cancel. Then we set the Cancel parameter to tell Windows to abort the attempted shutdown. Your application will continue to run as if Windows never tried to shut down.

### Comments

As mentioned, the Unload event occurs in several circumstances. You shouldn't assume that Windows is shutting down; it may just be that your user closed your application somehow (by double-clicking on the system menu icon or by using the End Task button on the Task Manager window, for example).

## 6.5 ⬤ How do I...

# Search an entire disk for a file?

### Problem

Although I try to keep my hard drive organized, sometimes files get placed in the wrong directory. Is there any way to have my Visual Basic application search the whole disk for specific files?

### Technique

You are probably accustomed to searching directories manually using Visual Basic's directory list box control. This project also uses this control but automatically steps it through the directory structure under program control. As each directory is found, the filenames in the directory are scanned against a search mask. Those that match are displayed in a list box on the form.

### Steps

Open and run FILEFIND.MAK. Enter a filename search mask in the file spec text box. Select the disk drive and starting directory, then click on the Go command button. All directories and any matching filenames are displayed in the list box.

To create the Filefind project, enter the objects and code as detailed in the following steps.

1. Create a new project called FILEFIND.MAK. Create a new form with the objects and properties shown in Table 6-5, and save it as FILEFIND.FRM. The appearance of the form should match Figure 6-4. Note that because the Dir2 control is never visible, its size and placement on the form are not critical.

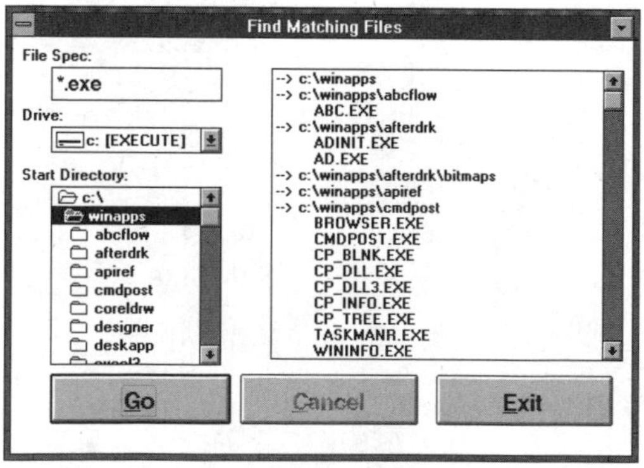

**Figure 6-4** The Filefind project in action

| Object | Property | Setting |
| --- | --- | --- |
| Form | FormName | Filefind |
| | Caption | Find Matching Files |
| | MaxButton | False |
| Label | Name | Label1 |
| | Caption | File Spec: |
| | Autosize | True |
| Label | Name | Label2 |
| | Caption | Drive: |
| | Autosize | True |
| Label | Name | Label3 |
| | Caption | Start    Directory: |
| | Autosize | True |
| | Alignment | 1 - Right Justify |
| Text box | Name | Text1 |
| | FontSize | 1 2 |
| | Text | * . * |
| Drive list box | Name | Drive1 |
| Directory list box | Name | Dir1 |
| Directory list box | Name | Dir2 |
| | Visible | False |
| Command button | Name | CmdGo |
| | Caption | &Go |
| | FontSize | 1 4 |
| | Default | True |
| Command button | Name | CmdCancel |
| | Caption | &Cancel |
| | FontSize | 1 4 |
| | Enabled | False |
| | Cancel | True |
| Command button | Name | CmdExit |
| | Caption | E&xit |
| | FontSize | 1 4 |
| List box | Name | List1 |

**Table 6-5** Filefind project form's objects and properties

2. Place the following variable declaration in the General section of the form.

```
Dim Abort As Integer                     ' Common Abort flag
```

3. Put the following code in the Dir2_Change event subroutine. This subroutine scans the current directory and all of its subdirectories for matching filenames.

```
Sub Dir2_Change ()
Dim DirCount As Integer, I As Integer, T As Integer
Dim Filename As String, Searchpath As String
'
'  Display directory name in list box.
'  Build Searchpath string, root directory already has "\".
'
   List1.AddItem "--> " + Dir2.Path ' Show directory
   Searchpath = Dir2.Path
   If Right$(Searchpath, 1) <> "\" Then Searchpath = Searchpath + "\"
   Searchpath = Searchpath + Text1.Text
'
'  Search and display matching files in current directory.
'
   Filename = Dir$(Searchpath)      ' Set initial search string
   Do While Filename <> ""
      List1.AddItem "        " + Filename
      Filename = Dir$                 ' No arguments to find next match
   Loop
'
'  Save all the directory names in current directory.
'
   DirCount = Dir2.ListCount
ReDim Dirlist(DirCount) As String
   For I = 0 To DirCount - 1
      Dirlist(I) = Dir2.List(I)
   Next I
'
'  For each directory in the list, processes their subdirectories.
'  This may take a while, so processes events in case user aborts.
   For I = 0 To DirCount - 1
      T = DoEvents()
      If Abort Then Exit Sub          ' Stop if requested
      Dir2.Path = Dirlist(I)
   Next I
End Sub
```

4. Put the following code in the Driv1_Change event subroutine. This code passes a drive change event to the Dir1, directory list box control.

```
Sub Drive1_Change ()
'
'  If we change the drive then we change the directory.
'
   Dir1.Path = Drive1.Drive
End Sub
```

5. Put the following code in the CmdGo_Click event subroutine. This code clears the list box of its contents and begins a new search.

```
Sub CmdGo_Click ()
Dim I As Integer
'
' Disable all controls (except CmdCancel) during the search.
'
    CmdGo.Enabled = 0
    Text1.Enabled = 0
    Drive1.Enabled = 0
    Dir1.Enabled = 0
    CmdCancel.Enabled = -1

' Clear ListBox. Let user know what we are doing.
'
    List1.Visible = 0
    CurrentX = List1.Left
    CurrentY = List1.Top + List1.Height / 2
    Print "Clearing List Box"
    For I = List1.ListCount - 1 To 0 Step -1
        List1.RemoveItem I
    Next I
    List1.Visible = -1

    Abort = 0          ' Clear abort flag from prior run
'
' Dir2_Change does recursive descent through directories.
' If Dir2 pointing to current directory, we need to trigger
' the change event ourselves.
'
    If Dir2.Path = Dir1.Path Then
        Dir2_Change
    Else
        Dir2.Path = Dir1.Path
    End If
'
' Enable controls after the search.
'
    CmdGo.Enabled = -1
    Text1.Enabled = -1
    Drive1.Enabled = -1
    Dir1.Enabled = -1
    CmdCancel.Enabled = 0
    CmdGo.SetFocus        ' Reset focus to Go button
End Sub
```

6. Put the following code in the Text1_GotFocus event subroutine. This code selects the search string when Text1 gets the focus.

```
Sub Text1_GotFocus ()
' Highlight all the contents of the TextBox.
    Text1.SelStart = 0
```

```
    Text1.SelLength = Len(Text1.Text)
End Sub
```

7. Put the following code in the CmdCancel_Click event subroutine. It sets a global variable, Abort, which will stop an active file search.

```
Sub CmdCancel_Click ()
    Abort = -1              ' Set abort flag
End Sub
```

8. Put the following code in the CmdExit_Click event subroutine. This button allows the users a graceful way to exit the application.

```
Sub CmdExit_Click ()
    End
End Sub
```

## How It Works

Although Visual Basic has the Dir$ function to return the filenames in a directory, there is no equivalent statement to return the list of directories on a drive. This project takes advantage of the way the Directory list box control works to have it inspect the branches of a directory tree.

The program begins the search process when the user clicks on the Go button invoking the CmdGo_Click event subroutine. We first disable the controls that were used to set up and initiate the search. If the controls were not disabled, parameters could be changed while a search was in progress, yielding misleading results. The Cancel button is enabled allowing the user to stop the search.

The list box containing the results from the prior search is cleared. Because this process can take a few seconds, the list box is made invisible, and an informational message is printed in its place. When the box is empty, it is made visible again covering the informational message.

This program uses two directory list box controls, Dir1 and Dir2. Dir1 is visible on screen and is used to select the starting directory branch for the search. Using Figure 6-4 as an example, the search would start at the selected subdirectory, C:\WINAPPS. Dir2 retrieves the directory names for us. Even though it is not visible on screen, it can still be manipulated and return data to the Visual Basic program.

The scan of directories begins with a Dir2_Change event. Note that in the Cmd_Go event subroutine we check whether Dir2 is already pointing to the selected directory. If it is, the Dir2_Change event subroutine is called directly. If not, the program initiates the directory change event by setting Dir2.Path to the desired starting point.

The Dir2_Change event subroutine searches the current directory and its subdirectories for filenames that match the search string. The current directory is searched for matching files using the Dir$ function. Dir$ is loaded with the name of the directory being searched and the file search mask located in the text box. Note the If...Then statement that is needed to handle the root directory. Subsequent Dir$ calls, with no parameters, will return the next matching filename. All matching files are displayed in the list box.

Looking at Figure 6-4, notice how subdirectories are displayed underneath the current directory. Each of the subdirectory names is copied from the directory list box to the DirList array. The property Dir2.ListCount returns the number of subdirectories. Finally, the Dir2_Change event subroutine changes the current path to each of the subdirectories, which will trigger a Dir2_Change event for the subdirectory and its subdirectories. This is called a recursive subroutine, because it calls itself to do additional work.

On a large and complex hard drive, a complete search can take quite a few seconds. The user can abort the process by clicking on the Cancel button. This action sets a global Abort flag that is checked by Dir2_Change and will cause it to exit the subroutine. The DoEvents function allows Visual Basic to respond to user actions while the search is progressing.

## 6.6  How do I...

**Complexity: Intermediate**

## Use the Shell function without causing run-time errors?

### Problem

Using Visual Basic's Shell function will cause a run-time error if the command to be executed can't be found. Is there some way to prevent these run-time errors without using On Error Goto?

### Technique

There's no way around the run-time error a Shell function causes if it can't find the program specified, unless you use an On Error Goto error-handling routine. The Shell function must be a file with an extension of .COM, .EXE, .BAT, or .PIF. Shell will look for a file in the following directories:

- The current directory

- The Windows directory (by default, C:\WINDOWS)

- The Windows system directory (by default, C:\WINDOWS\SYSTEM)

- The directories on your path

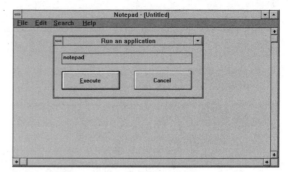

**Figure 6-5** The VBShell form in action

If Shell can't find a file in any of those directories, it will cause a Visual Basic run-time error. If your application doesn't have an active On Error Goto error-handling routine, the run-time error will cause Visual Basic to pop up a message box with a "File not found" error message. Then the program will abort—not a very user-friendly response.

Luckily, the Windows API library offers a function named WinExec, which works almost exactly the same as Visual Basic's Shell function, except it won't cause a run-time error. We can add a function that calls WinExec to the VBHOWTO.BAS module.

### Steps

Open and run VBSHELL.MAK. Type a command into the text box and press Enter or click on the Execute button. You can try running both DOS and Windows applications.

1. Create a new project called VBSHELL.MAK. Create a new form with the controls and properties listed in Table 6-6 and save it as VBSHELL.FRM. See Figure 6-5 for its appearance.

| Control | Property | Setting |
| --- | --- | --- |
| Form | Caption | Run an application |
| | MaxButton | False |
| | BackColor | &H00C0C0C0& |
| Text box | Name | Text1 |
| | Text | <blank> |
| Command button | Name | Execute |
| | Caption | Execute |
| | Default | True |

*continued on next page*

*continued from previous page*

| Control | Property | Setting |
|---------|----------|---------|
| Command button | Name | Cancel |
| | Caption | Cancel |
| | Cancel | True |

**Table 6-6** VBShell project form's objects and properties

2. Add the following to the Declarations section of the module. This is the declaration for the WinExec API function.

```
Declare Function WinExec Lib "Kernel" (ByVal lpCmdLine As String, ByVal ⇐
nCmdShow As Integer) As Integer
```

3. Add the following code to the VBHOWTO.BAS module.

```
Function VBHTShell (lpCmdLine$, nCmdShow As Integer)
   VBHTShell = WinExec(lpCmdLine$, nCmdShow)
End Function
```

4. Add the following code to the Cancel_Click event subroutine.

```
Sub Cancel_Click ()
   End
End Sub
```

5. Put the following code in the Execute_Click event subroutine. This code calls the VBHTShell function to execute the command the user entered in the text box.

```
Sub Execute_Click ()
   Cmd$ = Text1.Text
   Er% = VBHTShell(Cmd$, 1)
   If Er% < 32 Then
       MsgBox "Error" + Str$(Er%) + " executing your command!", 48
   End If
End Sub
```

### How It Works

The WinExec API function is almost identical to Visual Basic's Shell function. It even uses the same numbers for the second parameter (except that Shell calls the parameter "WindowStyle%" and WinExec calls it "nCmdShow").

Both Shell and WinExec return a number; Microsoft calls the number that Shell returns the "task ID." That ID is never used by any other Windows function, so it can be ignored. If WinExec returns a number less than 32, there was an error; if the number is greater than 32, it's the mythical task ID. Don't worry about storing this task ID.

### Comments

Unlike Visual Basic's Shell function, VBHTShell requires the second window style parameter. The default value for Shell is 1, so you could pass a 1 as the second parameter to VBHTShell to get the same effect as Visual Basic's Shell function.

## 6.7  How do I...

## Run a DOS internal command?

### Problem

Visual Basic's Shell function and the VBHTShell function that we've created won't execute an internal (non-EXE) DOS command like DIR or TYPE. Is there any way to run these commands within my applications?

### Technique

In the previous How-To, Use the Shell function without causing run-time errors, we created a custom shell called VBHTSHELL. Both the native Visual Basic Shell function and the WinExec API function (that our custom VBHTShell depends on) will only run .COM, .EXE, .BAT, and .PIF files. DOS commands like DIR and TYPE aren't any of these types of files. Instead they're internal to the DOS command processor COMMAND.COM.

Is there some way to get COMMAND.COM to execute its internal commands? A quick look at a DOS manual confirms that you can get COMMAND.COM to do just that by using the following format:

```
COMMAND /C command
```

In other words, we can write COMMAND/C DIR and we'll get a directory listing. So, are we all set? Unfortunately, no. DOS has always supported the ability to replace COMMAND.COM with another command processor. A shareware COMMAND.COM replacement/enhancement, 4DOS, is quite popular. Its filename is 4DOS.COM, so if we were to execute COMMAND.COM, and 4DOS was running instead, our program would still not work. How can you determine the name of the command processor so we run the correct one?

In DOS an environment variable named COMSPEC holds the name of the actual command processor being used by the system. You can get the value of the COMSPEC environment variable and execute it with the /C option of COMMAND.COM. (4DOS supports this option, too.) So, how can we get the COMSPEC environment variable value? The Visual Basic function Environ$ will return the value of a specified environment variable.

### Steps

Open and run DOSSHELL.MAK. You can type a DOS command in the text box and click Execute, the command processor will be invoked, and the command in the text box will be executed. If you don't type anything in the text box, a new DOS shell will be started. Then you can type multiple commands. Type EXIT and press (ENTER) to close the shell.

1. Create a new project called DOSSHELL.MAK and a new form with the controls and properties listed in Table 6-7. Save the form as DOS-SHELL.FRM.

| Control | Property | Setting |
|---------|----------|---------|
| Form | Caption | Do a DOS command |
| | MaxButton | False |
| Text box | Name | Text1 |
| | Text | <blank> |
| Command button | Name | Execute |
| | Caption | Execute |
| | Default | True |
| Command button | Name | Cancel |
| | Caption | Cancel |
| | Cancel | True |

**Table 6-7** DosShell project form's objects and properties

2. Add the VBHOWTO.BAS module to the project.

3. Put the following code in the Cancel_Click event subroutine.

```
Sub Cancel_Click ()
    End
End Sub
```

4. Put the following code in the Execute_Click event subroutine. This subroutine gets the name of the command processor from the COMSPEC environment variable, and then uses the /C option to execute the command in the text box, if there is one. Finally, a call to VBHTShell executes the command.

```
Sub Execute_Click ()
    DOSShell$ = Environ$("COMSPEC")
```

```
    If DOSShell$ = "" Then DOSShell$ = "COMMAND.COM"
    Cmd$ = DOSShell$
    If Len(Text1.Text) Then Cmd$ = Cmd$ + " /C " + Text1.Text

    Er% = VBHTShell(Cmd$, 1)
    If Er% < 32 Then
        MsgBox "Error" + Str$(Er%) + " executing your command!", 48
    End If
End Sub
```

### How It Works

A call to the Environ$ function returns the name of the command processor, including the directory. If there is no COMSPEC setting, Environ$ will return a null string, so we check for it and assume that the user is using COMMAND.COM. Then, if there's some text in the text box Text1, that command gets added to the command being executed. If there is no text, the command will just be the name of the command processor, which will start a DOS window where you can enter multiple commands. You must type "EXIT" to close the DOS window and return to your Visual Basic application.

### Comments

The settings in your _DEFAULT.PIF file will partially determine how the DOS window looks. If you're running Windows in 386 Enhanced mode, you can set up _DEFAULT.PIF to run either full screen or in a window. You can also change the appearance of the window with the nCmdShow parameter in the VBHTShell function call. See your Visual Basic documentation or the online Help for details on that second parameter.

## 6.8  How do I...

Complexity: Advanced

## Prevent multiple program instances from being loaded?

### Problem

I would like to be able to prevent multiple instances of my Visual Basic application from being loaded but this has proven to be more difficult than I had imagined. There appear to be a number of solutions, all of which are less than ideal, such as dynamic data exchange (DDE) and temporary files. Is there an easier way? Using the FindWindow API function requires that the application must never change the caption on the main window.

### Technique

There are a number of approaches, as you mention, including DDE, temporary files, and FindWindow. All of these are less than ideal, so we will examine a couple of alternatives. FindWindow seems to be the immediate choice, but it falls short of our needs here. This is because all Visual Basic forms have the same classname—ThunderForm—so using FindWindow will not do, unless we are willing to leave the main form's caption alone.

One possibility is simply to check the number of running instances of our application. There are two pertinent Windows API functions for this, GetModuleHandle and GetModuleUsage.

However, to get a little fancier, FindWindow can be broken down to manually step through the "window list." We can step through the window list using the GetWindow and GetNextWindow API functions.

### Steps

There are two examples for this How-To and, in each case, they must be run as .EXE files to test their functionality. Therefore, load the file MIP1.MAK into the Visual Basic editor and select Make EXE from the File menu. Just accept the defaults and click OK. Now do the same thing with the file MIP2.MAK. You now have two .EXE files that you can add to the Program Manager: MIP1.EXE and MIP2.EXE.

In both cases the idea is to simply try to launch each one more than once. Launch MIP1.EXE and then minimize the resulting form. Now, try to launch it again from the Program Manager. You should see a message box, similar to the one used by the File Manager, that says that the application is already loaded. The second instance of MIP1.EXE will then terminate.

When you launch MIP2.EXE, for the second time, there is no message box. Instead, the "original" instance of MIP2.EXE will be restored before the second instance terminates. Use the technique that better suits your needs.

To create MIP1, perform the following steps:

1. Create a new project called MIP1.MAK. and a new form with the objects and properties in Table 6-8.

| Object | Property | Setting |
|--------|----------|---------|
| Form | FormName | Form1 |
| | Caption | MIP |
| Picture box | Name | Picture1 |
| | Caption | I'm Here! |
| | BorderStyle | None |

**Table 6-8** Mip project form's objects and properties

> 2. Select New Module from the File menu.

> 3. Insert the following code in the new module.

```
DefInt A-Z

Declare Function GetModuleHandle Lib "Kernel" (ByVal lpProgName$)
Declare Function GetModuleUsage Lib "Kernel" (ByVal hModule)

Sub Main ()
    hModule = GetModuleHandle("MIP1.EXE")
    Count = GetModuleUsage(hModule)
    If Count > 1 Then
        MsgBox "Application Already Loaded!"
        End
    Else
        Form1.Show
    End if
End Sub
```

> 4. Select Save File from the File menu and save the form and the module as MIP1.FRM and MIP1.BAS, respectively. Save the project as MIP1.MAK.

> 5. Select Sub Main as your startup form. Create the .EXE file and run the application.

> To create MIP2.EXE, perform the following steps:

> 1. Create a new form same as above with the one label.

> 2. Insert the following code in the Form_Resize procedure.

```
Sub Form_Resize ()
    Label1.Caption = "I'm Back!"
End Sub
```

> 3. Create a new module named MIP2.BAS. Insert the following code into MIP2.BAS.

```
DefInt A-Z

Declare Sub ShowWindow Lib "User" (ByVal hWnd, ByVal nCmd)
Declare Sub SetActiveWindow Lib "User" (ByVal hWnd)

Const SW_SHOWNORMAL = 1

Sub Main ()
    Wnd = SearchWindow("multi")
    If Wnd <> 0 Then
        ShowWindow Wnd, SW_SHOWNORMAL
        SetActiveWindow Wnd
        End
    Else
        Form1.Show
    End If
End Sub
```

4. Create a new module named WNDFIND.BAS, and insert the following code.

```
DefInt A-Z

Declare Function FindWindow Lib "User" (ByVal Class&, ByVal Caption&)
Declare Function GetWindow Lib "User" (ByVal hWnd, ByVal wCmd)
Declare Function GetNextWindow Lib "User" (ByVal hWnd, ByVal wCmd)

Declare Function GetWindowText Lib "User" (ByVal hWnd, ByVal Buf$, ⇐
ByVal lBuf)

Const GW_HWNDFIRST = 0
Const GW_HWNDNEXT = 2

Dim Capt As String * 256

Function SearchWindow (Search$)
   Dest$ = UCase$(Search$)
   Wnd = FindWindow(0, 0)
   Wnd = GetWindow(Wnd, GW_HWNDFIRST)
   While Wnd <> 0
      TChars = GetWindowText(Wnd, Capt, 256)
      If TChars > 0 Then
         Source$ = UCase$(Left$(Capt, TChars))
         If InStr(Source$, Dest$) > 0 Then
            SearchWindow = Wnd
            Exit Function
         End If
      End If
      Wnd = GetNextWindow(Wnd, GW_HWNDNEXT)
   Wend
   SearchWindow = 0
End Function

Function WndCaption$ (hWnd)
   TChars = GetWindowText(hWnd, Capt, 256)
   WndCaption$ = Left$(Capt, TChars)
End Function
```

5. Set Sub Main as the startup form. Save the form and project as MIP2 and create the .EXE file.

### How They Work

MIP1 works by first finding the module handle of MIP1.EXE. Because code is reused under Windows, the module handle for both instances (if there are two) of the application will be the same. Therefore, it is a simple matter to find how many instances of the application are currently running by using the GetModuleUsage function. If there is more than one, the application crashes.

MIP2 is a little more sophisticated; we end up with the "other" instance of our application being restored. This is possible because the SearchWindow function returns the hWnd property of the main window of the other application. Using this value we can use the SetActiveWindow (equivalent to AppActivate but uses an hWnd) API function to activate the old instance of the application. Then to get really fancy, we use the ShowWindow API function to "restore" the other instance.

SearchWindow works by stepping through the system's window list of top-level windows. FindWindow is used to simply get a valid handle to any window. With each hWnd retrieved with GetWindow and GetNextWindow, the GetWindowText API function is used to retrieve the caption of that window (just as we do in WndPeek). Then Instr is used to find a match with the search string and, if one is found, it returns that hWnd as the function's result.

### Comments

You may notice that within the SearchWindow function we check whether TChars is greater than 0. GetWindowText returns the number of characters that were actually copied into our string buffer. There are, in fact, a number of hidden windows on the system at all times, and it is quicker to eliminate them numerically than by using Instr.

An additional function in WNDFIND.BAS returns the caption of a window, based on its hWnd. Although not used in the sample, this is useful if you want to use AppActivate or you want to present a selection for the user.

Finally, it should be obvious that SearchWindow could also easily find the window of another application instead of using FindWindow with the classname. SearchWindow might prove more useful if, for example, you wanted, not only to find any instance of Notepad, but the one that contained a particular file.

## 6.9  How do I...

**Complexity: Advanced**

## Find other running applications?

### Problem

I would like to be able to locate other applications so that I can send keystrokes to those applications. Of course, SendKeys sends keystrokes to the active application. Presumably, I should use AppActivate to make the desired "target application" the active one. However, AppActivate requires an explicit Window title. Very often, applications change the Window title to reflect the current workspace, making it impossible to predict what the current window title is for a particular application.

### Technique

You need to break a high-level function down into its component parts to accomplish this task. Most of the functions of Visual Basic are derived from one or more functions of the Windows API. Further, many of the high-level functions in the API are built using a number of low-level functions, also in the API. For example, by using SendMessage to send the LB_DIR message to a "normal" list box, you can populate the control with a list of files matching a specification, thus creating a File list. Visual Basic's DoEvents function is just a wrapper around the PeekMessage API function.

The AppActivate function is simply a combination of the FindWindow and SetActiveWindow API functions. Using these two functions instead of AppActivate gives more flexibility when searching for the window of another application, when used in tandem with the WndPeek utility, covered in How-To 6.16 Simulate SPY in Visual Basic. Using WndPeek, we can determine the "classname" of a window and with FindWindow, you have the choice to search for a window based on its class, rather than its caption. Because the class of a window will not change based on the current workspace of an application, this is a consistent way to search for a window.

### Steps

Open and run FINDAPP.MAK. In the text box, simply enter the classname of the window for which you want to search (such as Notepad). The classname is not case sensitive. Then either press (ENTER) or click on the Search button. If FindApp finds a match, it displays the window handle (hWnd) in the caption bar and activates the corresponding window, much the same way the Visual Basic AppActivate function does, using the caption.

To determine the classname of a particular window you can use WndPeek. Table 6-9 lists a few classnames to get you started. (Note that the classname used by WINVER.EXE and SETUP.EXE is the same.)

| Classname | Application |
|---|---|
| SciCalc | CALC.EXE |
| CalWndMain | CALENDAR.EXE |
| Cardfile | CARDFILE.EXE |
| Clipboard | CLIPBOARD.EXE |

| Classname | Application |
|-----------|-------------|
| Clock | CLOCK.EXE |
| CtlPanelClass | CONTROL.EXE |
| Session | MS-DOS.EXE |
| Notepad | NOTE.EXE |
| pbParent | PBRUSH.EXE |
| Pif | PIFEDIT.EXE |
| PrintManager | PRINTMAN.EXE |
| Recorder | RECORDER.EXE |
| Roversi | REVERSI.EXE |
| #32770 | SETUP.EXE |
| Solitaire | SOL.EXE |
| Terminal | TERMINAL.EXE |
| WFS_Frame | WINFILE.EXE |
| MW_WINHELP | WINHELP.EXE |
| #32770 | WINVER.EXE |
| MSWRITE_MENU | WRITE.EXE |

**Table 6-9** Determining the classname of a window

To create FindApp, perform the following steps:

1. Create a new project called FINDAPP.MAK. and a new form with the objects and properties in Table 6-10. Save thefform as FINDAPP.FRM. When complete, the form should resemble Figure 6-6.

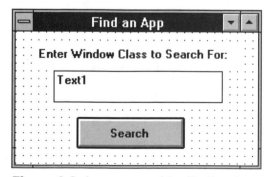

**Figure 6-6** Appearance of the FindApp form

| Object | Property | Setting |
|--------|----------|---------|
| Form | FormName | Form1 |
| | Caption | Find an App |
| Label | Name | Label1 |
| | Caption | Enter Class Name |
| Text box | Name | Text1 |
| Button | Name | Command1 |
| | Caption | Searh |
| | Default | TRUE |

**Table 6-10** FindApp project form's objects and properties

2. Insert the following code in the Declarations section of Form1.

```
DefInt A-Z

Declare Function FindWindow Lib "User" (ByVal lpClassName As Any, ByVal ⇐
lpCaption As Any)
Declare Sub SetActiveWindow Lib "User" (ByVal hWnd)

Const NULL = O&
```

3. Insert the following code in the Command1_Click procedure.

```
Sub Command1_Click ()
   ClassName$ = Text1.Text
   FoundhWnd = FindWindow(ClassName$, NULL)
   If FoundhWnd <> O Then
      Form1.Caption = "Found: " + Str$(FoundhWnd)
      SetActiveWindow (FoundhWnd)
   Else
      Form1.Caption = ClassName$ + " not found!"
   End If
End Sub
```

### How It Works

The FindWindow function will search for a window based either on its caption or its classname. It then returns the hWnd property of the window if there is a match, or a 0 if there is no match. By passing a classname with a NULL for a caption, we tell FindWindow that all captions should match. You can think of it like a file specification, where you can search for a file based on its extension or its filename.

### Comments

It is interesting to note that FindWindow is described in the Windows API reference as taking two "long pointers to strings" for parameters. Normally, this would imply that two strings must be passed using the ByVal directive.

However, declaring the function with ByVal in Visual Basic prevents passing a NULL pointer. If we were to pass a "null string" (that is, "") to this function, we would be passing a pointer to a "null string" and not a "null pointer." This would imply that we were searching for a window that had no caption or no classname. Instead we need to pass a Long with a value of zero, hence our NULL constant.

We accomplish this by declaring the parameters to FindWindow "As Any," thereby disabling parameter checking by Visual Basic. Use the As Any parameter type with care, because if you place an invalid variable type on the stack, your application will almost certainly visit the Twilight Zone.

## 6.10 ⬤ How do I...

Complexity: Easy

## Determine how many function keys are on my user's keyboard?

### Problem
I'd like to offer function keys for some of the common operations in my application (like saving a file, or printing a document). But different keyboards have a different number of function keys. How can I adapt my program to the type of keyboard a user has?

### Technique
Although you should avoid making your Windows applications hardware-specific, if you can adapt it to take advantage of the complete range of hardware present, that will make the application perform better.

You can determine how many function keys your user's keyboard includes by using the Windows API function GetKeyboardType. GetKeyboardType can return the make and model of keyboard installed for Windows (for example, the original PC keyboard, with the 10 function keys along the left or the Enhanced keyboard, with 12 function keys along the top) and can also return the number of function keys on that keyboard.

If the call to GetKeyboardType determines that the user has a keyboard with 12 function keys, for example, you can check in a KeyDown or KeyUp event subroutine for presses of function key (F11) or (F12), and respond accordingly.

### Steps
Open and run KEYBOARD.MAK. When you click on the form, a message box describing your keyboard will appear. See Figure 6-7 for an example of the message box.

**Figure 6-7** The Keyboard project in action

1. Create a new project called KEYBOARD.MAK and a new form. There are no controls on this form. Save the form as KEYBOARD.FRM. Put the following code in the Declarations section of the form. This Declare statement gives the form access to the GetKeyboardType API function.

```
Declare Function GetKeyboardType Lib "Keyboard" (ByVal nTypeFlag As ⇐
Integer) As Integer
```

2. Put the following code in the Form_Click event subroutine. This code calls GetKeyboardType to get the make and model of keyboard, and then again to get the number of function keys on the keyboard. Then it pops up a message box with that information.

```
Sub Form_Click ()
   Select Case GetKeyboardType(0)
      Case 1
         Msg$ = "IBM PC/XT or compatible"
      Case 2
         Msg$ = "Olivetti M24"
      Case 3
         Msg$ = "IBM AT or compatible"
      Case 4
         Msg$ = "IBM Enhanced or compatible"
      Case 5
         Msg$ = "Nokia 1050 or compatible"
      Case 6
         Msg$ = "Nokia 9140 or compatible"
   End Select

   FKeys = GetKeyboardType(2)

   MsgBox Msg$ + ", with" + Str$(FKeys) + " function keys"
End Sub
```

### How It Works

The GetKeyboardType API function returns some relatively low-level information about the keyboard that the user specified when installing Windows. The keyboard type may be changed by running the Windows Setup program.

GetKeyboardType accepts a parameter, nTypeFlag, that specifies what information about the keyboard GetKeyboardType is to return. If nType-Flag is 0, GetKeyboardType returns a code indicating the make and model of the keyboard. (See the Form_Click event subroutine for details on which code indicates which keyboard type.)

If nTypeFlag is 1, GetKeyboardType returns the "subtype" of the keyboard. This subtype is defined in the keyboard driver by the keyboard manufacturer. Unless you have specific information from the keyboard manufacturer, the subtype is meaningless.

If nTypeFlag is 2, GetKeyboardType returns the number of function keys on the installed keyboard. You may be thinking that it's redundant to have a separate call for the keyboard type when an nTypeFlag of 1 will tell you the keyboard type. However, the Olivetti keyboard, for example, can have either 12 or 18 function keys, and there's nothing stopping a keyboard manufacturer from coming out with a keyboard that's identical to an Enhanced keyboard, except with another row of 12 function keys, for a total of 24. If that manufacturer provided an updated keyboard driver for Windows, a call to GetKeyboardType with an nTypeFlag of 2 would properly reveal the presence of 24 function keys.

### Comments

To interpret the KeyCode parameter passed to a KeyDown or KeyUp event subroutine, you'll need to use the key codes defined in the CONSTANT.TXT file from your Visual Basic disks.

## 6.11 ⬤ How do I...

**Complexity: Intermediate**

## Determine the directory where Windows is installed?

### Problem

As I write my application's installation program, I realize that there are several auxiliary files that I must include, like the VBRUN300.DLL and several custom control VBX libraries. These files must be placed someplace where Windows can find them when the user goes to start my application. How do I find out the best place to put the files?

### Technique

Store files with .DLL and .VBX extensions in either the main Windows directory or Windows' own system directory. The default names for these directories are WINDOWS and WINDOWS\SYSTEM, respectively. However, the user is free to change the main Windows directory name, and can install Windows on any hard drive in the system, so using C:\WINDOWS as the directory name won't always work.

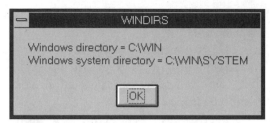

**Figure 6-8** The WinDirs project in action

Luckily, the Windows API offers two functions—GetWindowsDirectory and GetSystemDirectory—that return the names of the two Windows directories regardless of what the user called them. Your installation program could call these API functions and then copy all the needed .DLL and .VBX files to either of those two directories.

### Steps

Open and run WINDIRS.MAK. When you click on the form, a message box appears that shows the names of the two Windows directories. See Figure 6-8 for an example of that message box.

1. Create a new project called WINDIRS.MAK and a new form. There are no controls on this form. Save the form as WINDIRS.FRM.

2. Add the VBHOWTO.BAS module to the project. VBHOWTO.BAS contains the VBHTTrim$ function used in the Form_Click event subroutine. (This VBHTTrim$ function was added to the module in How-To 3.9 Trim null characters from a string.)

3. Put the following code in the Declarations section of the form. These Declare statements provide the form access to the Windows API functions.

```
Declare Function GetWindowsDirectory Lib "Kernel" (ByVal lpBuffer As ⇐
String, ByVal nSize As Integer) As Integer
Declare Function GetSystemDirectory Lib "Kernel" (ByVal lpBuffer As ⇐
String, ByVal nSize As Integer) As Integer
```

4. Put the following code in the Form_Click event subroutine. This code calls the GetWindowsDirectory and GetSystemDirectory API functions and uses the MsgBox statement to show them to the user. GetWindowsDirectory and GetSystemDirectory return 0 if there was an error, so we check for that and display a message box indicating there was an error.

```
Sub Form_Click ()
   WinDir$ = Space$(144)
```

```
    WinSysDir$ = Space$(144)

    If GetWindowsDirectory(WinDir$, 144) = 0 Or
GetSystemDirectory(WinSysDir$, 144) = 0 Then
        MsgBox "Unable to determine Windows directories", 16
    Else
        WinDir$ = VBHTTrim$(WinDir$)
        WinSysDir$ = VBHTTrim$(WinSysDir$)
        MsgBox "Windows directory = " + WinDir$ + Chr$(13) + Chr$(10) +
"Windows system directory = " + WinSysDir$
    End If
End Sub
```

### How It Works

First, the Form_Click event subroutine initializes the WinDir$ and WinSysDir$ variables to 144 spaces, which is the theoretical maximum length of the Windows directory names.

The GetWindowsDirectory and GetSystemDirectory API functions return 0 if there was some error processing the Windows directory names, so the If statement calls GetWindowsDirectory and GetSystemDirectory and compares their return values with 0. If either return value is 0, the MsgBox statement pops up a message.

This If statement is a little trick you can use if the return value of any function indicates an error condition. Normally, you might use code similar to the following:

```
I = GetWindowsDirectory(WinDir$, 144)
If I = 0 Then
    MsgBox "Unable to determine Windows directories", 16
    Exit Sub
End If

I = GetSystemDirectory(WinSysDir$, 144)
If I = 0 Then
    MsgBox "Unable to determine Windows directories", 16
    Exit Sub
End If
```

But if all you're doing is checking whether an error occurred and you won't be using the function's return value for anything else, you can call the function as the condition part of an If statement. You can even combine multiple calls using the logical Or operator, as in the Form_Click event subroutine.

If the GetWindowsDirectory and GetSystemDirectory API functions were both successful, a call to the VBHTTrim$ function removes the extra spaces from the strings, and the null characters that API functions put into strings.

### Comments

The GetWindowsDirectory and GetSystemDirectory API functions do not add a backslash at the end of the directory names, which can be useful when you need to copy files. The only directory name that the functions terminate with a backslash is the root directory, for example, C:\. The following code will ensure that the directory name ends in a single backslash.

```
If Right$(WinDir$, 1) <> "\" Then WinDir$ = WinDir$ + "\"
```

## 6.12 ⬤ How do I...

## Determine system resources?

### Problem

The About... dialog box of the Program Manager contains a value labeled Free System Resources. What are "resources"? I thought that resources included icons, bitmaps, and dialog boxes contained in program files. "System resources" seem to be something else. I know that when they get too low, applications cannot be loaded even though there is a lot of "Free Memory." How do I determine how many resources there are and how many my application needs?

### Technique

There are two different contexts in which the issue of resources comes up. When you discuss an .EXE file, resources refers to noncode or data such as icons, bitmaps, metafiles, dialog boxes, and cursors stored in the .EXE file. The number of these resources in a particular .EXE has absolutely no bearing on "System Resources."

System resources, however, refer to a number of objects that can be created by the system. There are two types of system resources—those in USER.EXE and those in the Graphics Device Interface DLL (GDI.EXE). USER.EXE is the system dynamic link library that manages the creation of windows and controls. Accordingly, "User" resources refer to the number of windows and controls that can be created. GDI.EXE is the system DLL that manages the creation of graphical objects such as brushes, pens, and display contexts (hDC).

One of the greatest benefits of Windows 3.0 is its virtual memory management, which allows for unlimited virtual RAM. Virtual RAM enables you to store local data and documents that are "larger than memory" with little or no special effort by using the hard disk to store sections of RAM. However, Windows 3 also introduced an incredible limitation in the form

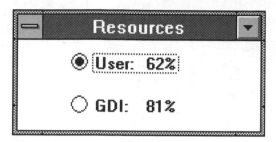

**Figure 6-9** System Resource Monitor at run time

**Figure 6-10** The minimized icon showing system resource status

of system resources. Simply put, User and GDI create arrays to hold the handles of different resources as they are created. Therefore, the entire system is limited to the number of elements in each of these arrays.

Determining the percentage of remaining system resources requires a call to an undocumented API function, GetHeapSpaces, which returns a long integer. The high-order word contains the total number of resources that can be created and the low-order word contains the number already in use. With their values we can determine the number of remaining resource "elements" as a percentage of the total. We can check available resources for both User and GDI. The number displayed by the Program Manager is the lower of these two percentages.

However, it is important to note that these figures are independent of each other. It is possible to "run out" of one sort of resource while plenty of the other remains. In fact, this is what almost always happens. Because windows and controls are more often used than graphic objects, the Program Manager is nearly always displaying the percentage of free User resources as the percentage of free GDI resources is almost always much higher.

This How-To creates a generalized function that returns the percentage of free resources for a given module (User or GDI). Our form will display both figures, as shown in Figure 6-9. Finally, when minimized, our utility will periodically check the system resources and paint the result on the icon, as you can see in Figure 6-10.

### Steps

Open and run RESOURCE.MAK. You will see the remaining resources in both User and GDI; the one that is smaller will be selected. When you minimize the utility, the little monitor icon will be updated with the current resource percentage available. To re-create the example, perform the following steps:

1. Create a new project called RESOURCE.MAK. Create a new form with the following objects and properties from Table 6-11, and save it as RESOURCE.FRM.

| Object | Property | Setting |
|--------|----------|---------|
| Form | FormName | Form1 |
| | Caption | Resources |
| | Icon | COMPUTER\MONITR01.ICO |
| | ScaleMode | Pixels |
| Radio button | Name | User |
| | Caption | User |
| Radio button | Name | GDI |
| | Caption | GDI |
| Timer | Name | Timer1 |
| | Interval | 2000 |
| | Enabled TRUE | |

**Table 6-11** Resource project form's objects and properties

2. Insert the following code in the Declarations section of the form.

```
DefInt A-Z
Declare Function GetModuleHandle Lib "Kernel" (ByVal ModName$)
Declare Function GetHeapSpaces& Lib "Kernel" (ByVal hModule)

Function GetFreeResources (ModuleName$)
    rInfo& = GetHeapSpaces&(GetModuleHandle(ModuleName$))
    Totalr& = HiWord&(rInfo&)
    FreeR& = LoWord(rInfo&)
    GetFreeResources = FreeR& * 100 \ Totalr&
End Function

Function HiWord& (LongInt&)
    Temp& = LongInt& \ &H10000
    If Temp& < 0 Then Temp& = Temp& + &H10000
    HiWord& = Temp&
End Function

Function LoWord& (LongInt&)
    Temp& = LongInt& Mod &H10000
    If Temp& < 0 Then Temp& = Temp& + &H10000
    LoWord& = Temp&
End Function

Function Min (P1, P2)
    If P1 < P2 Then Min = P1 Else Min = P2
End Function
```

3. Insert the following code in the Form_Paint event handler.

```
Sub Form_Paint ()
   UserFree = GetFreeResources("User")
   GDIFree = GetFreeResources("GDI")
   User.Caption = "User: " + Str$(UserFree) + "%"
   GDI.Caption = "GDI:  " + Str$(GDIFree) + "%"
   If UserFree < GDIFree Then
      User.Value = -1
   Else
      GDI.Value = -1
   End If
End Sub
```

4. Insert the following code in the Form_Resize procedure.

```
Sub Form_Resize ()
   If WindowState = 1 Then
      Timer1.Enabled = -1
   Else
      Timer1.Enabled = 0
   End If
End Sub
```

5. Insert the following code in the Timer1_Timer procedure.

```
Sub Timer1_Timer ()
    TFree = Min(GetFreeResources("User"), GetFreeResources("GDI"))
    If TFree <> OldTotal Then
       Text$ = Format$(TFree, "00") + "%"
       Cls
       CurrentX = 7
       CurrentY = 8
       Print Text$
       OldTotal = TFree
    End If
End Sub
```

### How It Works

Once you know about the undocumented GetHeapSpaces API function, the rest of the program is fairly straightforward. First a handle to the "module" for the library we are examining is required. We find this via the GetModuleHandle API function.

You might think it strange that our Visual Basic HiWord& and LoWord& functions are defined as long integer functions. This is because the only way to represent an "unsigned" integer is with a long integer. An unsigned integer is one that is always positive. As you know, the valid range of a signed integer is -32,767 to +32,768. However, the range of an unsigned short integer is 0 to 65,535. The only way to represent numbers greater than 32,768 in Visual Basic is with a long integer.

The Form_Paint procedure simply makes calls to GetFreeResources for User and GDI, fills in the caption properties of the corresponding radio buttons, and "clicks" the one that is smaller. Because the Form_Paint event will occur when the form is restored from an iconic posting, this information will be automatically updated whenever the resources icon is restored.

The Form_Resize procedure will be invoked whenever the form is resized either by directly manipulating the size border or by minimizing, restoring, or maximizing the form. Here we check whether the form is minimized (WindowState = 1) and if so, enable the timer, and if not, disable it.

The Timer1_Timer procedure begins determining the percentage of free system resources. Again, the Min function was constructed to make the code more readable. The value of TFree is compared to a static variable called OldTotal. Only if they are different do we proceed. This is just a small detail but it does serve to minimize flicker and, more importantly, drain on the CPU.

Cls clears our icon back to its original state so that we have a "clean slate," as it were, to draw our text. We then use CurrentX and CurrentY to position the "text cursor" to an appropriate location in our icon. (Note the values are hard-coded and may differ if you use another icon.) Finally, we use Print to print out the percentage of free resources.

### Comments

Resources are one of the most serious limitations of Windows 3.0, but much less serious under Windows 3.1 because the menus (one of the largest resource consumers) have been separated into their own array. In addition, Program Manager has been rewritten to mitigate its resource consumption.

In addition, the GetHeapSpaces function, although undocumented in version 3.0, is part of a documented TOOLHELP.DLL in version 3.1.

There are two relevant functions, GDIHeapInfo and UserHeapInfo, which fill record variables with information about the appropriate heaps.

```
Type HeapInfoStruc
    dwSize as Long
    wHeapFree as Integer
    wMaxHeap as Integer
    percentFree as Integer
    hSegment as Integer
End Type

DefInt A-Z

Declare Sub GDIHeapInfo Lib "ToolHelp.DLL" (HeapInfo as HeapInfoStruc)
Declare Sub UserHeapInfo Lib "ToolHelp.DLL" (HeapInfo as HeapInfoStruc)

Dim HeapInfo as HeapInfoStruc
```

```
GDIHeapInfo HeapInfo
GDIFree = HeapInfo.percentFree
UserHeapInfo HeapInfo
UserFree = HeapInfo.percentFree
FreeResources = Min (UserFree, GDIFree)
```

Strangely enough, like DOS, the undocumented function GetHeapSpaces appears to still work in Windows 3.1, but it reflects inaccurate information because the nature of resource usage has changed in Windows 3.1. It is therefore, better to make use of the documented API in future Windows releases.

The best way for you to control resource consumption in your application is to minimize the number of controls you use and the number of loaded forms. For example, you gain huge resource savings by using Print, along with CurrentX and CurrentY, instead of label controls.

## 6.13 ● How do I...

## Determine how much memory is available?

### Problem

I'd like my application to be able to tell the user how much memory is available in the system, like Windows' Program Manager. There is no Visual Basic function that gives the amount of memory. What can I do?

### Technique

Although QuickBASIC for DOS gives you the FRE function to check how much memory is in the system, Microsoft left that function out of Visual Basic. However, you can turn to the Windows API GetFreeSpace function, which returns the amount of available memory, in bytes.

**13672**

**Free memory**

**Figure 6-11**
The Memory project in action

### Steps

Open and run MEMORY.MAK. The Memory application runs itself as an icon and prints the amount of memory available on the top line of the icon as shown in Figure 6-11. Try opening another application and watch how the number goes down.

1. Create a new project called MEMORY.MAK and a new form with the objects and properties shown in Table 6-12. Save the form as MEMORY.FRM.

| Object | Property | Setting |
| --- | --- | --- |
| Form | BackColor | &H00000000& |
| | Caption | Free memory |
| | FontBold | False |
| | ForeColor | &H00FFFFFF& |
| | FormName | MemoryForm |
| | MaxButton | False |
| | MinButton | False |
| Timer | Name | Timer1 |
| | Enabled | True |
| | Interval | 1000 |

**Table 6-12** Memory project form's objects and properties

2. Put the following code in the Declarations section of the form. This Declare statement gives the form access to the GetFreeSpace API function.

```
Declare Function GetFreeSpace Lib "Kernel" (ByVal wFlags As Integer) As Long
```

3. Put the following code in the Form_Load event subroutine. This code clears the icon that would normally be displayed, then iconizes the form.

```
Sub Form_Load ()
   Icon = LoadPicture() 'clears default icon for form
   WindowState = 1        'sets form to minimized icon state
End Sub
```

4. Put the following code in the Timer1_Timer event subroutine. This code updates the display of the icon with the amount of free memory at the time the timer control is triggered.

```
Sub Timer1_Timer ()
   Static OldFreeSpace As Long, FreeSpace As Long

   FreeSpace = GetFreeSpace(0)

   If OldFreeSpace <> FreeSpace Then
      OldFreeSpace = FreeSpace
      Cls
      Print Format$(FreeSpace \ 1024);
   End If
End Sub
```

### How It Works

The GetFreeSpace API function returns the amount of memory in bytes Windows has available for use. The wFlags parameter is only used in Real mode Windows, which Visual Basic doesn't support. (Visual Basic applications and Visual Basic itself require Standard or 386 Enhanced mode Windows.)

The form has a timer control with an interval of 1000 (measured in milliseconds). The code in the timer's Timer event subroutine updates the icon's display of how much memory is available, if necessary. The code keeps a variable that stores how much memory was available the last time the icon's display was updated. If that variable and the current amount of available memory match, there's no reason to waste the time it would take to update the icon's display.

Because that variable is declared using the Static statement, Visual Basic initializes it to zero. GetFreeSpace will always return more than zero, so the two variables don't match the first time the timer is triggered and the amount of available memory will be printed on the icon's display.

The Cls method clears the icon to the background color (which was set with the BackColor property when the form was designed) and sets the CurrentX and CurrentY properties to 0.

The Print method then prints the amount of available memory on the icon, in kilobytes. Because the FontSize property of the form was set to 8.25, there is just enough room for the maximum number of digits that could appear.

### Comments

Note the use of the integer division operator(/) in the Timer1_Timer event subroutine. Because the GetFreeSpace API function returns a long integer, you can speed up your calculations by using pure integer operations on it, rather than the floating point division operator(/).

## 6.14 ⬤ How do I...

Complexity: Intermediate

## Determine which version of Windows my application is running on?

### Problem

My application will be run on a variety of machines. I'd like to ensure compatibility with future versions of Windows. If I could determine the current version of Windows, I could use certain features only if they exist in the version of Windows running on the machine.

### Technique

The Windows API library contains a function called GetVersion that returns the version number of Windows. You can use this function to restrict your program's use of certain features. For example, Windows 3.1 provides some common file dialog boxes in a DLL that you can access. If the user is running your application under Windows 3.0, though, those dialog boxes won't be available and you'll have to provide them yourself. If, however, GetVersion reveals that Windows 3.1 is running, you are free to make those calls.

### Steps

**Figure 6-12**
The Version project in action

Open and run VERSION.MAK. This project is based on the Memory project in How-To 6.13 Determine how much memory is available, but adds the Windows version number in the icon below the amount of available memory shown in Figure 6-12.

1. Create a new project called VERSION.MAK. and a new form with the objects and properties listed in Table 6-13. Save the form as VERSION.FRM.

| Object | Property | Setting |
|--------|----------|---------|
| Form | BackColor | &H00000000& |
| | Caption | Windows version |
| | FontBold | False |
| | ForeColor | &H00FFFFFF& |
| | FormName | VersionForm |
| | MaxButton | False |
| | MinButton | False |
| Timer | Name | Timer1 |
| | Enabled | True |
| | Interval | 1000 |

**Table 6-13** Version project form's objects and properties

2. Put the following code in the Declarations section of the form. This Declare statement gives the form access to the GetFreeSpace and GetVersion API functions and declares some variables.

```
Declare Function GetFreeSpace Lib "Kernel" (ByVal wFlags As Integer) As Long
Declare Function GetVersion Lib "Kernel" () As Integer

Dim MajorVersion As Integer, MinorVersion As Integer
```

3. Put the following code in the Form_Load event subroutine. This code clears the icon that would normally be displayed, then iconizes the form and gets the Windows version number using the GetVersion API function.

```
Sub Form_Load ()
   Icon = LoadPicture()
   WindowState = 1
   Version% = GetVersion()
   MajorVersion = Version% And &HFF
   MinorVersion = (Version% And &HFF00) \ 256
End Sub
```

4. Put the following code in the Timer1_Timer event subroutine. This code updates the display of the icon with the amount of free memory every one second and redisplays the Windows version number that was determined in the Form_Load event subroutine.

```
Sub Timer1_Timer ()
   Static OldFreeSpace As Long, FreeSpace As Long

   FreeSpace = GetFreeSpace(0)

   If OldFreeSpace <> FreeSpace Then
      OldFreeSpace = FreeSpace
      Cls
      Print Format$(FreeSpace \ 1024); "K"
      Print "Win"; Format$(MajorVersion); "."; Format$(MinorVersion)
   End If
End Sub
```

### How It Works

See How-To 6.13 Determine how much memory is available, for more information about the GetFreeSpace API function.

The GetVersion API function takes no arguments and just returns the Windows version number. The version is a fractional number, however. The number before the decimal point is called the major version number; the number after the decimal point is the minor version number. So, for example, for version 3.0, the major version number is 3 and the minor version number is 0.

GetVersion puts the major version number in the low-order byte of its return value, and the minor version number in the high-order byte. The Form_Load event subroutine plucks out the major and minor version numbers and stores them in the MajorVersion and MinorVersion variables.

Then in the Timer1_Timer event subroutine, the Windows version number is printed after the current amount of available memory. Because there is very little extra space on the icon, the Format$ function strips out the extra spaces.

### Comments

If you want your application to decide whether it should use the features of another version of Windows, the best place to check the Windows version number is in the Form_Load event subroutine. So you might have code like this:

```
Sub Form_Load ()
    Version% = GetVersion()
    MajorVersion = Version% And &HFF
    MinorVersion = (Version% And &HFF00) \ 256

    If MajorVersion = 3 And MinorVersion = 1 Then
        ' do Windows 3.1 stuff
    Else
        ' stick with Windows 3.0 stuff
    End If
End Sub
```

## 6.15 ● How do I...

## Find out everything about the system configuration?

### Problem

A well-behaved application should know about the system on which it is running. Information such as the version of Windows, the total available memory, and current directory is extremely helpful. How can I obtain this information in Visual Basic?

### Technique

This How-To ties together the previous couple of How-Tos in one larger project. In QuickBasic, it is possible to retrieve a lot of system information by using a "CALL Interrupt" construct. Interrupts, under DOS, are roughly equivalent to API calls under Windows. Unfortunately, although the Windows API is much richer than the DOS API, a huge number of functions that are present in DOS were omitted from Windows. Therefore, until an equivalent to CALL Interrupt is made available to Visual Basic programmers, much of the system information will remain unavailable, except through the use of dynamic linked libraries written in other languages.

However, there are a number of Windows API functions devoted to interrogating the system that can be used here. The available system information is sort of a mixed bag, and the importance of each piece of information is dependent on the application you have in mind. We will proceed a little differently in this How-To and put our system functions in a separate Visual Basic module that can then be included in any Visual Basic application.

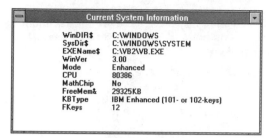

**Figure 6-13** Appearance of the Sysinfo form

### Steps

Open and run SYSINFO.MAK. You will see a dump of system information, as shown in Figure 6-13. The information is updated every time the screen is repainted, so if you minimize SysInfo, load a collection of programs, and restore SysInfo, you will see the changes to memory that result.

1. Create a new project called SYSINFO.MAK. Create a new module called SYSINFO.BAS. Insert the following code in that module.

```
DefInt A-Z
Declare Function GetWindowsDirectory Lib "Kernel" (ByVal Buff$, ⇐
ByVal sizeBuf)
Declare Function GetSystemDirectory Lib "Kernel" (ByVal Buff$, ⇐
ByVal sizeBuf)
Declare Function GetClassWord Lib "User" (ByVal hWnd, ByVal nIndex)
Declare Function GetModuleFileName Lib "Kernel" (ByVal hModule, ⇐
ByVal Buff$, ByVal sizeBuf)
Declare Function GetVersion Lib "Kernel" ()
Declare Function GetFreeSpace& Lib "Kernel" (ByVal wFlags)
Declare Function GetWinFlags& Lib "Kernel" ()
Declare Function GetKeyBoardType Lib "Keyboard" (ByVal nFlag)

'From Win.INI
Const GCW_HMODULE = -16

Const WF_CPU286 = &H2
Const WF_CPU386 = &H4
Const WF_CPU486 = &H8
Const WF_STANDARD = &H10
Const WF_ENHANCED = &H20
Const WF_8087 = &H400

'From CONSTANT.TXT
Const TRUE = -1
Const FALSE = 0

Function EXEName$ ()
   Wnd = Screen.ActiveForm.hWnd
   hModule = GetClassWord(Wnd, GCW_HMODULE)
```

*continued on next page*

*continued from previous page*

```
   Buff$ = Space$(255)
   TChars = GetModuleFileName(hModule, Buff$, 255)
   EXEName$ = Left$(Buff$, TChars)
End Function

Function WinDir$ ()
   Buff$ = Space$(255)
   TChars = GetWindowsDirectory(Buff$, 255)
   WinDir$ = Left$(Buff$, TChars)
End Function

Function SysDir$ ()
   Buff$ = Space$(255)
   TChars = GetSystemDirectory(Buff$, 255)
   SysDir$ = Left$(Buff$, TChars)
End Function

Function WinVer ()
   Version = GetVersion()
   WinVer = ((Version Mod 256) * 100) + Version \ 256
End Function

Function FreeMem& ()
   FreeMem& = GetFreeSpace(0)

End Function


Function CPU ()
   Flags& = GetWinFlags&()
   Match = 1
   Select Case Match
     Case (Flags& And WF_CPU486) \ WF_CPU486
        CPU = 486
     Case (Flags& And WF_CPU386) \ WF_CPU386
        CPU = 386
     Case Else
        CPU = 286
   End Select
End Function

Function Mode ()
   Flags& = GetWinFlags&
   If Flags& And WF_ENHANCED Then
     Mode = WF_ENHANCED
   Else
     Mode = WF_STANDARD
   End If
End Function

Function MathChip ()
   Flags& = GetWinFlags&
   If Flags& And WF_8087 Then
     MathChip = TRUE
```

```
      Else
         MathChip = FALSE
      End If
End Function

Function FKeys ()
   FKeys = GetKeyBoardType(2)
End Function

Function KBType ()
   KBType = GetKeyBoardType(0)
End Function

Function KBSubType ()
   KBSubType = GetKeyBoardType(1)
End Function
```

2. Create a new form and save it as SYSINFO.FRM.

3. In the Declarations section of the form, insert the following:

```
DefInt A-Z

Const WF_STANDARD = &H10
Const WF_ENHANCED = &H20

'Custom Constants
Const KB_XT = 1
Const KB_M24 = 2
Const KB_AT = 3
Const KB_Enhanced = 4
Const KB_N1050 = 5
Const KB_N9140 = 6
```

4. In the Form_Paint procedure, insert the following:

```
Sub Form_Paint ()
   Form1.Cls
   Print
   Print , "WinDIR$", WinDir$()
   Print , "SysDir$", SysDir$()
   Print , "EXEName$", EXEName$()
   Print , "WinVer", Format$(WinVer() / 100, "##.00")
   Print , "Mode",
   Select Case Mode()
      Case WF_ENHANCED
         Print "Enhanced"
      Case WF_STANDARD
         Print "Standard"
   End Select
   Print , "CPU", Format$(80000 + CPU())
```

*continued on next page*

*continued from previous page*

```
    Print , "MathChip",
    If MathChip() Then
        Print "Yes"
    Else
        Print "No"
    End If
    Print , "FreeMem&", Format$(FreeMem&() \ 1024); "KB"
    Print , "KBType",
    Select Case KBType()
        Case KB_XT
            Print "IBM PC/XT, or compatible (83-key)"
        Case KB_M24
            Print "Olivetti M24 'ICO' (102-key)"
        Case KB_AT
            Print "IBM AT or similar (84-key)"
        Case KB_Enhanced
            Print "IBM Enhanced (101- or 102-keys)"
        Case KB_N1050
            Print "Nokia 1050 or similar"
        Case KB_N9140
            Print "Nokia 9140 or similar"
    End Select
    Print , "FKeys", Format$(FKeys())
End Sub
```

5. Run the application. Minimize the application, open some applications, and restore your Sysinfo utility. You'll see the information on the form is updated.

### How It Works

Most of the API calls used in the SYSINFO.BAS module are self-explanatory but we will discuss those that are not. Essentially this is a semi-random assortment of system functions that can be called from any application that includes SYSINFO.BAS. You may add SYSINFO.BAS to a project by selecting Add File... from the File menu in Visual Basic.

### Name of the Currently Running Application

The EXEName$ function is a little tricky, but this information can be exceptionally useful to use from within an application. EXEName$ is the name of the currently running application, including the path in which the .EXE file can be found. This is useful for two reasons. First, the path eases the search for support, configuration, and data files that are found in the same directory as the .EXE file. Often an .EXE file will be launched without a change to the current directory. This happens when the program's directory is in the path and when the calling program uses an explicit path to your application. Normally, this is not a problem, but if you need to find other files in the same directory, your application needs some way to determine the directory in which it resides. Second, the name of the .EXE is useful when you want to provide special functionality based on the name that has been given to your program. For example, you might need the correct .EXE name to find other instances of your application running on the system.

The EXEName$ function first finds the hWnd property of the currently active window. This allows the function to be used more generically. Then GetClassWord is used to determine the current instance handle. This is the handle to the application itself, that is created when the application is launched by Windows. It is this handle that must be passed to the Get-ModuleFileName function to retrieve the exact name of the currently running process. The result of the function is the number of characters in the name, and this is used to assign the EXEName$ function result.

### Windows and SYSTEM Path Names

WinDir$ and SysDir$ are just shells around the Windows API functions GetWindowsDirectory and GetSystemDirectory. WinDir$ is the full path of the directory from which Windows was run. This is useful when you are trying to locate a support or initialization file stored there. SysDir$ returns the current "system" directory. This directory is usually named SYSTEM and branches off of the WinDir$ directory. This directory most often contains dynamic link libraries and support utilities.

### Windows Version, Flags, and Keyboard Type

The GetVersion API function returns an integer value for the version of Windows that is currently running. The high-order byte contains the "minor" version and the low-order byte contains the "major" version. The Mod function is used to retrieve the remainder of a division by 256, which returns the "major" version. The minor version, or "high byte," is retrieved through simple integer division. We multiply the major version by 100 so that the entire result can be expressed as an integer. This makes comparisons much faster. In other words, if you wanted to make sure that the current Windows version was at least 3.1 you could just check to see if WinVer => 310.

The GetWinFlags API function provides a wealth of information in a single long integer. The result contains a number of True/False values that correspond to bits in the number. CPU, Mode, and MathChip are simply checking the status of the relevant bits in Flags&.

The FKeys, KBType, and KBSubType are all shells around the API function, GetKeyBoardType, but with different parameters. Note that this function is found in a special kind of DLL called a driver. KEYBOARD.DRV will be specific on each system to the installed hardware. However, all keyboard drivers under Windows contain this function to retrieve the keyboard type.

SYSINFO.FRM is not very sophisticated but provides a means to display current system information. In the Declarations section of the Form, we have simply created some constants to make the code more readable.

The work is done in the Form_Paint event handler because this guarantees that the information will be updated when the Form is restored after being minimized. The code in Form_Paint is fairly self-explanatory.

### Comments

Note that, unlike QuickBasic, Visual Basic does not require you to declare routines that are in separate modules in your project. The Declare statement is reserved for the use of truly external routines contained in DLLs.

Note also that Format$ is often used instead of Str$. This prevents the addition of a leading space at the beginning of the created string.

## 6.16 ⬤ How do I...

## Simulate Spy in Visual Basic?

### Problem

A number of tricks involve knowing more about the windows in applications other than mine. To use FindWindow, SendMessage, and some other API calls, I need the name of the window class, its handle, and so on. I have seen an application that ships with the Software Development Kit (SDK) called Spy that accomplishes this. Can I accomplish the same thing using Visual Basic?

### Technique

While somewhat involved, this is certainly possible in Visual Basic. In fact, in the process of accomplishing this, we will examine a number of Windows API calls and their functions, many of which can be used in other contexts.

Spy is one of the most useful utilities that ships with the Software Developers' Kit. Its primary purpose is to trace messages sent to various controls at run time to help you test an application. While we will not be duplicating this functionality, we can duplicate its ability to "look at" other windows and determine their class and parent. Using the Class name, we can use the FindWindow API function to find another control at run time. It is also educational to see the overuse of controls and their effect on resources.

The key issue, tracking the mouse movements outside of your form, is also the easiest. While Visual Basic can only track mouse messages within your forms directly, when an API function called SetCapture is enabled, every mouse action on the system is sent to your window. This technique, used by screen capture programs and many specialized applications, will be central to WndPeek.

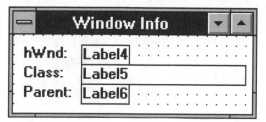

**Figure 6-14** Appearance of the Wndpeek form

In tracking the mouse movements, we need a way to find the current mouse location and learn whether it is over any windows. This is accomplished through calls to the GetMessagePos and WindowFromPoint API calls.

As the mouse pointer moves across different windows, the application can make a number of API calls to get information about each window.

Finally, you can add an aesthetic feature that "highlights" the window as the mouse cursor passes over it. This allows you to see just how many windows a number of applications contain.

### Steps

To try the example, run the WNDPEEK.EXE file from the Program Manager. The utility will automatically go into "peek" mode, so just start to move the mouse cursor around the screen. You should see various windows becoming highlighted and their details displayed in WndPeek's information box. You might want to load your favorite application before loading WndPeek so that you can examine the windows of that application. When you click the mouse, WndPeek releases the mouse and exits. To re-create the demo, perform the following steps:

1. Create a new project called WNDPEEK.MAK. Create a new form with the objects and properties in Table 6-14, and save it as WNDPEEK.FRM. It will look like Figure 6-14.

| Object | Property | Setting |
|--------|----------|---------|
| Form | FormName | Form1 |
| | Caption | Window Info |
| Label | Name | Label1 |
| | Caption | hWnd: |
| Label | Name | Label2 |
| | Caption | Class: |

*continued on next page*

*continued form previous page*

| Object | Property | Setting |
|--------|----------|---------|
| Label | Name | Label3 |
|       | Caption | Parent: |
| Label | Name | Label4 |
|       | Caption | Label4 |
| Label | Name | Label5 |
|       | Caption | Label5 |
| Label | Name | Label6 |
|       | Caption | Label6 |

**Table 6-14** Wndpeek project form's objects and properties

2. Open the Declarations section of Form1 and insert the following code.

```
DefInt A-Z

'Subs in USER.EXE
Declare Sub SetCapture Lib "User" (ByVal hWnd)
Declare Sub ReleaseCapture Lib "User" ()
Declare Sub GetWindowRect Lib "User" (ByVal hWnd, MyRect As Rect)
Declare Sub ReleaseDC Lib "User" (ByVal hWnd, ByVal hDC)

'Functions in USER.EXE
Declare Function GetMessagePos& Lib "User" ()
Declare Function WindowFromPoint Lib "User" (ByVal MPos&)
Declare Function GetParent Lib "User" (ByVal hWnd)
Declare Function GetClassName Lib "User" (ByVal hWnd, ByVal Buff$, ⇐
ByVal sizeBuff)
Declare Function GetWindowText Lib "User" (ByVal hWnd, ByVal Buff$, ByVal ⇐
sizeBuff)
Declare Function GetWindowDC Lib "User" (ByVal hWnd)

'Subs in GDI.EXE
Declare Sub SetROP2 Lib "GDI" (ByVal hDC, ByVal DrawMode)
Declare Sub SelectObject Lib "GDI" (ByVal hDC, ByVal hPen)
Declare Sub Rectangle Lib "GDI" (ByVal hDC, ByVal X1, ByVal Y1, ByVal ⇐
X2, ByVal Y2)
Declare Sub DeleteObject Lib "GDI" (ByVal hPen)

'Functions in GDI.EXE
Declare Function CreatePen Lib "GDI" (ByVal pStyle, ByVal pWidth, ⇐
ByVal pClr&)
Declare Function GetStockObject Lib "GDI" (ByVal nIndex)

Const R2_NOT = 6
Const PS_InsideFrame = 6
Const Null_Brush = 5

Dim OldWnd As Integer
```

```
Dim MyRect As Rect

Sub BoxWindow (Wnd)
    GetWindowRect Wnd, MyRect
    TargetDC = GetWindowDC(Wnd)
    SetROP2 TargetDC, R2_NOT
    hPen = CreatePen(PS_InsideFram, 5, 0)
    SelectObject TargetDC, hPen
    SelectObject TargetDC, GetStockObject(Null_Brush)
    X2 = MyRect.Right - MyRect.Left
    Y2 = MyRect.Bottom - MyRect.Top
    Rectangle TargetDC, 0, 0, X2, Y2
    ReleaseDC Wnd, TargetDC
    DeleteObject (hPen)
End Sub
```

3. In the Form_Load procedure, insert the following code.

```
Sub Form_Load ()
    SetCapture hWnd
End Sub
```

4. In the Form_MouseMove procedure, insert the following code.

```
Sub Form_MouseMove (Button As Integer, Shift As Integer, X As Single, ⇐
    Y As Single)
    MyPos& = GetMessagePos&()
    Wnd = WindowFromPoint(MyPos&)
    If Wnd <> OldWnd Then
        Label4.Caption = Str$(Wnd)
        Label6.Caption = Str$(GetParent(Wnd))
        Class$ = Space$(255)
        TChars = GetClassName(Wnd, Class$, 255)
        Class$ = Left$(Class$, TChars)
        Label5.Caption = Class$
        Capt$ = Space$(255)
        TChars = GetWindowText(Wnd, Capt$, 255)
        If TChars > 0 Then
            Form1.Caption = Left$(Capt$, TChars)
        Else
            Form1.Caption = "(No Caption)"
        End If
        BoxWindow OldWnd
        BoxWindow Wnd
        OldWnd = Wnd
    End If
End Sub
```

5. In the Form_MouseUp procedure, insert the following code.

```
Sub Form_MouseUp (Button As Integer, Shift As Integer, X As Single, ⇐
    Y As Single)
    BoxWindow OldWnd
    ReleaseCapture
    Unload Form1
End Sub
```

6. Place the following record variable declaration in the global module. It is required for the GetWindowRect API function to work. This function is used by the BoxWindow routine to draw a box around the window that currently has mouse focus in WndPeek.

```
Type Rect
    Left As Integer
    Top As Integer
    Right As Integer
    Bottom As Integer
End Type
```

Now, save the global module as MNDPEEK.GLB.

7. Now compile the program to a stand-alone .EXE for best results. Add your program as a Program Manager icon.

8. (Optional) Launch the program you want to examine.

9. Launch WndPeek, using File Open in Program Manager.

As you move the mouse around the screen, you should see the WndPeek form updated with the information corresponding to the window below the cursor, including the background.

If you use WndPeek to examine the Program Manager, you will see very quickly why so many "User" resources are gone before you load any programs!

**How It Works**

There are a number of interesting things going on in WndPeek. First, in the Form_Load procedure we are making a call to the Windows API function SetCapture. This function, when passed a valid hWnd, informs Windows that all following mouse messages should be sent to our window. This enables us to process these messages as though the mouse were inside our own form.

This technique is often used in applications like WndPeek—for example, Spy—that allow the user to dynamically select a window to examine.

The real work in WndPeek is done in the Form_MouseMove event handler. First, the GetMessagePos API function is used to retrieve the current mouse cursor location. GetMessagePos returns the location of the mouse cursor, the last time a message was generated. In this case, the last message was generated by the MouseMove event. At first glance, it might appear more efficient to use the X and Y parameters passed to the MouseMove procedure, but there are a couple of disadvantages to this approach. First, these figures are relative to the position of the form. In other words, if the form is in the lower right-hand corner of the screen and the mouse is in the upper left, X and Y will both be negative. Finding the true screen coordinates is then based on the location of the form on the screen.

Second, using GetMessagePos, we are able to more easily use the WindowFromPoint function. WindowFromPoint is actually expecting a record variable of the type POINT, used in a number of Windows Graphics Device Interface (GDI) routines.

```
Type PointStruc
     X as Integer
     Y as Integer
End Type
```

Normally, this record variable structure would have to be typed in the global module, and an instance of it dimensioned (Dim MyPoint As PointStruc) for use by the form. However, two short integers make a long integer, so a LONG can be passed to this routine as well. Conveniently, GetMessagePos returns a long integer with the X position in the LoWord and the Y position in the HiWord—in other words, identical to the POINT structure expected by WindowFromPoint. Therefore, using GetMessagePos will increase speed dramatically compared to the X and Y parameters passed to us by Visual Basic.

### Returning the Window's Handle

WindowFromPoint, as its name implies, returns the hWnd (or handle) of the window currently at the location specified in POINT. In our case, this is the current mouse cursor position. Obviously, this function would be of great value in the "drag 'n drop" situation as well.

Before going any further, we check to make certain that the hWnd that we are "over" is different from the last one we were examining. We compare Wnd to OldWnd, a static variable that we continuously update with our current window handle. This is done to increase program speed and reduce flicker.

Whenever the mouse moves to a new window, the window is updated. The hWnd of the current window is shown. This information is useful if you want to try to send messages to a specific window. Next, the parent of the current window is found and displayed. The parent of any window can be retrieved using the GetParent API call. To find the main window of an application, you should look for the window that does not have a parent.

Next the "class name" of the window being examined is retrieved. The class name is perhaps the most useful information, retrieved by WndPeek because it is the most accurate way to locate a window, using the Find-Window API call. The use of FindWindow is explained in How-To 6.9 Find other running applications. The GetClassName API function requires that you send it a buffer in which to place the classname, and the function returns the number of characters actually copied to the buffer. It is essential to preallocate space in strings being passed to API functions declared in this way. If the string is not big enough to hold all of the characters that will be copied to it by the GetClassName function, the result will be truncated.

Next, to make sure that the cursor is placed correctly, the Caption of the current window is retrieved and displayed.

Finally, the box around the old window is erased and a box is drawn around the new window being examined.

The Form_MouseUp event handler cleans up by releasing the mouse capture, using the ReleaseCapture API routine, erasing the last box we drew, and exiting from our application.

The BoxWindow routine is a self-contained procedure that draws a box around a window. This routine is purely aesthetic, but the box allows the user to see which window is being examined at a particular time. The Get-WindowRect API function determines the coordinates of the window in question. BoxWindow is implemented this way, so that a second call to the routine with the same hWnd erases the box that was previously drawn.

GetWindowDC is a specialized function that retrieves the display context of the entire window. You will use GetWindowDC very seldom, because most often you only need the display context of the client region of the window. However, because we want to enclose the entire window in a box, we need the display context of the whole window.

### Drawing Window Frames

SetRop2 is equivalent to setting DrawMode for an object in Visual Basic. In our case, we want to set it to R2_NOT, which is equivalent to DrawMode 2 in Visual Basic, or more specifically, inverting the current colors of the screen. This drawing mode is preferable to using a specific color, for two reasons. First, it is practically guaranteed to be visible on almost any background. Second, it facilitates erasing the box, because the box can simply be "inverted" to its original color.

Next, we create a pen with which to draw the box. The PS_INSIDEFRAME pen style draws a box inside of the window, without having to calculate a different position for the box. We can simply pass the coordinates of the window as retrieved by the GetWindowRect procedure. This is identical to setting the DrawStyle property of a control or form in Visual Basic to Inside_Solid.

Then the project calls the SelectObject API function to tell Windows to use the objects we specify when painting on the specified display context. First, we specify that our newly created pen should be used. Next, a NULL_BRUSH should be used to paint on TargetDC. This would normally be the handle to a brush of a certain color that was created with the CreateBrush function. However, in this case, we don't want the rectangle to be filled in, so we select one of Windows' "stock objects" as NULL (or invisible) brush. This is functionally equivalent to setting the FillStyle for a particular control to Invisible in Visual Basic.

Next our rectangle is drawn using the Rectangle API procedure. We calculate our width and height parameters and call Rectangle to draw the box. This is equivalent to using the Line method in Visual Basic.

Finally, the project's cleanup is handled, releasing the display context of the window and deleting the pen that the project created.

## Comments

The most important purpose of WndPeek as a utility is to find the class name of the window of a particular application so that it can be used in a call to FindWindow. It is also instructive to see how many windows various applications are creating to accomplish their tasks. You can see which applications are resource monsters and how. Every time WndPeek highlights a new area on the desktop, it is revealing the location of another window or control. Each one of these consumes valuable resources. Program Manager, for example, uses separate controls to display icons and their labels. It is also useful to examine your own application and attempt to minimize the number of controls that you use on your forms and the number of forms that are loaded at one time.

However, WndPeek demonstrates a number of important techniques, including the tracking of the mouse outside of your application, drawing on windows of other applications, even the desktop, and calling API functions.

In addition, we have looked here at a number of Windows API equivalents to Visual Basic functions—how they differ and how they are used. Although Visual Basic supplies equivalents to many functions in GDI (actually, Visual Basic is calling these functions) the Visual Basic routines are very specific to use with Visual Basic controls and forms. Therefore, if you want to accomplish some of the same functionality outside of your application, you need to use the equivalent API calls.

Note that the speed of BoxWindow could be increased if the pen was created only once and the Null_BRUSH was retrieved only once. Their handles could be stored in static variables by the Form_Load procedure and the pen could be released in the Form_Unload routine. BoxWindow was created to be self contained, in this instance for simplicity and to facilitate its use in other applications.

# CHAPTER 7

# PERIPHERALS: SCREEN, SPEAKER, AND SERIAL PORTS

# How do I...

Your computer's peripherals—including the monitor, printer, speaker, and serial port—may be thought of as its arms, legs, and voice. They allow your programs to communicate with the outside world. This chapter will show you how to get Visual Basic to control these various hardware extensions of your PC. You will see how to figure out the color capabilities of any user's video display and printer, how to create sound effects and attach them to your programs, how to create a phone dialer that works with a modem and serial port, and how to build your own Visual Basic communications program. Visual Basic lacks the great PLAY statement that came with QuickBASIC so we'll show you a way to simulate PLAY's complete macro language to play music.

Many of the familar hardware-addressing commands of QuickBASIC or DOS have been left out of Visual Basic. This is because Visual Basic programs are written to run in the Windows multitasking environment, where all hardware interrupts must be processed and parceled out by Windows. This chapter takes full advantage of a number of Windows APIs to manipulate computer peripherals.

## Windows APIs Covered

| | | |
|---|---|---|
| BuildCommDCB | midiInOpen | OpenSound |
| CloseComm | midiInReset | ReadComm |
| CloseSound | midiInStart | SendMessage |
| CountVoiceNotes | midiInStop | SetCommState |
| GetCommError | midiOutClose | SetVoiceAccent |
| GetDeviceCaps | midiOutGetDevCaps | SetVoiceNote |
| mciGetErrorString | midiOutGetErrorText | SetVoiceQueueSize |
| mciSendString | midiOutGetNumDevs | SetVoiceSound |
| midiInClose | midiOutOpen | StartSound |
| midiInGetDevCaps | midiOutReset | timeGetTime |
| midiInGetErrorText | midiOutShortMsg | WriteComm |
| midiInGetNumDev | OpenComm | |

### 7.1 Determine the color capabilities of a screen or printer

There is no straightforward way to guarantee the monitor or printer display characteristics of your users' systems and, therefore, that your program will generate the output you intend. This How-To shows how to determine the number of colors that a system can display or print. Since Visual Basic does not include this capability, we use the GetDeviceCaps Windows API to ascertain the number of bits per pixel and bits per color plane, which can then be used to figure out the colors available for display and hard-copy printing. These values are found in the device drivers that come with each video card and printer.

### 7.2 Make a replacement for QuickBASIC's SOUND statement

### 7.3 Make music in Visual Basic

Visual Basic's forerunner, QuickBASIC, includes sophisticated sound commands that can add fun and realism to your games and other applications. But the powerful Visual Basic language only includes a BEEP statement. Sound generation is dangerous in a multitasking environment like Windows because no application should directly access any hardware, including the speaker. Indeed, all messages to hardware should be directed by Windows to prevent more than one application from controlling the same hardware at the same time. How-To 7.2 uses four Windows APIs: OpenSound, CloseSound, SetVoiceSound, and StartSound, to produce a siren effect. The process shown can be modified to create a myriad of different sounds. How-To 7.3 expands the previous technique to play music just like Quick-BASIC's original PLAY statement using the additional Windows APIs SetVoiceQueueSize, SetVoiceAccent, and SetVoiceNote. All of the APIs found in a special Windows device driver called SOUND.DRV. The sample program demonstrates how to set voices, octaves, notes, sound duration, and accents—all the elements of standard music. You can add this module to any of your Visual Basic programs and it will process sound in the background.

**7.4      Create a phone dialer in Visual Basic**

Serial port communications is a hot topic in every programming language. This How-To uses Visual Basic's file I/O techniques to create a simple phone dialer that can be used with a modem and COM2 port. An interesting aspect of this How-To is that DOS does all the work—you will see that Windows still uses DOS file operations!

**7.5      Perform Serial I/O in Visual Basic**

Once again, we delve into the magical Windows API library to build a simple  serial communications program that allows you to choose a serial port, transmission speed, and communications parameters. Windows gives you a number of built-in functions for these purposes: OpenComm, SetCommState, ReadComm, WriteComm, CloseComm, BuildCommDCB, and GetCommError. Using Windows APIs for serial communications is superior to using Visual Basic's I/O statements because, as mentioned in How-To 7-4, simple I/O functions are still routed through DOS, which does not queue characters. This will cause characters to be lost in a multi-tasking environment, or in a high-transmission environment such as 2400 baud.

**7.6      Use the Media Control Interface with Visual Basic**

Windows 3.1 added Multimedia Extensions for Windows. The Multimedia Extensions include the Media-Control Interface (MCI). MCI has a command-string interface that makes it easy to control any MCI-compatible multimedia device. The project developed in this How-To provides a program that can be used to test MCI command strings before they are coded into a program. The project shows you everything you need to know to control MCI devices using Visual Basic.

**7.7**     **Write a MIDI recorder program using Visual Basic**

For reasons known only to Microsoft, MCI does not provide a way to record from external MIDI devices. This How-To uses the Waite Group's free custom control MsgHook and Windows' low-level Midi and Timer API functions to create a program that can record and play back using external MIDI devices.

## 7.1  ⚫  How do I...

## Determine the color capabilities of a screen or printer?

### Problem

My applications will be used with systems that have different display and printer characteristics. I need to determine the number of colors that can be displayed or printed for any given system.

### Technique

Visual Basic has no built-in statement or facility to determine a device's color capability, but a Windows API function can be used to provide your program with this data.

### Steps

Open and run GETCOLOR.MAK. The form will display the color parameters of the screen and default print as shown in Figure 7-1.

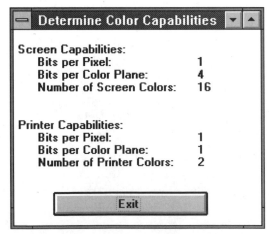

**Figure 7-1** The GetColor form displays screen and printer color parameters

The GetColor project may be created by entering the objects and code as detailed in the following steps.

1. Create a new project called GETCOLOR.MAK. Create a new form with the objects and properties shown in Table 7-1, and save it as GET-COLOR.FRM.

| Object | Property | Setting |
| --- | --- | --- |
| Form | FormName | GetColor |
| | Caption | Determine Color Capabilities |
| Command button | Name | Command1 |
| | Caption | Exit |

**Table 7-1** GetColor project form's objects and properties

2. Place the following code in the Declarations section of the form.

```
Const BITSPIXEL = 12        ' Number of bits per pixel
Const PLANES = 14           ' Number of planes
Declare Function GetDeviceCaps Lib "GDI" (ByVal hdc As Integer, ByVal ⇐
nIndex As Integer) As Integer
```

3. Place the following code in the Form_Paint event subroutine. Because Form_Paint is automatically called when a form is initially loaded, the user does not have to perform any action to display the data.

```
Sub Form_Paint ()
   Cls
'
' Get and display screen color capabilities.
'
   BPP = GetDeviceCaps(GetColor.hdc, BITSPIXEL)
   CPlanes = GetDeviceCaps(GetColor.hdc, PLANES)
   Print
   Print " Screen Capabilities:"
   Print Tab(5); "Bits per Pixel: "; Tab(32); BPP
   Print Tab(5); "Bits per Color Plane: "; Tab(32); CPlanes
   Print Tab(5); "Number of Screen Colors:"; Tab(32); (2 ^ BPP) ^ CPlanes

'
' Get and display printer color capabilities.
'
   BPP = GetDeviceCaps(Printer.hdc, BITSPIXEL)
   CPlanes = GetDeviceCaps(Printer.hdc, PLANES)
   Print
   Print
   Print " Printer Capabilities:"
   Print Tab(5); "Bits per Pixel: "; Tab(32); BPP
   Print Tab(5); "Bits per Color Plane: "; Tab(32); CPlanes
   Print Tab(5); "Number of Printer Colors:"; Tab(32); (2 ^ BPP) ^ CPlanes
End Sub
```

4. Place the following code in the Command1_Click event subroutine to allow for a graceful exit from the program.

```
Sub Command1_Click ()
    End
End Sub
```

## How It Works

Color in Windows can be a tricky issue. The capabilities differ for various display cards, printers, and other Windows-supported devices. Each device has an associated device driver that provides information about many of the supported capabilities, including number of colors. The screen or display drivers are defined in the SYSTEM.INI file, and the printer drivers can be selected through the Control Panel. We use the Windows API function GetDeviceCaps to have a device driver return information about its capabilities.

The two values from GetDeviceCaps that determine color capabilities are number of bits per pixel and number of color planes. The number of bits per pixel specifies how many bits are used in each color plane. The number of color planes determines the types of colors that a device can represent. The total number of shades per color is 2 raised to the bits per pixel. The total number of colors is this value raised to the number of color planes.

For instance, a standard VGA display has one bit per pixel and four color planes—red, green, blue, and intensity. This gives us a total of 16 pure colors. Non-pure or dithered colors are used when an RGB value specifies something other than these 16.

GetDeviceCaps retrieves information about a device by passing it the handle to a previously created device context, hDC. Visual Basic makes readily available two useful device contexts for us: the form's device context, FormName.hDC; and the printer's device context, Printer.hDC. The second parameter to GetDeviceCaps is a constant that specifies which piece of information to return.

## Comments

Making sense of the bits per pixel and number of color planes can be a bit confusing. Table 7-2 lists the values for some common Windows device drivers.

| Device | Bits Per Pixel | Number of Color Planes | Total Colors |
|---|---|---|---|
| Standard VGA | 1 | 4 | 16 |
| 256 Color VGA | 8 | 1 | 256 |
| Mono Adapter | 1 | 1 | 2 |
| LaserJet | 1 | 1 | 2 |

| Device | Bits Per Pixel | Number of Color Planes | Total Colors |
|---|---|---|---|
| Postscript Printer | 1 | 1 | 2 |
| HP PaintJet | 1 | 3 | 8 |

**Table 7-2** Color capabilities for selected Windows devices

## 7.2 ● How do I...

Complexity: Intermediate

## Make a replacement for QuickBASIC's SOUND statement?

### Problem

My QuickBASIC programs have some marvelous sound effects like police sirens and bloop sounds. Visual Basic, on the other hand, has only a Beep statement. What can I do?

### Technique

Sound is complicated in Windows because you can have many different programs running simultaneously. It would wreak havoc on your computer if any program could access hardware like the PC's speaker, so Windows programs have to cooperate with Windows to get access to the speaker and sound hardware. There are four Windows API functions that produce sound: CloseSound, OpenSound, SetVoiceSound, and StartSound. All these functions are stored in the SOUND.DRV device-driver DLL that comes with Windows.

### Steps

Open and run SOUND.MAK. There are no controls on this form. Just click on the form to produce a siren glissando effect. This project may be created by following these steps.

1. Create a new project called SOUND.MAK. Create a new form with no objects or properties and save it as SOUND.FRM. Put the following code in the Declarations section of the form. These Declare statements give access to the various sound functions needed to produce sounds in a Windows application.

```
DefInt A-Z

Declare Function CloseSound Lib "Sound.Drv" () As Integer
Declare Function OpenSound Lib "Sound.Drv" () As Integer
```

*continued on next page*

*continued from previous page*

```
Declare Function SetVoiceSound Lib "Sound.Drv" (ByVal nSource%, ByVal ⇐
Freq&, ByVal nDuration%) As Integer
Declare Function StartSound Lib "Sound.Drv" () As Integer
```

2. Put the following code in the general Sound subroutine. These statements call the SetVoiceSound and StartSound functions to play the specified tone for the specified duration.

```
Sub Sound (ByVal Frequency As Long, ByVal Duration As Integer)
    Frequency = Frequency * 65536
    I = SetVoiceSound(1, Frequency, Duration)
    I = StartSound()
End Sub
```

3. Put the following code in the Form_Click event subroutine. This code produces a police siren sound effect whenever you click on the form. (Dividing the frequency by 880 causes the higher frequencies to last longer, which produces a more realistic siren sound effect.)

```
Sub Form_Click ()
    For Freq& = 440 To 880 Step 4
        Call Sound(Freq&, Freq& / 880)
    Next

    For Freq& = 880 To 440 Step -4
        Call Sound(Freq&, Freq& / 880)
    Next
End Sub
```

4. Put the following code in the Form_Load event subroutine. This code calls the OpenSound function to tell Windows that the program will use sound.

```
Sub Form_Load ()
    I = OpenSound()
End Sub
```

5. Put the following code in the Form_Unload event subroutine. This code calls the CloseSound function to tell Windows that the program is done using sound. It's important to call this function so Windows can let other applications use sound.

```
Sub Form_Unload (Cancel As Integer)
    I = CloseSound()
End Sub
```

### How It Works

Creating sound in Windows applications is much more complex than it is in DOS applications, primarily because Windows is a multitasking environment that runs multiple applications simultaneously. Something the computer generally only has one of—like the speaker and sound hardware—must be requested and addressed by Windows to prevent several applications from trying to grab the same thing at the same time.

There are four steps involved in creating sound under Windows:

1. Request access to the sound hardware by calling OpenSound. (The Form_Load event subroutine does this.)

2. Enter a note to be played into Windows' sound queue. Windows maintains a queue of sounds that are to be played sequentially. (If you are familiar with QuickBASIC programming, this is similar to the queue used by the Play statement.)

3. Tell Windows to actually play the note that was entered into the sound queue.

4. Repeat Steps 2 and 3 for as many notes as you want to play. Then tell Windows you're finished using sound by calling CloseSound. (The Form_Unload event subroutine does this.)

The general Sound subroutine is called for each note you want to play. First, it moves the frequency you passed it as a parameter into the high-order word, since that's how Windows expects it. Because the frequency of each note is limited to a single word, the frequency can be anywhere between 0 and 32,767 hertz. Since most humans only hear between 20 and 20,000 hertz, that shouldn't be a problem.

### Comments

Be aware that after the OpenSound and before the CloseSound functions are called, no other application can use sound.

## 7.3 ● How do I...

Complexity: Intermediate

## Make music in Visual Basic?

### Problem

Visual Basic offers a number of functions that make the interface easier to use and to make programs fun for the user, including sophisticated graphics functions. In QuickBASIC, however, I can make sound effects, using the Sound and Play functions. Is Visual Basic really two steps forward and one step back, or can I have the best of both worlds? I would like to be able to create sound effects at various times in my application and to reuse all those QuickBASIC PLAY macros I spent so much time typing in.

### Technique

Don't delete those macros yet! Visual Basic can produce some very interesting sound effects, because of the sophisticated sound support built into the Windows API. The sound functions are contained in a device driver, which is a special DLL called SOUND.DRV. It can be called from Visual Basic, because the functions in a device driver can be accessed in the same way as functions in a normal DLL by just declaring them as external functions.

Under DOS, a program must jump through a lot of hoops to run the speaker, including speeding up the timer. This is certainly not a good idea under Windows for a number of reasons, not the least of which is that a lot of functions depend on the timer. With multiple applications running on the system at the same time, it is certainly not "well behaved" to speed up the timer. For this reason many device drivers exist that provide a layer between the application and the hardware and standardize the hardware access method.

### Steps

The sound effects sample, PLAYTEST.MAK, uses two subroutines that control the sound driver functions: a specialized replacement for the MsgBox function and a simple implementation of the Play statement. Each subroutine is in a separate module file, so you can use either one in your own programs.

Open and run PLAYTEST.MAK. If you click the button labeled "Music," the program will play a few bars from "Greensleeves." You will notice that you can minimize the application and even switch to another application, without disrupting the music. If you click on the button labeled "Error," you will see a specialized message box and hear music you can use in error situations.

Unlike many How-Tos in this book, we will first create separate module files that can be called from any Visual Basic program. Then to demonstrate them we'll build a new form that makes music.

1. Create the file EBOX.BAS, the module that provides support for the "enhanced" message box, and insert the following code.

```
DefInt A-Z

'Sound.DRV DLL routines.

Declare Function OpenSound Lib "SOUND.DRV" ()
Declare Sub CloseSound Lib "SOUND.DRV" ()
Declare Sub SetVoiceNote Lib "SOUND.DRV" (ByVal Voice, ByVal Note, ⇐
ByVal Length, ByVal Dots)
Declare Sub StartSound Lib "SOUND.DRV" ()

Function ErrBox (Message$, BoxType, Title$)
```

```
      CloseSound
      Voices = OpenSound()
      For I = 1 To 10
        SetVoiceNote 1, 40, 16, 0
        SetVoiceNote 1, 41, 16, 0
        SetVoiceNote 1, 40, 16, 0
        SetVoiceNote  1, 37, 16, 0
      Next I
      StartSound
      ErrBox = MsgBox(Message$, BoxType + 48, Title$)
      CloseSound
End Function
```

The ErrBox function is used exactly like the MsgBox function, with one exception. ErrBox automatically adds 48 to the box type that you specify to produce the exclamation point icon in the message box. Your application need only specify the base message box type. ErrBox returns the same values as the MsgBox function does, referring to the button that the user has selected. While the user reads the message box, the musical theme is playing in the background. The music is stopped, using the CloseSound function, as soon as the user makes a selection. This is a fairly simple implementation of sound from Visual Basic, but it is a good warm-up for our implementation of Play.

The following code creates the PLAY.BAS module, which you can include in your applications to add this sound functionality. The majority of the relevant code is simply parsing the string that is passed to it. Note that there are a number of occasions in which a number must be parsed from the string; the GoSub GetNote is used for this purpose. In addition, many characters in the PLAY macro do not immediately require a sound driver function to be called. For example, when the program sees a letter corresponding to a note on the scale, the code waits to find the length of the note and the number of dots before making a call to the SetVoiceNote function. Therefore, the SendNote subroutine is used to submit all the current information to the queue when a new note is encountered.

2. Insert the following code in a new file called PLAY.BAS.

```
DefInt A-Z

'Sound.DRV DLL routines.

Declare Function OpenSound Lib "SOUND.DRV" ()
Declare Sub CloseSound Lib "SOUND.DRV" ()
Declare Sub SetVoiceQueueSize Lib "SOUND.DRV" (ByVal Voice, ByVal Bytes)
Declare Sub SetVoiceAccent Lib "SOUND.DRV" (ByVal Voice, ByVal Tempo,_ ⇐
ByVal Volume, ByVal Mode, ByVal Pitch)
```

*continued on next page*

*continued from previous page*

```
Declare Sub SetVoiceNote Lib "SOUND.DRV" (ByVal Voice, ByVal Note,_ ⇐
ByVal Length, ByVal Dots)
Declare Sub StartSound Lib "SOUND.DRV" ()

Const Range$ = "PCzDzEFzGzAzB"
Const Numbers$ = "0123456789"

Const TRUE = -1
Const FALSE = 0

Sub Play (Song$)
    Voices = OpenSound()
    SetVoiceQueueSize 1, 1024
    SongString$ = UCase$(Song$)
    TChars = Len(SongString$)
    Tempo = 120
    Music = 0
    Octave = 3
    Length = 4
    NewNote = FALSE
    NewAccent = TRUE
    CharOff = 1
    Do
      Char$ = Mid$(SongString$, CharOff, 1)
      Select Case Char$
        Case "A" To "G", P
          GoSub SendNote
          Pitch = InStr(Range$, Char$) - 1
          NewNote = TRUE
        Case "+", "#"
          Pitch = Pitch + 1

        Case "-"
          Pitch = Pitch - 1

        Case "."
          Dots = Dots + 1

        Case "1" To "9"
          GoSub GetNum
          NoteLength = TempNum

        Case ">"
          GoSub SendNote
          Octave = Octave + 1

        Case "<"
          GoSub SendNote
          Octave = Octave - 1

        Case "M"
          GoSub SendNote
          CharOff = CharOff + 1
          Char$ = Mid$(SongString$, CharOff, 1)
          Select Case Char$
```

```
                    Case "N"
                       Music = 0
                    Case "S"
                       Music = 2
                    Case "L"
                       Music = 1
                End Select
                NewAccent = TRUE

          Case "N"
             GoSub SendNote
             CharOff = CharOff + 1
             GoSub GetNum
             Pitch = TempNum
             NewNote = TRUE
             GoSub SendNote

          Case "O"
             GoSub SendNote
             CharOff = CharOff + 1
             GoSub GetNum
             Octave = TempNum

          Case "T"
             GoSub SendNote
             CharOff = CharOff + 1
             GoSub GetNum
             Tempo = TempNum
             NewAccent = TRUE

          Case "L"
             GoSub SendNote
             CharOff = CharOff + 1
             GoSub GetNum
             Length = TempNum

          Case Else
       End Select
       CharOff = CharOff + 1
    Loop Until CharOff > TChars
    GoSub SendNote
    StartSound
Exit Sub

    SendNote:
    If NewAccent Then SetVoiceAccent 1, Tempo, 1, Music, 0
    If NewNote Then
    If Pitch > 0 Then Pitch = (Pitch + (Octave * 12)) - 1
       If NoteLength Then
          PlayLength = NoteLength
          NoteLength = 0
       Else
          PlayLength = Length
       End If
       SetVoiceNote 1, Pitch, PlayLength, Dots
```

*continued on next page*

*continued from previous page*

```
      Dots = 0
   End If
   NewNote = FALSE
   NewAccent = FALSE
Return

GetNum:
   TempNum = Val(Mid$(SongString$, CharOff, 1))
   If CharOff < TChars Then
     TestChar$ = Mid$(SongString$, CharOff + 1, 1)
     If InStr(Numbers, TestChar$) > 0 Then
        TempNum = TempNum * 10 + Val(TestChar$)
        CharOff = CharOff + 1
     Else
          Return
     End If
   End If
   If CharOff < TChars Then
     TestChar$ = Mid$(SongString$, CharOff + 1, 1)
     If InStr(Numbers, TestChar$) > 0 Then
        TempNum = TempNum * 10 + Val(TestChar$)
        CharOff = CharOff + 1
     End If
   End If
Return
End Sub
```

To make use of PLAY.BAS, simply add it to your application, using the Add File option of the File menu. You can then call the Play statement, passing a macro, similar to the one in QuickBasic. The only exception is that all music is played in the background, so MF and MB are simply ignored. If you want to force the sound driver into foreground mode, you can simply call the WaitSoundState sound driver function, like this:

```
WaitSoundState 0
```

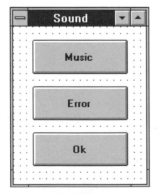

**Figure 7-2** Appearance of the Playtest form

However, it is recommended that you do not tie up the system in this way. To create the demo program shown in Figure 7-2, perform the following steps:

3. Create a new project called PLAYTEST.MAK. Create a new form with the objects and properties in Table 7-3 and save it as PLAYTEST.FRM.

| Object | Property | Setting |
|--------|----------|---------|
| Form | FormName | Form1 |
| | Caption | Sound |
| | BackColor | &H00FFFFFF& (White) |
| Button | Name | Command1 |
| | Caption | Music |
| Button | Name | Command2 |
| | Caption | Error |
| Button | Name | Command3 |
| | Caption | OK |

**Table 7-3** Playtest project's objects and properties

4. Using the Add File option on the File menu, add the EBOX.BAS and PLAY.BAS files to your project.

5. Insert the following code in the Declarations section of Form1.

```
DefInt A-Z

Declare Sub CloseSound Lib "SOUND.DRV" ()
```

6. Insert the following code in the Form_Unload procedure.

```
Sub Form_Unload (Cancel As Integer)
    CloseSound
End Sub
```

7. Insert the following code in the Command1_Click procedure to actually make music.

```
Sub Command1_Click ()
    Part1$ = "E8G4A8MLB8.>C16.MN<B8A4F#8MLD8.E16.MNF#8G4E8"
    Part2$ = "MLE8.D#16.MNE8F#4.<B4>"
    Green$ = "T24o2" + Part1$ + Part2$
    Play Green$
End Sub
```

8. Insert the following code in the Command2_Click procedure.

```
Sub Command2_Click ()
    Title$ = "You shouldn't have done that!"
    Mess$ = "You are now entering "
    Button = ErrBox(Mess$, 0, Title$)
End Sub
```

9. Insert the following code in the Command3_Click procedure.

```
Sub Command3_Click ()
    Unload Form1
End Sub
```

### How It Works

Although the Windows sound driver is still underdeveloped, to say the least, enough functions are operational to mimic the functionality of Sound and Play. The sound driver operates on a system of queues, much like Windows itself. You open a "voice" of the sound driver and insert notes, and other information, in the queue, then instruct the sound driver to begin processing the queue. The sound driver then processes the sound in the background, allowing your application to continue with other tasks.

You open a "voice queue" using the OpenSound function. This function returns the number of available voices. Currently, only one voice can be opened at once, but the API allows for future enhancements. If there is an error opening a queue, or the sound driver is already in use, OpenSound will return a -1. The SetVoiceQueueSize function is used to tell the sound driver to reserve enough space for the notes that you want to play. Determining the correct value to use is still a bit of a black art, but 1024 seems to do the trick in most cases.

The functions that allow us to place information in the voice queue are SetVoiceNote and SetVoiceAccent. SetVoiceNote enables us to place a note in the queue. This note corresponds to the number used in the N directive in BASIC's PLAY macro language. It is a value of 1 through 84, corresponding to the 84 keys—7 octaves—on a piano keyboard. A value of 0 is considered a pause. SetVoiceNote also enables us to set the length of the note we insert into the queue. These lengths, again, are specified the same way they are in BASIC. For example, 1 is a whole note, 2 is a half note, and 16 is a sixteenth note. You specify the reciprocal of the duration of the note. Finally, SetVoiceNote allows us to set the number of "dots" following the note directly.

SetVoiceAccent enables us to set the tempo, volume (not implemented), mode, and pitch. Again, tempo is specified exactly the way it is in BASIC, with values ranging from 32 to 255 and a default of 120.

When you are finished filling the queue, you start the sound driver processing the queue using the StartSound function.

### Comments

One nice aspect of the Windows 3 sound driver is the music can be processed in the background, even when the current task is modal. Such is the case with the message box example for this project.

As noted earlier, it is not wise to force the sound driver into foreground mode. If you want to keep the CPU free yet pause your program until the music has finished playing, insert the following code after each call to PLAY:

```
While DoEvents () and CountVoiceNotes (1) > 0
Wend
```

Of course, you will need to include the additional declaration for CountVoiceNotes in the Declarations section of the form:

```
Declare Function CountVoiceNotes Lib "Sound.DRV" (nVoice%)
```

The CountVoiceNotes will return the number of notes in the specified voice queue put there by the SetVoiceNote function. As always, the DoEvents function will allow other applications to proceed while your application pauses. This enables you to have the best of both worlds: foreground music and a "well-behaved" Windows application.

In addition, you will probably see a number of ways to improve on the string parsing in the Play subroutine. This routine is presented primarily for educational purposes and was written for readability. Perhaps the most important speed optimization enhancement would be to compare integers in the Select Case loop rather than strings. Integer comparisons are much faster than string comparisons. However, it is easier to see what is going on from the letters. Your new Select Case block would look something like this:

```
Select Case ASC (Char$)
    Case 65 - 71, 80
        etc.
```

This code will certainly improve the speed of your string parsing. Another technique that this implementation of Play uses is to create a look-up table, for note values, using a string constant, PCzDzEFzGzAzB. The Instr function is used to find which "note" should be inserted in the queue based on the character's position in this table. One possible alternative would be to create a look-up array, whose subscripts correspond to the ASC values of the characters. The result might look something like this:

```
NoteTable(65) = 10 ' A
NoteTable(66) = 12 ' B
NoteTable(67) = 1  ' C
NoteTable(68) = 3  ' D
NoteTable(69) = 5  ' E
NoteTable(70) = 6  ' F
NoteTable(71) = 8  ' G
```

So, as you can see, there are a number of places to go from here, but this should get you started.

## 7.4 How do I...

# Create a phone dialer in Visual Basic?

### Problem

I would like to create a simple phone dialer in Visual Basic, but Visual Basic doesn't seem to include communications functions. Is this true? Is there a way to access a modem from within Visual Basic?

### Technique

This can be accomplished using simple file I/O techniques. While it is possible to create a full terminal emulation program in Visual Basic using the Windows communications API, this is not necessary for creating a simple phone dialer.

### Steps

To try the sample program, open and run DIALER.MAK. Type a phone number into the text control and click the command button. Dialer will then dial the phone number and change the caption of the command button to Hangup. Once the other party has answered, and you have picked up the extension, you should click Hangup to hang up the modem.

The port is set to COM2 as a program default, because most people install their mouse on COM1. If your modem is on another port, simply change that line in the source code.

To create Dialer, perform the following steps:

1. Create a new project called DIALER.MAK. Create a new form with the objects and properties shown in Table 7-4 and save it as DIALER.FRM. When finished, the form should look like Figure 7-3.

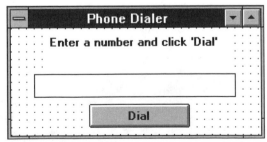

**Figure 7-3** Appearance of the Dialer form

| Object | Property | Setting |
|--------|----------|---------|
| Form | FormName | Form1 |
| | Caption | Phone Dialer |
| Label | Name | Label1 |
| | Caption | Enter a number and click 'Dial' |
| Text box | Name | Text1 |
| Button | Name | Command1 |
| | Cation | Dial |

**Table 7-4** Dialer project form's objects and properties

2. Insert the following code in the Command1_Click procedure.

```
Sub Command1_Click ()
   If Command1.Caption = "Dial" Then
      If Text1.Text <> "" Then
         Num$ = "ATDT" + Text1.Text
         Open "Com2" For Output As #1
         Print #1, Num$
         Label1.Caption = "Pick up the phone and click 'Hangup'"
         Command1.Caption = "Hangup"
      End If
   Else
      Num$ = "ATH"
      Print #1, Num$
      Close #1
      Label1.Caption = "Enter number and click 'Dial'"
      Command1.Caption = "Dial"
   End If
End Sub
```

### How It Works

The process is fairly simple. We open the communications port as a standard device supported by DOS. We then send command strings to the "file" using the Print # statement. This technique automatically appends the necessary carriage return to our command string.

A Hayes-compatible modem string is constructed by combining the phone number and the standard ATDT prefix of the Hayes command set. If your phone line is pulse dial, then the prefix would be ATDP.

The port then remains open until the user clicks the Hangup button. The label of the Command button is set and checked to determine whether to dial or hang up the phone.

## Comments

The most interesting aspect of this sample is that DOS does all the work. In fact, file operations are one of the few things that Windows still uses DOS to accomplish. While the DOS file system leaves quite a bit to be desired, it does have the capability to address a number of devices, including a communications port, as though it was a file. This technique is used to redirect output dynamically in a DOS application.

Although this simplistic example can be accomplished without using the standard Windows communications, we would have to move beyond these techniques to create something like a terminal emulation package. The functions exist in the Windows API to check for a modem and, in fact, to create an entire communications package.

## 7.5  How do I...

# Perform serial I/O in Visual Basic?

### Problem

I need to transfer data between a Visual Basic application and our corporate minicomputer using serial communcations. When I use the standard input/output functions such as Open, Get, and Put, with a communication port, my program often loses characters.

### Technique

Using standard I/O calls for serial communications has never worked properly, either under DOS or Windows. DOS-based applications usually require the assistance of a third party's programming library to assist in serial communications. Fortunately, Windows comes with a built-in serial communications library that Visual Basic applications can access.

### Steps

The Commfunc project demonstrates the use of the Windows communication functions by emulating a dumb terminal.

Open and run COMMFUNC.MAK. Check that the Commstring constant in the Declarations section of the form is set for the desired port, speed, and communication parameters. Change it to suit your particular hardware configuration.

Click on the Start menu to open the serial communications port. Characters entered from the keyboard will be sent to the COM port. Any characters received will be displayed on the form. Click on the End menu item to close the port, and exit the program.

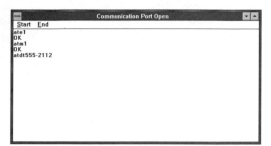

**Figure 7-4** The Commfunc form in action

1. Create a new project called COMMFUNC.MAK. Create a new form with the properties and settings shown in Table 7-5, and save it as COMMFUNC.FRM. The layout of the form will appear similar to Figure 7-4.

| Object | Property | Setting |
| --- | --- | --- |
| Form | AutoRedraw | False |
| | Caption | Communication Port Closed |
| | FormName | Commfunc |

**Table 7-5** Commfunc project form's properties and settings

2. Create a menu for the form using the Menu Design window with the captions and controls shown in Table 7-6.

| Caption | Name |
| --- | --- |
| &Start | Start |
| &End | End_Comm |

**Table 7-6** Menu for Commfunc form

3. Place the following constants and declarations in the Global module. Save them as COMMFUNC.BAS. The constants defined in this module are returned error codes. The user-defined types, DCB and COMSTAT, are passed as parameters to some of the API communications routines.

```
' Error Flags
Global Const CE_RXOVER = &H1      ' Receive Queue overflow
Global Const CE_OVERRUN = &H2     ' Receive Overrun Error
Global Const CE_RXPARITY = &H4    ' Receive Parity Error
Global Const CE_FRAME = &H8       ' Receive Framing error
Global Const CE_BREAK = &H10      ' Break Detected
```

*continued on next page*

*continued from previous page*

```
Global Const CE_CTSTO = &H20          ' CTS Timeout
Global Const CE_DSRTO = &H40          ' DSR Timeout
Global Const CE_RLSDTO = &H80         ' RLSD Timeout
Global Const CE_TXFULL = &H100        ' TX Queue is full
Global Const CE_PTO = &H200           ' LPTx Timeout
Global Const CE_IOE = &H400           ' LPTx I/O Error
Global Const CE_DNS = &H800           ' LPTx Device not selected
Global Const CE_OOP = &H1000          ' LPTx Out-of-Paper
Global Const CE_MODE = &H8000         ' Requested mode unsupported

Global Const IE_BADID = (-1)          ' Invalid or unsupported ID
Global Const IE_OPEN = (-2)           ' Device Already Open
Global Const IE_NOPEN = (-3)          ' Device Not Open
Global Const IE_MEMORY = (-4)         ' Unable to allocate queues
Global Const IE_DEFAULT = (-5)        ' Error in default parameters
Global Const IE_HARDWARE = (-10)      ' Hardware Not Present
Global Const IE_BYTESIZE = (-11)      ' Illegal Byte Size
Global Const IE_BAUDRATE = (-12)      ' Unsupported BaudRate

        Type DCB
        Id As String * 1
        BaudRate As Integer
        ByteSize As String * 1
        Parity As String * 1
        StopBits As String * 1
        RlsTimeout As Integer
        CtsTimeout As Integer
        DsrTimeout As Integer
        Bits1 As String * 1
        Bits2 As String * 1
        XonChar As String * 1
        XoffChar As String * 1
        XonLim As Integer
        XoffLim As Integer
        PeChar As String * 1
        EofChar As String * 1
        EvtChar As String * 1
        TxDelay As Integer
End Type

Type COMSTAT
        Bits As String * 1
        cbInQue As Integer
        cbOutQue As Integer
End Type

' COMM declarations
Declare Function OpenComm Lib "User" (ByVal lpComName As String, ByVal ⇐
wInQueue As Integer, ByVal wOutQueue As Integer) As Integer
Declare Function SetCommState Lib "User" (lpDCB As DCB) As Integer
Declare Function ReadComm Lib "User" (ByVal nCid As Integer, ByVal lpBuf ⇐
As String, ByVal nSize As Integer) As Integer
```

```
Declare Function WriteComm Lib "User" (ByVal nCid As Integer, ByVal lpBuf ⇐
As String, ByVal nSize As Integer) As Integer
Declare Function Closecomm Lib "User" (ByVal nCid As Integer) As Integer
Declare Function BuildCommDCB Lib "User" (ByVal lpDef As String, lpDCB ⇐
As DCB) As Integer
Declare Function GetCommError Lib "User" (ByVal nCid As Integer, lpStat ⇐
As COMSTAT) As Integer

' Functions for Scrolling a Window
'
Declare Sub ScrollWindow Lib "User" (ByVal hWnd As Integer, ByVal XAmount ⇐
As Integer, ByVal YAmount As Integer, lpRect As Any, lpClipRect As Any)
Declare Sub UpdateWindow Lib "User" (ByVal hWnd As Integer)
```

4. Enter the following code into the Declarations section of the form. The Commstring constant, which is in DOS mode format, should be changed to reflect the communication parameters of your hardware configuration. The example below is read as, COM port 2, 2400 baud, no parity, 7 data bits, and 1 stop bit.

```
Dim LpDCB As DCB
Dim nCid As Integer
Const Commstring = "COM2:2400,n,7,1"
```

5. Place the following code in the General section of the Commfunc form. This code, which is called from the Start_Click event subroutine, opens the communication port and sets the port parameters to those specified in the Comstring.

```
Sub Comm_open (Commstring$)
  Dim T As Integer
'----------------------------------------------------
' -- Close any previously open communication ports
'
   T = Closecomm(1)
   T = Closecomm(2)
'----------------------------------------------------
' -- Open the communication port, get nCid
' -- nCid < 0 if error, refer to IE_ constants.
' -- -2 = port already open, try closing it anyway.
'
   Commport$ = Left$(Commstring$, InStr(Commstring$, ":") - 1)
   nCid = OpenComm(Commport$, 1024, 1024)
   If nCid < 0 Then
      MsgBox "Unable to Open Comm Device: " + Str$(nCid), 16
      If nCid = -2 Then T = Closecomm(1)
      End
   End If


'----------------------------------------------------
' -- Load the CommDCB with parameters from Commstring
```

*continued on next page*

*continued from previous page*

```
'
    If (BuildCommDCB(Commstring$, lpDCB)) Then
        MsgBox "Unable to Build Comm DCB", 16
        End
    End If


'------------------------------------------------
' -- Set the port state
'
    lpDCB.Id = Chr$(nCid)
    If (SetCommState(lpDCB)) Then
        MsgBox "Unable to set Comm State", 16
        End
    End If
End Sub
```

6. Place the following code into the General section of the Commfunc form. This code will constantly check for incoming characters. If any are found, they will be sent to the Print_to_form subroutine for printing.

```
Sub Poll_comm ()
  Dim Nchars As Integer, Commerr As Integer, T As Integer
  Dim Readbuff As String * 1024, Lpstat As COMSTAT
    Do While nCid
        Nchars = ReadComm(nCid, Readbuff, Len(Readbuff))  ' Read buffer
        If Nchars < 0 Then Nchars = -Nchars               ' Ignore errors
        If Nchars Then Print_to_form Left$(Readbuff, Nchars)  ' Display data
        Commerr = GetCommError(nCid, Lpstat)          ' Need to poll for errors
        T = DoEvents()                                ' Let other people run
    Loop
End Sub
```

7. Place the following code into the General section of the Commfunc form. This subroutine closes the communication port.

```
Sub Close_comm ()
  Dim Ret As Integer
    Ret = Closecomm(nCid)
    If Ret < 0 Then
        MsgBox "Unable to Close comm port: " + Str$(Ret), 16
        End
    Else
        nCid = 0              ' Clear nCid to stop Poll_comm
    End If
End Sub
```

8. Enter the following code into the Form_KeyPress event subroutine. This subroutine sends characters entered from the keyboard to the communications port.

```
Sub Form_KeyPress (KeyAscii As Integer)
  Dim Ret As Integer, T As Integer
```

```
Dim Lpstat As COMSTAT                  ' Communication status block
Static Buffer$
  If nCid = 0 Then Exit Sub
  Buffer$ = Buffer$ + Chr$(KeyAscii)
  T = GetCommError(nCid, Lpstat)   ' Get current stats
  If Lpstat.cbOutQue < 1024 Then   ' Space left in buffer?
     Ret = WriteComm(nCid, Buffer$, Len(Buffer$)) ' Place chars in buffer
     If Ret <= 0 Then Ret = -Ret   ' Ret has # of chars output,
                                   ' <0 indicates error (ignored)
     Buffer$ = Mid$(Buffer$, Ret + 1)    ' Remove xmited chars from buffer
  End If
End Sub
```

9. Put the following code in the Start_Click menu event subroutine. This subroutine opens the COM port and changes the caption on the form to indicate that the port is open. The Poll_comm subroutine is then called to read incoming characters from the COM port.

```
Sub Start_Click ()
   Comm_open Commstring$
   If nCid Then Commfunc.Caption = "Communication Port Open"
   Poll_comm
End Sub
```

10. Put the following code in the End_Comm_Click menu event subroutine. It closes the COM port and exits the application.

```
Sub End_Comm_Click ()
   Close_comm
   Commfunc.Caption = "Communication Port Closed"
   End
End Sub
```

11. Place the following subroutine in the General section of the Commfunc form. This subroutine is used to print characters on the form. Unlike the standard Visual Basic Print statement, this code emulates the scrolling action of a dumb terminal. As a new line is printed at the bottom of the form, the previous lines are scrolled up to make room.

```
Sub Print_to_form (Buffer As String)
  Dim Yamount As Integer, Cnt As Integer
    Scalemode = 3                  ' Set to pixels
    Yamount = TextHeight("a")      ' Height of character
    For Cnt = 1 To Len(Buffer)     ' Process all characters
       C$ = Mid$(Buffer, Cnt, 1)
       If C$ = Chr$(10) And Currenty >= Scaleheight - 2 * Yamount Then ' do ⇐
         we scroll?
          ScrollWindow hwnd, 0, -Yamount, ByVal 0&, ByVal 0&
          UpdateWindow hwnd
          T% = DoEvents()
          Currentx = 0
       ElseIf C$ = Chr$(13) Then      ' Carriage returns reset line position
```

*continued on next page*

*continued from previous page*

```
            Currentx = 0
        Else
            Commfunc.Print C$;
        End If
    Next Cnt
End Sub
```

### How It Works

Using Windows communication functions isn't difficult once you realize how much of the work Windows does for you. If you try to open a communication port, such as COM1, and use standard I/O statements—such as Get and Put—on the port, your communications will be unreliable. Incoming characters are likely to be dropped, especially at line speeds of 2400 baud or greater. In addition, if Windows switches to another application, all characters received while the second application is in control will be lost. The reason is that Visual Basic I/O relies on DOS to do the work. DOS's COM port drivers were not designed for high-speed lines or multitasking environments like Windows.

The Windows communication functions are "interrupt driven." This means that incoming characters briefly interrupt the current program so that Windows can receive the character from the communication port. The character is then stored away in a queue, maintained by Windows, for later reading by the application.

Writing characters works much the same way. Windows takes the characters from your application program and stores them in its queue. When the communication port is ready to transmit the next character, Windows will transmit it for you. All this happens behind the scenes, very quickly, and without direct involvement on your part.

If you are familiar with the standard Visual Basic I/O statements, using the communications functions provided by the Windows API will not be much different. In fact, the important communication port API calls looks very similar to the standard Visual Basic I/O statements, as Table 7-7 shows.

| VB I/O Statement | Communications API Name | Function Performed |
|---|---|---|
| Open | OpenComm | Open a communication port |
| Close | CloseComm | Close a communication port |
| Get | ReadComm | Read data from receive buffer |
| Put | WriteComm | Write data to the COM transmit buffer |
| Err | GetCommError | Check for communication errors |
| n/a | SetCommState | Set COM port characteristics |
| n/a | BuildCommDCB | Build a Data Control Block |

**Table 7-7** Visual Basic's I/O statements and communication port API calls compared

Our sample terminal program starts by opening a communcation port with the OpenComm API call. The three parameters to OpenComm are the communication port name (such as COM2) and the sizes, in number of bytes, of the receive and transmit queues. These sizes are limited to 32,767 bytes per queue, although typical values range from 1K to 16K bytes. The OpenComm function returns a variable, nCid, which is used in subsequent communications API calls. The nCid variable is similar to a file number in the Visual Basic I/O statements. If the returned nCid is less than zero, then the COM port was not opened, and nCid represents an error code instead. The global constants IE_ will identify the type of error. For example, a returned value of (-2) is an IE_OPEN error, "Device Already Open."

Because a communications port is a hardware device, it has many different configurable attributes. Items like baud rate, parity, and bits per character can be set and changed. The functions BuildCommDCB and SetCommState are used to configure the COM port. The SetCommState function actually sets the communication port attributes. Its only parameter is a user-defined data type called the DCB, which contains all the information needed to configure the operation of the communication port and API functions. SetCommState is called with the DCB as its single parameter. The first byte of the DCB is set to the nCid value returned by OpenComm. The other bytes of the DCB can be set manually or by calling Build-CommDCB. The BuildCommDCB function interprets a standard DOS mode-style string into the proper byte and bit settings in the DCB.

### Processing Incoming Characters

The Poll_com subroutine processes incoming characters from the COM port. The ReadComm API function takes three parameters: the nCid from the OpenComm call, a string to store the incoming characters, and the total number of characters that the string can store. Its return value is the actual number of incoming characters transferred to the string parameter. If the returned value is negative, an error was detected, although the magnitude of the returned value still indicates the number of characters transferred.

We can ignore the sign of ReadComm's return value, because Get-CommError is always called after each read. GetCommError not only returns communication errors, but also clears any internal error indicators with the communication API functions. Until these indicators are cleared, ReadComm will not return additional characters to your application. Get-CommError return values are set according to the CE_ constant flags defined in the Global declarations. Note that these are bit flags; each bit in the return code corresponds to a different error. The lpStat contains the number of characters present in the receive and transmit buffer queues.

The Poll_comm subroutine calls DoEvents after each read to ensure that other Windows functions can process.

The Form_KeyPress event subroutine handles keyboard activity. As each character is typed, it is appended to a buffer within the subroutine itself. The GetComm function is called to determine whether any room is left in the communication port's output buffer. The variable lpStat.cbOutQue is checked against the maximum buffer size to ensure that there is some space left. The WriteComm function moves the number of characters specified in the third parameter to the transmit queue. Windows will then take care of sending these characters to the communication port. WriteComm returns the number of characters actually moved to the transmit queue. These characters can then be removed for the Buffer$ string.

Although it doesn't use a communications API function, the Print_to_form subroutine does make a different use of the Windows API. The purpose of the Print_to_form subroutine is to provide a scrolling window, much like you would see on a CRT or at the DOS command line. When the cursor is at the bottom of the screen and a line feed is received, the entire contents of the screen are scrolled up by one line. The ScrollWindow API function scrolls the window's contents vertically by the number of pixels specified in the third parameter, Yamount. Yamount is set to the height of a single line of text using Visual Basic's TextHeight function. Because the Scalemode was previously set to "3 - Pixels," Yamount will already be expressed in terms of screen pixels. Since we want the text to scroll up the screen, a negative value for Yamount is used in the ScrollWindow call. The UpdateWindow and DoEvents calls ensure that the scrolling takes place before the characters on the new line are printed.

### Comments

Although the code in this project will work for many communications applications, a truly robust and reliable system will require a more thorough understanding of the DCB than was presented in this project.

The ScrollWindow API function will not work properly if the Auto-Redraw property of the form is set to True. For additional information about this API function, see the Scrllwnd project in How-To 3.1 Scroll all the objects in a window.

To test this project, your system will need to be connected via a communcation port to another device, such as a modem, minicomputer, or printer. If so, ensure that the port and connection are operating properly using a commercial communications package such as the Terminal program supplied with Microsoft Windows. This step lets you isolate hardware, interface, and cabling issues prior to debugging the Commfunc project code.

## 7.6 ⬤ How do I...

# Use the Media Control Interface with Visual Basic?

### Problem

Windows 3.1 added new APIs that make multimedia capabilities available to Windows programmers. I've heard that among these APIs there is something called the Media Control Interface (MCI) that makes adding multimedia capabilities to programs relatively easy. How do I use the Media Control Interface from within Visual Basic programs? I'm especially interested in playing music in the background while my program continues to do other things, and I need to know when the music has finished playing.

### Technique

MCI does provide an easy way to add Multimedia to your programs. A single function in the Windows API, mciSendString, provides access to most of the multimedia capabilities in Windows 3.1. MciSendString accepts command strings that describe what you want done. For instance, to play a wave file, you would send the following two strings:

```
open \windows\mmdata\train.wav type waveaudio alias train
play train
```

When the file is finished playing, you would send the following string to close the device:

```
close train
```

While these three lines make it easy enough to open, play, and close a wave file, there is no way for your program to know when the play has completed. This makes it difficult to know when exactly to send the "close train" command.

Most MCI command strings accept the optional command "notify" which can be used to receive notification that a command has been completed. When the notify option is used, the fourth argument to mciSendString (HANDLE hCallback) tells Windows how to notify your application the command has been completed. An hCallback is either a window handle or a callback function. When hCallback is a window handle, MCI sends a message to the window when the command is complete. When hCallback is a callback function, address notification is made by calling the function. This presents a bit of a challenge to the programmer. Callback functions can't be used with Visual Basic programs, and messages that arrive for a Visual Basic window are ignored unless they correspond to a standard event.

This is where the Waite Group's MsgHook custom control comes in. By putting an instance of the MsgHook custom control on your form you can intercept any message sent to any window! A MsgHook control has an array with one element for each possible window message. When you set an element to True the MsgHook control will fire an event each time the corresponding window message is received. Each MsgHook control also has an hwndHook property. You set this property to the hWnd of the window whose messages you want to intercept. As you will see in this How-To, MsgHook makes it easy to know when an MCI command has been completed. MsgHook, included with the companion disk, is a fully functional free custom control that you can use and distribute with your applications.

## Steps

Open and run MCITEST.MAK. The program has two text boxes, as shown in Figure 7-5; the top box is used to enter command strings, and the bottom box displays the results. When the form is loaded, it puts a sequence of sample commands into the commands box. You may need to modify the path and filename to match the files on your system. Then you can press either the Go or Step command buttons to execute the list of command strings. MCITEST is a good way to learn about the MCI command-string interface. Interactively executing commands makes it is easy to experiment with MCI.

1. Create a new project named MCITEST.MAK. Create a new form with the objects and properties shown in Table 7-8.

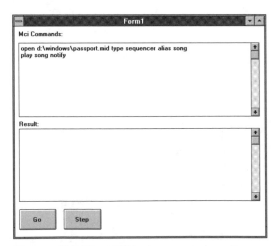

**Figure 7-5** The MCI test program in action

| Object | Property | Setting |
| --- | --- | --- |
| Form | Caption | "Form1" |
| | Height | 6630 |
| | Left | 1035 |
| | Name | "Form1" |
| | ScaleHeight | 6225 |
| | ScaleWidth | 7365 |
| | Top | 1140 |
| | Width | 7485 |
| Text box | Height | 2175 |
| | Left | 120 |
| | Name | "Text1" |
| | MultiLine | -1 'True |
| | ScrollBars | 2 'Vertical |
| | TabIndex | 0 |
| | Top | 3000 |
| | Width | 7095 |
| Text box | Height | 2175 |
| | Left | 120 |
| | MultiLine | -1 'True |
| | Name | "Text2" |
| | ScrollBars | 2 'Vertical |
| | TabIndex | 5 |
| | Top | 480 |
| | Width | 7095 |
| Command button | Caption | "Step" |
| | Height | 615 |
| | Left | 1440 |
| | Name | "StepCmd" |
| | TabIndex | 2 |
| | Top | 5400 |
| | Width | 1095 |
| Command button | Caption | "Go" |
| | Height | 615 |
| | Left | 120 |
| | Name | "GoCmd" |
| | TabIndex | 1 |
| | Top | 5400 |

*continued on next page*

continued from previous page

| Object | Property | Setting |
|--------|----------|---------|
|  | Width | 1095 |
| Label | Caption | "MCI Commands:" |
|  | Height | 255 |
|  | Left | 120 |
|  | Name | "Label1" |
|  | TabIndex | 4 |
|  | Top | 120 |
|  | Width | 1455 |
| Label | Caption | "Result:" |
|  | Height | 255 |
|  | Left | 120 |
|  | Name | "Label2" |
|  | TabIndex | 3 |
|  | Top | 2760 |
|  | Width | 735 |
| MsgHook | Height | 420 |
|  | Left | 2880 |
|  | Name | "MsgHook1" |
|  | Top | 5400 |
|  | Width | 420 |

**Table 7-8** Objects and properties for MCITEST

2. Add the following to the General Declarations section of Form1. This code declares global variables, Windows API functions, and constants used in this How-To.

```
Option explicit
'
' Newline is initialized during Form_Load to contain a crlf pair
'
Dim newline As String
'
' Declare Windows API functions used
'
Declare Function SendMessage Lib "User" (ByVal hWnd As Integer, ByVal ⇐
wMsg As Integer, ByVal wParam As Integer, ByVal lParam As Any) As Long
Declare Function mciSendString Lib "MMSystem" (ByVal lpstrCommand As ⇐
String, ByVal lpstrReturn As String, ByVal nSize As Integer, ByVal ⇐
hCallback As Integer) As Long
Declare Function mciGetErrorString Lib "MMSystem" (ByVal dwError As Long,⇐
ByVal lpstrBuffer As String, ByVal wLength As Integer) As Integer
```

```
'
' MCI notification constants
'
Const MM_MCINOTIFY = &H3B9
Const MCI_NOTIFY_SUCCESSFUL = 1
Const MCI_NOTIFY_SUPERSEDED = 2
Const MCI_NOTIFY_ABORTED = 4
Const MCI_NOTIFY_FAILURE = 8
'
' Messages used with the edit controls
'
Const WM_USER = 1024
Const EM_SETSEL = WM_USER + 1
Const EM_GETLINECOUNT = WM_USER + 10
Const EM_LINEINDEX = WM_USER + 11
Const EM_LINELENGTH = WM_USER + 17
Const EM_GETLINE = WM_USER + 20
Const EM_LINEFROMCHAR = WM_USER + 25
```

3. Add the following subroutine to the General section of Form1. This subroutine is used to append a line to the results text box.

```
Sub AddLineToResults (Text As String)
   text1.Text = text1.Text + newline + Text
End Sub
```

4. Add the following subroutine to the General section of Form1. This subroutine sends the message EM_LINEFROMCHAR to the control passed in. The wParam sent with this message tells the edit control what character you want the line number of. When wParam is -1, the edit control returns the line that the caret is on instead.

```
Function EditGetCurLine (ctl As Control) As Integer
   EditGetCurLine = SendMessage(ctl.hWnd, EM_LINEFROMCHAR, -1, 0&)
End Function
```

5. Add the following subroutine to the General section of Form1. This subroutine gets a single line of text from the edit control and returns it to the caller. A number of messages are sent to the edit control to accomplish this. First EM_LINEINDEX and EM_LINELENGTH are used to find the length of the current line. Then, after creating a buffer with the correct size, EM_GETLINE is used to get the line. Finally, the trailing NULL character is removed from the line and the line is returned to the caller.

```
Function EditGetLine (ctl As Control, lineNum As Integer) As String
   Dim lineLen      As Integer
   Dim charIndex    As Integer
   Dim hWnd         As Integer
   Dim buffer       As String
```

*continued on next page*

*continued from previous page*

```
    Dim dwReturn    As Long
    '
    ' Check number of lines in edit box and return empty line if none
    '
    If (EditGetLineCount(ctl) <= lineNum) Then
        EditGetLine$ = ""
        Exit Function
    End If
    '
    ' Get first character position of the current line
    '
    charIndex = SendMessage(ctl.hWnd, EM_LINEINDEX, lineNum, 0&)
    '
    ' And use it to get the length of the current line
    '
    lineLen = SendMessage(ctl.hWnd, EM_LINELENGTH, charIndex, 0&)
    '
    ' Allocate a buffer to put the line in
    '
   buffer = Chr$(lineLen Mod 256) + Chr$(lineLen / 256) + String$(lineLen ⇐
     + 1, 0)
    '
    ' Get the current line into our buffer
    '
    dwReturn = SendMessage(ctl.hWnd, EM_GETLINE, lineNum, buffer)
    '
    ' Strip the trailing null from the buffer and return
    ' it to the caller
    '
    EditGetLine = StripNull(buffer)
End Function
```

6. Add the following subroutine to the General section of Form1. This subroutine returns the total number of lines in a text box.

```
Function EditGetLineCount (ctl As Control)
    '
    ' Return the number of lines currently in the edit control
    '
    EditGetLineCount = SendMessage(ctl.hWnd, EM_GETLINECOUNT, 0&, 0&)
End Function
```

7. Add the following subroutine to the General section of Form1. This subroutine is used to set the current line of a text box.

```
Sub EditSetCurLine (ctl As Control, lineNum As Integer)
    Dim charIndex    As Long
    Dim setSelArg    As Long
    Dim lResult      As Long
    '
    ' Prevent the caller from trying to change to a non-existent
    ' line
    '
```

```
      If (lineNum < EditGetLineCount(ctl)) Then
          '
          ' Get char index of first char on line to move to
          '
          charIndex = SendMessage(ctl.hWnd, EM_LINEINDEX, lineNum, O&)
          '
          ' Set the start and end selection position to the first char on line
          '
          setSelArg = (charIndex * 65536) + charIndex
          lResult = SendMessage(ctl.hWnd, EM_SETSEL, O, setSelArg)
      End If
Fnd Sub
```

8. Add the following code to the Load event subroutine of Form1. The most important thing that happens here is the initialization of the MsgHook control. We set the array element indexed by MM_MCINOTIFY to True and put Form1's hwnd in the hwndHook property. As soon as the property hwndHook has been set, MsgHook1 begins receiving messages for Form1 before they are sent to the form.

```
Sub Form_Load ()
    '
    ' Initialize newline string
    '
    newline = Chr$(13) + Chr$(10)
    '
    ' Put some lines in the command list
    '
    text2.Text = "open \windows\passport.mid type sequencer alias song" +⇐
      newline + "play song notify"
    '
    ' Set the message interceptor up for the MM_MCINOTIFY message
    '
    MsgHook1.Message(MM_MCINOTIFY) = True
    MsgHook1.hwndHook = Form1.hWnd
End Sub
```

9. Add the following code to the Click event subroutine of the GoCmd command button. This subroutine selects and executes each line in the command-string list.

```
Sub GoCmd_Click ()
    Dim i       As Integer
    Dim nLines  As Integer
    Dim result  As String
    Dim cmd     As String


    '
    ' Set focus to list of commands
    '
    text2.SetFocus
```

*continued on next page*

*continued from previous page*

```
    nLines = EditGetLineCount(text2) - 1
    '
    ' Select and send each line
    '
    For i = 0 To nLines
        EditSetCurLine text2, i
        SendCurrentLine
    Next
End Sub
```

10. Add the following code to the Message event subroutine of MsgHook1. This subroutine executes each time the MM_MCINOTIFY message is sent to Form1. The wParam sent with the message is used to add an appropriate message to the results text box.

```
Sub MsgHook1_Message (msg As Integer, wParam As Integer, lParam As Long)
    '
    ' Got an MM_MCINOTIFY message, add string for notification
    ' type to results
    '
    Select Case wParam
        Case MCI_NOTIFY_ABORTED
            AddLineToResults "Notification: Aborted"
        Case MCI_NOTIFY_FAILURE
            AddLineToResults "Notification: Failure"
        Case MCI_NOTIFY_SUCCESSFUL
            AddLineToResults "Notification: Successful"
        Case MCI_NOTIFY_SUPERSEDED
            AddLineToResults "Notification: Superseded"
    End Select
End Sub
```

11. Add the following subroutine to the General section of Form1. This subroutine gets the current line from the commands text box and calls SendMciCommand to issue the command. If a result string is returned from SendMciCommand, it is added to the results text box.

```
Sub SendCurrentLine ()
    Dim cmd As String
    Dim result As String

    '
    ' Get the current line from the command list
    '
    cmd = EditGetLine(text2, EditGetCurLine(text2))
    If (cmd <> "") Then
        '
        ' Send the command to mci
        '
        result = SendMciCommand(cmd)
```

```
    '
    ' If mci had a result string add it to the results
    '
    If (result <> "") Then
        AddLineToResults result
    End If
  End If
End Sub
```

12. Add the following subroutine to the General section of Form1. This subroutine uses the Windows API function mciSendString to send a command string to the MCI subsystem of Windows. If an error is returned from the call to mciSendString, then mciGetErrorString is used to get the corresponding error message. The result string, containing either a normal response or an error message, is returned to the caller.

```
Function SendMciCommand (cmd As String) As String
  Dim result  As String
  Dim status  As Integer

  ' Create a buffer for the result string
  '
  result = String$(256, 0)
  '
  ' Send the command and retrieve error message if the command
  ' fails
  '
  status = mciSendString(cmd, result, Len(result), Form1.hWnd)
  If (status <> 0) Then
      status = mciGetErrorString(status, result, Len(result))
  End If
  '
  ' Return result or error string
  '
  SendMciCommand = StripNull(result)
End Function
```

13. Add the following code to the Click event subroutine of the StepCmd command button. This subroutine sends the current command string to MCI and advances the caret to the next line in the commands text box.

```
Sub StepCmd_Click ()
  '
  ' Step command, send current line
  '
  SendCurrentLine
  '
  ' Advance to next line
```

*continued on next page*

*continued from previous page*

```
    '
    EditSetCurLine text2, EditGetCurLine(text2) + 1
End Sub
```

14. Add the following code to the General section of Form1. Strings returned from the Windows API are terminated with a NULL character. This subroutine removes the trailing NULL from a string.

```
Function StripNull (from As String) As String
    Dim i As Integer

    i = InStr(from, Chr$(0))
    If (i <> 0) Then
        StripNull = Left$(from, i - 1)
    Else
        StripNull = from
    End If
End Function
```

### How It Works

The MCI function mciSendString sends command strings to the MCI subsystem of Windows, and has four arguments. The first argument is the command string to send. The second and third arguments are a buffer and its length that allow mciSendString to return information when appropriate. The last argument is either a window handle or a callback function. Command strings that use the "notify" option request MCI to provide notification when the command is complete.

In this How-To, Form1's hWnd is used as the last argument to mciSendString; this directs MCI to send notification messages to Form1. An instance of the MsgHook control is used to intercept messages sent to Form1. With the exception of MM_MCINOTIFY, all messages are simply sent on to Form1, and when the MM_MCINOTIFY message is sent, MsgHook fires its Message event. In a program that needed to know when an MCI command has been completed, you would simply wait until the MM_MCINOTIFY message arrived.

This How-To makes extensive use of the Windows API function SendMessage to get individual lines from the commands text box. Six of the 28 messages supported by the Windows text box are used to set the current line and retrieve individual lines of text. By using some of the other available messages you can add a number of useful features to this program, including cut-and-paste operations and undo.

### Comments

By combining the MCI command-string "notify" option with MsgHook, you can add a substantial number of Multimedia capabilities to your programs. The MCI command-string interface supports a number of commands that allow you to control virtually any Multimedia device. The full list of supported commands, occupying about twenty pages, can be found in *Microsoft's Multimedia Programmer's Reference.*

## 7.7 How do I...

## Write a MIDI recorder program using Visual Basic?

### Problem

I have an electronic keyboard that has a Musical Instrument Digital Interface (MIDI) port; my computer also has a MIDI port. I would like to be able to read the MIDI messages that my keyboard can send. I would also like to be able to play back what I've read. The only functions Windows provides for reading MIDI messages are low-level functions, which require either a callback function or the ability to receive special Windows messages. Callback functions cannot be written using Visual Basic, and unrecognized messages sent to a form are discarded.

### Technique

One of the free custom controls that comes with the Visual Basic How-To sample code diskette is MSGHOOK.VBX. This control gives you a way to intercept messages sent to a form or any other window in the system.

MSGHOOK is an extremely simple control to use, having only two properties and one event. The properties are Messages, an array with one element for each possible window message, and hwndHook, which identifies the window whose messages are to be intercepted. The single event supplied by MSGHOOK is Message(wMsg As Integer, wParam As Integer, lParam As Long, action As Integer, result As Long). The first two arguments to the Message event procedure, wParam and lParam, are the same arguments that are sent with every Windows message. The next to the last parameter, action, determines what will be done with a message after the Message event subroutine returns. If action is set to 0, the message is passed on to Visual Basic. If action is set to 1, the message is not passed on to Visual Basic and the value of the last parameter, result, is returned to Windows as the message response.

As you will see in this How-To, MSGHOOK makes it possible for the Visual Basic programmer to interact with windows at a level previously accessible only from within C programs.

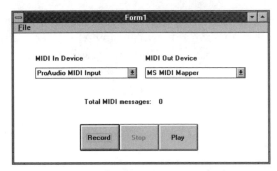

**Figure 7-6** The MIDIIO project in action

## Steps

Open and run MIDIIO.MAK. The two drop-down list boxes can be used to select input and output MIDI devices. After selecting the input and output devices, shown in Figure 7-6, you can either play or record by clicking on the appropriate command button.

**Note:** This How-To presumes that you have an external MIDI device connected to your computer, and that both it and Windows are correctly configured. If possible you should use a sequencer or other program to verify that the configuration and connections are correct.

A sample recording is included in the MIDIIO project directory. The sample recording, KATHYS.FOO, was recorded using MIDIIO and a Casio CT-460 keyboard. If you have a Casio CT-460 (or compatible) keyboard you will be able to play the sample file. Use the File Open dialog box to open KATHYS.FOO, then click on the Play command button.

If you don't have an external MIDI keyboard you may be able to play the sample file that comes with this How-To. Try selecting the MS MIDI Mapper and then use the File Open dialog box to open KATHYS.FOO, then click on the Play command button.

1. Create a new project named MIDIIO.MAK. Add the objects and properties shown in Table 7-9 to the form.

| Object | Property | Setting |
|--------|----------|---------|
| Form1  | Caption  | "Form1" |
|        | Height   | 4260    |
|        | Left     | 1035    |
|        | Name     | "Form1" |
|        | ScaleHeight | 3570 |
|        | ScaleWidth  | 6990 |

| Object | Property | Setting |
|--------|----------|---------|
| | Top | 1140 |
| | Width | 7110 |
| OpenDialog | CreatePrompt | 0 'False |
| | DefaultExt | "" |
| | DialogType | 0 'Open Dialog |
| | File | "" |
| | FileMustExist | 0 'False |
| | FileTitle | "" |
| | Filter | "" |
| | FilterIndex | 0 |
| | HideReadOnly | 0 'False |
| | InitialDir | "" |
| | Name | "OpenDialog1" |
| | OvorwritePrompt | -1 'True |
| | PathMustExist | -1 'True |
| | ReadOnly | 0 'False |
| | Title | "" |
| ComboBox | Height | 300 |
| | Left | 3600 |
| | Name | "OutList" |
| | Style | 2 'Dropdown List |
| | TabIndex | 6 |
| | Top | 960 |
| | Width | 2775 |
| ComboBox | Height | 300 |
| | Left | 600 |
| | Name | "InList" |
| | Style | 2 'Dropdown List |
| | TabIndex | 4 |
| | Top | 960 |
| | Width | 2775 |
| Command button | Caption | "Stop" |
| | Enabled | 0 'False |
| | Height | 735 |
| | Left | 2880 |
| | Name | "StopIt" |
| | TabIndex | 2 |

*continued on next page*

*continued from previous page*

| Object | Property | Setting |
|---|---|---|
| | Top | 2520 |
| | Width | 1095 |
| Command button | Caption | "Play" |
| | Height | 735 |
| | Left | 3960 |
| | Name | "PlayCmd" |
| | TabIndex | 1 |
| | Top | 2520 |
| | Width | 1095 |
| Command button | Caption | "Record" |
| | Height | 735 |
| | Left | 1800 |
| | Name | "RecordCmd" |
| | TabIndex | 0 |
| | Top | 2520 |
| | Width | 1095 |
| MsgHook | Height | 420 |
| | Left | 5880 |
| | Name | "Message1" |
| | Top | 1560 |
| | Width | 420 |
| Label | Caption | "0" |
| | Height | 255 |
| | Left | 3960 |
| | Name | "Label4" |
| | TabIndex | 8 |
| | Top | 1800 |
| | Width | 975 |
| Label | Caption | "Total MIDI messages:" |
| | Height | 255 |
| | Left | 1920 |
| | Name | "Label3" |
| | TabIndex | 7 |
| | Top | 1800 |
| | Width | 1935 |
| Label | Caption | "MIDI Out Device" |
| | Height | 255 |
| | Left | 3600 |

| Object | Property | Setting |
|--------|----------|---------|
|        | Name     | "Label2" |
|        | TabIndex | 5 |
|        | Top      | 600 |
|        | Width    | 2055 |
| Label  | Caption  | "MIDI In Device" |
|        | Height   | 255 |
|        | Left     | 600 |
|        | Name     | "Label1" |
|        | TabIndex | 3 |
|        | Top      | 600 |
|        | Width    | 1455 |

**Table 7-9** MIDIIO project's objects and properties

2. Select the Menu Design Window tool and create a menu with captions and names as shown in Table 7-10.

| Caption | Name |
|---------|------|
| &File | FileMenu |
| -File &New | FileNew |
| -File &Open | FileOpen |
| -File Save &As... | FileSaveAs |
| - | FileFoo |
| &Exit | FileExit |

**Table 7-10** MIDIIO menu

3. Create a new module and, after adding the following code to the module's General Declarations section, save it as MIDIIO.BAS. The code in this section defines the data types and functions used in MIDIIO.FRM.

```
'
' Data type used by windows to describe midi input device
' capabilities
'
Type MidiInCaps
    wMid            As Integer
    wPid            As Integer
    vDriverVersion  As Integer
    szPName         As String * 32
End Type
'
```

*continued on next page*

*continued from previous page*

```
' Data type used by windows to describe midi output device
' capabilities
'
Type MidiOutCaps
    wMid             As Integer
    wPid             As Integer
    vDriverVersion   As Integer
    szPName          As String * 32
    wTechnology      As Integer
    wVoices          As Integer
    wNotes           As Integer
    wChannelMask     As Integer
    dwSupport        As Integer
End Type
'
' Data type used by windows when sending short midi messages
'
Type MidiShortMsg
    dwTimestamp      As Long
    dwMidiMsg        As Long
End Type
'
' Midi output device functions
'
Declare Function midiOutGetNumDevs Lib "mmsystem" () As Integer
Declare Function midiOutGetDevCaps Lib "mmsystem" (ByVal uDeviceID As ⇐
Integer, lpCaps As MidiOutCaps, ByVal uSize As Integer) As Integer
Declare Function midiOutGetErrorText Lib "mmsystem" (ByVal uError As ⇐
Integer, lpText As String, ByVal uSize As Integer) As Integer
Declare Function midiOutOpen Lib "mmsystem" (lphMidiOut As Integer,⇐
ByVal uDeviceID As Integer, ByVal dwCallback As Long, ByVal notUsed As⇐
Long, ByVal dwFlags As Long) As Integer
Declare Function midiOutClose Lib "mmsystem" (ByVal hMidiOut As Integer)⇐
As Integer
Declare Function midiOutShortMsg Lib "mmsystem" (ByVal hMidiOut As ⇐
Integer, ByVal dwMsg As Long) As Integer
Declare Function midiOutReset Lib "mmsystem" (ByVal hMidiOut As Integer)⇐
As Integer
'
' Midi input device functions
'
Declare Function midiInOpen Lib "mmsystem" (lphMidiIn As Integer, ByVal⇐
uDeviceID As Integer, ByVal dwCallback As Long, ByVal notUsed As Long, ⇐
ByVal dwFlags As Long) As Integer
Declare Function midiInClose Lib "mmsystem" (ByVal hMidiIn As Integer) ⇐
As Integer
Declare Function midiInGetNumDevs Lib "mmsystem" () As Integer
Declare Function midiInGetDevCaps Lib "mmsystem" (ByVal uDeviceID As ⇐
Integer, lpCaps As MidiInCaps, ByVal uSize As Integer) As Integer
Declare Function midiInGetErrorText Lib "mmsystem" (ByVal uError As ⇐
Integer, lpText As String, uSize As Integer) As Integer
Declare Function midiInStart Lib "mmsystem" (ByVal hMidiIn As Integer) ⇐
As Integer
```

```
Declare Function midiInStop Lib "mmsystem" (ByVal hMidiIn As Integer) As⇐
Integer
Declare Function midiInReset Lib "mmsystem" (ByVal hMidiIn As Integer) ⇐
As Integer
'
' High-resolution Multimedia time function
'
Declare Function timeGetTime Lib "mmsystem" () As Long
```

4. Add the following code to the General Declarations section of Form1. This section declares the global variables used.

```
'
' This is new to VB 2.0, when this option is specified attempting to use an
' undefined variable will cause an error instead of creating a new variable.
'
Option Explicit
'
' Contains the handle of the currently open midi device
'
Dim hMidi As Integer
'
' While recording this variable contains the recording
' start time
'
Dim startTime As Long
'
' This array contains the current midi messages
'
Dim notes(10000) As MidiShortMsg
'
' Index into notes array
'
Dim note As Integer
'
' Total number of notes in notes array
'
Dim notesRecorded As Integer

'
' These constants are used to keep track of midi device
' open mode
'
Const OpenModeNOT = 0
Const OpenModeRecord = 1
Const OpenModePlay = 2

'
' Contains the current midi open mode. This variable contains
' OpenModeNOT when no midi device is open.
'
Dim openMode As Integer
```

*continued on next page*

*continued from previous page*

```
'
' Define the Midi input message we're interested in
'
Const MM_MIM_DATA = &H3C3
```

5. Add the following code to the Click event procedure of ExitMenu. This event is fired when the user selects Exit from the File menu.

```
Sub ExitMenu_Click ()
    End
End Sub
```

6. Add the following code to the Click event procedure FileNew. When the user selects File New from the menu we reset the number of notes recorded to 0 and update the size displayed in Label4.

```
Sub FileNew_Click ()
    notesRecorded = 0
    label4.Caption = 0
End Sub
```

7. Add the following code to the Click event procedure of FileOpen. This subroutine uses the Waite Group's free File Dialog custom control to prompt the user to select a file. If a file is selected, it is read into memory and the size displayed in Label4 is updated.

```
Sub FileOpen_Click ()
    '
    ' User wants to open an existing foo file. Set up the
    ' Waite Group's Open Dialog custom control
    '
    openDialog1.DialogType = 0
    openDialog1.Filter = "Foo Files(*.foo)|*.foo||"
    openDialog1.FilterIndex = 0
    openDialog1.DefaultExt = "foo"
    openDialog1.Title = "Open Foo File"
    '
    ' Go get a filename
    '
    openDialog1.DoIt = True
    '
    ' If a file was chosen go read it. If some non-foo file
    ' was chosen it's going to sound really strange when played!
    '
    If (openDialog1.File <> "") Then
        ReadFooFile (openDialog1.File)
    End If
End Sub
```

8. Add the following code to the Click event procedure of FileSaveAs. After checking to see that there is something to save, this subroutine uses the Waite Group's File Dialog custom control to select a filename to save to.

If a filename is selected, the current set of MIDI messages is written to it.

```
Sub FileSaveAs_Click ()
    '
    ' Let's not save a file if nothing is in the notes array
    '
    If (notesRecorded = 0) Then
        MsgBox "There is nothing to save", 32, "Error"
        Exit Sub
    End If
    '
    ' Otherwise set up the Waite Group's File Dialogs control
    '
    openDialog1.FileTitle = ""
    openDialog1.File = ""
    openDialog1.DialogType = 1
    openDialog1.Title = "Save As Foo File"
    openDialog1.Filter = "Foo Files(*.foo)|*.foo||"
    openDialog1.FilterIndex = 1
    openDialog1.DefaultExt = "foo"
    '
    ' Go get a filename to save the file as
    '
    openDialog1.DoIt = True
    '
    ' If we got a name then save the file
    '
    If (openDialog1.File <> "") Then
        SaveFooFile (openDialog1.File)
    End If
End Sub
```

9. Add the following code to the Load event procedure of Form1. This subroutine loads the drop-down list boxes with the names of all the MIDI input and output devices installed on the system. Notice that the MIDI Mapper is not, strictly speaking, a MIDI output device and must be added to the list explicitly.

```
Sub Form_Load ()
    Dim nDevices    As Integer
    Dim i           As Integer
    Dim wRtn        As Integer
    Dim inCaps      As MidiInCaps
    Dim outCaps     As MidiOutCaps
    '
    ' Get the number of midi input devices available
    '
    nDevices = midiInGetNumDevs()
    '
    ' Get the name of each midi input device and add it
    ' to the input devices list box
    '
    For i = 0 To nDevices - 1
```

*continued on next page*

*continued from previous page*

```
        wRtn = midiInGetDevCaps(i, inCaps, Len(inCaps))
        InList.List(i) = inCaps.szPName
    Next i
    '
    ' Select the first input device as the default
    '
    InList.ListIndex = 0
    '
    ' Get the number of midi output devices available
    '
    nDevices = midiOutGetNumDevs()
    '
    ' Add the MIDI Mapper which isn't treated like a midi out device
    '
    OutList.List(0) = "MS MIDI Mapper"
    '
    ' Now add each midi output device to the output device
    ' list box
    '
    For i = 0 To nDevices - 1
        wRtn = midiOutGetDevCaps(i, outCaps, Len(outCaps))
        OutList.List(i + 1) = outCaps.szPName
    Next i
    '
    ' Select the MIDI Mapper as the default output device
    '
    OutList.ListIndex = 0
End Sub
```

10. Add the following code to the Message event procedure of MsgHook1. MsgHook1 fires this event whenever a MM_MIM_DATA message is sent to Form1. This subroutine puts the MIDI data and a timestamp into the notes array.

```
Sub MsgHook1_Message (msg As Integer, wParam As Integer, lParam As Long)
    Dim timestamp As Long

    '
    ' A midi message has been received. If this is the first message
    ' the timestamp will be 0 otherwise it is the time elapsed since
    ' the first note was received
    '
    If (note = 0) Then
        timestamp = 0
        startTime = timeGetTime()
    Else
        timestamp = timeGetTime() - startTime
    End If

    notes(note).dwTimestamp = timestamp
    notes(note).dwMidiMsg = lParam
```

```
   note = note + 1
   label4.Caption = Str$(note)
End Sub
```

11. Add the following subroutine to the General section of Form1. This subroutine opens the currently selected output device and sends all of the MIDI messages in the notes array to that device.

```
Sub play ()
   Dim wRtn As Integer
   Dim outCaps As MidiOutCaps
   Dim outDev As Integer
   Dim errmsg As String * 256
   '
   ' If there's nothing to play we're outta here
   '
   If (notesRecorded = 0) Then Exit Sub
   '
   ' Get the output device id
   '
   outDev = OutList.ListIndex
   If (outDev = 0) Then
      outDev = -1
   Else
      outDev = outDev - 1
   End If
   '
   ' Open the output device, the last argument (&H10000) tells Windows
   ' that the third argement (Form1.hWnd) is a window handle.
   '
   wRtn = midiOutOpen(hMidi, outDev, Form1.hWnd, 0, &H10000)

   If (wRtn <> 0) Then
      wRtn = midiOutGetErrorText(wRtn, errmsg, Len(errmsg))
      MsgBox errmsg
      Exit Sub
   End If
   '
   ' Change buttons' enabled status
   '
   StopIt.Enabled = True
   RecordCmd.Enabled = False
   PlayCmd.Enabled = False
   '
   ' Flag that we're open to play
   '
   openMode = OpenModePlay
   '
   ' Initialize variables required for playback
   '
   note = 0
   startTime = timeGetTime()
```

*continued on next page*

*continued from previous page*

```
'
' Now for each note in the array
'
Do While (note < notesRecorded And StopIt.Enabled = True)
    '
    ' Wait until it's time to send the next message
    '
    Do While (timeGetTime() - startTime < notes(note).dwTimestamp)
        wRtn = DoEvents()
        If (StopIt.Enabled = False) Then
            Exit Do
        End If
    Loop
    '
    ' Send the next message and increment the notes array index
    '
    wRtn = midiOutShortMsg(hMidi, notes(note).dwMidiMsg)
    note = note + 1
Loop
'
' We're done, reset the output device (just for luck!)
'
wRtn = midiOutReset(hMidi)
'
' Close the output device
'
wRtn = midiOutClose(hMidi)
'
' Return buttons and variables to preplay state
'
StopIt.Enabled = False
RecordCmd.Enabled = True
PlayCmd.Enabled = True
openMode = OpenModeNOT
End Sub
```

12. Add the following code to the Click event procedure of PlayCmd.

```
Sub PlayCmd_Click ()
    Call play
End Sub
```

13. Add the following subroutine to the General section of Form1. This subroutine opens a file (which is presumed to be a FOO file) and reads its contents into the notes array.

```
Sub ReadFooFile (filepath As String)

    Open filepath For Binary As #1

    notesRecorded = 0

    Do While Not EOF(1)
        Get #1, , notes(notesRecorded + 1)
```

```
        notesRecorded = notesRecorded + 1
    Loop

    Close #1
    label4.Caption = Str$(notesRecorded)
End Sub
```

14. Add the following subroutine to the General section of Form1. This subroutine opens the currently selected MIDI input device and starts the input process.

```
Sub record ()
    Dim nDevices As Integer
    Dim i As Integer
    Dim wRtn As Integer
    Dim caps As MidiInCaps
    Dim errmsg As String * 256
    '
    ' Set up the MsgHook control so we get midi messages
    '
    MsgHook1.hwndHook = Form1.hWnd
    MsgHook1.Message(MM_MIM_DATA) = True
    '
    ' Open the midi input device, display error and
    ' return if the open fails. The last argument to
    ' midiInOpen tells midiInOpen that the third
    ' argument is a window handle.
    '
    wRtn = midiInOpen(hMidi, InList.ListIndex, Form1.hWnd, 0, &H10000)
    If (wRtn <> 0) Then
        wRtn = midiInGetErrorText(wRtn, errmsg, Len(errmsg))
        MsgBox errmsg
        Exit Sub
    End If
    '
    ' Start input, display error and return if an error
    ' occurs
    '
    wRtn = midiInStart(hMidi)
    If (wRtn <> 0) Then
        wRtn = midiInGetErrorText(wRtn, errmsg, Len(errmsg))
        MsgBox errmsg
        wRtn = midiInClose(hMidi)
        Exit Sub
    End If
    '
    ' All set ... change buttons enabled status and set up variables
    '
    PlayCmd.Enabled = False
    RecordCmd.Enabled = False
    StopIt.Enabled = True
    openMode = OpenModeRecord
    note = 0
End Sub
```

15. Add the following code to the Click event procedure of RecordCmd.

```
Sub RecordCmd_Click ()
    Call record
End Sub
```

16. Add the following subroutine to the General section of Form1. This subroutine writes the contents of notes to a file.

```
Sub SaveFooFile (filepath As String)
    Dim i As Integer

    Open filepath For Binary As #1

    For i = 0 To notesRecorded - 1
        Put #1, , notes(i)
    Next i

    Close #1
End Sub
```

17. Add the following code to the Click event procedure of StopIt. This subroutine uses the openMode variable to decide whether input or output is currently in progress and takes the required action to stop it.

```
Sub StopIt_Click ()
    Dim wRtn As Integer

    If (openMode = OpenModeRecord) Then
        wRtn = midiInClose(hMidi)
        notesRecorded = note
    End If

    openMode = OpenModeNOT

    StopIt.Enabled = False
    RecordCmd.Enabled = True
    PlayCmd.Enabled = True
End Sub
```

### How It Works

This How-To uses low-level MIDI functions. During Form_Load midiInGetNumDevs and midiInGetDevCaps is used to get a list of available input devices. Likewise, midiOutGetNumDevs and midiOutGetDevCaps get a list of available output devices.

Recording MIDI messages is really somewhat easy. First, the selected input device is opened with midiInOpen, and then the input process is started by calling midiInStart. After midiInStart is called, each MIDI message received from the selected device results in a window message being sent to Form1. Since the message/MsgHook control was initialized with a handle to Form1's window and the MM_MIM_DATA message was enabled, each MM_MIM_DATA message sent to Form1 causes Message1's Message event to be fired. Inside the Message event procedure we store the MIDI data and the time it arrived. You may have noticed that the Windows function timeGetTime is used. timeGetTime, which is new in Windows 3.1, returns the current system time in milliseconds and provides much better resolution than the standard time functions.

To play back recordings made with MIDIIO, it is only necessary to call midiOutOpen with a valid output device and then send the received messages at the right times. The only complication in the playback code results from the need to wait between messages. During playback the program basically wastes time between each midiOutShortMsg call. Without the call to DoEvents, while waiting to send the next message, this time would truly be wasted. Windows is a cooperative multitasking system. This means that each program must yield control to Windows frequently so other tasks can have a chance to run. In a Visual Basic program, DoEvents should be called periodically whenever a lengthy process is being performed.

You should be aware that the technique used in this How-To to playback a recording has a limitation. By calling DoEvents to share the CPU with other applications you run the risk that control of the CPU will not be returned to your application until after the next note should be played. This can cause playback to have intermittent pauses. One way to avoid this problem would be to convert the received MIDI messages to a MIDI file and use MCI to play the recording.

## Comments

The MIDI specification addresses hardware issues such as baud rate and signal characteristics, as well as defining the format and content of MIDI messages. This does not mean that you can record from one MIDI device and expect to hear the same thing, or even anything, when playing back the received MIDI messages on a different device. MIDI devices can send information on one or more "channels." There is no standard assignment of instruments to channels, so it is possible to record a piano on channel 1 of some device and get something that sounds like a foghorn or worse when played back on channel 1 of some other device.

The MIDI Mapper in Windows provides a way to translate messages intended for one device to the correct messages for some other device. Each MIDI message sent to the MIDI Mapper can go through three different mappings before being sent to the output device. The details of the MIDI Mapper are beyond the scope of this book; for an introduction to the issues, refer to Microsoft's *Multimedia Programmer's Workbook*.

# THE
# PROFESSIONAL
# TOOLKIT

# How do I...

Microsoft's Professional Toolkit for Visual Basic provides 22 custom controls, a Help Compiler, tools to create Setup programs, and the include files and library needed to create your own custom controls using C. The Professional Toolkit makes it even easier to create professional looking Windows applications using Visual Basic.

**Figure 8-1**

3-D controls

### 3-D Controls

The 3-D grayscale look, first made popular by the NeXT™, is commonly used in Windows programs to emphasize controls and groups of controls on the screen. 3-D controls that are intended to be clicked on appear to stand out from the background, like buttons on the form. Panels containing text or graphical information are often presented in a panel, which appears to be sunken into the background. These visual aids help users quickly locate controls and important information on your forms. The Professional Toolkit includes six 3-D controls: 3-D check box, 3-D command button, 3-D frame, 3-D ribbon button, 3-D option button, and 3-D panels.

**Figure 8-2**

Animated
Button
control

### Animated Button Control

The Animated Button control provides a way to animate the appearance of command buttons, as well as to create multistate buttons and multistate check boxes. Animated Button controls can contain a number of frames, like frames of a movie, which can be played using programmable speeds and sequences. The Animated Button control makes it easy to add interesting visual effects to your programs.

**Figure 8-3**

Communica-
tions control

### Communications Control

The Professional Toolkit's Communications control makes it easy to write Visual Basic applications containing sophisticated serial communicatons capabilities. The Communication control provides properties to control the baud rate, number of data bits, stop bits, and type of parity. There are also properties that can be used to set and monitor modem-control lines, such as CTS (Clear To Send) and DSR (Data Set Ready).

**Figure 8-4**

Gauge
control

### Gauge Control

Using the Gauge control, you can create a number of analog-like gauges and indicators. Thermometers, fuel indicators, percent complete bars, and similar types of gauges are easy to create and provide meaningful, easy to understand feedback for users.

**Figure 8-5**

Graph
control

### Graph Control

The Graph control provides the Visual Basic programmer with an easy way to create a virtually unlimited variety of charts and graphs. This is one of the most powerful and useful controls that comes with the Professional Toolkit. Bar charts, pie charts, scatter charts, high-low graphs, and a number of other chart and graph styles can be presented in either two or three dimensions. Titles and other annotations can be displayed, and colors are programmable. One of the nicer features of the Graph control is that it appears on the form at design time exactly as it will look at run time. This makes it easy to size the graph and pick the appropriate style for the type of data you're presenting to the user.

**Figure 8-6**

Key Status control

## Key Status Control

The Key Status control can be used to monitor the state of the (INS), (ALT), (SHIFT), (CTRL), (CAPS LOCK), (NUM LOCK), and (SCROLL LOCK) keys. As these keys change state, events notify your application of the change. This allows you to display the current key states on your form and respond appropriately to other keys as they arrive. For instance, the (INS) key can be used to toggle between insert and overwrite in a text box.

**Figure 8-7**

MAPI controls

## MAPI Controls

Microsoft's Messaging Applications Programming Interface (MAPI) provides access to e-mail and other messaging-related services provided by Microsoft and other software vendors. Windows for Workgroups provides a MAPI-compatible API that can be used to exchange mail with users of Microsoft Mail. Mail-enabled applications are applications that can send or receive information from mail systems. MAPI Session and MAPI Message make it easy to write mail-enabled applications using Visual Basic. Using the MAPI controls you can write a program that generates a report and automatically mails a copy to any number of e-mail users.

**Figure 8-8**

Masked Edit control

## Masked Edit Control

The Masked Edit control is deceptively simple. At first you may wonder why you need it, but later you will wonder how you ever got by without it. No application can be considered complete until code has been written to verify that user input is correct. Writing code to check entered strings is tedious and tends to be a source of bugs. The Masked Edit control helps solve this problem. You provide the control with a string describing acceptable characters, and the Masked Edit control takes care of the rest of the hard work!

**Figure 8-9**

Multimedia MCI control

## Multimedia MCI Control

The Multimedia Media Control Interface (MCI) control makes it easy to handle a wide variety of multimedia devices from within your Visual Basic program. The Multimedia MCI control provides access to all the functionality contained in Windows MCI API. Using this control you can easily record to and play back from all multimedia files and devices for which an MCI driver exists. There are MCI drivers for MIDI, WAVE, CDAUDIO, VIDEODISK, VCR, and AVI devices. The Multimedia MCI control also provides a VCR-like control panel that you can display on your forms.

**Figure
8-10**

Pen controls

### Pen Controls

The Pen controls—PenBEdit, PenHEdit, PenInk, and PenKbd—provide a
way to write pen-aware applications that run under the Microsoft Pen for
Windows environment. PenBEdit and PenHEdit provide a way for users to
enter information, the PenInk control allows users to draw over the top of
an existing bitmap, and the PenKbd control allows users to click on the keys
of a Pen Keyboard displayed on your form. If you plan to write pen-aware
applications using Visual Basic these controls will make the job much easier.

**Figure
8-11**

Common
Dialogs
control

### Common Dialogs Control

An important part of writing Windows applications is creating a user interface
that has the look and feel of other Windows applications. Maintaining consistency with other Windows applications makes it easier for users to learn how to
use your application. Windows 3.1 comes with COMMDLG.DLL, a library of
commonly used dialog boxes useful for most Windows applications.
COMMDLG.DLL has font selection, print, printer setup, file open, file save as,
and color selection dialog boxes. The Common Dialogs control lets you easily
use the Common Dialogs. By using the Common Dialogs control in your application, you can present the same dialog boxes used by other Windows programs,
while writing very little support code.

**Figure
8-12**

Picture Clip
control

### Picture Clip Control

Sometimes it is useful to have a number of bitmap images that are displayed
by your application. One way to do this is to place a number of picture boxes
on an invisible form and copy pictures from the picture boxes when needed.
While this approach works well enough for a few picture boxes, it is not a
good approach when you have a large number of images to display. Each
picture box consumes system resources and decreases the number of controls
available for other purposes. The Picture Clip control lets you place a number of images in a single Picture Clip control. This is a much more efficient
way to deal with large numbers of images. For example, many applications
make use of toolbars with a multitude of tool button faces. The Picture Clip
control efficiently stores all these toolfaces without gobbling up system resources.

**Figure
8-13**

Spin Button
control

### Spin Button control

The Spin Button control provides a visually compact control that can be
used to handle situations where you have variable information that the user
can select from, but a list box or combo box doesn't look quite right. Spin
buttons are usually used for numeric information that can be incremented
and decremented, although they can be used as an alternative to list boxes
and combo boxes for lists of items.

**8.1    Create a 3-D grayscale look on my Visual Basic forms**

The Professional Toolkit comes with a set of 3-D controls. You can use these controls to give a neat grayscale look to buttons and text, like those found in sophisticated computer systems such as the NeXTStep interface. Check boxes, options buttons, frames, and command buttons provide an outstanding shadowed effect with text that appears to be etched or raised from the surface of the form. You can use the frames to hold other controls in a 3-D box. The option buttons have an unusual circular appearance, while check boxes have an actual X mark with a slight shadow. A special Ribbon button control lets you create a group of buttons that mimic the functionality of the ribbon button in Microsoft Excel. The Panel control can be used to display text with a 3-D effect, or to wrap around list boxes, combo boxes, and scroll bars to give them a 3-D feeling. This How-To presents a demo project that shows off all these controls by letting you set document preferences.

**8.2    Add a color selection dialog to my application**

The Windows 3.1 Common Dialogs make it easy to present dialogs that look like, and are in fact identical to, dialogs used by other Windows applications and Windows itself. This How-To enhances the Shapes project, 5.16, by adding a color selection dialog box. The original project had only a small number of colors from which to choose the color for a particular shape. The color selection dialog box allows us to easily extend the Shapes project so that virtually any color can be used for any shape.

**8.3    Add printer dialogs to my applications**

The wide variety of printers, each with varying capabilities, makes writing print and printer setup dialogs an unpleasant prospect. With the Common Dialogs control's print and printer setup dialogs all of the details are handled for you. This How-To shows how to use the Common Dialogs control to access the print and printer setup dialogs.

**8.4    Add a status bar to my programs**

Windows programs often display a status bar along the bottom edge of the window. Various types of important information are placed on the status bar. In addition to application specific information, most status bars display the state of the (SCROLL), (CAPS LOCK), (NUM LOCK), and (INS) keys. Some applications also display the current time on the status bar. Using the 3-D controls and the Key Status control, this How-To demonstrates how to create a status bar containing a status message, states of various keys, and the current time.

**8.5**     **Write a professional quality Windows setup program**

The Professional Toolkit comes with tools and code to help write setup programs. Using these tools and code, you can write a setup program that correctly handles installation of DLLs, uncompresses files, creates directories and groups, and installs from multiple disks. This How-To is actually the setup program used for the sample disk.

# 8.1  How do I...     **Complexity: Easy**

## Create a 3-D grayscale look on my Visual Basic forms?

### Problem

I'd like to create Visual Basic forms that have a state-of-the-art 3-D look similar to the NeXTStep interface. Ideally, this 3-D look should involve no special Visual Basic code on my part, and should include 3-D versions of the standard controls I'm already used to working with, such as check boxes and option buttons.

---

**BY THE WAY: DESIGN-MODE ONLY VERSION OF PROFESSIONAL TOOLKIT 3-D CONTROLS PROVIDED ON DISK**

If you don't have the Visual Basic Professional Toolkit you can still run the 8.1 How-To. Sheridan Software, the author of Microsoft's 3-D Controls, has provided design-mode only versions of the 3-D Controls to use with this How-To. These are DESIGN-MODE ONLY controls which can be used when you are running Visual Basic in design mode, but not when running executables created with Visual Basic. To use the design-mode versions of the controls simply add SS3DDEMO.VBX to your project instead of THREED.VBX in Step 1.

---

### Technique

The Visual Basic Professional Toolkit includes a set of Custom Controls that provide 3-D versions of several standard Visual Basic controls, as well as some new ones. Figure 8-14 shows the Visual Basic Toolbox with the 3-D custom controls.

This How-To describes the steps required to produce the Document Preferences form shown in Figure 8-15. This form has a sampling of the kinds of visual elements that can be created with the 3-D tools.

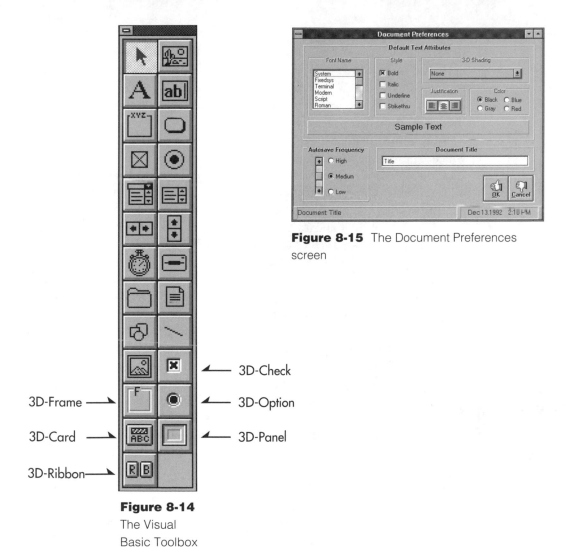

**Figure 8-15** The Document Preferences screen

**Figure 8-14**
The Visual
Basic Toolbox
with the 3-D
controls

### 3-D Grayscale Look Overview

The 3-D grayscale look, which is relatively new in Windows applications, has been in use for several years on UNIX-based machines such as the NeXT. User interfaces based on this look tend to be very effective because they provide an unobtrusive background on which to present an application, and still provide a clear indication of the groupings of controls on the application. And because the look tends to promote the selective use of color, the interface doesn't get in the way of the application.

### 3-D Controls Summary

In keeping with the grayscale look, the 3-D controls are designed to be used on Visual Basic forms that have the BackColor property set to light gray (&H00C0C0C0&). The BackColor property on most of the 3-D controls is set to light gray and cannot be changed. This allows the controls to look as though they are part of the background.

3-D controls that have a Caption property also have a Font3D property, which controls the amount and type of 3-D shading to be applied to the Caption text. By changing the setting of the Font3D property at design time or at run time, Caption text can be shaded to appear either raised or inset, and the shading can be light or heavy. The Font3D property works in conjunction with all the standard Visual Basic Font properties. Heavy shading (whether inset or raised) tends to look better with bigger, bolder fonts. The Font3D property and the resultant 3-D feel that can be applied to screen text adds to the impact of a Visual Basic form without being distracting to the user. This How-To shows how to use the Font3D property to subtly highlight key information on the form.

**Figure 8-16**

3-D check box

**Figure 8-17**

3-D option button

### Check Boxes and Option Buttons

The 3-D check boxes and options buttons emulate the functionality of their standard Visual Basic 3.0 counterparts, while sporting a 3-D look and a text alignment property. The appearance of the buttons is definitely 3-D, but they retain the basic feel of the standard Visual Basic buttons.

**Figure 8-18**

3-D frame

### Frames

The 3-D frame works just like the standard Visual Basic frame. It can have other controls placed inside it and can optionally have a caption. In addition, the Alignment property allows the caption text to be aligned to the left, right, or center of the frame.

**Figure 8-19**

3-D command button

### Command Buttons

The 3-D command button has all the functionality of the standard Visual Basic command button, with some interesting additions. Bitmap and icon images can be placed on the button, with or without text. And you can give the text a 3-D look by setting the button's Font3D property. In addition, the width of the button's beveled edges can be varied to fine-tune the 3-D look of the button.

**Figure
8-20**

3-D ribbon
button

### Ribbon Buttons

The 3-D ribbon buttons enable you to create a group of buttons that emulate the functionality of the ribbon in Microsoft Excel or the toolbar in Word for Windows. Think of ribbon buttons as looking like command buttons but acting like option buttons—when one button in a group is selected, the previously selected button in the group (if any) is deselected.

One of the things that makes ribbon buttons so effective is that a number of choices can be presented in a relatively small amount of space. Unlike option buttons, which have a caption to describe the options being selected, ribbon buttons use pictures instead. By assigning a carefully designed bitmap to the Picture property of the button, three options can be fit in the same space that a single option button would occupy. Of course, you will still need option buttons for those situations where a small picture cannot effectively convey the meaning of an option.

One of the convenient aspects of the 3-D ribbon buttons is that the control can draw a beveled border, which gives the button its 3-D look. In addition, a bitmap does not need to be specified for the down (pressed) state of the button. When a bitmap isn't specified for the PictureDn property, the ribbon button will create one automatically, based on the bitmap specified for the PictureUp property. It does this by either dithering or inverting (your choice via another property setting) the up bitmap, and offsetting it with proper shadow lines.

**Figure
8-21**

3-D panel

### Panels

A panel is basically a 3-D rectangle of variable size. It can be as large as the form itself, or just large enough to display a single line of text. The panel is the most versatile 3-D control. Panels can be used in a variety of ways:

- To display text (plain or 3-D) on a 3-D background.

- To group other controls on a 3-D background as an alternative to the frame control.

- To lend a 3-D appearance to standard controls such as list boxes, combo boxes, scroll bars, and so on.

While dramatic 3-D effects can be created with the panel, the panel itself only has four basic visual properties—BevelOuter, BevelInner, BevelWidth, and BorderWidth. By combining these properties in different ways, you can generate interesting backgrounds for text and other controls.

**Steps**

Open and run 3DWIGET.MAK to get a hands-on feel for the project and the 3-D controls. The form is designed to allow three categories of Document Preferences to be set: Default Text Attributes, Autosave Frequency, and Document Title. As you set the various Default Text Attributes, the program modifies the sample text to reflect the new changes.

When you set the Autosave Frequency option buttons, the program updates the adjacent scroll bar to reflect the new value. Conversely, when you change the Frequency via the scroll bar, the program sets the appropriate option button. If the document title is changed, the updated text is reflected in the status bar at the bottom of the screen.

1. Create a new project named 3DWIGETS.MAK. Add the 3-D controls file THREED.VBX to the project using the File menu's Add File command.

2. Create a new form and add the object and properties shown in Table 8-1.

| Object | Property | Setting |
| --- | --- | --- |
| Form | BackColor | &H00C0C0C0& |
| | Caption | "Document Preferences" |
| | ForeColor | &H00C0C0C0& |
| | Name | Form1 |
| SSFrame | Alignment | 2 - Center |
| | Caption | "Default Text Attributes" |
| | Font3D | 1 - Raised w/light shading |
| | Name | SSFrame1 |
| | ShadowStyle | 1 - Raised |

**Table 8-1** Form1 and first frame control

3. Add the objects and properties shown in Table 8-2 to SSFrame1. When adding the objects in Table 8-2, it is important to be sure that they are child controls of SSFrame1. To do this, first select the correct tool on the toolbar, then move the mouse pointer over SSFrame1. Finally, press and hold down the mouse button, and drag the sizing rectangle to create the new control. When you have finished this step, your form should look like the form shown in Figure 8-22.

| Object | Property | Setting |
| --- | --- | --- |
| SSFrame | Alignment | 2 - Center |
| | Caption | "Font Name" |
| | Font3D | 1 - Raised w/light shading |
| | Name | SSFrame2 |

| Object | Property | Setting |
| --- | --- | --- |
| SSFrame | Alignment | 2 - Center |
| | Caption | "Style" |
| | Font3D | 1 - Raised w/light shading |
| | Name | SSFrame3 |
| SSFrame | Alignment | 2 - Center |
| | Caption | "3-D Shading" |
| | Font3D | 1 - Raised w/light shading |
| | Name | SSFrame4 |
| SSFrame | Alignment | 2 - Center |
| | Caption | "Justification" |
| | Font3D | 1 - Raised w/light shading |
| | Name | SSFrame5 |
| SSFrame | Alignment | 2 - Center |
| | Caption | "Color" |
| | Font3D | 1 - Raised w/light shading |
| | Name | SSFrame6 |
| SSPanel | BorderWidth | 2 |
| | Font3D | 1 - Raised w/light shading |
| | FontBold | -1 - True |
| | Name | Sample |

**Table 8-2** Frame1's objects and properties

4. Add the objects and properties shown in Table 8-3 to Form1.

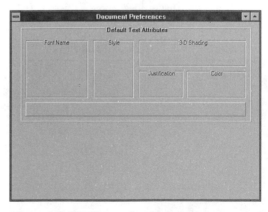

**Figure 8-22** Form after Step 3

| Object | Property | Setting |
|--------|----------|---------|
| SSFrame | Alignment | 2 - Center |
| | Caption | "Autosave Frequency" |
| | Font3D | 1 - Raised w/light shading |
| | ShadowStyle | 1 - Raised |
| | Name | SSFrame7 |
| SSFrame | Alignment | 2 - Center |
| | Caption | "Document Title" |
| | Font3D | 1 - Raised w/light shading |
| | Name | SSFrame8 |
| | ShadowStyle | 1 - Raised |

**Table 8-3** Objects and properties for Form1

5. Add the object and properties shown in Table 8-4 to SSFrame2. Be sure to create this object on top of SSFrame2.

| Object | Property | Setting |
|--------|----------|---------|
| SSPanel | AutoSize | 3 - AutoSize Child To Panel |
| | BackColor | &H00C0C0C0& |
| | BevelOuter | 1 - Inset |
| | BevelWidth | 2 |
| | BorderWidth | 2 |
| | Font3D | 1 - Raised w/light shading |
| | Name | SSPanel1 |

**Table 8-4** Object and properties for SSFrame2

6. Add the object and properties shown in Table 8-5 to SSFrame4. Be sure to create this object on top of SSFrame4.

| Object | Property | Setting |
|--------|----------|---------|
| SSPanel | AutoSize | 3 - AutoSize Child To Panel |
| | BackColor | &H00C0C0C0& |
| | BevelWidth | 2 |
| | BorderWidth | 2 |
| | Font3D | 1 - Raised w/light shading |
| | Name | SSPanel2 |

**Table 8-5** Object and properties for SSFrame4

7. Add the object and properties shown in Table 8-6 to SSFrame5. Be sure to create this object on top of SSFrame5.

| Object | Property | Setting |
|---|---|---|
| SSPanel | BackColor | &H00C0C0C0& |
| | BevelWidth | 2 |
| | BorderWidth | 2 |
| | Font3D | 1 - Raised w/light shading |
| | ForeColor | &H00800000& |
| | Name | SSPanel3 |

**Table 8-6** Object and properties for SSFrame5

8. Add the object and properties shown in Table 8-7 to SSFrame7. Be sure to create this object on top of SSFrame7.

| Object | Property | Setting |
|---|---|---|
| SSPanel | AutoSize | 3 - AutoSize Child To Panel |
| | BackColor | &H00C0C0C0& |
| | BevelOuter | 1 - Inset |
| | BevelWidth | 2 |
| | BorderWidth | 2 |
| | Font3D | 1 - Raised w/light shading |
| | Name | SSPanel4 |

**Table 8-7** SSFrame7's object and properties

9. Add the object and properties shown in Table 8-8 to SSFrame8. Be sure to create this object on top of SSFrame8.

| Object | Property | Setting |
|---|---|---|
| SSPanel | AutoSize | 3 - AutoSize Child To Panel |
| | BackColor | &H00C0C0C0& |
| | BevelOuter | 1 - Inset |
| | BevelWidth | 2 |
| | BorderWidth | 2 |
| | Name | SSPanel5 |

**Table 8-8** Panel for SSFrame8

10. Add the object and properties shown in Table 8-9 to Form1. When this step is completed, your form should look like the one shown in Figure 8-23.

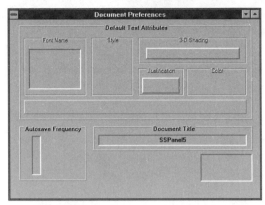

**Figure 8-23** Form1 after completion of Step 10

| Obejct | Property | Setting |
| --- | --- | --- |
| SSPanel | BackColor | &H00C0C0C0& |
| | BevelOuter | 1 - Inset |
| | BevelWidth | 2 |
| | BorderWidth | 2 |
| | Name | SSPanel6 |

**Table 8-9** Panel for Form1

11. Add the object shown in Table 8-10 to SSPanel1. Be sure to create this control on top of SSPanel1.

| Object | Property | Setting |
| --- | --- | --- |
| ListBox | Name | FontList |

**Table 8-10** ListBox for SSPanel1

12. Add the objects and properties shown in Table 8-11 to SSFrame3. Be sure to create these contols on top of SSFrame3.

| Object | Property | Setting |
| --- | --- | --- |
| SSCheck | Caption | "Bold" |
| | Name | StyleBold |
| SSCheck | Caption | "Italic" |
| | Name | StyleItalic |

| Object | Property | Setting |
|--------|----------|---------|
| SSCheck | Caption | "Underline" |
|  | Name | StyleUnderline |
| SSCheck | Caption | "Strikethru" |
|  | Name | StyleStrikethru |

**Table 8-11** Check boxes for SSFrame3

13. Add the object and properties listed in Table 8-12 to SSPanel2. Be sure to create this control on top of SSPanel2.

| Object | Property | Setting |
|--------|----------|---------|
| ComboBox | Name | Text3DStyle |
|  | Style | 2 - Dropdown List |

**Table 8-12** Drop down list box for SSPanel2

14. Add the objects and properties listed in Table 8-13 to SSPanel3. Be sure to create these controls on top of SSPanel3.

| Object | Property | Setting |
|--------|----------|---------|
| SSRibbon | BevelWidth | 0 |
|  | GroupAllowAllUp | 0 - False |
|  | Name | JustifyLeft |
|  | Outline | 0 - False |
|  | PictureDn | lft-dwn.bmp |
|  | PictureUp | lft-up.bmp |
| SSRibbon | BevelWidth | 0 |
|  | GroupAllowAllUp | 0 - False |
|  | Name | JustifyCenter |
|  | Outline | 0 - False |
|  | PictureDn | cnt-dwn.bmp |
|  | PictureUp | cnt-up.bmp |
| SSRibbon | BevelWidth | 0 |
|  | GroupAllowAllUp | 0 - False |
|  | Name | JustifyRight |
|  | Outline | 0 - False |
|  | PictureDn | rt-dwn.bmp |
|  | PictureUp | rt-up.bmp |

**Table 8-13** Ribbon buttons for SSPanel3

15. Add the objects and properties listed in Table 8-14 to SSFrame6. Be sure to create these controls on top of SSFrame6.

| Object | Property | Setting |
|--------|----------|---------|
| SSOption | Caption | "Black" |
| | Name | ColorBlack |
| SSOption | Caption | "Gray" |
| | Name | ColorGray |
| SSOption | Caption | "Blue" |
| | Name | ColorBlue |
| SSOption | Caption | "Red" |
| | Name | ColorRed |

**Table 8-14** Option buttons for SSFrame6

16. Add the object and properties listed in Table 8-15 to SSPanel4. Be sure to create this control on top of SSPanel 4.

| Object | Property | Setting |
|--------|----------|---------|
| VScrollBar | LargeChange | 1 |
| | Max | 2 |
| | Min | 0 |
| | Name | AutosaveScroll |
| | SmallChange | 1 |

**Table 8-15** Vertical scroll bar for SSPanel4

17. Add the objects and properties listed in Table 8-16 to SSFrame7. Be sure to create the controls on top of SSFrame7.

| Object | Property | Setting |
|--------|----------|---------|
| SSOption | Caption | "High" |
| | Index | 0 |
| | Name | Autosave |
| SSOption | Caption | "Medium" |
| | Index | 1 |
| | Name | Autosave |
| SSOption | Caption | "Low" |
| | Index | 2 |
| | Name | Autosave |

**Table 8-16** Option buttons for SSFrame7

18. Add the object listed in Table 8-17 to SSPanel5. Be sure to create this control on top of SSPanel5.

| Object | Property | Setting |
|---|---|---|
| TextBox | Name | DocTitle |

**Table 8-17** Text box for SSPanel5

19. Add the objects and properties listed in Table 8-18 to SSPanel6. Be sure to create the controls on top of SSPanel6.

| Object | Property | Setting |
|---|---|---|
| SSCommand | Caption | "&OK" |
| | Font3D | 3 - Inset w/light shading |
| | Name | SSCommand1 |
| | Picture | thumbsup.bmp |
| SSCommand | Caption | "&Cancel" |
| | Font3D | 3 - Inset w/light shading |
| | Name | SSCommand2 |
| | Picture | thumbsdn.bmp |

**Table 8-18** Command buttons for SSPanel6

20. Add the object and properties listed in Table 8-19 to Form1. When this step is complete, your form should look like the one shown in Figure 8-24.

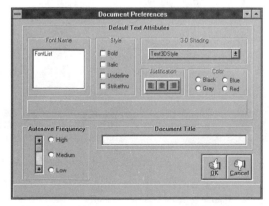

**Figure 8-24** Form1 after completion of Step 20

| Object | Property | Setting |
|--------|----------|---------|
| SSPanel | Name | SSPanel7 |
| | BorderWidth | 2 |
| | Font3D | 1 - Raised w/light shading |

**Table 8-19** Panel for Form1

21. Add the objects and properties shown in Table 8-20 to SSPanel7. Be sure to create the controls on top of SSPanel7.

| Object | Property | Setting |
|--------|----------|---------|
| SSPanel | BevelOuter | 1 - Inset |
| | BorderWidth | 2 |
| | Name | StatusDate |
| SSPanel | Alignment | 1 - Left Justify - MIDDLE |
| | BevelOuter | 1 - Inset |
| | BorderWidth | 2 |
| | Name | StatusDocTitle |

**Table 8-20** Panels for SSPanel7

22. Add the following code to the General Declarations section of Form1.

```
Option Explicit
```

23. Add the following code to the Click event procedure of the Autosave control array. This code changes the location of the scroll bar's thumb to match the selected check box.

```
Sub Autosave_Click (index As Integer, Value As Integer)
   AutosaveScroll.Value = index
End Sub
```

24. Add the following code to the Change event procedure of AutosaveScroll. This code selects the Autosave check box corresponding to the new value of the scroll bar.

```
Sub AutosaveScroll_Change ()
   Autosave(AutosaveScroll.Value).Value = True
End Sub
```

25. Add the following code to the Click event procedure of ColorBlack.

```
Sub ColorBlack_Click (Value As Integer)
   sample.ForeColor = RGB(0, 0, 0)
End Sub
```

26. Add the following code to the Click event procedure of ColorBlue.

```
Sub ColorBlue_Click (Value As Integer)
    sample.ForeColor = RGB(0, 0, 128)
End Sub
```

27. Add the following code to the Click event procedure of ColorGray.

```
Sub ColorGray_Click (Value As Integer)
    sample.ForeColor = RGB(128, 128, 128)
End Sub
```

28. Add the following code to the Click event procedure of ColorRed.

```
Sub ColorRed_Click (Value As Integer)
    sample.ForeColor = RGB(128, 0, 0)
End Sub
```

29. Add the following code to the Change event procedure of DocTitle. When the user changes the document title edit box the status bar reflects its new contents.

```
Sub DocTitle_Change ()
    StatusDocTitle.Caption = "Document: " + doctitle.Text
End Sub
```

30. Add the following code to the Click event procedure of FontList. This code assigns the selected font to the sample text. You may wonder why FontSize is reset here. This is because a previously selected font may not have had a 12 pt. size available and a different size would have been automatically assigned to the FontSize property.

```
Sub FontList_Click ()
    sample.FontName = FontList.Text
    sample.FontSize = 12
End Sub
```

31. Add the following code to the Load event procedure of Form1.

```
Sub Form_Load ()
    Dim i            As Integer
    Dim datetime     As Double
    '
    ' Load the font listbox
    '
    For i = 0 To screen.FontCount - 1
        FontList.AddItem screen.Fonts(i)
    Next i
    '
    ' Initialize the text 3D-Style combo box
    '
    Text3DStyle.AddItem "None"
    Text3DStyle.AddItem "Raised w/Light Shading"
```

*continued on next page*

*continued from previous page*

```
    Text3DStyle.AddItem "Raised w/Heavy Shading"
    Text3DStyle.AddItem "Inset w/Light Shading"
    Text3DStyle.AddItem "Inset w/Heavy Shading"
    Text3DStyle.ListIndex = 0
    '
    ' Initialize the other controls
    '
    JustifyCenter.Value = True
    StyleBold.Value = True
    ColorBlack.Value = True
    Autosave(1).Value = True
    doctitle.Text = "Title"
    sample.Caption = "Sample Text"
    '
    ' Display date/time
    datetime = Now
    statusdate.Caption = Format$(datetime, "mmm d,yyyy    h:mm AM/PM")
End Sub
```

32. Add the following code to the Click event subroutine of JustifyCenter.

```
Sub JustifyCenter_Click (Value As Integer)
    sample.Alignment = 7
End Sub
```

33. Add the following code to the Click event subroutine of JustifyLeft.

```
Sub JustifyLeft_Click (Value As Integer)
    sample.Alignment = 1
End Sub
```

34. Add the following code to the Click event subroutine of JustifyRight.

```
Sub JustifyRight_Click (Value As Integer)
    sample.Alignment = 4
End Sub
```

35. Add the following code to the Click event subroutine of SSCommand1.

```
Sub SSCommand1_Click ()
    Unload form1
End Sub
```

36. Add the following code to the Click event subroutine of SSCommand2.

```
Sub SSCommand2_Click ()
    Unload form1
End Sub
```

37. Add the following code to the Click event subroutine of StyleBold.

```
Sub StyleBold_Click (Value As Integer)
    sample.FontBold = Value
End Sub
```

38. Add the following code to the Click event subroutine of StyleItalic.

```
Sub StyleItalic_Click (Value As Integer)
    sample.FontItalic = Value
End Sub
```

39. Add the following code to the Click event subroutine of StyleStrikethru.

```
Sub StyleStrikethru_Click (Value As Integer)
    sample.FontStrikethru = Value
End Sub
```

40. Add the following code to the Click event subroutine of StyleUnderline.

```
Sub StyleUnderline_Click (Value As Integer)
    sample.FontUnderline = Value
End Sub
```

41. Add the following code to the Change event subroutine of Text3DStyle.

```
Sub Text3DStyle_Change ()
    sample.Font3D = Text3DStyle.ListIndex
End Sub
```

42. Add the following code to the Click event subroutine of Text3DStyle.

```
Sub Text3DStyle_Click ()
    sample.Font3D = Text3DStyle.ListIndex
End Sub
```

### How It Works

Getting the various controls to interact with the 3-D controls, such as the ribbon buttons used for the Justification options, is no more difficult than with standard controls. In fact, all the coding techniques used here to support the various controls are applicable to standard controls as well. For example, using a control array to handle the Autosave option buttons makes the coding for the interaction between the buttons and the scroll bar very clean.

### Comments

This How-To demonstrates an approach to designing a 3-D form that you could use when designing your own 3-D forms. First you place frames and panels on the form. Next you place panels on these frames and panels where needed, to create 3-D effects for controls that do not have their own. Finally you place the remaining controls on the various panels and frames.

## 8.2 How do I...

# Add a color selection dialog to my application?

### Problem

I would like to add a color selection dialog to my application. I want the dialog to look like the color selection dialogs used by other applications in Windows 3.1. How can I easily add such a dialog to my application?

### Technique

Windows provides a set of Common Dialogs for applications to use. There are dialogs for opening, saving, and printing files or selecting colors and fonts. These dialogs are contained in a single Windows DLL named COMMDLG.DLL. The Visual Basic Professional Toolkit provides a custom control named CMDialog in the file CMDIALOG.VBX. CMDialog controls provide access to the functionality of COMMDLG.DLL, making it easy for the Visual Basic programs to use the same dialogs commonly used by other Windows applications. Using the Common Dialogs where appropriate saves time because there is no need to design the layout of controls, write code to respond to user selections, and deal with error handling.

This How-To uses the Shapes project from How-To 5.16 to demonstrate using the CMDialog custom control to open a color select dialog. The existing Shapes program is modified so that the CMDialog's color selection dialog can be used to choose a shape's color.

### Steps

Open and run COLORDLG.MAK. Use the Add menu item to add a shape to the form. Figure 8-25 shows the COLORDLG project running. You can

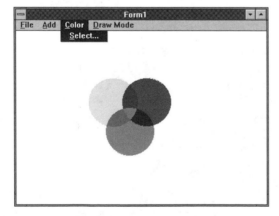

**Figure 8-25** ColorDlg project in action

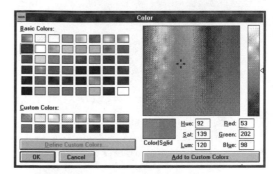

**Figure 8-26** Color selection dialog

experiment with the color select dialog, shown in Figure 8-26, by choosing the Color Select...menu item.

1. This program is a modification of How-To 5.16, SHAPES.MAK. Begin by copying \HOWTO\CHAPTER5\5.16\SHAPES.* to COLORDLG.* in the project directory. Use a text editor to change each occurrence of the word SHAPES in COLORDLG.MAK to COLORDLG and save the modified COLORDLG.MAK. Use the File Open Project... menu to open COLORDLG.MAK.

2. Add the following lines to the General Declarations section of COLORDLG.BAS.

```
'
' Value to assign to CMDialog control to start color dialog
'
Global Const DLG_COLOR = 3
'
' Color Dialog Flags
'
Global Const CC_RGBINIT = &H1&
Global Const CC_FULLOPEN = &H2&
Global Const CC_PREVENTFULLOPEN = &H4&
Global Const CC_SHOWHELP = &H8&
```

3. Open the Menu Design window and remove the color submenu items from the Color menu. Insert a new submenu item named ColorSelect between the Color and Draw Mode menus. Enter "Select..." as the new submenu's caption.

4. When a menu item or control is removed from a form, any event subroutines it had are moved to the General section of the form. Remove the Color_Click subroutine, which is now in the General section of Form1.

5. Remove the following lines from the General Declarations section of Form1.

```
'
' colorChecked contains the menu index of the currently selected color
'
Dim colorChecked As Integer

'
' This array is initialed during the Form1_Load event subroutine to
' contain the RGB values corresponding to the color menu indices
'
Dim fillColors(5) As Long
```

6. Remove the following lines from the Form_Load event subroutine of Form1.

```
'
' Pick black as the default color, copy pen as default draw mode
'
colorChecked = 4

Color(4).Checked = True

'
' Make table to translate menu selection to correct color
'
fillColors(0) = RGB(255, 0, 0)
fillColors(1) = RGB(0, 255, 0)
fillColors(2) = RGB(0, 0, 255)
fillColors(3) = RGB(255, 255, 255)
fillColors(4) = RGB(0, 0, 0)
```

7. Remove the following lines from the General Declarations subroutine Check_Menus.

```
'
' To check the correct color menu item we have to convert
' the RGB value into an array index
'
For i = 0 To 4
   If (shapes(selected).FillColor = fillColors(i)) Then
      Color(i).Checked = True
      Exit For
   End If
Next
```

8. Remove the following lines from the General Declarations subroutine Uncheck_Menus.

```
For i = 0 To 4
  Color(i).Checked = False
Next i
```

9. Use File Add to add CMDIALOG.VBX to the project. Create a CMDialog control by double-clicking the CMDialog icon on the Toolbar.

10. Add the following code to the ColorSelect_Click event subroutine of the Color Select... menu item.

```
Sub ColorSelect_Click ()
    '
    ' Load the control with the current (or last selected) shapes
    ' FillColor
    '
    CMDialog1.Color = shapes(selected).FillColor
    '
    ' Execute the color select dialog
    '
    CMDialog1.Flags = CC_RGBINIT Or CC_FULLOPEN
    CMDialog1.Action = DLG_COLOR
    '
    ' Assign the selected color to the shape's color properties
    '
    shapes(selected).BorderColor = CMDialog1.Color
    shapes(selected).FillColor = CMDialog1.Color
End Sub
```

### How It Works

The CMDialog control really makes color selection easy. First, the current shape's color is assigned to CMDialog1's color property. By assigning the color property and setting the CC_RGBINIT bit in CMDialog1's Flags property, the color select dialog box will be loaded with the shapes currently color selected. The CC_FULLOPEN bit is ORed in with CC_RGBINIT when the Flags property is set. CC_FULLOPEN starts the dialog box with the custom color select panel initially showing. When CC_FULLOPEN is not set, the user can still access custom colors by pressing a command button on the color select dialog. Not setting the CC_FULLOPEN bit has the advantage of allowing the color select dialog to open much faster than when the bit is set.

Once CMDialog1 is set up DLG_COLOR is assigned to its Action property. This causes the color select dialog to be displayed. When the user presses either the OK or Cancel buttons control returns to ColorSelect_Click event subroutine. The program then simply copies CMDialog1's color property to the shapes color properites. If the user pressed OK, a new color may be assigned. If the user pressed Cancel, the previous color is simply reassigned. The CMDialog control doesn't change its Color property when Cancel is pressed.

## Comments

This is Visual Basic programming at its best. We added a substantial new capability to the Shapes program by adding a custom control, and removing a lot of code!

## 8.3  How do I...

## Add printer dialogs to my application?

### Problem

I would like to add print and printer setup dialogs to my application. I want the dialog to look like the printer dialogs used by other applications, such as the Windows Write program, in Windows 3.1. How can I easily add the print dialogs to my application?

### Technique

Windows provides a set of common dialogs for applications to use. There are dialogs for opening, saving, and printing files or selecting colors and fonts. These dialogs are contained in a single Windows DLL named COMMDLG.DLL. The Visual Basic Professional Toolkit provides a custom control named CMDialog in the file CMDIALOG.VBX. CMDialog controls provide access to the functionality of COMMDLG.DLL, making it easy for the Visual Basic programs to use the same dialogs commonly used by other Windows applications. Using the common dialogs where appropriate saves a lot of time, since there is no need to design the layout of controls, write code to respond to user selections, and deal with error handling.

CMDialog makes it easy to add both the print and printer setup dialogs to a program. Setting CMDialog's Action property to DLG_PRINT starts one of the printer dialogs. Whether the print dialog or the printer setup dialog is displayed depends upon the value of the PD_PRINTSETUP bit in CMDialogs Flags property. When the bit is set, the printer setup dialog is displayed. When the bit is not set the print dialog is displayed.

### Steps

Open and run PRINTDLG.MAK. Select the File/Printer Setup menu item. The printer setup dialog box shown in Figure 8-27 will be displayed. If the printer setup is already correct then press Cancel, otherwise configure the printer and press the OK button. Next enter some text in the text box contained on Form1, and then either press the printer button on the toolbar or

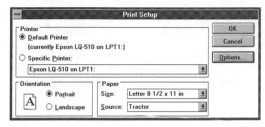

**Figure 8-27** Printer setup dialog

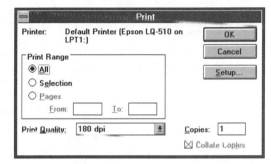

**Figure 8-28** Print dialog

select the File Print menu item. The Print dialog box shown in Figure 8-28 will be displayed. Press OK to print the text you've entered, or Cancel to abort the print operation.

1. Create a new project and use the File Save Project menu item to save it as PRINTDLG.MAK. Add the objects and properties shown in Table 8-21 to Form1. Panel3D1 creates a toolbar just beneath Form1's menu bar. Panel3D2 should fill the remainder of Form1's client area.

| Object | Property | Setting |
|---|---|---|
| Form | BorderStyle | 3 - 'Fixed Double |
| | Caption | "Form1" |
| | MaxButton | 0 'False |
| SSPanel | Name | Panel3D1 |
| SSPanel | AutoSize | 3 'Autosize Child To Panel |
| | Name | Panel3D2 |
| | BevelInner | 1 'Inset |

**Table 8-21** Objects and properties for Form1

2. Add the objects and properties shown in Table 8-22 to Panel3D1. Be sure to create the objects on Panel3D1.

| Object | Property | Setting |
|--------|----------|---------|
| CommonDialog | CancelError | -1 'True |
| | Name | CMDialog1 |
| SSRibbon | Name | PrintButton |
| | Outline | 0 'False |
| | PictureDisabled | prt-dis.bmp |
| | PictureDn | prt-dwn.bmp |
| | PictureUp | prt-up.bmp |

**Table 8-22** Objects and properties placed on Panel3D1

3. Add the text box with properties shown in Table 8-23 to Panel3D2. Be sure to create the text box on Panel3D2.

| Object | Property | Setting |
|--------|----------|---------|
| Text box | MultiLine | -1 'True |
| | Name | Text1 |
| | ScrollBars | 2 'Vertical |

**Table 8-23** Text box control placed on Panel3D2

4. Use File Add Module to add a new module named MODULE1.BAS to the project. Enter the following code in the General Declarations section of MODULE1.BAS.

```
'
' Setting for CMDialogs Action property to start a print dialog
'
Global Const DLG_PRINT = 5
'
'Printer Dialog Flags
'
Global Const PD_ALLPAGES = &H0&
Global Const PD_SELECTION = &H1&
Global Const PD_PAGENUMS = &H2&
Global Const PD_NOSELECTION = &H4&
Global Const PD_NOPAGENUMS = &H8&
Global Const PD_COLLATE = &H10&
Global Const PD_PRINTTOFILE = &H20&
Global Const PD_PRINTSETUP = &H40&
Global Const PD_NOWARNING = &H80&
Global Const PD_RETURNDC = &H100&
```

```
Global Const PD_RETURNIC = &H200&
Global Const PD_RETURNDEFAULT = &H400&
Global Const PD_SHOWHELP = &H800&
Global Const PD_USEDEVMODECOPIES = &H40000
Global Const PD_DISABLEPRINTTOFILE = &H80000
Global Const PD_HIDEPRINTTOFILE = &H100000
```

5. Use the Menu Design window to create a menu for Form1 with the menu names and captions shown in Table 8-24.

| Menu Name | Caption | Enabled |
|---|---|---|
| FileMenu | &File | |
| ---FilePrint | &Print... | False |
| ---FilePrinterSetup | P&rinter Setup... | |
| ---FileSep1 | - | |
| ---FileExit | E&xit | |

**Table 8-24** Menu for Form1

6. Add the following code to the General Declarations section of Form1.

```
Option Explicit
```

7. Add the following code to the Click event subroutine of menu item FileExit.

```
Sub FileExit_Click ()
    End
End Sub
```

8. Add the following code to the Click event subroutine of menu item FilePrint.

```
Sub FilePrint_Click ()
    '
    ' Skip the print code if the user presses cancel
    '
    On Error GoTo CancelPressed:

    CMDialog1.Flags = PD_NOPAGENUMS Or PD_HIDEPRINTTOFILE
    CMDialog1.Action = DLG_PRINT
    Printer.Print text1.Text
    Printer.EndDoc
CancelPressed:
    Exit Sub
End Sub
```

9. Add the following code to the Click event subroutine of the FilePrinterSetup menu item.

```
Sub FilePrinterSetup_Click ()
   On Error Resume Next

   CMDialog1.Flags = PD_PRINTSETUP
   CMDialog1.Action = DLG_PRINT
End Sub
```

10. Add the following code to the Click event subroutine of PrintButton.

```
Sub PrintButton_Click (Value As Integer)
   PrintButton.Value = False
   Call FilePrint_Click
End Sub
```

11. Add the following code to the Change event subroutine of Text1.

```
Sub Text1_Change ()
   If (text1.Text <> "" And PrintButton.Enabled = False) Then
      FilePrint.Enabled = True
      PrintButton.Enabled = True
   ElseIf (text1.Text = "" And PrintButton.Enabled = True) Then
      FilePrint.Enabled = False
      PrintButton.Enabled = False
   End If
End Sub
```

## How It Works

The code required to display the printer setup dialog differs from that required to display the print dialog only in the assignment of the Flags property. To display the printer setup dialog, the Flags property is set to PD_PRINTSETUP. The Flags property is set to the logical-OR of PD_NOPAGENUMS and PD_HIDEPRINTTOFILE when displaying the Print dialog. Setting these flags disables the start and end page number options, and hides the print to file option.

The CMDialog control has a property named CancelError that will generate an error when the user presses the Cancel button in either the print or printer setup dialog box. The FilePrint_Click event subroutine uses the On Error statement to skip the print code when the user presses Cancel. For the printer setup dialog, the error is simply ignored.

## Comments

This How-To and the previous one show how simple it is to use the CMDialog control. There are a number of other options that can be enabled by using various PD_ flag settings. By modifying the values assigned to

CMDialog's Flags property this project can serve as a test program to see what the various flags do. Table 8-25 lists the PD_ flag settings. Multiple flags may be set at one time by ORing the PD_ constants together. PD_ flag values are defined in CONSTANT.TXT.

| Flag Name | Effect |
| --- | --- |
| PD_ALLPAGES | Sets or returns the state of the All Pages option button. |
| PD_COLLATE | Sets or returns the state of the Collate check box. |
| PD_DISABLEPRINTTOFILE | Disables the Print to File check box. |
| PD_HIDEPRINTTOFILE | The Print to File check box is not displayed. |
| PD_NOPAGENUMS | Disables the Pages option button and the associated edit control. |
| PD_NOWARNING | Prevents a warning message from being displayed when there is no default printer. |
| PD_NOSELECTION | Disables the Selection option button. |
| PD_PAGENUMS | Sets or returns the state of the Pages option button. |
| PD_PRINTSETUP | Causes the system to display the print setup dialog box rather than the Print dialog box. |
| PD_PRINTTOFILE | Sets or returns the state of the Print to File check box. |
| PD_RETURNDC | Returns a device context for the printer selection made in the dialog box. The device context is returned in the dialog box's hDC property. |
| PD_RETURNIC | Returns an information context for the printer selection made in the dialog box. An information context provides a fast way to get information about the device without creating a device context. The information context is returned in the dialog box's hDC property. |
| PD_SELECTION | Sets or returns the state of the Selection option button. If neither PD_PAGENUMS nor PD_SELECTION are specified, the All option button is in the selected state. |
| PD_SHOWHELP | Causes the dialog box to display the Help button. |
| PD_USEDEVMODECOPIES | If a printer driver does not support multiple copies, setting this flag disables the copies edit control. If a driver does support multiple copies, setting this flag indicates that the dialog box should store the requested number of copies in the Copies property. |

**Table 8-25** Print Dialog flag settings

## 8.4 How do I...

# Add a status bar to my programs?

### Problem

Word for Windows and many other popular Windows programs have a status bar. Status bars display brief messages about the status of the program, and often also display the state of the CAPS, INS, NUM LOCK, and SCROLL LOCK keys. Some programs also display the time on their status bar. How can I add these features to my Visual Basic programs?

### Technique

This How-To uses two of the custom controls from the Visual Basic Professional Toolkit to aid the creation of a status bar. 3-D panel controls create the status bar and the KeyStatus control is used to track the state of the CAPS, INS, NUM LOCK, and SCROLL LOCK keys.

You can place KeyStatus controls directly on a form. When their Visible property is set to True, they will automatically display key status. Unfortunately the KeyStatus controls do not have an appearance that fits in well with the 3-D look used in status bars. For this reason the KeyStatus control's Visible property is set to False, requiring a small amount of code to display the actual key status in the status bar.

### Steps

Open and run KEYSTATS.MAK. The running program will resemble Figure 8-29. The status bar at the bottom of the screen will display a status message, the state of the CAPS, INS, NUM LOCK, and SCROLL LOCK keys, as well as the current time. The time is updated every second. You can press these keys to see their corresponding status display change. You can change the size of the form while it is running. The status bar size and position will be adjusted accordingly.

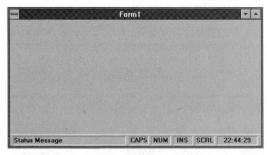

**Figure 8-29** The Keystat program

1. Create a new project named KEYSTATS.MAK. Add the custom control files KEYSTAT.VBX and THREED.VBX to the toolbar using the File menu's Add the File menu item.

2. Create a new form and add the objects and properties shown in Table 8-26 to the form.

| Object | Property | Setting |
|--------|----------|---------|
| Form | BackColor | &H00C0C0C0& |
| | Caption | "Form1" |
| | Name | Form1 |
| | ScaleMode | 3 - Pixel |
| Timer | Interval | 1000 |
| | Name | Timer1 |
| MhState | Index | 0 |
| | Name | KeyStat1 |
| | Style | 0 - Caps |
| | Tag | "CAPS" |
| | TimerInterval | 250 |
| | Visible | 0 - False |
| MhState | Index | 1 |
| | Name | KeyStat1 |
| | Style | 1 - Num Lock |
| | Tag | "NUM" |
| | TimerInterval | 250 |
| | Visible | 0 - False |
| MhState | Index | 2 |
| | Name | KeyStat1 |
| | Style | 2 - Insert State |
| | Tag | "INS" |
| | TimerInterval | 250 |
| | Visible | 0 - False |
| MhState | Index | 3 |
| | Name | KeyStat1 |
| | Style | 3 - Scroll Lock |
| | Tag | "SCRL" |
| | TimerInterval | 250 |
| | Visible | 0 - False |

*continued on next page*

*continued from previous page*

| Object | Property | Setting |
|---|---|---|
| SSPanel | RoundedCorners | 0 - False |
| | Name | StatusBarPanel |

**Table 8-26** Objects and properties for Form1

3. Add the objects and properties listed in Table 8-27 to StatusBarPanel. Be sure to create the controls on top of StatusBarPanel. The positioning of these controls is not critical, since they are positioned and sized whenever the form's Resize event procedure is called. The Resize event procedure is called after the form is loaded but before it is displayed, so the controls will already be positioned and sized when the form is first displayed.

| Object | Property | Setting |
|---|---|---|
| SSPanel | BevelInner | 1 - Inset |
| | Name | TimePanel |
| | Caption | "99:99:99" |
| SSPanel | Alignment | 1 - Left Justify - MIDDLE |
| | Name | StatusMessagePanel |
| | BevelInner | 1 - Inset |
| | Caption | "Status Message" |
| SSPanel | BevelInner | 1 - Inset |
| | Name | KeyStatusPanels |
| | Caption | "SCRL" |
| SSPanel | BevelInner | 1 - Inset |
| | Name | KeyStatusPanels |
| | Caption | "INS" |
| SSPanel | BevelInner | 1 - Inset |
| | Name | KeyStatusPanels |
| | Caption | "NUM" |
| SSPanel | BevelInner | 1 - Inset |
| | Name | KeyStatusPanels |
| | Caption | "CAPS" |

**Table 8-27** Panels placed on StatusBarPanel

4. Add the following code to the General Declarations section of Form1.

```
Option Explicit
```

5. Add the following code to the Load event procedure of Form1. This code fires the KeyStat_Change event so that the status bar reflects the initial states of the keys.

```
Sub Form_Load ()
    Dim i As Integer
    '
    ' Display the current state of the keys
    '
    For i = 0 To 3
        KeyStat1_change (i)
    Next
End Sub
```

6. Add the following code to the Resize event procedure of Form1. This code takes care of positioning the status bar and its controls whenever the form is resized. The Resize event is fired after the form is loaded and before the form is displayed so the status bar and its controls will be correct when the form is first displayed.

```
Sub Form_Resize ()
    Dim i As Integer
    Dim x As Integer
    '
    ' Position the status bar panels
    '
    StatusBarPanel.Height = StatusMessagePanel.Height / ⇐
      screen.TwipsPerPixelY
    StatusBarPanel.Top = form1.ScaleHeight - StatusBarPanel.Height
    StatusBarPanel.Left = -2
    StatusBarPanel.Width = form1.ScaleWidth + 4
    StatusMessagePanel.Left = 5 * screen.TwipsPerPixelX
    StatusMessagePanel.Top = screen.TwipsPerPixelY

    x = StatusMessagePanel.Left + StatusMessagePanel.Width
    '
    ' Position the KeyStatus panels
    '
    For i = 0 To 3
        KeyStatusPanels(i).Top = StatusMessagePanel.Top
        KeyStatusPanels(i).Height = StatusMessagePanel.Height
        KeyStatusPanels(i).Left = x
        x = x + KeyStatusPanels(i).Width - 2 * screen.TwipsPerPixelX
    Next
    '
    ' And position the time display panel
    '
    TimePanel.Top = StatusMessagePanel.Top
    TimePanel.Height = StatusMessagePanel.Height
    TimePanel.Left = x
End Sub
```

7. Add the following code to the Change event procedure of KeyStat1. This procedure is called whenever any one of the KeyStat controls has detected a change in the key it is monitoring. This procedure is also called during Form_Load to initialize the key status panels to the correct value.

```
Sub KeyStat1_change (index As Integer)
    '
    ' Some key has changed state, fix the text displayed for it
    '
    If (KeyStat1(index).Value = True) Then
        KeyStatusPanels(index).Caption = KeyStat1(index).Tag
    Else
        KeyStatusPanels(index).Caption = ""
    End If
End Sub
```

8. Add the following code to the Timer event procedure of Timer1. This procedure is called every second and updates the current time display in the status bar.

```
Sub Timer1_Timer ()
    '
    ' Another second gone ... update the display
    '
    TimePanel.Caption = Time$
End Sub
```

### How It Works

The KeyStatus control does the dirty work involved in tracking the state of the (CAPS), (INS), (NUM LOCK), and (SCROLL LOCK) keys. By setting the TimeInterval property to 250 milliseconds (1/4 of a second) a change in key state is reflected on the status bar quickly. Values larger than this can create enough of a lag between the time a key changes state and the time its change is reflected that a user might press the key again, thinking it hadn't been pressed all the way down on the first try. Values smaller than 1/4 of a second consume more CPU time due to the frequent checking of the key states, and doesn't improve the apparent response time noticeably.

The two control arrays, KeyStat1 and KeyStatusPanels, have index values that minimize the amount of code required to display the correct text whenever the key state changes. Assigning the text to be displayed when the KeyStatus Value property is True to the Tag property of the KeyStatus controls makes getting the right text into the right spot on the status bar a breeze.

### Comments

This How-To demonstrates an easy way to create a status bar using Visual Basic that is as good as any Windows program's status bar. Depending upon the nature of your application, many bits of useful information can be displayed in a status bar. You should display short bits of information regarding the status of your application in the status bar.

## 8.5 How Do I...

## Write a setup program?

### Problem

I would like to make it easy for users to install my program. I want to let the user select the program directory. Also, to save disk space, the user must be able to install only a subset of the files that are provided with my program. Finally, I need to create a new Program Manager Group and add my application to it. How do I write a setup program with these capabilities using Visual Basic?

### Technique

This project shows you how to write a complete setup program for Windows and can be used nearly as-is for a wide variety of application setup requirements. Writing a setup program from scratch can be a difficult job. Files may need to be installed in a number of different directories. Multiple diskettes may be required to hold all of the files to be installed. And there are a number of errors that need to be handled: the wrong diskette might be in the drive or the destination disk may be full, the list goes on and on. This project shows you how to create the setup program used to install the Visual Basic How-To sample code, shown in Figure 8-30. As you will see there is very little that needs to be changed in the code to use it to install your own applications.

**Figure 8-30** GetDestination form

The setup program developed in this How-To gets most of the information about what files to install, and where to install them, from a file named HTSETUP.INI, that is formatted like other Windows INI files. In a Windows INI file there are one or more *sections*. An INI file section contains lines that have *key-value* pairs. The key and its value are separated by an equal sign. The key appears to the left of the equal sign and its value appears to the right. The following two lines are from a typical WIN.INI file:

```
[ports]
COM1:=9600,n,8,1,x
```

A string enclosed by square brackets identifies the beginning of a section. In the example above, the name of the section is the square bracket delimited string [ports]. The second line shows what a key-value pair looks like. In this example "COM1:" is the key and "9600,n,8,1,x" is its value. The Windows API function GetProfileString takes a section name and key as arguments and returns the value of the key-value pair in the specified section of WIN.INI. Windows has an API function named GetPrivateProfileString that can be used to access key-value pairs in files other than WIN.INI. GetPrivateProfileString works exactly like GetProfileString except that you must specify a file to search for the specified section and key.

The file HTSETUP.INI used by the Visual Basic How-To Setup program contains a number of sections that describe global settings, the files to install, how much space each file requires, and more.

The first section, Settings, contains information of a general nature. The ProgramTitle key has as its value a string, "Visual Basic How-To Setup" in this case, that is displayed in the title bar of dialog and message boxes. The BackgroundTitle is displayed on the blue background of the main form while the setup program is running. DefaultDirectory has as its value the default installation directory, which will be displayed in a dialog box before any files are installed so that it may be changed.

```
[Settings]
ProgramTitle=Visual Basic How-To Setup
BackgroundTitle=Visual Basic How-To Setup
DefaultDirectory=C:\VBHOWTO
```

The next section of HTSETUP.INI is Source Media Descriptions. This section contains one line for each diskette that contains files to be installed. The Visual Basic How-To sample code comes on one disk so only one line is required. The assignment of keys in the Source Media Descriptions is important. The first key must be Disk1, the second must be Disk2, and so on. This naming scheme is important since the code that parses the INI file builds the keys inside a loop and expects the keys to be named Disk1, Disk2 ... Diskn.

The value of each key in the Source Media Descriptions section is two comma-separated strings. The first string, VB How-To Sample Code in the example below, is a user-friendly description of the diskette. This string will be displayed when prompting the user to insert the diskette. You will want to label your diskettes so that they match this string. The second of the comma-separated strings is the name of a file that can be found on the diskette. After the user has inserted a diskette the installation program will look for this file as confirmation that the correct diskette has been inserted. It doesn't matter much what file you use here, as long as it really exists on the diskette that's prompted for.

```
[Source Media Descriptions]
Disk1=VB How-To Sample Code,vbhowto\hotspots.fr_
```

The next section in HTSETUP.INI is Installation Sections. The Installation Sections provides a way to group files that may be installed. Depending upon the values in Installation Sections you can allow users to choose to install only a subset of all the files that might be installed.

In the Installation Sections section there are a number of key-value pairs. As with the naming of keys in the Source Media Descriptions section the naming of keys in this section is very important. The first key must be Section1 and subsequent keys must be Section2, Section3, and so on. The subroutine ParseSectionDescriptions that parses this section increments a counter and builds the keys using the value of the counter. If the keys are not consecutively numbered the ParseSectionDescriptions subroutine will terminate without parsing all of the key-value pairs.

The value of each key in the Installation Sections section is a string containing three comma-separated strings. The first of these strings "points to" another section in the INI file. All of the files being installed are listed as part of some section in the INI file. The second string has a user-friendly section description of the section. The third string determines whether the user has the option of either installing, or not installing, files in the corresponding section.

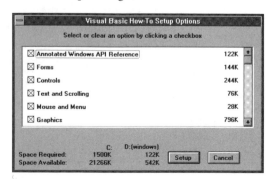

**Figure 8-31** Options form

Take a look at Figure 8-31. The second check box has Forms for its label. The check boxes are created, and labels assigned, during the Form_Load event subroutine of OPTIONS.FRM according to the contents of the Installation Sections section of HTSETUP.INI.

```
[Installation Sections]
Section1=Appendix A,Annotated Windows API Reference,OPTIONAL
Section2=Chapter 1,Forms,OPTIONAL
Section3=Chapter 2,Controls,OPTIONAL
Section4=Chapter 3,Text and Scrolling,OPTIONAL
Section5=Chapter 4,Mouse and Menu,OPTIONAL
Section6=Chapter 5,Graphics,OPTIONAL
Section7=Chapter 6,Environment and System,OPTIONAL
Section8=Chapter 7,Peripherals,OPTIONAL
Section9=Chapter 8,Professional Toolkit,OPTIONAL
Section10=Root,VB How-To,!OPTIONAL
```

Following the Installation Sections there are a number of sections, each containing one or more key-value pairs. This is where the installation files are listed. Below are some fragments of HTSETUP.INI. Three sections are shown: Appendix A, part of Chapter 1, and Root. The Section name of each group of files is the same as the first string of one of the Installation Sections values. This is how the setup program knows which files belong in which Installation Sections. As with the Installation Sections and Source Media Descriptions, the naming of keys is very important. The keys should be named File1 .... Filen within each section.

The value of each key-value pair contains four strings. Refer to the value of File1 in the section Appendix A. The third string—we'll get to the first and second strings in a moment—gives the destination directory and filename for one file to install. The destination directory and filename are concatenated with either the DefaultDirectory or a user-selected drive and directory to form the full destination filename. The first of the four strings is simply a 1. This identifies the diskette containing the file. The 1 can be concatenated to the string Disk to come up with the string Disk1 which when used as a key in the Source Media Descriptions identifies the diskette containing the file. The second string tells us what subdirectory on the installation diskette contains the file. The fourth string gives the file size in bytes. While parsing HTSETUP.INI the setup program accumulates the file sizes to determine the amount of disk space required to install all options.

```
[Appendix A]
File1=1,vbhowto,appxa\winapi.txt, 123753
```

The section Chapter 1 in HTSETUP.INI has a large number of files. Only a few of them are shown here. File1 identifies a file which is in the vbhowto subdirectory of Disk 1. The file autopos.frm which is 520 bytes in size will be installed in the chapter1\1.1 subdirectory.

Take a look at the destination directory of File27 in the section Chapter 1. The string $(SYSDIR) tells the installation program to install the file in the user's System directory. You can also use $(WINDIR) to install files in the Windows directory.

```
[Chapter 1]
File1=1,vbhowto,chapter1\1.1\autopos.frm, 520
File2=1,vbhowto,chapter1\1.1\autopos.mak, 56
File3=1,vbhowto,chapter1\1.10\gifview.mak, 190
.

.

.
File27=1,vbhowto,$(SYSDIR)\gifbox.vbx, 68476
```

The last section shown, Root, contains files that are always installed. This is because the section is flagged with !OPTIONAL in Installation Sections.

```
[Root]
File1=1,vbhowto,vbhowto.bas, 1864
File2=1,vbhowto,readme.txt, 1789
File3=1,vbhowto,readme.wri, 768
```

### Steps

Insert the Visual Basic Sample Code diskette in a floppy disk drive. Open and run SETUP.MAK. As you run the Visual Basic How-To Sample Code Setup program pay particular attention to the Setup Options dialog box. You may want to run SETUP.MAK more than once so you can try turning some of the options on and off. You should change the installation directory to something like C:\HTTEMP while trying the program out. This way you won't overwrite any files from the original installation that you may have modified.

1. Create a new project named SETUP.MAK. Create a new form named SETUP.FRM with the objects and properties in Table 8-28.

| Object | Property | Setting |
|--------|----------|---------|
| Form | Caption | "Setup" |
| | Icon | setup.ico |
| | Name | Setup |
| Label | Caption | "Used for DDE with Program Manager" |
| | Name | Label1 |
| | Visible | 0 'False |

**Table 8-28** Objects and properties for SETUP.FRM

2. Add the following code to the Global Declarations section of Setup.

```
Option Explicit
Dim SkipPaint As Integer
```

3. Add the following code to the Form_Load event subroutine of Setup. Setup.frm's Form_Load subroutine is somewhat unusual. Unlike most Form_Load subroutines, which do some initialization and then exit the event procedure, setup.frm's Form_Load event subroutine doesn't exit until the program ends. The entire setup program executes from within the Form_Load subroutine.

```
Sub Form_Load ()
    Dim result      As Integer
    Dim i           As Integer
    Dim version     As Long
    Dim verMinor    As Long

    ReDim files(1)
    '
    ' Get windows and system directories
    '
    WinDir = GetWindowsDir()
    WinSysDir = GetWindowsSysDir()
    '
    ' If the Windows \SYSTEM directory is a subdirectory
    ' of the Windows directory, the proper place for
    ' installation of .VBXs and shared .DLLs is the
    ' Windows \SYSTEM directory.
    '
    ' If the Windows \SYSTEM directory is *not* a subdirectory
    ' of the Windows directory, then the user is running a
    ' shared version of Windows, and the proper place for
    ' installation of .VBXs and shared .DLLs is the
    ' Windows directory.
    '
    If InStr(WinSysDir, WinDir) = 0 Then
        WinSysDir = WinDir
    End If
    '
    ' If this program was executed by setup.exe the command line
    ' will contain the source drive, otherwise we simply use the
    ' the current drive
    '
    If (Command$ <> "") Then
        SourceDrive = Command$
    Else
        SourceDrive = CurDir
    End If
    SourcePath = SourceDrive + "\"
    '
    ' Get allocation unit size
```

```
    '
    MinAlloc = AllocUnit()
    '
    ' Avoid double painting the screen during startup
    '
    SkipPaint = True
    Me.Move 0, 0, screen.Width, screen.Height * .85
    Me.Show
    DoEvents
    SkipPaint = False
    '
    ' Get installation settings
    '
    If (ParseSettings("HTSETUP.INI") = False) Then
        End
    End If
    '
    ' Now we've got the program caption ... display it
    '
    Setup.Caption = ProgramTitle
    DoEvents
    '
    ' Get destination drive
    '
    GetDestination.Show 1
    DoEvents
    If (AbortSetup = True) Then
        End
    End If
    '
    ' Read initialization file
    '
    result = ParseIniFile(SourcePath + "HTSETUP.INI")
    If (result = True) Then
        Options.Show 1
    End If
    DoEvents
    If (AbortSetup = True) Then
        End
    End If
    '
    ' Copy files
    '
    result = CopyFiles()
    '
    ' Install programs
    '
    CreateProgManGroup Me, "Visual Basic How-To", "vbhowto.grp"
    CreateProgManItem Me, WinDir + "htsetup.exe a:", "How-To Setup"
    CreateProgManItem Me, WinDir + "write.exe " + InstallDir + ⇐
"readme.wri", "How-To Readme"
    End
End Sub
```

4. Add the following code to the Form_Paint event subroutine of Setup. The global variable SkipPaint is used to prevent double repaints that can occur whenever the form is moved or resized.

```
Sub Form_Paint ()
   If (SkipPaint = False) Then
      FadeForm Me
   End If
End Sub
```

5. Add the following code to the Form_Resize event subroutine of Setup. After setting the SkipPaint flag to True, FadeForm is called to paint the background. Painting the background triggers a repaint which will be ignored since SkipPaint has been set to True. After the background has been repainted SkipPaint can be reset to False.

```
Sub Form_Resize ()
   SkipPaint = True
   FadeForm Me
   SkipPaint = False
End Sub
```

6. Create a new form named GETDESTI.FRM. Add the objects and properties in Table 8-29 to GETDESTI.FRM. Figure 8-30 shows the GetDestination form in action.

| Object | Property | Setting |
| --- | --- | --- |
| Form | BackColor | &H00C0C0C0& |
| | BorderStyle | 3 'Fixed Double |
| | Caption | "Visual Basic How-To Setup" |
| | Name | GetDestination |
| CommandButton | Caption | "Exit Setup" |
| | Name | Command2 |
| CommandButton | Caption | "Continue" |
| | Default | -1 'True |
| | Name | Command1 |
| TextBox | TabIndex | 4 |
| | Name | Text1 |
| Label | BackColor | &H00C0C0C0& |
| | Caption | "Install to:" |
| | Name | Label4 |
| Label | BackColor | &H00C0C0C0& |
| | Caption | "If you want to insall the sample code in a different directory and/or drive, type the name of the directory." |
| | Name | Label3 |

| Object | Property | Setting |
|--------|----------|---------|
| Label | BackColor | &H00C0C0C0& |
|  | Caption | "Setup will place the sample code into the following directory, which it will create on your hard disk." |
|  | Name | Label2 |
| Label | Alignment | 2 'Center |
|  | AutoSize | -1 'True |
|  | BackColor | &H00C0C0C0& |
|  | Caption | "Welcome to Visual Basic How-To Setup" |
|  | Name | Label1 |

**Table 8-29** GetDestination's objects and properties

7. Add the following code to the Click event subroutine of Command1. If the user has entered a syntactically correct path then GetDestination is unloaded, otherwise an error message is displayed and the user gets to try again.

```
Sub Command1_Click ()
    '
    ' Check to be sure a valid path has been entered.
    '
    If (IsValidPath(CStr(text1.Text), "c:")) Then
        '
        ' Path ok ... we're done
        '
        Unload Me
    Else
        '
        ' Invalid path ... give 'em another try
        '
        MsgBox "Invalid Path", 48, ProgramTitle + " Error"
    End If
End Sub
```

8. Add the following code to the Click event subroutine of Command2. When Command2 (Cancel) is pressed the global flag AbortSetup is set to True. This signals Setup to end the setup program.

```
Sub Command2_Click ()
    '
    ' Cancel button pressed ... abort setup
    '
    AbortSetup = True
    Unload Me
End Sub
```

9. Add the following code to the Load event subroutine of GetDestination. During Form_Load, text1's Text property is assigned the value of DefaultDirectory. DefaultDirectory is read from HTSETUP.INI when the file is parsed. To accept the default directory the user can simply press (ENTER) or click on the OK button.

```
Sub Form_Load ()
    '
    ' Set caption and default installation directory using
    ' information read from "HTSETUP.INI"
    '
    Caption = ProgramTitle
    Label1.Caption = "Welcome to " + ProgramTitle
    text1.Text = DefaultDirectory
    CenterOnSetupForm Me
End Sub
```

10. Add the following code to the Paint event subroutine of GetDestination. This ensures that the text box maintains its 3-D look.

```
Sub Form_Paint ()
    HighLight text1, CTLSUNKEN
End Sub
```

11. Add the following code to the Unload event subroutine of GetDestination. The contents of text1.Text must be checked during this subroutine since the user may have closed the form by using the system menu's Close item instead of clicking on either the OK or Cancel button. If the form is being unloaded without a valid path the global flag AbortSetup is set to True.

```
Sub Form_Unload (Cancel As Integer)
    '
    ' We're done ... make sure path is valid
    '
    If (IsValidPath(CStr(text1.Text), "c:")) Then
        '
        ' Path ok ... make sure it has a trailing "\"
        '
        InstallDir = UCase$(text1.Text)
        If (Right$(InstallDir, 1) <> "\") Then
            InstallDir = InstallDir + "\"
        End If
    Else
        '
        ' Unload without valid path ... abort setup
        '
        AbortSetup = True
    End If
End Sub
```

12. Create a new form named OPTION.FRM. Add the objects and properties in Table 8-30 to OPTION.FRM. The Option form allows the user to select which sections to install and displays the amount of disk space required and available. Figure 8-31 shows the Options form in action.

| Object | Property | Setting |
|---|---|---|
| Form | AutoRedraw | -1 'True |
| | BackColor | &H00C0C0C0& |
| | BorderStyle | 3 'Fixed Double |
| | Caption | "Visual Basic How-To Setup Options" |
| | FontName | "MS Sans Serif" |
| | FontSize | 8.25 |
| | Name | Options |
| | ScaleMode | 3 'Pixel |
| Command button | Caption | "Cancel" |
| | Name | Command2 |
| Command button | Caption | "Setup" |
| | Default | -1 'True |
| | Name | Command1 |
| Picture box | BackColor | &H00C0C0C0& |
| | BorderStyle | 0 'None |
| | Name | Picture1 |
| | ScaleMode | 3 'Pixel |
| Label | Alignment | 1 'Right Justify |
| | BackStyle | 0 'Transparent |
| | Name | WinSpaceAvail |
| Label | Alignment | 1 'Right Justify |
| | BackStyle | 0 'Transparent |
| | Name | WinSpaceReq |
| Label | Alignment | 1 'Right Justify |
| | BackStyle | 0 'Transparent |
| | Name | PrgSpaceAvail |
| Label | Alignment | 1 'Right Justify |
| | BackStyle | 0 'Transparent |
| | Name | PrgSpaceReq |
| Label | BackStyle | 0 'Transparent |
| | Caption | "Select or clear an option by clicking a checkbox" |

*continued on next page*

*continued from previous page*

| Object | Property | Setting |
|--------|----------|---------|
|        | Name | Label1 |
| Label  | BackStyle | 0 'Transparent |
|        | Caption | "Space Required:" |
|        | Name | Label2 |
| Label  | BackStyle | 0 'Transparent |
|        | Caption | "Space Available:" |
|        | Name | Label3 |
| Label  | Alignment | 1 'Right Justify |
|        | BackStyle | 0 'Transparent |
|        | Caption | "PrgDrv:" |
|        | Name | Label4 |
| Label  | BackStyle | 0 'Transparent |
|        | Caption | "x:(Windows)" |
|        | Name | Label5 |

**Table 8-30** Objects and properties for Options form

13. Add the picture box in Table 8-31 to Picture1. It is important that this picture box be created on top of Picture1.

| Object | Property | Setting |
|--------|----------|---------|
| Picture box | BorderStyle | 0 'None |
|        | Name | Picture2 |
|        | ScaleMode | 3 'Pixel |

**Table 8-31** Control created on Picture1

14. Add the objects and properties in Table 8-32 to Picture2. It is important that the objects in Table 8-32 be created on top of Picture2.

| Object | Property | Settings |
|--------|----------|----------|
| Check box | Caption | "Check1" |
|        | Name | OptionCheckBox |
| Label  | Alignment | 1 'Right Justify |
|        | Caption | "Label2" |
|        | Name | DiskSpace |
| VScrollBar | TabStop | 0 'False |
|        | Name | VScroll1 |

**Table 8-32** Controls created on Picture2

15. Add the following subroutine to the general section of Options. This subroutine goes through the Sections array and for each section enabled, the required disk space is accumulated. Next the subroutine updates the labels at the bottom of the Options form with the required and available disk space.

```
Sub CalcRequiredDiskSpace ()
    Dim i              As Integer
    Dim winTotal       As Long
    Dim prgTotal       As Long

    TotalBytes = 0
    '
    ' For each element in Sections array
    '
    For i = 0 To UBound(Sections) - 1
        '
        ' If this section is being installed update totals
        '
        If (Sections(i).install = True) Then
            winTotal = winTotal + Sections(i).reqDskWin
            prgTotal = prgTotal + Sections(i).reqDskPrg
            TotalBytes = TotalBytes + Sections(i).reqDskWin
            TotalBytes = TotalBytes + Sections(i).reqDskPrg
        End If
    Next
    '
    ' Display required and available byte counts
    '
    PrgSpaceReq.Caption = Str$((prgTotal + 1023) \ 1024) + "K"
    WinSpaceReq.Caption = Str$((winTotal + 1023) \ 1024) + "K"
    ChDrive Left$(InstallDir, 1)
    PrgSpaceAvail.Caption = Str$(DiskSpaceFree() \ 1024) + "K"
    ChDrive Left$(WinSysDir, 1)
    WinSpaceAvail.Caption = Str$(DiskSpaceFree() \ 1024) + "K"
    ChDrive InstallDrive
End Sub
```

16. Add the following code to the Click event subroutine of Command1.

```
Sub Command1_Click ()
    '
    ' Setup button pressed ... continue installation
    '
    AbortSetup = False
    Unload Me
End Sub
```

17. Add the following code to the Click event subroutine of Command2.

```
Sub Command2_Click ()
    '
    ' Cancel button pressed ... set global abort flag
```

*continued on next page*

*continued from previous page*

```
    '
    AbortSetup = True
    Unload Me
End Sub
```

18. Add the following code to the Load event subroutine of Options. Most of the code in this subroutine is needed to create and position check boxes and labels. One of each is required for each group of files that may optionally be installed. This subroutine also sizes Picture2 so that it will hold all of the check boxes and labels. If Picture2's height is greater than that of Picture1 after the check boxes and labels have been added, the scroll bar is positioned and made visible. The importance of creating Picture2 as a child (on top) of Picture1 should become clear now. Picture2 can often be taller than Picture1. Making Picture2 a child control causes it to be clipped to the boundaries of Picture1. When Picture2 is taller than Picture1, VScroll1's Max property is set to the value Picture2.Height - Picture1.Height which, as can be seen in the VScroll1_Change subroutine, makes scrolling Picture2 over Picture1 easy. This use of Picture1, Picture2, VScroll1, and the check boxes and labels creates the appearance of a list box containing check boxes and labels.

```
Sub Form_Load ()
    Dim nLines       As Integer
    Dim i            As Integer
    Dim picHeight    As Integer
    Dim labelDiff    As Integer
    Dim tabx         As Integer
    '
    ' Hourglass
    '
    Screen.MousePointer = 11

    CenterOnSetupForm Me
    '
    ' Size bottom picture for six lines
    '
    Picture1.Height = OptionCheckBox(0).Height * 6
    '
    ' Sink picture in background
    '
    HighLight Picture1, CTLSUNKEN
    '
    ' Load and initialize contents of check boxes and labels
    '
    tabx = 1
    For i = 0 To UBound(Sections) - 1
        If (Sections(i).optional = True) Then
            If (nLines > 0) Then
```

```
            Load OptionCheckBox(nLines)
            Load DiskSpace(nLines)
            OptionCheckBox(nLines).Visible = True
            OptionCheckBox(nLines).Caption = Sections(i).display
            DiskSpace(nLines).Caption = Str$((Sections(i).reqDskWin + ⇐
Sections(i).reqDskPrg + 1023) \ 1024) + "K"
            DiskSpace(nLines).Visible = True
        Else
            OptionCheckBox(0).Caption = Sections(i).display
            DiskSpace(0).Caption = Str$((Sections(i).reqDskWin + ⇐
Sections(i).reqDskPrg + 1023) \ 1024) + "K"
        End If
        OptionCheckBox(nLines).TabIndex = tabx
        tabx = tabx + 1
        nLines = nLines + 1
    End If
Next
Command1.TabIndex = tabx
Command2.TabIndex = tabx + 1
'
' Nlines should always be > 0 but we check here just in case
'
If (nLines = 0) Then
    Unload Me
    Exit Sub
End If
'
' Set the size of the second picture, the scroll bar is enabled and
' sized if needed.
'
If (nLines * OptionCheckBox(0).Height > Picture1.Height) Then
    VScroll1.Top = 0
    VScroll1.Left = Picture1.Width - VScroll1.Width
    VScroll1.Height = Picture1.Height
    Picture2.Move 0, 0, Picture1.Width - VScroll1.Width, nLines * ⇐
OptionCheckBox(0).Height
    VScroll1.Visible = True
    VScroll1.Max = Picture2.Height - Picture1.Height
    VScroll1.SmallChange = OptionCheckBox(0).Height
    VScroll1.LargeChange = Picture1.Height
Else
    Picture2.Move 0, 0, Picture1.Width, Picture1.Height
    VScroll1.Visible = False
End If
'
' This calculation assumes that the check boxes are taller than the
' labels. LabelDiff gives the distance from the check box top that a
' corresponding labels top needs to be set to.
'
labelDiff = (OptionCheckBox(0).Height - DiskSpace(0).Height) / 2
'
' Position the check boxes and labels
```

*continued on next page*

*continued from previous page*

```
'
    For i = 0 To nLines - 1
        OptionCheckBox(i).Move 10, i * OptionCheckBox(0).Height
        DiskSpace(i).Top = i * OptionCheckBox(0).Height + labelDiff
        DiskSpace(i).Left = Picture2.Width - DiskSpace(i).Width - 10
    Next
'
' Set up the available and required disk space labels
'
    label4.Caption = Left$(InstallDir, 2)
    label5.Caption = Left$(WinSysDir, 2) + "(windows)"
    CalcRequiredDiskSpace
'
' Get rid of the hourglass pointer
'
    Screen.MousePointer = 0
End Sub
```

19. Add the following code to the Click event subroutine of OptionCheckBox. This subroutine locates the section corresponding to the OptionCheckBox given by index by comparing the OptionCheckBox's Caption property to the Section's display variable. The OptionCheckBox index cannot be used as a direct index into the Sections array since non-optional sections do not have an OptionCheckBox.

```
Sub OptionCheckBox_Click (index As Integer)
    Dim i   As Integer
'
' Search sections for check box that has been changed then
' set its installation flag according to the state of the
' check box
'
    For i = 0 To UBound(Sections)
        If (Sections(i).display = OptionCheckBox(index).Caption) Then
            If (OptionCheckBox(index).Value = 1) Then
                Sections(i).install = True
            Else
                Sections(i).install = False
            End If
        End If
    Next
    CalcRequiredDiskSpace
End Sub
```

20. Add the following code to the Change event subroutine of VScroll1. Notice how simple it is to scroll Picture2 on top of Picture1 by calculating an appropriate Max property during Form_Load. This technique is useful in a wide variety of situations that require scroll bars.

```
Sub VScroll1_Change ()
    Picture2.Top = -VScroll1.Value
End Sub
```

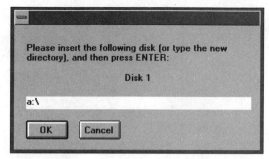

**Figure 8-32** PromptForDisk form

21. Create a new form named PRMTDISK.FRM. Add the objects and properties shown in Table 8-33. Figure 8-32 shows the PromptForDisk form in action.

| Object | Property | Setting |
|---|---|---|
| Form | AutoRedraw | -1 'True |
| | BackColor | &H00C0C0C0& |
| | BorderStyle | 3 'Fixed Double |
| | Name | PromptForDisk |
| Command button | Caption | "Cancel" |
| | TabIndex | 3 |
| | Name | CancelCmd |
| Command button | Caption | "OK" |
| | Default | -1 'True |
| | TabIndex | 2 |
| | Name | OkCmd |
| Text box | BorderStyle | 0 'None |
| | TabIndex | 1 |
| | Name | Text1 |
| Label | Alignment | 2 'Center |
| | BackColor | &H00C0C0C0& |
| | Name | Label2 |
| Label | BackColor | &H00C0C0C0& |
| | Caption | "Please insert the following disk (or type the new directory), and then press ENTER:" |
| | Name | Label1 |
| | WordWrap | -1 'True |

**Table 8-33** Objects and properties for PromptForDisk

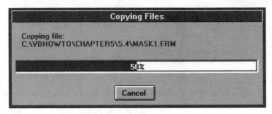

**Figure 8-33** STATUS.FRM

22. Add the following code to the Click event subroutine of OkCmd.

```
Sub OkCmd_Click ()
    AbortSetup = False
    Me.Hide
End Sub
```

23. Add the following code to the Click event subroutine of CancelCmd.

```
Sub CancelCmd_Click ()
    AbortSetup = True
    Me.Hide
End Sub
```

24. Add the following code to the Load event subroutine of PromptForDisk.

```
Sub Form_Load ()
    CenterOnSetupForm Me
    Beep
End Sub
```

25. Add the following code to the Paint event subroutine of PromptForDisk.

```
Sub Form_Paint ()
    HighLight Text1, CTLSUNKEN
End Sub
```

26. Create a new form named STATUS.FRM. Add the objects and properties in Table 8-34 to STATUS.FRM. Figure 8-33 shows STATUS.FRM in action.

| Object | Property | Setting |
|--------|----------|---------|
| Form | BackColor | &H00C0C0C0& |
| | BorderStyle | 3 'Fixed Double |
| | Caption | "StatusDlg" |
| | Name | StatusDlg |
| Picture box | AutoRedraw | -1 'True |
| | BorderStyle | 0 'None |
| | Name | Picture1 |

| Object | Property | Setting |
|---|---|---|
| Command button | Caption | "Cancel" |
| | Name | Cmd_Cancel |
| Picture box | AutoRedraw | -1 'True |
| | BackColor | &H00FF0000& |
| | ForeColor | &H00FFFFFF& |
| | Name | InvisGauge |
| | Visible | 0 'False |
| Picture box | AutoRedraw | -1 'True |
| | BackColor | &H00FFFFFF& |
| | ForeColor | &H00000000& |
| | Name | Gauge |
| Label | BackColor | &H00C0C0C0& |
| | ForeColor | &H00FF0000& |
| | Name | Label1 |

**Table 8-34** Objects and properties for StatusDlg

27. Add the following code to the Click event subroutine of Cmd_Cancel.

```
Sub Cmd_Cancel_Click ()
   AbortSetup = True
End Sub
```

28. Add the following code to the Load event subroutine of StatusDlg.

```
Sub Form_Load ()
   CenterOnSetupForm Me
End Sub
```

29. Add the following code to the Paint event subroutine of StatusDlg.

```
Sub Form_Paint ()
   HighLight Gauge, CTLSUNKEN
End Sub
```

30. Create a new module named 3DDRAW.BAS. Add the following code to the General Declarations section of 3DDRAW.BAS.

```
Option Explicit

Global Const CTLRAISED = 1
Global Const CTLSUNKEN = 2
```

31. Add the following subroutine to the general section of 3DDRAW.BAS. This subroutine is used by many of the forms in this project to create a 3-D frame around important controls.

```
Sub HighLight (C As Control, Style As Integer)
    Dim TLShade      As Long
    Dim BRShade      As Long
    Dim i            As Integer
    Dim T, L, W, H   As Integer
    Dim oldScale     As Integer
    '
    ' Save control parent's ScaleMode and change it to Pixel
    '
    oldScale = C.Parent.ScaleMode
    C.Parent.ScaleMode = 3
    '
    ' Initialize shade colors based on Style
    '
    If Style = CTLRAISED Then
        TLShade = RGB(255, 255, 255)
        BRShade = RGB(128, 128, 128)
    Else
        TLShade = RGB(128, 128, 128)
        BRShade = RGB(255, 255, 255)
    End If
    '
    ' Draw two pixel wide shadowed border
    '
    For i = 1 To 2
        T = C.Top - i
        L = C.Left - i
        H = C.Height + 2 * i
        W = C.Width + 2 * i
        '
        ' Draw left, top, right, bottom
        '
        C.Parent.Line (L, T)-Step(0, H), TLShade
        C.Parent.Line (L, T)-Step(W, 0), TLShade
        C.Parent.Line (L + W, T)-Step(0, H), BRShade
        C.Parent.Line (L, T + H)-Step(W, 0), BRShade
    Next i
    C.Parent.ScaleMode = oldScale
End Sub
```

32. Create a new module named SETUP.BAS. Add the following code to the General Declarations section of SETUP.BAS

```
'
' Used by the Windows API function OpenFile
'
Type OFStruct
    cBytes As String * 1
    fFixedDisk As String * 1
    nErrCode As Integer
    reserved As String * 4
    szPathName As String * 128
End Type
```

```
'
' Describes an installation disk
'
Type SourceMedia
    disknum   As Integer
    diskid    As String
    reffile   As String
End Type
'
' Describes an installation section
'
Type Section
    tag       As String
    display   As String
    optional  As Integer
    install   As Integer
    reqDskWin As Long
    reqDskPrg As Long
End Type
'
' Describes one file to install
'
Type FileInfo
    filename   As String
    filepath   As String
    filesize   As Long
    Section    As Integer
    sourceDisk As Integer
    sourceDir  As String
End Type
'
' One element for each installation disk
'
Global Media()      As SourceMedia
'
' One element for each installation section
'
Global Sections()   As Section
'
' One element for each file to install
'
Global files()      As FileInfo
'
' Total number of files to install
'
Global TotalFiles   As Integer
'
' Total number of bytes in files to install
'
Global TotalBytes   As Long
'
' These are read from the [Settings] section of HTSETUP.INI
'
```

*continued on next page*

*continued from previous page*

```
Global ProgramTitle      As String
Global BackgroundTitle   As String
Global DefaultDirectory  As String
Global InstallDir        As String
'
' Where we're installing from
'
Global SourceDrive       As String
Global SourcePath        As String
'
' Initialized at during Setup_Load with Windows and
' System directories
'
Global WinDir            As String
Global WinSysDir         As String
'
' MinAlloc is assigned the destination disks cluster-size
' during Setup_Load
'
Global MinAlloc          As Long
'
' Set to True whenever the user chooses Cancel
'
Global AbortSetup        As Integer
'
' Used to calculate percentage complete
'
Global BytesCopied       As Long
```

33. Create a new form named PARSE.BAS. The subroutines in PARSE.BAS are used to parse the HTSETUP.INI file. Add the following code to the General Declarations section of PARSE.BAS.

```
Option Explicit
'
' Windows API function used
'
Declare Function GetPrivateProfileString Lib "Kernel" (ByVal⇐
lpApplicationName As String, ByVal lpKeyName As String, ByVal lpDefault As⇐
String, ByVal lpReturnedString As String, ByVal nSize As Integer, ByVal ⇐
lpFileName As String) As Integer
Declare Function GetPrivateProfileInt Lib "Kernel" (ByVal ⇐
lpApplicationName As String, ByVal lpKeyName As String, ByVal nDefault As⇐
Integer, ByVal lpFileName As String) As Integer
Declare Function GetProfileString Lib "Kernel" (ByVal lpAppName As⇐
String, ByVal lpKeyName As String, ByVal lpDefault As String, ByVal ⇐
lpReturnedString As String, ByVal nSize As Integer) As Integer
Declare Function GetProfileInt Lib "Kernel" (ByVal lpAppName As String,⇐
ByVal lpKeyName As String, ByVal nDefault As Integer) As Integer
Declare Function WritePrivateProfileString Lib "Kernel" (ByVal ⇐
lpApplicationName As String, ByVal lpKeyName As String, ByVal lpString As ⇐
String, ByVal lplFileName As String) As Integer
Declare Function WriteProfileString Lib "Kernel" (ByVal lpApplicationName⇐
As String, ByVal lpKeyName As String, ByVal lpString As String) As Integer
```

34. Add the following subroutine to the General Declarations section of PARSE.BAS.

```
Function GetWindowsDir () As String
    Dim temp    As String
    Dim wRtn    As Integer

    temp = String$(145, 0)
    wRtn = GetWindowsDirectory(temp, 145)
    temp = Left$(temp, wRtn)

    If Right$(temp, 1) <> "\" Then
        GetWindowsDir = temp + "\"
    Else
        GetWindowsDir = temp
    End If
End Function
```

35. Add the following subroutine to the General Declarations section of PARSE.BAS.

```
Function GetWindowsSysDir () As String
    Dim temp    As String
    Dim wRtn    As Integer

    temp = String$(145, 0)
    wRtn = GetSystemDirectory(temp, 145)
    temp = Left$(temp, wRtn)

    If Right$(temp, 1) <> "\" Then
        GetWindowsSysDir = temp + "\"
    Else
        GetWindowsSysDir = temp
    End If
End Function
```

36. Add the following subroutine to the General Declarations section of PARSE.BAS. This subroutine parses the string of comma-delimited substrings in lpString, placing each in an element of the strings array.

```
Sub ParseString (ByVal lpString As String, strings() As String)
    Dim i As Integer
    Dim substring As String
    Dim commaPos As Integer

    lpString = Left$(lpString, InStr(lpString, Chr$(0)) - 1)
    '
    ' Parse a comma-delimited string returning it as
    ' an array of strings
    '
    i = 0
    Do While (Len(lpString) > 0)
        commaPos = InStr(lpString, ",")
```

*continued on next page*

*continued from previous page*

```
      If (commaPos <> 0) Then
          substring = Left$(lpString, commaPos - 1)
          lpString = Right$(lpString, Len(lpString) - commaPos)
      Else
          substring = lpString
          lpString = ""
      End If
      strings(i) = substring
      i = i + 1
   Loop
End Sub
```

37. Add the following subroutine to the General Declarations section of PARSE.BAS. This subroutine is called from Setup's Form_Load subroutine to get the program and background titles and the default installation directory.

```
Function ParseSettings (filename As String)
   Dim wRtn          As Integer
   Dim lpDefault     As String * 1
   Dim lpIniString   As String * 80
   '
   ' Get   [Settings]
   '       ProgramTitle=...
   '
   If (GetPrivateProfileString("Settings", "ProgramTitle", lpDefault, ⇐
lpIniString, Len(lpIniString), SourcePath + filename) = 0) Then
       If PromptForNextDisk(1, "", SourcePath, filename) Then
           If (Right$(SourcePath, 1) <> "\") Then
               SourcePath = SourcePath + "\"
           End If
           If (GetPrivateProfileString("Settings", "ProgramTitle", ⇐
lpDefault, lpIniString, Len(lpIniString), SourcePath + filename) = 0) ⇐
Then
               MsgBox "Cannot open " & filename & ".", 16, "SETUP"
               ParseSettings = False
               Exit Function
           End If
       Else
           ParseSettings = False
           Exit Function
       End If
   End If
   ProgramTitle = Left$(lpIniString, InStr(lpIniString, Chr$(0)) - 1)
   '
   ' Get   [Settings]
   '       BackgroundTitle=
   '
   If (GetPrivateProfileString("Settings", "BackgroundTitle", ⇐
lpDefault, lpIniString, Len(lpIniString), SourcePath + filename) = 0) ⇐
Then
       ParseSettings = False
```

```
        Exit Function
    End If
    BackgroundTitle = Left$(lpIniString, InStr(lpIniString, Chr$(0)) - 1)
    '
    ' Get   [Settings]
    '       DefaultDirectory=
    '
    If (GetPrivateProfileString("Settings", "DefaultDirectory", ⇐
lpDefault, lpIniString, Len(lpIniString), SourcePath + filename) = 0) ⇐
Then
        ParseSettings = False
        Exit Function
    End If
    DefaultDirectory = Left$(lpIniString, InStr(lpIniString, Chr$(0)) - 1)

    ParseSettings = True
End Function
```

38. Add the following subroutine to the General Declarations section of PARSE.BAS. This subroutine is called from Setup's Form_Load subroutine to parse everything but the Settings section.

```
Function ParseIniFile (filename As String)
    Dim lpszPath    As String * 128
    Dim lpszTemp    As String
    Dim wRtn        As Integer
    Dim nullPos     As Integer

    screen.MousePointer = 11
    If (ParseMediaDescriptions(filename) = False) Then
        ParseIniFile = False
    Else
        ParseIniFile = ParseSectionDescriptions(filename)
    End If
    screen.MousePointer = 0
End Function
```

39. Add the following subroutine to the General Declarations section of PARSE.BAS. This subroutine is called by ParseIniFile.

```
Function ParseMediaDescriptions (filename As String)
    Dim lpSection           As String * 80
    Dim lpKeyName           As String * 80
    Dim lpDefault           As String * 1
    Dim lpReturnedString    As String * 80
    Dim lpTrimedString      As String * 80
    Dim disknum             As Integer
    ReDim strings(20)        As String

    lpSection = "Source Media Descriptions"
    '
    ' For each item in [Source Media Descriptions] we get:
    '   diskid .... Displayable disk identifier
```

*continued on next page*

continued from previous page

```
'    reffile ... File we expect to find on the disk
'    disknum ... The sequential disk number (1 ... n)
'
    disknum = 1
    Do While True
        lpKeyName = "Disk" & Format$(disknum, "#")
        lpDefault = ""
        If (GetPrivateProfileString(lpSection, lpKeyName, lpDefault, ⇐
lpReturnedString, Len(lpReturnedString), filename) = 0) Then
            Exit Do
        End If
        lpTrimedString = Left$(lpReturnedString, InStr(lpReturnedString, ⇐
Chr$(0)) - 1)
        ParseString lpReturnedString, strings()
        ReDim Preserve media(disknum)
        media(disknum - 1).diskid = strings(0)
        media(disknum - 1).reffile = strings(1)
        media(disknum - 1).disknum = disknum
        disknum = disknum + 1
    Loop

    ParseMediaDescriptions = True
End Function
```

40. Add the following subroutine to the General Declarations section of PARSE.BAS. This subroutine is called by ParseIniFile and calls ParseFileDescriptions to get the file information for each section.

```
Function ParseSectionDescriptions (filename As String)
    Dim lpSection      As String * 80
    Dim lpKeyName      As String * 80
    Dim lpDefault      As String * 1
    Dim lpIniString    As String * 80
    Dim sectionNum     As Integer
    ReDim strings(20) As String

    lpSection = "Installation Sections"
    '
    ' For each section we get the following:
    '    tag ....... Identifies the section of HTSETUP.INI containing the
    '                files for this group of files
    '    display ... User friendly description of section (displayed
    '                in Options dialog box)
    '
    sectionNum = 1
    Do While True
        lpKeyName = "Section" & Format$(sectionNum, "##")
        If (GetPrivateProfileString(lpSection, lpKeyName, lpDefault, ⇐
lpIniString, Len(lpIniString), filename) = 0) Then
            Exit Do
        End If
        ParseString lpIniString, strings()
        ReDim Preserve Sections(sectionNum)
```

```
        Sections(sectionNum - 1).tag = strings(0)
        Sections(sectionNum - 1).display = strings(1)
        '
        ' Default is to install all sections
        '
        Sections(sectionNum - 1).install = True
        Select Case strings(2)
            '
            ' One or more sections may not be optional
            '
            Case "!OPTIONAL"
                Sections(sectionNum - 1).optional = False
            Case "OPTIONAL"
                Sections(sectionNum - 1).optional = True
        End Select
        '
        ' Read file descriptions for this section
        '
        If (ParseFileDescriptions(sectionNum - 1, filename) = False) Then
            ParseSectionDescriptions = False
            Exit Function
        End If

        sectionNum = sectionNum + 1
    Loop
    ParseSectionDescriptions = True
End Function
```

41. Add the following subroutine to the General Declarations section of PARSE.BAS. This subroutine parses the file descriptions for the files in a particular section.

```
Function ParseFileDescriptions (sectionNum As Integer, filename As ⇐
    String)
    Dim wRtn            As Integer
    Dim lpSection       As String * 80
    Dim lpKeyName       As String * 80
    Dim lpDefault       As String * 1
    Dim lpIniString     As String * 80
    Dim allocSize       As Long
    Dim slashPos        As Integer
    Dim filenum         As Integer
    ReDim strings(20) As String
    '
    ' Initialize bytes required for this section
    '
    Sections(sectionNum).reqDskWin = 0&
    Sections(sectionNum).reqDskPrg = 0&
    '
    ' Get section identifier
    '
    lpSection = Sections(sectionNum).tag
```

*continued on next page*

*continued from previous page*

```
    filenum = 0
    Do While True
        '
        ' Look for line starting with "Filenn=" in lpSection
        '
        lpKeyName = "File" + Format$(filenum + 1, "##")
        If (GetPrivateProfileString(lpSection, lpKeyName, lpDefault, ⇐
lpIniString, Len(lpIniString), filename) = 0) Then
            '
            ' String not found ... either we've reached the end
            ' of the list or there are one or more gaps in the
            ' sequence
            '
            Exit Do
        End If
        '
        ' Parse comma-delimited strings into array of strings
        '
        ParseString lpIniString, strings()
        '
        ' Enlarge the files info array to make room
        ' for the new element
        '
        ReDim Preserve files(TotalFiles + 1)
        '
        ' Store info in new element
        '
        files(TotalFiles).sourceDisk = Val(strings(0))
        files(TotalFiles).sourceDir = strings(1)
        files(TotalFiles).section = sectionNum
        slashPos = Len(strings(2))
        '
        ' Find position of rightmost "\"
        '
        Do While slashPos >= 1
            If (Mid$(strings(2), slashPos, 1) = "\") Then
                Exit Do
            End If
            slashPos = slashPos - 1
        Loop
        '
        ' If there was no slash the file is installed
        ' in the destinations root, otherwise we strip the path
        ' info and store it
        '
        If (slashPos = 0) Then
            files(TotalFiles).filename = strings(2)
            files(TotalFiles).filepath = InstallDir
        Else
            files(TotalFiles).filename = Right$(strings(2), ⇐
Len(strings(2)) - slashPos)
            files(TotalFiles).filepath = InstallDir + Left$(strings(2), ⇐
slashPos)
```

```
        End If
        '
        ' Get the size of this file
        '
        files(TotalFiles).filesize = Val(strings(3))
        '
        ' Round size up to an allocation unit boundary
        '
        allocSize = ((files(TotalFiles).filesize + (MinAlloc - 1)) \ ⇐
        MinAlloc) * MinAlloc
        '
        ' Check for installation to windows system directory
        '
        If (InStr(files(TotalFiles).filepath, "$($YSDIR)") <> 0) Then
            files(TotalFiles).filepath = WinSysDir
            Sections(sectionNum).reqDskWin = ⇐
Sections(sectionNum).reqDskWin + allocSize
        Else
            Sections(sectionNum).reqDskPrg = ⇐
Sections(sectionNum).reqDskPrg + allocSize
        End If
        filenum - filenum + 1
        TotalFiles = TotalFiles + 1
    Loop

    ParseFileDescriptions = True
End Function
```

42. Create a new module named INSTUTL.BAS. Add the following code to the General Declarations section of INSTUTL.BAS.

```
Option Explicit
'
' Windows API functions
'
Declare Function AllocUnit Lib "SETUPKIT.DLL" () As Long
Declare Function DiskSpaceFree Lib "SETUPKIT.DLL" () As Long
Declare Function SetTime Lib "SETUPKIT.DLL" (ByVal A As String, ByVal B ⇐
As String) As Integer
Declare Sub GetFileVersion Lib "SETUPKIT.DLL" (ByVal filename As ⇐
String, ByVal szBuf As String, ByVal LenBuf As Integer)
Declare Function GetWindowsDirectory Lib "Kernel" (ByVal lpBuffer As ⇐
String, ByVal nSize As Integer) As Integer
Declare Function GetSystemDirectory Lib "Kernel" (ByVal lpBuffer As ⇐
String, ByVal nSize As Integer) As Integer
Declare Function GetVersion Lib "Kernel" () As Long
Declare Function OpenFile Lib "Kernel" (ByVal lpFileName As String, ⇐
lpReOpenBuff As OFSTRUCT, ByVal wStyle As Integer) As Integer
Declare Function BitBlt Lib "GDI" (ByVal hDestDC As Integer, ByVal x As ⇐
Integer, ByVal Y As Integer, ByVal nWidth As Integer, ByVal nHeight As ⇐
Integer, ByVal hSrcDC As Integer, ByVal XSrc As Integer, ByVal YSrc As ⇐
Integer, ByVal dwRop As Long) As Integer
'
```

*continued on next page*

*continued from previous page*

```
' Ver API functions
'
Declare Function VerInstallFile& Lib "VER.DLL" (ByVal Flags%, ByVal ⇐
SrcFile$, ByVal DestFile$, ByVal SrcPath$, ByVal DestPath$, ByVal⇐
CurrDir$, ByVal TmpFile$, lpwTmpFileLen%)
'
' VerInstallFile() flags
'
Const VIFF_FORCEINSTALL% = &H1
Const VIFF_DONTDELETEOLD% = &H2

Const VIF_TEMPFILE& = &H1
Const VIF_MISMATCH& = &H2
Const VIF_SRCOLD& = &H4
Const VIF_DIFFLANG& = &H8
Const VIF_DIFFCODEPG& = &H10
Const VIF_DIFFTYPE& = &H20
Const VIF_WRITEPROT& = &H40
Const VIF_FILEINUSE& = &H80
Const VIF_OUTOFSPACE& = &H100
Const VIF_ACCESSVIOLATION& = &H200
Const VIF_SHARINGVIOLATION& = &H400
Const VIF_CANNOTCREATE& = &H800
Const VIF_CANNOTDELETE& = &H1000
Const VIF_CANNOTRENAME& = &H2000
Const VIF_CANNOTDELETECUR& = &H4000
Const VIF_OUTOFMEMORY& = &H8000
Const VIF_CANNOTREADSRC& = &H10000
Const VIF_CANNOTREADDST& = &H20000
Const VIF_BUFFTOOSMALL& = &H40000
'
' Misc. flags
'
Const OF_DELETE% = &H200

Const MB_OK = 0
Const MB_OKCANCEL = 1
Const MB_YESNOCANCEL = 3
Const MB_YESNO = 4
Const MB_ICONSTOP = 16
Const MB_ICONQUESTION = 32
Const MB_ICONEXCLAMATION = 48
Const MB_ICONINFORMATION = 64
Const MB_DEFBUTTON2 = 256

Const IDYES = 6
Const IDNO = 7

Global Const SRCCOPY = &HCC0020
```

43. Add the following subroutine to the General Declarations section of INSTUTL.BAS. This subroutine is called when it is appropriate to ask

the user whether installation of a file should be forced or not. There are a number of situations where this might be appropriate; see the subroutine VerInstallError.

```
Function AskAboutForce (Msg As String) As Integer
   Dim MBFlags As Integer
   Dim Res      As Integer

   Msg = Msg & Chr$(10) & Chr$(13) & "Do you want to "
   Msg = Msg & "replace this file?"
   MBFlags = MB_YESNO & MB_DEFBUTTON2 & MB_ICONQUESTION
   Res = MsgBox(Msg, 0, "SETUP")

   If Res = IDYES Then
      AskAboutForce = True
   Else
      AskAboutForce = False
   End If
End Function
```

44. Add the following subroutine to the General Declarations section of INSTUTL.BAS. This subroutine is called from the Form_Load subroutine of forms to center them over the background form Setup.

```
Sub CenterOnSetupForm (child As Form)
   Dim dh  As Integer
   Dim dw  As Integer

   dh = setup.Height - child.Height
   dw = setup.Width - child.Width

   child.Top = (dh / 2) * .85
   child.Left = dw / 2

End Sub
```

45. Add the following subroutine to the General Declarations section of INSTUTL.BAS. This subroutine is called by CopyFiles for each file to install.

```
Function CopyFile (ByVal SrcPath As String, ByVal SrcFile As String, ByVal⇐
   DstPath As String, ByVal DstFile As String)
      Dim CurrentDir  As String * 255
      Dim TempFile    As String * 255
      Dim result      As Long
      Dim TempStr     As String
      Dim TryAgain    As Integer
      Dim Force       As Integer

      On Error GoTo ErrorCopy
      Screen.MousePointer = 11
      '
```

*continued on next page*

*continued from previous page*

```
' Add ending \ symbols to path variables
'
If Right$(SrcPath, 1) <> "\" Then
    SrcPath = SrcPath + "\"
End If
If Right$(DstPath, 1) <> "\" Then
    DstPath = DstPath + "\"
End If
'
' Check the validity of the path and file
'
If Not FileExists(SrcPath + SrcFile) Then
    MsgBox "Error occurred while attempting to copy file. ⇐
Could not locate file: """ + SrcPath + SrcFile + """", 64, "SETUP"
    CopyFile = False
Else
'
' VerInstallFile installs the file. We need to initialize
' some arguments for the temp file that is created by the call
'
result = VerInstallFile(0, SrcFile, DstFile, SrcPath, DstPath, ⇐
    CurrentDir, TempFile, 255)
If (result <> 0) Then
    '
    ' Installation of file failed ... need path for it?
    '
    If (result = VIF_CANNOTCREATE) Then
    '
    ' Create path and try again
    '
    result = CreatePath(DstPath)
    result = VerInstallFile(0, SrcFile, DstFile, SrcPath, DstPath,⇐
    CurrentDir, TempFile, 255)
    End If
    '
    ' Still have an error?
    '
    If (result <> 0) Then
    '
    ' Display error message
    '
    VerInstallError result, SrcFile, DstFile, TryAgain, Force
    '
    ' Try again if required
    '
    If (TryAgain) Then
        If (Force) Then
            result = VerInstallFile(VIFF_FORCEINSTALL, SrcFile, ⇐
                DstFile, "\", DstPath, CurrentDir, TempFile, 255)
        Else
            result = VerInstallFile(0, SrcFile, DstFile, "\", ⇐
                DstPath, CurrentDir, TempFile, 255)
        End If
```

```
            End If
            '
            ' If we haven't copied the file by now give it up!
            '
            If (result <> 0) Then
                MsgBox "Error occurred while attempting to copy file.  ⇐
Could  not locate file: """ + SrcPath + SrcFile + """", 64, ProgramTitle
                CopyFile = False
            End If
          Else
            CopyFile = True
          End If
      Else
        CopyFile = True
      End If
    End If
    Screen.MousePointer = 0
    Exit Function

ErrorCopy:
    CopyFile = False
    Screen.MousePointer = 0
    Exit Function
End Function
```

46. Add the following subroutine to the General Declarations section of INSTUTL.BAS. This subroutine is called by Setup's Form_Load subroutine to install all the selected files.

```
Function CopyFiles () As Integer
    Dim sourceDisk  As Integer
    Dim i           As Integer
    Dim DestFile    As String
    Dim DestPath    As String
    Dim SourceFile  As String
    Dim DestSize    As Long
    Dim FilesCopied As Integer
    Dim BytesCopied As Long
    Dim DotPos      As Integer

    FilesCopied = 0
    '
    ' For each disk in installation set
    '
    For sourceDisk = 1 To UBound(Media)
      '
      ' Make sure correct disk is available
      '
      If Not PromptForNextDisk(sourceDisk, Media(sourceDisk - 1).diskid,⇐
        SourcePath, Media(sourceDisk - 1).reffile) Then
        CopyFiles = False
        Exit Function
      End If
```

*continued on next page*

*continued from previous page*

```
    '
    ' Display status dialog if not already showing
    '
    If (Not StatusDlg.Visible) Then
        DisplayStatusDialog "Copying Files"
        DoEvents
    End If
    '
    ' For each file to be installed
    '
    For i = 0 To UBound(files) - 1
        '
        ' If this file is on the current disk then install it
        '
        If (files(i).sourceDisk = sourceDisk And ⇐
          sections(files(i).section).install = True) Then
            '
            ' The setup file contains only the destination filename, we need
            ' to add an underscore to create the source filename
            '
            SourceFile = files(i).filename
            DotPos = InStr(SourceFile, ".")
            '
            ' If the source file has no extension or the extension is
            ' less than three characters long append the "_"
            '
            If (DotPos = 0) Then
                SourceFile = SourceFile + "._"
            ElseIf (Len(SourceFile) - DotPos < 3) Then
                SourceFile = SourceFile + "_"
            Else
                SourceFile = Left$(SourceFile, Len(SourceFile) - 1) + "_"
            End If
            '
            ' Prepend the source directory to the filename
            '
            SourceFile = files(i).sourceDir + "\" + SourceFile
            '
            ' Get destination info
            '
            DestSize = ((files(i).filesize + (MinAlloc - 1)) \ MinAlloc) * ⇐
                MinAlloc
            DestPath = files(i).filepath
            DestFile = files(i).filename
            '
            ' Update status dialog info
            '
            StatusDlg.Label1.Caption = "Copying file: " + Chr$(10) + ⇐
                Chr$(13) + UCase$(DestPath + DestFile)
            StatusDlg.Label1.Refresh
            DoEvents
            FilesCopied = FilesCopied + 1
            '
            ' Copy file ... if copy fails or StatusDlg's Cancel button is
```

```
     ' pressed we take an abnormal termination here
     '
     If (Not CopyFile(SourcePath, SourceFile, DestPath, DestFile) ⇐
       Or AbortSetup) Then
        CopyFiles = False
        Exit Function
     End If
     '
     ' Update percent complete indicator
     '
     BytesCopied = BytesCopied + DestSize
     UpdateStatus DestSize
    End If
   Next i
  Next sourceDisk
  '
  ' All files copied ... get rid of StatusDlg
  '
  CopyFiles = True
  Unload StatusDlg
End Function
```

47. Add the following subroutine to the General Declarations section of INSTUTL.BAS. This subroutine is called by CopyFile.

```
Function CreatePath (ByVal DestPath As String) As Integer
    Dim BackPos As Integer
    Dim ForePos As Integer
    Dim TempStr As String

    Screen.MousePointer = 11
    '
    ' Add slash to end of path if not there already
    '
    If Right$(DestPath, 1) <> "\" Then
         DestPath = DestPath + "\"
    End If
    '
    ' Change to the root dir of the drive
    '
    On Error Resume Next
    ChDrive DestPath
    If Err <> 0 Then GoTo errorOut
    ChDir "\"
    '
    ' Attempt to make each directory, then change to it
    '
    BackPos = 3
    ForePos = InStr(4, DestPath, "\")
    Do While ForePos <> 0
         TempStr = Mid$(DestPath, BackPos + 1, ForePos - BackPos - 1)

         Err = 0
         MkDir TempStr
```

*continued on next page*

*continued from previous page*

```
            If Err <> 0 And Err <> 75 Then GoTo errorOut

            Err = 0
            ChDir TempStr
            If Err <> 0 Then GoTo errorOut

            BackPos = ForePos
            ForePos = InStr(BackPos + 1, DestPath, "\")
    Loop
    '
    ' Path created ... return True
    '
    CreatePath = True
    Screen.MousePointer = 0
    Exit Function

errorOut:
    '
    ' Bummer dude couldn't create path ... display error and
    ' return False
    '
    MsgBox "Error While Attempting to Create Directories on Destination ⇐
        Drive.", 48, "SETUP"
    CreatePath = False
    Screen.MousePointer = 0
End Function
```

48. Add the following subroutine to the General Declarations section of INSTUTL.BAS. This subroutine is called by Setup's Form_Load subroutine to create the Visual Basic How-To group.

```
Sub CreateProgManGroup (x As Form, GroupName As String, GroupPath As ⇐
String)
    Dim i  As Integer
    '
    ' Hourglass
    '
    Screen.MousePointer = 11
    '
    ' Windows requires DDE in order to create a program group and item.
    ' Here, a Visual Basic label control is used to generate the DDE
    ' and
    ' messages
    '
    On Error Resume Next
    '
    ' Set LinkTopic to PROGRAM MANAGER
    '
    x.Label1.LinkTopic = "ProgMan|Progman"
    x.Label1.LinkMode = 2
    '
    ' Short loop to allow time for DDE Execute. This is really only needed
    ' when running debug windows.
    '
```

```
    For i = 1 To 10
      DoEvents
    Next
    x.Label1.LinkTimeout = 100
    '
    ' Create program group
    '
    x.Label1.LinkExecute "[CreateGroup(" + GroupName + Chr$(44) + ⇐
      GroupPath + ")]"
    '
    ' Reset properties
    '
    x.Label1.LinkTimeout = 50
    x.Label1.LinkMode = 0

    Screen.MousePointer = 0
End Sub
```

49. Add the following subroutine to the General Declarations section of INSTUTL.BAS. This subroutine is called by Setup's Form_Load subroutine to add HTSETUP.EXE and WRITE.EXE to the Visual Basic How-To group.

```
Sub CreateProgManItem (x As Form, CmdLine As String, IconTitle As String)
    Dim i As Integer

    Screen.MousePointer = 11
    '
    ' Windows requires DDE in order to create a program group and item.
    ' Here, a Visual Basic label control is used to generate the DDE
    ' messages
    '
    On Error Resume Next
    '
    ' Set LinkTopic to PROGRAM MANAGER
    '
    x.Label1.LinkTopic = "ProgMan|Progman"
    x.Label1.LinkMode = 2
    '
    ' Short loop to allow time for DDE Execute. This is really only needed
    ' when running debug windows.
    '
    For i = 1 To 10
      DoEvents
    Next
    x.Label1.LinkTimeout = 100
    '
    ' Create Program Item, one of the icons to launch
    ' an application from Program Manager
    '
    x.Label1.LinkExecute "[AddItem(" + CmdLine + Chr$(44) + IconTitle + ⇐
      Chr$(44) + ",,)]"
    '
```

*continued on next page*

*continued from previous page*

```
    ' Reset properties
    '
    x.Label1.LinkTimeout = 50
    x.Label1.LinkMode = 0

    Screen.MousePointer = 0
End Sub
```

50. Add the following subroutine to the General Declarations section of INSTUTL.BAS.

```
Sub DisplayStatusDialog (Title As String)
    Load StatusDlg
    StatusDlg.Caption = Title
    CenterOnSetupForm StatusDlg
    StatusDlg.Show 0
End Sub
```

51. Add the following subroutine to the General Declarations section of INSTUTL.BAS.

```
Function FileExists (filename As String) As Integer
    Dim x   As Integer

    x = FreeFile

    On Error Resume Next
    Open filename For Input As x
    If Err = 0 Then
      FileExists = True
      Close x
    Else
    FileExists = False
    End If
End Function
```

52. Add the following subroutine to the General Declarations section of INSTUTL.BAS. This subroutine verifies that a path is syntactically correct and that the specified drive exists. When IsValidPath is finished DestPath will be of the form "x:\dir\dir\".

```
Function IsValidPath (DestPath As String, ByVal DefaultDrive As String) ⇐
As Integer
    Dim temp As String
    Dim drive As String
    Dim legalChar As String
    Dim BackPos As Integer
    Dim ForePos As Integer
    Dim PeriodPos As Integer
    Dim i As Integer
    Dim length As Integer
    '
    ' Remove left and right spaces
```

```
'
DestPath = RTrim$(LTrim$(DestPath))
'
' Check Default Drive Parameter
'
If Right$(DefaultDrive, 1) <> ":" Or Len(DefaultDrive) <> 2 Then
  '
  ' This is a programming error ... check the calling function
  '
  MsgBox "Bad default drive parameter specified in IsValidPath ⇐
Function.", 64, ProgramTitle + "Error"
  GoTo parseErr
End If
'
' Insert default drive if path begins with root backslash
'
If Left$(DestPath, 1) = "\" Then
  DestPath = DefaultDrive + DestPath
End If
'
' check for invalid characters
'
On Error Resume Next
temp = Dir$(DestPath)
If Err <> 0 Then
  GoTo parseErr
End If
'
' Check for wildcard characters and spaces
'
If (InStr(DestPath, "*") <> 0) GoTo parseErr
If (InStr(DestPath, "?") <> 0) GoTo parseErr
If (InStr(DestPath, " ") <> 0) GoTo parseErr
'
' Make Sure colon is in second char position
'
If Mid$(DestPath, 2, 1) <> ":" Then GoTo parseErr
'
' Insert root backslash if needed
'
If Len(DestPath) > 2 Then
  If Right$(Left$(DestPath, 3), 1) <> "\" Then
    DestPath = Left$(DestPath, 2) + "\" + Right$(DestPath, ⇐
Len(DestPath) - 2)
  End If
End If
'
' Check drive to install on
'
drive = Left$(DestPath, 1)
ChDrive (drive)
If Err <> 0 Then GoTo parseErr
'
```

*continued on next page*

*continued from previous page*

```
' Add final \
'
If Right$(DestPath, 1) <> "\" Then
  DestPath = DestPath + "\"
End If
'
' Root dir is a valid dir
'
If Len(DestPath) = 3 Then
  If Right$(DestPath, 2) = ":\" Then
     GoTo ParseOK
  End If
End If
'
' Check for repeated Slash
'
If InStr(DestPath$, "\\") <> 0 Then
  GoTo parseErr
End If
'
' Check for illegal directory names
'
legalChar = "!#$%&'()-0123456789@ABCDEFGHIJKLMNOPQRSTUVWXYZ^_`{}~."
BackPos = 3
ForePos = InStr(4, DestPath, "\")
Do
  temp = Mid$(DestPath, BackPos + 1, ForePos - BackPos - 1)
  '
  ' Test for illegal characters
  '
  For i = 1 To Len(temp)
     If InStr(legalChar, UCase$(Mid$(temp, i, 1))) = 0 Then
       GoTo parseErr
     End If
  Next i
  '
  ' Check combinations of periods and lengths
  '
  PeriodPos = InStr(temp, ".")
  length = Len(temp)
  If PeriodPos = 0 Then
     If length > 8 Then GoTo parseErr
  Else
     If PeriodPos > 9 Then GoTo parseErr
     If length > PeriodPos + 3 Then GoTo parseErr
     If InStr(PeriodPos + 1, temp, ".") <> 0 Then GoTo parseErr
  End If

  BackPos = ForePos
  ForePos = InStr(BackPos + 1, DestPath, "\")
Loop Until ForePos = 0

ParseOK:
```

```
   IsValidPath = True
   Exit Function

parseErr:
   IsValidPath = False
End Function
```

53. Add the following subroutine to the General section of INSTUTL.BAS. Before loading the PromptForDisk subroutine, PromptForNextDisk first checks to see if the correct disk is already available, and if so the user is not prompted to insert it.

```
Function PromptForNextDisk (wDiskNum As Integer, diskid As String, Path ⇐
As String, FileToLookFor As String) As Integer
   Dim KeepTrying  As Integer
   Dim TempStr     As String
   Dim RetCode     As Integer
   Dim DiskIdStr   As String

   KeepTrying = True
   On Error Resume Next
   '
   ' Take initial look for file
   '
   TempStr = Dir$(Path + FileToLookFor)
   '
   ' File not found ... we'll have to prompt for the disk
   '
   If Err <> 0 Or Len(TempStr) = 0 Then
     While KeepTrying
       '
       ' Put up msg box
       '
       PromptForDisk.Caption = ProgramTitle
       PromptForDisk.Text1 = Path
       DiskIdStr = "Disk" + Str$(wDiskNum)
       If (diskid <> "") Then
         DiskIdStr = DiskIdStr + "(" + diskid + ")"
       End If
       PromptForDisk.Label2 = DiskIdStr
       PromptForDisk.Show 1
       DoEvents
       If (AbortSetup = True) Then
       '
       ' User pressed Cancel ... we're outta here
       '
       PromptForNextDisk = False
       Exit Function
       Else
       '
       ' User pressed OK, try to find the file again
       '
```

*continued on next page*

*continued from previous page*

```
        Path = PromptForDisk.Text1
        If (Right$(Path, 1) <> "\") Then
            Path = Path + "\"
        End If
        TempStr = Dir$(Path + FileToLookFor)
        If Err = 0 And Len(TempStr) <> 0 Then
            '
            ' File found now ... we're outta here
            '
            PromptForNextDisk = True
            KeepTrying = False
          End If
        End If
    Wend
  Else
    PromptForNextDisk = True
  End If

ExitProc:

End Function
```

54. Add the following subroutine to the General Declarations section of INSTUTL.BAS. This subroutine updates the percentage complete bar on the StatusDlg form.

```
Sub UpdateStatus (pFileLen As Long)
    Static Position  As Integer
    Static BytesCopied As Long
    Dim Percent      As String
    Dim OldScaleMode As Integer
    Dim wRtn         As Integer
    '
    ' Update total bytes copied
    '
    BytesCopied = BytesCopied + pFileLen
    '
    ' Calculate percent complete
    '
    Position = (BytesCopied / TotalBytes) * 100
    If Position > 100 Then
      Position = 100
    End If
    Percent = Format$(CLng(Position)) & "%"
    StatusDlg.Gauge.Cls
    StatusDlg.InvisGauge.Cls
    '
    ' Place percent complete string in center of both labels
    '
    StatusDlg.Gauge.CurrentX = (StatusDlg.Gauge.Width − ⇐
StatusDlg.Gauge.TextWidth(Percent)) / 2
    StatusDlg.InvisGauge.CurrentX = StatusDlg.Gauge.CurrentX
    StatusDlg.Gauge.CurrentY = (StatusDlg.Gauge.Height − ⇐
```

```
StatusDlg.Gauge.TextHeight(Percent)) / 2
   StatusDlg.InvisGauge.CurrentY = StatusDlg.Gauge.CurrentY
   StatusDlg.Gauge.Print Percent
   StatusDlg.InvisGauge.Print Percent
   OldScaleMode = StatusDlg.Gauge.Parent.ScaleMode
   StatusDlg.Gauge.Parent.ScaleMode = 3
   wRtn = BitBlt(StatusDlg.Gauge.hDC, 0, 0, StatusDlg.InvisGauge.Width ⇐
* Position% \ 100, StatusDlg.InvisGauge.Height, ⇐
StatusDlg.InvisGauge.hDC, 0, 0, SRCCOPY)
   StatusDlg.Gauge.Parent.ScaleMode = OldScaleMode
   StatusDlg.Gauge.Refresh
End Sub
```

55. Add the following subroutine to the General Declarations section of INSTUTL.BAS. This subroutine is called by CopyFile when VerInstallFile returns an error. The error code "result" is used to determine what type of error occurred and an error message is displayed. There are some types of errors, such as VIF_SRCOLD that are not fatal. In the case of VIF_SRCOLD this can happen when the user is reinstalling files that have been modified since they were first installed. The flags TryAgain and Force are set by VerInstallError and examined by CopyFile after VerInstallError returns. The TryAgain flag causes CopyFile to try the call to VerInstallFile again. The Force flag causes CopyFile to try the call to VerInstallFile again with the VIFF_FORCEINSTALL flag set.

```
Sub VerInstallError (result As Long, SrcFile As String, DstFile As ⇐
   String, TryAgain As Integer, Force As Integer)
   Dim MBFlags  As Integer
   Dim Msg      As String
   '
   ' VerInstall error ... display an appropriate error message
   '
   If result = (result And VIF_SRCOLD&) = VIF_SRCOLD& Then
      TryAgain = True
      Msg = "The file you are about to install is older than "
      Msg = Msg & "the pre-existing file."
      Force = AskAboutForce(Msg)
   ElseIf (result And VIF_DIFFLANG&) = VIF_DIFFLANG& Then
      TryAgain = True
      Msg = "The file you are about to install has a different "
      Msg = Msg & "language or code-page value than the "
      Msg = Msg & "pre-existing file."
      Force = AskAboutForce(Msg)
   ElseIf (result And VIF_DIFFCODEPG&) = VIF_DIFFCODEPG& Then
      TryAgain = True
      Msg = "The file you are about to install requires "
      Msg = Msg & "a code-page that cannot be displayed by "
      Msg = Msg & "the currently running version of Windows."
      Force = AskAboutForce(Msg)
```

*continued on next page*

*continued from previous page*

```
    ElseIf (result And VIF_DIFFTYPE&) = VIF_DIFFTYPE& Then
      TryAgain = True
      Msg = "The file you are about to install has a "
      Msg = Msg & "different type, sub-type, or operating "
      Msg = Msg & "system than the pre-existing file."
      Force = AskAboutForce(Msg)
    ElseIf (result And VIF_WRITEPROT&) = VIF_WRITEPROT& Then
      TryAgain = False
      Force = False
      Msg = "The file, " & UCase$(DstFile) & " is write-protected.  "
      Msg = Msg & "Please change the attributes of this file "
      Msg = Msg & "and re-install the program."
      MBFlags = MB_OK & MB_ICONEXCLAMATION
      MsgBox Msg, MBFlags, "SETUP"
    ElseIf (result And VIF_FILEINUSE&) = VIF_FILEINUSE& Then
      TryAgain = False
      Force = False
      Msg = "The file, " & UCase$(DstFile) & " is in use.  Please "
      Msg = Msg & "close all applications and re-attempt Setup."
      MBFlags = MB_OK & MB_ICONEXCLAMATION
      MsgBox Msg, MBFlags, "SETUP"
    ElseIf (result And VIF_OUTOFSPACE&) = VIF_OUTOFSPACE& Then
      TryAgain = False
      Force = False
      Msg = "Cannot create a temporary file, " & UCase$(DstFile)
      Msg = Msg & "on the " & UCase$(Mid$(DstFile, 1, 1)) & " drive."
      MBFlags = MB_OK & MB_ICONEXCLAMATION
      MsgBox Msg, MBFlags, "SETUP"
    ElseIf (result And VIF_ACCESSVIOLATION&) = VIF_ACCESSVIOLATION& Then
      TryAgain = False
      Force = False
      Msg = "An access violation occured while creating, deleting, "
      Msg = Msg & "or renaming the file " & UCase$(DstFile) & "."
      MBFlags = MB_OK & MB_ICONEXCLAMATION
      MsgBox Msg, MBFlags, "SETUP"
    ElseIf (result And VIF_SHARINGVIOLATION&) = VIF_SHARINGVIOLATION& Then
      TryAgain = False
      Force = False
      Msg = "An sharing violation occured while creating, deleting, "
      Msg = Msg & "or renaming the file " & UCase$(DstFile) & "."
      MBFlags = MB_OK & MB_ICONEXCLAMATION
      MsgBox Msg, MBFlags, "SETUP"
    ElseIf (result And VIF_CANNOTDELETE&) = VIF_CANNOTDELETE& Then
      TryAgain = False
      Force = False
    If (result And VIF_TEMPFILE&) = VIF_TEMPFILE& Then
      Msg = "The destination file,  " & UCase$(DstFile)
      Msg = Msg & " cannot be deleted."
      MBFlags = MB_OK & MB_ICONEXCLAMATION
      MsgBox Msg, MBFlags, "SETUP"
    End If
    ElseIf (result And VIF_CANNOTRENAME&) = VIF_CANNOTRENAME& Then
      TryAgain = False
      Force = False
```

```
      Msg = "An access violation occured while creating, deleting, "
      Msg = Msg & "or renaming the file " & UCase$(DstFile) & "."
      MBFlags = MB_OK & MB_ICONEXCLAMATION
      MsgBox Msg, MBFlags, "SETUP"
   ElseIf (result And VIF_OUTOFMEMORY&) = VIF_OUTOFMEMORY& Then
      TryAgain = False
      Force = False
      Msg = "The installation utility ran out of memory while "
      Msg = Msg & "trying to uncompress the file, " & UCase$(DstFile)
      Msg = Msg & ".  Please close some of your applications "
      Msg = Msg & "and try again."
      MBFlags = MB_OK & MB_ICONEXCLAMATION
      MsgBox Msg, MBFlags, "SETUP"
   ElseIf (result And VIF_CANNOTREADSRC&) = VIF_CANNOTREADSRC& Then
      TryAgain = False
      Force = False
      Msg = "Cannot read the source file, " & UCase$(SrcFile) & "."
      MBFlags = MB_OK & MB_ICONEXCLAMATION
      MsgBox Msg, MBFlags, "SETUP"
   ElseIf (result And VIF_CANNOTREADDST&) = VIF_CANNOTREADDST& Then
      TryAgain = False
      Force = False
      Msg = "Cannot read the destination file, " & UCase$(DstFile) & "."
      MBFlags = MB_OK & MB_ICONEXCLAMATION
      MsgBox Msg, MBFlags, "SETUP"
   ElseIf (result And VIF_BUFFTOOSMALL&) = VIF_BUFFTOOSMALL& Then
      TryAgain = False
      Force = False
      Msg = "Internal error, buffer too small for temporary source "
      Msg = Msg & "file.  This error should not happen!"
      MBFlags = MB_OK & MB_ICONEXCLAMATION
      MsgBox Msg, MBFlags, "SETUP"
   Else
      TryAgain = False
      Force = False
      Msg = "Unknow error while copying the file " & UCase$(DstFile) & "."
      MBFlags = MB_OK & MB_ICONEXCLAMATION
      MsgBox Msg, MBFlags, "SETUP"
   End If
End Sub
```

56. Create a new module named FADE.BAS. Add the following code to the General Declarations section of FADE.BAS.

```
Option Explicit

Type RECT
   Left As Integer
   Top As Integer
   Right As Integer
   Bottom As Integer
End Type
'
' Windows API functions used
```

continued on next page

*continued from previous page*

```
'
Declare Function CreateSolidBrush Lib "GDI" (ByVal crColor As Long) As ⇐
Integer
Declare Function FillRect Lib "User" (ByVal hDC As Integer, lpRect As ⇐
RECT, ByVal hBrush As Integer) As Integer
Declare Function DeleteObject Lib "GDI" (ByVal hObject As Integer) As ⇐
Integer
```

57. Add the following subroutine to the General Declarations section of
    FADE.BAS. This subroutine is called by the form Setup to create the
    setup program's background. FadeForm first paints the background
    and then displays the program's background title. The background title
    is printed on the background twice—first in black and then at a slightly
    different location in white. This creates a shadowed effect for the
    background title.

```
Sub FadeForm (TheForm As Form)
    Dim FormHeight      As Integer
    Dim Blue            As Integer
    Dim StepInterval    As Integer
    Dim X               As Integer
    Dim RetVal          As Integer
    Dim OldMode         As Integer
    Dim hBrush          As Integer
    Dim FillArea        As RECT
    '
    ' Save current ScaleMode, change to Pixel
    '
    OldMode = TheForm.ScaleMode
    TheForm.ScaleMode = 3
    FormHeight = TheForm.ScaleHeight
    '
    ' Divide the form into 63 regions
    '
    StepInterval = FormHeight \ 63
    Blue = 255
    FillArea.Left = 0
    FillArea.Right = TheForm.ScaleWidth
    FillArea.Top = 0
    FillArea.Bottom = StepInterval
    For X = 1 To 63
        hBrush = CreateSolidBrush(RGB(0, 0, Blue))
        RetVal = FillRect(TheForm.hDC, FillArea, hBrush)
        RetVal = DeleteObject(hBrush)
        Blue = Blue - 4
        FillArea.Top = FillArea.Bottom
        FillArea.Bottom = FillArea.Bottom + StepInterval + 1
    Next
    '
    ' Fill the remainder of the form with black
    '
    FillArea.Bottom = FillArea.Bottom + 63
```

```
    hBrush% = CreateSolidBrush(RGB(0, 0, 0))
    RetVal% = FillRect(TheForm.hDC, FillArea, hBrush)
    RetVal% = DeleteObject(hBrush)
    '
    ' To eliminate program ending if can't find
    '   a particular font
    '
    On Error Resume Next
    TheForm.FontName = "Helv"
    TheForm.FontSize = 24
    TheForm.FontBold = True
    '
    ' Print background title in black
    '
    TheForm.ForeColor = RGB(0, 0, 0)
    TheForm.CurrentY = 9
    TheForm.CurrentX = 9
    TheForm.Print BackgroundTitle
    TheForm.CurrentY = 5
    TheForm.CurrentX = 5
    '
    ' Print background title in white
    '
    TheForm.ForeColor = RGB(255,255,255)
    TheForm.Print BackgroundTitle
    On Error GoTo 0
    '
    ' Restore parent form's ScaleMode
    '
    TheForm.ScaleMode = OldMode
End Sub
```

### How It Works

The Setup program begins in Setup's Form_Load event subroutine. After some preliminary initialization the Form_Load event subroutine calls ParseSettings, which parses the ProgramTitle, BackgroundTitle, and DefaultDrive settings from HTSETUP.INI. Having retrieved the titles and default drive settings the user can be prompted for the installation directory. After an installation directory has been selected the remainder of HTSETUP.INI is parsed by the subroutine ParseIniFile. Parsing HTSETUP.INI is broken into these two phases for two reasons: first to minimize the amount of time required to display the GetDestination form, and second so that the destination directory is available prior to building the files array.

After HTSETUP.INI has been parsed the Options form is displayed. The Options form has been designed to adapt to the contents of HTSETUP.INI. An array of check boxes and labels is used to display each section's user-friendly description and number of bytes required. During

Form_Load, elements of the OptionsCheckBox and DiskSpace control arrays are initialized using the contents of the Sections array. Picture1, Picture2, VScroll1, and the OptionsCheckBox and DiskSpace control arrays work together to create what appears to be a list box containing check boxes and labels. Picture1 provides a boundary for Picture2. By creating Picture2 on top of Picture1 the image painted for Picture2 will be clipped to Picture1. During the Options Form_Load subroutine a member of the OptionsCheckBox and DiskSpace control arrays is created for each OPTIONAL section. Picture2 is made tall enough to display all of the check boxes and labels. Picture2 is then sized so that it is tall enough to display all of the lines, but not shorter than Picture1. If Picture2 is taller than Picture1 VScroll1 is made visible and its Max property is set to Picture2.Height - Picture1.Height. When Picture2's Top property is set to 0 this expression gives the total vertical distance that Picture2 must be moved to fully display the last line. This arrangement of controls easily creates a complex type of list box.

Labels on the bottom part of the Options form display the amount of disk space required and the amount available. Whenever the user clicks on an OptionsCheckBox the CalcRequiredSpace subroutine is called to update the label's captions.

After the user has finished selecting sections to install the CopyFiles subroutine is called. For each file to be installed, CopyFiles checks to see if the file's section is selected for installation. Files in selected sections are installed by calling the CopyFile subroutine. Although it is a little more work for the computer to look at each file for each disk being copied from, it minimizes the number of disk swaps required of the user.

### Comments

This How-To expands on the sample setup program supplied with the Visual Basic Professional Toolkit and should provide a good foundation upon which to build your own setup programs. For many programs you will simply need to create installation disks and build a HTSETUP.INI file. Other setup programs may require modification of WIN.INI or SYSTEM.INI or other Windows INI files. Modifications to INI files can be made using the Windows API functions WritePrivateProfileString and WriteProfileString.

### Thanks

Thanks to L.J. Johnson (Compuserve ID 70700, 1334) for many useful subroutines and ideas borrowed from VINST6 in Compuserve's MSBASIC forum. And thanks to Brian Stine (Compuserve ID 73617,323) for providing FADE.BAS in Compuserve's MSBASIC forum.

# CHAPTER 9

# USING VISUAL BASIC WITH DLLs

One of the most powerful aspects of Visual Basic is its ability to use custom dynamic link libraries (DLLs) that greatly extend the power of what you can do. This chapter will show you how to take a DLL written in another language, such as C, and get it working for Visual Basic. It will also point out the advantages of a DLL, how it can be used as a black box, and the power of Visual Basic to serve as an interface that is completely independent of the DLL's operation (adaptive programming).

The chapter is based on a fractal-generating DLL. Fractals are beautiful mathematical patterns that occur frequently in nature and can be generated on a computer screen from simple recursive formulas. Fractals occur in nature as clouds, ferns, waves, and any physical process where there is a noticeable degree of what is called self-similarity. You can learn much more about fractals by referring to *The Waite Group's Fractal Creations*, by Tim Wegner and Mark Peterson, a book/disk package that includes the fabulous Fractint program, a foldout fractal poster, and a set of 3-D glasses for seeing fractals in three dimensions. The fractal DLL in this chapter was written in Borland C++ and some 386 assembly language. Details on it can be found in *The Waite Group's Borland C++ Developer's Bible* by Mark Peterson. Borland C++ is an object-oriented language suitable for developing complex applications that must run at the highest possible speed. The purpose of the DLL is to allow the Visual Basic user to select from a set of its built-in formulas, and then have it return a color given a certain pixel location on the screen. Visual Basic must supply the screen location to plot and the menu structure for accessing its fractal formulas. The DLL uses a concept called atoms which allow Visual Basic to poll it and find out what formulas it supports. The names of these formulas are returned to Visual Basic and used to fill its menu items. That way the DLL can be extended and no changes need to be made in the interface.

In addition you'll learn how to convert between Visual Basic's data types and the data types found in the C language and the extended data types in Windows.

## Introducing DLLs

One of the great features of Windows is its dynamic link libraries (DLLs). A DLL is a library of functions that Windows reads in and executes as the .EXE program requires them. The opposite of a dynamic link library is a static link library, where the functions and subroutines are copied from the static library into your .EXE executable program when it's compiled. There are many advantages to DLLs and only a few disadvantages.

A big advantage to DLLs is that since they're separate from your program, you can update the DLL itself without changing your compiled .EXE program. Another advantage is that since Windows manages the DLL, it's possible for several applications to use routines from the same DLL, saving memory and disk space.

The biggest disadvantage to using DLLs is that Windows must take time to load the routines from the DLL when they're needed, while routines that are linked statically to your .EXE are already in memory when the program is loaded. Another disadvantage of DLLs is that usually an entire DLL must be distributed with your .EXE program, even though you may use only a small portion of its routines. With a static link library, on the other hand, only the functions that are used by your application are included.

DLLs are so useful that they form the entire foundation of Windows itself. In the Windows SYSTEM directory, you'll find many different types of files: .DLL, .DRV, and .EXE. Contrary to the .DRV and .EXE extensions, many of them are actually DLLs that act as hardware drivers, which means that you can just plug in newer, updated versions if the manufacturer of your video board, for example, updates its video driver, or when Microsoft releases new versions of Windows.

### Visual Basic and DLLs

The Visual Basic Declare statement is used primarily to provide access to the routines in a DLL. In the Declare statement, you'll find a Lib keyword that specifies the DLL that actually contains the routine. Many of the How-Tos in this book deal with using functions from Windows' own application programming interface (API). The API functions are available in the Kernel,

GDI, and User libraries. The DLLs for those functions are in KER-NEL.EXE, GDI.EXE, and USER.EXE in the Windows SYSTEM directory, respectively.

Visual Basic custom controls are actually implemented as DLLs (regardless of the normal .VBX extension).

What about DLLs that aren't part of Windows? Visual Basic can use almost any routine from any DLL. Third-party companies that want to offer extensions to Visual Basic that aren't custom controls will offer standard DLLs.

But the truly exciting thing is that Visual Basic can use DLLs created in any language, for any language, with few exceptions. A third party could write a DLL in Pascal that's usable by Pascal, C, and Visual Basic programmers. The third-party doesn't need to do anything special to support so many languages. Novell, for example, offers a DLL version of its Btrieve Record Manager that's usable by almost any Windows programming language, including Visual Basic.

All is not perfect, however. Since C has dominated Windows programming for so long, the majority of DLLs available to help Windows developers is geared toward C. Indeed the DLL documentation uses C code to show how to use the DLL and even how to access the routines in the DLL. What's a non-C person to do?

## A Mini C Primer

Since Visual Basic is so popular, many companies are providing Visual Basic code examples and Declare statements for their DLLs. The problem, of course, comes up when such declarations aren't available in Visual Basic form but only C code is provided. It would seem overkill to learn C just to be able to interface your Visual Basic application with a DLL.

Luckily, you don't have to go to that extreme. By following a few simple rules, you should be able to convert declarations from C to their Visual Basic equivalents.

### C-Style Function Declarations

We'll begin with the declaration for the SendMessage function from the WINDOWS.H header file from the Windows Software Development Kit (SDK). Here is the C declaration for the SendMessage API function:

```
DWORD SendMessage(HWND hWnd, WORD wMsg, WORD wParam, DWORD lParam)
```

1. The first step in converting the declaration to Visual Basic format is to give a Declare keyword:

```
Declare
```

2. The first word in the C declaration tells you the type of value that function returns. For SendMessage, it's a DWORD. In C, some functions can be of type void, which means they don't actually return a value. In that case, Visual Basic calls them subroutines, not functions, so the next step would be to declare them as such.

`Declare Sub`

Most functions, including SendMessage, do return a value, so we must tell Visual Basic so.

`Declare Function`

We'll come back to the type of value of the function, since Visual Basic specifies the return value later.

3. The next part is easy. Just type the name of the function.

`Declare Function SendMessage`

There is a possible problem with function names. Sometimes a Visual Basic built-in statement, function, method, or property name will conflict with a function in a DLL. For example, there is an API function SetFocus, but there's also Visual Basic's SetFocus method. If there is a conflict, see Step 5.

4. The next step is to tell Visual Basic in which DLL the function resides. This information isn't part of the C function declaration but it is usually part of the documentation for the DLL. SendMessage, for example, is located in the User library. (That's the USER.EXE in your WINDOWS\SYSTEM directory.) The way to specify the library is with the Lib keyword.

`Declare Function SendMessage Lib "USER"`

5. If the function name conflicts with a Visual Basic built-in statement, function, method, or property (see Step 3), here's where you need to work around the conflict. The Visual Basic Alias keyword lets you "rename" the function. For example, the API function SetFocus (which conflicts with the Visual Basic SetFocus method) could be declared like this.

`Declare Function SetFocusAPI Lib "User" Alias "SetFocus"...`

Now the name you would use to execute the function is "SetFocusAPI." With the Alias keyword, Visual Basic knows that it's really called "SetFocus" in the DLL.

6. The next step is to translate each of the parameters of the function. In C, the type of the parameter is first, followed by the parameter name. SendMessage's first parameter is

```
HWND hWnd
```

so the type is HWND and the name is hWnd. In Visual Basic a parameter is declared as

```
name As type
```

so we can say

```
hWnd As ...
```

but what would we use as the HWND type? There doesn't seem to be such a Visual Basic type.

### Windows Types

The WINDOWS.H header file defines several types that aren't native to pure C. As you've seen in other chapters, much of Windows operates on handles, which are actually just integer numbers. WINDOWS.H defines types for the various types of handles that are available—handles to windows, menus, bitmaps, etc. The idea is that it makes C programming for Windows easier.

WINDOWS.H also defines new names for some of the standard variable types, like Integer, Long, and String. Table 9-1 lists the new types that WINDOWS.H defines, along with their C and Visual Basic equivalents.

| Windows Type | C Type | Visual Basic Type | Declaration Character |
|---|---|---|---|
| BOOL | int | ByVal Integer | % |
| BYTE | unsigned char | n/a | |
| WORD | unsigned int | ByVal Integer | % |
| DWORD | unsigned long | ByVal Long | & |
| LPSTR | char far * | ByVal String | $ |
| ATOM | WORD | ByVal Integer | % |
| HANDLE | WORD | ByVal Integer | % |
| HWND | HANDLE | ByVal Integer | % |
| HICON | HANDLE | ByVal Integer | % |
| HDC | HANDLE | ByVal Integer | % |
| HMENU | HANDLE | ByVal Integer | % |
| HBITMAP | HANDLE | ByVal Integer | % |
| COLORREF | DWORD | ByVal Long | & |

**Table 9-1** Some common Windows types

Using Table 9-1, we can now complete the parameter declaration by saying

```
ByVal hWnd As Integer
```

or

```
ByVal hWnd%
```

Using the table, the rest of the parameters are also easily translated:

```
ByVal wMsg As Integer, ByVal wParam As Integer, ByVal lParam As Long
```

or

```
ByVal wMsg%, ByVal wParam%, ByVal lParam&
```

so the Visual Basic declaration for SendMessage so far is

```
Declare Function SendMessage Lib "USER" (ByVal hWnd As Integer, ByVal wMsg⇐
As Integer, ByVal wParam As Integer, ByVal lParam As Long)
```

7. As we saw in Step 2, SendMessage returns a DWORD. From Table 9-1, we know that a DWORD is a Long integer. There are two ways to tell Visual Basic what type a function returns: You can either add

```
As type
```

to the end of the declaration, as follows:

```
Declare Function SendMessage Lib "USER" (ByVal hWnd As Integer, ByVal wMsg ⇐
As Integer, ByVal wParam As Integer, ByVal lParam As Long) As Long
```

Or you can add the type specification character (for DWORD, it's an ampersand) to the function name:

```
Declare Function SendMessage& Lib "USER" (ByVal hWnd As Integer, ByVal ⇐
wMsg As Integer, ByVal wParam As Integer, ByVal lParam As Long)
```

Note that you can use either the "As *type*" method or the appropriate type specification character interchangably. They both have the same result. Which you use is mostly a matter of personal preference. Using "As *type*" can be easier to read, but the type specification character method uses less space, which can be important if you're declaring a function that takes many parameters.

As you can see, translating C-style function declarations to Visual Basic is mostly mechanical; you should be able to convert most DLL function declarations from C using the steps outlined above. There may be some more exotic declarations that don't follow the above steps. Also remember that some C parameters don't have exact matches or equivalents in Visual Basic. That's the 0.01% of DLL functions that you may not be able to use with Visual Basic. Always check with the supplier of the DLL for compatibility information.

# The Fractal DLL

How can we put our newfound knowledge to work? On the disk accompanying this book, you'll find a DLL called FRACTDLL.DLL. This DLL is developed in *The Waite Group's Borland C++ Developer's Bible,* by Mark Peterson.

FRACTDLL is a DLL that a Windows application can call to display a fractal image. We won't go into a lot of detail here about fractals, except to say that fractals are some of the most interesting and beautiful images you can create on your computer. For more information about fractals and how they're created, see *Fractal Creations,* another Waite Group Press book.

Looking at the chapter in the *Borland C++ Developer's Bible* that discusses the fractal DLL, we see that it's implemented as a series of files written in C++ and assembly language. The fractal DLL can perform its calculation using normal floating point math, or two special math formats: QFloat, or fixed 16-bit. The latter two math types are implemented using 386 assembly language, which means you must have a 386 (or i486) machine to use them.

How can Visual Basic use a DLL written in C++ or 386 assembly language? After all, Visual Basic doesn't have any of those features. The beauty of DLLs is that it doesn't matter how they were written. It's easiest to think of a DLL as a black box: The "internal" implementation details are hidden from view. You just throw some numbers into the box, shake it up, and the proper results come out.

The fractal DLL has an external API (application program interface), much like the Windows API. Calling one of the fractal API functions sets it in motion, executing the C++ or assembly code. As long as you stick to the fractal's API functions, it doesn't matter *how* it's done internally. Mr. Peterson could entirely rewrite how the DLL does what it does, but as long as he keeps the external API the same, your application would continue to work. The same thing holds true for any other DLLs, including those that make up Windows itself. Microsoft might very well rewrite the internals of Windows (to speed it up or make it more reliable), but as long as they keep the same external API, your application will continue to work as before.

### The Fractal DLL's API

Here's an abbreviated version of how an application using the fractal DLL should work:

●     Call the NumberFractals function to determine how many fractals the DLL supports.

This is an example of adaptive programming: If a future version of the fractal DLL supports more fractals than the original version, your application will automatically be able to use them.

⬤ Call the FractalName function to get the name of each fractal.

We call FractalName to build a Fractal menu that contains the name of every fractal the DLL supports. The value returned by NumberFractals tells you how many times to call FractalName.

⬤ When the user has selected a fractal, call the FractalDefaults function to get the default values for the fractal.

⬤ A fractal has parameters that tell what part of the fractal to display and how to display it. Again, that kind of detail isn't covered here, but *Fractal Creations* is an excellent resource to learn all about fractals. One interesting parameter is a fractal's symmetry; some fractals are symmetrical and have parts that are mirror images of other parts so we can speed up the fractal display by only calculating the needed parts.

⬤ Call the CreateFractal function to have the DLL initialize the fractal.

CreateFractal actually allocates the memory needed to calculate the fractal. Mercifully, the detail is taken care of by the DLL.

⬤ Call the ActivateFractal function to start calculating the fractal.

ActivateFractal has the DLL tell Windows it will be using the memory allocated in CreateFractal. After ActivateFractal is called, the memory used for the fractal is reserved and can't be used by another application, so you should only call ActivateFractal when you're ready to begin displaying the fractal.

⬤ Call IdleFractal if you're temporarily not going to be displaying the fractal.

IdleFractal lets Windows have the memory that was allocated in CreateFractal. You should call IdleFractal if you call Visual Basic's DoEvent function or if you exit a subroutine.

⬤ Call the FractalPoint function to have the DLL calculate the color of a given point.

In essence, a fractal is created by calculating how long a given point takes to exceed some formula. The specific formula actually depends on the fractal type and there are many different fractal types. Calling FractalPoint tells the fractal DLL to calculate the formula for the given point. The number returned by FractalPoint tells how long it took the point to exceed the formula for the fractal. That number is then used to pick a color for the point.

The number FractalPoint returns also indicates how long the DLL spent calculating, so the higher the number, the longer it took. Since it's not proper Windows style to "hog" the machine for a long period of time, the application should return control to Windows after it has spent a while calculating.

● Finally, when the application is done displaying the fractal, it should call the DestroyFractal function to tell the DLL it's done.

DestroyFractal releases the memory the DLL used to calculate the fractal.

We will follow all these steps to create a Visual Basic application that calls the fractal DLL to create some beautiful images.

### The Fractal DLL's Functions

Here's where we get to test out the translation steps discussed at the beginning of this chapter. The C declarations of the fractal DLL's functions are.

```
BOOL ActivateFractal(FRACTAL Fractal);
FRACTAL CreateFractal(unsigned FractNum, unsigned xdots, unsigned ydots,
   MATHTYPE MathType, double Left, double Right, double Top, double
Bottom,
   unsigned long maxit, double p1x, double p1y, double p2x, double p2y);
BOOL DestroyFractal(FRACTAL Fractal);
ATOM FractalDefaults(unsigned FractNum);
ATOM FractalName(unsigned FractNum);
unsigned long FractalPoint(FRACTAL Fractal, unsigned x, unsigned y);
BOOL IdleFractal(FRACTAL Fractal);
unsigned NumberFractals();
```

It looks like some types are missing from Table 9-1. "unsigned," "double," FRACTAL, and MATHTYPE aren't listed. "unsigned" and "double" are easy: they're other C types. "unsigned" is the same as "unsigned int," which means it translates to the Visual Basic type ByVal Integer. "double" is the Visual Basic type ByVal Double.

FRACTAL and MATHTYPE are defined by the fractal DLL. FRACTAL is the same as a Visual Basic ByVal Long and MATHTYPE is ByVal Integer.

So using this information and Table 9-1, we can translate the above C declarations to their Visual Basic equivalents:

```
Declare Function ActivateFractal Lib "FRACTDLL.DLL" (ByVal hFractal As ⇐
Long) As Integer
Declare Function CreateFractal Lib "FRACTDLL.DLL" (ByVal fractNum%, ⇐
ByVal xDots%, ByVal yDots%, ByVal mathType%, ByVal fLeft#, ByVal fRight#, ⇐
ByVal fTop#, ByVal fBottom#, ByVal maxIt&, ByVal p1x#, ByVal p1y#, ByVal ⇐
p2x#, ByVal p2y#) As Long
Declare Function DestroyFractal Lib "FRACTDLL.DLL" (ByVal hFractal As ⇐
Long) As Integer
Declare Function FractalDefaults Lib "FRACTDLL.DLL" (ByVal fractNum As ⇐
Integer) As Integer
Declare Function FractalName Lib "FRACTDLL.DLL" (ByVal fractNum As ⇐
Integer) As Integer
Declare Function FractalPoint Lib "FRACTDLL.DLL" (ByVal hFractal ⇐
As Long, ByVal x As Integer, ByVal y As Integer) As Long
Declare Function IdleFractal Lib "FRACTDLL.DLL" (ByVal hFractal As ⇐
Long) As Integer
Declare Function NumberFractals Lib "FRACTDLL.DLL" () As Integer
```

Note that in the Declare statement for CreateFractal we had to use Visual Basic's type declaration characters so the entire statement would fit on one line. Also, all the functions are in the file named FRACTDLL.DLL, so that's what we used for the Lib keyword.

So where do we go from here? Let's plunge right into creating a Visual Basic fractal interface.

### Steps

Open and run VFRACTAL.MAK. Select a fractal type from the Fractal menu. Sit back and enjoy! A sample fractal is shown in Figure 9-1. Try some of the other fractal types to see how they look.

1. Create a new project called VFRACTAL.MAK. Since the VFRACTAL project uses the WhichCPU function, add the VBHOWTO.BAS

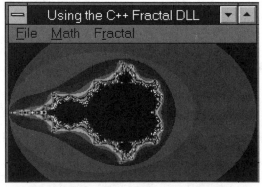

**Figure 9-1** The VFRACTAL project showing the Mandelbrot fractal

module to the project. Create a new form with the properties listed in Table 9-2 and save it as VFRACTAL.FRM.

| Control | Property | Setting |
|---------|----------|---------|
| Form | AutoRedraw | True |
| | Caption | Using the C++ Fractal DLL |
| | FormName | fractalForm |
| | Icon | WINFRACT.ICO |

**Table 9-2** VFractal form's controls and properties

2. Give VFRACTAL.FRM a menu using the Menu Design Window and the commands listed in Table 9-3.

| Caption | Name | Index |
|---------|------|-------|
| &File | FileMenu | |
| &About... | FileAbout | |
| E&xit | FileExit | |
| &Math | MathMenu | |
| &Fixed point | MathFixed | |
| &Quick float | MathQuick | |
| F&loating point | MathFloat | |
| F&ractal | FractalMenu | |
| First | Fractals | 0 |

**Table 9-3** VFractal form's menu

3. Put the following code in the Declarations section of VFRACTAL.FRM. This code declares some Windows and Fractal API functions and declares some global variables.

```
DefInt A-Z

' Fractal DLL functions -----------------
Declare Function ActivateFractal Lib "fractdll.dll" (ByVal hFractal As ⇐
Long) As Integer
Declare Function CreateFractal Lib "fractdll.dll" (ByVal fractNum%, ⇐
ByVal xDots%, ByVal yDots%, ByVal mathType%, ByVal fLeft#, ⇐
ByVal fRight#, ByVal fTop#, ByVal fBottom#, ByVal maxIt&, ByVal p1x#, ⇐
ByVal p1y#, ByVal p2x#, ByVal p2y#) As Long
Declare Function DestroyFractal Lib "fractdll.dll" (ByVal hFractal As ⇐
Long) As Integer
```

*continued on next page*

*continued form previous page*

```
Declare Function FractalDefaults Lib "fractdll.dll" (ByVal fractNum As ⇐
Integer) As Integer
Declare Function FractalName Lib "fractdll.dll" (ByVal fractNum As ⇐
Integer) As Integer
Declare Function FractalPoint Lib "fractdll.dll" (ByVal hFractal As ⇐
Long, ByVal x As Integer, ByVal y As Integer) As Long
Declare Function IdleFractal Lib "fractdll.dll" (ByVal hFractal As Long) ⇐
As Integer
Declare Function NumberFractals Lib "fractdll.dll" () As Integer

Const ORIGIN = 1, X_AXIS = 2, XY_AXIS = 3

' Windows API functions -----------------
Declare Function GlobalGetAtomName Lib "User" (ByVal nAtom As Integer, ⇐
ByVal lpbuffer As String, ByVal nSize As Integer) As Integer
Const FALSE = 0, TRUE = 1, NULL = 0&

' Globals ----------------------
Const MB_ICONASTERISK = 64
Const SCALE_PIXELS = 3

Dim mathType As Integer
Dim fractal As Long
Dim numFractals As Integer
```

4. Put the following code in the StopFractal general subroutine. This code calls the fractal DLL function DestroyFractal when you're finished using it.

```
Sub StopFractal ()
    If fractal <> NULL Then
        i = DestroyFractal(fractal)
        fractal = NULL
    End If

    Cls
End Sub
```

5. Put the following line in the FileAbout_Click event subroutine. The Show method will just display the About box that we'll design in Steps 13 and 14.

```
Sub FileAbout_Click ()
    AboutForm.Show
End Sub
```

6. Put the following code in the FileExit_Click event subroutine.

```
Sub FileExit_Click ()
    End
End Sub
```

7. Put the following code in the Form_Load event subroutine. This code puts the name of every fractal that the DLL supports into the Fractal menu and selects the fastest math type that the computer can support.

```
Sub Form_Load ()
   ScaleMode = SCALE_PIXELS
   temp$ = Space$(32)

   numFractals = NumberFractals()
   For i = 0 To numFractals - 1
      atom = FractalName(i)
      If atom = NULL Then Exit For

      j = GlobalGetAtomName(atom, temp$, Len(temp$))
      If i Then Load Fractals(i)
      Fractals(i).Caption = temp$
   Next

   If WhichCPU() = 386 Or WhichCPU() = 486 Then
      MathFixed_Click
   Else
      MathFloat_Click
   End If

   ' pull down the Fractal menu
   SendKeys "%R"
End Sub
```

8. Put the following code in the Form_Unload event subroutine. Calling the StopFractal function ensures that the DLL releases its memory.

```
Sub Form_Unload (Cancel As Integer)
   StopFractal
End Sub
```

9. Put the following code in the Fractals_Click event subroutine. This code does all the work of calling the fractal DLL functions to calculate the fractal.

```
Sub Fractals_Click (Index As Integer)
   Dim fLeft As Double, fRight As Double, fTop As Double, fBottom As ⇐
   Double, maxIt As Long, p1x As Double, p1y As Double, p2x As Double, ⇐
   p2y As Double
   Dim fColor As Long

   fractNum = Index

   For i = 0 To numFractals - 1
      Fractals(i).Checked = FALSE
   Next
   Fractals(fractNum).Checked = TRUE

   StopFractal
   temp$ = Space$(240)

   atom = FractalDefaults(fractNum)
   j = GlobalGetAtomName(atom, temp$, Len(temp$))
```

*continued on next page*

*continued form previous page*

```
file = FreeFile
Open "VFRACTAL.DAT" For Output As #file
Print #file, temp$
Close #file

file = FreeFile
Open "VFRACTAL.DAT" For Input As #file
Input #file, availMathTypes, fLeft, fRight, fTop, fBottom, maxIt, ⇐
  p1x, p1y, p2x, p2y, symmetry
Close #file

If (mathType And availMathTypes) = 0 Then
    MathFloat_Click
  MsgBox "The current math type is not supported by this fractal type.⇐
  Floating point math has been selected", MB_ICONASTERISK, "Note!"
End If

fractalIsIdle = TRUE
n = 0
xMax = CInt(fractalForm.ScaleWidth)
yMax = CInt(fractalForm.ScaleHeight)

Select Case symmetry
    Case ORIGIN, X_AXIS
        xLimit = xMax
        yLimit = yMax \ 2
    Case XY_AXIS
        xLimit = xMax \ 2
        yLimit = yMax \ 2
End Select

fractal = CreateFractal(fractNum, xMax, yMax, mathType, fLeft, fRight,⇐
        fTop, fBottom, maxIt, p1x, p1y, p2x, p2y)
  If fractal = NULL Then
    MsgBox "Unable to create fractal", MB_ICONASTERISK, "Note!"
  Else
    For y = 0 To yLimit - 1
        For x = 0 To xLimit - 1
            If fractalIsIdle Then
                If ActivateFractal(fractal) = FALSE Then
                    MsgBox "Unable to activate fractal", MB_ICONASTERISK,⇐
                        "Note!"
                    End
                Else
                    fractalIsIdle = FALSE
                    n = 0
                End If
            End If

            fColor = FractalPoint(fractal, x, y)
            n = n + fColor
```

```
            If fColor = maxIt Then
                fColor = 1
            Else
                fColor = fColor Mod 16
            End If
            fColor = QBColor(fColor)

            PSet (x, y), fColor

            Select Case symmetry
                Case ORIGIN
                    PSet (xMax - x - 1, yMax - y - 1), fColor
                Case X_AXIS
                    PSet (x, yMax - y - 1), fColor
                Case XY_AXIS
                    PSet (xMax - x - 1, yMax - y - 1), fColor
                    PSet (xMax - x - 1, y), fColor
                    PSet (x, yMax - y - 1), fColor
            End Select

            If n >= 1000 Then
                i = IdleFractal(fractal)
                i = DoEvents()
                fractalIsIdle = TRUE
            End If
        Next
    Next
    End If
End Sub
```

10. Put the following code in the MathFixed_Click event subroutine. This code sets the mathType variable to the fixed floating point math type and checks the menu item.

```
Sub MathFixed_Click ()
    mathType = 2
    MathFixed.Checked = TRUE
    MathQuick.Checked = FALSE
    MathFloat.Checked = FALSE
End Sub
```

11. Put the following code in the MathFloat_Click event subroutine. This code sets the mathType variable to the normal floating point math type and checks the menu item.

```
Sub MathFloat_Click ()
    mathType = 1
    MathFixed.Checked = FALSE
    MathQuick.Checked = FALSE
    MathFloat.Checked = TRUE
End Sub
```

12. Put the following code in the MathQuick_Click event subroutine. This code sets the mathType variable to the quick floating point math type and checks the menu item.

```
Sub MathQuick_Click ()
    mathType = 4
    MathFixed.Checked = FALSE
    MathQuick.Checked = TRUE
    MathFloat.Checked = FALSE
End Sub
```

13. Create a new form with the properties listed in Table 9-4 and save it as VFABOUT.FRM. Figure 9-2 shows how it looks.

| Control | Property | Setting |
|---|---|---|
| Form | BorderStyle | 3 - Fixed Double |
| | Caption | About... |
| | FormName | AboutForm |
| | Icon | WINFRACT.ICO |
| | MaxButton | False |
| | MinButton | False |
| Picture box | AutoSize | True |
| | Name | Picture1 |
| | Picture | WINFRACT.ICO |
| Label | Alignment | 2 - Center |
| | Caption | Using the C++ Fractal DLL |
| | FontBold | True |
| | FontSize | 9 |
| Label | Alignment | 2 - Center |
| | Caption | The Waite Group's Visual Basic How-To |
| | FontBold | True |
| | FontItalic | True |
| | FontName | Helv |
| | FontSize | 9 |
| Label | Alignment | 2 - Center |
| | Caption | Robert Arnson |
| | FontBold | True |
| | FontName | Helv |
| | FontSize | 9 |
| Label | Alignment | 2 - Center |
| | Caption | Fractal DLL by Mark Peterson |
| | FontBold | True |

| Control | Property | Setting |
|---------|----------|---------|
| Command button | FontSize | 9 |
| | Caption | OK |
| | Name | Command1 |
| | Default | True |

**Table 9-4**  AboutForm's controls and properties

14. Add the following code to the Command1_Click event subroutine. This code just unloads the About box and returns to the main fractal application.

```
Sub Command1_Click ()
    Unload AboutForm
End Sub
```

### How It Works

In the Declarations section of the VFRACTAL form, there are several global variables. The mathType variable stores the currently selected math type as a global variable so the MathFixed, MathFloat, and MathQuick Click event subroutines can set it.

The fractal variable stores the FRACTAL handle type that the DLL function CreateFractal returns. Then that variable can be passed to the fractal DLL whenever we want to refer to the fractal.

The numFractals variable stores the number of fractals that the DLL supports, as the NumberFractals function returned.

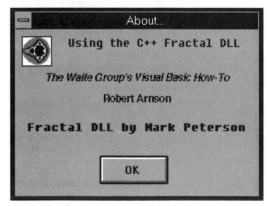

**Figure 9-2** The AboutForm displaying with the fractal icon

The StopFractal function calls the DLL function DestroyFractal function to release the memory the DLL was using to create the fractal. The Form_Unload calls this function when the application ends.

The first thing the Form_Load event subroutine does is to set the ScaleMode property to pixels. We have to do that because the fractal DLL doesn't support Visual Basic's twips. Then, the For loop goes through each fractal the DLL supports and gets its name. The FractalName function returns a Windows atom. What the heck's an atom? An atom is a string that Windows stores globally, so any application can read it. The DLL makes an atom so that the application can read it. There's a little bit of extra work, but it also means that the DLL doesn't have to understand how Visual Basic stores strings. The Windows API function GlobalGetAtomName reads the string atom.

Since the index of the Fractal menu item is 0, it's an element of a menu control array. The Load statement makes an element in the control array for each fractal type, then Caption property is set to the fractal's name.

Calling the WhichCPU function tells us whether or not the machine will support the 386 math types. If it won't, normal floating point is selected.

Finally, using the SendKeys statement, the Fractal menu is pulled down.

The Fractals_Click event subroutine is the biggie: It's the subroutine that's executed when the user selects one of the fractal types. Since the Fractals menu is in a menu control array, Fractals_Click has the Index parameter indicating which fractal was picked.

The first For loop makes sure that the fractal that was picked is the only one with a check mark next to it.

FractalDefaults returns the fractal parameters. Again, GlobalGetAtomName is used to read the string atom. The atom that FractalDefaults returns has all the fractal default parameters in a single string, separated by commas. We cheat a little here by writing that string to a text file and reading it back in. Visual Basic's Input statement will automatically separate each part of the string and read it into a numeric variable.

Since some fractals don't support all the math types, we check to make sure. If it isn't supported by the math type selected from the Math menu, normal floating point math is selected, which all fractals support.

The symmetry parameter of the fractal is checked next to see if we really need to calculate all of the fractal. Here's what the following symmetries mean:

ORIGIN    The fractal is symmetrical about the origin. With this type of symmetry, the bottom half of the image is upside-down and leftside-right to the top half of the image.

| X_AXIS | The fractal is symmetrical about the x axis. This means the bottom half is a mirror image of the top half. |
|--------|-----------------------------------------------------------------------------------------------------------|
| Y_AXIS | The fractal is symmetrical about the y axis. This means the right half is a mirror image of the left half. |
| XY_AXIS | The fractal is symmetrical about both the x and y axes. This means the upper left quarter of the image can be used to generate the remaining three quarters. |

Finally, the real work begins by calling the CreateFractal function with the default parameters. There's a For loop for each point along the x and y axes. If we haven't already called ActivateFractal, we do so (and display an error if it couldn't be activated).

The FractalPoint function is then called to get the color of the given x/y point in the fractal. The variable $n$ is used to keep track of how long the fractal DLL has been calculating, so we can release control to Windows after a while.

The maxIt parameter is returned if the point exceeded the maximum of the formula. Here, we then set the color to 1, which is blue. Otherwise, since Visual Basic only supports 16-color images, we use the Mod operator so a color above 15 won't cause an "Illegal function call" error. Then we display the point in the right color using the QBColor function.

For example, if the symmetry is XY_AXIS, we plot four points for every one point calculated. Using symmetry is a great time saver!

Finally, we check the $n$ variable to see if we should release control to Windows. Since we're in two tight For…Next loops, Windows would normally not get control until the subroutine ends. This would make calculating the fractal faster, but would mean that all other applications would be stopped in their tracks. We call IdleFractal before releasing control to Windows with Visual Basic's DoEvents so the memory is available. The fractalIsIdle variable keeps track of whether the fractal is idle. If it is, we call ActivateFractal to reactivate it.

### Comments

It's important to call DoEvents for more than just letting other applications get a chance to run. We set the form's AutoRedraw property to True so that we don't have to totally repaint the form, but when AutoRedraw is True, the form isn't displayed until Windows gets control. If we didn't call DoEvents, the form wouldn't be displayed until the entire fractal was created.

# DATABASE CONTROLS

# How do I...

Most real-world programs have database requirements that are difficult to implement using Visual Basic's built-in file I/O capabilities. Visual Basic 3.0 adds an important new custom control, the DataControl, to the Visual Basic programmer's bag of tricks. Using the DataControl and other standard Visual Basic controls you can now easily implement sophisticated database storage and retrieval capabilites in your applications.

The DataControl acts as an intermediary between your application and Microsoft's Access database engine. With Visual Basic 3.0, you get DLLs that contain the Access database engine. The core set of DLLs, VBDB300.DLL, MSAES110.DLL and MSAJT110.DLL, allow your programs to work with data in Access databases. You can distribute the DLLs and a database with your application. So it is not necessary for your users to buy a copy of Access to run your application.

Access is a relational database. A relational database stores data in *tables,* which are made up of *rows* and *columns.* Rows and columns are often referred to as records and fields, especially when talking about a particular row/column. In this chapter, the terms rows and records will be used interchangeably, and the terms columns and fields will be used interchangeably. A database can contain more than one table; the maximum number of tables in a database depends upon the database implementation. Relational databases are so named because values from a column in one table can be matched with values in another table's column, and one or more columns from the collection of both table's columns can be extracted to create a new table. In other words, a relation is established between the two tables.

The following sections contain an introduction to the fundamentals of using the DataControl. If you are already familiar with the DataControl, you might want to skip ahead to the How-Tos.

### Opening a Database

The first thing you'll need to do when using the DataControl is to open a database. Opening a database with the DataControl is really very simple. In fact, in many cases all you need to do is set two properties, DatabaseName and RecordSource. The DataControl will automatically open the database and locate the first record from the RecordSource during the Form_Load event subroutine.

The DatabaseName property is used by the DataControl to locate the database you want to use. During design-time, you set the DatabaseName property so that it contains the path and filename of your database. The RecordSource property is used to specify the source of records to be used by the DataControl.

There are two different types of settings for the RecordSource property. The first, and simplest, way of selecting records from the database is to specify one of the database table's names as the setting of the RecordSource property. After you have set the DatabaseName property, a list of tables in the database will be available in the Properties Window when the RecordSource property is selected.

The second, and much more powerful, way of selecting a source of records is to assign an SQL (Structured Query Language) query to the RecordSource property. A thorough explanation of SQL is beyond the scope of this book—in fact, you should probably get at least two books about SQL. With SQL you can use fields from one or more tables to create a third table. Fields from source tables can be tested for values, or ranges of values, as a precondition to inclusion in the result table. Mathematical functions such as Sum and Average can be applied to

| ForestId | ForestName | ForestState |
|----------|------------|-------------|
| 1 | Olympic National Park | WA |
| 2 | Black Hills National Forest | SD |
| 3 | Gifford Pinchot National Forest | WA |
| 4 | Rio Grand National Forest | CO |

**Figure 10-1** ForestsTable

the result columns. The result table can be sorted on any field and grouped by field values. If this seems like a lot, it's not. SQL is a very powerful database query language that is capable of doing all this and much more.

As an example of how simple a SQL query works, consider a database that has a table named ForestsTable. Figure 10-1 shows the format of the ForestsTable. To create a table containing a list of all forests in Washington, you would assign

```
SELECT ForestName FROM ForestsTable WHERE ForestsState = 'WA'
```

to the DataControl's RecordSource property. The result of this query will be a table with one column that contains the name of each forest in the database.

For a more complex example of what you can do using SQL, we'll add a couple new tables to the Forests database. Figures 10-2 and 10-3 show the two new tables, PermitsTable and ForestPermits.

| PermitNumber | BoardFeet |
|--------------|-----------|
| 1 | 14000000 |
| 2 | 23500000 |
| 3 | 40000000 |
| 4 | 15000000 |
| 5 | 5000000 |

**Figure 10-2** PermitsTable

| ForestId | PermitNumber |
|----------|--------------|
| 1 | 1 |
| 2 | 2 |
| 1 | 3 |
| 3 | 4 |
| 4 | 5 |

**Figure 10-3** ForestPermits

To create a table containing the total number of board feet of logging permitted in each state's forests, you would assign the following string to the RecordSource property of a DataControl:

```
SELECT DISTINCTROW ForestsTable.ForestState, Sum(PermitsTable.BoardFeet) AS⇐
  SumOfBoardFeet
    FROM ForestPermits, ForestsTable, PermitsTable, PermitsTable
    INNER JOIN ForestPermits ON PermitsTable.Permit Number =
    ForestsTable.PermitNumber, ForestPermits
    INNER JOIN ForestsTable ON ForestPermits.ForestId = ⇐
forestsTable.ForestId
    GROUP BY ForestsTable.ForestState
    ORDER BY Sum(PermitsTable.BoardFeet) DESC
```

When this query is run on the database shown in Figures 10-1 through 10-3, the resulting table will have the rows and columns shown in Figure 10-4.

This SQL query is substantially more complex than the previous one, and still it is somewhat simple by SQL standards! Having such a powerful database query language at your disposal when writing Visual Basic programs will allow you to easily add sophisticated query capabilities to your applications.

By the way, if the above example looks somewhat overwhelming to write, don't worry about it: I didn't actually have to write the query and neither do you. The way I did this was to create the query using Access. First, I created the query using a point-and-click tool. Then I used Access's View menu to look at the SQL code generated for the query. You can use Access to design your query, and then simply copy the SQL code to your Visual Basic application!

### Accessing Records in a Database

Once you've selected a source of records for the DataControl, you are ready to begin accessing the records. The DataControl contains an object named RecordSet. Once you've opened the database and specified a record source, the RecordSet object will provide access to the specified rows. The RecordSet object provides a rich set of methods that you can use to manipulate the records it contains.

| SumOfBoardFee | ForestState |
|---|---|
| 69000000 | WA |
| 23500000 | SD |
| 5000000 | CO |

**Figure 10-4** Total board feet by state

When you're using the DataControl's RecordSet object, you can only access one record at a time. This record is called the *current record*. The RecordSet has a number of methods that you can use to select the current record. Among them are MoveFirst, MoveNext, MoveLast, and MovePrevious. These methods do exactly what their names imply. MoveFirst selects the first row in the database as the current record, MoveNext moves to the next row, and so on.

In addition to the methods implemented by the RecordSet, this object also provides access to the fields of the current record through its Fields collection. The Fields collection provides a number of different ways to retrieve the value of a field in the current record. The most verbose way to access a field is to use a statement like the following:

```
Data1.RecordSet.Fields("ForestName").Value
```

This statement returns the value of the field named ForestName from the current record. In the Forests database, where ForestName is the second field, another way to retrieve the same value is to use one of the following statements:

```
Data1.RecordSet.Fields(1).Value
Data1.RecordSet.Fields(1)
```

You might wonder why the second example works, since it appears to be missing the Value property. The second example works because Value is the default return value of a RecordSet's Fields collection.

A RecordSet also has a default object that will be used as its value, the Fields collection object. Because of this, the following two statements are equivalent to the previous three:

```
Data1.RecordSet(1)
Data1.RecordSet(1).Value
```

Careful use of default values can significantly reduce the amout of code you need to write. On the other hand, careless use of default values can create some rather annoying bugs!

### Adding New Records to a Database

Adding new records to a database is a three-step process. First, you create a new record using the AddNew method. Next, you assign a value to each of the fields in the database. And finally, you append the new record to the database by using the Update method. The following code fragment demonstrates how this is done:

```
'
' Create a new record
'
```

*continued on next page*

*continued from previous page*

```
Data1.RecordSet.AddNew
'
' Assign values to the new record's fields
'
Data1.RecordSet("PermitNumber") = 6
Data1.RecordSet("BoardFeet") = 1500000
'
' Add the new record to the database
'
Data1.RecordSet.Update
```

### Editing Existing Records in the Database

Editing an existing database record is similar to adding a new record, except you don't need to invoke the AddNew method. All you need to do is locate the record to be edited, change one or more fields, and invoke the Update method to update the record in the database. The following code fragment shows how to locate and edit a particular database record:

```
Dim Found As Integer
'
' Select the PermitsTable
'
Data1.RecordSource = "PermitsTable"
'
' Find permit number 3
'
Found = False
Data1.RecordSet.MoveFirst
Do While Data1.RecordSet.EOF = False And Found = False
    If Data1.RecordSet("PermitNumber") = 3 Then
        Found = True
    Else
        Data1.RecordSet.MoveNext
    End If
Loop
If (Found = True) Then
    '
    ' Record Found ... change BoardFeet
    '
    Data1.RecordSet("BoardFeet") = 0
    Data1.RecordSet.Update
Else
    MsgBox "Record Not Found"
End If
```

### Using Transactions

When you are changing data in a database, you will probably need to change records in more than one table. For example, let's say that you want to delete permit number 3 from the ForestPermits table. You wouldn't want to leave the reference to permit number 3 in the PermitsTable, since the database would then be inconsistent, so you need to remove a record from each of the tables. Now consider what would happen if power failed, or your machine crashed, after the ForestPermits table was changed but before the PermitsTable table was changed. You would be left with the very situation you were trying to avoid. This is the type of problem *transaction processing* is designed to handle. When you use transaction processing, you can ensure that either both changes are made, or neither change is made. This way, regardless of when the machine might fail, you still have a consistent database. The following example shows how to use a transaction when deleting a permit from the ForestPermits table:

```
'
' When we arrive here Data1.RecordSet's current record contains a record in
' the ForestPermtis table, and Data2.RecordSet's current record contains
' the corresponding record in the PermitsTable.
'
BeginTrans
Data1.RecordSet.Delete
Data2.RecordSet.Delete
CommitTrans
```

After the BeginTrans statement is executed, database changes are not actually made permanently in the database until the CommitTrans statement is executed. And even then the database commits the changes in such a way that it is guaranteed that if one of the records is deleted, the other one will be deleted also.

This is a very simple example of transaction processing. A more realistic example would require changes to a number of tables. Sometimes it happens that you are in the middle of changing a number of records when your program determines that the current set of changes must be abandoned. When this happens, you can use the RollBack statement. The RollBack statement discards any changes made since the last BeginTrans was executed and ends the current transaction. Thus there are two ways to end a transaction: you can end the transaction and commit changes to the database by executing the CommitTrans statement, or you can end the transaction and abandon changes by executing the RollBack statement.

## Bound Controls

Often you want to present the contents of records to your users so that the records can be viewed and edited. While it would be possible to retrieve fields from records and change the contents of text boxes and such each time a new record was selected, a considerable amount of code would be required.

For example, if you wanted to create a data-entry program for a table that had ten columns, you would need to write code to put field values into the edit boxes. And you would need to keep track of which edit boxes had changed so the database fields could be updated. This would clearly not be in the spirit of Visual Basic!

To make writing database applications easier, Visual Basic 3.0 comes with a number of *bound controls*. A bound control has two new properties that let you specify a database field that is bound with the control. You use the DataSource property to specify a particular DataControl, PermitsTable for instance, and the DataField property to specify that a particular field, like BoardFeet, from PermitsTable's RecordSet be bound to the control. A bound control will automatically display its field from the RecordSet's current record, and changes made to the bound control can be automatically commited to the database when the current record changes.

Five bound controls come with the standard edition of Visual Basic 3.0: Check box, Image, Label, Picture box, and Text box. When you're using fields that can be displayed in one of the five bound controls, you really don't have to do much work. This will not always be the case; you might want, for instance, to have a group of option buttons where each button is used to display and modify a database field. How-Tos 10.2, 10.3, and 10.4 show you how to create your own bound controls using Visual Basic.

### 10.1    Write a database structure browser

Databases can contain a large number of tables, and each table can contain a large number of fields. How-To 10.1 shows you how to write a database structure browser. Using the program built in this How-To you can quickly and easily  locate table and field names, and field sizes and datatypes.

### 10.2    Use non-bound controls with the DataControl

Many of the standard Visual Basic 3.0 controls cannot be bound to a database field. This How-To shows you how to update non-bound controls as a RecordSet's current record changes.

### 10.3    Bind an option button to a database field

Databases often contain fields that can contain any one of a fixed number of values. Option buttons are the natural way to represent the contents of such a field. Unfortunately, Visual Basic doesn't provide a bound option button. How-To 10.3 shows you how to make option buttons behave as if they were bound controls.

**10.4    Use the Grid control to view database tables**

Displaying a list of records from a database is a common requirement. Since the Grid control is not one of the bound controls, you need to do some work to use it to display records. How-To 10.4 shows you how to use the Grid control with records from a RecordSet.

**10.5    Store pictures in a database**

Databases can be used for more than just keeping track of social-security numbers! How-To 10.5 shows you how to build a database of bitmaps. By adding information about the stored images, and possibly creating some relational tables for searching, you can store all your favorite bitmaps in a database and easily find them without needing to remember the filenames.

**10.6    Detect when a database record is locked**

In addition to ensuring that changes to a database are made as a unit, transactions can also be used to prevent multiple users from simultaneously modifying a given record or records. In How-To 10.6, you will see how to let two programs access the same database simultaneously without making inconsistent changes.

# 10.1 ● How do I...

Complexity: Intermediate

## Write a database structure browser?

### Problem

When I'm writing applications that use a database, I often want to know what tables and fields are in a database. How can I write a simple program that will show me the tables and fields in a database?

### Solution

A DataControl is associated with a database on disk. This control has a Database object that has properties you can use to access different elements of a database. It is important to keep in mind the way Visual Basic thinks of objects.

With the DataControl, you specify which database to open by assigning a string containing the path and name of the database to the Database property. However, if you use the debug window to print the value of the DataControl's Database property, the database's name will not be printed.

This is because the value of the DataControl's Database property is a *database object,* not a string.

It is important to note that the Database property contains a database object, and that this object contains properties that you can use to access other objects. The objects of interest for this How-To are the TableDefs and FieldDefs objects. Both TableDefs and FieldDefs are *object collections.* The individual objects in a collection can be referenced by using an index number, as in the following code fragment:

```
Data1.RecordSource = Data1.Database.TableDefs(0)
```

In addition to specifying a collection member by index, you can also locate a collection member by using its name. Assuming that Data1.Database contains a table named "Pictures", the Pictures TableDef object can be referenced as follows:

```
Data1.RecordSource = Data1.Database.TableDefs("Pictures")
```

The previous line assigns the TableDef object named Pictures to the RecordSource property of Data1. Once a TableDef object has been assigned to the RecordSource property, the Data1.RecordSource.Fields collection can be used to retrieve information about the fields in the table, such as the field name and size.

Each collection also contains a Count property, which contains the number of objects in the collection. The following code fragment will print the name of all of the tables and fields in a database:

```
'
' For each table in the database
'
For t = 0 To Data1.Database.TableDefs.Count - 1
    '
    ' Print the current TableDefs name
    '
    Debug.Print Data1.Databse.TableDefs(t).Name
    '
    ' Select the current table as Data1's record source
    '
    Data1.RecordSource = Data1.Database.TableDefs(t)
    '
    ' For each field in the table
    '
    For f = 0 To Data1.RecordSet.Fields.Count - 1
        '
        ' Print the field's name
        '
        Debug.Print chr$(9) & Data1.RecordSet.Fields(r).Name
    Next
Next
```

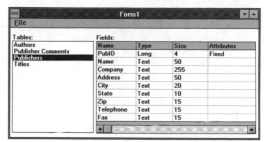

**Figure 10-5** Schema project in action

As you can see, it is really easy to find all of the tables and fields in a database. Using the approach shown above, it is simply a matter of filling in the details to create a useful database structure browser.

By the way, it isn't uncommon for the definition of a database to be refered to as a database *schema*. A database schema is simply a description, or schematic, of a database. I call this project Schema because it lets you examine database schemas.

### Steps

Open and run SCHEMA.MAK. The running program appears as shown in Figure 10-5. Use the File Open menu to open a database. Once you have opened a database, the Tables list box will contain a list of the tables in your database. The first table in the list will be highlighted, and its fields will be listed in the grid. The grid displays the name, size, type, and attributes of each field in the selected table. You can see the fields defined in any table by double-clicking on the table name in the tables list box.

1. Create a new project called SCHEMA.MAK. Add the objects and properties listed in Table 10-1 to Form1 and save the form as SCHEMA.FRM.

| Object | Property | Setting |
| --- | --- | --- |
| Form | Caption | "Form1" |
|  | Name | "Form1" |
|  | ScaleMode | 3 'Pixel |
| List box | Name | TablesListBox |
|  | TabIndex | 1 |
| OpenDialog | CreatePrompt | 0 'False |
|  | DefaultExt | ".MDB" |
|  | DialogType | 0 'Open Dialog |
|  | FileMustExist | -1 'True |

*continued on next page*

*continued from previous page*

| Object | Property | Setting |
|--------|----------|---------|
|  | Filter | "Database Files (*.mdb)|*.mdb|" |
|  | HideReadOnly | -1 'True |
|  | Name | "OpenDialog1" |
|  | PathMustExist | -1 'True |
|  | Title | "Open Database" |
| Grid | FixedCols | 0 |
|  | HighLight | 0 'False |
|  | Name | "Grid1" |
| Data | Autoload | -1 'True |
|  | Name | "Data1" |
|  | ReadOnly | -1 'True |
|  | Visible | 0 'False |
| Label | Caption | "Fields:" |
|  | Name | Label2 |
| Label | Caption | "Tables:" |
|  | Name | Label1 |

**Table 10-1** SCHEMA.FRM objects and properties

2. Select the menu design window tool and create a menu for SCHEMA.FRM with captions and names, as shown in Table 10-2.

| Control Name | Caption |
|--------------|---------|
| FileMenu | "&File" |
| ---FileOpenDatabase | "&Open Database..." |
| ---FileSep1 | "-" |
| ---FileExit | "E&xit" |

**Table 10-2** SCHEMA.FRM menu

3. Create a new module named SCHEMA.BAS. Add the following code to the General Declarations section of SCHEMA.BAS. This module declares the Windows API functions and constants used by the schema program.

```
'
' Windows API Functions
'
Declare Function GetTextExtent Lib "GDI" (ByVal hDC As Integer, ByVal ⇐
lpString As String, ByVal nCount As Integer) As Long
```

```
Declare Function GetDC Lib "User" (ByVal hWnd As Integer) As Integer
Declare Function SendMessage Lib "User" (ByVal hWnd As Integer, ByVal ⇐
wMsg As Integer, ByVal wParam As Integer, lParam As Any) As Long

Global Const WM_USER = &H400
Global Const LB_RESETCONTENT = (WM_USER + 5)
```

4. Add the following code to the General Declarations section of SCHEMA.FRM. The TypeDescriptions array is initialized during the Form_Load event subroutine and is used to quickly locate the string description of an Access datatype.

```
Option Explicit
'
' The following array is initialized during form load to
' contain a string describing each of the possible Access data
' types. The value of the field's data type is used as an index
' into the array.
'
Dim TypeDescriptions(12) As String
```

5. Add the following code to the FileExit menu's Click event subroutine.

```
Sub FileExit_Click ()
    End
End Sub
```

6. Add the following code to the FileOpenDatabase menu's Click event subroutine. This subroutine is called when the user selects Open Database... from the File menu. OpenDialog1 is used to prompt the user for a database filename. If a database file is selected, the database is opened by setting the DatabaseName property and invoking the Refresh method. Next, the previous contents, if any, of the TablesListBox is cleared by using the Windows API function SendMessage. Finally, the list box is loaded with the name of each table in the database.

```
Sub FileOpenDatabase_Click ()
    Dim tableIndex  As Integer
    Dim ListIndex   As Integer
    Dim wRtn        As Integer
    '
    ' Clear the filename so we can tell if Cancel was pressed
    '
    OpenDialog1.File = ""
    '
    ' Start open dialog
    '
    OpenDialog1.DoIt = True
    '
    ' Bail out if no file specified
```

*continued on next page*

*continued from previous page*

```
    '
    If (OpenDialog1.File = "") Then
        Exit Sub
    End If
    '
    ' Got a database filename
    '
    Data1.DatabaseName = OpenDialog1.File
    '
    ' Let form repaint where dialog box was removed
    '
    DoEvents
    '
    ' Executing Refresh opens the database
    '
    Data1.Refresh
    '
    ' Clear tables list
    '
    wRtn = SendMessage(TablesListBox.hWnd, LB_RESETCONTENT, 0, 0)
    For tableIndex = 0 To Data1.Database.TableDefs.Count - 1
        '
        ' Don't add Access's private tables to the list box
        '
        If (Left$(Data1.Database.TableDefs(tableIndex).Name, 4) <> "MSys") Then
            TablesListBox.AddItem Data1.Database.TableDefs(tableIndex).Name
            ListIndex = ListIndex + 1
        End If
    Next
    '
    ' Select first table in list
    '
    TablesListBox.ListIndex = 0
    '
    ' Load fields from first table
    '
    TablesListBox_DblClick
End Sub
```

7. Add the following code to Form1's Form_Load event subroutine. After calling InitializeTypeDescriptions, this subroutine assigns column headings to the grid, and adjusts the columns to fit within the design-time size of the grid. The Grid control doesn't allow design-time assignment of the text for cells, not even for the fixed rows and columns. So the Form_Load event subroutine takes care of sizing and assigning text to columns headings.

```
Sub Form_Load ()
    Dim Col        As Integer
    Dim ColWidth   As Integer
```

```
    Dim colTitle     As String
    Dim hDC          As Integer
    Dim totalWidth   As Integer
    '
    ' Load type descriptions array for easy access later
    '
    InitializeTypeDescriptions
    '
    ' Get the grid's device-context
    '
    hDC = GetDC(grid1.hWnd)
    '
    ' There are four columns: Name, Type, Size, and Attributes
    '
    grid1.Cols = 4
    '
    ' Put column titles in the fixed row (row = 0)
    '
    grid1.Row = 0
    For Col = 0 To 3
        '
        ' Move to next column
        '
        grid1.Col = Col
        '
        ' Get column title
        '
        colTitle = Mid$("Name     Type     Size     Attributes", Col * 10 + 1, 10)
        colTitle = RTrim$(colTitle)
        grid1.Text = colTitle
        '
        ' Get column width in pixels
        '
        ColWidth = GetTextExtent(hDC, colTitle, Len(colTitle)) And &HFFFF&
        '
        ' Convert to twips for grid's column width
        '
        grid1.ColWidth(Col) = ColWidth * Screen.TwipsPerPixelX
        '
        ' Accumulate total width
        '
        totalWidth = totalWidth + ColWidth
    Next
    '
    ' If there's extra room in the grid adjust each column
    '
    ColWidth = (grid1.Width - totalWidth) * Screen.TwipsPerPixelX / 4
    If (ColWidth > 0) Then
        For Col = 0 To 3
            grid1.ColWidth(Col) = grid1.ColWidth(Col) + ColWidth
        Next
    End If
End Sub
```

8. Add the following subroutine to the General Declarations section of Form1. Access datatypes are retrieved from the Type property of a Field object. The datatypes are represented by integers between 0 and 11. By using a datatype value as an index into the TypeDescriptions array, it is easy to get a text description of a particular datatype.

```
Sub InitializeTypeDescriptions ()
    TypeDescriptions(0) = "Boolean"
    TypeDescriptions(1) = "Byte"
    TypeDescriptions(2) = "Integer"
    TypeDescriptions(3) = "Long"
    TypeDescriptions(4) = "Currency"
    TypeDescriptions(5) = "Single"
    TypeDescriptions(6) = "Double"
    TypeDescriptions(7) = "Date"
    TypeDescriptions(8) = "Binary"
    TypeDescriptions(9) = "Text"
    TypeDescriptions(10) = "Long Binary"
    TypeDescriptions(11) = "Memo"
End Sub
```

9. Add the following code to the DblClick event subroutine of TablesListBox. First, this subroutine assigns the selected table to the RecordSource property of Data1. Next the name, size, type, and attributes of each field in Data1.RecordSet's Fields collection are loaded into the Grid control.

```
Sub TablesListBox_DblClick ()
    Dim Row          As Integer
    Dim Attributes   As Integer
    Dim attribString As String
    '
    ' Change pointer to hourglass
    '
    Screen.MousePointer = 11
    '
    ' Set record source to selected table name
    '
    Data1.RecordSource = Data1.Database.TableDefs(TablesListBox.Text)
    Data1.Refresh
    '
    ' Get the number of fields
    '
    grid1.Rows = Data1.RecordSet.Fields.Count + 1
    '
    ' For each field
    '
    For Row = 1 To grid1.Rows - 1
        '
        ' Put Name, type, size, and attributes in grid
        '
```

```
        grid1.Row = Row
        grid1.Col = 0
        grid1.Text = Data1.RecordSet.Fields(Row - 1).Name
        grid1.Col = 1
        grid1.Text = TypeDescriptions(Data1.RecordSet.Fields(Row - 1).Type - 1)
        grid1.Col = 2
        grid1.Text = Data1.RecordSet.Fields(Row - 1).Size
        grid1.Col = 3

        Attributes = Data1.RecordSet.Fields(Row - 1).Attributes
        If (Attributes And (512 Or 32 Or 16 Or 4 Or 1)) Then
            If (Attributes And 1) Then
                attribString = "Fixed,"
            End If
            If (Attributes And 4) Then
                attribString = attribString & "NotNull,"
            End If
            If (Attributes And 16) Then
                attribString = attribString & "Counter,"
            End If
            If (Attributes And 32) Then
                attribString = attribString & "Updatable,"
            End If
            If (Attributes And 512) Then
                attribString = attribString & "Graphic,"
            End If
            grid1.Text = Left$(attribString, Len(attribString) - 1)
        Else
            grid1.Text = ""
        End If
    Next
    Screen.MousePointer = 0
End Sub
```

### How It Works

There are three major subroutines in the Schema project: Form_Load, FileOpenDatabase_Click, and TablesListBox_Click. The Form_Load subroutine is mostly concerned with initializing the Grid control. The Grid control does not allow design-time assignment of text to grid cells, or sizing the rows and columns. During Form_Load the length of the text assigned to each column heading is obtained by calling the Windows API function GetTextExtent. The label's length is then used to size the column so that all of the text will be visible. The length of each text string is also accumulated in the variable totalWidth. After the columns have been sized, the Form_Load subroutine checks to see if totalWidth is less than the width of the Grid; if so the remaining space is distributed evenly among the columns.

After initialization is finished, the user can select the File Open Database... menu item to open a database. The first job for the FileOpenDatabase_Click routine is to initialize the OpenDialog1 control and invoke the Common Dialog file open dialog box. If the user selects a database file, the File property of OpenDialog1 will contain the name of a database. Opening the database is as simple as assigning the File property of OpenDialog1 to Data1's DatabaseName property and invoking Data1's Refresh method. Once the database has been opened, Data1's TableDefs collection can be accessed. The Count property of Data1.TableDefs gives the total number of tables contained in the database. The FileOpenDatabase_Click routine accesses each member of the TableDefs collection by using an index that ranges from 0 to Data1.TableDefs.Count - 1. Each TableDef object has a name property. With the exception of table names that begin with "MSys," each table's name is loaded into the TablesListBox. The tables that begin with "MSys" are used internally by the Access engine and cannot be examined by Visual Basic programs. Any attempt to reference the fields of the system tables results in a run-time error, so these tables are not loaded into TablesListBox.

At the end of the FileOpenDatabase_Click subroutine, the first item in TablesListBox is selected and the TablesListBox_DblClick subroutine is called. When the TablesListBox_DblClick subroutine is called, either directly or by the user double-clicking an item in the list, the grid control is loaded with the information about the fields in the selected table. To accomplish this, a TableDef object is assigned to Data1's RecordSet property. The correct TableDef object is easily retrieved from Data1 by using the table name as an index into the TableDefs collection. The ability to reference a member of a collection by name instead of by using an index number is an important feature of collections. Without this feature, it would be necessary to keep track of the correspondence between items in the list box and the index of a TableDef object. Once a TableDef object has been assigned to Data1's RecordSet property, the Fields collection can be used. Like the TableDefs collection, the Fields collection also has a Count property that lets you know how many fields are in a table. Each Field object in the collection gives the name, size, datatype, and attributes of one field in the table. The TablesListBox_DblClick routine accesses each of the members of the Fields collection and loads the name, size, datatype, and attributes into one row of the grid.

## Comments

When writing an application that uses a database, it is necessary to know what tables and fields are available, and what type of data is stored in the fields. The Schema project provides a handy utility that can be used to browse through a database schema. While you could certainly use Access itself for browsing, the Schema project will load and execute much more quickly, and use considerably less system resources. An interesting variation on this project would be to add an option to list the database schema on the printer. Another useful feature that could be added would be to change the size of the columns based both upon the length of the text string in the column heading and the length of the longest string occurring in the column, choosing the larger of these as the width of the column.

## 10.2 How do I...

## Use non-bound controls with the DataControl?

### Problem

A number of controls, such as the Shape control, do not have DataSource and DataField properties. Is there some way I can easily make non-Bound controls behave as if they were bound controls?

### Solution

Yes, there is an easy way to simulate the behavior of bound controls. The DataControl's Reposition event procedure is called whenever the current record changes. In the Reposition event procedure, you can use fields from the new current record to change properties of one or more controls. To change the contents of the current record, you can use the DataControl's Edit and Update methods.

This How-To uses a database named SMPLBIND.MDB. The database contains a single table named Shapes. The Shapes table's fields are shown in Figure 10-6. Each row in the table specifies a shape and its size, position, and color.

### Steps

Open and run SMPLBIND.MAK. When the project runs, you will see the DataControls record navigation buttons at the bottom of the form. In the

| Field Name | Data Type |
| --- | --- |
| Shape | Text |
| Top | Number |
| Left | Number |
| Width | Number |
| Height | Number |
| Color | Number |

**Figure 10-6** SMPLBIND.MDB's shapes table

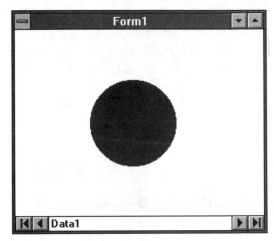

**Figure 10-7** SMPLBIND.MAK in action

center of the form, a shape is displayed. You can use the record navigation buttons to change the current record. The shape displayed on the form will be changed as the current record changes.

You can move the shape around on the form by first pressing, and holding down, the left mouse button when it is over the shape. With the left mouse button held down, you can move the shape around on the form. When you release the button, the shape's new position is entered into the database. You can also change the shape's color by clicking the right button on the shape. Shape colors are also updated in the database.

1. Create a new project named SMPLBIND.MAK. Add the objects and properties listed in Table 10-3 to Form1 and save the form as SMPLBIND.FRM, as shown in Figure 10-7.

| Object | Property | Setting |
| --- | --- | --- |
| Form | Caption | "Form1" |
| | Name | Form1 |
| | ScaleMode | 3 'Pixel |
| | | |
| Data | Caption | "Data1" |
| | Name | Data1 |
| | Connect | "" |
| | DatabaseName | "GRAPHICS.MDB" |
| | Exclusive | 0 'False |
| | Height | 270 |
| | Left | 0 |

| Object | Property | Setting |
|--------|----------|---------|
|  | Options | 0 |
|  | ReadOnly | 0 'False |
|  | RecordSource | "Shapes" |
|  | Top | 3240 |
|  | Width | 4335 |
|  |  |  |
| Shape | FillStyle | 0 'Solid |
|  | Name | Shape1 |

**Table 10-3** Objects and properties for Form1

2. Create a new module named SMPLBIND.BAS. Add the following code to the General Section of SMPLBIND.BAS.

```
'
' Windows data types used
'
Type RECT
    left As Integer
    top As Integer
    right As Integer
    bottom As Integer
End Type
'
' Windows API functions used
'
Declare Function PtInRect Lib "User" (lpRect As RECT, ByVal ptRect As Any) As ⇐
Integer
'
' Masks for mouse button testing
'
Global Const LEFT_MOUSEBUTTON_MASK = 1
Global Const RIGHT_MOUSEBUTTON_MASK = 2
```

3. Add the following code to the General Declarations section of Form1.

```
'
' True when the Shape control should follow mouse moves
'
Dim Tracking    As Integer
'
' True when the Shape's color should be changed on button up
'
Dim ChangeColor As Integer
'
' Used to keep track of mouse movements
'
Dim prevX       As Integer
Dim prevY       As Integer
```

4. Add the following function to the General Declarations section of Form1. PointInShape uses the Windows API function PtInRect to detect when the mouse pointer is over the shape.

```
Function pointInShape (x As Integer, y As Integer) As Integer
    Dim shapeRect    As RECT
    Dim pt           As Long

    pt = (y * 65536) + x
    shapeRect.Top = Shape1.Top
    shapeRect.Left = Shape1.Left
    shapeRect.bottom = Shape1.Top + Shape1.Height
    shapeRect.right = Shape1.Left + Shape1.Width
    pointInShape = PtInRect(shapeRect, pt)
End Function
```

5. Add the following code to the Reposition event of Data1. The current record's fields are used to modify the Shape control's properties.

```
Sub Data1_Reposition ()
    '
    ' Set type of shape
    '
    Select Case Data1.Recordset!Shape
        Case "Rectangle"
            Shape1.Shape = 0
        Case "Square"
            Shape1.Shape = 1
        Case "Oval"
            Shape1.Shape = 2
        Case "Circle"
            Shape1.Shape = 3
        Case "Rounded Rectangle"
            Shape1.Shape = 4
        Case "Rounded Square"
            Shape1.Shape = 5
    End Select
    '
    ' Set shape's position and size
    '
    Shape1.Top = Data1.Recordset!Top
    Shape1.Left = Data1.Recordset!Left
    Shape1.Width = Data1.Recordset!Width
    Shape1.Height = Data1.Recordset!Height
    '
    ' Set shape's color
    '
    Shape1.FillColor = QBColor(Data1.Recordset!Color)
    Shape1.BorderColor = Shape1.FillColor
End Sub
```

6. Add the following code to the MouseDown event subroutine of Form1. If the mouse pointer is over the shape when either the left or right button is pressed, this subroutine either starts tracking or prepares to change the Shape's color.

```
Sub Form_MouseDown (Button As Integer, Shift As Integer, x As Single, y As Single)
    '
    ' Check for mouse in shape's rectangle
    '
    If pointInShape(CInt(x), CInt(y)) Then
        '
        ' Mouse over shape, is it the left button?
        '
        If (Button And LEFT_MOUSEBUTTON_MASK) Then
            '
            ' Yes ... shape tracks mouse
            '
            Tracking = True
            prevX = x
            prevY = y
            Shape1.FillStyle = 7
        Else
            '
            ' Right button, we're going to change colors
            '
            ChangeColor = True
        End If
    End If
End Sub
```

7. Add the following code to the Move event subroutine of Form1. If Tracking is True, then the Shape control is moved the same direction and distance as the mouse moved since the last MouseMove event.

```
Sub Form_MouseMove (Button As Integer, Shift As Integer, x As Single, y As Single)
    Dim dx As Integer
    Dim dy As Integer
    '
    ' Move shape with mouse?
    '
    If (Tracking = True) Then
        '
        ' Yes ...
        '
        Shape1.Left = Shape1.Left + (x - prevX)
        Shape1.Top = Shape1.Top + (y - prevY)
        prevX = x
        prevY = y
    End If
End Sub
```

8. Add the following code to the MouseUp event procedure of Form1. If the mouse is still over the Shape control, then the current record is modified to reflect either the Shape's new position or color.

```
Sub Form_MouseUp (Button As Integer, Shift As Integer, x As Single, y As Single)
    '
    ' Mouse up over shape?
    '
    If (pointInShape(CInt(x), CInt(y))) Then
        '
        ' Yes ... is it the left button?
        '
        If (Tracking And (Button And LEFT_MOUSEBUTTON_MASK)) Then
            '
            ' Yes ... start record edit
            '
            Data1.Recordset.Edit
            '
            ' Change Top and Left fields
            '
            Data1.Recordset!Top = Shape1.Top
            Data1.Recordset!Left = Shape1.Left
            '
            ' Make changes to database
            '
            Data1.Recordset.Update
            Shape1.FillStyle = 0
            Tracking = False
        Else
            '
            ' Right button up over shape, change color?
            '
            If (ChangeColor) Then
                '
                ' Yes ... start record edit
                '
                Data1.Recordset.Edit
                '
                ' Change color
                '
                Data1.Recordset!Color = (Data1.Recordset!Color + 1) Mod 16
                '
                ' Update record
                '
                Data1.Recordset.Update
                Shape1.FillColor = QBColor(Data1.Recordset!Color)
                ChangeColor = False
            End If
        End If
    End If
End Sub
```

### How It Works

The DataControl's Reposition event makes it easy to know when the current record has been changed. The Reposition event is fired regardless of what caused the current record to change. For instance, when the database is first opened (during Form_Load), the first record in the table becomes the current record. This causes the Reposition event to be fired during Form_Load. Also, when you use the DataControl's Move methods in your code, the Reposition event will be fired.

### Comments

The techniques used in this How-To can be used with any non bound control. The basic idea will always be the same. Code in the Reposition event detects changes in the current record and updates one or more controls; changes in control properties can be made to the database as they occur.

## 10.3 ● How do I...

## Bind an option button to a database field?

### Problem

I often have database fields that can contain one of some fixed number of values. A typical way to present this type of data to a user is to use a group of option buttons. An example of this type of field would be a field that can contain a number from 0 to 6, where 0 represents Sunday, 1 represents Monday, and so on. Naturally, users of my programs wouldn't be pleased if they had to enter numbers to represent days. So, for situations like this, I usually use a group of Option buttons so users can easily select one of the valid choices. A number of controls, like labels and check boxes, can be "bound" to some field in a database. Unfortunately, option buttons are not capable of being bound to database fields. Is there some way to simulate the binding of a group of option buttons to a field?

### Solution

Fortunately, there is a fairly straightforward way to simulate the binding of option buttons to a field. The basic idea is to bind a hidden Label control to the field of interest. Then, as each record is selected, the label's caption property will be updated. This fires the label's Change event, and the Caption properties value can be used to select the correct option button. Similarly,

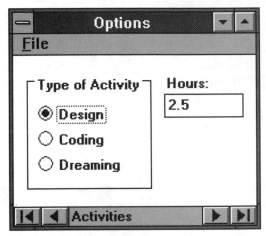

**Figure 10-8** The Options project in action

whenever the user selects one of the options, the option button's Change event is fired, and the appropriate value can be placed in the label's caption. Since the label is a bound control, it will take care of making sure the database is updated with the new value.

OPTIONS.MDB, the sample database for this How-To, contains two tables: Activities and Activity Types. Table 10-4 lists the database tables and fields in the OPTIONS.MDB.

| Table | Field | Datatype |
|---|---|---|
| Activities | Record ID | Counter |
| | Activity Type Code | Number |
| | Activity Hours | Number |
| Activity Types | Activity Type Code | Number |
| | Activity Description | Text |

**Table 10-4** OPTIONS.MDB tables and fields

The Options database implements a simple database to track activities. There are three types of activities: dreaming, design, and coding. The number of hours devoted to each type of activity are recorded in the activities table.

### Steps

Open and run OPTIONS.MAK. Figure 10-8 shows the Options project in action. There are three records in the sample database. You can use the

DataControl buttons, located at the bottom of the form, to move back and forth through the records in the database. As you move from record to record, the option button's values change to reflect the values of the underlying data. There is also a bound text box that contains the time devoted to each activity. You can change any of the records by selecting a different option or changing the contents of the text box.

1. Create a new project named OPTIONS.MAK. Add the objects and properties shown in Table 10-5 to Form1.

| Object | Property | Setting |
|--------|----------|---------|
| Form | Caption | "Options" |
| | Name | Form1 |
| Text box | DataField | "" |
| | DataSource | "Data1" |
| | Name | Text1 |
| Data | Autoload | -1 'True |
| | BackColor | &H00C0C0C0& |
| | Caption | "Activities" |
| | DatabaseName | "OPTIONS.MDB" |
| | Name | Data1 |
| | RecordSource | "Activity Types" |
| Label | Caption | "Label1" |
| | Name | Label1 |
| | DataField | "Activity Type Description" |
| | DataSource | "Data1" |
| Label | Caption | "Hours:" |
| | Name | Label2 |
| Frame | Caption | "Type of Activity" |
| | Name | Frame1 |

**Table 10-5** Form1's objects and properties

2. Create the option buttons shown in Table 10-6 on Frame1. Be sure to create the option buttons as child windows of Frame1. To do this, you select the option button tool from the toolbox with a single-click. Next, move the mouse pointer until it is over Frame1, press the left button, and hold it down. Finally, drag the mouse toward the bottom right corner of the screen and release the button when the option button is the right size.

| Object | Property | Setting |
|---|---|---|
| Option button | Caption | "Option1" |
| | Index | 0 |
| | Name | Option1 |
| Option button | Caption | "Option1" |
| | Index | 1 |
| | Name | Option1 |
| Option button | Caption | "Option1" |
| | Index | 2 |
| | Name | Option1 |

**Table 10-6** Frame1's option buttons

3. Use the menu design window to create the menu and menu items shown in Table 10-7.

| Object | Property |
|---|---|
| FileMenu | "&File" |
| —FileExit | "E&xit" |

**Table 10-7** Form1's menu

4. Add the following code to the General Declarations section of Form1.

```
Option Explicit
'
' The variable Loading is used to avoid acting on Label1's
' change events during form load.
'
Dim Loading As Integer
```

5. Add the following code to the Load event subroutine of Form1. During the Form_Load event subroutine, the option buttons have their caption property set to an Activity Description. After the captions are set, Data1's RecordSource is changed to Activities, Label1's DataField is changed to Activity Type Code.

```
Sub Form_Load ()
    Dim i As Integer
    '
    ' Set flag so Label1_Change won't do anything during form
    ' load.
    '
    Loading = True
    '
```

```
' Open the database and load records
'
Data1.Refresh
'
' Get the captions for option boxes
'
Do Until Data1.Recordset.EOF
    option1(i).Caption = Label1.Caption
    i = i + 1
    Data1.Recordset.MoveNext
Loop
'
' Switch record source to Activities Table ...
' label1's DataField needs to be removed so we
' don't get an error when the RecordSource changes
'
Label1.DataField = ""
Data1.RecordSource = "Activities"
'
' Refresh is required to create the new table view
'
Data1.Refresh
Text1.DataField = "Activity Hours"
Label1.DataField = "Activity Type Code"
Loading = False
End Sub
```

6. Add the following code to the Change event subroutine of Label1. Label1 serves two purposes in this program. During form load, Label1 is bound to the Activity Types table's Activity Type Description field. The form load routine accesses each row from the Activity Types table so that the options button's captions can be retrieved. Thus, when the form is loading the variable, Loading is set to True so that this subroutine does not try to set the option buttons captions.

```
Sub Label1_Change ()
    '
    ' During Form_Load this caption is used to retrieve the
    ' Description fields from Activity Types. While this
    ' is happening we ignore changes to caption1.
    '
    If (Loading = False) Then
        option1(Val(Label1.Caption) - 1).Value = True
    End If
End Sub
```

7. Add the following code to the Click event subroutine of Option1. This subroutine is called when the user clicks one of the option buttons. Setting Label1's Caption property will result in the bound field being changed when the current record changes.

```
Sub Option1_Click (index As Integer)
    Label1.Caption = Str(index + 1)
End Sub
```

8. Add the following code to the Click event subroutine of menu item FileExit.

```
Sub FileExit_Click ()
    End
End Sub
```

### How It Works

During design time, Data1's RecordSource property is set to Activity Types and Lable1's DataField is set to Activity Description. So when the Form_Load event subroutine executes we're all set to get the Activity Descriptions loaded into the option button's caption property.

Once the captions are loaded, Data1's RecordSource property is changed to Activities and Label1's DataField property is changed to Activty Type Code. Since the Activity Type Code contains values that are confined to either 1, 2, or 3, it is easy to determine which option button value to set to True. As the current record changes, Label1's change event subroutine is called. Label1's Caption property is converted to an integer and used as an index into the array of option buttons.

### Comments

Using hidden controls can be useful in a number of different situations. The technique used in this How-To to deal with controls that cannot be bound to database fields can be used for other types of controls just as easily. An example of this would be binding a scrollbar to a multivalued numeric field that had a wide range of possible values.

## 10.4 ● How do I...

**Complexity: Intermediate**

## Use the Grid control to view database tables?

### Problem

Relational database managers, like Access, organize data in tables. Tables can have rows and columns. The Grid control also has rows and columns, so it would appear to be an appropriate control to use for displaying database tables. Many of the standard Visual Basic controls can be bound to a field in a table. A bound control automatically displays fields in a database. Unfortunately, the Grid control is not a bound control. What do I need to do to display database tables using the Grid control?

### Solution

There is a reasonably straightforward way to use the Grid control as a database table viewer. The first thing you have to do is to create a Dynaset containing the rows and columns of interest. A Dynaset is a set of records that are accessed through the DataControl's RecordSet property. All you need to do to create a Dynaset is assign a database name to the DataControl's DatabaseName property, and specify a source of records by assigning either a database table name, database query, or SQL query to the RecordSource property of the DataControl.

After you've created a Dynaset you can use the DataControl.RecordSet's MoveFirst, MoveNext, MoveLast, and MovePrevious methods to access the individual rows in the set. At any given time there will be no more than one "current row" in a Dynaset. The RecordSet's Move methods determine what the current row is. The RecordSet's Fields property lets you access the fields in the current record. The MoveNext method is used to iterate over the records in a Dynaset. Then each record in the Dynaset and the Fields collection is used to load Grid cells.

### Steps

Open and run DBGRID.MAK. Figure 10-9 shows the Dbgrid project in action. Use the File Open... menu item to select a database. The database's tables are listed in the list box that appears on the left side of the form. You can display the contents of a table by double-clicking its name in the tables list box.

1. Create a new project named DBGRID.MAK. Add the objects and properties shown in Table 10-8 to Form1.

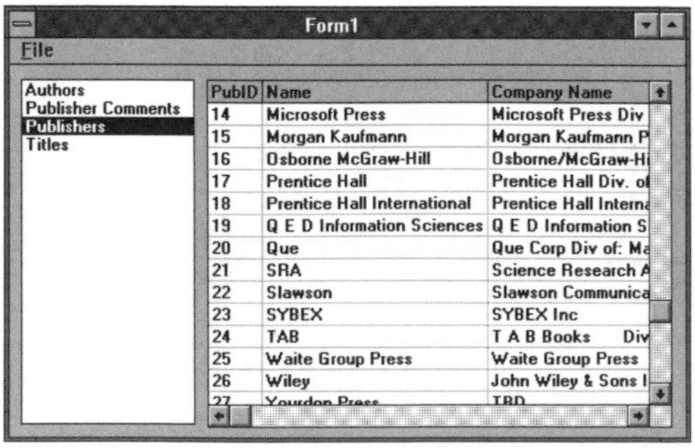

**Figure 10-9** The DBGRID program in action

| Object | Property | Setting |
|--------|----------|---------|
| Form | Caption | "Form1" |
| | Name | Form1 |
| OpenDialog | Prop1234 | 228 |
| | DefaultExt | "*.mdb" |
| | DialogType | 0 'Open Dialog |
| | FileMustExist | -1 'True |
| | Filter | "Access Database (*.mdb)\|*.mdb\|" |
| | Name | Grid1 |
| | PathMustExist | -1 'True |
| | ReadOnly | -1 'True |
| | Title | "Open Database" |
| Data | Autoload | -1 'True |
| | Name | Data1 |
| | Visible | 0 'False |
| List box | Height | 2565 |
| | Name | TablesListBox |
| Grid | Cols | 10 |
| | FixedCols | 0 |
| | FixedRows | 1 |
| | Name | Grid1 |
| | Rows | 10 |

**Table 10-8** Objects and properties for Form1

2. Use the menu design window to create the menu and menu items shown in Table 10-9.

| Name | Caption | Shortcut |
|------|---------|----------|
| FileMenu | "&File" | |
| ---FileOpen | "&Open Database..." | F2 |
| ---FileMenuSep1 | "-" | |
| ---FileExit | "E&xit" | |

**Table 10-9** DBGRID menu

3. Create a new module named DBGRID.BAS. Add the following code to the Global Declarations section of DBGRID.BAS.

```
'
' Windows API functions used
'
Declare Function GetTextExtent Lib "GDI" (ByVal hDC As Integer, ByVal ⇐
lpString As String, ByVal nCount As Integer) As Long
Declare Function GetDC Lib "User" (ByVal hWnd As Integer) As Integer
Declare Function ReleaseDC Lib "User" (ByVal hWnd As Integer, ByVal hDC ⇐
As Integer) As Integer
```

4. Add the following code to the Global Declarations section of Form1.

```
Option Explicit
```

5. Add the following code to the Click event subroutine of menu item FileOpen. When the user selects a database this subroutine clears the existing contents of TablesListBox and then adds table names from the database to it.

```
Sub FileOpen_Click ()
    Dim tableIndex   As Integer
    Dim wRtn         As Integer
    '
    ' Execute the file open dialog
    '
    OpenDialog1.File = ""
    OpenDialog1.DoIt = True
    '
    ' Bail out if no file specified
    '
    If (OpenDialog1.File = "") Then
       Exit Sub
    End If
    '
    ' Let form repaint where dialog box was removed
    '
    DoEvents
    '
    ' Assign database name
    '
    Data1.DatabaseName = OpenDialog1.File
    '
    ' Create DynaSet
    '
    Data1.Refresh
    '
    ' Clear the list of tables
    '
    TablesListBox.Clear
    '
    ' Load list with tables from current database
    '
```

*continued on next page*

*continued from previous page*

```
    For tableIndex = 0 To Data1.Database.TableDefs.Count - 1
        '
        ' Skip Acess's private tables
        '
        If (Left$(Data1.Database.TableDefs(tableIndex).Name, 4) <> "MSys") ⇐
Then
            TablesListBox.AddItem Data1.Database.TableDefs(tableIndex).Name
        End If
    Next
    '
    ' Select first item in the list
    '
    TablesListBox.ListIndex = 0
End Sub
```

6. Add the following code to the Click event subroutine of TablesListBox. This subroutine first empties the Grid control and then refills it with rows from the selected table. As the column titles and text are loaded the width required for each column is calculated so that the user will be able to view the contents of each field in the database without resizing the columns manually.

```
Sub TablesListBox_Click ()
    Dim i           As Integer
    Dim attribs     As Integer
    Dim textLen     As Long
    Dim fieldName   As String
    Dim hdcGrid     As Integer
    Dim wRtn        As Integer
    Dim rowText     As String
    Dim colText     As String
    Dim firstRow    As Integer
    Dim colWidths() As Integer
    '
    ' This could take a while, display hourglass
    '
    Screen.MousePointer = 11
    '
    ' Use name of table as index into TableDefs collection
    '
    Data1.RecordSource = Data1.Database.TableDefs(TablesListBox.Text)
    Data1.Refresh
    Grid1.Cols = Data1.RecordSet.Fields.Count
    '
    ' Toss old contents of grid
    '
    Grid1.Rows = 2
    '
    ' Select row 0 so the column titles can be loaded
    '
    Grid1.Row = 0
```

```
'
' Size the colWidths array
'
ReDim colWidths(Grid1.Cols) As Integer
'
' Get device context for the Grid
'
hdcGrid = GetDC(Grid1.hWnd)
'
' Put column titles in first row and keep track of
' the width of each so that the columns can be sized
' later
'
For i = 0 To Grid1.Cols - 1
   Grid1.Col = i
   fieldName = Data1.RecordSet.Fields(i).Name
   Grid1.Text = fieldName
   colWidths(i) = GetTextExtent(hdcGrid, fieldName, Len(fieldName)) And ⇐
&HFFFF&
Next
'
' Set flag for special handling of first row
'
firstRow = True
'
' Load records from the current table into the grid
'
Do While Data1.RecordSet.EOF = False
   rowText = ""
   For i = 0 To Grid1.Cols - 1
      '
      ' If there is no value assigned to the current row's
      ' field supply a blank string
      '
      If (IsNull(Data1.RecordSet.Fields(i).Value)) Then
         colText = " "
      '
      ' Otherwise use the field's value
      '
      Else
         colText = Data1.RecordSet.Fields(i).Value
      End If
      rowText = rowText & colText & Chr$(9)
      '
      ' Keep track of the length of the longest string seen
      ' in each column
      '
      textLen = GetTextExtent(hdcGrid, colText, Len(colText)) And &HFFFF&
      If (textLen > colWidths(i)) Then
         colWidths(i) = textLen
      End If
   Next
```

*continued on next page*

*continued from previous page*

```
        '
        ' Add new row to grid, the first non-fixed row has to
        ' be handled as a special case
        '
        If (firstRow = True) Then
            Grid1.SelStartRow = 1
            Grid1.SelEndRow = 1
            Grid1.SelStartCol = 0
            Grid1.SelEndCol = Grid1.Cols - 1
            Grid1.Clip = rowText
            firstRow = False
        Else
            Grid1.AddItem Left$(rowText, Len(rowText) - 1)
        End If
        '
        ' Move to the next row
        '
        Data1.RecordSet.MoveNext
    Loop
    '
    ' Now size each column so that the contents of each row
    ' will be visible
    '
    For i = 0 To Grid1.Cols - 1
        Grid1.ColWidth(i) = colWidths(i) * Screen.TwipsPerPixelX
    Next
    '
    ' Release the Grid's device context
    '
    wRtn = ReleaseDC(Grid1.hWnd, hdcGrid)
    '
    ' Return the mouse pointer to normal
    '
    Screen.MousePointer = 0
End Sub
```

7. Add the following code to the Click event subroutine of the FileExit menu item.

```
Sub FileExit_Click ()
    End
End Sub
```

### How It Works

The DataControl makes it easy to iterate over the rows of a Dynaset. After setting the DatabaseName and RecordSource properties, it's really simple to access each row by using the MoveNext method. When iterating over a Dynaset like this, there are a couple of important points to be aware of. First, after the DataControl's Refresh method has been executed, the current row will be the first row in the RecordSet, so the fields for the first row are ready to be accessed. Second, the DataControl.RecordSet's EOF property will be set to True if the current row is the last row in the Dynaset and the MoveNext method is executed. The basic strategy for iterating over a set of rows therefore involves four steps:

1. Select the first row as the current row.
2. Access the fields of the current row.
3. Move to the next row.
4. If EOF is not True, repeat starting from step 2.

The Grid control requires a little attention to make it perform as required by this project. The Grid control demands that the total number of rows always be one more than the number of fixed rows. This makes it impossible to delete all of the non-fixed rows from a grid by setting the Rows property to 1. So, when loading the Grid with rows, the first non-fixed row is handled differently than the rest. The first row is loaded by selecting all of its columns and assigning values to the columns, using the Clip property. The remaining rows can easily be added by using the Grid's AddItem method.

### Comments

This How-To demonstrates the basic techniques required to access the rows and fields of a Dynaset, as well as showing how to use the Grid control to display the contents of a Dynaset. This How-To also shows how to use the Windows API function GetTextExtent to determine the length of text fields.

## 10.5  How do I...

**Complexity: Easy**

### Store pictures in a database?

### Problem

I have a large number of bitmaps and icons that I would like to keep track of. It would be ideal if I could easily browse through the bitmaps and icons. I would also like to have a description, and perhaps other information, stored with them. Can I use VB to store pictures in a database?

### Solution

It's quite easy to store pictures in a database using the DataControl and a Picture control. Bound controls, like the Picture, Text, and Label controls, take care of displaying and modifying fields in a table. To bind a control to a table's field, you simply set the control's DataSource and DataField properties. As you move around in the database, the current record changes. Whenever the current record changes, the bound control will update its contents from the new current record.

This How-To uses a simple database with one table, named "Pictures". The Pictures table has only three fields: PictureID, Picture, and Description. The first field, PictureID, is a 32-bit Counter field. In Access Counters are used to generate unique identifiers for records. When you create a new record, the Access engine automatically creates a unique value for each Counter field in the record. It is often useful to use a Counter as the primary key for a table. There are two reasons for this. First, by using a Counter, you guarantee that each record has a unique value for its primary key (which is required). Second, the relatively short 32-bit field makes a good key to use for joining tables.

The second field in the Pictures table is named Picture. The Picture field is a long binary field. Long binary fields can store virtually any type of data. In this How-To, the contents of a bound picture control will be stored in the Picture field.

The third field in the Pictures table is named Description. The Description field is a text field capable of holding up to 64 bytes. The contents of the Description field are bound to a text control. Changes to the contents of the text edit control are written to the database.

### Steps

Open and run PICTBASE.MAK. Figure 10-10 shows the Pictbase project running. Click on the New... button on the right side of the toolbar. You can then select a bitmap, icon, or metafile. After you select a file, the program creates a new record. The new record's description is initially set to the name of the file from which the record's picture was created. You can change the description by changing the contents of the textbox on the left side of the toolbar.

1. Create a new project named PICTBASE.MAK. Add the objects and properties shown in Table 10-10 to Form1 and save it as PICTBASE.FRM.

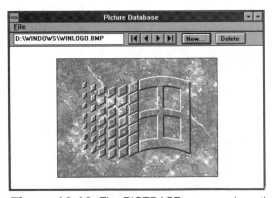

**Figure 10-10** The PICTBASE program in action

| Object | Property | Setting |
|---|---|---|
| Form | Caption | "Picture Database" |
| | Name | Form1 |
| Picture box | BackColor | &H00C0C0C0& |
| | FillColor | &H00C0C0C0& |
| | FillStyle | 0 'Solid |
| | Name | Picture1 |
| Picture box | AutoRedraw | -1 'True |
| | AutoSize | -1 'True |
| | DataField | "Picture" |
| | DataSource | "Data1" |
| | Name | Pic |
| OpenDialog | CreatePrompt | 0 'False |
| | DefaultExt | "*.bmp,*.ico,*.wmf" |
| | DialogType | 0 'Open Dialog |
| | File | "" |
| | FileMustExist | -1 'True |
| | Filter | "Bitmap (*.bmp)\|*.bmp\|Icon(*.ico)\|*.ico\|Metafile (*.wmf)\|*.wmf\|" |
| | HideReadOnly | -1 'True |
| | Name | OpenDialog1 |
| | Title | "Open Picture" |

**Table 10-10** Objects and property settings for Form1

2. Create the objects and properties shown in Table 10-11 on top of Picture1. It is important that these objects be created on top of Picture1 so that they will be child windows of Picture1.

| Object | Property | Setting |
|---|---|---|
| Text box | DataField | "Description" |
| | DataSource | "Data1" |
| | Name | Text1 |
| Data | Autoload | -1 'True |
| | DatabaseName | "PICTBASE.MDB" |
| | Name | Data1 |
| | RecordSource | "Pictures" |
| Command button | Caption | "Delete" |
| | Name | DeleteRecord |

*continued on next page*

*continued from previous page*

| Object | Property | Setting |
| --- | --- | --- |
| Command button | Caption | "New..." |
| | Name | NewRecord |

**Table 10-11** Objects and properties for Picture1

3. Use the menu design window to create the menu shown in Table 10-12.

| Menu Name | Menu Caption |
| --- | --- |
| FileMenu | "&File" |
| —FileExit | "E&xit" |

**Table 10-12** Menu for PICTBASE

4. Add the following code to the Global Declarations section of Form1.

```
Option Explicit
```

5. Add the following code to the Load event subroutine of Form1.

```
Sub Form_Load ()
    '
    ' Make sure that the pic control is never displayed on top of the toolbar
    '
    Picture1.ZOrder 0
    pic.Top = Picture1.Height
    pic.Left = 0
    Data1.Refresh
    '
    ' If there aren't any pictures in the database disable the
    ' DeleteRecord command and hide the picture box which looks dumb without
    ' anything in it
    '
    If (Data1.Recordset.BOF = True And Data1.Recordset.EOF = True) Then
        DeleteRecord.Enabled = False
        pic.Visible = False
    End If
End Sub
```

6. Add the following code to the Resize event subroutine of Form1. Whenever the form's size changes, we make sure that Picture1 covers the entire width of the client area. Picture1 is placed slightly to the left of the client area, and made slightly larger so that the one pixel border won't be visible on either the right or the left. The border has been left on the top and bottom since toolbars almost always have a thin line across the top and bottom.

```
Sub Form_Resize ()
   Picture1.Left = -Screen.TwipsPerPixelX
   Picture1.Width = Form1.ScaleWidth + (2 * Screen.TwipsPerPixelX)
   Pic_Resize
End Sub
```

7. Add the following code to the Resize event subroutine of Pic. This subroutine centers each record's picture on Form1's client area.

```
Sub Pic_Resize ()
   Dim useableWidth As Integer
   Dim useableHeight As Integer

   useableWidth = Form1.ScaleWidth
   useableHeight = Form1.ScaleHeight - Picture1.Height

   pic.Left = (useableWidth - pic.Width) / 2
   pic.Top = ((useableHeight - pic.Height) / 2) + Picture1.Height
End Sub
```

8. Add the following code to the Click event subroutine of the NewRecord command button. This is where new records are added to the database. First, the common dialog's Open dialog is used to select a bitmap, icon, or metafile. If the user selects a file the AddNew method is invoked, the new record's fields are set and the database is updated. New records are always added at the end of the Dynaset, so MoveLast is invoked to display the newly created record.

```
Sub NewRecord_Click ()
   '
   ' Get filename from user
   '
   OpenDialog1.File = ""
   OpenDialog1.DoIt = True
   '
   ' Bail out, no filename specified
   '
   If (OpenDialog1.File = "") Then
      Exit Sub
   End If
   '
   ' Redraw form now that dialog box is gone, otherwise
   ' we might see a partially painted screen for quite a
   ' while as the database does its thing
   '
   Form1.Refresh
   '
   ' Create new record
   '
   Data1.Recordset.AddNew
   Data1.Recordset!Description = OpenDialog1.File
```

*continued on next page*

*continued from previous page*

```
    pic.Picture = LoadPicture(OpenDialog1.File)
    Data1.Recordset.Update
    Data1.Recordset.MoveLast
    '
    ' We've got at least one record so deletion is OK
    '
    DeleteRecord.Enabled = True
    pic.Visible = True
End Sub
```

9. Add the following code to the Click event subroutine of the DeleteRecord command button. In this subroutine, it is important to determine two things: whether the deleted record was at the end of the Dynaset, and whether the deleted record was the last record in the Dynaset. If the deleted record was not the last record in the Dynaset, then the MoveNext method will succeed and we'll be done. However, if the deleted record was last in the Dynaset, we need to back up to the new last record. The MoveLast method will take care of this, except in the case where the Dynaset has become empty. In this case the MoveLast method will generate an error; when this happens, we know the Dynaset is empty so the RecordDelete command button is disabled and the picture box is hidden.

```
Sub DeleteRecord_Click ()
    Data1.RecordSet.Delete
    On Error Resume Next
    Data1.RecordSet.MoveNext
    If (Err) Then
        If (Data1.RecordSet.EOF = True) Then
            Data1.RecordSet.MoveLast
            If (Data1.RecordSet.EOF = True) Then
                DeleteRecord.Enabled = False
                pic.Visible = False
            End If
        Else
            MsgBox Error$
        End If
    End If
End Sub
```

10. Add the following code to the Error event subroutine of Data1. When the database is first opened, an error is generated if there are no rows in Data1's Dynaset. This will be the case when the database has no records. By intercepting this error we can display a more informative error message than the default message.

```
Sub Data1_Error (DataErr As Integer, Response As Integer)
    If (DataErr = 3021) Then
        MsgBox "There are no pictures in the database"
```

```
      Response = 0
   End If
End Sub
```

11. Add the following code to the Click event subroutine of the FileExit menu item.

```
Sub FileExit_Click ()
   End
End Sub
```

### How It Works

It's interesting to note that there is almost no code in this project to actually deal with reading and writing database records. It is all handled automatically by the two bound controls, Pic and Text1. Almost all of the code in this project deals with handling the user interface, and exceptional conditions that may arise. Some care in handling record deletions is required. When a record is deleted the current record becomes undefined. Either a MoveNext, MovePrevious, MoveFirst, or MoveLast can be used to establish a new current record. Regardless of which method you choose, you still need to handle a couple of special cases. In this project, when a record is deleted, we try to move to the next record. This won't work if the record deleted was the last record in the set. When this happens, we try to move to the last record in the set; if this fails there are no more records so the DeleteRecord command button is disabled.

### Comments

With a few enhancements, this project could become a useful way to organize bitmaps and other graphical images. Probably the most immediate enhancement needed is some way to get a copy of an image out of the database so it can be used. One way to do this is by using the clipboard. You could add an Edit Copy menu item to the menu. Then, when the user selects the Edit Copy menu item, you can use standard clipboard techniques to copy the image to the clipboard. Finally, with the image on the clipboard, you can paste into a number of different programs, save it in a file, and so on.

Another useful enhancement would be to add a keyword search capability. Basically, the idea is this: Create a new table named Keywords with two fields, Keyword and PictureId. Then add to the user interface the ability to associate one or more keywords with a picture. For each keyword the user assigns to a picture, add the keyword and the picture id to the new table. Later, a simple SQL statement like

```
SELECT PictureID FROM Keywords WHERE Keyword = 'Environment'
```

can be used to find the pictures that have been associated with the keyword Environment.

## 10.6 ● How do I...

**Complexity: Easy**

## Detect when a database record is locked?

### Problem

I'm writing an application that will allow users on more than one machine to edit records in a networked database simultaneously. Sometimes one user will be editing a record when another user accesses it. Is there some way that my program can detect that a record is locked by another user?

### Solution

Visual Basic's DataControl does not provide any way to directly test whether a record is in use by another user. One way to detect that a record is in use is to start an edit using the RecordSet's Edit method. The Edit method returns an error if the current record is already being edited by another program.

In this How-To, the Edit method is executed each time a new record becomes the current record. If the new current record is locked by another program, the Edit method returns an error that lets us know.

### Steps

You will need to run two instances of the Locktest project in order to see how record locking works. Since you can run only one instance of an application in design mode, you will need to compile this project before running it.

Open LOCKTEST.MAK. Select Make Exe File... from the File menu and make an executable file named LOCKTEST.EXE. Use the Program Manager's File Run menu to run LOCKTEST.EXE. After LOCKTEST.EXE begins running, move it to a new location on the desktop. Use the Program Manager's File Run menu to start a second instance of LOCKTEST.EXE. Figure 10-11 shows two instances of LOCKTEST running.

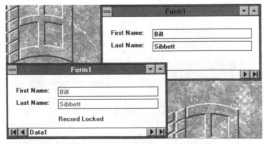

**Figure 10-11** Record locking example

The first instance of Locktest that you run will look like the one shown in the upper-right corner of Figure 10-11. The second instance of Locktest, shown in the lower-left corner of Figure 10-11, will display a flashing Record Locked message. Select the first instance of Locktest and use the DataControl's MoveNext button to move through the database records until the second instance stops flashing the Record Locked message.

Now, select the second instance of Locktest again and use the DataContol's MoveNext button to select the same record that is selected by the first instance. Once again you will see the flashing record locked message. Select the first instance of LOCKTEST and change the contents of one of the two text boxes, then press the MovePrevious button. The second instance's record locked message will stop flashing and its edit boxes will be updated to reflect the edits made with the first instance.

1. Create a new project named LOCKTEST.MAK. Add the objects and properties shown in Table 10-13 to Form1.

| Object | Property | Setting |
| --- | --- | --- |
| Form | Caption | "Form1" |
| | Name | Form1 |
| Timer | Name | Timer1 |
| Text box | DataField | "First Name" |
| | DataSource | "Data1" |
| | Name | Text1 |
| | Text | "" |
| Text box | DataField | "Last Name" |
| | DataSource | "Data1" |
| | Name | Text2 |
| | Text | "" |
| Data | Caption | "Data1" |
| | Connect | "" |
| | DatabaseName | "MULTUSER.MDB" |
| | Exclusive | 0 'False |
| | Name | Data1 |
| | Options | 0 |
| | ReadOnly | 0 'False |
| | RecordSource | "Select ID, [First Name], [Last Name] FROM Names ORDER BY City" |
| Label | Caption | "First Name:" |

*continued on next page*

*continued from previous page*

| Object | Property | Setting |
|--------|----------|---------|
|        | Name     | Label1  |
| Label  | Caption  | "Last Name:" |
|        | Name     | Label2  |
| Label  | Caption  | "Record Locked" |
|        | ForeColor | &H00FF0000& |
|        | Name     | Label3  |

**Table 10-13** Objects and properties for Form1

2. Add the following code to the Global Declarations section of Form1.

```
Option Explicit
Dim IgnoreReposition As Integer
```

3. Add the following code to Data1's Reposition event procedure. The Reposition event is fired each time the current record changes. Executing the Edit method will result in an error if the new current record is already locked, otherwise the current record is locked. The IgnoreReposition variable is needed here so that the current record's contents can be refreshed during the Timer1_Timer event procedure without testing to see if the current record is locked. The timer wouldn't be enabled unless we already knew the record was locked!

```
Sub Data1_Reposition ()
   '
   ' If we're searching for a specific record then
   ' ignore the reposition event
   '
   If (IgnoreReposition = True) Then
      Exit Sub
   End If
   '
   ' Trap errors
   '
   On Error Resume Next
   '
   ' Try to start an edit on the current record
   '
   Data1.Recordset.Edit
   If (Err = 3260) Then
      '
      ' The record is locked, disable text boxes
      '
      Text1.Enabled = False
      Text2.Enabled = False
      '
```

```
    ' Start the timer so we can flash the Locked
    ' message and retry
    '
    Timer1.Interval = 900
    Timer1.Enabled = True
    '
    ' Display record locked message
    '
    Label3.Visible = True
Else
    '
    ' We got the record ... enable the edit boxes
    '
    Text1.Enabled = True
    Text2.Enabled = True
    '
    ' Make sure the timer isn't running
    '
    Timer1.Enabled = False
    '
    ' Make sure record locked message isn't showing
    '
    Label3.Visible = False
End If
End Sub
```

4. Add the following code to Timer1's Timer event procedure. The timer is enabled whenever the current record is locked by another user. The timer does two jobs: flashing the record locked message with a duty cycle of 9/10 on and 1/10 off, and checking once a second to see if the record is still locked. Once the current record becomes unlocked, this subroutine refreshes the current record's contents, which may have been altered by the other application.

```
Sub Timer1_Timer ()
    '
    ' Each time the 900 millisecond timer runs out
    ' we check to see if the record is still locked
    '
    If Timer1.Interval = 900 Then
        On Error Resume Next
        Data1.Recordset.Edit
        If (Err = 3260) Then
            '
            ' When the record is still locked we hide
            ' the label for a tenth of a second
            '
            Timer1.Interval = 100
            Label3.Visible = False
        Else
```

*continued on next page*

*continued from previous page*

```
            '
            ' The record isn't locked any longer
            '
            Timer1.Enabled = False
            Label3.Visible = False
            Text1.Enabled = True
            Text2.Enabled = True
            '
            ' Refresh the current record by moving away from it and then back again
            '
            IgnoreReposition = True
            If (Data1.Recordset.EOF) Then
                Data1.Recordset.MoveNext
                Data1.Recordset.MovePrevious
            Else
                Data1.Recordset.MovePrevious
                Data1.Recordset.MoveNext
            End If
            IgnoreReposition = False
            '
            ' Invoke reposition just in case the record became
            ' locked again while we were fooling around with the
            ' current record
            '
            Data1_Reposition
            Screen.MousePointer = 0
        End If
    Else
        '
        ' The record locked off-time has expired, show the
        ' label again.
        '
        Timer1.Interval = 900
        Label3.Visible = True
    End If
End Sub
```

### How It Works

When the current record changes, the Reposition event is fired. In the Reposition event subroutine, an attempt is made to execute the Edit method. After the Edit method executes without error, the current record will be locked by the Access database engine. The current record remains locked until another record becomes the current record. If the current record is locked by another application, the Edit method will fail. When this happens, Timer1 is enabled. The Timer1 Timer event procedure flashes a message to indicate that the record is locked and checks once a second to see if the record is still locked. Once the record is unlocked, it is necessary to refresh our view of the current record. This is necessary since the other application may have changed its contents.

## Comments

You may have noticed that although LOCKTEST.EXE only invokes the Edit method on one record at a time a large number of records become locked. This is because internally, the database engine uses page locking instead of record locking. Page sizes are currently 4K bytes, although that could change in a future version of the database, and with records less than 4K bytes a number of them may be on one page. So, whenever the Edit method is executed for a given record, all of the other records on the same page are locked.

CHAPTER

# 11

# PROFESSIONAL
# EDITION
# DATA ACCESS

# How do I...

The Professional Edition of Visual Basic 3.0 provides a number of important database-related extensions. Using the Professional Edition you can create databases, add tables and fields, easily search for specific records, and more. Also, with the Professional Edition, you can use *object variables* containing various database objects, such as Dynasets, Snapshots, QueryDefs, Tables, TableDefs, and Indexes. You are probably already familiar with object variables; forms and most controls can be stored in object variables.

Object variables are defined just like any other Visual Basic variable. The following are examples of database object variable definitions:

```
Dim db       As Database
Dim ds       As Dynaset
Dim snap     As Snapshot
```

Database object variables can contain any valid database object. Assigning values to object variables has a slightly different syntax than assigning values to other variables. When you assign a value to an object variable, you use the Set keyword. The following example opens a database and assigns the database object to a Database object variable:

```
Set db = OpenDatabase( "mydb.db")
```

Once you've created a database object, you can use it to access the database. For example, the following code uses SQL to create a Dynaset using the db database object:

```
Set ds = CreateDynaset( "SELECT [Last Name], [First Name] FROM Tables" )
```

Likewise, you can use the object variable ds to access records in a database, as in the following example:

```
ds.FindFirst "'Last Name' = Thompson"
```

Dynasets have a filter property that you can use to create another Dynaset or a Snapshot. Snapshots are like Dynasets except that they reflect a view of the underlying table(s) at a given point in time, the time the Snapshot was created. Snapshots are faster to create than Dynasets, but their contents do not change if the underlying data changes. The following example creates a Snapshot containing a list of records all having the same value in the State field:

```
Set ds = CreateDynaset( "SELECT * FROM AddressTable" )
ds.Filter = "STATE = WA"
Set snap = ds.CreateSnapshot()
```

The Professional Edition also lets you manipulate the database definition objects TableDefs, FieldDefs, and Indexes. A database's TableDefs object describes each table in the database. Similarly, a FieldDefs object describes the fields in a given table. The Indexes collection contains the indexes that have been defined for a table. With the Professional edition you can modify any of these database object collections. The Append method is used to add a new table, field, or index, and the Delete method is used to delete them.

The How-Tos in this chapter show you how to use all of these features of the Visual Basic 3.0 Professional Edition and more.

## 11.1 Create a database

With the Professional Edition, it is not necessary to have Microsoft's Access database program to create databases. This can be important if you are planning on creating programs that will be used on machines that do not have Access installed. This How-To shows you the fundamentals of creating a database using Visual Basic only.

**11.2    Create a database from a text file description**

There's more than one way to create a database to use with Visual Basic. One way, as shown in How-To 11.1 Create a database, is to write a program that creates exactly the database you want. Another way to create a database is to use Microsoft's Access. Both of these approaches have drawbacks. In either case, there is too much manual labor involved, and too much room for error. This How-To shows you how to write a general-purpose database creation program that uses a simple text file to describe the database to create.

**11.3    Import text records into a database**

Another common requirement for database programs is the ability to import data into a database. How-To 11.3 shows you how to write a database import program.

**11.4    Find incorrectly spelled names in a database**

It is not unusual to use a person's name to find a record in a database. Unfortunately, it is also not unusual for a name to be misspelled. There have been a number of algorithms developed to get around this problem. This How-To uses the Soundex algorithm to help locate records containing people's names.

# 11.1  How do I...

## Create a database?

Complexity: Easy

### Problem

I would like to use the DataControl and Visual Basic's other data access capabilities in my applications. However, users who do not have Access installed on their machines have no way to create a database for my application to use. And even for those who do, I would rather not require that users of my application create a database using Access. What I'd really like to do is write a program that creates the database. How do I write a program to create a database using Visual Basic?

### Solution

The Professional Edition of Visual Basic 3.0 gives you all the tools you need to easily create a database for your application to use. You can declare new instances of database object variables using the New keyword. For instance, the following line declares a new database object variable named newDb:

```
Dim newDb As New Database
```

Once you've declared an object variable, you can assign it a value using the Set keyword. The following example creates a new database and assigns the database object to the newDb object variable:

```
Set newDb = CreateDatabase("mydb.mdb",language,options)
```

CreateDatabase accepts three arguments. The first argument to CreateDatabase, mydb.mdb in the example, contains the name of the database to create. Language, the second argument to CreateDatabase, specifies the language and code page to use with the new database. The third argument to CreateDatabase, options, contains bits that can be set to select various database creation options. The options available when using CreateDatabase are:

| Option Value | Meaning |
|---|---|
| 0 | Create Access 1.1 format database without encryption |
| 1 | Create Access 1.0 format database without encryption |
| 2 | Create Access 1.1 format database with encryption |
| 3 | Create Access 1.0 format database with encryption |

When the value of option is either 2 or 3, the database is encrypted when it is stored on disk. Encrypted databases can only be read by Access or Visual Basic.

### Steps

Open and run MAKEDB.MAK. The running program looks like Figure 11-1. You can experiment with creating databases by selecting options on the form and clicking on the Create button. Before creating the database a second time, you must delete the previous version using the Delete button.

1. Create a new project named MAKEDB.MAK. Add the objects and properties shown in Table 11-1 to Form1.

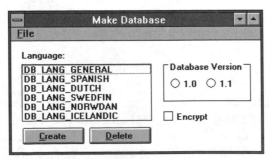

**Figure 11-1** Makedb in action

| Object | Property | Setting |
|--------|----------|---------|
| Form | Caption | "Make Database" |
| | Height | 3015 |
| | Left | 1335 |
| | Name | Form1 |
| | ScaleHeight | 2325 |
| | ScaleWidth | 5175 |
| | Top | 1905 |
| | Width | 5295 |
| Check box | Caption | "Encrypt" |
| | Height | 210 |
| | Left | 3135 |
| | Name | Check1 |
| | TabIndex | 4 |
| | Top | 1485 |
| | Width | 1815 |
| Frame | Caption | "Database Version" |
| | Height | 870 |
| | Left | 3135 |
| | Name | Frame1 |
| | TabIndex | 7 |
| | Top | 405 |
| | Width | 1830 |
| Command button | Caption | "&Create" |
| | Height | 345 |
| | Left | 225 |
| | Name | CmdCreate |
| | TabIndex | 5 |
| | Top | 1815 |
| | Width | 1280 |
| Command button | Caption | "&Delete" |
| | Height | 345 |
| | Left | 1605 |
| | Name | CmdDelete |
| | TabIndex | 6 |
| | Top | 1815 |
| | Width | 1280 |

*continued on next page*

*continued from previous page*

| Object | Property | Setting |
|---|---|---|
| Label | Caption | "Language:" |
| | Height | 225 |
| | Left | 210 |
| | Name | Label1 |
| | TabIndex | 3 |
| | Top | 195 |
| | Width | 1710 |
| List box | Height | 1200 |
| | Left | 210 |
| | Name | List1 |
| | TabIndex | 0 |
| | Top | 480 |
| | Width | 2685 |

**Table 11-1** Objects and properties for Form1

2. Add the objects and properties shown in Table 11-2 to Frame1.

| Object | Property | Setting |
|---|---|---|
| Option button | Caption | "1.1" |
| | Height | 240 |
| | Index | 1 |
| | Left | 900 |
| | Name | Option1 |
| | TabIndex | 2 |
| | Top | 375 |
| | Width | 675 |
| Option button | Caption | "1.0" |
| | Height | 240 |
| | Index | 0 |
| | Left | 150 |
| | Name | Option1 |
| | TabIndex | 1 |
| | Top | 375 |
| | Width | 660 |

**Table 11-2** Objects and properties for Frame1

3. Use the menu design window to add the menu shown in Table 11-3 to Form1.

| Menu Name | Caption |
| --- | --- |
| FileMenu | "&File" |
| ---FileExit | "E&xit" |

**Table 11-3** Form1's Menu

4. Create a new module named DATACONS.BAS. Add the following code to the General Declarations section of DATACONS.BAS. DATACONS.BAS contains definitions for all of the database constants. While not all of the constants declared here are used in this project, you will be able to use this file in applications you write.

```
'
' Data Access constants
'

'
' Option argument values (CreateDynaset, etc)
'
Global Const DB_DENYWRITE = &H1
Global Const DB_DENYREAD = &H2
Global Const DB_READONLY = &H4
Global Const DB_APPENDONLY = &H8
Global Const DB_INCONSISTENT = &H10
Global Const DB_CONSISTENT = &H20
Global Const DB_SQLPASSTHROUGH = &H40
'
' SetDataAccessOption
'
Global Const DB_OPTIONINIPATH = 1
'
' Field Attributes
'
Global Const DB_FIXEDFIELD = &H1
Global Const DB_VARIABLEFIELD = &H2
Global Const DB_AUTOINCRFIELD = &H10
Global Const DB_UPDATABLEFIELD = &H20
'
' Field Data Types
'
Global Const DB_BOOLEAN = 1
Global Const DB_BYTE = 2
Global Const DB_INTEGER = 3
Global Const DB_LONG = 4
Global Const DB_CURRENCY = 5
Global Const DB_SINGLE = 6
Global Const DB_DOUBLE = 7
```

*continued on next page*

*continued from previous page*

```
Global Const DB_DATE = 8
Global Const DB_TEXT = 10
Global Const DB_LONGBINARY = 11
Global Const DB_MEMO = 12
'
' TableDef Attributes
'
Global Const DB_ATTACHEXCLUSIVE = &H10000
Global Const DB_ATTACHSAVEPWD = &H20000
Global Const DB_SYSTEMOBJECT = &H80000002
Global Const DB_ATTACHEDTABLE = &H40000000
Global Const DB_ATTACHEDODBC = &H20000000
'
' ListTables TableType
'
Global Const DB_TABLE = 1
Global Const DB_QUERYDEF = 5
'
' ListTables Attributes (for QueryDefs)
'
Global Const DB_QACTION = &HF0
Global Const DB_QCROSSTAB = &H10
Global Const DB_QDELETE = &H20
Global Const DB_QUPDATE = &H30
Global Const DB_QAPPEND = &H40
Global Const DB_QMAKETABLE = &H50
'
' ListIndexes IndexAttributes values
'
Global Const DB_UNIQUE = 1
Global Const DB_PRIMARY = 2
Global Const DB_PROHIBITNULL = 4
Global Const DB_IGNORENULL = 8
'
' ListIndexes FieldAttributes value
'
Global Const DB_DESCENDING = 1  'For each field in Index
'
' CreateDatabase and CompactDatabase Language constants
'
Global Const DB_LANG_GENERAL = ";LANGID=0x0809;CP=1252;COUNTRY=0"
Global Const DB_LANG_SPANISH = ";LANGID=0x040A;CP=1252;COUNTRY=0"
Global Const DB_LANG_DUTCH = ";LANGID=0x0413;CP=1252;COUNTRY=0"
'
'            VB3 and Access 1.1 Databases
'
Global Const DB_LANG_SWEDFIN = ";LANGID=0x040C;CP=1252;COUNTRY=0"
Global Const DB_LANG_NORWDAN = ";LANGID=0x0414;CP=1252;COUNTRY=0"
Global Const DB_LANG_ICELANDIC = ";LANGID=0x040F;CP=1252;COUNTRY=0"
'
'            Access 1.0 Databases only
'
```

```
Global Const DB_LANG_NORDIC = ";LANGID=0x041D;CP=1252;COUNTRY=0"
'
' CreateDatabase and CompactDatabase options
'
Global Const DB_VERSION10 = 1      ' Microsoft Access Version 1.0
Global Const DB_ENCRYPT = 2        ' Make database encrypted.
Global Const DB_DECRYPT = 4        ' Decrypt database while compacting.
'
'Collating order values
'
' Sort by EFGPI rules (English, French, German,Portuguese, Italian)
Global Const DB_SORTGENERAL = 256
' Sort by Spanish rules
Global Const DB_SORTSPANISH = 258
' Sort by Dutch rules
Global Const DB_SORTDUTCH = 259
' Sort by Swedish, Finnish rules
Global Const DB_SORTSWEDFIN = 260
' Sort by Norwegian, Danish rules
Global Const DB_SORTNORWDAN = 261
' Sort by Icelandic rules
Global Const DB_SORTICELANDIC = 262
' Sort by Paradox international rules
Global Const DB_SORTPDXINTL = 4096
' Sort by Paradox Swedish, Finnish rules
Global Const DB_SORTPDXSWE = 4097
' Sort by Paradox Norwegian, Danish rules
Global Const DB_SORTPDXNOR = 4098
' Sort rules are undefined or unknown
Global Const DB_SORTUNDEFINED = -1
```

5. Add the following code to the General Declarations section of Form1.

```
Option Explicit
```

6. Add the following code to CmdCreate's Click event subroutine. Here's where the action is. First, the language and options variables are set using the values of List1, the option buttons, and Check1. Next, CreateDatabase is used to create the new database. After the database is created, a new table, with two fields, and an index, are added to the database.

```
Sub CmdCreate_Click ()
    Dim language           As String
    Dim options            As Integer
    Dim newDb              As Database
    Dim newTable           As New TableDef
    Dim custName           As New Field
    Dim custNumber         As New Field
    Dim custNumberIndex    As New Index
    '
    ' Get language identifier string
```

*continued on next page*

*continued from previous page*

```
'
Select Case List1.ListIndex
    Case 0: Case -1
        language = ";LANGID=0x0809;CP=1252;COUNTRY=0"
    Case 1:
        language = ";LANGID=0x040A;CP=1252;COUNTRY=0"
    Case 2:
        language = ";LANGID=0x0413;CP=1252;COUNTRY=0"
    Case 3:
        language = ";LANGID=0x040C;CP=1252;COUNTRY=0"
    Case 4:
        language = ";LANGID=0x0414;CP=1252;COUNTRY=0"
    Case 5:
        language = ";LANGID=0x040F;CP=1252;COUNTRY=0"
End Select
'
' Set option, 0 = Access 1.1 format, DB_VERSION10 = Access 1.0 format
'
If (option1(0).Value = True) Then
    options = DB_VERSION10
Else
    options = 0
End If
'
' Encrypt database?
'
If (Check1.Value = 1) Then
    options = options + DB_ENCRYPT
End If
'
' Create database
'
On Error Resume Next
Set newDb = CreateDatabase("makedb.mdb", language, options)
If (Err) Then
    MsgBox "Database Create Failed: " & Error$
    On Error GoTo 0
Else
    '
    ' We'll let Visual Basic handle any errors here
    '
    On Error GoTo 0
    '
    ' Creation ok ... set new table's name
    '
    newTable.Name = "Customers"
    '
    ' Create fields
    '
    custName.Name = "Customer Name"
    custName.Type = DB_TEXT
    custName.Size = 40
```

```
        custNumber.Name = "Customer Number"
        custNumber.Type = DB_LONG
        '
        ' Add fields to table
        '
        newTable.Fields.Append custName
        newTable.Fields.Append custNumber
        '
        ' Create an index for the table
        '
        custNumberIndex.Name = "Customer Number Index"
        custNumberIndex.Fields = "Customer Number"
        custNumberIndex.Primary = True
        '
        ' Add index to table
        '
        newTable.Indexes.Append custNumberIndex
        '
        ' Add table to database
        '
        newDb.TableDefs.Append newTable
        '
        ' Database created ... close it
        '
        newDb.Close
        '
        ' All's well that ends well
        '
        MsgBox "Database Created"
    End If
End Sub
```

7. Add the following code to CmdDelete's Click event subroutine.

```
Sub CmdDelete_Click ()
    Kill "makedb.mdb"
End Sub
```

8. Add the following code to Form1's Load event subroutine.

```
Sub Form_Load ()
    List1.AddItem "DB_LANG_GENERAL"
    List1.AddItem "DB_LANG_SPANISH"
    List1.AddItem "DB_LANG_DUTCH"
    List1.AddItem "DB_LANG_SWEDFIN"
    List1.AddItem "DB_LANG_NORWDAN"
    List1.AddItem "DB_LANG_ICELANDIC"
End Sub
```

### How It Works

As you can see from reading the CmdCreate_Click event subroutine code, creating a database and adding tables, fields, and indexes is really pretty simple. CreateDatabase creates a new, empty database. New tables, fields, and indexes are easily created by assigning values to objects created with the New keyword.

The database object, newDb in this project, has a collection named TableDefs. New tables are added to a database by simply assigning the table a name and executing the database object's Append method. Adding fields and indexes to a table is just as easy. For each field you want to add to a table, you simply create a new field object, using the New keyword, assign values to a few properties and use the table's Fields.Append method to add the field to the table. Indexes are also easily added to a table. As with fields, all you need to do is create a new instance of an index object, assign a few properties, and add the index to the table using the table's Indexes.Append method.

### Comments

This project shows how to easily create a database using Visual Basic. You can use this project as a template to create your own customized databases. All you need to do is copy the CmdCreate_Click subroutine into your application and add code to create the tables, fields and indexes you need. While this technique works well enough for simple databases, it can get tedious to create large databases this way. The next project, How-To 11.2 Create a database from a text file description, shows you how to create a more powerful, general-purpose program that you can use to create databases.

## 11.2 How do I...

## Create a database from a text file description?

### Problem

I often need to create a database from scratch. This happens frequently during program development, since my program fills the database with test data that must be purged before the next test can be run. Also, during program development I often want to change the structure of the database.

One way to re-create a database is to keep an empty copy of the database handy and simply copy it over the database that I've been using. This works well enough when I simply need an empty database, but doesn't help at all when I want to change the database structure. Using Access or writing a code every time I want to change the database structure is tedious and slow. How can I write a program that will create a database from a text-file description?

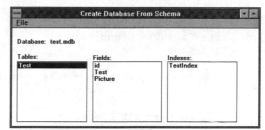

**Figure 11-2** Sample database schema file

### Solution

The Professional Edition of Visual Basic 3.0 provides the CreateDatabase function to create a database. As you will see later in this How-To, Visual Basic also provides a way to create new tables, fields, and indexes in your database.

Writing a new program, or modifying an old one, for each database you want to create would get old soon! So this How-To shows you how to read the contents of a text file containing a description of the database to create. Once you've got the project running, there's no end to the variety of databases you can easily create by writing a simple text file. The text file shown in Figure 11-2 contains a database *schema* that can be used with this project. A database schema is simply a description, or schematic, of a database.

```
'
' Schema file comments work just like Visual Basic comments
'
' First define the database name
'
Database VbHowTo.mdb
(
    '
    ' A table definition begins with the keyword Table followed by
    ' tables name
    '
    Table Customers
    (
        '
        ' Each table has one or more fields
        '
        ' Valid field types are:
        '
        '       Boolean      Byte        Integer       Long
        '       Currency     Single      Double        Date
        '       Binary       Text        LongBinary    Memo
        '
        Field ID (Long Counter)
        Field LastName (Text 20)
        Field FirstName (Text 20)
```

*continued on next page*

*continued from previous page*

```
    Field Married (Boolean)
    Field DOB (DAte)
    Field Picture (LongBinary)
    Field Notes (Memo)
    '
    ' Tables can also have indexes, an Index can provide a Unique key or
    ' a Primary key. Only one primary key is allowed per table.
    '
    Index IDIndex (ID Primary)
    Index LastNameIndex (LastName)
    Index FullNameIndex (LastName;FirstName Unique)
  )
  Table CustomerAddresses
  (
    Field CustomerID (Long Counter)
    Field Addr1 (Text 32)
    Field Addr2 (Text 32)
    Field City (Text 32)
    Field State (Text 2)
    Field Zip (Text 9)
    Index Zip (Zip)
    Index CustomerID (CustomerID Primary)
  )
)
```

### Steps

Open and run DBCREATE.MAK. Use Dbcreate's File Open... menu item to open the sample schema DBCREATE.SCH. The list boxes on Dbcreate's form show you which tables are defined, and for the currently selected table, which fields and indexes are defined for that table. After you've opened a schema you can create the new database by selecting the File Create Database menu item.

1. Create a new project named DBCREATE.MAK. Add the objects and properties shown in Table 11-4 to Form1. Position the controls so that the program will resemble Figure 11-3 when it is running.

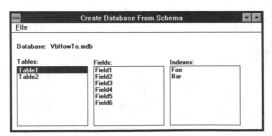

**Figure 11-3** The DBCREATE
project in action

| Object | Property | Setting |
|--------|----------|---------|
| Form | Caption | "Create Database From Schema" |
| | Name | Form1 |
| List box | Name | IndexesListBox |
| CommonDialog | DefaultExt | "*.sch" |
| | Name | CMDialog1 |
| | DialogTitle | "Open Schema" |
| | Filter | "Schema (*.sch)|*.sch" |
| List box | Name | FieldsListBox |
| List box | Name | TablesListBox |
| Label | Caption | "Indexes:" |
| | Name | Label1 |
| Label | Name | DbNameLabel |
| Label | Caption | "Database:" |
| | Name | Label1 |
| Label | Caption | "Fields:" |
| | Name | Label1 |
| Label | Caption | "Tables:" |
| | Name | Label1 |

**Table 11-4** Objects and properties for Form1

2. Use the menu design window to create the menu shown in Table 11-5.

| Menu Name | Caption |
|-----------|---------|
| FileMenu | "&File" |
| ---FileOpenSchema | "&Open Schema..." |
| ---FileSep1 | "-" |
| ---FileCreateDatabase | "&Create Database" |
| ---FileSep2 | "-" |
| ---FileExit | "E&xit" |

**Table 11-5** Form1's Menu

3. Create a new module named DBCREATE.BAS. Add the following code to the General Declarations section of DBCREATE.BAS.

```
Option Explicit
'
' Used during parsing as a single char pushback buffer
'
```

*continued on next page*

*continued from previous page*

```
Dim savedChar       As String
'
' Source line
'
Dim curLine         As String
'
' Current position in source line
'
Dim curLineIndex    As Integer
'
' Source line number, useful when printing error messages
'
Dim curLineNumber   As Integer
'
' Arbitrary limits on data structure sizes
'
Global Const MaxIndexesPerTable = 10
Global Const MaxFieldsPerTable = 32
Global Const MaxTablesPerDatabase = 32
'
' Information retrieved when parsing an Index statement
'
Type IndexDesc
    Name        As String
    Fields      As String
    Unique      As Integer
    Primary     As Integer
End Type
'
' Information retrieved when parsing a Field statement
'
Type FieldDesc
    Name        As String
    Type        As Integer
    Size        As Integer
    Attributes As Integer
End Type
'
' Information retrieved when parsing a Table statement
'
Type TableDesc
    Name                       As String
    fieldCount                 As Integer
    Fields(MaxFieldsPerTable)  As FieldDesc
    indexCount                 As Integer
    Indexes(MaxIndexesPerTable) As IndexDesc
End Type
'
' Used to keep track of the current position in various
' tables
'
Dim tableIndex As Integer
```

```
Dim fieldIndex As Integer
Dim indexesIndex As Integer
'
' After a successful schema parse these vars will be set
'
Global dbName As String
Global dbTablesCount As Integer
Global dbTables(MaxTablesPerDatabase) As TableDesc
'
' Windows API Functions
'
Declare Function SendMessage Lib "User" (ByVal hWnd As Integer, ByVal wMsg As ⇐
Integer, ByVal wParam As Integer, lParam As Any) As Long
'
' SendMessage constants
'
Global Const WM_USER = &H400
Global Const LB_RESETCONTENT = (WM_USER + 5)
'
' Visual Basic Data Access constants
'
' OPTIONS values
Global Const DB_DENYWRITE = &H1
Global Const DB_DENYREAD = &H2
Global Const DB_READONLY = &H4
Global Const DB_APPENDONLY = &H8
Global Const DB_INCONSISTENT = &H10
Global Const DB_CONSISTENT = &H20
Global Const DB_SQLPASSTHROUGH = &H40

' RecordSet Attributes
Global Const DB_UPDATABLE = &H1
Global Const DB_BOOKMARKABLE = &H2
Global Const DB_ROLLBACKABLE = &H4
Global Const DB_RESTARTABLE = &H8
Global Const DB_NOINSERTS = &H10

' SetDataAccessOption
Global Const DB_INITPATH = 1

' Field Attributes
Global Const DB_FIELDFIXED = &H1
Global Const DB_FIELDTAGGED = &H2
Global Const DB_FIELDNOTNULL = &H4
Global Const DB_FIELDVERSION = &H8
Global Const DB_FIELDCOUNTER = &H10
Global Const DB_FIELDUPDATABLE = &H20
Global Const DB_FIELDGRAPHIC = &H200

' Field Data Types
Global Const DB_BOOLEAN = 1
Global Const DB_BYTE = 2
```

*continued on next page*

*continued from previous page*

```
Global Const DB_INTEGER = 3
Global Const DB_LONG = 4
Global Const DB_CURRENCY = 5
Global Const DB_SINGLE = 6
Global Const DB_DOUBLE = 7
Global Const DB_DATE = 8
Global Const DB_BINARY = 9
Global Const DB_TEXT = 10
Global Const DB_LONGBINARY = 11
Global Const DB_MEMO = 12

' ListTables Attributes
Global Const DB_SYSTEMOBJECT = &H80000002
Global Const DB_TABLE = 1
Global Const DB_ATTACHEDTABLE = 6
Global Const DB_ATTACHEDODBC = 4
Global Const DB_QUERYDEF = 5
Global Const DB_QACTION = &HF0
Global Const DB_ATTACHEXCLUSIVE = &H40000000
Global Const DB_ATTACHSAVEPWD = &H20000000

' Query types
Global Const DB_QCROSSTAB = &H10
Global Const DB_QDELETE = &H20
Global Const DB_QUPDATE = &H30
Global Const DB_QAPPEND = &H40
Global Const DB_QMAKETABLE = &H50

' Index Attributes
Global Const DB_UNIQUE = 1
Global Const DB_PRIMARY = 2
Global Const DB_NONULLS = 3
Global Const DB_DESCENDING = 1

' CreateDatabase Language constants
Global Const DB_CREATE_GENERAL = ";LANGID=0x0809;CP=1252;COUNTRY=0"
Global Const DB_CREATE_SPANISH = ";LANGID=0x040A;CP=1252;COUNTRY=0"
Global Const DB_CREATE_DUTCH = ";LANGID=0x0413;CP=1252;COUNTRY=0"
'VB3 and Access 1.1 Databases
Global Const DB_CREATE_SWEDFIN = ";LANGID=0x040C;CP=1252;COUNTRY=0"
'VB3 and Access 1.1 Databases
Global Const DB_CREATE_NORWDAN = ";LANGID=0x0414;CP=1252;COUNTRY=0"
'VB3 and Access 1.1 Databases
Global Const DB_CREATE_ICELANDIC = ";LANGID=0x040F;CP=1252;COUNTRY=0"
'Access 1.0 Databases only
Global Const DB_CREATE_NORDIC = ";LANGID=0x041D;CP=1252;COUNTRY=0"
```

4. Add the following subroutine to the General Declarations section of DBCREATE.BAS. This subroutine is where the schema parsing starts. The first thing we expect to find in the schema file, ignoring comments and whitespace, is a Database statement. The Database statement must

be followed by a database name. The database name should be followed by an open-paren. Between the open-paren and the expected close-paren there may be one or more Table statements.

```
Function ParseSchema (filenum As Integer) As Integer
    Dim Token As String
    Dim result As Integer
    '
    ' Reset the current line number and table index
    '
    curLineNumber = 0
    tableIndex = 0
    '
    ' The first thing we expect in the source file (excluding
    ' whitespace and comments) is the DATABASE statement.
    '
    If (ExpectToken(filenum, "DATABASE") = False) Then
        ParseSchema = False
        Exit Function
    End If
    '
    ' Assume that the next token contains a valid database name
    '
    dbName = GetToken(filenum)
    '
    ' No tables are defined yet
    '
    dbTablesCount = 0
    '
    ' Next we expect to see an open paren.
    '
    If (ExpectToken(filenum, "(") = False) Then
        ParseSchema = False
        Exit Function
    End If
    '
    ' Assume success
    '
    result = True
    '
    ' We now expect to see zero or more Table statements
    '
    Do While Token <> ")" And result = True
        Token = UCase(GetToken(filenum))
        Select Case Token
            Case "TABLE"
                    result = ParseTable(filenum)
            Case ")"
            Case Else
                MsgBox "Error at line " & Format(curLineNumber) & ". ⇐
Expected either 'Table' or ')', got '" & Token & ".'"
                    result = False
```

*continued on next page*

*continued from previous page*

```
          End Select
     Loop
     '
     ' If there were no parsing errors save the number of tables
     ' parsed in dbTablesCount
     '
     If (result = True) Then
          dbTablesCount = tableIndex
     End If
     ParseSchema = result
End Function
```

5. Add the following function to the Global Declarations section of DBCREATE.BAS. This function is called from ParseSchema whenever the Table keyword is parsed out of the input file. The next token in the file is assumed to be the table's name. Following the table name we expect an open-paren, followed by one or more Field and Index statements, followed by a close-paren. When either a Field or Index keyword is found, the ParseField or ParseIndex function is called.

```
Function ParseTable (filenum As Integer) As Integer
     Dim Token     As String
     Dim result    As Integer
     Dim tableName As String
     '
     ' Assume that the next token is a valid table name
     '
     dbTables(tableIndex).Name = GetToken(filenum)
     dbTables(tableIndex).fieldCount = 0
     '
     ' We expect to see an open paren next
     '
     If (ExpectToken(filenum, "(") = False) Then
          ParseTable = False
          Exit Function
     End If
     '
     ' Assume success for the rest of the table parse
     '
     result = True
     fieldIndex = 0
     indexesIndex = 0
     '
     ' Each table contains zero or more Field or Index
     ' statements.
     '
     Do While Token <> ")" And result = True
          Token = UCase(GetToken(filenum))
          Select Case Token
             Case ")"
```

```
            Case "FIELD"
                    result = ParseField(filenum)
                    If (result = True) Then
                        fieldIndex = fieldIndex + 1
                    End If
            Case "INDEX"
                    result = ParseIndex(filenum)
                    If (result = True) Then
                        indexesIndex = indexesIndex + 1
                    End If
            Case Else
                    MsgBox "Error at line " & Format(curLineNumber) & ". ⇐
Expected either 'Field' or ')', got '" & Token & ".'"
                    result = False
        End Select
    Loop
    '
    ' If the parse was without error update the database
    ' tables information
    '
    If (result = True) Then
        dbTables(tableIndex).fieldCount = fieldIndex
        dbTables(tableIndex).indexCount = indexesIndex
        tableIndex = tableIndex + 1
    End If

    ParseTable = result
End Function
```

6. Add the following function to the General Declarations section of DBCREATE.BAS. This function is called by ParseTable when the Field keyword is read from the schema file. Each field definition consists of at least a Field name and a datatype. Text fields must also have a size parameter. Also, there are a number of field attributes that may be specified.

```
Function ParseField (filenum As Integer) As Integer
    Dim Token      As String
    Dim result     As Integer
    Dim fldSize    As Integer
    Dim fldType    As Integer
    Dim fldAttrib  As Integer
    '
    ' The next token is assumed to be a valid field name
    '
    dbTables(tableIndex).Fields(fieldIndex).Name = GetToken(filenum)
    '
    ' Field names must be followed by an open paren
    '
    If (ExpectToken(filenum, "(") = False) Then
```

*continued on next page*

*continued from previous page*

```
            ParseField = False
            Exit Function
        End If
        '
        ' Get the field type
        '
        result = True
        Token = UCase(GetToken(filenum))
        Select Case Token
            Case "BOOLEAN"
                fldType = DB_BOOLEAN
                fldSize = 1
            Case "BYTE"
                fldType = DB_BYTE
                fldSize = 1
            Case "INTEGER"
                fldType = DB_INTEGER
                fldSize = 2
            Case "LONG"
                fldType = DB_LONG
                fldSize = 4
            Case "CURRENCY"
                fldType = DB_CURRENCY
                fldSize = 8
            Case "SINGLE"
                fldType = DB_SINGLE
                fldSize = 4
            Case "DOUBLE"
                fldType = DB_DOUBLE
                fldSize = 8
            Case "DATE"
                fldType = DB_DATE
                fldSize = 8
            Case "BINARY"
                fldType = DB_BINARY
                fldSize = 0
            Case "TEXT"
                Token = GetToken(filenum)
                fldType = DB_TEXT
                fldSize = Val(Token)
            Case "LONGBINARY"
                fldType = DB_LONGBINARY
                fldSize = 0
            Case "MEMO"
                fldType = DB_MEMO
                fldSize = 0
            Case Else
                MsgBox "Invalid field type '" & Token & "', line " & ⇐
Format(curLineNumber) & "."
                result = False
        End Select

        Do While (result = True And Token <> ")")
```

```
        '
        ' Didn't get a close paren, so we should have a field
        ' attribute
        '
        Token = UCase(GetToken(filenum))
        Select Case Token
            Case "FIXED"
                fldAttrib = fldAttrib Or DB_FIELDFIXED
            Case "NOTNULL"
                fldAttrib = fldAttrib Or DB_FIELDNOTNULL
            Case "COUNTER"
                fldAttrib = fldAttrib Or DB_FIELDCOUNTER
            Case "UPDATABLE"
                fldAttrib = fldAttrib Or DB_FIELDUPDATABLE
            Case "GRAPHICS"
                fldAttrib = fldAttrib Or DB_FIELDGRAPHIC
            Case ")"
            Case Else
                MsgBox "Invalid Field Attribute: " & Token & " in line" &⇐
Str(curLineNumber) & "."
                result = False
        End Select
    Loop
    '
    ' Save definition of this field
    '
    If (result = True) Then
        dbTables(tableIndex).Fields(fieldIndex).Size = fldSize
        dbTables(tableIndex).Fields(fieldIndex).Type = fldType
        dbTables(tableIndex).Fields(fieldIndex).Attributes = fldAttrib
    End If
    ParseField = result
End Function
```

7. Add the following code to the General Declarations section of DBCREATE.BAS. This function is called by ParseTable when the Index keyword is found. An index definition must have a name and one or more key field names. The Unique and Primary attributes may also be specified for a field.

```
Function ParseIndex (filenum As Integer) As Integer
    Dim Token      As String
    Dim result     As Integer
    '
    ' The next token is assumed to be a valid index name
    '
    dbTables(tableIndex).Indexes(indexesIndex).Name = GetToken(filenum)
    '
    ' We expect an open paren to follow the index name
    '
    If (ExpectToken(filenum, "(") = False) Then
        ParseIndex = False
```

*continued on next page*

*continued from previous page*

```
            Exit Function
    End If
    '
    ' Assume that all goes well
    '
    result = True
    '
    ' The next token is assumed to be one or more fields to be
    ' used as the index key. Multiple fields are joined by a ';'
    ' and have no spaces between them.
    '
    Token = GetToken(filenum)
    dbTables(tableIndex).Indexes(indexesIndex).Fields = Token
    Token = GetToken(filenum)
    '
    ' If the current token is not a ')' then we expect to
    ' it to be an index attribute.
    '
    If (Token <> ")") Then
        Select Case UCase(Token)
            Case "UNIQUE"
                dbTables(tableIndex).Indexes(indexesIndex).Unique = True
            Case "PRIMARY"
                dbTables(tableIndex).Indexes(indexesIndex).Primary = ⇐
True
            Case Else
                MsgBox "Invalid token '" & Token & "'. Line number" & ⇐
Str(curLineNumber)
                result = False
        End Select
        '
        ' One index attribute is allowed. It must be followed by a close
        ' paren.
        '
        Token = GetToken(filenum)
        If (Token <> ")") Then
            MsgBox "Invalid token '" & Token & "'. Line number" & ⇐
Str(curLineNumber) & ". Expected token ')'."
            result = False
        End If
    End If
    ParseIndex = result
End Function
```

8. Add the following function to the General Declarations section of DBCREATE.BAS. The GetToken function is called whenever another token is needed.

```
Function GetToken (filenum As Integer) As String
    Dim Token As String
    Dim char  As String
    '
    ' Skip leading whitespace
```

```
    '
    SkipWhitespace filenum
    '
    ' Get the next character
    '
    char = GetChar(filenum)
    '
    ' Skip comment lines
    '
    Do While char = "'"
        FlushLine (filenum)
        char = GetChar(filenum)
    Loop
    '
    ' The '(' and ')' characters are  tokens
    '
    If (char = "(" Or char = ")") Then
        GetToken = char
    Else
        '
        ' Any string of characters followed by space, ', (, ),
        ' or tab is a token.
        '
        Do While char <> "" And InStr(" '()" & Chr$(9), char) = 0
            Token = Token & char
            char = GetChar(filenum)
        Loop
        '
        ' Push the character following the token back onto
        ' the character stream.
        '
        UngetChar (char)
        GetToken = Token
    End If
End Function
```

9. Add the following function to the General Declarations section of DBCREATE.BAS. ExpectToken is called whenever we know what token should be next in the input file. If the next token parsed from the input file does not match the expected token, an error message is displayed and an error is returned to the calling function.

```
Function ExpectToken (filenum As Integer, expected As String) As Integer
    Dim i        As Integer
    Dim Token    As String
    '
    ' Get the next token
    '
    Token = UCase(GetToken(filenum))
    '
    ' If no token is returned we've reached the end-of-file
    '
```

*continued on next page*

*continued from previous page*

```
    If (Token = "") Then
        MsgBox "Unexpected end of file"
        ExpectToken = False
        '
        ' Got a token, see if it was what we expected
        '
    ElseIf (UCase(expected) <> Token) Then
        MsgBox "Expected " & expected & " at line " & Str(curLineNumber)
        ExpectToken = False
    Else
        ExpectToken = True
    End If
End Function
```

10. Add the following code to the General Declarations section of DBCREATE.BAS. GetChar is called by GetToken to get the next character from the input stream.

```
Function GetChar (filenum As Integer) As String
    '
    ' If a character has been pushed back return it
    '
    If (savedChar <> "") Then
        GetChar = savedChar
        savedChar = ""
        Exit Function
    End If
    '
    ' If the current line is empty read a new one
    '
    If (curLine = "" Or curLineIndex > Len(curLine)) Then
        If (GetLine(filenum) = False) Then
            GetChar = ""
            Exit Function
        End If
    End If
    '
    ' Return the next char from the current line
    '
    GetChar = Mid$(curLine, curLineIndex, 1)
    curLineIndex = curLineIndex + 1
End Function
```

11. Add the following function to the General Declarations section of DBCREATE.BAS. GetLine is called by GetChar when current line is empty. Leading spaces, tabs, and other irrelevant characters are discarded before this function returns.

```
Function GetLine (filenum)
    Do While (Not EOF(filenum)) And (curLine = "" Or curLineIndex > ⇐
Len(curLine))
```

```
        Line Input #filenum, curLine
        curLineNumber = curLineNumber + 1
        curLineIndex = 1
        '
        ' Trim leading spaces, tabs, and other meaningless chars from
        ' the line
        '
        Do While curLineIndex < Len(curLine) And Mid$(curLine, ⇐
curLineIndex, 1) <= " "
            curLineIndex = curLineIndex + 1
        Loop
    Loop
    GetLine = Not curLine = ""
End Function
```

12. Add the following subroutine to the General Declarations section of DBCREATE.BAS. FlushLine is called by GetToken whenever a comment character is seen. This subroutine changes the curLineIndex so that the remaining characters on the line are skipped. The next call to GetChar will find an empty line, and so a call will be made to GetLine to read in the next line of the file.

```
Sub FlushLine (filenum)
    '
    ' Advance to the end of the current line. The next
    ' call to GetChar will cause a new line to be read.
    '
    savedChar = ""
    curLineIndex = Len(curLine) + 1
End Sub
```

13. Add the following subroutine to the General Declarations section of DBCREATE.BAS. This subroutine is called by GetToken to skip any whitespace that may precede a token in the input file.

```
Sub SkipWhitespace (filenum As Integer)
    Dim char As String
    '
    ' Skip characters until either eof (char = "") or
    ' we've got a char > space
    '
    char = GetChar(filenum)
    Do While char <> "" And char <= " "
        char = GetChar(filenum)
    Loop
    '
    ' Put the first non-space character back in the input
    ' stream
    '
    UngetChar (char)
End Sub
```

14. Add the following subroutine to the General Declarations section of DBCREATE.BAS. UngetChar is called whenever a character has been read that isn't needed yet. This happens when searching for the end of a token, and when skipping whitespace in the input stream.

```
Sub UngetChar (char As String)
    '
    ' Push char back onto input stream
    '
    savedChar = char
End Sub
```

15. Add the following code to the General Declarations section of Form1.

```
Option Explicit
```

16. Add the following code to the FileOpenSchema menu item's Click event subroutine. When the user chooses the File Open... menu item, this event procedure is called. If the user selects a schema filename, the file is opened and ParseSchema is called. If the schema was successfully parsed, the tables defined by the schema will be loaded into the TablesListBox.

```
Sub FileOpenSchema_Click ()
    Dim fileNum     As Integer
    Dim result      As Integer
    Dim t, f        As Integer
    Dim fd          As FieldDesc
    Dim wRtn        As Integer
    '
    ' Get a filenumber to use
    '
    fileNum = FreeFile
    '
    ' Get the schema filename from the user
    '
    CMDialog1.Filename = ""
    CMDialog1.Action = 1
    If (CMDialog1.Filename = "") Then
        Exit Sub
    End If
    '
    ' Allow the background to repaint after the dialog box
    ' goes away
    '
    DoEvents
    '
    ' Open the schema file
    '
    Open CMDialog1.Filename For Input As fileNum
    '
    ' Go parse the schema
```

```
    result = ParseSchema(fileNum)
    '
    ' Zap the TablesListBox contents
    '
    wRtn = SendMessage(TablesListBox.hWnd, LB_RESETCONTENT, 0, 0)
    '
    ' If we got a useable schema add table names to the
    ' TablesListBox
    '
    If (result = True) Then
        DbNameLabel.Caption = dbName
        For t = 0 To dbTablesCount - 1
            TablesListBox.AddItem dbTables(t).Name
        Next
        TablesListBox.ListIndex = 0
    Else
        '
        ' Bad schema, clear out the Fields and Indexes list boxes also
        '
        wRtn = SendMessage(FieldsListBox.hWnd, LB_RESETCONTENT, 0, 0)
        wRtn = SendMessage(IndexesListBox.hWnd, LB_RESETCONTENT, 0, 0)
    End If
    Close fileNum
End Sub
```

17. Add the following code to the Click event subroutine of TablesListBox. Whenever a table name is selected in the TablesListBox, its fields and indexes are listed in the FieldsListBox and IndexesListBox.

```
Sub TablesListBox_Click ()
    Dim fd      As FieldDesc
    Dim f       As Integer
    Dim i       As Integer
    Dim t       As Integer
    Dim wRtn    As Integer
    '
    ' Clear Fields and Indexes listboxs
    '
    wRtn = SendMessage(FieldsListBox.hWnd, LB_RESETCONTENT, 0, 0)
    wRtn = SendMessage(IndexesListBox.hWnd, LB_RESETCONTENT, 0, 0)
    t = TablesListBox.ListIndex
    '
    ' Fill FieldsListBox with current tables field names
    '
    For f = 0 To dbTables(t).fieldCount - 1
        fd = dbTables(t).Fields(f)
        FieldsListBox.AddItem fd.Name
    Next
    '
    ' Fill IndexesListBox with current tables index names
    '
    For i = 0 To dbTables(t).indexCount - 1
        IndexesListBox.AddItem dbTables(t).Indexes(i).Name
    Next
End Sub
```

18.  Add the following code to the FileCreateDatabase menu item's Click event subroutine. When the user selects the Create Database menu item, this subroutine is called. First, the CreateDatabase function is used to create a new database. If an invalid database name was specified in the schema file's Database statement, an error will be generated here. An error will also be generated if the database already exists. Code to handle these possibilities could be added to the parser functions. Once the database has been created, it is a simple matter to create the fields and indexes using information that was parsed from the schema file.

```
Sub FileCreateDatabase_Click ()
    Dim db          As Database
    Dim tbl()       As New TableDef
    Dim fld()       As New field
    Dim idx()       As New index
    Dim f           As Integer
    Dim t           As Integer
    Dim i           As Integer
    '
    ' This will take a while so turn the mouse pointer into
    ' an hourglass
    '
    Screen.MousePointer = 11
    '
    ' Trap errors from CreateDatabase
    '
    On Error Resume Next
    Set db = CreateDatabase(dbName, DB_CREATE_GENERAL, 1)
    If (Err) Then
            MsgBox "Could not create " & dbName & ". " & Error
            Screen.MousePointer = 0
            Exit Sub
    End If
    On Error GoTo 0
    '
    ' Create an array of TableDef objects, one for each
    ' table.
    '
    ReDim tbl(dbTablesCount) As New TableDef
    '
    ' For each table in the new database
    '
    For t = 0 To dbTablesCount - 1
            '
            ' Assign the tables Name property
            '
            tbl(t).Name = dbTables(t).Name
            '
            ' Create new Field and Index objects for each
            ' new field and index
            '
```

```
      ReDim fld(dbTables(t).fieldCount) As New field
      ReDim idx(dbTables(t).indexCount) As New index
      '
      ' Set each field's properties
      '
      For f = 0 To dbTables(t).fieldCount - 1
         fld(f).Name = dbTables(t).Fields(f).Name
         fld(f).Type = dbTables(t).Fields(f).Type
         fld(f).Size = dbTables(t).Fields(f).Size
         fld(f).Attributes = dbTables(t).Fields(f).Attributes
         tbl(t).Fields.Append fld(f)
      Next
      '
      ' Set each indexes properties
      '
      For i = 0 To dbTables(t).indexCount - 1
         idx(i).Name = dbTables(t).Indexes(i).Name
         idx(i).Fields = dbTables(t).Indexes(i).Fields
         idx(i).Unique = dbTables(t).Indexes(i).Unique
         idx(i).Primary = dbTables(t).Indexes(i).Primary
         tbl(t).Indexes.Append idx(i)
      Next
      '
      ' Add the new table to the database
      '
      db.TableDefs.Append tbl(t)
      '
      ' Be nice to other applications!
      '
      DoEvents
   Next
   '
   ' We're done. Restore the mouse pointer to normal.
   '
   Screen.MousePointer = 0
   db.Close
End Sub
```

19. Add the following subroutine to the FileExit menu item's Click event subroutine.

```
Sub FileExit_Click ()
   End
End Sub
```

## How It Works

There are two major aspects to the Dbcreate project: parsing the schema and creating the database.

Quite a bit of code is required to parse the schema file, but for the most part, it is quite straightforward. At the heart of the parser is the *token extraction* process. In the schema file, a token is either an open-paren, a close-paren, or any string of non-blank characters delimited by blanks. The identification and extraction of tokens is done in GetToken, with help from the called routines SkipWhitespace, GetChar, and UngetChar.

Whether a particular token is appropriate or not is left up to the routines that call GetToken. The ParseSchema function, for instance, expects the first token read from the schema file to be the string "Database". If this token is not found, ParseSchema will return an error to the caller. If the Database token is found, ParseSchema reads the next token and saves it as the database name. Next, ParseSchema expects to get the token '(' which indicates the start of Table definitions. If the open paren is found, a loop is entered. Within the loop only the tokens 'Table' and ')' are expected. If a Table token is read, the ParseTable function is called. When the ')' token is read, the database statement is complete. Similar logic is used to parse the Table, Field, and Index statements.

Compared with the parsing routines, creating the database, tables, fields, and indexes is really easy. The first step is to call the CreateDatabase function. CreateDatabase returns a Database object, which is assigned to the variable db. Tables are added to the database by using the db.TableDefs.Append method. Similarly, fields and indexes are added to a table by using the a TableDef objects Fields.Append and Indexes.Append methods.

When you're adding objects such as fields and indexes to a table, it is important that you create a new instance of each object. Visual Basic's New keyword creates a new instance of an object. The following example shows how to use ReDim and New to create a set of Field objects to add to a Fields object collection:

```
ReDim fld(dbTables(t).fieldCount) As New field
```

If you try something like this:

```
Dim fld As New field

fld.ID = 1
table.Fields(0).Append fld
fld.ID = 2
table.Fields(1).Append fld
```

an error will be generated when the second Append executes. This is because the Fields collection does not make a copy of the Field objects during the Append, but instead simply stores a reference to the Field object. So when you modify the field object a second time, the Fields collection's copy is also modified. An error is generated at the second Append because the field you're trying to add already is in the collection.

### Comment

This project provides a handy database utility. You could embed the code from this project in your own applications, thus enabling them to recreate a database from scratch. This way you'll seldom need to write an application-specific database create program!

There is room for improvement in this project's parser. For instance, it would be nice if the names of various objects such as tables and indexes were checked to ensure that they are syntactically correct. Also, it would be nice to extend the syntax to include QueryDef statements.

## 11.3 How do I...

## Import a text file into a database?

### Problem

Users often need to be able to import data from text files into a database. A commonly used text file format contains one line per record, with fields separated by commas. This format is often referred to as comma-delimited text. How can I import comma-delimited text files into a database using Visual Basic?

### Solution

Fundamentally, loading comma-delimited records into a database is a simple, two-step process. First, the text record must be parsed into its individual fields, and then a new database record must be created using these fields.

Realistically, the requirements are usually more complex than this. It is important to avoid making any changes to the database until all of the text records are known to be valid; otherwise, the database may be left in an inconsistent state. Using Visual Basic and the Access database, it is easy to ensure that no records are added to the database until they have all been verified. The Visual Basic statements BeginTrans and CommitTrans can be used to bracket any number of changes to a database. Between the time that BeginTrans and CommitTrans are executed, all database changes are treated as a unit, called a *transaction*. Changes are not actually made to the database until CommitTrans is executed, at which time all of the changes are made at once. If, during loading the text records, you need to abort the operation, you can use the Rollback statement. The Rollback statement returns the

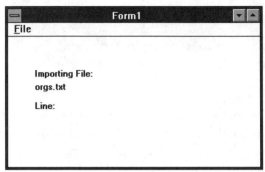

**Figure 11-4** LOADTEXT.MDB database schema

database to the state that existed prior to the execution of the last BeginTrans statement.

This How-To shows you how to load text from three different text files into a database. The database schema for the sample database, loadtext.mdb, is shown in Figure 11-4. The sample database contains three tables: Organizations, Members, and OrganizationMembers. The Organizations table contains information about organizations, the Members table has a list of members of the various organizations, and the OrganizationMembers table is a relational table that instantiates the relationships between members and organizations.

```
'
' Sample database schema for loadtext.mak
'
database loadtext.mdb
(
   Table Organizations
   (
      Field ID (Long Counter)
      Field Name (Text 40)
      Field Street_Address (Text 40)
      Field City (Text 20)
      Field State (Text 2)
      Field Zip (Text 9)
      Index OrgIdIndex (ID Primary)
      Index OrgName (Name Unique)
   )
   Table Members
   (
      Field ID (Long Counter)
      Field Name (Text 20)
```

```
    Index MemberIdIndex (ID Primary)
    Index MemberNameIndex (Name Unique)
)
Table OrganizationMembers
(
    Field Organization_ID (Long)
    Field Member_Id(Long)
    Index MemberOrganizationIndex(Member_ID;Organization_ID Primary)
    Index MemberIndex(Member_ID)
    Index OrganizationIndex(Organization_ID)
)
)
```

Three text files will be used to load the contents of LOADTEXT.MDB: ORGS.TXT, MEMBERS.TXT, and MEMBSHIP.TXT. ORGS.TXT contains records with the following format:

```
1000 Friends of Washington,1224 Fourth Ave.,Seattle,WA,98101
```

ORGS.TXT has fields for the organization name, street address, city, state, and zip-code. MEMBERS.TXT is simply a list of names; there is only one field in each record of MEMBERS.TXT. MEMBSHIP.TXT lists the members of each organization in the database. The records in MEMBSHIP.TXT have the following format:

```
Eleanor Bauxdale,Washington State Audobon Society
Eleanor Bauxdale,1000 Friends of Washington
```

There are two fields in each record of MEMBSHIP.TXT. The first field lists the member's name, and the second field lists an organization. Some people may be members of more than one organization.

### Steps

Before running the Loadtext project, you will need to create the sample database loadtext.mdb using the Dbcreate program from How-To 11.1, Create a database using Visual Basic.

After LOADTEXT.MDB has been created, open and run LOADTEXT.MAK. Select the File Import menu item to load the database. If the current directory is not the same as the project directory when you execute Loadtext, the database file LOADTEXT.MDB will not be found. When this happens, the program displays a dialog box that you can use to select the LOADTEXT.MDB in the project directory.

1. Create a new project named DBCREATE.MAK. Add the objects and properties shown in Table 11-6 to Form1.

| Object | Property | Setting |
|--------|----------|---------|
| Form | Caption | "Form1" |
| | Name | Form1 |
| CommonDialog | DefaultExt | "*.txt" |
| | Name | CMDialog1 |
| | DialogTitle | "Import Text" |
| | Filter | "Text Files (*.txt)|*.txt" |
| Label | Name | LineLabel |
| Label | Caption | "Line:" |
| | Name | Label3 |
| Label | Name | FileNameLabel |
| Label | Caption | "Importing File:" |
| | Name | Label1 |

**Table 11-6** Objects and properties for Form1

2. Use the menu design window to create the menu for Form1 as shown in Table 11-7.

| Menu name | Caption |
|-----------|---------|
| FileMenu | "&File" |
| ---FileImport | "&Import" |
| ---FileSep1 | "-" |
| ---FileExit | "E&xit" |

**Table 11-7** Menu for Form1

3. Add the following code to the General Declarations section of Form1.

```
'
' Generate error for undeclared variables
'
Option Explicit
'
' Global variable to hold database object
'
Dim db As Database
```

4. Add the following code to the Click event subroutine of the FileImport menu item. This is where the action begins. After opening the database, a transaction is started with BeginTrans. Next each of the three text files is loaded into a table by calling the appropriate routine. If all of the text files were successfully loaded, then CommitTrans is used to commit changes

to the database; otherwise, Rollback is used to undo partial changes that may have been made.

```
Sub FileImport_Click ()
    Dim success As Integer
    Dim db      As Database
    '
    ' Change mouse pointer to hourglass
    '
    Screen.MousePointer = 11
    '
    ' Open database
    '
    If (OpenDB("loadtext.mdb")) Then
        '
        ' Database opened, start a transaction. The subsequent
        ' table modifications are contained within thier own
        ' transactions.
        '
        BeginTrans
        If (ImportOrgs()) Then
            '
            ' Organization info imported
            '
            If (ImportMembers()) Then
                '
                ' Member info imported
                '
                success = CreateRelations()
            End If
        End If
        '
        ' If the entire import completed successfully then commit
        ' the changes otherwise roll the database back to its prior
        ' state
        '
        If (success) Then
            CommitTrans
        Else
            Rollback
        End If
    End If
    '
    ' Restore mouse pointer to normal
    '
    Screen.MousePointer = 0
    If (success) Then
        MsgBox "Data imported."
    Else
        MsgBox "Data import failed."
    End If
End Sub
```

5. Add the following subroutine to the General Declarations section of Form1. This subroutine creates one new record in the Organization table for each record in ORGS.TXT. Preceding the While Loop within which new records are created is a BeginTrans statement. Following the While Loop is a CommitTrans statement. If an error is encountered before EOF is reached, Rollback is executed and the function exits. Within the While Loop records are created by using the Table's AddNew and Update methods.

```
Function ImportOrgs ()As Integer
    Dim filenum        As Integer
    Dim strings()      As String
    Dim tbl            As table
    Dim orgId          As Integer
    '
    ' Organization source file has 5 fields:
    '     Name
    '     Street address
    '     City
    '     State
    '     Zip
    '
    ReDim strings(5) As String
    '
    ' Open source text file
    '
    If (OpenTextFile("orgs.txt", filenum) = True) Then
        '
        ' Open table to modify
        '
        Set tbl = db.OpenTable("Organizations")
        '
        ' Each organization gets a unique id
        '
        orgId = 1
        '
        ' Start transaction
        '
        BeginTrans
        '
        ' Read each line from source file
        '
        Do While (Not EOF(filenum))
            If (GetLine(filenum, strings(), 5) = True) Then
                '
                ' Create new record
                '
                tbl.AddNew
                tbl!ID = orgId
                tbl!Name = strings(0)
```

```
                    tbl!Street_Address = strings(1)
                    tbl!City = strings(2)
                    tbl!State = strings(3)
                    tbl!Zip = strings(4)
                    tbl.Update
                    orgId = orgId + 1
            Else
                '
                ' Woops...error in source file, abort transaction
                '
                MsgBox "Error reading text file. Changes have been ⇐
discarded."
                Rollback
                ImportOrgs = False
                Exit Function
            End If
        Loop
        '
        ' All done commit changes
        '
        CommitTrans
        ImportOrgs = True
    Else
        ImportOrgs = False
    End If
    Close filenum
End Function
```

6. Add the following routine to the General Declarations section of Form1. ImportMembers imports the contents of MEMBERS.TXT into the database. Transactions are used here, as with ImportOrganizations, to ensure that database consistency is maintained.

```
Function ImportMembers () As Integer
    Dim filenum     As Integer
    Dim strings()   As String
    Dim tbl         As table
    Dim memberID    As Integer
    '
    ' Members source file has only one field: Name
    '
    ReDim strings(1) As String
    '
    ' Open source file
    '
    If (OpenTextFile("members.txt", filenum) = True) Then
        '
        ' Open table to load
        '
        Set tbl = db.OpenTable("Members")
        '
        ' Unique id for each member
```

*continued on next page*

*continued from previous page*

```
        '
        memberID = 1
        '
        ' Start transaction
        '
        BeginTrans
        '
        ' Read each line from source file
        '
        Do While (Not EOF(filenum))
            '
            ' Parse fields out of line and create new record
            '
            If (GetLine(filenum, strings(), 1) = True) Then
                tbl.AddNew
                tbl!ID = memberID
                tbl!Name = strings(0)
                tbl.Update
                memberID = memberID + 1
            Else
                '
                ' Woops...error reading source file, abort transaction.
                '
                MsgBox "Error reading text file. Changes have been ⇐
discarded."
                Rollback
                ImportMembers = False
                Exit Function
            End If
        Loop
        '
        ' All done ... commit changes
        '
        CommitTrans
        ImportMembers = True
    Else
        ImportMembers = False
    End If
    Close filenum
End Function
```

7. Add the following subroutine to the General Declarations section of Form1. LOADTEXT.MDB, the sample database, contains a table named OrganizationMembers. The OrganizationMembers table can be used to quickly locate all members of a particular organization, or to quickly determine which organizations an individual belongs to.

```
Function CreateRelations () As Integer
    Dim filenum     As Integer
    Dim strings()   As String
    Dim tbl         As table
    Dim members     As Dynaset
```

```
Dim orgs            As Dynaset
'
' Create sets for ID retrieval
'
Set members = db.CreateDynaset("Members")
Set orgs = db.CreateDynaset("Organizations")
'
' Each line of 'membship.txt' has two fields:
'    Member name
'    Organization name
'
ReDim strings(2) As String
'
' Open source file
'
If (OpenTextFile("membship.txt", filenum) = True) Then
    '
    ' Open destination table
    '
    Set tbl = db.OpenTable("OrganizationMembers")
    '
    ' Start transaction ... this transaction is nested inside
    ' of the transactaion started in FileImport_Click
    '
    BeginTrans
    '
    ' For each line in source file
    '
    Do While (Not EOF(filenum))
        '
        ' Get comma-delimited line from file into strings() array
        '
        If (GetLine(filenum, strings(), 2) = True) Then
            '
            ' Find correct row in members and organizations tables
            '
            members.FindFirst "[Name] = '" & strings(0) & "'"
            orgs.FindFirst "[Name] = '" & strings(1) & "'"
            '
            ' Create a new record
            '
            tbl.AddNew
            tbl!Organization_ID = orgs!ID
            tbl!Member_ID = members!ID
            tbl.Update
        Else
            '
            ' Woops ... something's wrong in source file, abort ⇐
transaction.
            '
            MsgBox "Error reading text file. Changes have been ⇐
discarded."
            Rollback
```

*continued on next page*

*continued from previous page*

```
                        CreateRelations = False
                        '
                        ' Function failed ... we're done
                        '
                        Exit Function
                End If
        Loop
        '
        ' Got to end of source file, commit changes
        '
        CommitTrans
        CreateRelations = True
    Else
        CreateRelations = False
    End If
    Close filenum
End Function
```

8. Add the following function to the General Declarations section of Form1. GetLine reads the next line from a text file, and returns each comma-delimited field as a separate string in Strings array that is passed to GetLine.

```
Function GetLine (filenum, strings() As String, nfields As Integer)
    Dim buffer      As String
    Dim i           As Integer
    Dim curComma    As Integer
    Dim prevComma   As Integer
    '
    ' Read next line from source file
    '
    Line Input #filenum, buffer
    '
    ' Display line
    '
    LineLabel.Caption = buffer
    LineLabel.Refresh
    '
    ' Add trailing comma to simplify parsing
    '
    buffer = buffer & ","
    prevComma = 0
    '
    ' Pick apart comma-delimited fields
    '
    For i = 0 To nfields - 1
        curComma = InStr(Right$(buffer, Len(buffer) - prevComma), ",") + ⇐
prevComma
        strings(i) = Mid$(buffer, prevComma + 1, curComma - prevComma - 1)
        prevComma = curComma
    Next
    GetLine = True
End Function
```

9. Add the following code to the General Declarations Section of Form1. This subroutine is called from FileImport_Click to open the database.

```
Function OpenDB (Filename As String) As Integer
    '
    ' Assume success
    '
    OpenDB = True
    On Error Resume Next
    Set db = OpenDatabase(Filename)
    If (Err) Then
        '
        ' Couldn't open file on first try ... path may be wrong
        ' Let user try with Open Dialog
        '
        Filename = PromptForFilename(Filename, "Open Database", "Access ⇐
Files (*.mdb)|*.mdb", "*.mdb")
        If (Filename = "") Then
            '
            ' No filename specified, return error indicator
            '
            OpenDB = False
        Else
            Err = 0
            Set db = OpenDatabase(Filename)
            If (Err) Then
                MsgBox "Could not open database '" & Filename & "'."
                OpenDB = False
            End If
        End If
    End If
End Function
```

10. Add the following code to the General Declarations section of Form1. This subroutine is called to open text files.

```
Function OpenTextFile (Filename As String, filenum As Integer) As Integer
    '
    ' Assume success
    '
    OpenTextFile = True
    FileNameLabel.Caption = Filename
    filenum = FreeFile
    On Error Resume Next
    Open Filename For Input As #filenum
    If (Err) Then
        '
        ' Couldn't open file ... path may be incorrect so let
        ' the user take a shot at it.
        '
        Filename = PromptForFilename(Filename, "Open Text File", "Text ⇐
Files (*.txt)|*.txt", "*.txt")
```

*continued on next page*

*continued from previous page*

```
            If (Filename = "") Then
                OpenTextFile = False
            Else
                Err = 0
                Open Filename For Input As #filenum
                If (Err) Then
                    MsgBox "Could not open file '" & Filename & "'."
                    OpenTextFile = False
                End If
            End If
        End If
    End If
End Function
```

11. Add the following subroutine to the General Declarations section of Form1. PromptForFilename is called when a file open fails; the Common Dialog control is used to let the user locate the file to open.

```
Function PromptForFilename (Filename As String, title As String, Filter As ⇐
String, defext As String) As String
    '
    ' Load properties
    '
    CMDialog1.DialogTitle = title
    CMDialog1.Filter = Filter
    CMDialog1.DefaultExt = defext
    CMDialog1.Filename = Filename
    '
    ' Set CancelError = True so that we can tell if the
    ' user is giving up
    '
    CMDialog1.CancelError = True
    On Error Resume Next
    CMDialog1.Action = 1
    If (Err) Then
        '
        ' No file specified
        '
        PromptForFilename = ""
    Else
        '
        ' File specified, return name as value of this function
        '
        PromptForFilename = CMDialog1.Filename
    End If
End Function
```

### How It Works

The import operation begins when the user selects the File Import menu item, which fires the FileImport_Click event. FileImport_Click opens the database and begins a transaction. Next, the functions ImportOrgs, ImportMembers, and CreateRelations are called.

ImportOrgs and ImportMembers are similar in structure. After opening the source text file and the destination table, each record from the source file is read from disk and added to the table. The Organizations and Members tables each have a counter field named ID. The ID field serves two purposes. First, it ensures that each record is unique; this can be important where two members have the same names. Second, it provides a short, unique identifier for each record. These unique record identifiers can be used in other tables to efficiently create relations between members and organizations. In this simple example, the ID numbers always begin at 1. This approach probably wouldn't work in a database that already had records in it, because it is likely that one or more IDs would already be used. What you will need to do in a real program is find an unused ID for each new record. One way to do this is to simply find the highest numbered ID in the table and increment it before adding each record. You can easily find the highest numbered ID in a table using code like the following:

```
Set MyQuery = DB.CreateQueryDef("Find Max ID")
MyQuery.SQL - "SELECT DISTINCTROW Max(Members.ID) As MaxOfID From Members;"
Set MySnapshot = MyQuery.CreateSnapshot()
```

The snapshot will have a single row with one field named MaxOfID that contains the highest numbered ID in the table.

Once the Members and Organizations tables have been loaded, the function CreateRelations is called. CreateRelations builds a third table that contains the relationship between members and organizations. Each member in the database may be a member of more than one organization. In the sample database, this relationship is expressed directly in the table named OrganizationMembers. Each row in the OrganizationMembers table contains two fields; an organization and a member. So the OrganizationMembers table shows which organizations have which members.

### Comments

Using the techniques in this How-To, you can easily write database import utilities. Comma-delimited text is a commonly used import/export format. Another common format is tab-delimited text, where a (TAB) is used to separate fields. To modify the code in this How-To to use tab-delimited text records, you need only modify a few lines of code in the GetLine function so that:

```
buffer = buffer & ","
prevComma = 0
'
' Pick apart comma-delimited fields
'
```

*continued on next page*

*continued from previous page*

```
    For i = 0 To nfields - 1
        curComma = InStr(Right$(buffer, Len(buffer) - prevComma), ",") + ⇐
prevComma
```

becomes:

```
buffer = buffer & chr$(9)
prevTab = 0
'
' Pick apart comma-delimited fields
'
For i = 0 To nfields - 1
    curTab = InStr(Right$(buffer, Len(buffer) - prevTab), chr$(9)) + ⇐
prevTab
```

## 11.4 ● How do I...

**Complexity: Intermediate**

# Find incorrectly spelled names in a database?

### Problem

I'm designing an application where customer records are retrieved using the customer's last name. It is not uncommon for the last name to be misspelled, either in the database or when entered in the record retrieval application. How can I locate records in a database using names that may be spelled incorrectly?

### Solution

You're in luck! The Soundex algorithm was designed to solve precisely this problem. According to Donald Knuth, in his classic *The Art of Programming, Vol. 3, Searching and Sorting,* the Soundex algorithm was originally developed by Margaret K. Odell and Robert C. Russell [cf. U.S. Patents 1261167 (1918), 1435663 (1922)]. The Soundex algorithm changes a string containing a person's last name into a string containing a letter followed by three numeric characters. The characters of the resulting string will often be the same for similar sounding names.

This How-To implements the Soundex algorithm as described by Knuth and shows how to use the algorithm to locate database records.

### Steps

Open and run SOUNDEX.BAS. The running program looks like Figure 11-5. It may take a number of seconds for the form to load the first time you run it, since it builds a database if one does not yet exist.

You can experiment with the Soundex algorithm by entering a name in the Last Name text box and clicking on the Search button. All of the names

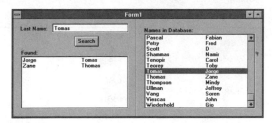

**Figure 11-5** Soundex in action

in the database are listed on the right side of the form. Select a name from the right list box and enter it into the text box. You can then try various misspellings of the name. Each time you press the Search button, the database will be searched for names that have the same Soundex code as the name you entered. Each name with a matching Soundex code will be shown in the list box on the left side of the form.

1. Create a new project named SOUNDEX.MAK. Enter the objects and properties shown in Table 11-8 to form1.

| Object | Property | Setting |
| --- | --- | --- |
| Form | BackColor | &H00C0C0C0& |
| | Caption | "Form1" |
| | Height | 3795 |
| | Left | 645 |
| | Name | Form1 |
| | Top | 1185 |
| | Width | 8850 |
| SSCommand | Caption | "Search" |
| | Font3D | 0 'None |
| | Height | 375 |
| | Left | 2160 |
| | Name | Command3D1 |
| | TabIndex | 2 |
| | Top | 600 |
| | Width | 855 |
| SSPanel | AutoSize | 3 'AutoSize Child To Panel |
| | BackColor | &H00C0C0C0& |
| | BevelInner | 1 'Inset |
| | BevelOuter | 0 'None |
| | Caption | "Panel3D1" |

*continued on next page*

*continued from previous page*

| Object | Property | Setting |
|--------|----------|---------|
|  | Font3D | 0 'None |
|  | Height | 405 |
|  | Left | 1320 |
|  | Name | Panel3D1 |
|  | Top | 120 |
|  | Width | 2775 |
| SSPanel | AutoSize | 3 'AutoSize Child To Panel |
|  | BackColor | &H00C0C0C0& |
|  | BevelInner | 1 'Inset |
|  | BevelOuter | 0 'None |
|  | Caption | "Panel3D3" |
|  | Font3D | 0 'None |
|  | Height | 1905 |
|  | Left | 225 |
|  | Name | Panel3D2 |
|  | Top | 1260 |
|  | Width | 3855 |
| SSPanel | AutoSize | 3 'AutoSize Child To Panel |
|  | BackColor | &H00C0C0C0& |
|  | BevelInner | 1 'Inset |
|  | BevelOuter | 0 'None |
|  | Caption | "Panel3D4" |
|  | Font3D | 0 'None |
|  | Height | 2685 |
|  | Name | Panel3D3 |
|  | Left | 4560 |
|  | Top | 480 |
|  | Width | 3975 |
| Line | BorderColor | &H00808080& |
|  | Index | 1 |
|  | Name | Line1 |
|  | X1 | 4305 |
|  | X2 | 4305 |
|  | Y1 | -105 |
|  | Y2 | 3375 |
| Label | BackColor | &H00C0C0C0& |
|  | Caption | "Names in Database:" |
|  | Height | 255 |

| Object | Property | Setting |
|--------|----------|---------|
|  | Left | 4590 |
|  | Name | Label4 |
|  | Top | 300 |
|  | Width | 2055 |
| Line | BorderColor | &H00FFFFFF& |
|  | Index | 0 |
|  | Name | Line1 |
|  | X1 | 4320 |
|  | X2 | 4320 |
|  | Y1 | 0 |
|  | Y2 | 3480 |
| Label | BackColor | &H00C0C0C0& |
|  | Caption | "Found:" |
|  | Height | 255 |
|  | Left | 270 |
|  | Name | Label3 |
|  | Top | 1080 |
|  | Width | 1575 |
| Label | BackColor | &H00C0C0C0& |
|  | Caption | "Last Name:" |
|  | Height | 255 |
|  | Left | 240 |
|  | Name | Label1 |
|  | Top | 240 |
|  | Width | 975 |

**Table 11-8**  Objects and properties for Form1

2. Add the control shown in Table 11-9 to Panel3D1.

| Object | Property | Setting |
|--------|----------|---------|
| Text box | Height | 285 |
|  | Name | Text1 |
|  | Left | 60 |
|  | TabIndex | 1 |
|  | Top | 60 |
|  | Width | 2655 |

**Table 11-9**  Objects and properties for Panel3D1

3. Add the control shown in Table 11-10 to Panel3D2.

| Object | Property | Setting |
|--------|----------|---------|
| List box | Height | 1785 |
| | Name | List1 |
| | Left | 60 |
| | TabStop | 0  'False |
| | Top | 60 |
| | Width | 3735 |

**Table 11-10** Objects and properties for Panel3D2

4. Add the control shown in Table 11-11 to Panel3D3.

| Object | Property | Setting |
|--------|----------|---------|
| List box | Height | 2565 |
| | Left | 60 |
| | Name | List2 |
| | TabStop | 0  'False |
| | Top | 60 |
| | Width | 3855 |

**Table 11-11** Objects and properties for Panel3D3

5. Create a new module named SOUNDEX.BAS. Add the following code to the General Declarations section of SOUNDEX.BAS.

```
'
' Windows API functions and constants
'
Declare Function SendMessage Lib "User" (ByVal hWnd As Integer, ByVal wMsg As ⇐
Integer, ByVal wParam As Integer, lParam As Any) As Long
Global Const WM_USER = &H400
Global Const LB_SETTABSTOPS = (WM_USER + 19)


'
' Visual Basic Data Access constants
'

' Field Data Types
Global Const DB_BOOLEAN = 1
Global Const DB_BYTE = 2
Global Const DB_INTEGER = 3
Global Const DB_LONG = 4
Global Const DB_CURRENCY = 5
Global Const DB_SINGLE = 6
```

```
Global Const DB_DOUBLE = 7
Global Const DB_DATE = 8
Global Const DB_TEXT = 10
Global Const DB_LONGBINARY = 11
Global Const DB_MEMO = 12



' CreateDatabase and CompactDatabase Language constants
Global Const DB_LANG_GENERAL = ";LANGID=0x0809;CP=1252;COUNTRY=0"
Global Const DB_LANG_SPANISH = ";LANGID=0x040A;CP=1252;COUNTRY=0"
Global Const DB_LANG_DUTCH = ";LANGID=0x0413;CP=1252;COUNTRY=0"
Global Const DB_LANG_SWEDFIN = ";LANGID=0x040C;CP=1252;COUNTRY=0"  'VB3 ⇐
and Access 1.1 Databases
Global Const DB_LANG_NORWDAN = ";LANGID=0x0414;CP=1252;COUNTRY=0"  'VB3 ⇐
and Access 1.1 Databases
Global Const DB_LANG_ICELANDIC = ";LANGID=0x040F;CP=1252;COUNTRY=0" 'VB3 ⇐
and Access 1.1 Databases
Global Const DB_LANG_NORDIC = ";LANGID=0x041D;CP=1252;COUNTRY=0"   'Access⇐
1.0 Databases only
' CreateDatabase and CompactDatabase options
Global Const DB_VERSION10 = 1        ' Microsoft Access Version 1.0
Global Const DB_ENCRYPT = 2          ' Make database encrypted.
Global Const DB_DECRYPT = 4          ' Decrypt database while compacting.
'
' Soundex code table
'
Dim codes(26) As Integer
```

6. Add the following subroutine to the General Declarations section of SOUNDEX.BAS. InitSoundexCodes is called once, the first time MakeSoundex is called. InitSoundexCodes initializes the contents of the codes array. MakeSoundex uses the codes array to turn a letter into its soundex code.

```
Sub InitSoundexCodes ()
   codes(0) = 0
   codes(1) = 1
   codes(2) = 2
   codes(3) = 3
   codes(4) = 0
   codes(5) = 1
   codes(6) = 2
   codes(7) = 0
   codes(8) = 0
   codes(9) = 2
   codes(10) = 2
   codes(11) = 4
   codes(12) = 5
   codes(13) = 5
   codes(14) = 0
   codes(15) = 1
```

*continued on next page*

*continued from previous page*

```
    codes(16) = 2
    codes(17) = 6
    codes(18) = 2
    codes(19) = 3
    codes(20) = 0
    codes(21) = 1
    codes(22) = 0
    codes(23) = 2
    codes(24) = 0
    codes(25) = 2
End Sub
```

7. Add the following subroutine to the General Declarations section of SOUNDEX.BAS. The Soundex algorithm returns a four-character string that is constructed according to the following rules:

   a. Retain the first letter of the name, and drop all other occurrences of A, E, H, I, O, U, W, and Y.

   b. Assign the following numbers to the remaining letters:

   | | |
   |---|---|
   | B,F,P,V | 1 |
   | E,G,I,K,Q,S,X,Z | 2 |
   | D,T | 3 |
   | L | 4 |
   | M,N | 5 |
   | R | 6 |

   c. Retain only one occurrence of duplicate adjacent codes

   d. If the result is less than four characters long, add enough trailing zeros to make the result four characters long. Otherwise, if the result is longer than four characters retain only the first four.

```
Function MakeSoundex (from As String) As String
    Dim pval, cval   As Integer
    Dim i, j         As Integer
    Dim c            As Integer
    Dim soundx       As String
    Dim A, Z         As Integer

    If (codes(1) = 0) Then
        InitSoundexCodes
    End If

    If (Len(from) = 0) Then
        MakeSoundex = ""
        Exit Function
    Else
        soundx = UCase$(Left$(from, 1))
    End If
```

```
    Z = Asc("Z")
    A = Asc("A")

    pval = codes(Asc(Left$(from, 1)) - Asc("A"))
    i = 1
    Do While (i < Len(from)) And Len(soundx) < 4
        c = Asc(UCase$(Mid$(from, i + 1, 1)))
        If (c >= A And c <= Z) Then
            cval = codes(c - A)
            If (cval <> 0) Then
                If (cval <> pval) Then
                    soundx = soundx & Format$(cval)
                End If
            End If
            pval = cval
        End If
        i = i + 1
    Loop
    Do While (Len(soundx) < 4)
        soundx = soundx & "0"
    Loop
    MakeSoundex = soundx
End Function
```

8. Add the following code to the General Declarations section of Form1.

```
Option Explicit
'
' Set during form load
'
Dim db As Database
```

9. Add the following code to Form1's Load event subroutine. The Load event subroutine creates the sample database if it does not exist.

```
Sub Form_Load ()
    '
    ' Display form right away since opening the
    ' database will take a while
    '
    Form1.Show
    Form1.Refresh
    '
    ' Set pointer to hourglass
    '
    Screen.MousePointer = 11
    '
    ' See if the database exisits
    '
    On Error Resume Next
    Set db = CreateDatabase("soundex.mdb", DB_LANG_GENERAL, 1)
    If (Err <> 0) Then
      If (Err <> 3204) Then
```

*continued on next page*

*continued from previous page*

```
      '
      ' Unknown error
      '
      Screen.MousePointer = 0
      MsgBox Error, 48
      End
   End If
   '
   ' Database already exists ... open it
   '
   Set db = OpenDatabase("soundex.mdb")
 Else
   '
   ' Database didn't exist yet ...
   On Error GoTo 0
   '
   ' Create table
   '
   createTable
   '
   ' Add names to table
   '
   loadTable
 End If
 '
 ' Load records into list box
 '
 LoadListOfAllRecords
 '
 ' We're done ... return mouse pointer to normal
 '
 Screen.MousePointer = 0
End Sub
```

10. Add the following code to Command3D1's Click event subroutine. The Click event subroutine first creates a Dynaset containing all of the records in the Names table. Then a filter is set that will select only the records with a Soundex code that matches that of the text box, and a Snapshot containing only these records is created. Finally, all of the records in the result set are added to list1.

```
Sub Command3D1_Click ()
    Dim ds      As dynaset
    Dim snap    As snapshot
    Dim tabstop As Long
    Dim wRtn    As Integer
    '
    ' Clear search results list box
    '
    list1.Clear
    '
```

```
    ' Set tab stops
    '
    tabstop = 4 * 20
    wRtn = SendMessage(list1.hWnd, LB_SETTABSTOPS, 1, tabstop)
    '
    ' Create a dynaset containing all of the Names table's records
    '
    Set ds = db.CreateDynaset("Names")
    '
    ' Set a filter, the filter will look something like:  Soundex = 'T324'
    '
    ds.Filter = "Soundex = " & "'" & MakeSoundex(CStr(text1.Text)) & "'"
    '
    ' Create a snapshot of the filtered table
    '
    Set snap = ds.CreateSnapshot()
    '
    ' Add result set to list1
    '
    Do While (snap.EOF = False)
      list1.AddItem snap![First Name] & Chr$(9) & snap![Last Name]
      snap.MoveNext
    Loop
End Sub
```

11. Add the following code to the General Declarations section of Form1.
CreateTable is called during Form_Load after the sample database is
created.

```
Sub createTable ()
    Dim tbl            As New TableDef
    Dim fldID          As New field
    Dim fldLastName    As New field
    Dim fldFirstName   As New field
    Dim fldSoundex     As New field
    Dim idxID          As New index
    Dim idxSoundex     As New index
    '
    ' Give table a name
    '
    tbl.Name = "Names"
    '
    ' Add id field
    '
    fldID.Name = "ID"
    fldID.Type = DB_LONG
    fldID.Size = 4
    tbl.Fields.Append fldID
    '
    ' Add Last Name field
    '
```

*continued on next page*

*continued from previous page*

```
    fldLastName.Name = "Last Name"
    fldLastName.Type = DB_TEXT
    fldLastName.Size = 20
    tbl.Fields.Append fldLastName
    '
    ' Add First name field
    '
    fldFirstName.Name = "First Name"
    fldFirstName.Type = DB_TEXT
    fldFirstName.Size = 20
    tbl.Fields.Append fldFirstName
    '
    ' Add Soundex code field
    '
    fldSoundex.Name = "Soundex"
    fldSoundex.Type = DB_TEXT
    fldSoundex.Size = 4
    tbl.Fields.Append fldSoundex
    '
    ' Create a primary index on the id field
    '
    idxID.Name = "IdIndex"
    idxID.Fields = "ID"
    idxID.Unique = True
    idxID.Primary = True
    tbl.Indexes.Append idxID
    '
    ' Create another index for the Soundex field, this
    ' will speed up searches
    '
    idxSoundex.Name = "SoundexIndex"
    idxSoundex.Fields = "Soundex"
    idxSoundex.Unique = False
    idxSoundex.Primary = False
    tbl.Indexes.Append idxSoundex
    '
    ' Add new table to database
    '
    db.TableDefs.Append tbl
End Sub
```

12. Add the following subroutine to the General Declarations section of Form1. LoadTable reads the text file NAMES.TXT and creates one record in the Names table for each line in NAMES.TXT.

```
Sub loadTable ()
    Dim filenum      As Integer
    Dim strings()    As String
    Dim tbl          As table
    Dim id           As Integer
    '
    ' Names.txt file has 2 fields:
```

```
'   Last Name
'   First Name
'
ReDim strings(2) As String
'
' Open source text file
'
filenum = FreeFile
Open "c:\howto2e\chapterb\11.3\names.txt" For Input As #filenum
'
' Open table to modify
'
Set tbl = db.OpenTable("Names")
'
' Each name gets a unique id
'
id = 1
'
' Read each line from source file
'
Do While (Not EOF(filenum))
  GetLine filenum, strings(), 2
    '
    ' Create new record
    '
    tbl.AddNew
    tbl!id = id
    tbl![Last Name] = strings(0)
    tbl![First Name] = strings(1)
    tbl!Soundex = MakeSoundex(strings(0))
    tbl.Update
    id = id + 1
Loop
Close filenum
End Sub
```

13. Add the following subroutine to the General Declarations section of
Form1. GetLine is called by LoadTable each time data is needed for a
new record. GetLine expects to read comma-delimited records from the
input file, and returns an array of string.

```
Sub GetLine (filenum, strings() As String, nfields As Integer)
    Dim buffer      As String
    Dim i           As Integer
    Dim curComma    As Integer
    Dim prevComma   As Integer
    '
    ' Read next line from source file
    '
    Line Input #filenum, buffer
    '
    ' Add trailing comma to simplify parsing
```

*continued on next page*

continued from previous page

```
    '
    buffer = buffer & ","
    prevComma = 0
    '
    ' Pick apart comma-delimited fields
    '
    For i = 0 To nfields - 1
      curComma = InStr(Right$(buffer, Len(buffer) - prevComma), ",") + prevComma
      strings(i) = Mid$(buffer, prevComma + 1, curComma - prevComma - 1)
      prevComma = curComma
    Next
End Sub
```

14. Add the following subroutine to the General Declarations section of Form1. LoadListOfAllRecords is called during Form_Load and lists the first and last names from each record in list2.

```
Sub LoadListOfAllRecords ()
    Dim ds        As dynaset
    Dim tabstop   As Long
    Dim wRtn      As Integer
    '
    ' Create two columns in the list box
    '
    tabstop = 4 * 20
    wRtn = SendMessage(list2.hWnd, LB_SETTABSTOPS, 1, tabstop)
    '
    ' Get a dynaset containing all of the records in
    ' the Names table
    '
    Set ds = db.CreateDynaset("Names")
    ds.MoveFirst
    '
    ' Add each record in the dynaset to list2
    '
    Do While (ds.EOF = False)
      list2.AddItem ds![Last Name] & Chr$(9) & ds![First Name]
      ds.MoveNext
    Loop
End Sub
```

### How It Works

When records are added to the Names table, the Soundex code for the person's last name is computed and stored in the Soundex field of the record. Later, when a name is entered in the text box and the Search command button is pressed, the Soundex code for the string in Text1 is generated. Text1's Soundex code is used to create a filter, and then a Snapshot of the table is made using the filter. The filter selects only those records with a Soundex code that matches Text1's Soundex code, so the resulting Snapshot contains only records with matching Soundex codes.

## Comments

Storing the Soundex code with each record and providing an index for it are important performance optimizations. If the Soundex code wasn't included in each record, you would have to look at every record in the table and compute its Soundex code each time the table is searched. The index created for the Soundex field in the Names table serves a similar purpose. Without this index the database engine would need to access each record in the table to retrieve the value of its Soundex field. The index allows the database engine to quickly determine which records contain a particular value in the Soundex field without actually reading the records.

# APPENDIX A

## The Annotated
## Windows API Text Files

Many of the How-To solutions in this book rely on Windows API functions to extend the capabilities of Visual Basic. As you have seen, you must declare every Windows API function before you can use it, and you've probably noticed that the Declarations statements are long and cryptic. How do you know the parameters of each function and in which library the function can be found?

### The Windows API Text Files Explained

Fortunately, Microsoft has provided two files: WIN30API.TXT, and WIN31EXT.TXT.

WIN30API.TXT contains Declare statements for almost all of the original Windows 3.0 API functions (close to 600 of them!). There are a few API functions that Visual Basic can't use because they require support for pointers to functions, something that Visual Basic doesn't provide. WIN31EXT.TXT provides the Declare statements for the Windows 3.1 extensions.

The best way to use the Windows API text files is to copy the statements that relate to the API functions you intend to use to the global module of your Visual Basic program, or the Declarations section of your form. Note, however, that no single form or module in a Visual Basic application can hold over 64K of code. Since the WIN30API.TXT file is over 120K, you can't load the whole thing into a single module.

This appendix is an annotated version of the Windows API text files; throughout we have provided helpful information, tips, and references to solutions in this book that demonstrate the use of APIs.

### Global Const Statements

In addition to API function Declare statements, there are hundreds of Global Const statements to declare some mnemonic constants for the Windows messages in the text file. For example, the LB_RESETCONTENT message is declared as follows:

```
Global Const LB_RESETCONTENT = (WM_USER+5)
```

WM_USER is another constant declared as follows:

```
Global Const WM_USER = &H400
```

So the value of the constant LB_RESETCONTENT is actually &H400 + 5, which equals &H405 in hexadecimal, or 1029 in decimal. So you could actually use 1029 every time instead of LB_RESETCONTENT, but the constant LB_RESETCONTENT gives you at least a hint of what it will actually do. 1029 doesn't tell you much of anything at all!

If you're using control messages such as LB_RESETCONTENT with the SendMessageToControl function in How-To 1.6 Quickly clear a list box, you can simply use these Global Const statements in your Global module. A couple of hints: Many messages depend on the value of another; LB_RESETCONTENT, for example, depends on the value of the WM_USER constant. Be sure to include the Global Const statements for both WM_USER and LB_RESETCONTENT. The other hint: If you don't use a Global module in your Visual Basic application, you must remove the "Global" from the Const statements. Global Const statements are allowed only in the Global module.

Some other useful parts of WINAPI.TXT:

- Look for Global Const statements with WF_… constants. These constants are used in How-To 6.15 Find out everything about the system configuration.

- Look for the section entitled "GDI Section." There are several Declare and Global Const statements used in How-Tos throughout this book.

- The section entitled "Virtual Keys, Standard Set" contains Global Const statements for all the key codes used in the Visual Basic KeyDown and KeyUp event subroutines.

- The section entitled "MessageBox() Flags" contains several Global Const statements for the MsgBox statement and function. For example, instead of trying to remember which number to use to display an icon in a message box, just use one of the MB_ICON… constants.

- There are several MF_ constants used in How-To 4.5 Draw a bitmapped picture in a menu, and How-To 4.6 Place font typefaces in a menu.

- There are many LB_ constants used to send messages to list boxes.

  ●    There are several HELP_ constants you can use if your Visual Basic application supports online Help.

It is almost mandatory that you use a Windows reference guide; an excellent one is *The Waite Group's Windows API Bible*, James Conger, Waite Group Press, 1992.

```
' -----------------------------------
'
'   WIN30API.TXT -- Windows 3.0 API Declarations for Visual Basic
'
'       Copyright (C) 1993 Microsoft Corporation
'
'
' This file contains the Const, Type, and Declare statements for
' Windows 3.0 APIs. Use WIN31EXT.TXT for Windows 3.1 APIs.
'
' The Global Constants ABORTDOC, STARTUPDOC, and ENDDOCAPI are
' Windows 3.0 specific and have been superseded by the ABORTDOC,
' STARTDOC, and ENDDOCAPI functions in Windows 3.1. These constants
' have been made into comments in this file. In order to use them you will
' need to remove the comment symbol preceding each constant.
'
' You have a royalty-free right to use, modify, reproduce and distribute
' this file (and/or any modified version) in any way you find useful,
' provided that you agree that Microsoft has no warranty, obligation or
' liability for its contents.  Refer to the Microsoft Windows Programmer's
' Reference for further information.
'
' -----------------------------------


'   General Purpose Defines
```

  NULL is used throughout the API to indicate zero or an empty string.

```
Global Const NULL = 0
```

  RECT is a structure holding the four corners of a rectangular screen region. Note that the coordinates are in pixels, not twips.

```
Type RECT
     left As Integer
     top As Integer
     right As Integer
     bottom As Integer
End Type
```

  POINTAPI is a structure that holds the coordinates of a pixel. Note that, like the RECT structure, the coordinates are in pixels, not twips. The name of this structure in C is POINT, but that conflicts with the Visual Basic Point method.

```
Type POINTAPI
    x As Integer
    y As Integer
End Type

' ------------------------------------
'  Kernel Section
' ------------------------------------


' ParameterBlock description structure for use with LoadModule
Type PARAMETERBLOCK
    wEnvSeg As Integer
    lpCmdLine As Long
    lpCmdShow As Long
    dwReserved As Long
End Type

' Loader Routines
```

GetVersion is used in How-To 6.10 Determine which version of Windows my application is running on. GetNumTasks is used in How-To 6.1 Run a DOS program and find out when it's done. The other functions in this section are used to load other applications or DLLs and find out information about them.

```
Declare Function GetVersion Lib "Kernel" () As Integer
Declare Function GetNumTasks Lib "Kernel" () As Integer
Declare Function GetModuleHandle Lib "Kernel" (ByVal lpModuleName As ⇐
String) As Integer
Declare Function GetModuleUsage Lib "Kernel" (ByVal hModule As Integer) ⇐
As Integer
Declare Function GetModuleFileName Lib "Kernel" (ByVal hModule As Integer, ⇐
ByVal lpFilename As String, ByVal nSize As Integer) As Integer
Declare Function GetInstanceData Lib "Kernel" (ByVal hInstance As Integer, ⇐
ByVal pData As Integer, ByVal nCount As Integer) As Integer
Declare Function LoadLibrary Lib "Kernel" (ByVal lpLibFileName As String) ⇐
As Integer
Declare Function LoadModule Lib "Kernel" (ByVal lpModuleName As String, ⇐
lpParameterBlock As PARAMETERBLOCK) As Integer
Declare Sub FreeModule Lib "Kernel" (ByVal hModule As Integer)
Declare Sub FreeLibrary Lib "Kernel" (ByVal hLibModule As Integer)
Declare Function SetHandleCount Lib "Kernel" (ByVal wNumber As Integer) ⇐
As Integer
```

GetFreeSpace is used in How-To 6.13 Determine how much memory is available.

```
Declare Function GetFreeSpace Lib "Kernel" (ByVal wFlags As Integer) As Long
```

WinExec is used to create the VBHTShell function in How-To 6.7 Use the Shell function without causing run-time errors. The DebugBreak and OutputDebugString functions are used with the debugging version of Windows that comes with the SDK to aid in debugging of C and Pascal Windows applications. SwitchStackTo, SwitchStackBack, and GetCurrentPDB are used in DLLs.

```
Declare Function WinExec Lib "Kernel" (ByVal lpCmdLine As String, ByVal ⇐
nCmdShow As Integer) As Integer
Declare Sub DebugBreak Lib "Kernel" ()
Declare Sub OutputDebugString Lib "Kernel" (ByVal lpOutputString As ⇐
String)
Declare Sub SwitchStackBack Lib "Kernel" ()
Declare Sub SwitchStackTo Lib "Kernel" (ByVal wStackSegment As Integer, ⇐
ByVal wStackPointer As Integer, ByVal wStackTop As Integer)
Declare Function GetCurrentPDB Lib "Kernel" () As Integer
```

The Visual Basic Open statement can duplicate all the functionality of the OpenFile structures, constants, and functions. But if you use the Open statement and an error occurs, Visual Basic will cause a run-time error that you will have to use a trap to catch; OpenFile simply returns an error code that you can process without needing an error handler.

```
' OpenFile() Structure
Type OFSTRUCT
    cBytes As String * 1
    fFixedDisk As String * 1
    nErrCode As Integer
    reserved As String * 4
    szPathName As String * 128
End Type

' OpenFile() Flags
Global Const OF_READ = &H0
Global Const OF_WRITE = &H1
Global Const OF_READWRITE = &H2
Global Const OF_SHARE_COMPAT = &H0
Global Const OF_SHARE_EXCLUSIVE = &H10
Global Const OF_SHARE_DENY_WRITE = &H20
Global Const OF_SHARE_DENY_READ = &H30
Global Const OF_SHARE_DENY_NONE = &H40
Global Const OF_PARSE = &H100
Global Const OF_DELETE = &H200
Global Const OF_VERIFY = &H400
Global Const OF_CANCEL = &H800
Global Const OF_CREATE = &H1000
Global Const OF_PROMPT = &H2000
Global Const OF_EXIST = &H4000
Global Const OF_REOPEN = &H8000

Declare Function OpenFile Lib "Kernel" (ByVal lpFileName As String, ⇐
lpReOpenBuff As OFSTRUCT, ByVal wStyle As Integer) As Integer
```

These functions would be useful if you needed to create a temporary file, for sorting, for example.

```
' GetTempFileName() Flags
'
Global Const TF_FORCEDRIVE = &H80

Declare Function GetTempDrive Lib "Kernel" (ByVal cDriveLetter as Integer) ⇐
As Integer
Declare Function GetTempFileName Lib "Kernel" (ByVal cDriveLetter as ⇐
Integer, ByVal lpPrefixString As String, ByVal wUnique As Integer, ByVal ⇐
lpTempFileName As String) As Integer
```

GetDriveType returns one of the three DRIVE_ constants for the drive you specify. It would be useful if you wanted your application to know that files are being stored on a network drive (DRIVE_REMOTE), for example.

```
Declare Function GetDriveType Lib "Kernel" (ByVal nDrive As Integer) ⇐
As Integer

' GetDriveType return values
Global Const DRIVE_REMOVABLE = 2
Global Const DRIVE_FIXED = 3
Global Const DRIVE_REMOTE = 4
```

It's usually far easier to use Visual Basic's Dim and ReDim statements to allocate memory, but the Global… and Local… memory API functions are available if you need to allocate a special type of memory for a custom DLL, for example.

```
' Global Memory Flags
Global Const GMEM_FIXED = &H0
Global Const GMEM_MOVEABLE = &H2
Global Const GMEM_NOCOMPACT = &H10
Global Const GMEM_NODISCARD = &H20
Global Const GMEM_ZEROINIT = &H40
Global Const GMEM_MODIFY = &H80
Global Const GMEM_DISCARDABLE = &H100
Global Const GMEM_NOT_BANKED = &H1000
Global Const GMEM_SHARE = &H2000
Global Const GMEM_DDESHARE = &H2000
Global Const GMEM_NOTIFY = &H4000
Global Const GMEM_LOWER = GMEM_NOT_BANKED

Global Const GHND = (GMEM_MOVEABLE Or GMEM_ZEROINIT)
Global Const GPTR = (GMEM_FIXED Or GMEM_ZEROINIT)

Declare Function GlobalAlloc Lib "Kernel" (ByVal wFlags As Integer, ⇐
ByVal   dwBytes As Long) As Integer
Declare Function GlobalCompact Lib "Kernel" (ByVal dwMinFree As Long) ⇐
As  Long
Declare Function GlobalFree Lib "Kernel" (ByVal hMem As Integer) As ⇐
Integer
Declare Function GlobalHandle Lib "Kernel" (ByVal wMem As Integer) As Long
Declare Function GlobalLock Lib "Kernel" (ByVal hMem As Integer) As Long
Declare Function GlobalReAlloc Lib "Kernel" (ByVal hMem As Integer, ⇐
```

```
ByVal dwBytes As Long, ByVal wFlags As Integer) As Integer

'NOTE: instead of declaring the function GlobalDiscard and calling
'     GlobalDiscard(hMem), call GlobalReAlloc(hMem, 0, GMEM_MOVEABLE)

Declare Function GlobalSize Lib "Kernel" (ByVal hMem As Integer) As Long
Declare Function GlobalUnlock Lib "Kernel" (ByVal hMem As Integer) As Integer
Declare Function UnlockResource Lib "Kernel" Alias "GlobalUnlock" (ByVal ⇐
 hMem As Integer) As Integer
Declare Function GlobalFlags Lib "Kernel" (ByVal hMem As Integer) As Integer
Declare Function GlobalWire Lib "Kernel" (ByVal hMem As Integer) As Long
Declare Function GlobalUnWire Lib "Kernel" (ByVal hMem As Integer) As Integer
Declare Function GlobalUnlock Lib "Kernel" (ByVal hMem As Integer) As Integer
Declare Function GlobalLRUNewest Lib "Kernel" (ByVal hMem As Integer) As ⇐
Integer
Declare Function GlobalLRUOldest Lib "Kernel" (ByVal hMem As Integer) As ⇐
Integer
Declare Function GlobalPageLock Lib "Kernel" (ByVal wSelector As Integer) ⇐
As Integer
Declare Function GlobalPageUnlock Lib "Kernel" (ByVal wSelector As Integer) ⇐
As Integer
Declare Sub GlobalFix Lib "Kernel" (ByVal hMem As Integer)
Declare Function GlobalUnfix Lib "Kernel" (ByVal hMem As Integer) As ←
Integer

'  Flags returned by GlobalFlags (in addition to GMEM_DISCARDABLE)
Global Const GMEM_DISCARDED = &H4000
Global Const GMEM_LOCKCOUNT = &HFF

Declare Function LockSegment Lib "Kernel" (ByVal wSegment As Integer) ⇐
As Integer
Declare Function UnlockSegment Lib "Kernel" (ByVal wSegment As Integer) ⇐
As Integer

'  Local Memory Flags
Global Const LMEM_FIXED = &H0
Global Const LMEM_MOVEABLE = &H2
Global Const LMEM_NOCOMPACT = &H10
Global Const LMEM_NODISCARD = &H20
Global Const LMEM_ZEROINIT = &H40
Global Const LMEM_MODIFY = &H80
Global Const LMEM_DISCARDABLE = &HF00

Global Const LHND = (LMEM_MOVEABLE+LMEM_ZEROINIT)
Global Const LPTR = (LMEM_FIXED+LMEM_ZEROINIT)

Global Const NONZEROLHND = (LMEM_MOVEABLE)
Global Const NONZEROLPTR = (LMEM_FIXED)

Global Const LNOTIFY_OUTOFMEM = 0
Global Const LNOTIFY_MOVE = 1
Global Const LNOTIFY_DISCARD = 2
```

*continued on next page*

*continued from previous page*

```
Declare Function LocalAlloc Lib "Kernel" (ByVal wFlags As Integer, ⇐
ByVal wBytes As Integer) As Integer
Declare Function LocalCompact Lib "Kernel" (ByVal wMinFree As Integer) ⇐
As Integer
Declare Function LocalFree Lib "Kernel" (ByVal hMem As Integer) As Integer
Declare Function LocalHandle Lib "Kernel" (ByVal wMem As Integer) As ⇐
Integer
Declare Function LocalInit Lib "Kernel" (ByVal wSegment As Integer, ⇐
ByVal pStart As Integer, ByVal pEnd As Integer) As Integer
Declare Function LocalLock Lib "Kernel" (ByVal hMem As Integer) As Integer
'(returns a near pointer)
Declare Function LocalReAlloc Lib "Kernel" (ByVal hMem As Integer, ⇐
ByVal wBytes As Integer, ByVal wFlags As Integer) As Integer

'NOTE: instead of declaring the function LocalDiscard and calling
'      LocalDiscard(hMem), call LocalReAlloc(hMem, 0, LMEM_MOVEABLE)

Declare Function LocalSize Lib "Kernel" (ByVal hMem As Integer) As Integer
Declare Function LocalUnlock Lib "Kernel" (ByVal hMem As Integer) As
Integer
Declare Function LocalFlags Lib "Kernel" (ByVal hMem As Integer) As
Integer
Declare Function LocalShrink Lib "Kernel" (ByVal hSeg As Integer, ByVal ⇐
wSize As Integer) As Integer

' Flags returned by LocalFlags (in addition to LMEM_DISCARDABLE)
Global Const LMEM_DISCARDED = &H4000
Global Const LMEM_LOCKCOUNT = &HFF
```

These are low-level functions that Microsoft recommends against using.

```
Declare Function SetSwapAreaSize Lib "Kernel" (ByVal rsSize As Integer) As ⇐
Long
Declare Function ValidateFreeSpaces Lib "Kernel" () As Long
Declare Sub LimitEmsPages Lib "Kernel" (ByVal dwKbytes As Long)
Declare Function SetErrorMode Lib "Kernel" (ByVal wMode As Integer) As ⇐
Integer
Declare Sub ValidateCodeSegments Lib "Kernel" ()
Declare Function AllocDStoCSAlias Lib "Kernel" (ByVal wSelector As Integer) ⇐
As Integer
Declare Function AllocSelector Lib "Kernel" (ByVal wSelector As Integer) ⇐
As Integer
Declare Function ChangeSelector Lib "Kernel" (ByVal wDestSelector ⇐
As Integer, ByVal wSourceSelector As Integer) As Integer
Declare Function FreeSelector Lib "Kernel" (ByVal wSelector As Integer) As ⇐
Integer
```

GetDOSEnvironment returns the strings in an application's environment, just like Visual Basic's Environ$ function.

```
Declare Function GetDOSEnvironment Lib "Kernel" () As Long
```

These functions and constants are used when accessing the resources (such as bitmaps and icons) from an executable application or DLL.

```
Declare Function FindResource Lib "Kernel" (ByVal hInstance As Integer, ⇐
ByVal lpName As String, ByVal lpType As Any) As Integer
Declare Function LoadResource Lib "Kernel" (ByVal hInstance As Integer, ⇐
ByVal hResInfo As Integer) As Integer
Declare Function FreeResource Lib "Kernel" (ByVal hResData As Integer) ⇐
As Integer
Declare Function LockResource Lib "Kernel" (ByVal hResData As Integer) ⇐
As Long
Declare Function AllocResource Lib "Kernel" (ByVal hInstance As Integer, ⇐
ByVal hResInfo As Integer, ByVal dwSize As Long) As Integer
Declare Function SizeofResource Lib "Kernel" (ByVal hInstance As Integer, ⇐
ByVal hResInfo As Integer) As Integer
Declare Function AccessResource Lib "Kernel" (ByVal hInstance As Integer, ⇐
ByVal hResInfo As Integer) As Integer

'  Predefined Resource Types
Global Const RT_CURSOR = 1&
Global Const RT_BITMAP = 2&
Global Const RT_ICON = 3&
Global Const RT_MENU = 4&
Global Const RT_DIALOG = 5&
Global Const RT_STRING = 6&
Global Const RT_FONTDIR = 7&
Global Const RT_FONT = 8&
Global Const RT_ACCELERATOR = 9&
Global Const RT_RCDATA = 10&

'  OEM Resource Ordinal Numbers
Global Const OBM_CLOSE = 32754
Global Const OBM_UPARROW = 32753
Global Const OBM_DNARROW = 32752
Global Const OBM_RGARROW = 32751
Global Const OBM_LFARROW = 32750
Global Const OBM_REDUCE = 32749
Global Const OBM_ZOOM = 32748
Global Const OBM_RESTORE = 32747
Global Const OBM_REDUCED = 32746
Global Const OBM_ZOOMD = 32745
Global Const OBM_RESTORED = 32744
Global Const OBM_UPARROWD = 32743
Global Const OBM_DNARROWD = 32742
Global Const OBM_RGARROWD = 32741
Global Const OBM_LFARROWD = 32740
Global Const OBM_MNARROW = 32739
Global Const OBM_COMBO = 32738

Global Const OBM_OLD_CLOSE = 32767
Global Const OBM_SIZE = 32766
Global Const OBM_OLD_UPARROW = 32765
Global Const OBM_OLD_DNARROW = 32764
Global Const OBM_OLD_RGARROW = 32763
Global Const OBM_OLD_LFARROW = 32762
Global Const OBM_BTSIZE = 32761
```

*continued on next page*

*continued from previous page*

```
Global Const OBM_CHECK = 32760
Global Const OBM_CHECKBOXES = 32759
Global Const OBM_BTNCORNERS = 32758
Global Const OBM_OLD_REDUCE = 32757
Global Const OBM_OLD_ZOOM = 32756
Global Const OBM_OLD_RESTORE = 32755

Global Const OCR_NORMAL = 32512
Global Const OCR_IBEAM = 32513
Global Const OCR_WAIT = 32514
Global Const OCR_CROSS = 32515
Global Const OCR_UP = 32516
Global Const OCR_SIZE = 32640
Global Const OCR_ICON = 32641
Global Const OCR_SIZENWSE = 32642
Global Const OCR_SIZENESW = 32643
Global Const OCR_SIZEWE = 32644
Global Const OCR_SIZENS = 32645
Global Const OCR_SIZEALL = 32646
Global Const OCR_ICOCUR = 32647

Global Const OIC_SAMPLE = 32512
Global Const OIC_HAND = 32513
Global Const OIC_QUES = 32514
Global Const OIC_BANG = 32515
Global Const OIC_NOTE = 32516
```

Yield is similar to Visual Basic's DoEvent function, and gives Windows a chance to let other applications do some processing. Microsoft recommends against using Yield.

```
Declare Sub Yield Lib "Kernel" ()
Declare Function GetCurrentTask Lib "Kernel" () As Integer
```

Windows supports global atoms which are strings of information that applications can share with each other. The fractal DLL presented in Chapter 9 uses global atoms to inform applications what kinds of fractals it can do.

```
Declare Function InitAtomTable Lib "Kernel" (ByVal nSize As Integer) As ⇐
Integer
Declare Function AddAtom Lib "Kernel" (ByVal lpString As String) As ⇐
Integer
Declare Function DeleteAtom Lib "Kernel" (ByVal nAtom As Integer) As Integer
Declare Function FindAtom Lib "Kernel" (ByVal lpString As String) As Integer
Declare Function GetAtomName Lib "Kernel" (ByVal nAtom As Integer, ByVal ⇐
lpBuffer As String, ByVal nSize As Integer) As Integer
Declare Function GlobalAddAtom Lib "Kernel" (ByVal lpString As String) As ⇐
Integer
Declare Function GlobalDeleteAtom Lib "Kernel" (ByVal nAtom As Integer) As ⇐
Integer
Declare Function GlobalFindAtom Lib "Kernel" (ByVal lpString As String) As ⇐
Integer
Declare Function GlobalGetAtomName Lib "Kernel" (ByVal nAtom As Integer, ⇐
```

```
ByVal lpbuffer As String, ByVal nSize As Integer) As Integer
Declare Function GetAtomHandle Lib "Kernel" (ByVal wAtom As Integer) As ⇐
Integer
```

The profile functions are used to read and write information from .INI
files. See How-To 1.3 Save program settings to a file and How-To 1.4 Remember the sizes and locations of my forms, for information about using
these functions.

```
' User Profile Routines
Declare Function GetProfileInt Lib "Kernel" (ByVal lpAppName As String, ⇐
ByVal lpKeyName As String, ByVal nDefault As Integer) As Integer
Declare Function GetProfileString Lib "Kernel" (ByVal lpAppName As String, ⇐
ByVal lpKeyName As String, ByVal lpDefault As String, ByVal lpReturnedString
As String, ByVal nSize As Integer) As Integer
Declare Function WriteProfileString Lib "Kernel" (ByVal lpApplicationName ⇐
As String, ByVal lpKeyName As String, ByVal lpString As String) As Integer
Declare Function GetPrivateProfileInt Lib "Kernel" (ByVal ⇐
lpApplicationName As String, ByVal lpKeyName As String, ByVal nDefault ⇐
As Integer, ByVal lpFileName As String) As Integer
Declare Function GetPrivateProfileString Lib "Kernel" (ByVal ⇐
lpApplicationName As String, ByVal lpKeyName As String, ByVal lpDefault ⇐ As
String, ByVal lpReturnedString As String, ByVal nSize As Integer, ByVal ⇐
lpFileName As String) As Integer
Declare Function WritePrivateProfileString Lib "Kernel" (ByVal ⇐
lpApplicationName As String, ByVal lpKeyName As String, ByVal lpString As ⇐
String, ByVal lplFileName As String) As Integer
```

The Get…Directory functions return the directory in which Windows
was installed, and where Windows' system files are, respectively. See How-
To 6.11 Determine the directory where Windows is installed.

```
Declare Function GetWindowsDirectory Lib "Kernel" (ByVal lpBuffer As ⇐
String, ByVal nSize As Integer) As Integer
Declare Function GetSystemDirectory Lib "Kernel" (ByVal lpBuffer As ⇐
String, ByVal nSize As Integer) As Integer
```

Catch and Throw are low-level and should be avoided in Visual Basic
application.

```
'NOTE: Catch/Throw expect a long pointer to an 18-byte buffer (lpCatchBuf)
' eg:
'    Dim Buffer(1 To 9) As Integer
'    result% = Catch (Buffer(1))

Declare Function Catch Lib "Kernel" (lpCatchBuf As Any) As Integer
Declare Sub Throw Lib "Kernel" (lpCatchBuf As Any, ByVal nThrowBack As ⇐
Integer)
```

FatalExit and SwapRecording are used while debugging with the debugging version of Windows from the SDK.

```
Declare Sub FatalExit Lib "Kernel" (ByVal Code As Integer)
Declare Sub SwapRecording Lib "Kernel" (ByVal wFlag As Integer)
```

These functions translate between the ANSI character set that Windows usually uses and the OEM character set that the PC uses when in DOS. DOS uses the OEM character set to store filenames, for example, so these functions ensure that foreign characters are translated to their OEM equivalents (if they exist).

```
' Character Translation Routines
Declare Function AnsiToOem Lib "Keyboard" (ByVal lpAnsiStr As String, ByVal ⇐
lpOemStr As String) As Integer
Declare Function OemToAnsi Lib "Keyboard" (ByVal lpOemStr As String, ByVal ⇐
lpAnsiStr As String) As Integer
Declare Sub AnsiToOemBuff Lib "Keyboard" (ByVal lpAnsiStr As String, ByVal ⇐
lpOemStr As String, ByVal nLength As Integer)
Declare Sub OemToAnsiBuff Lib "Keyboard" (ByVal lpOemStr As String, ByVal ⇐
lpAnsiStr As String, ByVal nLength as Integer)
```

These functions convert between upper- and lowercase using the ANSI character set, so international characters are properly converted.

```
Declare Function AnsiUpper Lib "User" (ByVal lpString As String) As String
Declare Function AnsiUpperBuff Lib "User" (ByVal lpString As String, ByVal ⇐
aWORD As Integer) As Integer
Declare Function AnsiLower Lib "User" (ByVal lpString As String) As Long
Declare Function AnsiLowerBuff Lib "User" (ByVal lpString As String, ByVal ⇐
aWORD As Integer) As Integer
Declare Function AnsiNext Lib "User" (ByVal lpString As String) As Long
Declare Function AnsiPrev Lib "User" (ByVal lpString As String, ByVal ⇐
lpString As String) As Long
```

These functions return information about the keyboard installed on the user's machine. See How-To 6.10 Determine how many function keys are on my user's keyboard.

```
' Keyboard Information Routines
Declare Function OemKeyScan Lib "Keyboard" (ByVal wOemChar As Integer) ⇐
As Long
Declare Function VkKeyScan Lib "Keyboard" (ByVal cChar As Integer) As ⇐
Integer
Declare Function GetKeyboardType Lib "Keyboard" (ByVal nTypeFlag As ⇐
Integer) As Integer
Declare Function MapVirtualKey Lib "Keyboard" (ByVal wCode As Integer, ⇐
ByVal wMapType As Integer) As Integer
Declare Function GetKBCodePage Lib "Keyboard" ()
Declare Function GetKeyNameText Lib "Keyboard" (ByVal lParam As Long, ⇐
ByVal lpBuffer As String, ByVal nSize As Integer) As Integer
Declare Function ToAscii Lib "Keyboard" (ByVal wVirtKey As Integer, ByVal ⇐
wScanCode As Integer, lpKeyState As Any, lpChar As Any, Byval wFlags As ⇐
Integer) As Integer
```

The IsChar... functions indicate the characteristics of a given character. These functions let the language driver that Windows is using determine the characteristics, so they're essentially language-independent.

```
' Language dependent Routines
Declare Function IsCharAlpha Lib "User" (ByVal cChar As Integer) As ⇐
Integer
Declare Function IsCharAlphaNumeric Lib "User" (ByVal cChar As Integer) ⇐
As  Integer
Declare Function IsCharUpper Lib "User" (ByVal cChar As Integer) As ⇐
Integer
Declare Function IsCharLower Lib "User" (ByVal cChar As Integer) As ⇐
Integer
```

GetWinFlags returns information about how Windows is configured and the hardware it's running on. See How-To 6.15 Find out everything about the system configuration.

```
Declare Function GetWinFlags Lib "Kernel" () As Long

Global Const WF_PMODE = &H1
Global Const WF_CPU286 = &H2
Global Const WF_CPU386 = &H4
Global Const WF_CPU486 = &H8
Global Const WF_STANDARD = &H10
Global Const WF_WIN286 = &H10
Global Const WF_ENHANCED = &H20
Global Const WF_WIN386 = &H20
Global Const WF_CPU086 = &H40
Global Const WF_CPU186 = &H80
Global Const WF_LARGEFRAME = &H100
Global Const WF_SMALLFRAME = &H200
Global Const WF_80x87 = &H400
```

These constants are used by DLLs when they exit. Since Visual Basic can't create DLLs, they can't be used.

```
' WEP fSystemExit flag values
Global Const WEP_SYSTEM_EXIT = 1
Global Const WEP_FREE_DLL = 0


'------------------------------------
'  GDI Section
' ------------------------------------
```

These constants are used for setting the DrawMode property setting.

```
' Binary raster ops
Global Const R2_BLACK = 1        '  0
Global Const R2_NOTMERGEPEN = 2      ' DPon
Global Const R2_MASKNOTPEN = 3       ' DPna
Global Const R2_NOTCOPYPEN = 4       ' PN
Global Const R2_MASKPENNOT = 5       ' PDna
```

*continued on next page*

*continued from previous page*

```
Global Const R2_NOT = 6          '  Dn
Global Const R2_XORPEN = 7      '  DPx
Global Const R2_NOTMASKPEN = 8          '  DPan
Global Const R2_MASKPEN = 9    '  DPa
Global Const R2_NOTXORPEN = 10          '  DPxn
Global Const R2_NOP = 11         '  D
Global Const R2_MERGENOTPEN = 12        '  DPno
Global Const R2_COPYPEN = 13 '  P
Global Const R2_MERGEPENNOT = 14        '  PDno
Global Const R2_MERGEPEN = 15          '  DPo
Global Const R2_WHITE = 16      '    1
```

Some of these constants are used in How-To 5.4 Draw a transparent picture or icon on a form.

```
'   Ternary raster operations
Global Const SRCCOPY = &HCC0020      ' (DWORD) dest = source
Global Const SRCPAINT = &HEE0086     ' (DWORD) dest = source OR dest
Global Const SRCAND = &H8800C6       ' (DWORD) dest = source AND dest
Global Const SRCINVERT = &H660046    ' (DWORD) dest = source XOR dest
Global Const SRCERASE = &H440328     ' (DWORD) dest = source AND (NOT dest )
Global Const NOTSRCCOPY = &H330008   ' (DWORD) dest = (NOT source)
Global Const NOTSRCERASE = &H1100A6  ' (DWORD) dest = (NOT src) AND (NOT dest)
Global Const MERGECOPY = &HC000CA    ' (DWORD) dest = (source AND pattern)
Global Const MERGEPAINT = &HBB0226   ' (DWORD) dest = (NOT source) OR dest
Global Const PATCOPY = &HF00021      ' (DWORD) dest = pattern
Global Const PATPAINT = &HFB0A09     ' (DWORD) dest = DPSnoo
Global Const PATINVERT = &H5A0049    ' (DWORD) dest = pattern XOR dest
Global Const DSTINVERT = &H550009    ' (DWORD) dest = (NOT dest)
Global Const BLACKNESS = &H42&       ' (DWORD) dest = BLACK
Global Const WHITENESS = &HFF0062    ' (DWORD) dest = WHITE

'  StretchBlt() Modes
Global Const BLACKONWHITE = 1
Global Const WHITEONBLACK = 2
Global Const COLORONCOLOR = 3

'  PolyFill() Modes
Global Const ALTERNATE = 1
Global Const WINDING = 2
```

See How-To 3.5, Align text automatically for an example of using the TA_ constants to align text.

```
'  Text Alignment Options
Global Const TA_NOUPDATECP = 0
Global Const TA_UPDATECP = 1

Global Const TA_LEFT = 0
Global Const TA_RIGHT = 2
Global Const TA_CENTER = 6

Global Const TA_TOP = 0
Global Const TA_BOTTOM = 8
Global Const TA_BASELINE = 24
```

```
Global Const ETO_GRAYED = 1
Global Const ETO_OPAQUE = 2
Global Const ETO_CLIPPED = 4

Global Const ASPECT_FILTERING = &H1
```

These constants are used when creating Windows metafiles with the CreateMetaFile function. If you're only going to use metafiles (and not create them), you can use Visual Basic's LoadPicture function, which understands icons, bitmaps, and metafiles automatically.

```
' Metafile Functions
Global Const META_SETBKCOLOR = &H201
Global Const META_SETBKMODE = &H102
Global Const META_SETMAPMODE = &H103
Global Const META_SETROP2 = &H104
Global Const META_SETRELABS = &H105
Global Const META_SETPOLYFILLMODE = &H106
Global Const META_SETSTRETCHBLTMODE = &H107
Global Const META_SETTEXTCHAREXTRA = &H108
Global Const META_SETTEXTCOLOR = &H209
Global Const META_SETTEXTJUSTIFICATION = &H20A
Global Const META_SETWINDOWORG = &H20B
Global Const META_SETWINDOWEXT = &H20C
Global Const META_SETVIEWPORTORG = &H20D
Global Const META_SETVIEWPORTEXT = &H20E
Global Const META_OFFSETWINDOWORG = &H20F
Global Const META_SCALEWINDOWEXT = &H400
Global Const META_OFFSETVIEWPORTORG = &H211
Global Const META_SCALEVIEWPORTEXT = &H412
Global Const META_LINETO = &H213
Global Const META_MOVETO = &H214
Global Const META_EXCLUDECLIPRECT = &H415
Global Const META_INTERSECTCLIPRECT = &H416
Global Const META_ARC = &H817
Global Const META_ELLIPSE = &H418
Global Const META_FLOODFILL = &H419
Global Const META_PIE = &H81A
Global Const META_RECTANGLE = &H41B
Global Const META_ROUNDRECT = &H61C
Global Const META_PATBLT = &H61D
Global Const META_SAVEDC = &H1E
Global Const META_SETPIXEL = &H41F
Global Const META_OFFSETCLIPRGN = &H220
Global Const META_TEXTOUT = &H521
Global Const META_BITBLT = &H922
Global Const META_STRETCHBLT = &HB23
Global Const META_POLYGON = &H324
Global Const META_POLYLINE = &H325
Global Const META_ESCAPE = &H626
Global Const META_RESTOREDC = &H127
Global Const META_FILLREGION = &H228
Global Const META_FRAMEREGION = &H429
Global Const META_INVERTREGION = &H12A
Global Const META_PAINTREGION = &H12B
```

*continued on next page*

*continued from previous page*

```
Global Const META_SELECTCLIPREGION = &H12C
Global Const META_SELECTOBJECT = &H12D
Global Const META_SETTEXTALIGN = &H12E
Global Const META_DRAWTEXT = &H62F

Global Const META_CHORD = &H830
Global Const META_SETMAPPERFLAGS = &H231
Global Const META_EXTTEXTOUT = &Ha32
Global Const META_SETDIBTODEV = &Hd33
Global Const META_SELECTPALETTE = &H234
Global Const META_REALIZEPALETTE = &H35
Global Const META_ANIMATEPALETTE = &H436
Global Const META_SETPALENTRIES = &H37
Global Const META_POLYPOLYGON = &H538
Global Const META_RESIZEPALETTE = &H139

Global Const META_DIBBITBLT = &H940
Global Const META_DIBSTRETCHBLT = &Hb41
Global Const META_DIBCREATEPATTERNBRUSH = &H142
Global Const META_STRETCHDIB = &Hf43

Global Const META_DELETEOBJECT = &H1f0

Global Const META_CREATEPALETTE = &Hf7
Global Const META_CREATEBRUSH = &HF8
Global Const META_CREATEPATTERNBRUSH = &H1F9
Global Const META_CREATEPENINDIRECT = &H2FA
Global Const META_CREATEFONTINDIRECT = &H2FB
Global Const META_CREATEBRUSHINDIRECT = &H2FC
Global Const META_CREATEBITMAPINDIRECT = &H2FD
Global Const META_CREATEBITMAP = &H6FE
Global Const META_CREATEREGION = &H6FF
```

These constants are useful if you need to directly communicate with the printer. It's far easier to use Visual Basic's Printer object to manage printing.

```
' GDI Escapes
Global Const NEWFRAME = 1
Global Const ABORTDOC = 2
Global Const NEXTBAND = 3
Global Const SETCOLORTABLE = 4
Global Const GETCOLORTABLE = 5
Global Const FLUSHOUTPUT = 6
Global Const DRAFTMODE = 7
Global Const QUERYESCSUPPORT = 8
Global Const SETABORTPROC = 9
Global Const STARTDOC = 10
Global Const ENDDOCAPI = 11
Global Const GETPHYSPAGESIZE = 12
Global Const GETPRINTINGOFFSET = 13
Global Const GETSCALINGFACTOR = 14
Global Const MFCOMMENT = 15
Global Const GETPENWIDTH = 16
Global Const SETCOPYCOUNT = 17
Global Const SELECTPAPERSOURCE = 18
Global Const DEVICEDATA = 19
```

```
Global Const PASSTHROUGH = 19
Global Const GETTECHNOLGY = 20
Global Const GETTECHNOLOGY = 20
Global Const SETENDCAP = 21
Global Const SETLINEJOIN = 22
Global Const SETMITERLIMIT = 23
Global Const BANDINFO = 24
Global Const DRAWPATTERNRECT = 25
Global Const GETVECTORPENSIZE = 26
Global Const GETVECTORBRUSHSIZE = 27
Global Const ENABLEDUPLEX = 28
Global Const GETSETPAPERBINS = 29
Global Const GETSETPRINTORIENT = 30
Global Const ENUMPAPERBINS = 31
Global Const SETDIBSCALING = 32
Global Const EPSPRINTING = 33
Global Const ENUMPAPERMETRICS = 34
Global Const GETSETPAPERMETRICS = 35
Global Const POSTSCRIPT_DATA = 37
Global Const POSTSCRIPT_IGNORE = 38
Global Const GETEXTENDEDTEXTMETRICS = 256
Global Const GETEXTENTTABLE = 257
Global Const GETPAIRKERNTABLE = 258
Global Const GETTRACKKERNTABLE = 259
Global Const EXTTEXTOUT = 512
Global Const ENABLERELATIVEWIDTHS = 768
Global Const ENABLEPAIRKERNING = 769
Global Const SETKERNTRACK = 770
Global Const SETALLJUSTVALUES = 771
Global Const SETCHARSET = 772

Global Const STRETCHBLT = 2048
Global Const BEGIN_PATH = 4096
Global Const CLIP_TO_PATH = 4097
Global Const END_PATH = 4098
Global Const EXT_DEVICE_CAPS = 4099
Global Const RESTORE_CTM = 4100
Global Const SAVE_CTM = 4101
Global Const SET_ARC_DIRECTION = 4102
Global Const SET_BACKGROUND_COLOR = 4103
Global Const SET_POLY_MODE = 4104
Global Const SET_SCREEN_ANGLE = 4105
Global Const SET_SPREAD = 4106
Global Const TRANSFORM_CTM = 4107
Global Const SET_CLIP_BOX = 4108
Global Const SET_BOUNDS = 4109
Global Const SET_MIRROR_MODE = 4110

'   Spooler Error Codes
Global Const SP_NOTREPORTED = &H4000
Global Const SP_ERROR = (-1)
Global Const SP_APPABORT = (-2)
Global Const SP_USERABORT = (-3)
Global Const SP_OUTOFDISK = (-4)
```

*continued on next page*

*continued from previous page*

```
Global Const SP_OUTOFMEMORY = (-5)

Global Const PR_JOBSTATUS = &H0
```

These structures and constants are used to read .BMP bitmap files and .WMF metafiles. If all you need to do is display such a file in a picture box, use Visual Basic's LoadPicture function.

```
'  Bitmap Header Definition
Type BITMAP '14 bytes
     bmType As Integer
     bmWidth As Integer
     bmHeight As Integer
     bmWidthBytes As Integer
     bmPlanes As String * 1
     bmBitsPixel As String * 1
     bmBits As Long
End Type

Type RGBTRIPLE
     rgbtBlue As String * 1
     rgbtGreen As String * 1
     rgbtRed As String * 1
End Type

Type RGBQUAD
     rgbBlue as String * 1
     rgbGreen As String * 1
     rgbRed As String * 1
     rgbReserved As String * 1
End Type

'  structures for defining DIBs
Type BITMAPCOREHEADER '12 bytes
     bcSize as Long
     bcWidth As Integer
     bcHeight As Integer
     bcPlanes As Integer
     bcBitCount As Integer
End Type

Type BITMAPINFOHEADER '40 bytes
     biSize As Long
     biWidth As Long
     biHeight As Long
     biPlanes As Integer
     biBitCount As Integer
     biCompression As Long
     biSizeImage As Long
     biXPelsPerMeter As Long
     biYPelsPerMeter As Long
     biClrUsed As Long
     biClrImportant As Long
End Type

'  constants for the biCompression field
```

```
Global Const BI_RGB = O&
Global Const BI_RLE8 = 1&
Global Const BI_RLE4 = 2&

Type BITMAPINFO
    bmiHeader as BITMAPINFOHEADER
    bmiColors As String * 128 ' Array length is arbitrary; may be changed
End Type

Type BITMAPCOREINFO
    bmciHeader As BITMAPCOREHEADER
    bmciColors As String * 96 ' Array length is arbitrary; may be changed
End Type

Type BITMAPFILEHEADER
    bfType As Integer
    bfSize As Long
    bfReserved1 As Integer
    bfReserved2 As Integer
    bfOffBits As Long
End Type

' Clipboard Metafile Picture Structure
Type HANDLETABLE
    objectHandle As String * 512 ' Array length is arbitrary; may be ⇐
    changed
End Type

Type METARECORD
    rdSize As Long
    rdFunction As Integer
    rdParm As String * 512 ' Array length is arbitrary; may be changed
End Type

Type METAFILEPICT
    mm As Integer
    xExt As Integer
    yExt As Integer
    hMF As Integer
End Type

Type METAHEADER
    mtType As Integer
    mtHeaderSize As Integer
    mtVersion As Integer
    mtSize As Long
    mtNoObjects As Integer
    mtMaxRecord As Long
    mtNoParameters As Integer
End Type
```

These structures and functions are used to determine font characteristics. It's easier to use a Visual Basic function such as TextHeight and TextWidth and properties such as FontName, FontBold, FontItalic, and FontUnderline to determine most font characteristics.

```
Type TEXTMETRIC
     tmHeight As Integer
     tmAscent As Integer
     tmDescent As Integer
     tmInternalLeading As Integer
     tmExternalLeading As Integer
     tmAveCharWidth As Integer
     tmMaxCharWidth As Integer
     tmWeight As Integer
     tmItalic As String * 1
     tmUnderlined As String * 1
     tmStruckOut As String * 1
     tmFirstChar As String * 1
     tmLastChar As String * 1
     tmDefaultChar As String * 1
     tmBreakChar As String * 1
     tmPitchAndFamily As String * 1
     tmCharSet As String * 1
     tmOverhang As Integer
     tmDigitizedAspectX As Integer
     tmDigitizedAspectY As Integer
End Type

' Logical Font
Global Const LF_FACESIZE = 32

Type LOGFONT
     lfHeight As Integer
     lfWidth As Integer
     lfEscapement As Integer
     lfOrientation As Integer
     lfWeight As Integer
     lfItalic As String * 1
     lfUnderline As String * 1
     lfStrikeOut As String * 1
     lfCharSet As String * 1
     lfOutPrecision As String * 1
     lfClipPrecision As String * 1
     lfQuality As String * 1
     lfPitchAndFamily As String * 1
     lfFaceName As String * LF_FACESIZE
End Type

Global Const OUT_DEFAULT_PRECIS = 0
Global Const OUT_STRING_PRECIS = 1
Global Const OUT_CHARACTER_PRECIS = 2
Global Const OUT_STROKE_PRECIS = 3

Global Const CLIP_DEFAULT_PRECIS = 0
Global Const CLIP_CHARACTER_PRECIS = 1
Global Const CLIP_STROKE_PRECIS = 2

Global Const DEFAULT_QUALITY = 0
Global Const DRAFT_QUALITY = 1
```

```
Global Const PROOF_QUALITY = 2

Global Const DEFAULT_PITCH = 0
Global Const FIXED_PITCH = 1
Global Const VARIABLE_PITCH = 2

Global Const ANSI_CHARSET = 0
Global Const SYMBOL_CHARSET = 2
Global Const SHIFTJIS_CHARSET = 128
Global Const OEM_CHARSET = 255

'  Font Families
'
Global Const FF_DONTCARE = 0 '  Don't care or don't know.
Global Const FF_ROMAN = 16    '  Variable stroke width, serifed.

'  Times Roman, Century Schoolbook, etc.
Global Const FF_SWISS = 32    '  Variable stroke width, sans-serifed.

'  Helvetica, Swiss, etc.
Global Const FF_MODERN = 48  '  Constant stroke width, serifed or sans- ⇐
serifed.

'  Pica, Elite, Courier, etc.
Global Const FF_SCRIPT = 64 '  Cursive, etc.
Global Const FF_DECORATIVE = 80     '  Old English, etc.

'  Font Weights
Global Const FW_DONTCARE = 0
Global Const FW_THIN = 100
Global Const FW_EXTRALIGHT = 200
Global Const FW_LIGHT = 300
Global Const FW_NORMAL = 400
Global Const FW_MEDIUM = 500
Global Const FW_SEMIBOLD = 600
Global Const FW_BOLD = 700
Global Const FW_EXTRABOLD = 800
Global Const FW_HEAVY = 900

Global Const FW_ULTRALIGHT = FW_EXTRALIGHT
Global Const FW_REGULAR = FW_NORMAL
Global Const FW_DEMIBOLD = FW_SEMIBOLD
Global Const FW_ULTRABOLD = FW_EXTRABOLD
Global Const FW_BLACK = FW_HEAVY

'  Background Modes
Global Const TRANSPARENT = 1
Global Const OPAQUE = 2
```

Logical brushes and pens can be specified in Visual Basic drawing methods like Line without using these types.

```
'  GDI Logical Objects:

'  Pel Array
Type PELARRAY
```

*continued on next page*

*continued from previous page*

```
        paXCount As Integer
        paYCount As Integer
        paXExt As Integer
        paYExt As Integer
        paRGBs As Integer
End Type

'  Logical Brush (or Pattern)
Type LOGBRUSH
        lbStyle As Integer
        lbColor As Long
        lbHatch As Integer
End Type

'  Logical Pen
Type LOGPEN
        lopnStyle As Integer
        lopnWidth As POINTAPI
        lopnColor As Long
End Type
```

Windows' palettes are used to support images with more than sixteen colors, something that Visual Basic itself doesn't support.

```
Declare Function CreatePalette Lib "GDI" (lpLogPalette As LOGPALETTE) As ⇐
Integer
Declare Function SelectPalette Lib "GDI" (ByVal hDC As Integer, ByVal ⇐
hPalette as Integer, ByVal bForceBackground as Integer) As Integer
Declare Function RealizePalette Lib "GDI" (ByVal hDC As Integer) As
Integer
Declare Function UpdateColors Lib "GDI" (ByVal hDC As Integer) As Integer
Declare Sub AnimatePalette Lib "GDI" (ByVal hPalette As Integer, ByVal ⇐
wStartIndex As Integer, ByVal wNumEntries As Integer, lpPaletteColors As ⇐
PALETTEENTRY)
Declare Function SetPaletteEntries Lib "GDI" (ByVal hPalette As Integer, ⇐
ByVal wStartIndex As Integer, ByVal wNumEntries As Integer, ⇐
lpPaletteEntries As PALETTEENTRY) As Integer
Declare Function GetPaletteEntries Lib "GDI" (ByVal hPalette As Integer, ⇐
ByVal wStartIndex As Integer, ByVal wNumEntries As Integer, ⇐
lpPaletteEntries As PALETTEENTRY) As Integer
Declare Function GetNearestPaletteIndex Lib "GDI" (ByVal hPalette As ⇐
Integer, ByVal crColor As Long) As Integer
Declare Function ResizePalette Lib "GDI" (ByVal hPalette As Integer, ByVal ⇐
nNumEntries As Integer) As Integer

Declare Function GetSystemPaletteEntries Lib "GDI" (ByVal hDC As Integer, ⇐
ByVal wStartIndex As Integer, ByVal wNumEntries As Integer, ⇐
lpPaletteEntries As PALETTEENTRY) As Integer
Declare Function GetSystemPaletteUse Lib "GDI" (ByVal hDC As Integer) As ⇐
Integer
Declare Function SetSystemPaletteUse Lib "GDI" (ByVal hDC As Integer, ⇐
ByVal wUsage As Integer) As Integer

Type PALETTEENTRY
```

```
        peRed As String * 1
        peGreen As String * 1
        peBlue As String * 1
        peFlags As String * 1
End Type


'  Logical Palette
Type LOGPALETTE
        palVersion As Integer
        palNumEntries As Integer
        palPalEntry As String * 252 ' Array length is arbitrary; may be
changed
End Type


'  palette entry flags
Global Const PC_RESERVED = &H1      '  palette index used for animation
Global Const PC_EXPLICIT = &H2      '  palette index is explicit to device
Global Const PC_NOCOLLAPSE = &H4    '  do not match color to system palette


'  constants for Get/SetSystemPaletteUse()
Global Const SYSPAL_STATIC = 1
Global Const SYSPAL_NOSTATIC = 2


'  Mapping Modes
Global Const MM_TEXT = 1
Global Const MM_LOMETRIC = 2
Global Const MM_HIMETRIC = 3
Global Const MM_LOENGLISH = 4
Global Const MM_HIENGLISH = 5
Global Const MM_TWIPS = 6
Global Const MM_ISOTROPIC = 7
Global Const MM_ANISOTROPIC = 8


'  Coordinate Modes
Global Const ABSOLUTE = 1
Global Const RELATIVE = 2


'  Stock Logical Objects
Global Const WHITE_BRUSH = 0
Global Const LTGRAY_BRUSH = 1
Global Const GRAY_BRUSH = 2
Global Const DKGRAY_BRUSH = 3
Global Const BLACK_BRUSH = 4
Global Const NULL_BRUSH = 5
Global Const HOLLOW_BRUSH = NULL_BRUSH
Global Const WHITE_PEN = 6
Global Const BLACK_PEN = 7
Global Const NULL_PEN = 8
Global Const OEM_FIXED_FONT = 10
Global Const ANSI_FIXED_FONT = 11
Global Const ANSI_VAR_FONT = 12
Global Const SYSTEM_FONT = 13
Global Const DEVICE_DEFAULT_FONT = 14
```

*continued on next page*

*continued from previous page*

```
Global Const DEFAULT_PALETTE = 15
Global Const SYSTEM_FIXED_FONT = 16

'  Brush Styles
Global Const BS_SOLID = 0
Global Const BS_NULL = 1
Global Const BS_HOLLOW = BS_NULL
Global Const BS_HATCHED = 2
Global Const BS_PATTERN = 3
Global Const BS_INDEXED = 4
Global Const BS_DIBPATTERN = 5
```

These hatch styles can be used with the FillStyle property.

```
'  Hatch Styles
Global Const HS_HORIZONTAL = 0       '  ----
Global Const HS_VERTICAL = 1         '  |||||
Global Const HS_FDIAGONAL = 2        '  \\\\\
Global Const HS_BDIAGONAL = 3        '  /////
Global Const HS_CROSS = 4            '  +++++
Global Const HS_DIAGCROSS = 5        '  xxxxx
```

These pen styles can be used with the DrawStyle property.

```
'  Pen Styles
Global Const PS_SOLID = 0
Global Const PS_DASH = 1             '  ------
Global Const PS_DOT = 2             '  .......
Global Const PS_DASHDOT = 3         '  _._._._
Global Const PS_DASHDOTDOT = 4      '  _.._.._
Global Const PS_NULL = 5
Global Const PS_INSIDEFRAME = 6
```

These constants are used in calls to GetDeviceCaps, generally when communicating with a printer driver or other output device. See How-To 7.1 Determine the color capabilities of a screen or printer, for an example. Using Visual Basic's Printer object is much easier and is highly recommended.

```
'  Device Parameters for GetDeviceCaps()
Declare Function GetDeviceCaps Lib "GDI" (ByVal hDC As Integer, ByVal ⇐
nIndex As Integer) As Integer

Global Const DRIVERVERSION = 0       '  Device driver version
Global Const TECHNOLOGY = 2          '  Device classification
Global Const HORZSIZE = 4            '  Horizontal size in millimeters
Global Const VERTSIZE = 6            '  Vertical size in millimeters
Global Const HORZRES = 8             '  Horizontal width in pixels
Global Const VERTRES = 10            '  Vertical width in pixels
Global Const BITSPIXEL = 12          '  Number of bits per pixel
Global Const PLANES = 14             '  Number of planes
Global Const NUMBRUSHES = 16         '  Number of brushes the device has
Global Const NUMPENS = 18            '  Number of pens the device has
Global Const NUMMARKERS = 20         '  Number of markers the device has
Global Const NUMFONTS = 22           '  Number of fonts the device has
```

```
Global Const NUMCOLORS = 24          ' Number of colors the device supports
Global Const PDEVICESIZE = 26        ' Size required for device descriptor
Global Const CURVECAPS = 28          ' Curve capabilities
Global Const LINECAPS = 30           ' Line capabilities
Global Const POLYGONALCAPS = 32      ' Polygonal capabilities
Global Const TEXTCAPS = 34           ' Text capabilities
Global Const CLIPCAPS = 36           ' Clipping capabilities
Global Const RASTERCAPS = 38         ' Bitblt capabilities
Global Const ASPECTX = 40            ' Length of the X leg
Global Const ASPECTY = 42            ' Length of the Y leg
Global Const ASPECTXY = 44           ' Length of the hypotenuse

Global Const LOGPIXELSX = 88         ' Logical pixels/inch in X
Global Const LOGPIXELSY = 90         ' Logical pixels/inch in Y

Global Const SIZEPALETTE = 104       ' Number of entries in physical
palette
Global Const NUMRESERVED = 106       ' Number of reserved entries in
palette
Global Const COLORRES = 108          ' Actual color resolution


' Device Capability Masks:

' Device Technologies
Global Const DT_PLOTTER = 0          ' Vector plotter
Global Const DT_RASDISPLAY = 1       ' Raster display
Global Const DT_RASPRINTER = 2       ' Raster printer
Global Const DT_RASCAMERA = 3        ' Raster camera
Global Const DT_CHARSTREAM = 4       ' Character-stream, PLP
Global Const DT_METAFILE = 5         ' Metafile, VDM
Global Const DT_DISPFILE = 6         ' Display-file


' Curve Capabilities
Global Const CC_NONE = 0             ' Curves not supported
Global Const CC_CIRCLES = 1          ' Can do circles
Global Const CC_PIE = 2              ' Can do pie wedges
Global Const CC_CHORD = 4            ' Can do chord arcs
Global Const CC_ELLIPSES = 8         ' Can do ellipese
Global Const CC_WIDE = 16            ' Can do wide lines
Global Const CC_STYLED = 32          ' Can do styled lines
Global Const CC_WIDESTYLED = 64      ' Can do wide styled lines
Global Const CC_INTERIORS = 128      ' Can do interiors


' Line Capabilities
Global Const LC_NONE = 0             ' Lines not supported
Global Const LC_POLYLINE = 2         ' Can do polylines
Global Const LC_MARKER = 4           ' Can do markers
Global Const LC_POLYMARKER = 8       ' Can do polymarkers
Global Const LC_WIDE = 16            ' Can do wide lines
Global Const LC_STYLED = 32          ' Can do styled lines
Global Const LC_WIDESTYLED = 64      ' Can do wide styled lines
Global Const LC_INTERIORS = 128      ' Can do interiors
```

*continued on next page*

*continued from previous page*

```
' Polygonal Capabilities
Global Const PC_NONE = 0          ' Polygonals not supported
Global Const PC_POLYGON = 1       ' Can do polygons
Global Const PC_RECTANGLE = 2     ' Can do rectangles
Global Const PC_WINDPOLYGON = 4   ' Can do winding polygons
Global Const PC_TRAPEZOID = 4     ' Can do trapezoids
Global Const PC_SCANLINE = 8      ' Can do scanlines
Global Const PC_WIDE = 16         ' Can do wide borders
Global Const PC_STYLED = 32       ' Can do styled borders
Global Const PC_WIDESTYLED = 64   ' Can do wide styled borders
Global Const PC_INTERIORS = 128   ' Can do interiors

' Polygonal Capabilities
Global Const CP_NONE = 0          ' No clipping of output
Global Const CP_RECTANGLE = 1     ' Output clipped to rects

' Text Capabilities
Global Const TC_OP_CHARACTER = &H1 ' Can do OutputPrecision   CHARACTER
Global Const TC_OP_STROKE = &H2    ' Can do OutputPrecision   STROKE
Global Const TC_CP_STROKE = &H4    ' Can do ClipPrecision     STROKE
Global Const TC_CR_90 = &H8        ' Can do CharRotAbility     90
Global Const TC_CR_ANY = &H10      ' Can do CharRotAbility     ANY
Global Const TC_SF_X_YINDEP = &H20 ' Can do ScaleFreedom       X_YINDEPENDENT
Global Const TC_SA_DOUBLE = &H40   ' Can do ScaleAbility       DOUBLE
Global Const TC_SA_INTEGER = &H80  ' Can do ScaleAbility       INTEGER
Global Const TC_SA_CONTIN = &H100  ' Can do ScaleAbility       CONTINUOUS
Global Const TC_EA_DOUBLE = &H200  ' Can do EmboldenAbility    DOUBLE
Global Const TC_IA_ABLE = &H400    ' Can do ItalisizeAbility   ABLE
Global Const TC_UA_ABLE = &H800    ' Can do UnderlineAbility   ABLE
Global Const TC_SO_ABLE = &H1000   ' Can do StrikeOutAbility   ABLE
Global Const TC_RA_ABLE = &H2000   ' Can do RasterFontAble     ABLE
Global Const TC_VA_ABLE = &H4000   ' Can do VectorFontAble     ABLE
Global Const TC_RESERVED = &H8000

' Raster Capabilities
Global Const RC_BITBLT = 1         ' Can do standard BLT.
Global Const RC_BANDING = 2        ' Device requires banding support
Global Const RC_SCALING = 4        ' Device requires scaling support
Global Const RC_BITMAP64 = 8       ' Device can support >64K bitmap
Global Const RC_GDI20_OUTPUT = &H10' has 2.0 output calls
Global Const RC_DI_BITMAP = &H80   ' supports DIB to memory
Global Const RC_PALETTE = &H100    ' supports a palette
Global Const RC_DIBTODEV = &H200   ' supports DIBitsToDevice
Global Const RC_BIGFONT = &H400    ' supports >64K fonts
Global Const RC_STRETCHBLT = &H800 ' supports StretchBlt
Global Const RC_FLOODFILL = &H1000 ' supports FloodFill
Global Const RC_STRETCHDIB = &H2000' supports StretchDIBits
```

These constants are used when creating device-independent bitmaps manually. Visual Basic picture boxes provide the same capabilities.

```
' DIB color table identifiers
Global Const DIB_RGB_COLORS = 0    ' color table in RGBTriples
```

```
Global Const DIB_PAL_COLORS = 1       ' color table in palette indices

' constants for CreateDIBitmap
Global Const CBM_INIT = &H4& '  initialize bitmap
Declare Function CreateBitmap Lib "GDI" (ByVal nWidth As Integer, ByVal ⇐
nHeight As Integer, ByVal nPlanes As Integer, ByVal nBitCount As Integer, ⇐
ByVal lpBits As Any) As Integer
Declare Function CreateBitmapIndirect Lib "GDI" (lpBitmap As BITMAP) As ⇐
Integer
Declare Function CreateCompatibleBitmap Lib "GDI" (ByVal hDC As Integer, ⇐
ByVal nWidth As Integer, ByVal nHeight As Integer) As Integer
Declare Function CreateDiscardableBitmap Lib "GDI" (ByVal hDC As Integer, ⇐
ByVal nWidth As Integer, ByVal nHeight As Integer) As Integer

Declare Function SetBitmapBits Lib "GDI" (ByVal hBitmap As Integer, ByVal ⇐
dwCount As Long, ByVal lpBits As Any) As Long
Declare Function GetBitmapBits Lib "GDI" (ByVal hBitmap As Integer, ByVal ⇐
dwCount As Long, ByVal lpBits As Any) As Long
Declare Function SetBitmapDimension Lib "GDI" (ByVal hBitmap As Integer, ⇐
ByVal X As Integer, ByVal Y As Integer) As Long
Declare Function GetBitmapDimension Lib "GDI" (ByVal hBitmap As Integer) ⇐
As Long
```

Using these constants and the DrawText function is one way to display text in a window. In Visual Basic, you can also use the Print method or label controls, both of which are easier than using DrawText.

```
' DrawText() Format Flags
Global Const DT_TOP = &H0
Global Const DT_LEFT = &H0
Global Const DT_CENTER = &H1
Global Const DT_RIGHT = &H2
Global Const DT_VCENTER = &H4
Global Const DT_BOTTOM = &H8
Global Const DT_WORDBREAK = &H10
Global Const DT_SINGLELINE = &H20
Global Const DT_EXPANDTABS = &H40
Global Const DT_TABSTOP = &H80
Global Const DT_NOCLIP = &H100
Global Const DT_EXTERNALLEADING = &H200
Global Const DT_CALCRECT = &H400
Global Const DT_NOPREFIX = &H800
Global Const DT_INTERNAL = &H1000

Declare Function DrawText Lib "GDI" (ByVal hDC As Integer, ByVal lpStr As ⇐
String, ByVal nCount As Integer, lpRect As RECT, ByVal wFormat As Integer) ⇐
As Integer
Declare Function DrawIcon Lib "GDI" (ByVal hDC As Integer, ByVal X As ⇐
Integer, ByVal Y As Integer, ByVal hIcon As Integer) As Integer
```

The constants and functions in this rather large section comprise the majority of Windows' Graphics Device Interface (GDI). The GDI is extremely powerful in that it offers many built-in graphic images, such as lines, rectangles, ellipses, arcs, chord, and even pie segments. Better yet, they're device-independent—an ellipse is an ellipse on a lowly CGA and a high-tech XGA. Visual Basic offers most of the GDI in its graphical methods: Cls, Circle, Line, Point, Print, and PSet. If you need a visual effect that Visual Basic doesn't provide, you can use API functions.

Remember that GDI requires a device context which you must provide by calling the GetDC GDI function. Also remember that device contexts are a limited resource; you should release them as soon as you're finished drawing by calling the ReleaseDC GDI function.

Various GDI functions are used in How-To 4.7 Start my applications with an animated look, How-To 3.1 Scroll all the objects in a window, How-To 3.2 Scroll text and graphics in a form or picture box, How-To 3.3 Make text and graphics roll up the screen, How-To 3.5 Align text automatically, and almost all of Chapter 5.

```
' ExtFloodFill style flags
Global Const FLOODFILLBORDER = 0
Global Const FLOODFILLSURFACE = 1

Declare Function GetWindowDC Lib "GDI" (ByVal hWnd As Integer) As Integer
Declare Function GetDC Lib "USER" (ByVal hWnd As Integer) As Integer
Declare Function ReleaseDC Lib "GDI" (ByVal hWnd As Integer, ByVal hDC As ⇐
Integer) As Integer
Declare Function CreateDC Lib "GDI" (ByVal lpDriverName As String, ByVal ⇐
lpDeviceName As String, ByVal lpOutput As String, ByVal lpInitData As ⇐
String) As Integer
Declare Function CreateIC Lib "GDI" (ByVal lpDriverName As String, ByVal ⇐
lpDeviceName As String, ByVal lpOutput As String, ByVal lpInitData ⇐
As String) As Integer
Declare Function CreateCompatibleDC Lib "GDI" (ByVal hDC As Integer) As ⇐
Integer
Declare Function DeleteDC Lib "GDI" (ByVal hDC As Integer) As Integer
Declare Function SaveDC Lib "GDI" (ByVal hDC As Integer) As Integer
Declare Function RestoreDC Lib "GDI" (ByVal hDC As Integer, ByVal nSavedDC ⇐
As Integer) As Integer
Declare Function MoveTo Lib "GDI" (ByVal hDC As Integer, ByVal X ⇐
As Integer, ByVal Y As Integer) As Long
Declare Function GetCurrentPosition Lib "GDI" (ByVal hDC As Integer) As Long
Declare Function LineTo Lib "GDI" (ByVal hDC As Integer, ByVal X ⇐
As Integer, ByVal Y As Integer) As Integer
Declare Function GetDCOrg Lib "GDI" (ByVal hDC As Integer) As Long

Declare Function MulDiv Lib "GDI" (ByVal nNumber As Integer, ByVal ⇐
nNumerator As Integer, ByVal nDenominator As Integer) As Integer

Declare Function ExtTextOut Lib "GDI" (ByVal hDC As Integer, ByVal X As ⇐
Integer, ByVal Y As Integer, ByVal wOptions As Integer, lpRect As Any, ⇐
ByVal lpString As String, ByVal nCount As Integer, lpDx As Any) As Integer

Declare Function Polyline Lib "GDI" (ByVal hDC As Integer, lpPoints As ⇐
```

```
POINTAPI, ByVal nCount As Integer) As Integer
Declare Function Polygon Lib "GDI" (ByVal hDC As Integer, lpPoints As ⇐
POINTAPI, ByVal nCount As Integer) As Integer
Declare Function PolyPolygon Lib "GDI" (ByVal hDC As Integer, lpPoints As ⇐
POINTAPI, lpPolyCounts As Integer, ByVal nCount As Integer) As Integer

Declare Function Rectangle Lib "GDI" (ByVal hDC As Integer, ByVal X1 As ⇐
Integer, ByVal Y1 As Integer, ByVal X2 As Integer, ByVal Y2 As Integer) As ⇐
Integer
Declare Function RoundRect Lib "GDI" (ByVal hDC As Integer, ByVal X1 As ⇐
Integer, ByVal Y1 As Integer, ByVal X2 As Integer, ByVal Y2 As Integer, ⇐
ByVal X3 As Integer, ByVal Y3 As Integer) As Integer
Declare Function Ellipse Lib "GDI" (ByVal hDC As Integer, ByVal X1 ⇐
As Integer, ByVal Y1 As Integer, ByVal X2 As Integer, ByVal Y2 As Integer) ⇐
As Integer
Declare Function Arc Lib "GDI" (ByVal hDC As Integer, ByVal X1 As Integer, ⇐
ByVal Y1 As Integer, ByVal X2 As Integer, ByVal Y2 As Integer, ByVal X3 As ⇐
Integer, ByVal Y3 As Integer, ByVal X4 As Integer, ByVal Y4 As Integer) As ⇐
Integer
Declare Function Chord Lib "GDI" (ByVal hDC As Integer, ByVal X1 As Integer, ⇐
ByVal Y1 As Integer, ByVal X2 As Integer, ByVal Y2 As Integer, ByVal X3 As ⇐
Integer, ByVal Y3 As Integer, ByVal X4 As Integer, ByVal Y4 As Integer) As ⇐
Integer
Declare Function Pie Lib "GDI" (ByVal hDC As Integer, ByVal X1 As Integer, ⇐
ByVal Y1 As Integer, ByVal X2 As Integer, ByVal Y2 As Integer, ByVal X3 As ⇐
Integer, ByVal Y3 As Integer, ByVal X4 As Integer, ByVal Y4 As Integer) As ⇐
Integer
Declare Function PatBlt Lib "GDI" (ByVal hDC As Integer, ByVal X As Integer, ⇐
ByVal Y As Integer, ByVal nWidth As Integer, ByVal nHeight As Integer, ByVal ⇐
dwRop As Long) As Integer
Declare Function BitBlt Lib "GDI" (ByVal hDestDC As Integer, ByVal X As ⇐
Integer, ByVal Y As Integer, ByVal nWidth As Integer, ByVal nHeight As ⇐
Integer, ByVal hSrcDC As Integer, ByVal XSrc As Integer, ByVal YSrc As ⇐
Integer, ByVal dwRop As Long) As Integer
Declare Function StretchBlt% Lib "GDI" (ByVal hDC%, ByVal X%, ByVal Y%, ⇐
ByVal nWidth%, ByVal nHeight%, ByVal hSrcDC%, ByVal XSrc%, ByVal YSrc%, ⇐
ByVal nSrcWidth%, ByVal nSrcHeight%, ByVal dwRop&)
Declare Function TextOut Lib "GDI" (ByVal hDC As Integer, ByVal X As ⇐
Integer, ByVal Y As Integer, ByVal lpString As String, ByVal nCount As ⇐
Integer) As Integer
Declare Function TabbedTextOut Lib "GDI" (ByVal hDC As Integer, ByVal X As ⇐
Integer, ByVal Y As Integer, ByVal lpString As String, ByVal nCount As ⇐
Integer, ByVal nTabPositions As Integer, lpnTabStopPositions As Integer, ⇐
ByVal nTabOrigin As Integer) As Long
Declare Function GetCharWidth Lib "GDI" (ByVal hDC As Integer, ByVal ⇐
wFirstChar As Integer, ByVal wLastChar As Integer, lpBuffer As Integer) As ⇐
Integer
Declare Function SetPixel Lib "GDI" (ByVal hDC As Integer, ByVal X As ⇐
Integer, ByVal Y As Integer, ByVal crColor As Long) As Long
Declare Function GetPixel Lib "GDI" (ByVal hDC As Integer, ByVal X As ⇐
Integer, ByVal Y As Integer) As Long
Declare Function FloodFill Lib "GDI" (ByVal hDC As Integer, ByVal X As ⇐
Integer, ByVal Y As Integer, ByVal crColor As Long) As Integer
```

*continued on next page*

*continued from previous page*

```
Declare Function ExtFloodFill Lib "GDI" (ByVal hDC As Integer, ByVal X As ⟸
Integer, ByVal Y As Integer, ByVal crColor As Long, ByVal wFillType As ⟸
Integer) As Integer

Declare Function GetStockObject Lib "GDI" (ByVal nIndex As Integer) As ⟸
Integer

Declare Function CreatePen Lib "GDI" (ByVal nPenStyle As Integer, ByVal ⟸
nWidth As Integer, ByVal crColor As Long) As Integer
Declare Function CreatePenIndirect Lib "GDI" (lpLogPen As LOGPEN) As Integer

Declare Function CreateSolidBrush Lib "GDI" (ByVal crColor As Long) As ⟸
Integer
Declare Function CreateHatchBrush Lib "GDI" (ByVal nIndex As Integer, ByVal ⟸
crColor As Long) As Integer
Declare Function SetBrushOrg Lib "GDI" (ByVal hDC As Integer, ByVal X As ⟸
Integer, ByVal Y As Integer) As Long
Declare Function GetBrushOrg Lib "GDI" (ByVal hDC As Integer) As Long
Declare Function CreatePatternBrush Lib "GDI" (ByVal hBitmap As Integer) As ⟸
Integer
Declare Function CreateBrushIndirect Lib "GDI" (lpLogBrush As LOGBRUSH) As ⟸
Integer

Declare Function CreateFont% Lib "GDI" (ByVal H%, ByVal W%, ByVal E%, ByVal ⟸
O%, ByVal W%, ByVal I%, ByVal U%, ByVal S%, ByVal C%, ByVal OP%, ByVal CP%, ⟸
ByVal Q%, ByVal PAF%, ByVal F$)
Declare Function CreateFontIndirect Lib "GDI" (lpLogFont As LOGFONT) As ⟸
Integer

Declare Function SelectClipRgn Lib "GDI" (ByVal hDC As Integer, ByVal hRgn ⟸
As Integer) As Integer
Declare Function CreateRectRgn Lib "GDI" (ByVal X1 As Integer, ByVal Y1 As ⟸
Integer, ByVal X2 As Integer, ByVal Y2 As Integer) As Integer
Declare Sub SetRectRgn Lib "GDI" (ByVal hRgn As Integer, ByVal X1 As ⟸
Integer, ByVal Y1 As Integer, ByVal X2 As Integer, ByVal Y2 As Integer)
Declare Function CreateRectRgnIndirect Lib "GDI" (lpRect As RECT) As Integer
Declare Function CreateEllipticRgnIndirect Lib "GDI" (lpRect As RECT) As ⟸
Integer
Declare Function CreateEllipticRgn Lib "GDI" (ByVal X1 As Integer, ByVal Y1 ⟸
As Integer, ByVal X2 As Integer, ByVal Y2 As Integer) As Integer
Declare Function CreatePolygonRgn Lib "GDI" (lpPoints As POINTAPI, ByVal ⟸
nCount As Integer, ByVal nPolyFillMode As Integer) As Integer
Declare Function CreatePolyPolygonRgn Lib "GDI" (lpPoints As POINTAPI, ⟸
lpPolyCounts As Integer, ByVal nCount As Integer, ByVal nPolyFillMode As ⟸
Integer) As Integer
Declare Function CreateRoundRectRgn Lib "GDI" (ByVal X1 As Integer, ByVal ⟸
Y1 As Integer, ByVal X2 As Integer, ByVal Y2 As Integer, ByVal X3 As ⟸
Integer, ByVal Y3 As Integer) As Integer

Declare Function GetObject Lib "GDI" (ByVal hObject As Integer, ByVal ⟸
nCount As Integer, ByVal lpObject As Long) As Integer
Declare Function DeleteObject Lib "GDI" (ByVal hObject As Integer) As Integer
Declare Function SelectObject Lib "GDI" (ByVal hDC As Integer, ByVal ⟸
hObject As Integer) As Integer
```

```
Declare Function UnrealizeObject Lib "GDI" (ByVal hObject As Integer) As ⇐
Integer

Declare Function SetBkColor Lib "GDI" (ByVal hDC As Integer, ByVal crColor ⇐
As Long) As Long
Declare Function GetBkColor Lib "GDI" (ByVal hDC As Integer) As Long
Declare Function SetBkMode Lib "GDI" (ByVal hDC As Integer, ByVal nBkMode As ⇐
Integer) As Integer
Declare Function GetBkMode Lib "GDI" (ByVal hDC As Integer) As Integer
Declare Function SetTextColor Lib "GDI" (ByVal hDC As Integer, ByVal ⇐
crColor As Long) As Long
Declare Function GetTextColor Lib "GDI" (ByVal hDC As Integer) As Long
Declare Function SetTextAlign Lib "GDI" (ByVal hDC As Integer, ByVal wFlags ⇐
As Integer) As Integer
Declare Function GetTextAlign Lib "GDI" (ByVal hDC As Integer) As Integer
Declare Function SetMapperFlags Lib "GDI" (ByVal hDC As Integer, ByVal ⇐
dwFlag As Long) As Long
Declare Function GetAspectRatioFilter Lib "GDI" (ByVal hDC As Integer) As ⇐
Long
Declare Function GetNearestColor Lib "GDI" (ByVal hDC As Integer, ByVal ⇐
crColor As Long) As Long
Declare Function SetROP2 Lib "GDI" (ByVal hDC As Integer, ByVal nDrawMode ⇐
As Integer) As Integer
Declare Function GetROP2 Lib "GDI" (ByVal hDC As Integer) As Integer
Declare Function SetStretchBltMode Lib "GDI" (ByVal hDC As Integer, ByVal ⇐
nStretchMode As Integer) As Integer
Declare Function GetStretchBltMode Lib "GDI" (ByVal hDC As Integer) As ⇐
Integer
Declare Function SetPolyFillMode Lib "GDI" (ByVal hDC As Integer, ByVal ⇐
nPolyFillMode As Integer) As Integer
Declare Function GetPolyFillMode Lib "GDI" (ByVal hDC As Integer) As Integer
Declare Function SetMapMode Lib "GDI" (ByVal hDC As Integer, ByVal nMapMode ⇐
As Integer) As Integer
Declare Function GetMapMode Lib "GDI" (ByVal hDC As Integer) As Integer
Declare Function SetWindowOrg Lib "GDI" (ByVal hDC As Integer, ByVal X As ⇐
Integer, ByVal Y As Integer) As Long
Declare Function GetWindowOrg Lib "GDI" (ByVal hDC As Integer) As Long
Declare Function SetWindowExt Lib "GDI" (ByVal hDC As Integer, ByVal X As ⇐
Integer, ByVal Y As Integer) As Long
Declare Function GetWindowExt Lib "GDI" (ByVal hDC As Integer) As Long
Declare Function SetViewportOrg Lib "GDI" (ByVal hDC As Integer, ByVal X As ⇐
Integer, ByVal Y As Integer) As Long
Declare Function GetViewportOrg Lib "GDI" (ByVal hDC As Integer) As Long
Declare Function SetViewportExt Lib "GDI" (ByVal hDC As Integer, ByVal X As ⇐
Integer, ByVal Y As Integer) As Long
Declare Function GetViewportExt Lib "GDI" (ByVal hDC As Integer) As Long
Declare Function OffsetViewportOrg Lib "GDI" (ByVal hDC As Integer, ByVal X ⇐
As Integer, ByVal Y As Integer) As Long
Declare Function ScaleViewportExt Lib "GDI" (ByVal hDC As Integer, ByVal ⇐
Xnum As Integer, ByVal Xdenom As Integer, ByVal Ynum As Integer, ByVal ⇐
Ydenom As Integer) As Long
Declare Function OffsetWindowOrg Lib "GDI" (ByVal hDC As Integer, ByVal X ⇐
As Integer, ByVal Y As Integer) As Long
Declare Function ScaleWindowExt Lib "GDI" (ByVal hDC As Integer, ByVal ⇐
```

*continued on next page*

*continued from previous page*

```
Xnum As Integer, ByVal Xdenom As Integer, ByVal Ynum As Integer, ByVal ⇐
Ydenom As Integer) As Long


Declare Function GetClipBox Lib "GDI" (ByVal hDC As Integer, lpRect As ⇐
RECT) As Integer
Declare Function IntersectClipRect Lib "GDI" (ByVal hDC As Integer, ByVal ⇐
X1 As Integer, ByVal Y1 As Integer, ByVal X2 As Integer, ByVal Y2 As ⇐
Integer) As Integer
Declare Function OffsetClipRgn Lib "GDI" (ByVal hDC As Integer, ByVal X As ⇐
Integer, ByVal Y As Integer) As Integer
Declare Function ExcludeClipRect Lib "GDI" (ByVal hDC As Integer, ByVal ⇐
X1  As Integer, ByVal Y1 As Integer, ByVal X2 As Integer, ByVal Y2 As ⇐
Integer) As Integer
Declare Function PtVisible Lib "GDI" (ByVal hDC As Integer, ByVal X As ⇐
Integer, ByVal Y As Integer) As Integer
Declare Function CombineRgn Lib "GDI" (ByVal hDestRgn As Integer, ByVal ⇐
hSrcRgn1 As Integer, ByVal hSrcRgn2 As Integer, ByVal nCombineMode As ⇐
Integer) As Integer
Declare Function EqualRgn Lib "GDI" (ByVal hSrcRgn1 As Integer, ByVal ⇐
hSrcRgn2 As Integer) As Integer
Declare Function OffsetRgn Lib "GDI" (ByVal hRgn As Integer, ByVal X As ⇐
Integer, ByVal Y As Integer) As Integer
Declare Function GetRgnBox Lib "GDI" (ByVal hRgn As Integer, lpRect As ⇐
RECT) As Integer


Declare Function SetTextJustification Lib "GDI" (ByVal hDC As Integer, ⇐
ByVal nBreakExtra As Integer, ByVal nBreakCount As Integer) As Integer
Declare Function GetTextExtent Lib "GDI" (ByVal hDC As Integer, ByVal ⇐
lpString As String, ByVal nCount As Integer) As Long
Declare Function GetTabbedTextExtent Lib "GDI" (ByVal hDC As Integer, ⇐
ByVal lpString As String, ByVal nCount As Integer, ByVal nTabPositions As ⇐
Integer, lpnTabStopPositions As Integer) As Long
Declare Function SetTextCharacterExtra Lib "GDI" (ByVal hDC As Integer, ⇐
ByVal nCharExtra As Integer) As Integer
Declare Function GetTextCharacterExtra Lib "GDI" (ByVal hDC As Integer) ⇐
As Integer


Declare Function GetMetaFile Lib "GDI" (ByVal lpFilename As String) As ⇐
Integer
Declare Function DeleteMetaFile Lib "GDI" (ByVal hMF As Integer) As ⇐
Integer
Declare Function CopyMetaFile Lib "GDI" (ByVal hMF As Integer, ByVal ⇐
lpFilename As String) As Integer


Declare Function PlayMetaFile Lib "GDI" (ByVal hDC As Integer, ByVal hMF ⇐
As Integer) As Integer
Declare Sub PlayMetaFileRecord Lib "GDI" (ByVal hDC As Integer, ⇐
lpHandletable As Integer, lpMetaRecord As METARECORD, ByVal nHandles As ⇐
Integer)


Declare Function Escape Lib "GDI" (ByVal hDC As Integer, ByVal nEscape As ⇐
Integer, ByVal nCount As Integer, lplnData As Any, lpOutData As Any) As ⇐
Integer
Declare Function GetTextFace Lib "GDI" (ByVal hDC As Integer, ByVal ⇐
```

```
nCount As Integer, ByVal lpFacename As String) As Integer

Declare Function GetTextMetrics Lib "GDI" (ByVal hDC As Integer, lpMetrics ⇐
As TEXTMETRIC) As Integer

Declare Function SetEnvironment Lib "GDI" (ByVal lpPortName As String, ⇐
ByVal lpEnviron As String, ByVal nCount As Integer) As Integer
Declare Function GetEnvironment Lib "GDI" (ByVal lpPortName As String, ⇐
lpEnviron As Any, ByVal nMaxCount As Integer) As Integer

Declare Function DPtoLP Lib "GDI" (ByVal hDC As Integer, lpPoints As ⇐
POINTAPI, ByVal nCount As Integer) As Integer
Declare Function LPtoDP Lib "GDI" (ByVal hDC As Integer, lpPoints As ⇐
POINTAPI, ByVal nCount As Integer) As Integer

Declare Function CreateMetaFile Lib "GDI" (lpString As Any) As Integer
Declare Function CloseMetaFile Lib "GDI" (ByVal hMF As Integer) As Integer
Declare Function GetMetaFileBits Lib "GDI" (ByVal hMF As Integer) As ⇐
Integer
Declare Function SetMetaFileBits Lib "GDI" (ByVal hMem As Integer) As ⇐
Integer

Declare Function SetDIBits Lib "GDI" (ByVal aHDC As Integer, ByVal hBitmap ⇐
As Integer, ByVal nStartScan As Integer, ByVal nNumScans As Integer, ByVal ⇐
lpBits As String, lpBI As BITMAPINFO, ByVal wUsage As Integer) As Integer

Declare Function GetDIBits Lib "GDI" (ByVal aHDC As Integer, ByVal hBitmap ⇐
As Integer, ByVal nStartScan As Integer, ByVal nNumScans As Integer, ByVal ⇐
lpBits As String, lpBI As BITMAPINFO, ByVal wUsage As Integer) As Integer

Declare Function SetDIBitsToDevice% Lib "GDI" (ByVal hDC#, ByVal X#, ByVal ⇐
Y#, ByVal dX#, ByVal dY#, ByVal SrcX#, ByVal SrcY#, ByVal Scan#, ByVal ⇐
NumScans#, ByVal Bits As String, BitsInfo As BITMAPINFO, ByVal wUsage#)

Declare Function CreateDIBitmap Lib "GDI" (ByVal hDC As Integer, ⇐
lpInfoHeader As BITMAPINFOHEADER, ByVal dwUsage As Long, ByVal lpInitBits ⇐
As String, lpInitInfo As BITMAPINFO, ByVal wUsage As Integer) As Integer

Declare Function CreateDIBPatternBrush Lib "GDI" (ByVal hPackedDIB As ⇐
Integer, ByVal wUsage As Integer) As Integer

Declare Function StretchDIBits# Lib "GDI" (ByVal hDC#, ByVal X#, ByVal Y#, ⇐
ByVal dX#, ByVal dY#, ByVal SrcX#, ByVal SrcY#, ByVal wSrcWidth#, ByVal ⇐
wSrcHeight#, ByVal lpBits As String, lpBitsInfo As BITMAPINFO, ByVal ⇐
wUsage#, ByVal dwRop&)

' -------------------------------------
'    USER Section
' -------------------------------------
```

wvsprintf provides formatted outputs for numbers and strings. Visual Basic provides almost all the same capabilities with the Format$ function.

```
Declare Function wvsprintf Lib "User" (ByVal lpOutput As String, ByVal ⇐
lpFormat As String, lpArglist As Integer) As Integer
```

These are some miscellaneous constants for managing windows and controls. Visual Basic users generally don't need to worry about them.

```
' Scroll Bar Constants
Global Const SB_HORZ = 0
Global Const SB_VERT = 1
Global Const SB_CTL = 2
Global Const SB_BOTH = 3

' Scroll Bar Commands
Global Const SB_LINEUP = 0
Global Const SB_LINEDOWN = 1
Global Const SB_PAGEUP = 2
Global Const SB_PAGEDOWN = 3
Global Const SB_THUMBPOSITION = 4
Global Const SB_THUMBTRACK = 5
Global Const SB_TOP = 6
Global Const SB_BOTTOM = 7
Global Const SB_ENDSCROLL = 8

' ShowWindow() Commands
Global Const SW_HIDE = 0
Global Const SW_SHOWNORMAL = 1
Global Const SW_NORMAL = 1
Global Const SW_SHOWMINIMIZED = 2
Global Const SW_SHOWMAXIMIZED = 3
Global Const SW_MAXIMIZE = 3
Global Const SW_SHOWNOACTIVATE = 4
Global Const SW_SHOW = 5
Global Const SW_MINIMIZE = 6
Global Const SW_SHOWMINNOACTIVE = 7
Global Const SW_SHOWNA = 8
Global Const SW_RESTORE = 9

' Old ShowWindow() Commands
Global Const HIDE_WINDOW = 0
Global Const SHOW_OPENWINDOW = 1
Global Const SHOW_ICONWINDOW = 2
Global Const SHOW_FULLSCREEN = 3
Global Const SHOW_OPENNOACTIVATE = 4

' Identifiers for the WM_SHOWWINDOW message
Global Const SW_PARENTCLOSING = 1
Global Const SW_OTHERZOOM = 2
Global Const SW_PARENTOPENING = 3
Global Const SW_OTHERUNZOOM = 4

' Region Flags
Global Const ERRORAPI = 0
Global Const NULLREGION = 1
Global Const SIMPLEREGION = 2
Global Const COMPLEXREGION = 3

' CombineRgn() Styles
Global Const RGN_AND = 1
Global Const RGN_OR = 2
Global Const RGN_XOR = 3
```

```
Global Const RGN_DIFF = 4
Global Const RGN_COPY = 5
```

The following constants are key codes passed to KeyDown and KeyUp event subroutines. They're the same as the constants in the CONSTANT.TXT file.

```
' Virtual Keys, Standard Set
Global Const VK_LBUTTON = &H1
Global Const VK_RBUTTON = &H2
Global Const VK_CANCEL = &H3
Global Const VK_MBUTTON = &H4          '  NOT contiguous with L & RBUTTON
Global Const VK_BACK = &H8
Global Const VK_TAB = &H9
Global Const VK_CLEAR = &HC
Global Const VK_RETURN = &HD
Global Const VK_SHIFT = &H10
Global Const VK_CONTROL = &H11
Global Const VK_MENU = &H12
Global Const VK_PAUSE = &H13
Global Const VK_CAPITAL = &H14
Global Const VK_ESCAPE = &H1B
Global Const VK_SPACE = &H20
Global Const VK_PRIOR = &H21
Global Const VK_NEXT = &H22
Global Const VK_END = &H23
Global Const VK_HOME = &H24
Global Const VK_LEFT = &H25
Global Const VK_UP = &H26
Global Const VK_RIGHT = &H27
Global Const VK_DOWN = &H28
Global Const VK_SELECT = &H29
Global Const VK_PRINT = &H2A
Global Const VK_EXECUTE = &H2B
Global Const VK_SNAPSHOT = &H2C
'Global Const VK_COPY = &H2C not used by keyboards.
Global Const VK_INSERT = &H2D
Global Const VK_DELETE = &H2E
Global Const VK_HELP = &H2F

'  VK_A thru VK_Z are the same as their ASCII equivalents: 'A' thru 'Z'
'  VK_0 thru VK_9 are the same as their ASCII equivalents: '0' thru '9'

Global Const VK_NUMPAD0 = &H60
Global Const VK_NUMPAD1 = &H61
Global Const VK_NUMPAD2 = &H62
Global Const VK_NUMPAD3 = &H63
Global Const VK_NUMPAD4 = &H64
Global Const VK_NUMPAD5 = &H65
Global Const VK_NUMPAD6 = &H66
Global Const VK_NUMPAD7 = &H67
Global Const VK_NUMPAD8 = &H68
Global Const VK_NUMPAD9 = &H69
Global Const VK_MULTIPLY = &H6A
Global Const VK_ADD = &H6B
```

*continued on next page*

*continued from previous page*

```
Global Const VK_SEPARATOR = &H6C
Global Const VK_SUBTRACT = &H6D
Global Const VK_DECIMAL = &H6E
Global Const VK_DIVIDE = &H6F
Global Const VK_F1 = &H70
Global Const VK_F2 = &H71
Global Const VK_F3 = &H72
Global Const VK_F4 = &H73
Global Const VK_F5 = &H74
Global Const VK_F6 = &H75
Global Const VK_F7 = &H76
Global Const VK_F8 = &H77
Global Const VK_F9 = &H78
Global Const VK_F10 = &H79
Global Const VK_F11 = &H7A
Global Const VK_F12 = &H7B
Global Const VK_F13 = &H7C
Global Const VK_F14 = &H7D
Global Const VK_F15 = &H7E
Global Const VK_F16 = &H7F

Global Const VK_NUMLOCK = &H90
```

These constants and structures are used to install hooks or intercepts into Windows. Hooking into Windows is an advanced technique that can only be done in a more tranditional language like C or Pascal.

```
' SetWindowsHook() codes
Global Const WH_MSGFILTER = (-1)
Global Const WH_JOURNALRECORD = 0
Global Const WH_JOURNALPLAYBACK = 1
Global Const WH_KEYBOARD = 2
Global Const WH_GETMESSAGE = 3
Global Const WH_CALLWNDPROC = 4
Global Const WH_CBT = 5
Global Const WH_SYSMSGFILTER = 6
Global Const WH_WINDOWMGR = 7

' Hook Codes
Global Const HC_LPLPFNNEXT = (-2)
Global Const HC_LPFNNEXT = (-1)
Global Const HC_ACTION = 0
Global Const HC_GETNEXT = 1
Global Const HC_SKIP = 2
Global Const HC_NOREM = 3
Global Const HC_NOREMOVE = 3
Global Const HC_SYSMODALON = 4
Global Const HC_SYSMODALOFF = 5

' CBT Hook Codes
Global Const HCBT_MOVESIZE = 0
Global Const HCBT_MINMAX = 1
Global Const HCBT_QS = 2

' WH_MSGFILTER Filter Proc Codes
Global Const MSGF_DIALOGBOX = 0
```

```
Global Const MSGF_MESSAGEBOX = 1
Global Const MSGF_MENU = 2
Global Const MSGF_MOVE = 3
Global Const MSGF_SIZE = 4
Global Const MSGF_SCROLLBAR = 5
Global Const MSGF_NEXTWINDOW = 6

' Window Manager Hook Codes
Global Const WC_INIT = 1
Global Const WC_SWP = 2
Global Const WC_DEFWINDOWPROC = 3
Global Const WC_MINMAX = 4
Global Const WC_MOVE = 5
Global Const WC_SIZE = 6
Global Const WC_DRAWCAPTION = 7

' Message Structure used in Journaling
Type EVENTMSG
    message As Integer
    paramL As Integer
    paramH As Integer
    time As Long
End Type
```

These constants and functions are used with the GetWindowLong, GetWindowWord, GetClassLong, GetClassWord, SetWindowLong, SetWindowWord, SetClassLong, and SetClassWord functions to determine and set various characteristics of a window or control. See How-To 1.8 Prevent text typed into a text box from appearing on screen, for an example of how to use them.

```
' Window field offsets for GetWindowLong() and GetWindowWord()
Global Const GWL_WNDPROC = (-4)
Global Const GWW_HINSTANCE = (-6)
Global Const GWW_HWNDPARENT = (-8)
Global Const GWW_ID = (-12)
Global Const GWL_STYLE = (-16)
Global Const GWL_EXSTYLE = (-20)

' Class field offsets for GetClassLong() and GetClassWord()
Global Const GCL_MENUNAME = (-8)
Global Const GCW_HBRBACKGROUND = (-10)
Global Const GCW_HCURSOR = (-12)
Global Const GCW_HICON = (-14)
Global Const GCW_HMODULE = (-16)
Global Const GCW_CBWNDEXTRA = (-18)
Global Const GCW_CBCLSEXTRA = (-20)
Global Const GCL_WNDPROC = (-24)
Global Const GCW_STYLE = (-26)

Declare Function GetWindowWord Lib "User" (ByVal hWnd As Integer, ByVal ⇐
nIndex As Integer) As Integer
Declare Function SetWindowWord Lib "User" (ByVal hWnd As Integer, ByVal ⇐
nIndex As Integer, ByVal wNewWord As Integer) As Integer
```

*continued on next page*

*continued from previous page*

```
Declare Function GetWindowLong Lib "User" (ByVal hWnd As Integer, ByVal ⇐
nIndex As Integer) As Long
Declare Function SetWindowLong Lib "User" (ByVal hWnd As Integer, ByVal ⇐
nIndex As Integer, ByVal dwNewLong As Long) As Long
Declare Function GetClassWord Lib "User" (ByVal hWnd As Integer, ByVal ⇐
nIndex As Integer) As Integer
Declare Function SetClassWord Lib "User" (ByVal hWnd As Integer, ByVal ⇐
nIndex As Integer, ByVal wNewWord As Integer) As Integer
Declare Function GetClassLong Lib "User" (ByVal hWnd As Integer, ByVal ⇐
nIndex As Integer) As Long
Declare Function SetClassLong Lib "User" (ByVal hWnd As Integer, ByVal ⇐
nIndex As Integer, ByVal dwNewLong As Long) As Long
```

These messages are sent by Windows to the window procedure of a traditional C or Pascal Windows application. In Visual Basic, some of them trigger a Visual Basic event subroutine. When a user moves the mouse pointer over a form, for example, Windows sends a WM_MOUSEMOVE message. Visual Basic interprets that and executes that form's MouseMove event subroutine, if one exists. Since it all happens automatically, you don't need to worry about these constants.

```
'  Window Messages
Global Const WM_NULL = &H0
Global Const WM_CREATE = &H1
Global Const WM_DESTROY = &H2
Global Const WM_MOVE = &H3
Global Const WM_SIZE = &H5
Global Const WM_ACTIVATE = &H6
Global Const WM_SETFOCUS = &H7
Global Const WM_KILLFOCUS = &H8
Global Const WM_ENABLE = &HA
Global Const WM_SETREDRAW = &HB
Global Const WM_SETTEXT = &HC
Global Const WM_GETTEXT = &HD
Global Const WM_GETTEXTLENGTH = &HE
Global Const WM_PAINT = &HF
Global Const WM_CLOSE = &H10
Global Const WM_QUERYENDSESSION = &H11
Global Const WM_QUIT = &H12
Global Const WM_QUERYOPEN = &H13
Global Const WM_ERASEBKGND = &H14
Global Const WM_SYSCOLORCHANGE = &H15
Global Const WM_ENDSESSION = &H16
Global Const WM_SHOWWINDOW = &H18
Global Const WM_CTLCOLOR = &H19
Global Const WM_WININICHANGE = &H1A
Global Const WM_DEVMODECHANGE = &H1B
Global Const WM_ACTIVATEAPP = &H1C
Global Const WM_FONTCHANGE = &H1D
Global Const WM_TIMECHANGE = &H1E
Global Const WM_CANCELMODE = &H1F
Global Const WM_SETCURSOR = &H20
```

```
Global Const WM_MOUSEACTIVATE = &H21
Global Const WM_CHILDACTIVATE = &H22
Global Const WM_QUEUESYNC = &H23
Global Const WM_GETMINMAXINFO = &H24
Global Const WM_PAINTICON = &H26
Global Const WM_ICONERASEBKGND = &H27
Global Const WM_NEXTDLGCTL = &H28
Global Const WM_SPOOLERSTATUS = &H2A
Global Const WM_DRAWITEM = &H2B
Global Const WM_MEASUREITEM = &H2C
Global Const WM_DELETEITEM = &H2D
Global Const WM_VKEYTOITEM = &H2E
Global Const WM_CHARTOITEM = &H2F
Global Const WM_SETFONT = &H30
Global Const WM_GETFONT = &H31

Global Const WM_QUERYDRAGICON = &H37

Global Const WM_COMPAREITEM = &H39
Global Const WM_COMPACTING = &H41

Global Const WM_NCCREATE = &H81
Global Const WM_NCDESTROY = &H82
Global Const WM_NCCALCSIZE = &H83
Global Const WM_NCHITTEST = &H84
Global Const WM_NCPAINT = &H85
Global Const WM_NCACTIVATE = &H86
Global Const WM_GETDLGCODE = &H87
Global Const WM_NCMOUSEMOVE = &HA0
Global Const WM_NCLBUTTONDOWN = &HA1
Global Const WM_NCLBUTTONUP = &HA2
Global Const WM_NCLBUTTONDBLCLK = &HA3
Global Const WM_NCRBUTTONDOWN = &HA4
Global Const WM_NCRBUTTONUP = &HA5
Global Const WM_NCRBUTTONDBLCLK = &HA6
Global Const WM_NCMBUTTONDOWN = &HA7
Global Const WM_NCMBUTTONUP = &HA8
Global Const WM_NCMBUTTONDBLCLK = &HA9

Global Const WM_KEYFIRST = &H100
Global Const WM_KEYDOWN = &H100
Global Const WM_KEYUP = &H101
Global Const WM_CHAR = &H102
Global Const WM_DEADCHAR = &H103
Global Const WM_SYSKEYDOWN = &H104
Global Const WM_SYSKEYUP = &H105
Global Const WM_SYSCHAR = &H106
Global Const WM_SYSDEADCHAR = &H107
Global Const WM_KEYLAST = &H108

Global Const WM_INITDIALOG = &H110
Global Const WM_COMMAND = &H111
Global Const WM_SYSCOMMAND = &H112
Global Const WM_TIMER = &H113
Global Const WM_HSCROLL = &H114
```

*continued on next page*

*continued from previous page*

```
Global Const WM_VSCROLL = &H115
Global Const WM_INITMENU = &H116
Global Const WM_INITMENUPOPUP = &H117
Global Const WM_MENUSELECT = &H11F
Global Const WM_MENUCHAR = &H120
Global Const WM_ENTERIDLE = &H121

Global Const WM_MOUSEFIRST = &H200
Global Const WM_MOUSEMOVE = &H200
Global Const WM_LBUTTONDOWN = &H201
Global Const WM_LBUTTONUP = &H202
Global Const WM_LBUTTONDBLCLK = &H203
Global Const WM_RBUTTONDOWN = &H204
Global Const WM_RBUTTONUP = &H205
Global Const WM_RBUTTONDBLCLK = &H206
Global Const WM_MBUTTONDOWN = &H207
Global Const WM_MBUTTONUP = &H208
Global Const WM_MBUTTONDBLCLK = &H209
Global Const WM_MOUSELAST = &H209

Global Const WM_PARENTNOTIFY = &H210
Global Const WM_MDICREATE = &H220
Global Const WM_MDIDESTROY = &H221
Global Const WM_MDIACTIVATE = &H222
Global Const WM_MDIRESTORE = &H223
Global Const WM_MDINEXT = &H224
Global Const WM_MDIMAXIMIZE = &H225
Global Const WM_MDITILE = &H226
Global Const WM_MDICASCADE = &H227
Global Const WM_MDIICONARRANGE = &H228
Global Const WM_MDIGETACTIVE = &H229
Global Const WM_MDISETMENU = &H230

Global Const WM_CUT = &H300
Global Const WM_COPY = &H301
Global Const WM_PASTE = &H302
Global Const WM_CLEAR = &H303
Global Const WM_UNDO = &H304
Global Const WM_RENDERFORMAT = &H305
Global Const WM_RENDERALLFORMATS = &H306
Global Const WM_DESTROYCLIPBOARD = &H307
Global Const WM_DRAWCLIPBOARD = &H308
Global Const WM_PAINTCLIPBOARD = &H309
Global Const WM_VSCROLLCLIPBOARD = &H30A
Global Const WM_SIZECLIPBOARD = &H30B
Global Const WM_ASKCBFORMATNAME = &H30C
Global Const WM_CHANGECBCHAIN = &H30D
Global Const WM_HSCROLLCLIPBOARD = &H30E
Global Const WM_QUERYNEWPALETTE = &H30F
Global Const WM_PALETTEISCHANGING = &H310
Global Const WM_PALETTECHANGED = &H311

' NOTE: All Message Numbers below 0x0400 are RESERVED.
```

WM_USER is the first of the "user" messages, that an application can define for its own use to send to another window or control.

```
' Private Window Messages Start Here:
Global Const WM_USER = &H400
```

These constants identify task switches used internally by Windows. You won't have to worry about them.

```
' WM_SYNCTASK Commands
Global Const ST_BEGINSWP = 0
Global Const ST_ENDSWP = 1
```

These constants are used with the undocumented WinWhere function, so you should avoid them (and the function).

```
' WinWhere() Area Codes
Global Const HTERROR = (-2)
Global Const HTTRANSPARENT = (-1)
Global Const HTNOWHERE = 0
Global Const HTCLIENT = 1
Global Const HTCAPTION = 2
Global Const HTSYSMENU = 3
Global Const HTGROWBOX = 4
Global Const HTSIZE = HTGROWBOX
Global Const HTMENU = 5
Global Const HTHSCROLL = 6
Global Const HTVSCROLL = 7
Global Const HTREDUCE = 8
Global Const HTZOOM = 9
Global Const HTLEFT = 10
Global Const HTRIGHT = 11
Global Const HTTOP = 12
Global Const HTTOPLEFT = 13
Global Const HTTOPRIGHT = 14
Global Const HTBOTTOM = 15
Global Const HTBOTTOMLEFT = 16
Global Const HTBOTTOMRIGHT = 17
Global Const HTSIZEFIRST = HTLEFT
Global Const HTSIZELAST = HTBOTTOMRIGHT

' WM_MOUSEACTIVATE Return Codes
Global Const MA_ACTIVATE = 1
Global Const MA_ACTIVATEANDEAT = 2
Global Const MA_NOACTIVATE = 3

Declare Function RegisterWindowMessage Lib "User" (ByVal lpString As ⇐
String) As Integer

' Size Message Commands
Global Const SIZENORMAL = 0
Global Const SIZEICONIC = 1
Global Const SIZEFULLSCREEN = 2
Global Const SIZEZOOMSHOW = 3
Global Const SIZEZOOMHIDE = 4
```

These constants specify which button(s) (left, middle, and right) and
(SHIFT) and (CTRL) keys were pressed in a mouse message. In Visual Basic,
they're passed to MouseMove, MouseUp, and MouseDown event subroutines.

```
' Key State Masks for Mouse Messages
Global Const MK_LBUTTON = &H1
Global Const MK_RBUTTON = &H2
Global Const MK_SHIFT = &H4
Global Const MK_CONTROL = &H8
Global Const MK_MBUTTON = &H10
```

These constants specify the appearance of a window—whether it has a
Control-menu box or a caption (title) bar—and what kind of frame (border)
it has. In Visual Basic, you can change a form's appearance at design-time by
changing the following properties: MaxButton, MinButton, Visible, Enabled, BorderStyle, ControlBox, and WindowState.

```
' Window Styles
Global Const WS_OVERLAPPED = &H00000&
Global Const WS_POPUP = &H80000000&
Global Const WS_CHILD = &H40000000&
Global Const WS_MINIMIZE = &H20000000&
Global Const WS_VISIBLE = &H10000000&
Global Const WS_DISABLED = &H8000000&
Global Const WS_CLIPSIBLINGS = &H4000000&
Global Const WS_CLIPCHILDREN = &H2000000&
Global Const WS_MAXIMIZE = &H1000000&
Global Const WS_CAPTION = &HC00000&'  WS_BORDER Or WS_DLGFRAME
Global Const WS_BORDER = &H800000&
Global Const WS_DLGFRAME = &H400000&
Global Const WS_VSCROLL = &H200000&
Global Const WS_HSCROLL = &H100000&
Global Const WS_SYSMENU = &H80000&
Global Const WS_THICKFRAME = &H40000&
Global Const WS_GROUP = &H20000&
Global Const WS_TABSTOP = &H10000&

Global Const WS_MINIMIZEBOX = &H20000&
Global Const WS_MAXIMIZEBOX = &H10000&

Global Const WS_TILED = WS_OVERLAPPED
Global Const WS_ICONIC = WS_MINIMIZE
Global Const WS_SIZEBOX = WS_THICKFRAME

' Common Window Styles
Global Const WS_OVERLAPPEDWINDOW = (WS_OVERLAPPED Or WS_CAPTION Or ⇐
WS_SYSMENU Or WS_THICKFRAME Or WS_MINIMIZEBOX Or WS_MAXIMIZEBOX)
Global Const WS_POPUPWINDOW = (WS_POPUP Or WS_BORDER Or WS_SYSMENU)
Global Const WS_CHILDWINDOW = (WS_CHILD)
Global Const WS_TILEDWINDOW = (WS_OVERLAPPEDWINDOW)

' Extended Window Styles
Global Const WS_EX_DLGMODALFRAME = &H00001&
```

```
Global Const WS_EX_NOPARENTNOTIFY = &H00004&

' Class styles
Global Const CS_VREDRAW = &H1
Global Const CS_HREDRAW = &H2
Global Const CS_KEYCVTWINDOW = &H4
Global Const CS_DBLCLKS = &H8
Global Const CS_OWNDC = &H20
Global Const CS_CLASSDC = &H40
Global Const CS_PARENTDC = &H80
Global Const CS_NOKEYCVT = &H100
Global Const CS_NOCLOSE = &H200
Global Const CS_SAVEBITS = &H800
Global Const CS_BYTEALIGNCLIENT = &H1000
Global Const CS_BYTEALIGNWINDOW = &H2000
Global Const CS_GLOBALCLASS = &H4000          ' Global window class
```

These constants are used to determine and set the data in the Windows Clipboard. In Visual Basic, you can use the Clipboard object to ease use of the Windows Clipboard.

```
' Predefined Clipboard Formats
Global Const CF_TEXT = 1
Global Const CF_BITMAP = 2
Global Const CF_METAFILEPICT = 3
Global Const CF_SYLK = 4
Global Const CF_DIF = 5
Global Const CF_TIFF = 6
Global Const CF_OEMTEXT = 7
Global Const CF_DIB = 8
Global Const CF_PALETTE = 9

Global Const CF_OWNERDISPLAY = &H80
Global Const CF_DSPTEXT = &H81
Global Const CF_DSPBITMAP = &H82
Global Const CF_DSPMETAFILEPICT = &H83

' "Private" formats don't get GlobalFree()'d
Global Const CF_PRIVATEFIRST = &H200
Global Const CF_PRIVATELAST = &H2FF

' "GDIOBJ" formats do get DeleteObject()'d
Global Const CF_GDIOBJFIRST = &H300
Global Const CF_GDIOBJLAST = &H3FF

' Clipboard Manager Functions
Declare Function OpenClipboard Lib "User" (ByVal hWnd As Integer) As ⇐
Integer
Declare Function CloseClipboard Lib "User" () As Integer
Declare Function GetClipboardOwner Lib "User" () As Integer
Declare Function SetClipboardViewer Lib "User" (ByVal hWnd As Integer) As ⇐
Integer
Declare Function GetClipboardViewer Lib "User" () As Integer
Declare Function ChangeClipboardChain Lib "User" (ByVal hWnd As Integer, ⇐
ByVal hWndNext As Integer) As Integer
```

*continued on next page*

*continued from previous page*

```
Declare Function SetClipboardData Lib "User" (ByVal wFormat As Integer, ⇐
ByVal hMem As Integer) As Integer
Declare Function GetClipboardData Lib "User" (ByVal wFormat As Integer) As ⇐
Integer
Declare Function RegisterClipboardFormat Lib "User" (ByVal lpString As ⇐
String) As Integer
Declare Function CountClipboardFormats Lib "User" () As Integer
Declare Function EnumClipboardFormats Lib "User" (ByVal wFormat As ⇐
Integer) As Integer
Declare Function GetClipboardFormatName Lib "User" (ByVal wFormat As ⇐
Integer, ByVal lpString As String, ByVal nMaxCount As Integer) As Integer
Declare Function EmptyClipboard Lib "User" () As Integer
Declare Function IsClipboardFormatAvailable Lib "User" (ByVal wFormat As ⇐
Integer) As Integer
Declare Function GetPriorityClipboardFormat Lib "User" (lpPriorityList As ⇐
Integer, ByVal nCount As Integer) As Integer
```

PAINTSTRUCT is a structure used for responding to the WM_PAINT message; in Visual Basic, you can simply write a Paint event subroutine.

```
Type PAINTSTRUCT
    hdc As Integer
    fErase As Integer
    rcPaint As RECT
    fRestore As Integer
    fIncUpdate As Integer
    rgbReserved As String * 16
End Type
```

CREATESTRUCT is a structure used for responding to the WM_CREATE message; the Visual Basic form Load event is similar to this message.

```
Type CREATESTRUCT
    lpCreateParams As Long
    hInstance As Integer
    hMenu As Integer
    hwndParent As Integer
    cy As Integer
    cx As Integer
    y As Integer
    x As Integer
    style As Long
    lpszName As Long
    lpszClass As Long
    ExStyle As Long
End Type
```

These constants and structures are used to support owner-drawn or customized controls. Visual Basic supports custom controls to achieve the same effect. See Chapter 8 for more information about custom controls.

```
' Owner draw control types
Global Const ODT_MENU = 1
```

```
Global Const ODT_LISTBOX = 2
Global Const ODT_COMBOBOX = 3
Global Const ODT_BUTTON = 4

'  Owner draw actions
Global Const ODA_DRAWENTIRE = &H1
Global Const ODA_SELECT = &H2
Global Const ODA_FOCUS = &H4

'  Owner draw state
Global Const ODS_SELECTED = &H1
Global Const ODS_GRAYED = &H2
Global Const ODS_DISABLED = &H4
Global Const ODS_CHECKED = &H8
Global Const ODS_FOCUS = &H10

'  MEASUREITEMSTRUCT for ownerdraw
Type MEASUREITEMSTRUCT
     CtlType As Integer
     CtlID As Integer
     itemID As Integer
     itemWidth As Integer
     itemHeight As Integer
     itemData As Long
End Type

'  DRAWITEMSTRUCT for ownerdraw
Type DRAWITEMSTRUCT
     CtlType As Integer
     CtlID As Integer
     itemID As Integer
     itemAction As Integer
     itemState As Integer
     hwndItem As Integer
     hDC As Integer
     rcItem As RECT
     itemData As Long
End Type

'  DELETEITEMSTRUCT for ownerdraw
Type DELETEITEMSTRUCT
     CtlType As Integer
     CtlID As Integer
     itemID As Integer
     hwndItem As Integer
     itemData As Long
End Type

'  COMPAREITEMSTRUCT for ownerdraw sorting
Type COMPAREITEMSTRUCT
     CtlType As Integer
     CtlID As Integer
     hwndItem As Integer
     itemID1 As Integer
     itemData1 As Long
```

*continued on next page*

*continued from previous page*

```
     itemID2 As Integer
     itemData2 As Long
End Type
```

These functions, constants, and types are vital parts of the message processing of a C or Pascal Windows application. You generally don't need to worry about it in a Visual Basic application.

```
' Message structure
Type MSG
     hwnd As Integer
     message As Integer
     wParam As Integer
     lParam As Long
     time As Long
     pt As POINTAPI
End Type

' Message Function Templates
Declare Function GetMessage Lib "User" (lpMsg As MSG, ByVal hWnd As ⇐
Integer, ByVal wMsgFilterMin As Integer, ByVal wMsgFilterMax As Integer) ⇐
As Integer
Declare Function TranslateMessage Lib "User" (lpMsg As MSG) As Integer
Declare Function DispatchMessage Lib "User" (lpMsg As MSG) As Long
Declare Function PeekMessage Lib "User" (lpMsg As MSG, ByVal hWnd As ⇐
Integer, ByVal wMsgFilterMin As Integer, ByVal wMsgFilterMax As Integer, ⇐
ByVal wRemoveMsg As Integer) As Integer

' PeekMessage() Options
Global Const PM_NOREMOVE = &H0
Global Const PM_REMOVE = &H1
Global Const PM_NOYIELD = &H2
```

The lstr... functions provide the C or Pascal programmer a way to manipulate strings. The standard Visual Basic string operators (=, <, <=, >, >=, and <>) work just as well.

```
Declare Function lstrcmp Lib "User" (ByVal lpString1 As Any, ByVal ⇐
lpString2 As Any) As Integer
Declare Function lstrcmpi Lib "User" (ByVal lpString1 As Any, ByVal ⇐
lpString2 As Any) As Integer
Declare Function lstrcpy Lib "Kernel" (ByVal lpString1 As Any, ByVal ⇐
lpString2 As Any) As Long
Declare Function lstrcat Lib "Kernel" (ByVal lpString1 As Any, ByVal ⇐
lpString2 As Any) As Long
Declare Function lstrlen Lib "Kernel" (ByVal lpString As Any) As Integer
```

The following functions are used to perform disk I/O. The Visual Basic disk I/O statements perform the same functions, but you might want to use these functions to avoid Visual Basic error trapping.

```
Declare Function lopen Lib "Kernel" Alias "_lopen" (ByVal lpPathName As ⇐
String, ByVal iReadWrite As Integer) As Integer
```

```
Declare Function lclose Lib "Kernel" Alias "_lclose" (ByVal hFile As ⇐
Integer) As Integer
Declare Function lcreat Lib "Kernel" Alias "_lcreat" (ByVal lpPathName As ⇐
String, ByVal iAttribute As Integer) As Integer
Declare Function llseek Lib "Kernel" Alias "_llseek" (ByVal hFile As ⇐
Integer, ByVal lOffset As Long, ByVal iOrigin As Integer) As Long
Declare Function lread Lib "Kernel" Alias "_lread" (ByVal hFile As Integer, ⇐
ByVal lpBuffer As String, ByVal wBytes As Integer) As Integer
Declare Function lwrite Lib "Kernel" Alias "_lwrite" (ByVal hFile As ⇐
Integer, ByVal lpBuffer As String, ByVal wBytes As Integer) As Integer

Global Const READAPI = 0       ' Flags for _lopen
Global Const WRITEAPI = 1
Global Const READ_WRITE - 2
```

ExitWindows is used in How-To 6.3 Exit Windows and return to DOS. It is used to shut down Windows.

```
Declare Function ExitWindows Lib "User" (ByVal dwReserved As Long, ⇐
wReturnCode) As Integer

Declare Function SwapMouseButton Lib "User" (ByVal bSwap As Integer) As ⇐
Integer
Declare Function GetMessagePos Lib "User" () As Long
Declare Function GetMessageTime Lib "User" () As Long

Declare Function GetSysModalWindow Lib "User" () As Integer
Declare Function SetSysModalWindow Lib "User" (ByVal hWnd As Integer) As ⇐
Integer
```

SendMessage is used in many How-Tos throughout this book to manipulate controls by sending messages to them.

```
Declare Function SendMessage Lib "User" (ByVal hWnd As Integer, ByVal ⇐
wMsg As Integer, ByVal wParam As Integer, lParam As Any) As Long
Declare Function PostMessage Lib "User" (ByVal hWnd As Integer, ByVal ⇐
wMsg As Integer, ByVal wParam As Integer, lParam As Any) As Integer
Declare Function PostAppMessage Lib "User" (ByVal hTask As Integer, ByVal ⇐
wMsg As Integer, ByVal wParam As Integer, lParam As Any) As Integer
Declare Sub ReplyMessage Lib "User" (ByVal lReply As Long)
Declare Sub WaitMessage Lib "User" ()
Declare Function DefWindowProc Lib "User" (ByVal hWnd As Integer, ByVal ⇐
wMsg As Integer, ByVal wParam As Integer, lParam As Any) As Long
Declare Sub PostQuitMessage Lib "User" (ByVal nExitCode As Integer)
Declare Function InSendMessage Lib "User" () As Integer
```

As their names indicate, these functions are used to retrieve and set the delay for double-clicking a mouse button. Your application shouldn't use these functions; instead, let the user use the Control Panel to change the double-click delay.

```
Declare Function GetDoubleClickTime Lib "User" () As Integer
Declare Sub SetDoubleClickTime Lib "User" (ByVal wCount As Integer)
```

These functions are used to create and destroy windows. They're not required for Visual Basic programmers, since Visual Basic takes care of creating and destroying windows for us.

```
Declare Function UnregisterClass Lib "User" (ByVal lpClassName As String, ⇐
ByVal hInstance As Integer) As Integer

Declare Function SetMessageQueue Lib "User" (ByVal cMsg As Integer) As ⇐
Integer

Global Const CW_USEDEFAULT = &H8000

Declare Function CreateWindow% Lib "User" (ByVal lpClassName$, ByVal ⇐
lpWindowName$, ByVal dwStyle&, ByVal X%, ByVal Y%, ByVal nWidth%, ByVal ⇐
nHeight%, ByVal hWndParent%, ByVal hMenu%, ByVal hInstance%, ByVal ⇐
lpParam$)
Declare Function CreateWindowEx% Lib "User" (ByVal dwExStyle&, ByVal ⇐
lpClassName$, ByVal lpWindowName$, ByVal dwStyle&, ByVal X%, ByVal Y%, ⇐
ByVal nWidth%, ByVal nHeight%, ByVal hWndParent%, ByVal hMenu%, ByVal ⇐
hInstance%, ByVal lpParam$)
Declare Function IsWindow Lib "User" (ByVal hWnd As Integer) As Integer
Declare Function IsChild Lib "User" (ByVal hWndParent As Integer, ByVal ⇐
hWnd As Integer) As Integer
Declare Function DestroyWindow Lib "User" (ByVal hWnd As Integer) As ⇐
Integer

Declare Function ShowWindow Lib "User" (ByVal hWnd As Integer, ByVal ⇐
nCmdShow As Integer) As Integer
```

FlashWindow is used in How-To 1.5 Flash the title bar of my forms, as a way of attracting attention.

```
Declare Function FlashWindow Lib "User" (ByVal hWnd As Integer, ByVal ⇐
bInvert As Integer) As Integer
Declare Sub ShowOwnedPopups Lib "User" (ByVal hWnd As Integer, ByVal fShow ⇐
As Integer)
Declare Function OpenIcon Lib "User" (ByVal hWnd As Integer) As Integer
Declare Sub CloseWindow Lib "User" (ByVal hWnd As Integer)
```

MoveWindow is one way to move a form; you can also use Visual Basic's Move method.

```
Declare Sub MoveWindow Lib "User" (ByVal hWnd As Integer, ByVal X As ⇐
Integer, ByVal Y As Integer, ByVal nWidth As Integer, ByVal nHeight As ⇐
Integer, ByVal bRepaint As Integer)
Declare Sub SetWindowPos Lib "User" (ByVal hWnd As Integer, ByVal ⇐
hWndInsertAfter As Integer, ByVal X As Integer, ByVal Y As Integer, ByVal ⇐
cx As Integer, ByVal cy As Integer, ByVal wFlags As Integer)

Declare Function BeginDeferWindowPos Lib "User" (ByVal nNumWindows As ⇐
Integer)
Declare Function DeferWindowPos Lib "User" (ByVal hWinPosInfo As ⇐
Integer,  ByVal hWnd as Integer, ByVal hWndInsertAfter as Integer, ByVal⇐
```

```
x, ByVal y, ByVal cx, ByVal cy, ByVal wFlags as Integer)
Declare Sub EndDeferWindowPos Lib "User" (ByVal hWinPosInfo As Integer)

Declare Function IsWindowVisible Lib "User" (ByVal hWnd As Integer) As ⇐
Integer
Declare Function IsIconic Lib "User" (ByVal hWnd As Integer) As Integer
Declare Function AnyPopup Lib "User" () As Integer
Declare Sub BringWindowToTop Lib "User" (ByVal hWnd As Integer)
Declare Function IsZoomed Lib "User" (ByVal hWnd As Integer) As Integer
```

These constants and functions are used to manipulate the controls in a dialog box. In Visual Basic, you can simply manipulate the properties of a control directly.

```
' SetWindowPos Flags
Global Const SWP_NOSIZE = &H1
Global Const SWP_NOMOVE = &H2
Global Const SWP_NOZORDER = &H4
Global Const SWP_NOREDRAW = &H8
Global Const SWP_NOACTIVATE = &H10
Global Const SWP_DRAWFRAME = &H20
Global Const SWP_SHOWWINDOW = &H40
Global Const SWP_HIDEWINDOW = &H80
Global Const SWP_NOCOPYBITS = &H100
Global Const SWP_NOREPOSITION = &H200

Declare Sub EndDialog Lib "User" (ByVal hDlg As Integer, ByVal nResult As ⇐
Integer)
Declare Function GetDlgItem Lib "User" (ByVal hDlg As Integer, ByVal ⇐
nIDDlgItem As Integer) As Integer
Declare Sub SetDlgItemInt Lib "User" (ByVal hDlg As Integer, ByVal ⇐
nIDDlgItem As Integer, ByVal wValue As Integer, ByVal bSigned As Integer)
Declare Function GetDlgItemInt Lib "User" (ByVal hDlg As Integer, ByVal ⇐
nIDDlgItem As Integer, lpTranslated As Integer, ByVal bSigned As Integer) ⇐
As Integer
Declare Sub SetDlgItemText Lib "User" (ByVal hDlg As Integer, ByVal ⇐
nIDDlgItem As Integer, ByVal lpString As String)
Declare Function GetDlgItemText Lib "User" (ByVal hDlg As Integer, ByVal ⇐
nIDDlgItem As Integer, ByVal lpString As String, ByVal nMaxCount As ⇐
Integer) As Integer
Declare Sub CheckDlgButton Lib "User" (ByVal hDlg As Integer, ByVal ⇐
nIDButton As Integer, ByVal wCheck As Integer)
Declare Sub CheckRadioButton Lib "User" (ByVal hDlg As Integer, ByVal ⇐
nIDFirstButton As Integer, ByVal nIDLastButton As Integer, ByVal ⇐
nIDCheckButton As Integer)
Declare Function IsDlgButtonChecked Lib "User" (ByVal hDlg As Integer, ⇐
ByVal nIDButton As Integer) As Integer
Declare Function SendDlgItemMessage Lib "User" (ByVal hDlg As Integer, ⇐
ByVal nIDDlgItem As Integer, ByVal wMsg As Integer, ByVal wParam As ⇐
Integer, lParam As Any) As Long
Declare Function GetNextDlgGroupItem Lib "User" (ByVal hDlg As Integer, ⇐
ByVal hCtl As Integer, ByVal bPrevious As Integer) As Integer
Declare Function GetNextDlgTabItem Lib "User" (ByVal hDlg As Integer, ⇐
```

*continued on next page*

*continued from previous page*

```
ByVal hCtl As Integer, ByVal bPrevious As Integer) As Integer
Declare Function GetDlgCtrlID Lib "User" (ByVal hWnd As Integer) As
Integer
Declare Function GetDialogBaseUnits Lib "User" () As Long
Declare Function DefDlgProc Lib "User" (ByVal hDlg As Integer, ByVal ⇐
wMsg As Integer, ByVal wParam As Integer, lParam As Any) As Long

Global Const DLGWINDOWEXTRA = 30    ' Window extra bytes needed for
private dialog classes

Declare Function CallMsgFilter Lib "User" (lpMsg As MSG, ByVal nCode As ⇐
Integer) As Integer
```

Using the Visual Basic SetFocus method (or the API function SetFocus, which here is aliased to SetFocusAPI) followed by a call to the GetFocus API function is one way of returning the window handle of a control. See How-To 2.5 Quickly send a Windows message to a control.

```
Declare Function SetFocusAPI Lib "User" Alias "SetFocus" (ByVal hWnd As ⇐
Integer) As Integer
Declare Function GetFocus Lib "User" () As Integer
```

These functions are used to determine the status of Windows, such as which window is active.

```
Declare Function GetActiveWindow Lib "User" () As Integer
Declare Function GetKeyState Lib "User" (ByVal nVirtKey As Integer) As ⇐
Integer
Declare Function GetAsyncKeyState Lib "User" (ByVal vKey As Integer) As ⇐
Integer
Declare Sub GetKeyboardState Lib "User" (LpKeyState As Any)
Declare Sub SetKeyboardState Lib "User" (lpKeyState As Any)
Declare Function EnableHardwareInput Lib "User" (ByVal bEnableInput As ⇐
Integer) As Integer
Declare Function GetInputState Lib "User" () As Integer
Declare Function GetCapture Lib "User" () As Integer
Declare Function SetCapture Lib "User" (ByVal hWnd As Integer) As Integer
Declare Sub ReleaseCapture Lib "User" ()

' Windows Functions
Declare Function KillTimer Lib "User" (ByVal hWnd As Integer, ByVal ⇐
nIDEvent As Integer) As Integer
```

EnableWindow is used to enable and disable a window or control, and IsWindowEnabled returns whether a window or control is currently enabled. In Visual Basic, you can set the value of the Enabled property and query it instead.

```
Declare Function EnableWindow Lib "User" (ByVal hWnd As Integer, ByVal ⇐
aBOOL As Integer) As Integer
Declare Function IsWindowEnabled Lib "User" (ByVal hWnd As Integer) As ⇐
Integer
```

In Visual Basic, accelerators are defined in the Menu Design window and don't have to be explicitly loaded.

```
Declare Function LoadAccelerators Lib "User" (ByVal hInstance As Integer, ⇐
ByVal lpTableName As String) As Integer
```

```
Declare Function TranslateAccelerator Lib "User" (ByVal hWnd As Integer, ⇐
ByVal hAccTable As Integer, lpMsg As MSG) As Integer
```

These constants, when used with the GetSystemMetrics function, let you determine many system-wide characteristics, such as screen size. Many such characteristics can be determined by checking the properties of the Screen object.

```
' GetSystemMetrics() codes
Global Const SM_CXSCREEN = 0
Global Const SM_CYSCREEN = 1
Global Const SM_CXVSCROLL = 2
Global Const SM_CYHSCROLL = 3
Global Const SM_CYCAPTION = 4
Global Const SM_CXBORDER = 5
Global Const SM_CYBORDER = 6
Global Const SM_CXDLGFRAME = 7
Global Const SM_CYDLGFRAME = 8
Global Const SM_CYVTHUMB = 9
Global Const SM_CXHTHUMB = 10
Global Const SM_CXICON = 11
Global Const SM_CYICON = 12
Global Const SM_CXCURSOR = 13
Global Const SM_CYCURSOR = 14
Global Const SM_CYMENU = 15
Global Const SM_CXFULLSCREEN = 16
Global Const SM_CYFULLSCREEN = 17
Global Const SM_CYKANJIWINDOW = 18
Global Const SM_MOUSEPRESENT = 19
Global Const SM_CYVSCROLL = 20
Global Const SM_CXHSCROLL = 21
Global Const SM_DEBUG = 22
Global Const SM_SWAPBUTTON = 23
Global Const SM_RESERVED1 = 24
Global Const SM_RESERVED2 = 25
Global Const SM_RESERVED3 = 26
Global Const SM_RESERVED4 = 27
Global Const SM_CXMIN = 28
Global Const SM_CYMIN = 29
Global Const SM_CXSIZE = 30
Global Const SM_CYSIZE = 31
Global Const SM_CXFRAME = 32
Global Const SM_CYFRAME = 33
Global Const SM_CXMINTRACK = 34
Global Const SM_CYMINTRACK = 35
Global Const SM_CMETRICS = 36
```

*continued on next page*

*continued from previous page*

```
Declare Function GetSystemMetrics Lib "User" (ByVal nIndex As Integer) As ⇐
Integer
```

You can change a window's menu by using these functions. In Visual Basic, you create a form's menu using the Menu Design Window. How-To 4.3 Make a floating pop-up menu, How-To 4.4 Modify a form's system menu, How-To 4.5 Draw a bitmapped picture in a menu, and How-To 4.6 Place font typefaces in a menu, show how to use these API functions to modify a menu after you've created it.

```
Declare Function LoadMenu Lib "User" (ByVal hInstance As Integer, ByVal ⇐
lpString As String) As Integer
Declare Function LoadMenuIndirect Lib "User" (lpMenuTemplate As ⇐
MENUITEMTEMPLATE) As Integer
Declare Function GetMenu Lib "User" (ByVal hWnd As Integer) As Integer
Declare Function SetMenu Lib "User" (ByVal hWnd As Integer, ByVal hMenu As ⇐
Integer) As Integer
Declare Function ChangeMenu Lib "User" (ByVal hMenu As Integer, ByVal ⇐
wID As Integer, ByVal lpszNew As String, ByVal wIDNew As Integer, ByVal ⇐
wChange As Integer) As Integer
Declare Function HiliteMenuItem Lib "User" (ByVal hWnd As Integer, ByVal ⇐
hMenu As Integer, ByVal wIDHiliteItem As Integer, ByVal wHilite As ⇐
Integer) As Integer
Declare Function GetMenuString Lib "User" (ByVal hMenu As Integer, ByVal ⇐
wIDItem As Integer, ByVal lpString As String, ByVal nMaxCount As Integer, ⇐
ByVal wFlag As Integer) As Integer
Declare Function GetMenuState Lib "User" (ByVal hMenu As Integer, ByVal ⇐
wId As Integer, ByVal wFlags As Integer) As Integer
Declare Sub DrawMenuBar Lib "User" (ByVal hWnd As Integer)
Declare Function GetSystemMenu Lib "User" (ByVal hWnd As Integer, ByVal ⇐
bRevert As Integer) As Integer
Declare Function CreateMenu Lib "User" () As Integer
Declare Function CreatePopupMenu Lib "User" () As Integer
Declare Function DestroyMenu Lib "User" (ByVal hMenu As Integer) As ⇐
Integer
Declare Function CheckMenuItem Lib "User" (ByVal hMenu As Integer, ByVal ⇐
wIDCheckItem As Integer, ByVal wCheck As Integer) As Integer
Declare Function EnableMenuItem Lib "User" (ByVal hMenu As Integer, ByVal ⇐
wIDEnableItem As Integer, ByVal wEnable As Integer) As Integer
Declare Function GetSubMenu Lib "User" (ByVal hMenu As Integer, ByVal nPos ⇐
As Integer) As Integer
Declare Function GetMenuItemID Lib "User" (ByVal hMenu As Integer, ByVal ⇐
nPos As Integer) As Integer
Declare Function GetMenuItemCount Lib "User" (ByVal hMenu As Integer) As ⇐
Integer

Declare Function InsertMenu Lib "User" (ByVal hMenu As Integer, ByVal ⇐
nPosition As Integer, ByVal wFlags As Integer, ByVal wIDNewItem As Integer, ⇐
ByVal lpNewItem As Any) As Integer
Declare Function AppendMenu Lib "User" (ByVal hMenu As Integer, ByVal ⇐
wFlags As Integer, ByVal wIDNewItem As Integer, ByVal lpNewItem As Any) As ⇐
Integer
Declare Function ModifyMenu Lib "User" (ByVal hMenu As Integer, ByVal ⇐
```

```
nPosition As Integer, ByVal wFlags As Integer, ByVal wIDNewItem As Integer, ⇐
ByVal lpString As Any) As Integer
Declare Function RemoveMenu Lib "User" (ByVal hMenu As Integer, ByVal ⇐
nPosition As Integer, ByVal wFlags As Integer) As Integer
Declare Function DeleteMenu Lib "User" (ByVal hMenu As Integer, ByVal ⇐
nPosition As Integer, ByVal wFlags As Integer) As Integer
Declare Function SetMenuItemBitmaps Lib "User" (ByVal hMenu As Integer, ⇐
ByVal nPosition As Integer, ByVal wFlags As Integer, ByVal ⇐
hBitmapUnchecked As Integer, ByVal hBitmapChecked As Integer) As Integer
Declare Function GetMenuCheckMarkDimensions Lib "User" () As Long
Declare Function TrackPopupMenu Lib "User" (ByVal hMenu As Integer, ByVal ⇐
wFlags As Integer, ByVal x As Integer, ByVal y As Integer, ByVal nReserved ⇐
As Integer, ByVal hWnd As Integer, lpReserved As Any) As Integer

'  Menu flags for Add/Check/EnableMenuItem()
Global Const MF_INSERT = &H0
Global Const MF_CHANGE = &H80
Global Const MF_APPEND = &H100
Global Const MF_DELETE = &H200
Global Const MF_REMOVE = &H1000

Global Const MF_BYCOMMAND = &H0
Global Const MF_BYPOSITION = &H400

Global Const MF_SEPARATOR = &H800

Global Const MF_ENABLED = &H0
Global Const MF_GRAYED = &H1
Global Const MF_DISABLED = &H2

Global Const MF_UNCHECKED = &H0
Global Const MF_CHECKED = &H8
Global Const MF_USECHECKBITMAPS = &H200

Global Const MF_STRING = &H0
Global Const MF_BITMAP = &H4
Global Const MF_OWNERDRAW = &H100

Global Const MF_POPUP = &H10
Global Const MF_MENUBARBREAK = &H20
Global Const MF_MENUBREAK = &H40

Global Const MF_UNHILITE = &H0
Global Const MF_HILITE = &H80

Global Const MF_SYSMENU = &H2000
Global Const MF_HELP = &H4000
Global Const MF_MOUSESELECT = &H8000

'  Menu item resource format
Type MENUITEMTEMPLATEHEADER
     versionNumber As Integer
     offset As Integer
End Type

Type MENUITEMTEMPLATE
     mtOption As Integer
     mtID As Integer
```

*continued on next page*

*continued from previous page*

```
    mtString As Long
End Type

Global Const MF_END = &H80

'  System Menu Command Values
Global Const SC_SIZE = &HF000
Global Const SC_MOVE = &HF010
Global Const SC_MINIMIZE = &HF020
Global Const SC_MAXIMIZE = &HF030
Global Const SC_NEXTWINDOW = &HF040
Global Const SC_PREVWINDOW = &HF050
Global Const SC_CLOSE = &HF060
Global Const SC_VSCROLL = &HF070
Global Const SC_HSCROLL = &HF080
Global Const SC_MOUSEMENU = &HF090
Global Const SC_KEYMENU = &HF100
Global Const SC_ARRANGE = &HF110
Global Const SC_RESTORE = &HF120
Global Const SC_TASKLIST = &HF130

Global Const SC_ICON = SC_MINIMIZE
Global Const SC_ZOOM = SC_MAXIMIZE
```

These functions are used to update a window when it's uncovered or needs to be repainted.

```
Declare Sub UpdateWindow Lib "User" (ByVal hWnd As Integer)
Declare Function SetActiveWindow Lib "User" (ByVal hWnd As Integer) As ⇐
Integer

Declare Function BeginPaint Lib "User" (ByVal hWnd As Integer, lpPaint As ⇐
PAINTSTRUCT) As Integer
Declare Sub EndPaint Lib "User" (ByVal hWnd As Integer, lpPaint As ⇐
PAINTSTRUCT)
Declare Function GetUpdateRect Lib "User" (ByVal hWnd As Integer, lpRect ⇐
As RECT, ByVal bErase As Integer) As Integer
Declare Function GetUpdateRgn Lib "User" (ByVal hWnd As Integer, ByVal ⇐
hRgn As Integer, ByVal fErase As Integer) As Integer

Declare Function ExcludeUpdateRgn Lib "User" (ByVal hDC As Integer, ByVal ⇐
hWnd As Integer) As Integer

Declare Sub InvalidateRect Lib "User" (ByVal hWnd As Integer, lpRect As ⇐
RECT, ByVal bErase As Integer)
Declare Sub ValidateRect Lib "User" (ByVal hWnd As Integer, lpRect As ⇐
RECT)

Declare Sub InvalidateRgn Lib "User" (ByVal hWnd As Integer, ByVal hRgn As ⇐
Integer, ByVal bErase As Integer)
Declare Sub ValidateRgn Lib "User" (ByVal hWnd As Integer, ByVal hRgn As ⇐
Integer)
```

How-To 3.1 Scroll all the objects in a window, shows you how to use ScrollWindow.

```
Declare Sub ScrollWindow Lib "User" (ByVal hWnd As Integer, ByVal XAmount ⇐
As Integer, ByVal YAmount As Integer, lpRect As RECT, lpClipRect As RECT)
```

```
Declare Function ScrollDC Lib "User" (ByVal hDC As Integer, ByVal dx As ⇐
Integer, ByVal dy As Integer, lprcScroll As RECT, lprcClip As RECT, ByVal ⇐
hRgnUpdate As Integer, lprcUpdate As RECT) As Integer

Declare Function SetScrollPos Lib "User" (ByVal hWnd As Integer, ByVal ⇐
nBar As Integer, ByVal nPos As Integer, ByVal bRedraw As Integer) As ⇐
Integer
Declare Function GetScrollPos Lib "User" (ByVal hWnd As Integer, ByVal ⇐
nBar As Integer) As Integer
Declare Sub SetScrollRange Lib "User" (ByVal hWnd As Integer, ByVal nBar ⇐
As Integer, ByVal nMinPos As Integer, ByVal nMaxPos As Integer, ByVal ⇐
bRedraw As Integer)
Declare Sub GetScrollRange Lib "User" (ByVal hWnd As Integer, ByVal nBar ⇐
As Integer, lpMinPos As Integer, lpMaxPos As Integer)
Declare Sub ShowScrollBar Lib "User" (ByVal hWnd As Integer, ByVal wBar ⇐
As Integer, ByVal bShow As Integer)
```

These functions control aspects of a window, such as its property data and its caption. Visual Basic programmers can directly manipulate most of that data using properties like Caption.

```
Declare Function SetProp Lib "User" (ByVal hWnd As Integer, ByVal lpString ⇐
As String, ByVal hData As Integer) As Integer
Declare Function GetProp Lib "User" (ByVal hWnd As Integer, ByVal lpString ⇐
As Any) As Integer
Declare Function RemoveProp Lib "User" (ByVal hWnd As Integer, ByVal ⇐
lpString As String) As Integer
Declare Sub SetWindowText Lib "User" (ByVal hWnd As Integer, ByVal ⇐
lpString As String)
Declare Function GetWindowText Lib "User" (ByVal hWnd As Integer, ByVal ⇐
lpString As String, ByVal aint As Integer) As Integer
Declare Function GetWindowTextLength Lib "User" (ByVal hWnd As Integer) ⇐
As Integer

Declare Sub GetClientRect Lib "User" (ByVal hWnd As Integer, lpRect As ⇐
RECT)
Declare Sub GetWindowRect Lib "User" (ByVal hWnd As Integer, lpRect As ⇐
RECT)
Declare Sub AdjustWindowRect Lib "User" (lpRect As RECT, ByVal dwStyle As ⇐
Long, ByVal bMenu As Integer)
Declare Sub AdjustWindowRectEx Lib "User" (lpRect As RECT, ByVal dsStyle ⇐
As Long, ByVal bMenu As Integer, ByVal dwEsStyle As Long)
```

The API function MessageBox is the same as Visual Basic's MsgBox statement and function. You can use these constants to give mnemonic names to the values you pass to the MsgBox statement and function for the command buttons and icons.

```
' MessageBox() Flags
Global Const MB_OK = &H0
Global Const MB_OKCANCEL = &H1
Global Const MB_ABORTRETRYIGNORE = &H2
Global Const MB_YESNOCANCEL = &H3
Global Const MB_YESNO = &H4
```

*continued on next page*

*continued from previous page*

```
Global Const MB_RETRYCANCEL = &H5

Global Const MB_ICONHAND = &H10
Global Const MB_ICONQUESTION = &H20
Global Const MB_ICONEXCLAMATION = &H30
Global Const MB_ICONASTERISK = &H40

Global Const MB_ICONINFORMATION = MB_ICONASTERISK
Global Const MB_ICONSTOP = MB_ICONHAND

Global Const MB_DEFBUTTON1 = &H0
Global Const MB_DEFBUTTON2 = &H100
Global Const MB_DEFBUTTON3 = &H200

Global Const MB_APPLMODAL = &H0
Global Const MB_SYSTEMMODAL = &H1000
Global Const MB_TASKMODAL = &H2000

Global Const MB_NOFOCUS = &H8000

Global Const MB_TYPEMASK = &HF
Global Const MB_ICONMASK = &HF0
Global Const MB_DEFMASK = &HF00
Global Const MB_MODEMASK = &H3000
Global Const MB_MISCMASK = &HC000

' Dialog Box Command IDs
Global Const IDOK = 1
Global Const IDCANCEL = 2
Global Const IDABORT = 3
Global Const IDRETRY = 4
Global Const IDIGNORE = 5
Global Const IDYES = 6
Global Const IDNO = 7

Declare Function MessageBox Lib "User" (ByVal hWnd As Integer, ByVal lpText ⇐
As String, ByVal lpCaption As String, ByVal wType As Integer) As Integer
Declare Sub MessageBeep Lib "User" (ByVal wType As Integer)

Declare Function ShowCursor Lib "User" (ByVal bShow As Integer) As Integer
Declare Sub SetCursorPos Lib "User" (ByVal X As Integer, ByVal Y As ⇐
Integer)
Declare Function SetCursor Lib "User" (ByVal hCursor As Integer) As ⇐
Integer
Declare Sub GetCursorPos Lib "User" (lpPoint As POINTAPI)
Declare Sub ClipCursor Lib "User" (lpRect As Any)
```

How-To 3.10 Determine and modify the rate at which a text box's caret
blinks, uses GetCaretBlinkTime and SetCaretBlinkTime.

```
Declare Function GetCaretBlinkTime Lib "User" () As Integer
Declare Sub SetCaretBlinkTime Lib "User" (ByVal wMSeconds As Integer)
Declare Sub CreateCaret Lib "User" (ByVal hWnd As Integer, ByVal hBitmap ⇐
As Integer, ByVal nWidth As Integer, ByVal nHeight As Integer)
Declare Sub DestroyCaret Lib "User" ()
Declare Sub HideCaret Lib "User" (ByVal hWnd As Integer)
Declare Sub ShowCaret Lib "User" (ByVal hWnd As Integer)
Declare Sub SetCaretPos Lib "User" (ByVal X As Integer, ByVal Y As ⇐
```

```
Integer)
Declare Sub GetCaretPos Lib "User" (lpPoint As POINTAPI)
```

These functions convert between screen units and window coordinates; in Visual Basic, both are measured in twips by default.

```
Declare Sub ClientToScreen Lib "User" (ByVal hWnd As Integer, lpPoint As ⇐
POINTAPI)
Declare Sub ScreenToClient Lib "User" (ByVal hWnd As Integer, lpPoint As ⇐
POINTAPI)

Declare Function WindowFromPoint Lib "User" (ByVal Point As Any) As ⇐
Integer
Declare Function ChildWindowFromPoint Lib "User" (ByVal hWnd As Integer, ⇐
ByVal Point As Any) As Integer
```

These constants and functions can be used to determine and set the colors Windows uses to display parts of a window, such as the background color or the border color.

```
' Color Types
Global Const CTLCOLOR_MSGBOX = 0
Global Const CTLCOLOR_EDIT = 1
Global Const CTLCOLOR_LISTBOX = 2
Global Const CTLCOLOR_BTN = 3
Global Const CTLCOLOR_DLG = 4
Global Const CTLCOLOR_SCROLLBAR = 5
Global Const CTLCOLOR_STATIC = 6
Global Const CTLCOLOR_MAX = 8          ' three bits max

Global Const COLOR_SCROLLBAR = 0
Global Const COLOR_BACKGROUND = 1
Global Const COLOR_ACTIVECAPTION = 2
Global Const COLOR_INACTIVECAPTION = 3
Global Const COLOR_MENU = 4
Global Const COLOR_WINDOW = 5
Global Const COLOR_WINDOWFRAME = 6
Global Const COLOR_MENUTEXT = 7
Global Const COLOR_WINDOWTEXT = 8
Global Const COLOR_CAPTIONTEXT = 9
Global Const COLOR_ACTIVEBORDER = 10
Global Const COLOR_INACTIVEBORDER = 11
Global Const COLOR_APPWORKSPACE = 12
Global Const COLOR_HIGHLIGHT = 13
Global Const COLOR_HIGHLIGHTTEXT = 14
Global Const COLOR_BTNFACE = 15
Global Const COLOR_BTNSHADOW = 16
Global Const COLOR_GRAYTEXT = 17
Global Const COLOR_BTNTEXT = 18
Global Const COLOR_ENDCOLORS = COLOR_BTNTEXT

Declare Function GetSysColor Lib "User" (ByVal nIndex As Integer) As Long
Declare Sub SetSysColors Lib "User" (ByVal nChanges As Integer, lpSysColor ⇐
As Integer, lpColorValues As Long)
```

*continued on next page*

*continued from previous page*

These functions are used when painting regions; Visual Basic's graphics methods can be used more easily.

```
Declare Function FillRgn Lib "User" (ByVal hDC As Integer, ByVal hRgn As ⇐
Integer, ByVal hBrush As Integer) As Integer
Declare Function FrameRgn Lib "User" (ByVal hDC As Integer, ByVal hRgn As ⇐
Integer, ByVal hBrush As Integer, ByVal nWidth As Integer, ByVal nHeight ⇐
As Integer) As Integer
Declare Function InvertRgn Lib "User" (ByVal hDC As Integer, ByVal hRgn As ⇐
Integer) As Integer
Declare Function PaintRgn Lib "User" (ByVal hDC As Integer, ByVal hRgn As ⇐
Integer) As Integer
Declare Function PtInRegion Lib "User" (ByVal hRgn As Integer, ByVal X As ⇐
Integer, ByVal Y As Integer) As Integer

Declare Sub DrawFocusRect Lib "User" (ByVal hDC As Integer, lpRect As ⇐
RECT)
Declare Function FillRect Lib "User" (ByVal hDC As Integer, lpRect As RECT, ⇐
ByVal hBrush As Integer) As Integer
Declare Function FrameRect Lib "User" (ByVal hDC As Integer, lpRect As ⇐
RECT, ByVal hBrush As Integer) As Integer
Declare Sub InvertRect Lib "User" (ByVal hDC As Integer, lpRect As RECT)
Declare Sub SetRect Lib "User" (lpRect As RECT, ByVal X1 As Integer, ByVal ⇐
Y1 As Integer, ByVal X2 As Integer, ByVal Y2 As Integer)
Declare Sub SetRectEmpty Lib "User" (lpRect As RECT)
Declare Function CopyRect Lib "User" (lpDestRect As RECT, lpSourceRect As ⇐
RECT) As Integer
Declare Sub InflateRect Lib "User" (lpRect As RECT, ByVal X As Integer, ⇐
ByVal Y As Integer)
Declare Function IntersectRect Lib "User" (lpDestRect As RECT, lpSrc1Rect ⇐
As RECT, lpSrc2Rect As RECT) As Integer
Declare Function UnionRect Lib "User" (lpDestRect As RECT, lpSrc1Rect As ⇐
RECT, lpSrc2Rect As RECT) As Integer
Declare Sub OffsetRect Lib "User" (lpRect As RECT, ByVal X As Integer, ⇐
ByVal Y As Integer)
Declare Function IsRectEmpty Lib "User" (lpRect As RECT) As Integer
Declare Function EqualRect Lib "User" (lpRect1 As RECT, lpRect2 As RECT) As ⇐
Integer
Declare Function PtInRect Lib "User" (lpRect As RECT, ByVal Point As Any) As ⇐
Integer
Declare Function RectVisible Lib "User" (ByVal hDC As Integer, lpRect As ⇐
RECT) As Integer
Declare Function RectInRegion Lib "User" (ByVal hRgn As Integer, lpRect As ⇐
RECT) As Integer

Declare Function GetCurrentTime Lib "User" () As Long
Declare Function GetTickCount Lib "User" () As Long
```

See How-To 5.8 Arrange the icons on the Windows desktop, for one use of GetDesktopWindow.

```
Declare Function GetDesktopHwnd Lib "User" () As Integer
Declare Function GetDesktopWindow Lib "User" () As Integer
```

These functions are used when manipulating parent and child windows.

```
Declare Function GetParent Lib "User" (ByVal hWnd As Integer) As Integer
Declare Function SetParent Lib "User" (ByVal hWndChild As Integer, ByVal ⇐
hWndNewParent As Integer) As Integer
Declare Function FindWindow Lib "User" (lpClassName As Any, lpWindowName ⇐
As Any) As Integer
Declare Function GetClassName Lib "User" (ByVal hWnd As Integer, ByVal ⇐
lpClassName As String, ByVal nMaxCount As Integer) As Integer
Declare Function GetTopWindow Lib "User" (ByVal hWnd As Integer) As ⇐
Integer
Declare Function GetNextWindow Lib "User" (ByVal hWnd As Integer, ByVal ⇐
wFlag As Integer) As Integer
Declare Function GetWindowTask Lib "User" (ByVal hWnd As Integer) As Integer
Declare Function GetLastActivePopup Lib "User" (ByVal hwndOwnder As ⇐
Integer) As Integer

' GetWindow() Constants
Global Const GW_HWNDFIRST = 0
Global Const GW_HWNDLAST = 1
Global Const GW_HWNDNEXT = 2
Global Const GW_HWNDPREV = 3
Global Const GW_OWNER = 4
Global Const GW_CHILD = 5

Declare Function GetWindow Lib "User" (ByVal hWnd As Integer, ByVal wCmd As ⇐
Integer) As Integer
```

These cursor ID constants aren't the right values for changing the MousePointer property. Use the values 0 through 11 instead.

```
' Standard Cursor IDs
Global Const IDC_ARROW = 32512&
Global Const IDC_IBEAM = 32513&
Global Const IDC_WAIT = 32514&
Global Const IDC_CROSS = 32515&
Global Const IDC_UPARROW = 32516&
Global Const IDC_SIZE = 32640&
Global Const IDC_ICON = 32641&
Global Const IDC_SIZENWSE = 32642&
Global Const IDC_SIZENESW = 32643&
Global Const IDC_SIZEWE = 32644&
Global Const IDC_SIZENS = 32645&
```

Since Visual Basic .EXE applications don't contain normal resources like bitmaps, the only way to use these functions and constants is when loading resources from a custom DLL.

```
' Resource Loading Routines
Declare Function LoadBitmap Lib "User" (ByVal hInstance As Integer, ByVal ⇐
lpBitmapName As Any) As Integer
Declare Function LoadCursor Lib "User" (ByVal hInstance As Integer, ByVal ⇐
lpCursorName As Any) As Integer
Declare Function CreateCursor Lib "User" (ByVal hInstance%, ByVal ⇐
```

*continued on next page*

*continued from previous page*

```
nXhotspot%, ByVal nYhotspot%, ByVal nWidth%, ByVal nHeight%, ByVal ⇐
lpANDbitPlane As Any, ByVal lpXORbitPlane As Any) As Integer
Declare Function DestroyCursor Lib "User" (ByVal hCursor As Integer) As ⇐
Integer
Declare Function LoadIcon Lib "User" (ByVal hInstance As Integer, ByVal ⇐
lpIconName As Any) As Integer
Declare Function CreateIcon Lib "User" (ByVal hInstance%, ByVal nWidth%, ⇐
ByVal nHeight%, ByVal nPlanes%, ByVal nBitsPixel%, ByVal lpANDbits As Any, ⇐
ByVal lpXORbits As Any) As Integer
Declare Function DestroyIcon Lib "User" (ByVal hIcon As Integer) As ⇐
Integer

Global Const ORD_LANGDRIVER = 1      ' The ordinal number for the entry ⇐
point of
     ' language drivers.

' Standard Icon IDs
Global Const IDI_APPLICATION = 32512&
Global Const IDI_HAND = 32513&
Global Const IDI_QUESTION = 32514&
Global Const IDI_EXCLAMATION = 32515&
Global Const IDI_ASTERISK = 32516&

Declare Function LoadString Lib "User" (ByVal hInstance As Integer, ByVal ⇐
wID As Integer, ByVal lpBuffer As Any, ByVal nBufferMax As Integer) As ⇐
Integer

Declare Function AddFontResource Lib "GDI" (ByVal lpFilename As Any) As ⇐
Integer
Declare Function RemoveFontResource Lib "GDI" (ByVal lpFilename As Any) ⇐
As  Integer
```

```
' Control Manager Structures and Definitions
```

In this section, the constants with comments "Notification Codes" and that start with EN_, BN_, LBN_, and CBN_ are notification messages that Visual Basic handles with event subroutines.

```
' Edit Control Styles
```

See How-To 1.8 Prevent text typed into a text box from appearing on screen, and How-To 1.9 Prevent user access to a window or file, for examples of the ES_PASSWORD style.

```
Global Const ES_LEFT = &H0&
Global Const ES_CENTER = &H1&
Global Const ES_RIGHT = &H2&
Global Const ES_MULTILINE = &H4&
Global Const ES_UPPERCASE = &H8&
Global Const ES_LOWERCASE = &H10&
Global Const ES_PASSWORD = &H20&
Global Const ES_AUTOVSCROLL = &H40&
Global Const ES_AUTOHSCROLL = &H80&
Global Const ES_NOHIDESEL = &H100&
```

```
Global Const ES_OEMCONVERT = &H400&

'  Edit Control Notification Codes
Global Const EN_SETFOCUS = &H100
Global Const EN_KILLFOCUS = &H200
Global Const EN_CHANGE = &H300
Global Const EN_UPDATE = &H400
Global Const EN_ERRSPACE = &H500
Global Const EN_MAXTEXT = &H501
Global Const EN_HSCROLL = &H601
Global Const EN_VSCROLL = &H602

'  Edit Control Messages
```

See How-To 3.4 Scroll a text box under program control, for an example of how to use the EM_LINESCROLL message and How-To 1.8 Prevent text typed into a text box from appearing on screen, for an example of using the EM_SETPASSWORDCHAR message.

```
Global Const EM_GETSEL = WM_USER+0
Global Const EM_SETSEL = WM_USER+1
Global Const EM_GETRECT = WM_USER+2
Global Const EM_SETRECT = WM_USER+3
Global Const EM_SETRECTNP = WM_USER+4
Global Const EM_SCROLL = WM_USER+5
Global Const EM_LINESCROLL = WM_USER+6
Global Const EM_GETMODIFY = WM_USER+7
Global Const EM_SETMODIFY = WM_USER+8
Global Const EM_GETLINECOUNT = WM_USER+9
Global Const EM_LINEINDEX = WM_USER+10
Global Const EM_SETHANDLE = WM_USER+12
Global Const EM_GETHANDLE = WM_USER+13
Global Const EM_GETTHUMB = WM_USER+14
Global Const EM_LINELENGTH = WM_USER+17
Global Const EM_REPLACESEL = WM_USER+18
Global Const EM_SETFONT = WM_USER+19
Global Const EM_GETLINE = WM_USER+20
Global Const EM_LIMITTEXT = WM_USER+21
Global Const EM_CANUNDO = WM_USER+22
Global Const EM_UNDO = WM_USER+23
Global Const EM_FMTLINES = WM_USER+24
Global Const EM_LINEFROMCHAR = WM_USER+25
Global Const EM_SETWORDBREAK = WM_USER+26
Global Const EM_SETTABSTOPS = WM_USER+27
Global Const EM_SETPASSWORDCHAR = WM_USER+28
Global Const EM_EMPTYUNDOBUFFER = WM_USER+29
Global Const EM_MSGMAX = WM_USER+30

'  Button Control Styles
Global Const BS_PUSHBUTTON = &H0&
Global Const BS_DEFPUSHBUTTON = &H1&
Global Const BS_CHECKBOX = &H2&
Global Const BS_AUTOCHECKBOX = &H3&
Global Const BS_RADIOBUTTON = &H4&
```

*continued on next page*

*continued from previous page*

```
Global Const BS_3STATE = &H5&
Global Const BS_AUTO3STATE = &H6&
Global Const BS_GROUPBOX = &H7&
Global Const BS_USERBUTTON = &H8&
Global Const BS_AUTORADIOBUTTON = &H9&
Global Const BS_PUSHBOX = &HA&
Global Const BS_OWNERDRAW = &HB&
Global Const BS_LEFTTEXT = &H20&

' User Button Notification Codes
Global Const BN_CLICKED = 0
Global Const BN_PAINT = 1
Global Const BN_HILITE = 2
Global Const BN_UNHILITE = 3
Global Const BN_DISABLE = 4
Global Const BN_DOUBLECLICKED = 5

' Button Control Messages
Global Const BM_GETCHECK = WM_USER+0
Global Const BM_SETCHECK = WM_USER+1
Global Const BM_GETSTATE = WM_USER+2
Global Const BM_SETSTATE = WM_USER+3
Global Const BM_SETSTYLE = WM_USER+4

' Static Control Constants
Global Const SS_LEFT = &H0&
Global Const SS_CENTER = &H1&
Global Const SS_RIGHT = &H2&
Global Const SS_ICON = &H3&
Global Const SS_BLACKRECT = &H4&
Global Const SS_GRAYRECT = &H5&
Global Const SS_WHITERECT = &H6&
Global Const SS_BLACKFRAME = &H7&
Global Const SS_GRAYFRAME = &H8&
Global Const SS_WHITEFRAME = &H9&
Global Const SS_USERITEM = &HA&
Global Const SS_SIMPLE = &HB&
Global Const SS_LEFTNOWORDWRAP = &HC&
Global Const SS_NOPREFIX = &H80&    ' Don't do "&" character translation
```

C and Pascal programmers use these functions to manipulate dialog boxes; in Visual Basic, a form's methods can be used instead.

```
' Dialog Manager Routines
Declare Function IsDialogMessage Lib "User" (ByVal hDlg As Integer, lpMsg ⇐
As MSG) As Integer

Declare Sub MapDialogRect Lib "User" (ByVal hDlg As Integer, lpRect As ⇐
RECT)

Declare Function DlgDirList Lib "User" (ByVal hDlg As Integer, ByVal ⇐
lpPathSpec As String, ByVal nIDListBox As Integer, ByVal nIDStaticPath As ⇐
Integer, ByVal wFiletype As Integer) As Integer ⇐
Declare Function DlgDirSelect Lib "User" (ByVal hDlg As Integer, ByVal ⇐
lpString As String, ByVal nIDListBox As Integer) As Integer
```

```
Declare Function DlgDirListComboBox Lib "User" (ByVal hDlg As Integer, ⇐
ByVal lpPathSpec As String, ByVal nIDComboBox As Integer, ByVal ⇐
nIDStaticPath As Integer, ByVal wFileType As Integer) As Integer
Declare Function DlgDirSelectComboBox Lib "User" (ByVal hDlg As Integer, ⇐
ByVal lpString As String, ByVal nIDComboBox As Integer) As Integer

'  Dialog Styles
Global Const DS_ABSALIGN = &H1&
Global Const DS_SYSMODAL = &H2&
Global Const DS_LOCALEDIT = &H20&        '  Edit items get Local storage.
Global Const DS_SETFONT = &H40&          '  User specified font for Dlg ⇐
controls
Global Const DS_MODALFRAME = &H80&       '  Can be combined with WS_CAPTION
Global Const DS_NOIDLEMSG = &H100&       '  WM_ENTERIDLE message will not be ←
sent

Global Const DM_GETDEFID = WM_USER+0
Global Const DM_SETDEFID = WM_USER+1
Global Const DC_HASDEFID = &H534%     '0x534B

'  Dialog Codes
Global Const DLGC_WANTARROWS = &H1      '  Control wants arrow keys
Global Const DLGC_WANTTAB = &H2         '  Control wants tab keys
Global Const DLGC_WANTALLKEYS = &H4     '  Control wants all keys
Global Const DLGC_WANTMESSAGE = &H4     '  Pass message to control
Global Const DLGC_HASSETSEL = &H8       '  Understands EM_SETSEL message
Global Const DLGC_DEFPUSHBUTTON = &H10      '  Default pushbutton
Global Const DLGC_UNDEFPUSHBUTTON = &H20 '  Non-default pushbutton
Global Const DLGC_RADIOBUTTON = &H40 '  Radio button
Global Const DLGC_WANTCHARS = &H80 '  Want WM_CHAR messages
Global Const DLGC_STATIC = &H100     '  Static item: don't include
Global Const DLGC_BUTTON = &H2000    '  Button item: can be checked

Global Const LB_CTLCODE = 0&

'  Listbox Return Values
Global Const LB_OKAY = 0
Global Const LB_ERR = (-1)
Global Const LB_ERRSPACE = (-2)

'
'  The idStaticPath parameter to DlgDirList can have the following values
'  ORed if the list box should show other details of the files along with
'  the name of the files;

'  all other details also will be returned

'  Listbox Notification Codes
Global Const LBN_ERRSPACE = (-2)
Global Const LBN_SELCHANGE = 1
Global Const LBN_DBLCLK = 2
Global Const LBN_SELCANCEL = 3
Global Const LBN_SETFOCUS = 4
Global Const LBN_KILLFOCUS = 5

'  Listbox messages
```

*continued on next page*

*continued from previous page*

```
Global Const LB_ADDSTRING = (WM_USER+1)
Global Const LB_INSERTSTRING = (WM_USER+2)
Global Const LB_DELETESTRING = (WM_USER+3)
Global Const LB_RESETCONTENT = (WM_USER+5)
Global Const LB_SETSEL = (WM_USER+6)
Global Const LB_SETCURSEL = (WM_USER+7)
Global Const LB_GETSEL = (WM_USER+8)
Global Const LB_GETCURSEL = (WM_USER+9)
Global Const LB_GETTEXT = (WM_USER+10)
Global Const LB_GETTEXTLEN = (WM_USER+11)
Global Const LB_GETCOUNT = (WM_USER+12)
Global Const LB_SELECTSTRING = (WM_USER+13)
```

The project in How-To 1.5 Make a file dialog box using APIs, uses the LB_DIR message to fill list boxes with file and directory names.

```
Global Const LB_DIR = (WM_USER+14)
Global Const LB_GETTOPINDEX = (WM_USER+15)
Global Const LB_FINDSTRING = (WM_USER+16)
Global Const LB_GETSELCOUNT = (WM_USER+17)
Global Const LB_GETSELITEMS = (WM_USER+18)
Global Const LB_SETTABSTOPS = (WM_USER+19)
Global Const LB_GETHORIZONTALEXTENT = (WM_USER+20)
Global Const LB_SETHORIZONTALEXTENT = (WM_USER+21)
Global Const LB_SETCOLUMNWIDTH = (WM_USER+22)
Global Const LB_SETTOPINDEX = (WM_USER+24)
Global Const LB_GETITEMRECT = (WM_USER+25)
Global Const LB_GETITEMDATA = (WM_USER+26)
Global Const LB_SETITEMDATA = (WM_USER+27)
Global Const LB_SELITEMRANGE = (WM_USER+28)
Global Const LB_MSGMAX = (WM_USER+33)

' Listbox Styles
Global Const LBS_NOTIFY = &H1&
Global Const LBS_SORT = &H2&
Global Const LBS_NOREDRAW = &H4&
Global Const LBS_MULTIPLESEL = &H8&
Global Const LBS_OWNERDRAWFIXED = &H10&
Global Const LBS_OWNERDRAWVARIABLE = &H20&
Global Const LBS_HASSTRINGS = &H40&
Global Const LBS_USETABSTOPS = &H80&
Global Const LBS_NOINTEGRALHEIGHT = &H100&
Global Const LBS_MULTICOLUMN = &H200&
Global Const LBS_WANTKEYBOARDINPUT = &H400&
Global Const LBS_EXTENDEDSEL = &H800&
Global Const LBS_STANDARD = (LBS_NOTIFY Or LBS_SORT Or WS_VSCROLL Or ⇐
WS_BORDER)

' Combo Box return Values
Global Const CB_OKAY = 0
Global Const CB_ERR = (-1)
Global Const CB_ERRSPACE = (-2)

' Combo Box Notification Codes
Global Const CBN_ERRSPACE = (-1)
```

```
Global Const CBN_SELCHANGE = 1
Global Const CBN_DBLCLK = 2
Global Const CBN_SETFOCUS = 3
Global Const CBN_KILLFOCUS = 4
Global Const CBN_EDITCHANGE = 5
Global Const CBN_EDITUPDATE = 6
Global Const CBN_DROPDOWN = 7

'  Combo Box styles
Global Const CBS_SIMPLE = &H1&
Global Const CBS_DROPDOWN = &H2&
Global Const CBS_DROPDOWNLIST = &H3&
Global Const CBS_OWNERDRAWFIXED = &H10&
Global Const CBS_OWNERDRAWVARIABLE = &H20&
Global Const CBS_AUTOHSCROLL = &H40&
Global Const CBS_OEMCONVERT = &H80&
Global Const CBS_SORT = &H100&
Global Const CBS_HASSTRINGS = &H200&
Global Const CBS_NOINTEGRALHEIGHT = &H400&

'  Combo Box messages
Global Const CB_GETEDITSEL = (WM_USER+0)
Global Const CB_LIMITTEXT = (WM_USER+1)
Global Const CB_SETEDITSEL = (WM_USER+2)
Global Const CB_ADDSTRING = (WM_USER+3)
Global Const CB_DELETESTRING = (WM_USER+4)
Global Const CB_DIR = (WM_USER+5)
Global Const CB_GETCOUNT = (WM_USER+6)
Global Const CB_GETCURSEL = (WM_USER+7)
Global Const CB_GETLBTEXT = (WM_USER+8)
Global Const CB_GETLBTEXTLEN = (WM_USER+9)
Global Const CB_INSERTSTRING = (WM_USER+10)
Global Const CB_RESETCONTENT = (WM_USER+11)
Global Const CB_FINDSTRING = (WM_USER+12)
Global Const CB_SELECTSTRING = (WM_USER+13)
Global Const CB_SETCURSEL = (WM_USER+14)
Global Const CB_SHOWDROPDOWN = (WM_USER+15)
Global Const CB_GETITEMDATA = (WM_USER+16)
Global Const CB_SETITEMDATA = (WM_USER+17)
Global Const CB_GETDROPPEDCONTROLRECT = (WM_USER+18)
Global Const CB_MSGMAX = (WM_USER+19)

'  Scroll Bar Styles
Global Const SBS_HORZ = &H0&
Global Const SBS_VERT = &H1&
Global Const SBS_TOPALIGN = &H2&
Global Const SBS_LEFTALIGN = &H2&
Global Const SBS_BOTTOMALIGN = &H4&
Global Const SBS_RIGHTALIGN = &H4&
Global Const SBS_SIZEBOXTOPLEFTALIGN = &H2&
Global Const SBS_SIZEBOXBOTTOMRIGHTALIGN = &H4&
Global Const SBS_SIZEBOX = &H8&
```

Sound is much more complicated in a multitasking environment like Windows than normal single-tasking DOS. See How-To 7.2 Make a replacement for QuickBASIC's Sound statement, and How-To 7.3 Make music in Visual Basic.

```
'  Sound Functions
'
Declare Function OpenSound Lib "Sound" () As Integer
Declare Sub CloseSound Lib "Sound" ()
Declare Function SetVoiceQueueSize Lib "Sound" (ByVal nVoice As Integer, ⇐
ByVal nBytes As Integer) As Integer
Declare Function SetVoiceNote Lib "Sound" (ByVal nVoice As Integer, ByVal ⇐
nValue As Integer, ByVal nLength As Integer, ByVal nCdots As Integer) As ⇐
Integer
Declare Function SetVoiceAccent Lib "Sound" (ByVal nVoice As Integer, ⇐
ByVal nTempo As Integer, ByVal nVolume As Integer, ByVal nMode As Integer, ⇐
ByVal nPitch As Integer) As Integer
Declare Function SetVoiceEnvelope Lib "Sound" (ByVal nVoice As Integer, ⇐
ByVal nShape As Integer, ByVal nRepeat As Integer) As Integer
Declare Function SetSoundNoise Lib "Sound" (ByVal nSource As Integer, ⇐
ByVal nDuration As Integer) As Integer
Declare Function SetVoiceSound Lib "Sound" (ByVal nVoice As Integer, ⇐
ByVal lFrequency As Long, ByVal nDuration As Integer) As Integer
Declare Function StartSound Lib "Sound" () As Integer
Declare Function StopSound Lib "Sound" () As Integer
Declare Function WaitSoundState Lib "Sound" (ByVal nState As Integer) As ⇐
Integer
Declare Function SyncAllVoices Lib "Sound" () As Integer
Declare Function CountVoiceNotes Lib "Sound" (ByVal nVoice As Integer) As ⇐
Integer
Declare Function GetThresholdEvent Lib "Sound" () As Integer
Declare Function GetThresholdStatus Lib "Sound" () As Integer
Declare Function SetVoiceThreshold Lib "Sound" (ByVal nVoice As Integer, ⇐
ByVal nNotes As Integer) As Integer

'  WaitSoundState() Constants
Global Const S_QUEUEEMPTY = 0
Global Const S_THRESHOLD = 1
Global Const S_ALLTHRESHOLD = 2

'  Accent Modes
Global Const S_NORMAL = 0
Global Const S_LEGATO = 1
Global Const S_STACCATO = 2

'  SetSoundNoise() Sources
Global Const S_PERIOD512 = 0    '  Freq = N/512 high pitch, less coarse hiss
Global Const S_PERIOD1024 = 1   '  Freq = N/1024
Global Const S_PERIOD2048 = 2   '  Freq = N/2048 low pitch, more coarse hiss
Global Const S_PERIODVOICE = 3  '  Source is frequency from voice channel ⇐
(3)
Global Const S_WHITE512 = 4     '  Freq = N/512 high pitch, less coarse hiss
Global Const S_WHITE1024 = 5    '  Freq = N/1024
Global Const S_WHITE2048 = 6    '  Freq = N/2048 low pitch, more coarse hiss
Global Const S_WHITEVOICE = 7   '  Source is frequency from voice channel ⇐
(3)
```

```
Global Const S_SERDVNA = (-1)    '  Device not available
Global Const S_SEROFM = (-2)     '  Out of memory
Global Const S_SERMACT = (-3)    '  Music active
Global Const S_SERQFUL = (-4)    '  Queue full
Global Const S_SERBDNT = (-5)    '  Invalid note
Global Const S_SERDLN = (-6)     '  Invalid note length
Global Const S_SERDCC = (-7)     '  Invalid note count
Global Const S_SERDTP = (-8)     '  Invalid tempo
Global Const S_SERDVL = (-9)     '  Invalid volume
Global Const S_SERDMD = (-10)    '  Invalid mode
Global Const S_SERDSH = (-11)    '  Invalid shape
Global Const S_SERDPT = (-12)    '  Invalid pitch
Global Const S_SERDFQ = (-13)    '  Invalid frequency
Global Const S_SERDDR = (-14)    '  Invalid duration
Global Const S_SERDSR = (-15)    '  Invalid source
Global Const S_SERDST = (-16)    '  Invalid state
```

Communication is also more complex in Windows than in DOS. See How-To 7.4 Create a phone dialer in Visual Basic, and How-To 7.5 Perform serial I/O in Visual Basic.

```
'  COMM declarations
'
Global Const NOPARITY = 0
Global Const ODDPARITY = 1
Global Const EVENPARITY = 2
Global Const MARKPARITY = 3
Global Const SPACEPARITY = 4

Global Const ONESTOPBIT = 0
Global Const ONE5STOPBITS = 1
Global Const TWOSTOPBITS = 2

Global Const IGNORE = 0          '  Ignore signal
Global Const INFINITE = &HFFFF      '  Infinite timeout

'  Error Flags
Global Const CE_RXOVER = &H1 '  Receive Queue overflow
Global Const CE_OVERRUN = &H2        '  Receive Overrun Error
Global Const CE_RXPARITY = &H4       '  Receive Parity Error
Global Const CE_FRAME = &H8  '  Receive Framing error
Global Const CE_BREAK = &H10 '  Break Detected
Global Const CE_CTSTO = &H20 '  CTS Timeout
Global Const CE_DSRTO = &H40 '  DSR Timeout
Global Const CE_RLSDTO = &H80        '  RLSD Timeout
Global Const CE_TXFULL = &H100       '  TX Queue is full
Global Const CE_PTO = &H200  '  LPTx Timeout
Global Const CE_IOE = &H400  '  LPTx I/O Error
Global Const CE_DNS = &H800  '  LPTx Device not selected
Global Const CE_OOP = &H1000 '  LPTx Out-Of-Paper
Global Const CE_MODE = &H8000        '  Requested mode unsupported

Global Const IE_BADID = (-1) '  Invalid or unsupported id
Global Const IE_OPEN = (-2)  '  Device Already Open
```

*continued on next page*

*continued from previous page*

```
Global Const IE_NOPEN = (-3)'  Device Not Open
Global Const IE_MEMORY = (-4)        ' Unable to allocate queues
Global Const IE_DEFAULT = (-5)       ' Error in default parameters
Global Const IE_HARDWARE = (-10)     ' Hardware Not Present
Global Const IE_BYTESIZE = (-11)     ' Illegal Byte Size
Global Const IE_BAUDRATE = (-12)     ' Unsupported BaudRate

'  Events
Global Const EV_RXCHAR = &H1 '  Any Character received
Global Const EV_RXFLAG = &H2 '  Received certain character
Global Const EV_TXEMPTY = &H4        ' Transmitt Queue Empty
Global Const EV_CTS = &H8     '  CTS changed state
Global Const EV_DSR = &H10    '  DSR changed state
Global Const EV_RLSD = &H20   '  RLSD changed state
Global Const EV_BREAK = &H40 '  BREAK received
Global Const EV_ERR = &H80    '  Line status error occurred
Global Const EV_RING = &H100 '  Ring signal detected
Global Const EV_PERR = &H200 '  Printer error occured

'  Escape Functions
Global Const SETXOFF = 1      '  Simulate XOFF received
Global Const SETXON = 2       '  Simulate XON received
Global Const SETRTS = 3       '  Set RTS high
Global Const CLRRTS = 4       '  Set RTS low
Global Const SETDTR = 5       '  Set DTR high
Global Const CLRDTR = 6       '  Set DTR low
Global Const RESETDEV = 7     '  Reset device if possible

Global Const LPTx = &H80      '  Set if ID is for LPT device

Type DCB
     Id As String * 1
     BaudRate As Integer
     ByteSize As String * 1
     Parity As String * 1
     StopBits As String * 1
     RlsTimeout As Integer
     CtsTimeout As Integer
     DsrTimeout As Integer

     Bits1 As String * 1 ' The fifteen actual DCB bit-sized data fields
     Bits2 As String * 1 ' within these two bytes can be manipulated by
                         ' bitwise logical And/Or operations.  Refer to
                         ' SDKWIN.HLP for location/meaning of specific bits

     XonChar As String * 1
     XoffChar As String * 1
     XonLim As Integer
     XoffLim As Integer
     PeChar As String * 1
     EofChar As String * 1
     EvtChar As String * 1
     TxDelay As Integer
End Type

Type COMSTAT
```

```
    Bits As String * 1 ' For specific bit flags and their
                  ' meanings, refer to SDKWIN.HLP.
    cbInQue As Integer
    cbOutQue As Integer
End Type

Declare Function OpenComm Lib "User" (ByVal lpComName As String, ByVal ⇐
wInQueue As Integer, ByVal wOutQueue As Integer) As Integer
Declare Function SetCommState Lib "User" (lpDCB as DCB) As Integer
Declare Function GetCommState Lib "User" (ByVal nCid As Integer, lpDCB As ⇐
DCB) As Integer
Declare Function ReadComm Lib "User" (ByVal nCid As Integer, ByVal lpBuf
As String, ByVal nSize As Integer) As Integer
Declare Function UngetCommChar Lib "User" (ByVal nCid As Integer, ByVal ⇐
cChar As Integer) As Integer
Declare Function WriteComm Lib "User" (ByVal nCid As Integer, ByVal lpBuf ⇐
As String, ByVal nSize As Integer) As Integer
Declare Function CloseComm Lib "User" (ByVal nCid As Integer) As Integer
Declare Function BuildCommDCB Lib "User" (ByVal lpDef As String, lpDCB As ⇐
DCB) As Integer
Declare Function TransmitCommChar Lib "User" (ByVal nCid As Integer, ByVal ⇐
cChar As Integer) As Integer
Declare Function SetCommEventMask Lib "User" (ByVal nCid as Integer, ⇐
nEvtMask as Integer) As Long
Declare Function GetCommEventMask Lib "User" (ByVal nCid As Integer, ByVal ⇐
nEvtMask As Integer) As Integer
Declare Function SetCommBreak Lib "User" (ByVal nCid As Integer) As
Integer
Declare Function ClearCommBreak Lib "User" (ByVal nCid As Integer) As ⇐
Integer
Declare Function FlushComm Lib "User" (ByVal nCid As Integer, ByVal nQueue ⇐
As Integer) As Integer
Declare Function EscapeCommFunction Lib "User" (ByVal nCid As Integer, ⇐
ByVal nFunc As Integer) As Integer
```

Multiple Document Interface (MDI) windows are Windows' standard way of providing multiple windows in a single application. A word processor, for example, might provide MDI windows to let you open multiple documents simultaneously. Visual Basic, unfortunately, doesn't provide MDI windows, though a custom control might provide that functionality to Visual Basic applications.

```
Type MDICREATESTRUCT
    szClass As Long
    szTitle As Long
    hOwner As Integer
    x As Integer
    y As Integer
    cx As Integer
    cy As Integer
    style As Long
    lParam As Long
End Type
```

*continued on next page*

*continued from previous page*

```
Type CLIENTCREATESTRUCT
    hWindowMenu As Integer
    idFirstChild As Integer
End Type

Declare Function DefFrameProc Lib "User" (ByVal hWnd As Integer, ByVal ⇐
hWndMDIClient As Integer, ByVal wMsg As Integer, ByVal wParam As Integer, ⇐
ByVal lParam As Long) As Long
Declare Function DefMDIChildProc Lib "User" (ByVal hWnd As Integer, ByVal ⇐
wMsg As Integer, ByVal wParam As Integer, ByVal lParam As Long) As Long

Declare Function TranslateMDISysAccel Lib "User" (ByVal hWndClient As ⇐
Integer, lpMsg As MSG) As Integer

Declare Function ArrangeIconicWindows Lib "User" (ByVal hWnd As Integer) ⇐
As Integer
```

As your applications get more complex, your users will demand some form of online Help so they're not stuck when they come to a problem. Microsoft provides an add-on Help compiler kit that allows you to design and write online Help.

```
'  Help engine section.

'  Commands to pass WinHelp()
Global Const HELP_CONTEXT = &H1      ' Display topic in ulTopic
Global Const HELP_QUIT = &H2 ' Terminate help
Global Const HELP_INDEX = &H3        ' Display index
Global Const HELP_HELPONHELP = &H4 ' Display help on using help
Global Const HELP_SETINDEX = &H5     ' Set the current Index for multi ⇐
index help
Global Const HELP_KEY = &H101                ' Display topic for keyword ⇐
in offabData
Global Const HELP_MULTIKEY = &H201

Declare Function WinHelp Lib "User" (ByVal hWnd As Integer, ByVal ⇐
lpHelpFile As String, ByVal wCommand As Integer, dwData As Any) As Integer

Type MULTIKEYHELP
    mkSize As Integer
    mkKeylist As String * 1
    szKeyphrase As String * 253 ' Array length is arbitrary; may be ⇐
changed
End Type
```

Microsoft provides a profiler in the Windows SDK and Borland offers its Turbo Profiler for Windows. A profiler helps you pinpoint areas in your application that take too long to execute. Once you know where a "bottleneck" exists you can work on speeding it up.

```
' function declarations for profiler routines contained in Windows ⇐
libraries
Declare Function ProfInsChk Lib "User" () As Integer
Declare Sub ProfSetup Lib "User" (ByVal nBufferSize As Integer, ByVal ⇐
```

```
nSamples As Integer)
Declare Sub ProfSampRate Lib "User" (ByVal nRate286 As Integer, ByVal ⇐
nRate386 As Integer)
Declare Sub ProfStart Lib "User" ()
Declare Sub ProfStop Lib "User" ()
Declare Sub ProfClear Lib "User" ()
Declare Sub ProfFlush Lib "User" ()
Declare Sub ProfFinish Lib "User" ()
```

## The WIN31EXT.TXT adds the Windows extensions:

```
' -------------------------------------
'
'   WIN31EXT.TXT -- Windows 3.1 API Declarations for Visual Basic
'
'        Copyright (C) 1993 Microsoft Corporation
'
'
' This file contains the Const, Type, and Declare statements for
' Windows 3.1 APIs.  If you only want to reference Windows 3.0 APIs,
' use WIN30API.TXT.
'
' You must use this file together with WIN30API.TXT in Visual Basic
' if you want the references to match up properly.
'
' You have a royalty-free right to use, modify, reproduce and distribute
' this file (and/or any modified version) in any way you find useful,
' provided that you agree that Microsoft has no warranty, obligation or
' liability for its contents.  Refer to the Microsoft Windows Programmer's
' Reference for further information.
'
'*********************** Windows 3.1 Extensions ***********************
' Window 3.1 commands to pass WinHelp()
Global Const HELP_CONTENTS = &H3      ' Display Help for a particular topic
Global Const HELP_SETCONTENTS = &H5   ' Display Help contents topic
Global Const HELP_CONTEXTPOPUP = &H8  ' Display Help topic in popup window
Global Const HELP_FORCEFILE = &H9     ' Ensure correct Help file is displayed
Global Const HELP_COMMAND = &H102     ' Execute Help macro
Global Const HELP_PARTIALKEY = &H105  ' Display topic found in keyword list
Global Const HELP_SETWINPOS = &H203   ' Display and position Help window
```

You can use GetFreeSystemResources to determine what percentage of a various types of system resources are free.

```
Declare Function GetFreeSystemResources Lib "User" (ByVal fuSysResource ⇐
As Integer) As Integer

Global Const GFSR_SYSTEMRESOURCES = &H0000
Global Const GFSR_GDIRESOURCES = &H0001
Global Const GFSR_USERRESOURCES = &H0002
```

LogError and LogParamError are used by interrupt callback functions to retrieve information about system errors. Visual Basic handles error trapping and error return values for you.

```
Declare Sub LogError Lib "Kernel" (ByVal uErr As Integer, lpvInfo As Any)


' ***** LogParamError/LogError values *****

' Error modifier bits
Global Const ERR_WARNING = &H8000
Global Const ERR_PARAM = &H4000

Global Const ERR_SIZE_MASK = &H3000
Global Const ERR_BYTE = &H1000
Global Const ERR_WORD = &H2000
Global Const ERR_DWORD = &H3000


' ***** LogParamError() values *****

' Generic parameter values
Global Const ERR_BAD_VALUE = &H6001
Global Const ERR_BAD_FLAGS = &H6002
Global Const ERR_BAD_INDEX = &H6003
Global Const ERR_BAD_DVALUE = &H7004
Global Const ERR_BAD_DFLAGS = &H7005
Global Const ERR_BAD_DINDEX = &H7006
Global Const ERR_BAD_PTR = &H7007
Global Const ERR_BAD_FUNC_PTR = &H7008
Global Const ERR_BAD_SELECTOR = &H6009
Global Const ERR_BAD_STRING_PTR = &H700a
Global Const ERR_BAD_HANDLE = &H600b

' KERNEL parameter errors
Global Const ERR_BAD_HINSTANCE = &H6020
Global Const ERR_BAD_HMODULE = &H6021
Global Const ERR_BAD_GLOBAL_HANDLE = &H6022
Global Const ERR_BAD_LOCAL_HANDLE = &H6023
Global Const ERR_BAD_ATOM = &H6024
Global Const ERR_BAD_HFILE = &H6025

' USER parameter errors
Global Const ERR_BAD_HWND = &H6040
Global Const ERR_BAD_HMENU = &H6041
Global Const ERR_BAD_HCURSOR = &H6042
Global Const ERR_BAD_HICON = &H6043
Global Const ERR_BAD_HDWP = &H6044
Global Const ERR_BAD_CID = &H6045
Global Const ERR_BAD_HDRVR = &H6046

' GDI parameter errors
Global Const ERR_BAD_COORDS = &H7060
```

```
Global Const ERR_BAD_GDI_OBJECT = &H6061
Global Const ERR_BAD_HDC = &H6062
Global Const ERR_BAD_HPEN = &H6063
Global Const ERR_BAD_HFONT = &H6064
Global Const ERR_BAD_HBRUSH = &H6065
Global Const ERR_BAD_HBITMAP = &H6066
Global Const ERR_BAD_HRGN = &H6067
Global Const ERR_BAD_HPALETTE = &H6068
Global Const ERR_BAD_HMETAFILE = &H6069


' ***** LogError() values *****

' KERNEL errors
Global Const ERR_GALLOC = &H0001
Global Const ERR_GREALLOC = &H0002
Global Const ERR_GLOCK = &H0003
Global Const ERR_LALLOC = &H0004
Global Const ERR_LREALLOC = &H0005
Global Const ERR_LLOCK = &H0006
Global Const ERR_ALLOCRES = &H0007
Global Const ERR_LOCKRES = &H0008
Global Const ERR_LOADMODULE = &H0009


' USER errors
Global Const ERR_CREATEDLG = &H0040
Global Const ERR_CREATEDLG2 = &H0041
Global Const ERR_REGISTERCLASS = &H0042
Global Const ERR_DCBUSY = &H0043
Global Const ERR_CREATEWND = &H0044
Global Const ERR_STRUCEXTRA = &H0045
Global Const ERR_LOADSTR = &H0046
Global Const ERR_LOADMENU = &H0047
Global Const ERR_NESTEDBEGINPAINT = &H0048
Global Const ERR_BADINDEX = &H0049
Global Const ERR_CREATEMENU = &H004a


' GDI errors
Global Const ERR_CREATEDC = &H0080
Global Const ERR_CREATEMETA = &H0081
Global Const ERR_DELOBJSELECTED = &H0082
Global Const ERR_SELBITMAP = &H0083
```

Visual Basic provides its own debugging environment so you will find little use for the Windows debugging functions.

```
' Debugging support (DEBUG SYSTEM ONLY)
Type WINDEBUGINFO
    flags As Integer
    dwOptions As Long
    dwFilter As Long
    achAllocModule As String * 8
    dwAllocBreak As Long
```

*continued on next page*

*continued from previous page*

```
      dwAllocCount As Long
End Type

Declare Function GetWinDebugInfo Lib "Kernel" (lpwdi As WINDEBUGINFO, ⇐
ByVal flags As Integer) As Integer
Declare Function SetWinDebugInfo Lib "Kernel" (lpwdi As WINDEBUGINFO) As ⇐
Integer
Declare Sub DebugOutput Lib "Kernel" (flags As Integer, ByVal lpszFmt As ⇐
String)

' WINDEBUGINFO flags values
Global Const WDI_OPTIONS = &H0001
Global Const WDI_FILTER = &H0002
Global Const WDI_ALLOCBREAK = &H0004

' dwOptions values
Global Const DBO_CHECKHEAP = &H0001
Global Const DBO_BUFFERFILL = &H0004
Global Const DBO_DISABLEGPTRAPPING = &H0010
Global Const DBO_CHECKFREE = &H0020
Global Const DBO_SILENT = &H8000
Global Const DBO_TRACEBREAK = &H2000
Global Const DBO_WARNINGBREAK = &H1000
Global Const DBO_NOERRORBREAK = &H0800
Global Const DBO_NOFATALBREAK = &H0400
Global Const DBO_INT3BREAK = &H0100

' DebugOutput flags values
Global Const DBF_TRACE = &H0000
Global Const DBF_WARNING = &H4000
Global Const DBF_ERROR = &H8000
Global Const DBF_FATAL = &Hc000

' dwFilter values
Global Const DBF_KERNEL = &H1000
Global Const DBF_KRN_MEMMAN = &H0001
Global Const DBF_KRN_LOADMODULE = &H0002
Global Const DBF_KRN_SEGMENTLOAD = &H0004
Global Const DBF_USER = &H0800
Global Const DBF_GDI = &H0400
Global Const DBF_MMSYSTEM = &H0040
Global Const DBF_PENWIN = &H0020
Global Const DBF_APPLICATION = &H0008
Global Const DBF_DRIVER = &H0010

Global Const EW_REBOOTSYSTEM = &H43

Declare Function ExitWindowsExec Lib "User" (ByVal lpszExe As String, ⇐
ByVal lpszParams As String) As Integer
Declare Function IsBadReadPtr Lib "Kernel" (ByVal lp As String, ByVal cb ⇐
As Integer) As Integer
Declare Function IsBadWritePtr Lib "Kernel" (ByVal lp As String, ByVal cb ⇐
As Integer) As Integer
```

```
Declare Function IsBadStringPtr Lib "Kernel" (ByVal lpsz As String, ByVal ⇐
cchMax As Integer) As Integer
Declare Function IsTask Lib "Kernel" (ByVal htask As Integer) As Integer

Global Const OBM_UPARROWI = 32737
Global Const OBM_DNARROWI = 32736
Global Const OBM_RGARROWI = 32735
Global Const OBM_LFARROWI = 32734
```

You can use lstrcpyn to copy the contents of one C-style string to another. The cChars parameter specifies the maximum number of characters that will be copied. Regardless of the value of cChars, lstrcpyn will copy characters only until the first 0 byte is seen.

```
Declare Function lstrcpyn Lib "Kernel" (ByVal lpszString1 As String, ⇐
ByVal lpszString2 As String, ByVal cChars As Integer) As String
```

The IsDBCSLeadByte function determines whether a character is the first byte of a double-byte character set.

```
Declare Function IsDBCSLeadByte Lib "Kernel" (ByVal bTestChar As Integer) ⇐
As Integer
```

The SIZE structure is passed to many of the new GDI functions to indicate width (cx) and height (cy) where required.

```
Type SIZE
    cx As Integer
    cy As Integer
End Type
```

Windows 3.1 added a number of new GDI functions, these are listed below. Many of these functions can be used by Visual Basic programmers.

```
' Drawing bounds accumulation APIs
Declare Function SetBoundsRect Lib "GDI" (ByVal hdc As Integer, lprcBounds ⇐
As RECT, ByVal flags As Integer) As Integer
Declare Function GetBoundsRect Lib "GDI" (ByVal hdc As Integer, lprcBounds ⇐
As RECT, ByVal flags As Integer) As Integer

Global Const DCB_RESET = &H0001
Global Const DCB_ACCUMULATE = &H0002
Global Const DCB_DIRTY = DCB_ACCUMULATE
Global Const DCB_SET = (DCB_RESET Or DCB_ACCUMULATE)
Global Const DCB_ENABLE = &H0004
Global Const DCB_DISABLE = &H0008

Declare Function SetWindowOrgEx Lib "GDI" (ByVal hdc As Integer, ByVal nX ⇐
As Integer, ByVal nY As Integer, lpPoint As POINTAPI) As Integer
Declare Function GetWindowOrgEx Lib "GDI" (ByVal hdc As Integer, lpPoint ⇐
As POINTAPI) As Integer
Declare Function SetWindowExtEx Lib "GDI" (ByVal hdc As Integer, ByVal nX ⇐
As Integer, ByVal nY As Integer, lpSize As SIZE) As Integer
```

*continued on next page*

*continued from previous page*

```
Declare Function GetWindowExtEx Lib "GDI" (ByVal hdc As Integer, lpSize ⇐
As SIZE) As Integer
Declare Function OffsetWindowOrgEx Lib "GDI" (ByVal hdc As Integer, ByVal ⇐
nX As Integer, ByVal nY As Integer, lpPoint As POINTAPI) As Integer
Declare Function ScaleWindowExtEx% Lib "GDI" (ByVal hdc%, ByVal nXnum%, ⇐
ByVal nXdenom%, ByVal nYnum%, ByVal nYdenom%, lpSize As SIZE)
Declare Function SetViewportExtEx Lib "GDI" (ByVal hdc As Integer, ByVal ⇐
nX As Integer, ByVal nY As Integer, lpSize As SIZE) As Integer
Declare Function GetViewportExtEx Lib "GDI" (ByVal hdc As Integer, lpSize ⇐
As SIZE) As Integer
Declare Function SetViewportOrgEx Lib "GDI" (ByVal hdc As Integer, ByVal ⇐
nX As Integer, ByVal nY As Integer, lpPoint As POINTAPI) As Integer
Declare Function GetViewportOrgEx Lib "GDI" (ByVal hdc As Integer, ⇐
lpPoint As POINTAPI) As Integer
Declare Function OffsetViewportOrgEx Lib "GDI" (ByVal hdc As Integer, ⇐
ByVal nX As Integer, ByVal nY As Integer, lpPoint As POINTAPI) As Integer
Declare Function ScaleViewportExtEx% Lib "GDI" (ByVal hdc%, ByVal nXnum%, ⇐
ByVal nXdenom%, ByVal nYnum%, ByVal nYdenom%, lpSize As SIZE)

Global Const COLOR_INACTIVECAPTIONTEXT = 19
Global Const COLOR_BTNHIGHLIGHT = 20

Declare Function GetBrushOrgEx Lib "GDI" (ByVal hdc As Integer, lpPoint ⇐
As POINTAPI) As Integer
Declare Function MoveToEx Lib "GDI" (ByVal hdc As Integer, ByVal x As ⇐
Integer, ByVal y As Integer, lpPoint As POINTAPI) As Integer
Declare Function GetCurrentPositionEx Lib "GDI" (ByVal hdc As Integer, ⇐
lpPoint As POINTAPI) As Integer
Declare Function GetTextExtentPoint Lib "GDI" (ByVal hdc As Integer, ⇐
ByVal lpszString As String, ByVal cbString As Integer, lpSize As SIZE) ⇐
As Integer

Global Const OUT_TT_PRECIS = 4
Global Const OUT_DEVICE_PRECIS = 5
Global Const OUT_RASTER_PRECIS = 6
Global Const OUT_TT_ONLY_PRECIS = 7

Global Const CLIP_LH_ANGLES = &H10
Global Const CLIP_TT_ALWAYS = &H20
Global Const CLIP_EMBEDDED = &H80

Declare Function GetAspectRatioFilterEx Lib "GDI" (ByVal hdc As Integer, ⇐
lpAspectRatio As SIZE) As Integer

Global Const TMPF_TRUETYPE = &H04

Type PANOSE
    bFamilyType As String * 1
    bSerifStyle As String * 1
    bWeight As String * 1
    bProportion As String * 1
    bContrast As String * 1
    bStrokeVariation As String * 1
```

```
        bArmStyle As String * 1
        bLetterform As String * 1
        bMidline As String * 1
        bXHeight As String * 1
End Type


Type OUTLINETEXTMETRIC
        otmSize As Integer
        otmTextMetrics As TEXTMETRIC
        otmFiller As String * 1
        otmPanoseNumber As PANOSE
        otmfsSelection As Integer
        otmfsType As Integer
        otmsCharSlopeRise As Integer
        otmsCharSlopeRun As Integer
        otmItalicAngle As Integer
        otmEMSquare As Integer
        otmAscent As Integer
        otmDescent As Integer
        otmLineGap As Integer
        otmsCapEmHeight As Integer
        otmsXHeight As Integer
        otmrcFontBox As RECT
        otmMacAscent As Integer
        otmMacDescent As Integer
        otmMacLineGap As Integer
        otmusMinimumPPEM As Integer
        otmptSubscriptSize As POINTAPI
        otmptSubscriptOffset As POINTAPI
        otmptSuperscriptSize As POINTAPI
        otmptSuperscriptOffset As POINTAPI
        otmsStrikeoutSize As Integer
        otmsStrikeoutPosition As Integer
        otmsUnderscorePosition As Integer
        otmsUnderscoreSize As Integer
        otmpFamilyName As Long
        otmpFaceName As Long
        otmpStyleName As Long
        otmpFullName As Long
    End Type


Declare Function GetOutlineTextMetrics Lib "GDI" (ByVal hdc As Integer, ⇐
ByVal cbData As Integer, lpotm As OUTLINETEXTMETRIC) As Integer


' Structure passed to FONTENUMPROC
' NOTE: NEWTEXTMETRIC is the same as TEXTMETRIC plus 4 new fields
Type NEWTEXTMETRIC
        tmHeight As Integer
        tmAscent As Integer
        tmDescent As Integer
        tmInternalLeading As Integer
        tmExternalLeading As Integer
        tmAveCharWidth As Integer
```

*continued on next page*

*continued from previous page*

```
        tmMaxCharWidth As Integer
        tmWeight As Integer
        tmItalic As String * 1
        tmUnderlined As String * 1
        tmStruckOut As String * 1
        tmFirstChar As String * 1
        tmLastChar As String * 1
        tmDefaultChar As String * 1
        tmBreakChar As String * 1
        tmPitchAndFamily As String * 1
        tmCharSet As String * 1
        tmOverhang As Integer
        tmDigitizedAspectX As Integer
        tmDigitizedAspectY As Integer
        ntmFlags As Long
        ntmSizeEM As Integer
        ntmCellHeight As Integer
        ntmAvgWidth As Integer
End Type

' ntmFlags field flags
Global Const NTM_REGULAR = &H00000040&
Global Const NTM_BOLD = &H00000020&
Global Const NTM_ITALIC = &H00000001&

Global Const LF_FULLFACESIZE = 64

Global Const TRUETYPE_FONTTYPE = &H0004

Declare Function GetFontData& Lib "GDI" (ByVal hdc%, ByVal dwTable&, ⇐
ByVal dwOffset&, ByVal lpvBuffer$, ByVal cbData&)
Declare Function CreateScalableFontResource% Lib "GDI" (ByVal fHidden%, ⇐
ByVal lpszResourceFile$, ByVal lpszFontFile$, ByVal lpszCurrentPath$)

Type GLYPHMETRICS
        gmBlackBoxX As Integer
        gmBlackBoxY As Integer
        gmptGlyphOrigin As POINTAPI
        gmCellIncX As Integer
        gmCellIncY As Integer
End Type

Type FIXED
        fract As Integer
        value As Integer
End Type

Type MAT2
        eM11 As FIXED
        eM12 As FIXED
        eM21 As FIXED
        eM22 As FIXED
End Type
```

```
Declare Function GetGlyphOutline& Lib "GDI" (ByVal hdc%, ByVal uChar%, ⇐
ByVal fuFormat%, lpgm As GLYPHMETRICS, ByVal cbBuffer&, ByVal lpBuffer$, ⇐
lpmat2 As MAT2)

' GetGlyphOutline constants
Global Const GGO_METRICS = 0
Global Const GGO_BITMAP = 1
Global Const GGO_NATIVE = 2

Global Const TT_POLYGON_TYPE = 24

Global Const TT_PRIM_LINE = 1
Global Const TT_PRIM_QSPLINE = 2

Type POINTFX
     x As FIXED
     y As FIXED
End Type

Type TTPOLYCURVE
     wType As Integer
     cpfx As Integer
     apfx As POINTFX
End Type

Type TTPOLYGONHEADER
     cb As Long
     dwType As Long
     pfxStart As POINTFX
End Type

Type ABC
     abcA As Integer
     abcB As Integer
     abcC As Integer
End Type

Declare Function GetCharABCWidths Lib "GDI" (ByVal hdc As Integer, ByVal ⇐
uFirstChar As Integer, ByVal uLastChar As Integer, lpabc As ABC) As ⇐
Integer

Type KERNINGPAIR
     wFirst As Integer
     wSecond As Integer
     iKernAmount As Integer
End Type

Declare Function GetKerningPairs Lib "GDI" (ByVal hdc As Integer, ByVal ⇐
cPairs As Integer, lpkrnpair As KERNINGPAIR) As Integer

Type RASTERIZER_STATUS
     nSize As Integer
     wFlags As Integer
```

*continued on next page*

*continued from previous page*

```
     nLanguageID As Integer
End Type


' bits defined in wFlags of RASTERIZER_STATUS
Global Const TT_AVAILABLE = &H0001
Global Const TT_ENABLED = &H0002

Declare Function GetRasterizerCaps Lib "GDI" (lpraststat As ⇐
RASTERIZER_STATUS, ByVal cb As Integer) As Integer
Declare Function SetBitmapDimensionEx Lib "GDI" (ByVal hbm As Integer, ⇐
ByVal nX As Integer, ByVal nY As Integer, lpSize As SIZE) As Integer
Declare Function GetBitmapDimensionEx Lib "GDI" (ByVal hBitmap As ⇐
Integer, lpDimension As SIZE) As Integer
Declare Function SetMetaFileBitsBetter Lib "GDI" (ByVal hmt As Integer) ⇐
As Integer


Type DOCINFO
     cbSize As Integer
     lpszDocName As Long
     lpszOutput As Long
End Type

Declare Function StartDoc Lib "GDI" (ByVal hdc As Integer, lpdi As ⇐
DOCINFO) As Integer
Declare Function StartPage Lib "GDI" (ByVal hdc As Integer) As Integer
Declare Function EndPage Lib "GDI" (ByVal hdc As Integer) As Integer
Declare Function EndDocAPI Lib "GDI" Alias "EndDoc" (ByVal hdc As Integer) ⇐
As Integer
Declare Function AbortDoc Lib "GDI" (ByVal hdc As Integer) As Integer
Declare Function SpoolFile Lib "GDI" (ByVal lpszPrinter As String, ByVal ⇐
lpszPort As String, ByVal lpszJob As String, ByVal lpszFile As String) As ⇐
Integer
```

The SystemParametersInfo function is used to query or set system-wide parameters. If you pass SPIF_UPDATEINIFILE as the last argument to the function, the corresponding entry in WIN.INI will be modified.

```
Global Const SM_CXDOUBLECLK = 36
Global Const SM_CYDOUBLECLK = 37
Global Const SM_CXICONSPACING = 38
Global Const SM_CYICONSPACING = 39
Global Const SM_MENUDROPALIGNMENT = 40
Global Const SM_PENWINDOWS = 41
Global Const SM_DBCSENABLED = 42

Declare Function SystemParametersInfo Lib "User" (ByVal uAction As ⇐
Integer, ByVal uParam As Integer, lpvParam As Any, ByVal fuWinIni As ⇐
Integer) As Integer

Global Const SPI_GETBEEP = 1
Global Const SPI_SETBEEP = 2
Global Const SPI_GETMOUSE = 3
Global Const SPI_SETMOUSE = 4
```

```
Global Const SPI_GETBORDER = 5
Global Const SPI_SETBORDER = 6
Global Const SPI_GETKEYBOARDSPEED = 10
Global Const SPI_SETKEYBOARDSPEED = 11
Global Const SPI_LANGDRIVER = 12
Global Const SPI_ICONHORIZONTALSPACING = 13
Global Const SPI_GETSCREENSAVETIMEOUT = 14
Global Const SPI_SETSCREENSAVETIMEOUT = 15
Global Const SPI_GETSCREENSAVEACTIVE = 16
Global Const SPI_SETSCREENSAVEACTIVE = 17
Global Const SPI_GETGRIDGRANULARITY = 18
Global Const SPI_SETGRIDGRANULARITY = 19
Global Const SPI_SETDESKWALLPAPER = 20
Global Const SPI_SETDESKPATTERN = 21
Global Const SPI_GETKEYBOARDDELAY = 22
Global Const SPI_SETKEYBOARDDELAY = 23
Global Const SPI_ICONVERTICALSPACING = 24
Global Const SPI_GETICONTITLEWRAP = 25
Global Const SPI_SETICONTITLEWRAP = 26
Global Const SPI_GETMENUDROPALIGNMENT = 27
Global Const SPI_SETMENUDROPALIGNMENT = 28
Global Const SPI_SETDOUBLECLKWIDTH = 29
Global Const SPI_SETDOUBLECLKHEIGHT = 30
Global Const SPI_GETICONTITLELOGFONT = 31
Global Const SPI_SETDOUBLECLICKTIME = 32
Global Const SPI_SETMOUSEBUTTONSWAP = 33
Global Const SPI_SETICONTITLELOGFONT = 34
Global Const SPI_GETFASTTASKSWITCH = 35
Global Const SPI_SETFASTTASKSWITCH = 36

' SystemParametersInfo flags
Global Const SPIF_UPDATEINIFILE = &H0001
Global Const SPIF_SENDWININICHANGE = &H0002
```

These two functions are not useful in Visual Basic programs, since the message queue is handled by Visual Basic.

```
Declare Function GetMessageExtraInfo Lib "User" () As Long
Declare Function GetQueueStatus Lib "User" (ByVal fuFlags As Integer) As ⇐
Long

' GetQueueStatus flags
Global Const QS_KEY = &H0001
Global Const QS_MOUSEMOVE = &H0002
Global Const QS_MOUSEBUTTON = &H0004
Global Const QS_MOUSE = (QS_MOUSEMOVE Or QS_MOUSEBUTTON)
Global Const QS_POSTMESSAGE = &H0008
Global Const QS_TIMER = &H0010
Global Const QS_PAINT = &H0020
Global Const QS_SENDMESSAGE = &H0040

Global Const QS_ALLINPUT = &H007f
```

Power management messages can be intercepted using the MsgHook control.

```
' ***** Power management *****

Global Const WM_POWER = &H0048

' wParam for WM_POWER window message and DRV_POWER driver notification
Global Const PWR_OK = 1
Global Const PWR_FAIL = -1
Global Const PWR_SUSPENDREQUEST = 1
Global Const PWR_SUSPENDRESUME = 2
Global Const PWR_CRITICALRESUME = 3

Global Const GCW_ATOM = -32


Global Const WS_EX_TOPMOST = &H00000008&
Global Const WS_EX_ACCEPTFILES = &H00000010&
Global Const WS_EX_TRANSPARENT = &H00000020&

Type WINDOWPLACEMENT
    length As Integer
    flags As Integer
    showCmd As Integer
    ptMinPosition As POINTAPI
    ptMaxPosition As POINTAPI
    rcNormalPosition As RECT
End Type

Global Const WPF_SETMINPOSITION = &H0001
Global Const WPF_RESTORETOMAXIMIZED = &H0002
```

You can use a form's properties to manipulate WINDOWPLACEMENT values.

```
Declare Function GetWindowPlacement Lib "User" (ByVal hwnd As Integer, ⇐
lpwndpl As WINDOWPLACEMENT) As Integer
Declare Function SetWindowPlacement Lib "User" (ByVal hwnd As Integer, ⇐
lpwndpl As WINDOWPLACEMENT) As Integer

Global Const WM_WINDOWPOSCHANGING = &H0046
Global Const WM_WINDOWPOSCHANGED = &H0047

' WM_WINDOWPOSCHANGING/CHANGED struct pointed to by lParam
Type WINDOWPOS
    hwnd As Integer
    hwndInsertAfter As Integer
    x As Integer
    y As Integer
    cx As Integer
    cy As Integer
    flags As Integer
End Type
```

```
Declare Sub MapWindowPoints Lib "User" (ByVal hwndFrom As Integer, ByVal ⇐
hwndTo As Integer, lppt As POINTAPI, ByVal cPoints As Integer)
Declare Function GetDCEx Lib "User" (ByVal hwnd As Integer, ByVal ⇐
hrgnclip As Integer, ByVal fdwOptions As Long) As Integer

Global Const DCX_WINDOW = &H00000001&
Global Const DCX_CACHE = &H00000002&
Global Const DCX_CLIPCHILDREN = &H00000008&
Global Const DCX_CLIPSIBLINGS = &H00000010&
Global Const DCX_PARENTCLIP = &H00000020&
Global Const DCX_EXCLUDERGN = &H00000040&
Global Const DCX_INTERSECTRGN = &H00000080&
Global Const DCX_LOCKWINDOWUPDATE = &H00000400&
Global Const DCX_USESTYLE = &H00010000&

Declare Function LockWindowUpdate Lib "User" (ByVal hwndLock As Integer) ⇐
As Integer
Declare Function RedrawWindow Lib "User" (ByVal hwnd As Integer, ⇐
lprcUpdate As RECT, ByVal hrgnUpdate As Integer, ByVal fuRedraw As ⇐
Integer) As Integer

Global Const RDW_INVALIDATE = &H0001
Global Const RDW_INTERNALPAINT = &H0002
Global Const RDW_ERASE = &H0004
Global Const RDW_VALIDATE = &H0008
Global Const RDW_NOINTERNALPAINT = &H0010
Global Const RDW_NOERASE = &H0020
Global Const RDW_NOCHILDREN = &H0040
Global Const RDW_ALLCHILDREN = &H0080
Global Const RDW_UPDATENOW = &H0100
Global Const RDW_ERASENOW = &H0200
Global Const RDW_FRAME = &H0400
Global Const RDW_NOFRAME = &H0800

Declare Function ScrollWindowEx% Lib "User" (ByVal hwnd%, ByVal dx%, ⇐
ByVal dy%, lprcScroll As RECT, lprcClip As RECT, ByVal hrgnUpdate%, ⇐
lprcUpdate As RECT, ByVal fuScroll%)

Global Const SW_SCROLLCHILDREN = &H0001
Global Const SW_INVALIDATE = &H0002
Global Const SW_ERASE = &H0004

' WM_NCCALCSIZE return flags
Global Const WVR_ALIGNTOP = &H0010
Global Const WVR_ALIGNLEFT = &H0020
Global Const WVR_ALIGNBOTTOM = &H0040
Global Const WVR_ALIGNRIGHT = &H0080
Global Const WVR_HREDRAW = &H0100
Global Const WVR_VREDRAW = &H0200
Global Const WVR_REDRAW = (WVR_HREDRAW Or WVR_VREDRAW)
Global Const WVR_VALIDRECTS = &H0400

' WM_NCCALCSIZE parameter structure
```

*continued on next page*

*continued from previous page*

```
Type NCCALCSIZE_PARAMS
     rgrc As Long
     lppos As Long
End Type

Global Const MA_NOACTIVATEANDEAT = 4

Declare Function IsMenu Lib "User" (ByVal hmenu As Integer) As Integer

Global Const TPM_RIGHTBUTTON = &H0002
Global Const TPM_LEFTALIGN = &H0000
Global Const TPM_CENTERALIGN = &H0004
Global Const TPM_RIGHTALIGN = &H0008

Declare Function GetOpenClipboardWindow Lib "User" () As Integer
Declare Function CopyCursor Lib "User" (ByVal hinst As Integer, ByVal ⇐
hcur As Integer) As Integer
Declare Function GetCursor Lib "User" () As Integer
Declare Sub GetClipCursor Lib "User" (lprc As RECT)
Declare Function CopyIcon Lib "User" (ByVal hinst As Integer, ByVal hicon⇐
As Integer) As Integer

Global Const MDIS_ALLCHILDSTYLES = &H0001

' wParam values for WM_MDITILE and WM_MDICASCADE messages.
Global Const MDITILE_VERTICAL = &H0000
Global Const MDITILE_HORIZONTAL = &H0001
Global Const MDITILE_SKIPDISABLED = &H0002

' Static Control Mesages
Global Const STM_SETICON = (WM_USER+0)
Global Const STM_GETICON = (WM_USER+1)

Global Const ES_READONLY = &H00000800&
Global Const ES_WANTRETURN = &H00001000&

Global Const EM_GETFIRSTVISIBLELINE = (WM_USER+30)
Global Const EM_SETREADONLY = (WM_USER+31)
Global Const EM_SETWORDBREAKPROC = (WM_USER+32)
Global Const EM_GETWORDBREAKPROC = (WM_USER+33)
Global Const EM_GETPASSWORDCHAR = (WM_USER+34)

' EDITWORDBREAKPROC code values
Global Const WB_LEFT = 0
Global Const WB_RIGHT = 1
Global Const WB_ISDELIMITER = 2

Global Const LBS_DISABLENOSCROLL = &H1000&

Global Const LB_SETITEMHEIGHT = (WM_USER+33)
Global Const LB_GETITEMHEIGHT = (WM_USER+34)
Global Const LB_FINDSTRINGEXACT = (WM_USER+35)
```

```
Declare Function DlgDirSelectEx% Lib "User" (ByVal hwndDlg%, ByVal ⇐
lpszPath$, ByVal cbPath%, ByVal idListBox%)
Declare Function DlgDirSelectComboBoxEx% Lib "User" (ByVal hwndDlg%,⇐
ByVal lpszPath$, ByVal cbPath%, ByVal idComboBox%)
```

Visual Basic programmers cannot use the Windows Hook functions directly.

```
Global Const CBS_DISABLENOSCROLL = &H0800&

Global Const CB_SETITEMHEIGHT = (WM_USER+19)
Global Const CB_GETITEMHEIGHT = (WM_USER+20)
Global Const CB_SETEXTENDEDUI = (WM_USER+21)
Global Const CB_GETEXTENDEDUI = (WM_USER+22)
Global Const CB_GETDROPPEDSTATE = (WM_USER+23)
Global Const CB_FINDSTRINGEXACT = (WM_USER+24)

Global Const CBN_CLOSEUP = 8
Global Const CBN_SELENDOK = 9
Global Const CBN_SELENDCANCEL = 10

Declare Function UnhookWindowsHookEx Lib "User" (ByVal hHook As Integer) ⇐
As Integer
Declare Function CallNextHookEx Lib "User" (ByVal hHook As Integer, ByVal ⇐
ncode As Integer, ByVal wParam As Integer, lParam As Any) As Long

' HCBT_CREATEWND parameters pointed to by lParam
Type CBT_CREATEWND
     lpcs As Long
     hwndInsertAfter As Integer
End Type

' HCBT_ACTIVATE structure pointed to by lParam
Type CBTACTIVATESTRUCT
     fMouse As Integer
     hWndActive As Integer
End Type


Global Const WH_HARDWARE = 8

Type HARDWAREHOOKSTRUCT
     hWnd As Integer
     wMessage As Integer
     wParam As Integer
     lParam As Long
End Type

' SetWindowsHook() Shell hook code
Global Const WH_SHELL = 10

Global Const HSHELL_WINDOWCREATED = 1
Global Const HSHELL_WINDOWDESTROYED = 2
Global Const HSHELL_ACTIVATESHELLWINDOW = 3
```

*continued on next page*

*continued from previous page*

```
' SetWindowsHook debug hook support
Global Const WH_DEBUG = 9

Type DEBUGHOOKINFO
     hModuleHook As Integer
     reserved As Long
     lParam As Long
     wParam As Integer
     code As Integer
End Type

Declare Function QuerySendMessage Lib "User" (ByVal hreserved1 As ⇐
Integer, ByVal hreserved2 As Integer, ByVal hreserved3 As Integer, ByVal ⇐
lpMessage As String) As Integer
Declare Function LockInput Lib "User" (ByVal hReserved As Integer, ByVal ⇐
hwndInput As Integer, ByVal fLock As Integer) As Integer
Declare Function GetSystemDebugState Lib "User" () As Long

' Flags returned by GetSystemDebugState.
Global Const SDS_MENU = &H0001
Global Const SDS_SYSMODAL = &H0002
Global Const SDS_NOTASKQUEUE = &H0004
Global Const SDS_DIALOG = &H0008
Global Const SDS_TASKLOCKED = &H0010

' new escape functions
Global Const GETMAXLPT = 8
Global Const GETMAXCOM = 9
Global Const GETBASEIRQ = 10

' Comm Baud Rate indices
Global Const CBR_110 = &HFF10
Global Const CBR_300 = &HFF11
Global Const CBR_600 = &HFF12
Global Const CBR_1200 = &HFF13
Global Const CBR_2400 = &HFF14
Global Const CBR_4800 = &HFF15
Global Const CBR_9600 = &HFF16
Global Const CBR_14400 = &HFF17
Global Const CBR_19200 = &HFF18
Global Const CBR_38400 = &HFF1B
Global Const CBR_56000 = &HFF1F
 Global Const CBR_128000 = &HFF23
Global Const CBR_256000 = &HFF27

' notifications passed in low word of lParam on WM_COMMNOTIFY messages
Global Const CN_RECEIVE = &H0001
Global Const CN_TRANSMIT = &H0002
Global Const CN_EVENT = &H0004

Declare Function EnableCommNotification Lib "User" (ByVal idComDev As ⇐
Integer, ByVal hwnd As Integer, ByVal cbWriteNotify As Integer, ByVal ⇐
OutQueue As Integer) As Integer
```

```
Global Const WM_COMMNOTIFY = &H0044

' Driver messages
Global Const DRV_LOAD = &H0001
Global Const DRV_ENABLE = &H0002
Global Const DRV_OPEN = &H0003
Global Const DRV_CLOSE = &H0004
Global Const DRV_DISABLE = &H0005
Global Const DRV_FREE = &H0006
Global Const DRV_CONFIGURE = &H0007
Global Const DRV_QUERYCONFIGURE = &H0008
Global Const DRV_INSTALL = &H0009
Global Const DRV_REMOVE = &H000A
Global Const DRV_EXITSESSION = &H000B
Global Const DRV_EXITAPPLICATION = &H000C
Global Const DRV_POWER = &H000F
Global Const DRV_RESERVED = &H0800
Global Const DRV_USER = &H4000

' LPARAM of DRV_CONFIGURE message
Type DRVCONFIGINFO
     dwDCISize As Long
     lpszDCISectionName As Long
     lpszDCIAliasName As Long
End Type

' Supported return values for DRV_CONFIGURE message
Global Const DRVCNF_CANCEL = &H0000
Global Const DRVCNF_OK = &H0001
Global Const DRVCNF_RESTART = &H0002

' Supported lParam1 of DRV_EXITAPPLICATION notification
Global Const DRVEA_NORMALEXIT = &H0001
Global Const DRVEA_ABNORMALEXIT = &H0002

Declare Function DefDriverProc Lib "User" (ByVal dwDriverIdentifier As ⇐
Long, ByVal hdrvr As Integer, ByVal umsg As Integer, lParam1 As Any, ⇐
lParam2 As Any) As Long
Declare Function OpenDriver Lib "User" (ByVal lpDriverName As String, ⇐
ByVal lpSectionName As String, lParam As Any) As Integer
Declare Function CloseDriver Lib "User" (ByVal hdrvr As Integer, lParam1 ⇐
As Any, lParam2 As Any) As Long
Declare Function SendDriverMessage Lib "User" (ByVal hdrvr As Integer, ⇐
ByVal msg As Integer, lParam1 As Any, lParam2 As Any) As Long
Declare Function GetDriverModuleHandle Lib "User" (ByVal hdrvr As ⇐
Integer) As Integer
Declare Function GetNextDriver Lib "User" (ByVal hdrvr As Integer, ByVal ⇐
fdwFlag As Long) As Integer

' GetNextDriver flags
Global Const GND_FIRSTINSTANCEONLY = &H00000001

Global Const GND_FORWARD = &H00000000
```

*continued on next page*

*continued from previous page*

```
Global Const GND_REVERSE = &H00000002

Type DRIVERINFOSTRUCT
    length As Integer
    hDriver As Integer
    hModule As Integer
    szAliasName As String * 128
End Type

Declare Function GetDriverInfo Lib "User" (ByVal hdrvr As Integer, lpdis ⇐
As DRIVERINFOSTRUCT) As Integer
```

The LZ group of functions can be useful when writing custom installation programs.

```
' ***** LZEXPAND error return codes *****

Global Const LZERROR_BADINHANDLE = (-1)  ' invalid input handle
Global Const LZERROR_BADOUTHANDLE = (-2) ' invalid output handle
Global Const LZERROR_READ = (-3)         ' corrupt compressed file format
Global Const LZERROR_WRITE = (-4)        ' out of space for output file
Global Const LZERROR_GLOBALLOC = (-5)    ' insufficient memory for LZFile⇐
struct
Global Const LZERROR_GLOBLOCK = (-6)     ' bad global handle
Global Const LZERROR_BADVALUE = (-7)     ' input parameter out of range
Global Const LZERROR_UNKNOWNALG = (-8)   ' compression algorithm not ⇐
recognized

Declare Function LZStart Lib "LZexpand.dll" () As Integer
Declare Sub LZDone Lib "LZexpand.dll" ()
Declare Function CopyLZFile Lib "LZexpand.dll" (ByVal hfSource As ⇐
Integer, ByVal hfDest As Integer) As Long
Declare Function LZCopy Lib "LZexpand.dll" (ByVal hfSource As Integer, ⇐
ByVal hfDest As Integer) As Long
Declare Function LZInit Lib "LZexpand.dll" (ByVal hfSrc As Integer) As ⇐
Integer
Declare Function GetExpandedName Lib "LZexpand.dll" (ByVal lpszSource As ⇐
String, ByVal lpszBuffer As String) As Integer
Declare Function LZOpenFile Lib "LZexpand.dll" (ByVal lpszFile As String, ⇐
lpOf As OFSTRUCT, ByVal style As Integer) As Integer
Declare Function LZSeek Lib "LZexpand.dll" (ByVal hfFile As Integer, ByVal ⇐
lOffset As Long, ByVal nOrigin As Integer) As Long
Declare Function LZRead Lib "LZexpand.dll" (ByVal hfFile As Integer, ByVal ⇐
lpvBuf As String, ByVal cb As Integer) As Integer
Declare Sub LZClose Lib "LZexpand.dll" (ByVal hfFile As Integer)


' ***** Windows Network support *****

Global Const WN_SUCCESS = &H0000
Global Const WN_NOT_SUPPORTED = &H0001
Global Const WN_NET_ERROR = &H0002
Global Const WN_MORE_DATA = &H0003
```

```
Global Const WN_BAD_POINTER = &H0004
Global Const WN_BAD_VALUE = &H0005
Global Const WN_BAD_PASSWORD = &H0006
Global Const WN_ACCESS_DENIED = &H0007
Global Const WN_FUNCTION_BUSY = &H0008
Global Const WN_WINDOWS_ERROR = &H0009
Global Const WN_BAD_USER = &H000A
Global Const WN_OUT_OF_MEMORY = &H000B
Global Const WN_CANCEL = &H000C
Global Const WN_CONTINUE = &H000D


Global Const WN_NOT_CONNECTED = &H0030
Global Const WN_OPEN_FILES = &H0031
Global Const WN_BAD_NETNAME = &H0032
Global Const WN_BAD_LOCALNAME = &H0033
Global Const WN_ALREADY_CONNECTED = &H0034
Global Const WN_DEVICE_ERROR = &H0035
Global Const WN_CONNECTION_CLOSED = &H0036


Declare Function WNetAddConnection Lib "User" (ByVal lpszNetPath As ⇐
String, ByVal lpszPassword As String, ByVal lpszLocalName As String) As ⇐
Integer
Declare Function WNetCancelConnection Lib "User" (ByVal lpszName As ⇐
String, ByVal bForce As Integer) As Integer
Declare Function WNetGetConnection Lib "User" (ByVal lpszLocalName As ⇐
String, ByVal lpszRemoteName As String, cbRemoteName As Integer) As ⇐
Integer
```

# APPENDIX B

# The Visual Basic How-To Disk

This appendix lists the directories and files that the Visual Basic How-To setup program creates on your hard disk.

The disk is organized by chapters and numbered How-Tos. You will find directories labeled CHAPTER1, CHAPTER2, CHAPTER3 and so on. Within those directories you will find subdirectories labeled 1.1, 1.2, 1.3, etc. These subdirectories correspond to the numbered How-To solutions throughout the book and contain all the .MAK files, forms, bitmaps, DLLs and custom controls found in these pages.

See the Introduction of this book for complete information on how to install the disk. There is also a README file on the disk that details any last minute changes.

**C:\VBHOWTO**
VBHOWTO.BAS

README.WRI

**CHAPTER 1**

| | | | | | | |
|---|---|---|---|---|---|---|
| **1.1** | AUTOPOS.FRM | **1.8** | PASSWORD.MAK | | | CLEARAL2.FRM |
| | AUTOPOS.MAK | | PASSWORD.FRM | **2.5** | FILEDLG2.MAK |
| **1.2** | AUTOSIZE.MAK | **1.9** | PASSLOCK.MAK | | TESTFDIA.FRM |
| | AUTOSIZE.FRM | | PASSLOCK.FRM | | FILEDLG2.FRM |
| **1.3** | PROFILE1.MAK | **1.10** | GIFVIEW.MAK | **2.6** | EDITOR.MAK |
| | PROFILE1.FRM | | GIFVIEW.FRM | | HWND.BAS |
| **1.4** | PROFILE2.MAK | | MDIGIF.FRM | | TEXTBOX.BAS |
| | PROFILE2.FRM | | GIFVIEW.BAS | | EDITOR.FRM |
| **1.5** | FLASH.FRM | | | **2.7** | FILEDLG.MAK |
| | FLASH.MAK | **CHAPTER 2** | | | FILEDLG.FRM |
| **1.6** | TOPWIN.BAS | **2.1** | CHECKOFF.BMP | **2.8** | TASKS.FRM |
| | TOPWIN.MAK | | CHECKON.BMP | | TASKS.MAK |
| | TOPWIN.FRM | | CHECKPRS.BMP | | TASKS.BAS |
| **1.7** | EXPLODE.BAS | | CUSTOM.MAK | **2.9** | SEARCH.MAK |
| | EXPLODE.MAK | | CUSTOM.FRM | | SEARCH.FRM |
| | EXPLODIT.BAS | **2.2** | ADDCTL.MAK | **2.10** | SEARCH2.MAK |
| | EXPLODE.FRM | | ADDCTL.FRM | | SEARCH2.FRM |
| | | **2.3** | FILEBOX.FRM | **2.11** | COUNTER.MAK |
| | | | FILEBOX.MAK | | COUNTER.FRM |
| | | **2.4** | CLEARAL2.MAK | | |

# APPENDIX C

## ANSI Table

| | | | | | | | | | | | | | | | |
|---|---|---|---|---|---|---|---|---|---|---|---|---|---|---|---|
| 0 | | 32 | | 64 | @ | 96 | ` | 128 | ■ | 160 | | 192 | À | 224 | à |
| 1 | ■ | 33 | ! | 65 | A | 97 | a | 129 | ■ | 161 | ¡ | 193 | Á | 225 | á |
| 2 | ■ | 34 | " | 66 | B | 98 | b | 130 | ■ | 162 | ¢ | 194 | Â | 226 | â |
| 3 | ■ | 35 | # | 67 | C | 99 | c | 131 | ■ | 163 | £ | 195 | Ã | 227 | ã |
| 4 | ■ | 36 | $ | 68 | D | 100 | d | 132 | ■ | 164 | ¤ | 196 | Ä | 228 | ä |
| 5 | ■ | 37 | % | 69 | E | 101 | e | 133 | ■ | 165 | ¥ | 197 | Å | 229 | å |
| 6 | ■ | 38 | & | 70 | F | 102 | f | 134 | ■ | 166 | ¦ | 198 | Æ | 230 | æ |
| 7 | ■ | 39 | ' | 71 | G | 103 | g | 135 | ■ | 167 | § | 199 | Ç | 231 | ç |
| 8 | * | 40 | ( | 72 | H | 104 | h | 136 | ■ | 168 | ¨ | 200 | È | 232 | è |
| 9 | * | 41 | ) | 73 | I | 105 | i | 137 | ■ | 169 | © | 201 | É | 233 | é |
| 10 | * | 42 | * | 74 | J | 106 | j | 138 | ■ | 170 | ª | 202 | Ê | 234 | ê |
| 11 | ■ | 43 | + | 75 | K | 107 | k | 139 | ■ | 171 | « | 203 | Ë | 235 | ë |
| 12 | ■ | 44 | , | 76 | L | 108 | l | 140 | ■ | 172 | ¬ | 204 | Ì | 236 | ì |
| 13 | * | 45 | - | 77 | M | 109 | m | 141 | ■ | 173 | - | 205 | Í | 237 | í |
| 14 | ■ | 46 | . | 78 | N | 110 | n | 142 | ■ | 174 | ® | 206 | Î | 238 | î |
| 15 | ■ | 47 | / | 79 | O | 111 | o | 143 | ■ | 175 | ¯ | 207 | Ï | 239 | ï |
| 16 | ■ | 48 | 0 | 80 | P | 112 | p | 144 | ■ | 176 | ° | 208 | Ð | 240 | ð |
| 17 | ■ | 49 | 1 | 81 | Q | 113 | q | 145 | ' | 177 | ± | 209 | Ñ | 241 | ñ |
| 18 | ■ | 50 | 2 | 82 | R | 114 | r | 146 | ' | 178 | ² | 210 | Ò | 242 | ò |
| 19 | ■ | 51 | 3 | 83 | S | 115 | s | 147 | ■ | 179 | ³ | 211 | Ó | 243 | ó |
| 20 | ■ | 52 | 4 | 84 | T | 116 | t | 148 | ■ | 180 | ´ | 212 | Ô | 244 | ô |
| 21 | ■ | 53 | 5 | 85 | U | 117 | u | 149 | ■ | 181 | µ | 213 | Õ | 245 | õ |
| 22 | ■ | 54 | 6 | 86 | V | 118 | v | 150 | ■ | 182 | ¶ | 214 | Ö | 246 | ö |
| 23 | ■ | 55 | 7 | 87 | W | 119 | w | 151 | ■ | 183 | · | 215 | × | 247 | ÷ |
| 24 | ■ | 56 | 8 | 88 | X | 120 | x | 152 | ■ | 184 | , | 216 | Ø | 248 | ø |
| 25 | ■ | 57 | 9 | 89 | Y | 121 | y | 153 | ■ | 185 | ¹ | 217 | Ù | 249 | ù |
| 26 | ■ | 58 | : | 90 | Z | 122 | z | 154 | ■ | 186 | º | 218 | Ú | 250 | ú |
| 27 | ■ | 59 | ; | 91 | [ | 123 | { | 155 | ■ | 187 | » | 219 | Û | 251 | û |
| 28 | ■ | 60 | < | 92 | \ | 124 | \| | 156 | ■ | 188 | ¼ | 220 | Ü | 252 | ü |
| 29 | ■ | 61 | = | 93 | ] | 125 | } | 157 | ■ | 189 | ½ | 221 | Ý | 253 | ý |
| 30 | ■ | 62 | > | 94 | ^ | 126 | ~ | 158 | ■ | 190 | ¾ | 222 | Þ | 254 | þ |
| 31 | ■ | 63 | ? | 95 | _ | 127 | ■ | 159 | ■ | 191 | ¿ | 223 | β | 255 | ÿ |

■ Indicates that this character is not supported by Windows.

* Values 8, 9, 10, and 13 convert to tab, backspace, linefeed, and carriage return characters, respectively. They have no graphical representation but they do behave appropriately in some contexts.

# APPENDIX D

## ASCII Table

| DEC | HEX | Symbol | Key | | DEC | HEX | Symbol | Key |
|-----|-----|--------|-----|---|-----|-----|--------|-----|
| | | **IBM Character Codes** | | | | | **IBM Character Codes** | |
| 0 | 00 | (NULL) | CTRL 2 | | 29 | 1D | ↔ | CTRL ] |
| 1 | 01 | ☺ | CTRL A | | 30 | 1E | ▲ | CTRL 6 |
| 2 | 02 | ☻ | CTRL B | | 31 | 1F | ▼ | CTRL - |
| 3 | 03 | ♥ | CTRL C | | 32 | 20 | | SPACEBAR |
| 4 | 04 | ♦ | CTRL D | | 33 | 21 | ! | ! |
| 5 | 05 | ♣ | CTRL E | | 34 | 22 | " | " |
| 6 | 06 | ♠ | CTRL F | | 35 | 23 | # | # |
| 7 | 07 | • | CTRL G | | 36 | 24 | $ | $ |
| 8 | 08 | ◘ | BACKSPACE | | 37 | 25 | % | % |
| 9 | 09 | | TAB | | 38 | 26 | & | & |
| 10 | 0A | ◙ | CTRL J | | 39 | 27 | ' | ' |
| 11 | 0B | ♂ | CTRL K | | 40 | 28 | ( | ( |
| 12 | 0C | ♀ | CTRL L | | 41 | 29 | ) | ) |
| 13 | 0D | ♪ | ENTER | | 42 | 2A | * | * |
| 14 | 0E | ♫ | CTRL N | | 43 | 2B | + | + |
| 15 | 0F | ¤ | CTRL O | | 44 | 2C | , | , |
| 16 | 10 | ► | CTRL P | | 45 | 2D | - | - |
| 17 | 11 | ◄ | CTRL Q | | 46 | 2E | . | . |
| 18 | 12 | ↕ | CTRL R | | 47 | 2F | / | / |
| 19 | 13 | ‼ | CTRL S | | 48 | 30 | 0 | 0 |
| 20 | 14 | ¶ | CTRL T | | 49 | 31 | 1 | 1 |
| 21 | 15 | § | CTRL U | | 50 | 32 | 2 | 2 |
| 22 | 16 | ■ | CTRL V | | 51 | 33 | 3 | 3 |
| 23 | 17 | ↨ | CTRL W | | 52 | 34 | 4 | 4 |
| 24 | 18 | ↑ | CTRL X | | 53 | 35 | 5 | 5 |
| 25 | 19 | ↓ | CTRL Y | | 54 | 36 | 6 | 6 |
| 26 | 1A | → | CTRL Z | | 55 | 37 | 7 | 7 |
| 27 | 1B | ← | ESC | | 56 | 38 | 8 | 8 |
| 28 | 1C | ∟ | CTRL \ | | 57 | 39 | 9 | 9 |

## IBM Character Codes

| DEC | HEX | Symbol | Key | DEC | HEX | Symbol | Key |
|-----|-----|--------|-----|-----|-----|--------|-----|
| 58 | 3A | : | (:) | 97 | 61 | a | (a) |
| 59 | 3B | ; | (;) | 98 | 62 | b | (b) |
| 60 | 3C | < | (<) | 99 | 63 | c | (c) |
| 61 | 3D | = | (=) | 100 | 64 | d | (d) |
| 62 | 3E | > | (>) | 101 | 65 | e | (e) |
| 63 | 3F | ? | (?) | 102 | 66 | f | (f) |
| 64 | 40 | @ | (@) | 103 | 67 | g | (g) |
| 65 | 41 | A | (A) | 104 | 68 | h | (h) |
| 66 | 42 | B | (B) | 105 | 69 | i | (i) |
| 67 | 43 | C | (C) | 106 | 6A | j | (j) |
| 68 | 44 | D | (D) | 107 | 6B | k | (k) |
| 69 | 45 | E | (E) | 108 | 6C | l | (l) |
| 70 | 46 | F | (F) | 109 | 6D | m | (m) |
| 71 | 47 | G | (G) | 110 | 6E | n | (n) |
| 72 | 48 | H | (H) | 111 | 6F | o | (o) |
| 73 | 49 | I | (I) | 112 | 70 | p | (p) |
| 74 | 4A | J | (J) | 113 | 71 | q | (q) |
| 75 | 4B | K | (K) | 114 | 72 | r | (r) |
| 76 | 4C | L | (L) | 115 | 73 | s | (s) |
| 77 | 4D | M | (M) | 116 | 74 | t | (t) |
| 78 | 4E | N | (N) | 117 | 75 | u | (u) |
| 79 | 4F | O | (O) | 118 | 76 | v | (v) |
| 80 | 50 | P | (P) | 119 | 77 | w | (w) |
| 81 | 51 | Q | (Q) | 120 | 78 | x | (x) |
| 82 | 52 | R | (R) | 121 | 79 | y | (y) |
| 83 | 53 | S | (S) | 122 | 7A | z | (z) |
| 84 | 54 | T | (T) | 123 | 7B | { | ({) |
| 85 | 55 | U | (U) | 124 | 7C | ¦ | (¦) |
| 86 | 56 | V | (V) | 125 | 7D | } | (}) |
| 87 | 57 | W | (W) | 126 | 7E | ~ | (~) |
| 88 | 58 | X | (X) | 127 | 7F | Δ | (CTRL) (←) |
| 89 | 59 | Y | (Y) | 128 | 80 | Ç | (ALT) 128 |
| 90 | 5A | Z | (Z) | 129 | 81 | ü | (ALT) 129 |
| 91 | 5B | [ | ([) | 130 | 82 | é | (ALT) 130 |
| 92 | 5C | \ | (\) | 131 | 83 | â | (ALT) 131 |
| 93 | 5D | ] | (]) | 132 | 84 | ä | (ALT) 132 |
| 94 | 5E | ^ | (^) | 133 | 85 | à | (ALT) 133 |
| 95 | 5F | _ | (_) | 134 | 86 | å | (ALT) 134 |
| 96 | 60 | ` | (`) | 135 | 87 | ç | (ALT) 135 |

## IBM Character Codes

| DEC | HEX | Symbol | Key | | DEC | HEX | Symbol | Key |
|-----|-----|--------|-----|---|-----|-----|--------|-----|
| 136 | 88 | ê | (ALT) 136 | | 175 | AF | » | (ALT) 175 |
| 137 | 89 | ë | (ALT) 137 | | 176 | B0 | ▓ | (ALT) 176 |
| 138 | 8A | è | (ALT) 138 | | 177 | B1 | ▒ | (ALT) 177 |
| 139 | 8B | ï | (ALT) 139 | | 178 | B2 | █ | (ALT) 178 |
| 140 | 8C | î | (ALT) 140 | | 179 | B3 | │ | (ALT) 179 |
| 141 | 8D | ì | (ALT) 141 | | 180 | B4 | ┤ | (ALT) 180 |
| 142 | 8E | Ä | (ALT) 142 | | 181 | B5 | ╡ | (ALT) 181 |
| 143 | 8F | Å | (ALT) 143 | | 182 | B6 | ╢ | (ALT) 182 |
| 144 | 90 | É | (ALT) 144 | | 183 | B7 | ╖ | (ALT) 183 |
| 145 | 91 | æ | (ALT) 145 | | 184 | B8 | ╕ | (ALT) 184 |
| 146 | 92 | Æ | (ALT) 146 | | 185 | B9 | ╣ | (ALT) 185 |
| 147 | 93 | ô | (ALT) 147 | | 186 | BA | ║ | (ALT) 186 |
| 148 | 94 | ö | (ALT) 148 | | 187 | BB | ╗ | (ALT) 187 |
| 149 | 95 | ò | (ALT) 149 | | 188 | BC | ╝ | (ALT) 188 |
| 150 | 96 | û | (ALT) 150 | | 189 | BD | ╜ | (ALT) 189 |
| 151 | 97 | ù | (ALT) 151 | | 190 | BE | ╛ | (ALT) 190 |
| 152 | 98 | ÿ | (ALT) 152 | | 191 | BF | ┐ | (ALT) 191 |
| 153 | 99 | Ö | (ALT) 153 | | 192 | C0 | └ | (ALT) 192 |
| 154 | 9A | Ü | (ALT) 154 | | 193 | C1 | ┴ | (ALT) 193 |
| 155 | 9B | ¢ | (ALT) 155 | | 194 | C2 | ┬ | (ALT) 194 |
| 156 | 9C | £ | (ALT) 156 | | 195 | C3 | ├ | (ALT) 195 |
| 157 | 9D | ¥ | (ALT) 157 | | 196 | C4 | ─ | (ALT) 196 |
| 158 | 9E | P₊ | (ALT) 158 | | 197 | C5 | ┼ | (ALT) 197 |
| 159 | 9F | ƒ | (ALT) 159 | | 198 | C6 | ╞ | (ALT) 198 |
| 160 | A0 | á | (ALT) 160 | | 199 | C7 | ╟ | (ALT) 199 |
| 161 | A1 | í | (ALT) 161 | | 200 | C8 | ╚ | (ALT) 200 |
| 162 | A2 | ó | (ALT) 162 | | 201 | C9 | ╔ | (ALT) 201 |
| 163 | A3 | ú | (ALT) 163 | | 202 | CA | ╩ | (ALT) 202 |
| 164 | A4 | ñ | (ALT) 164 | | 203 | CB | ╦ | (ALT) 203 |
| 165 | A5 | Ñ | (ALT) 165 | | 204 | CC | ╠ | (ALT) 204 |
| 166 | A6 | ª | (ALT) 166 | | 205 | CD | ═ | (ALT) 205 |
| 167 | A7 | º | (ALT) 167 | | 206 | CE | ╬ | (ALT) 206 |
| 168 | A8 | ¿ | (ALT) 168 | | 207 | CF | ╧ | (ALT) 207 |
| 169 | A9 | ⌐ | (ALT) 169 | | 208 | D0 | ╨ | (ALT) 208 |
| 170 | AA | ¬ | (ALT) 170 | | 209 | D1 | ╤ | (ALT) 209 |
| 171 | AB | ½ | (ALT) 171 | | 210 | D2 | ╥ | (ALT) 210 |
| 172 | AC | ¼ | (ALT) 172 | | 211 | D3 | ╙ | (ALT) 211 |
| 173 | AD | ¡ | (ALT) 173 | | 212 | D4 | ╘ | (ALT) 212 |
| 174 | AE | « | (ALT) 174 | | 213 | D5 | ╒ | (ALT) 213 |

## IBM Character Codes

| DEC | HEX | Symbol | Key | DEC | HEX | Symbol | Key |
|-----|-----|--------|-----|-----|-----|--------|-----|
| 214 | D6 | ⊓ | (ALT) 214 | 235 | EB | δ | (ALT) 235 |
| 215 | D7 | ╫ | (ALT) 215 | 236 | EC | ∞ | (ALT) 236 |
| 216 | D8 | ╪ | (ALT) 216 | 237 | ED | φ | (ALT) 237 |
| 217 | D9 | ⌐ | (ALT) 217 | 238 | EE | ε | (ALT) 238 |
| 218 | DA | ⌐ | (ALT) 218 | 239 | EF | ∩ | (ALT) 239 |
| 219 | DB | ■ | (ALT) 219 | 240 | F0 | ≡ | (ALT) 240 |
| 220 | DC | ▬ | (ALT) 220 | 241 | F1 | ± | (ALT) 241 |
| 221 | DD | ▌ | (ALT) 221 | 242 | F2 | ≥ | (ALT) 242 |
| 222 | DE | ▐ | (ALT) 222 | 243 | F3 | ≤ | (ALT) 243 |
| 223 | DF | ▬ | (ALT) 223 | 244 | F4 | ⌠ | (ALT) 244 |
| 224 | E0 | α | (ALT) 224 | 245 | F5 | ⌡ | (ALT) 245 |
| 225 | E1 | β | (ALT) 225 | 246 | F6 | ÷ | (ALT) 246 |
| 226 | E2 | Γ | (ALT) 226 | 247 | F7 | ≈ | (ALT) 247 |
| 227 | E3 | π | (ALT) 227 | 248 | F8 | ° | (ALT) 248 |
| 228 | E4 | Σ | (ALT) 228 | 249 | F9 | • | (ALT) 249 |
| 229 | E5 | σ | (ALT) 229 | 250 | FA | · | (ALT) 250 |
| 230 | E6 | μ | (ALT) 230 | 251 | FB | √ | (ALT) 251 |
| 231 | E7 | τ | (ALT) 231 | 252 | FC | η | (ALT) 252 |
| 232 | E8 | Φ | (ALT) 232 | 253 | FD | ² | (ALT) 253 |
| 233 | E9 | Θ | (ALT) 233 | 254 | FE | ■ | (ALT) 254 |
| 234 | EA | Ω | (ALT) 234 | 255 | FF | (blank) | (ALT) 255 |

Note that IBM Extended ASCII charcters can be displayed by pressing the (ALT) key and then typing the decimal code of the character on the keypad.

# INDEX

## Y

Books have a substantial influence on the destruction of the forests of the Earth. For example, it takes 17 trees to produce one ton of paper. A first printing of 30,000 copies of a typical 480-page book consumes 108,000 pounds of paper which will require 918 trees!

      Waite Group Press™ is against the clear-cutting of forests and supports reforestation of the Pacific Northwest of the United States and Canada, where most of this paper comes from. As a publisher with several hundred thousand books sold each year, we feel an obligation to give back to the planet. We will, therefore, support and contribute a percentage of our proceeds to organizations which seek to preserve the forests of planet Earth.

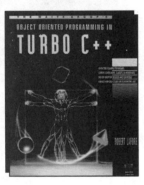

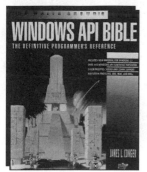

This is a legal agreement between you, the end user and purchaser, and The Waite Group®, Inc., and the authors of the programs contained in the disk. By opening the sealed disk package, you are agreeing to be bound by the terms of this Agreement. If you do not agree with the terms of this Agreement, promptly return the unopened disk package and the accompanying items (including the related book and other written material) to the place you obtained them for a refund.

## SOFTWARE LICENSE

1.  The Waite Group, Inc. grants you the right to use one copy of the enclosed software programs (the programs) on a single computer system (whether a single CPU, part of a licensed network, or a terminal connected to a single CPU). Each concurrent user of the program must have exclusive use of the related Waite Group, Inc. written materials.

2.  The program, including the copyrights in each program, is owned by the respective author and the copyright in the entire work is owned by The Waite Group, Inc. and they are therefore protected under the copyright laws of the United States and other nations, under international treaties. You may make only one copy of the disk containing the programs exclusively for backup or archival purposes, or you may transfer the programs to one hard disk drive, using the original for backup or archival purposes. You may make no other copies of the programs, and you may make no copies of all or any part of the related Waite Group, Inc. written materials.

3.  You may not rent or lease the programs, but you may transfer ownership of the programs and related written materials (including any and all updates and earlier versions) if you keep no copies of either, and if you make sure the transferee agrees to the terms of this license.

4.  You may not decompile, reverse engineer, disassemble, copy, create a derivative work, or otherwise use the programs except as stated in this Agreement.

## GOVERNING LAW

This Agreement is governed by the laws of the State of California.

# SATISFACTION REPORT CARD

Please fill out this card if you wish to know of future updates to
*Visual Basic How-To Second Edition,* or to receive our catalog.

**WAITE GROUP PRESS**™

Company Name:

Division/Department:           Mail Stop:

Last Name:           First Name:           Middle Initial:

Street Address:

City:           State:           Zip:

Daytime telephone: ( )

Date product was acquired: Month     Day     Year     Your Occupation:

**Overall, how would you rate *Visual Basic How-To Second Edition?***
☐ Excellent    ☐ Very Good    ☐ Good
☐ Fair    ☐ Below Average    ☐ Poor

**What did you like MOST about this book?**

**What did you like LEAST about this book?**

**How did you use this book (problem-solver, tutorial, reference...)?**

**What version of Visual Basic are you using?**

**What is your level of computer expertise?**
☐ New    ☐ Dabbler    ☐ Hacker
☐ Power User    ☐ Programmer    ☐ Experienced Professional

**What computer languages are you familiar with?**

**Please describe your computer hardware:**
Computer _____    Hard disk _____
5.25" disk drives _____    3.5" disk drives _____
Video card _____    Monitor _____
Printer _____    Peripherals _____
Sound Board _____    CD ROM _____

**Where did you buy this book?**
☐ Bookstore (name): _____
☐ Discount store (name): _____
☐ Computer store (name): _____
☐ Catalog (name): _____
☐ Direct from WGP    ☐ Other _____

**What price did you pay for this book?**

**What influenced your purchase of this book?**
☐ Recommendation    ☐ Advertisement
☐ Magazine review    ☐ Store display
☐ Mailing    ☐ Book's format
☐ Reputation of Waite Group Press    ☐ Other _____

**Do you own the first edition of this book?**

**How many other Waite Group books do you own?**

**What is your favorite Waite Group book?**

**Is there any program or subject you would like to see Waite Group Press cover in a similar approach?**

**Additional comments?**

☐ **Check here for a free Waite Group catalog**

**Send to: Waite Group Press, 200 Tamal Plaza Corte Madera, CA 94925**

*Visual Basic How-To Second Edition*

**Waite Group Press, Inc.**
**Attention:** *Visual Basic How-To Second Edition*
**200 Tamal Plaza**
**Corte Madera, CA 94925**

**FOLD HERE**